D1254233

RECORDS MANAGEMENT

INTEGRATED INFORMATION SYSTEMS

Third Edition

Dr. Patricia E. Wallace, CRM

Trenton State College

Jo Ann Lee, Ed.D

Pasadena City College

Dexter R. Schubert

University of Arizona

PRENTICE HALL, Englewood Cliffs, New Jersey 07632

Library of Congress Cataloging-in-Publication Data

Records management : integrated information systems / Patricia E.
Wallace . . . [et al.]. — 3rd ed.
p. cm.
Includes bibliographical references and index.
ISBN 0-13-769936-0
1. Archives—Administration. 2. Public records. I. Wallace,
Patricia E.
CD950.R383 1992 91-19338
651.5—dc20 CIP

Editorial/production supervision: *Anthony Calcara*
Designer: *David Levy*
Cover design: *Richard Dombrowski*
Acquisition editor: *Elizabeth Kendall*
Prepress buyer: *Ilene Levy*
Manufacturing buyer: *Ed O'Dougherty*
Marketing manager: *Robert Kern*
Editorial assistant: *Renee Pelletier*

© 1992 by Prentice-Hall, Inc.
A Simon & Schuster Company
Englewood Cliffs, New Jersey 07632

All rights reserved. No part of this book may be
reproduced, in any form or by any means,
without permission in writing from the publisher.

Printed in the United States of America

10 9 8 7 6 5 4 3 2 1

ISBN 0-13-769936-0

Prentice-Hall International (UK) Limited, *London*
Prentice-Hall of Australia Pty. Limited, *Sydney*
Prentice-Hall Canada Inc., *Toronto*
Prentice-Hall Hispanoamericana, S.A., *Mexico*
Prentice-Hall of India Private Limited, *New Delhi*
Prentice-Hall of Japan, Inc., *Tokyo*
Simon & Schuster Asia Pte. Ltd., *Singapore*
Editora Prentice-Hall do Brasil, Ltda., *Rio de Janeiro*

CONTENTS

6

RECORDS STORAGE AND RETRIEVAL SYSTEMS 119

7

RECORDS CLASSIFICATION SYSTEMS 168

8

RECORDS MAINTENANCE AND CONTROL 216

9

ELECTRONIC RECORDS STORAGE AND RETRIEVAL 236

10

MANAGING VITAL RECORDS AND DISASTER RECOVERY 271

11

Planning and Managing the Records Center 289

12

Managing the Archives 309

13

Correspondence and Reports Control 328

17

AUDITING THE RECORDS MANAGEMENT PROGRAM AND WRITING MANUALS 447

18

RECORDS MANAGEMENT TECHNOLOGY AND TRENDS 477

PREFACE

RECORDS MANAGEMENT: INTEGRATED INFORMATION SYSTEMS is intended to give the reader—whether professor, student, or records management practitioner—an understanding of the scope and complexities of the administrative management of records.

The third edition of the textbook focuses on the systems approach to managing information recorded in any form. Paper, microform, and electronic records are emphasized throughout the text, since records generally fall into one of these three categories. Practical guidelines are presented—from establishing a records management system to handling paper and electronic media—and issues relevant to records management are discussed. Emphasis is placed on managing and controlling documents from time of their creation until their disposition. The book presents the concepts in a logical, step-by-step manner, progressing from fundamental ideas to more complex concepts.

This third edition presents expanded coverage of all components of records management, to provide the reader with a comprehensive background in the subject. Specifically, the following improvements have been made in the third edition:

- A new chapter titled, "Electronic Records Storage and Retrieval," describes characteristics of electronic records, storage media, and retrieval systems.
- Vital Records and Records Centers are now separate chapters in the third edition, reflecting the expanded coverage given to these important topics.
- Disaster Recovery concepts have been included in the new Vital Records chapter signaling the importance of disaster recovery to the records management profession.
- A reorganization of chapters on Records Management Manuals and Auditing the Records Management Program was achieved by combining these topics into a new, improved chapter.
- The technology chapters have been updated to reflect the latest advances in the records management field including imaging systems, bar code scanning, and CAR systems.

- All five Appendices have been updated to reflect current information on Records Management Software, Organizations, and Publications including ARMA and CRM examination data.

Professors and students in universities, community colleges, and proprietary schools will find the book to be a relevant and thorough teaching tool for records management courses. In addition, individuals working in Records Management will find it a valuable resource for answering day-to-day questions that arise on the job.

In addition to this comprehensive textbook, a student workbook with databases exercises, correlated to the eighteen chapters in this third edition, provides both objective review questions and practical exercises for the records management student. The instructor's manual that accompanies this instructional package contains chapter outlines, teaching suggestions, answers to review questions and case studies, a test bank, and transparency masters for overhead projectors. Finally, a package of color slides on records management is available to teachers, to help highlight concepts presented throughout the textbook.

The authors gratefully acknowledge the assistance and guidance of our Editor, Elizabeth Kendall, and her Assistant, Jane Baumann. We also thank the many individuals who shared their expertise at the various stages in the development of the manuscript especially Dr. Paula Williams of Northern Illinois University; the business persons who contributed generously their knowledge, experience, and materials; and our famlies, who have been supportive of our writing.

Since paper, microfilm, and electronic records abound in the business offices of the 90s, this textbook prepares the reader to deal with the integration of these records. Regardless of the medium, current and future records managers need to be able to create a system that incorporates all storage media. This textbook endeavors to prepare records managers to meet this challenge.

Patricia E. Wallace, CRM
Jo Ann Lee

To the Student

A workbook to use with this textbook is available through your college bookstore. The workbook title is *Records Management Applications,* by Patricia E. Wallace. This workbook can help you learn the course material, by reinforcing the topics presented in the text. If the workbook is not in stock, ask the bookstore manager to order a copy for you.

The Role of Records Management and Administrative Services

OBJECTIVES

Upon completion of this chapter, the student should be able to:

1. Define the scope of records management.
2. Describe the "life cycle" of a business record.
3. Explain the role of the records manager.
4. Describe the career opportunities in records management.
5. Identify the professional organizations and literature germane to records management.
6. Describe how records management has evolved through the centuries.

Information is a vital business tool, as well as an essential business resource. Transmitting and receiving information occurs every minute of every business day. For information to be truly effective, it must be recorded in some form, stored in an appropriate system, and retrieved in an efficient manner. Information that is recorded in some form is known as a **record.**

Records are the memory of an organization. They document information for management decisions, provide litigation support, show compliance with government regulations, and supply a historical reference of transactions and events. Organizations in the 90s must face the challenge of setting corporate-wide records standards by utilizing the right mix of media, technologies, and people in records and information management.

RECORDS MANAGEMENT: CONTROLLING RECORDED INFORMATION

One of the most important functions in an office is the management of records. A business office would be greatly disorganized if it had to rely on memory for preserving every transaction. There would be no letters, cards, memos, invoices, computer tapes, personnel records, microforms, or other types of records to support the office functions. Recorded information is vital to the survival of the office. Moreover, records must be properly controlled and managed if they are to serve their purpose in an organization.

Information can be recorded in a paper-based format (such as letters, reports, or memos); in a microform-based format (such as microfiche); or in an electronic-based format (such as magnetic tapes and optical disks). A recent study by the Association of Information and Image Management indicates that paper is the dominant choice for 95 percent of all information storage in the United Sates in 1990. The remaining 5 percent is divided into microform storage (4 percent) and electronic storage (a mere 1 percent). Projections through 1999 reveal that paper storage will decrease only slightly to about 92 percent; information storage on microforms will also decrease slightly to approximately 3 percent. Electronic media (both magnetic and optical disks) will grow from a mere 1 percent to a projected 5 percent of all information storage technologies. The current use of information storage technologies as well as predictions for future growth are shown in Figure 1.1.

Records management is defined as the systematic control placed over the life cycle of recorded information—from creation to ultimate disposition or permanent storage of a record. The life cycle of a record—whether it is stored on paper, microform, or electronic media—is depicted in Figure 1-2.

FIGURE 1.1
Information
Storage Trends
1989–1999

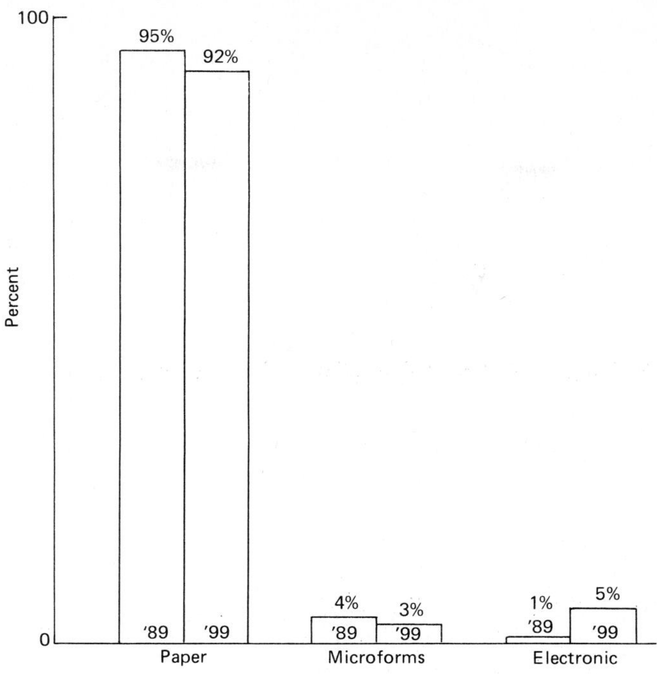

Source: AIIM, "Information and Image Management: The State of the Industry," 1989.

Records Creation

The creation stage in a record's life cycle is the point at which information is collected and captured. Thus, a record is created. Currently, records can be created in the following forms:

1. *PAPER-BASED RECORDS*—Information recorded on any form of paper is considered a paper document. Business forms, letterhead stationery, index cards, memos, purchase orders, maps, and blueprints are all examples of paper records. A paper record is also referred to as a **hard copy.** Figure 1-3 shows several examples of paper records.
2. *MICROFORM-BASED RECORDS*—Information recorded on any type of microform is considered a microform-based record. Hard-copy records that have been filmed and reduced in size are called *microimages or microforms.* Categories of microforms include roll film, microfiche, aperture cards, jackets, and ultrafiche. Examples of microform-based records are shown in Figure 1-4.
3. *ELECTRONIC-BASED RECORDS*—Information recorded in a digital form, such as computer tapes, floppy disks, magnetic tape, hard disks, and more recently, optical disks, are considered electronic-based records. Digital data may also be stored internally in a computer (on-line) or externally

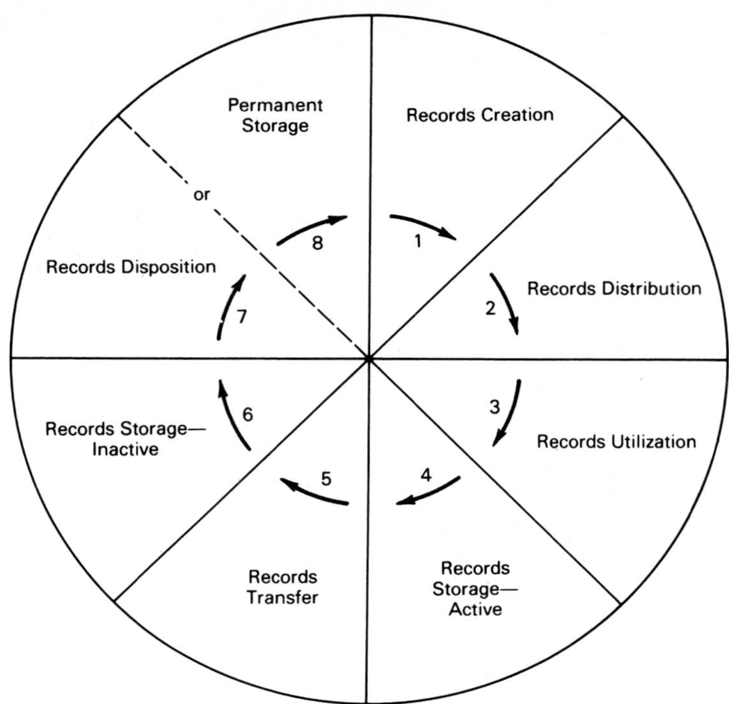

FIGURE 1-2 Life cycle of a record.

(off-line) on floppy disks or other magnetic media. Digital data is retrieved and stored through microcomputers, mainframe computers, computer-assisted retrieval systems, and electronic image management systems. Digital-based records are also called electronic files. Refer to Figure 1-5 for examples of electronic-based records.

Records Distribution

To make information readily available, the distribution of recorded information must take place as rapidly as possible. Traditional means of distributing information include both internal (interoffice) and external (U.S. Postal Service) mail delivery services. In addition, distribution via electronic mail has been made available to organizations with such equipment as *facsimile machines,* communicating information processors, and local area networks (LANS). The distribution of recorded information also involves deciding what reprographics process to use, who should receive a record, and how many copies are needed.

FIGURE 1-3
Paper-based records.

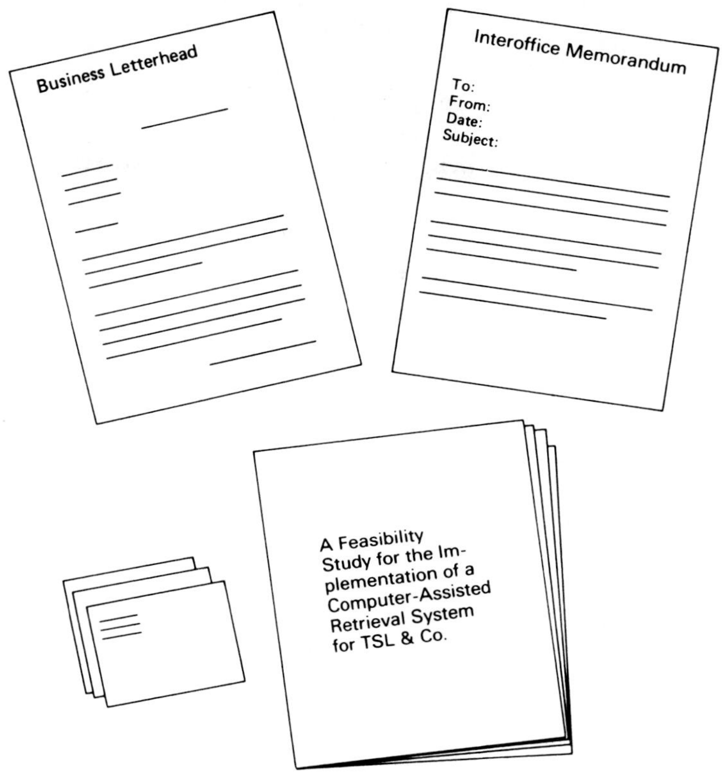

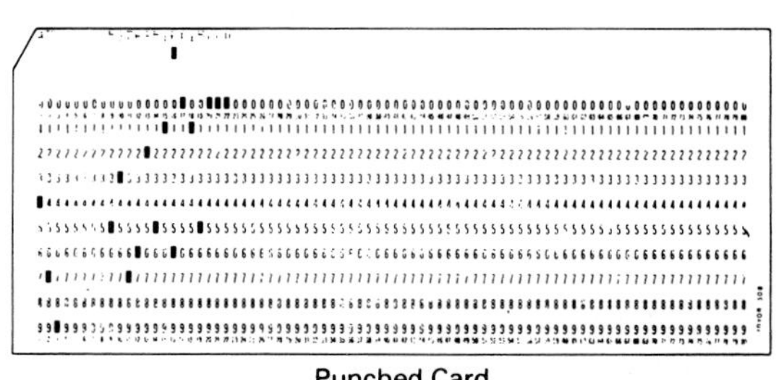
Punched Card

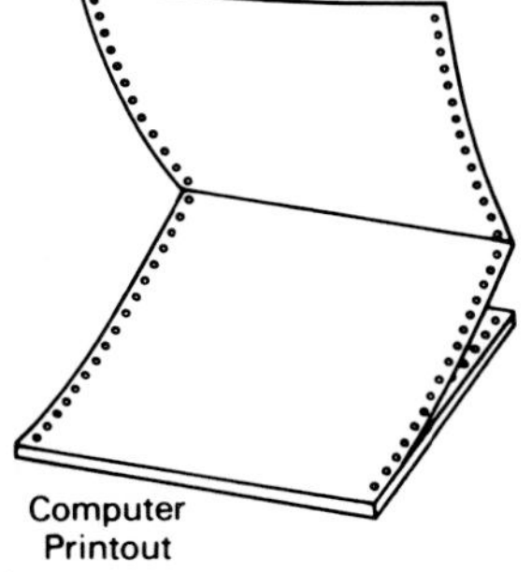
Computer Printout

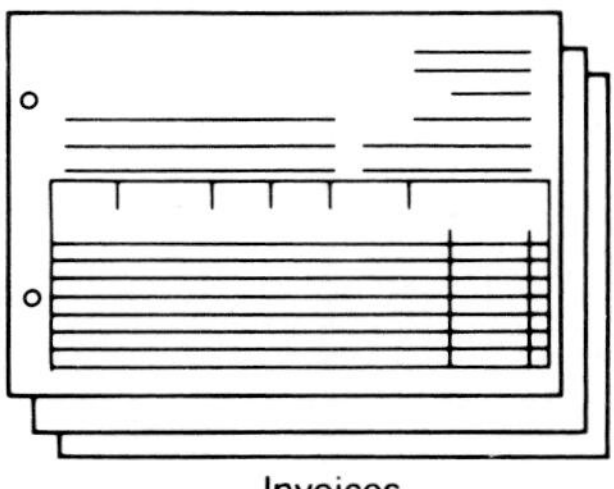
Invoices

FIGURE 1-4
Microform-based records.

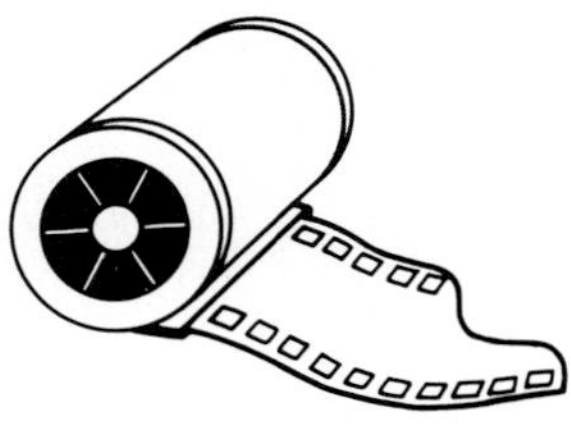
Roll Film

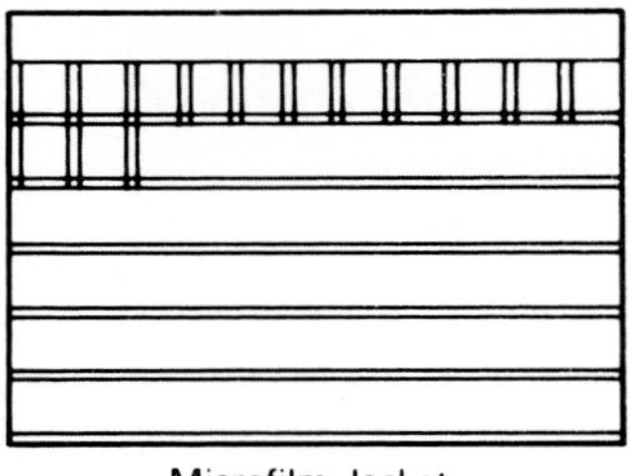
Microfilm Jacket

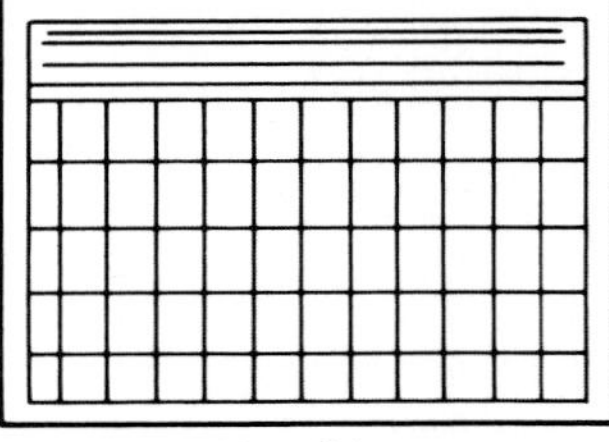
Microfiche

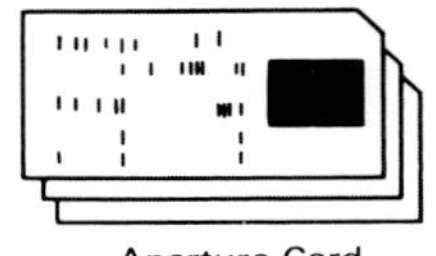
Aperture Card

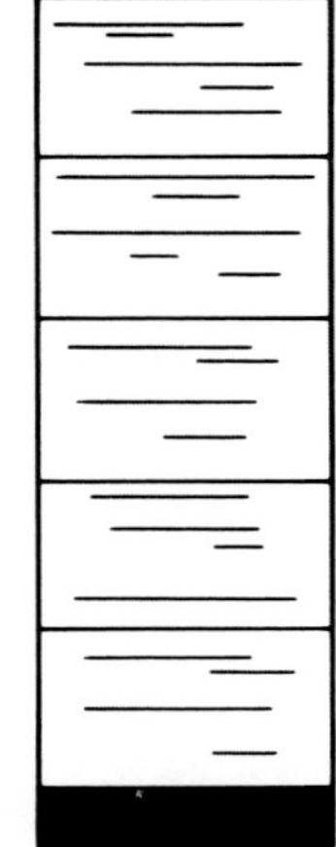
Ultrastrip

Records Utilization

Once received, records provide the recipient with the information needed to transact an organization's business. Records are generally classified into the following categories:

1. *FINANCIAL*—created for accounting and fiscal use (financial statements, tax forms, and so on)
2. *LEGAL*—created for evidence of business transactions or legal decisions (contracts, agreements, leases)
3. *ADMINISTRATIVE*—created for documenting policy, procedures, and guidelines (directive, manuals, reports)
4. *RESEARCH*—created to determine trends, recent developments, or new information related to an organization's products or services (market surveys, studies)
5. *HISTORICAL*—created to provide a record of an organization's past and current activities; also referred to as archival records (articles of incorporation, deeds)

FIGURE 1-5
Electronic-based records.

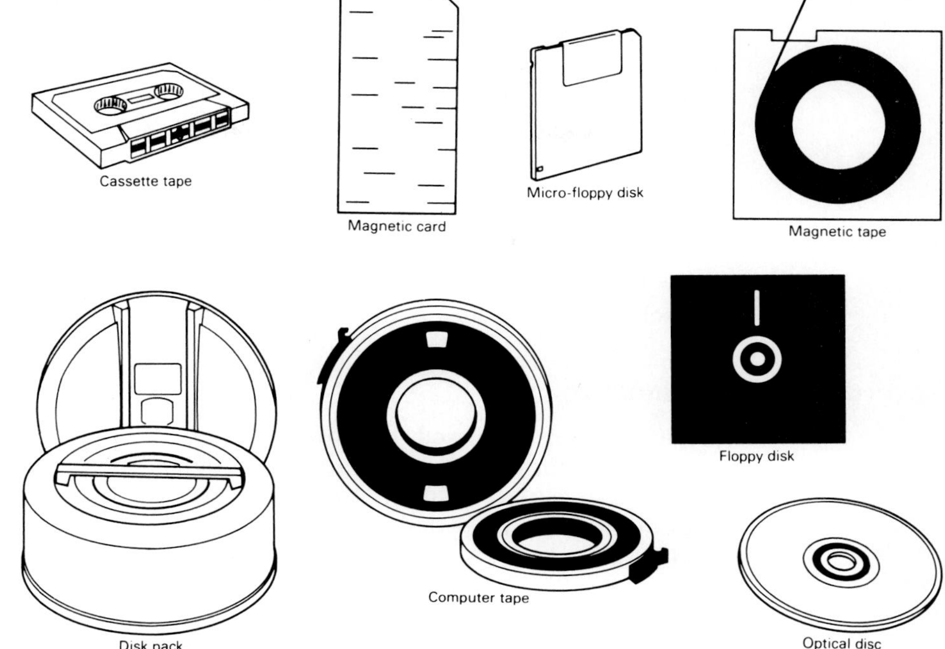

Records Storage—Active

Active records must be in close proximity to the people using them and must be available on a moment's notice. Active files may be centralized, decentralized, or a combination of both. Active files operations include equipment and supplies selection, layout, records classification, and establishing procedures for filing and access restriction.

Since records vary in media type as well as size, special storage requirements may be required. Typically, the following storage equipment is utilized:

Paper-based records: vertical cabinets, lateral or open-shelf files, and mobile or mechanized filing units.

Microform-based records: vertical cabinets, trays, ring binders, special storage cabinets or internally in a computer-assisted retrieval system (CAR).

Electronic-based records: special file folders with sleeves or protective pockets, albums, binders, lateral or open-shelf files, and hanging or canister racks. They can also be stored on-line through a database management system.

Non-standard size items: audio-visual records, maps, cards, engineering drawings, and continuous paper records must be stored in special cabinets, hanging files, binders, shelves, trays and boxes. Such nonstandard storage devices are illustrated in Chapter 6.

Records Transfer

Records are transferred from active to inactive storage as specified in a records retention schedule that is based on legal requirements and administrative decisions. A master records retention schedule indicates how long a record should be kept in both active and inactive storage, and at what point, if any, it should be destroyed. Records transfer includes moving recorded information—in any form—to inactive records storage. Records storage could be in the same building, at an off-site company-owned records center, or at a commercial records center. Records transfer can be periodic or continuous. Records transfer includes transfer list approval, boxing records for transfer, and scheduling pickups.

Records Storage—Inactive

Storing records in a well-run, low-cost records center results in substantial monetary savings to an organization, through economical use of both equipment and space. In addition, transferring inactive records to a records center frees up valuable office floor space, which can be used more effectively than by storing outdated records.

Factors to consider when storing inactive records include site location, security and safety, and control procedures. Managing and operating a records center requires that indexing methods be utilized and that records retention requirements are adhered to.

Care must be taken to distinguish between the terms **archive** and **records center.** An archive is a place for storing records that are deemed historical and, therefore, expected to be of interest to researchers. A company archive would store records that describe a company's origins, its growth, and its present business activities.

Records Disposition or Permanent Storage

The final stage of a record's life cycle concludes with either disposition or permanent storage. Paper records are disposed of by burning, shredding, pulverizing, or pulping. Disposition of microform-based records is accomplished by shredding or pulverizing. Electronic-based records are erased or pulverized.

It is important to note that a record can be disposed of at any point during its life cycle. Not all records will complete the "birth to death" cycle in the same order. In addition, some records are kept permanently, owing to the value the recorded information has for the organization. Such decisions regarding records are made systematically by companies with comprehensive records management programs. Thus records management is a scientific approach to managing the creation, distribution, use, storage, retrieval, preservation, retention, and disposition of recorded information.

Comprehensive Records Management Systems

Developing a comprehensive records management system requires an organized approach to the management of recorded information. A **system** can be defined as a group of interrelated components working together to achieve a desired outcome or goal. Records management's overall goal is to provide the right information, at the right time, in the right order, to the right person, at the lowest possible cost. Such requirements demand a total organizational approach towards records management, incorporating all forms of recorded information.

Other important objectives of records management programs include:

1. To provide needed documentation in the event of litigation
2. To serve as the "memory bank" of information for an organization
3. To retain records as required by federal, state, and other regulatory agencies
4. To preserve records that are vital—those needed for the continuation of operations of an organization in the event of a disaster
5. To maintain records that reflect an organization's history
6. To retain records as a basis for decision making by management

To accomplish these objectives, it is necessary to take an organized approach to records management. Such an organized approach to records management is illustrated by the flowchart in Figure 1-6. This systematic approach to records management will be described in this textbook to permit the student to understand the "systems approach" to developing a comprehensive organizational records management program. Each chapter of this textbook can be considered a subsystem or component that contributes to the overall goal of providing information to individuals in a timely fashion.

Subsystems of Records Management

The major subsystems or components of records management are links in a chain that together form the records management system (see Figure 1-7). To better understand the subsystems that will be presented in this textbook, consider the following definitions:

1. *RECORDS INVENTORY*—a complete and accurate listing of file contents, including the type of equipment, the classification system, descriptive data on the records, location of the records, and the cubic feet of space used (see Chapter 4).
2. *RECORDS RETENTION SCHEDULE*—a document that specifies how long each record will be held in active storage, how long in inactive storage,

FIGURE 1-6
Developing an integrated records management system—paper-based, microform-based, and electronic-based records.

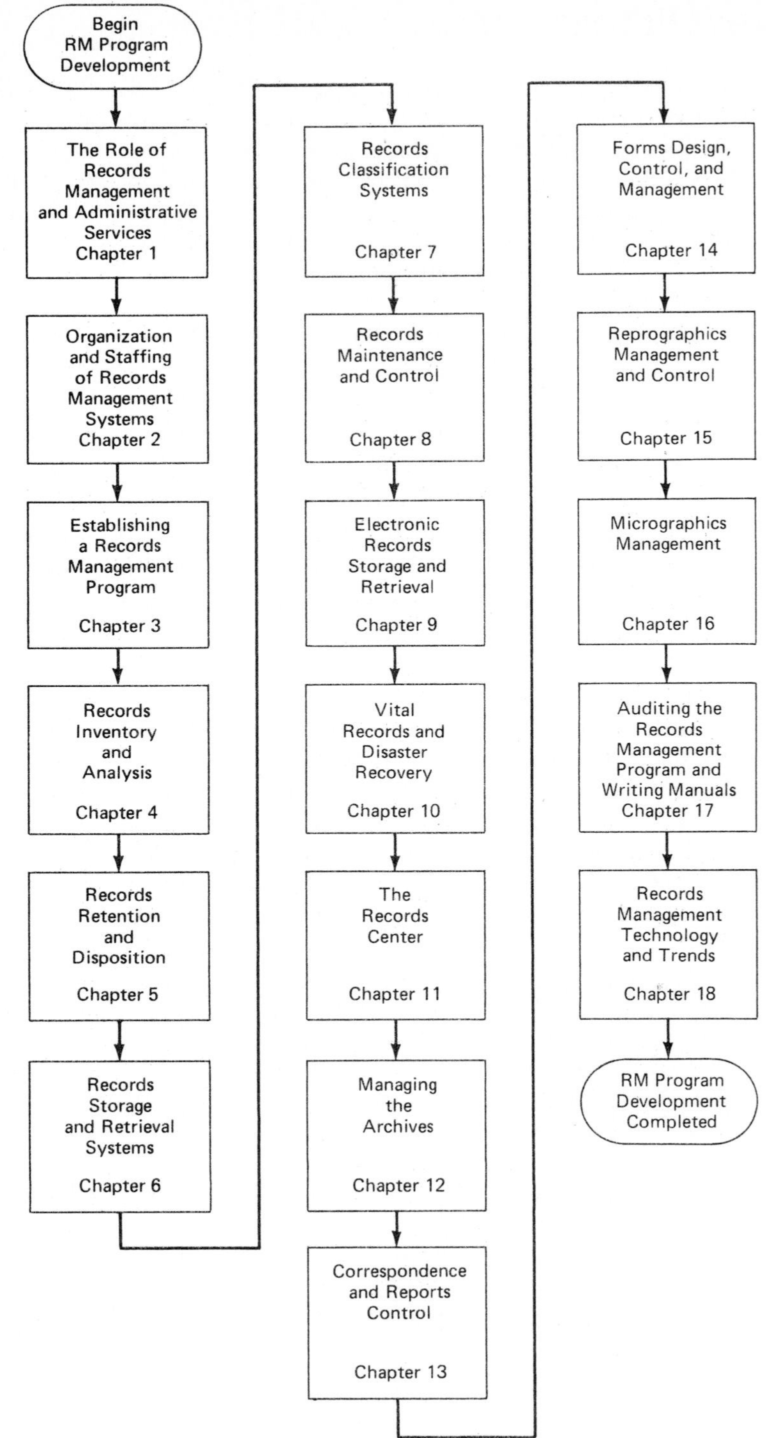

FIGURE 1-7
Subsystems of records management—"links in a chain."

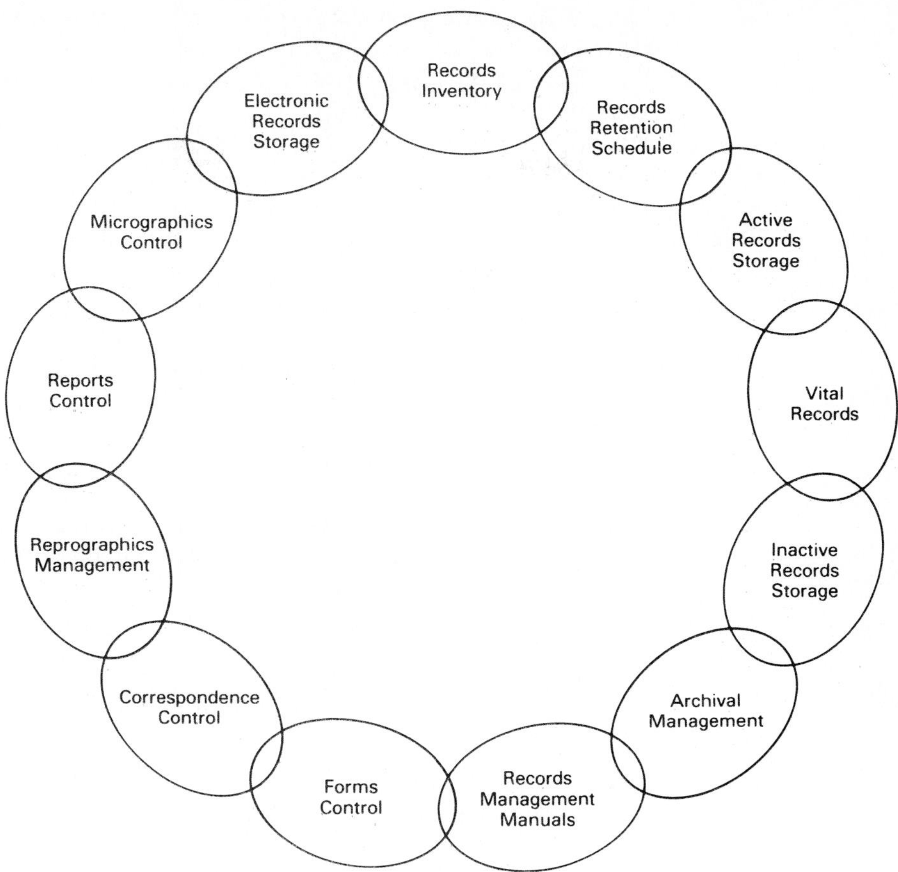

and the date of destruction. In some cases, records are kept permanently owing to their vital or archival status (see Chapter 5).

3. *ACTIVE RECORDS STORAGE*—using an appropriate records classification system; selecting appropriate records storage equipment; and developing effective controls for indexing, coding, and storing active records (see Chapter 6, 7, and 8).
4. *VITAL RECORDS*—records that are essential for the continuous operation of a business and must be specially protected against possible disasters, both natural and man-made (see Chapter 10).
5. *INACTIVE RECORDS STORAGE*—storing records in a low-cost storage facility, such as a records center, during the inactive part of their life cycle. Such facilities can be company-owned or commercial centers that offer storage, security, microfilming, copying, and other services (see Chapter 11).

6. *ARCHIVAL MANAGEMENT*—protecting records that are retained for their historical or research value, by providing appropriate preservation techniques, storage facilities, and protection from various elements (see Chapter 12).
7. *CORRESPONDENCE AND REPORTS CONTROL*—managing the creation, use, distribution, and storage of memos, letters and reports to improve their appearance and to save money, space, and time (see Chapter 13).
8. *FORMS CONTROL*—managing the designing, ordering, and stocking of forms, including the use of forms control files to monitor all forms used by an organization, resulting in better forms design as well as cost savings (see Chapter 14).
9. *REPROGRAPHICS MANAGEMENT*—selecting appopriate duplicating, copying, and/or printing processes, based on copy appearance, number of copies needed, and cost per copy (see Chapter 15).
10. *MICROGRAPHICS CONTROL*—managing the various micrographic components; using the appropriate microform, cameras, readers, and printers. In addition, it includes understanding the effective use of microforms in an organization, including computer-output microfilm and computer-assisted retrieval (see Chapter 16).
11. *RECORDS MANAGEMENT MANUALS*—publications that clearly set forth the objectives of the records management program, the procedures and guidelines to be adhered to, the organization chart for the department, and the duties and responsibilities of individual staff members (see Chapter 17).
12. *ELECTRONIC RECORDS STORAGE*—the use of information processing systems and various types of computer-assisted and non-computer-assisted storage and retrieval systems, and the integration of automated office technologies in records/information management system (see Chapters 9 and 18).

Career Opportunities

Good jobs are readily available for persons who are highly qualified records managers. Salaries for records managers are comparable to the pay of office administrators. As with other business careers, however, most individuals do not begin at the top. A 1987 compensation and benefits survey of records management positions sponsored by (ARMA The Association of Records Managers and Administrators International) revealed an average base salary for the position Records and Information Manager to be $44,000 annually. The participants in the ARMA survey fitting the description of records manager reported a range of salaries from a low of approximately $30,000 to a high of $60,000. (Source: ARMA, Compensation and Benefits Survey of Records Management Positions, 1987)

A more recent study by the Louisville National Records Management Corporation in 1990 reveals a salary range of approximately $20,000 to $70,000 for CRMs. In addition, this survey revealed that 52 percent of Certified Records Managers were earning between $30,000 and $45,000 annually. Figure 1.8 below further illustrates the earning capacity of the CRMs that responded to this study.

FIGURE 1.8
CRM compensation

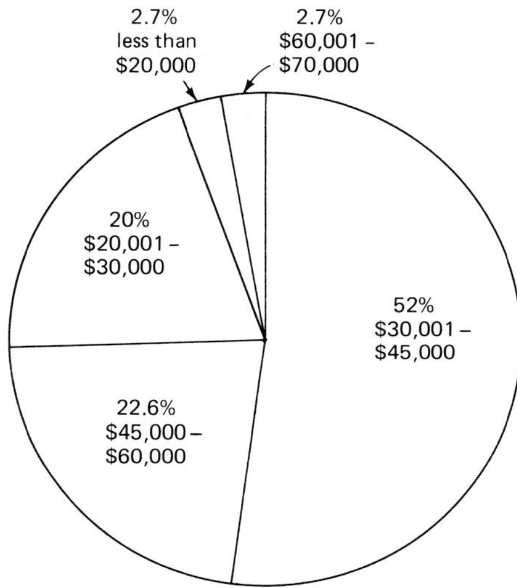

Source: Louisville National Records Mgt. Corp., 1990.

As the pie chart illustrates, approximately 25 percent of CRMs in this study made salaries in the range of $45,001 to $70,000 while 23 percent earned salaries of less than $30,000. The midpoint of $44,000 in the ARMA study on compensation appears to correlate with the statistics reported in the 1990 Louisville National Records Management Corporation study. (Source: Louisville National Records Management Corporation, "Certified Records Managers: Responsibilities; Influence; Future Prospects." May, 1990.)

Records/Information Management Career Ladder

As an educational service, the Association of Records Managers and Administrators (ARMA) has developed the Records and Information Management Career Ladder shown in Figure 1-9. This graphic representation of a typical job ladder, prepared by the Job Descriptions and Salary Guidelines Committee of ARMA, shows various job titles in records and information management that students and current records personnel can aspire to. The committee's goal was to provide a set of generic job titles and descriptions; these job titles were not intended to reflect any one industry.

The generic job descriptions for the job titles shown in Figure 1-9 are re-

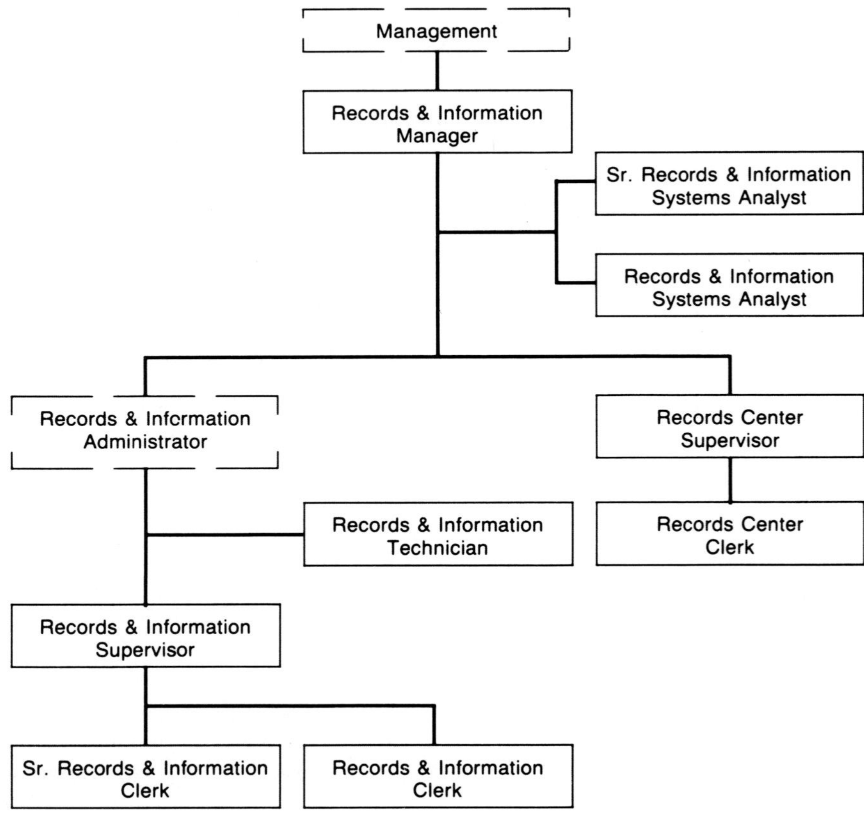

FIGURE 1-9 Records and information management career ladder. (Courtesy of ARMA, 4200 Somerset Drive, Suite 215, Prairie Village, KS 66208.)

printed in abbreviated form in Appendix A. The complete job descriptions (available from ARMA) contain the position titles, functions, duties and responsibilities, principal contacts, position requirements, education/experience requirements, jobs previously held, and career mobility information. Chapter 2 presents more detailed information on staffing records management systems.

Professional Organizations

Outstanding professional trade organizations are available to records management personnel. Many benefits accrue to those who join these organizations, such as attending seminars, workshops, and annual meetings, and obtaining subscriptions to the records management periodicals. The programs for the seminars and meetings usually attract equipment dealers who are eager to display the latest systems or machines. Book publishers are also on hand to display up-to-date textbooks and resource materials. Appendix C lists professional organizations available to records management professionals.

The Institute of Certified Records Managers (ICRM) Founded in 1975, the Institute of Certified Records Managers (ICRM) is the official certifying organization of professional records managers and administrative officers who specialize in the field of records and information management. Celebrating its 15th anniversary in 1990, the ICRM has certified over 600 individuals as Certified Records Managers (CRMs). Membership is international including CRMs from the United States as well as Canada, Europe, Africa, and Australia. Figure 1.10 illustrates the certificate an individual is awarded upon successfully passing all six parts of the CRM examination.

Candidates interested in becoming certified must apply to the ICRM Certification Standards Committee and must meet the criteria established for both education and professional work experience. In order to become a CRM, a candidate must have a minimum of three years of full-time professional experience in records management, must have a baccalaureate degree from an accredited four-year institution, and must pass all parts of the Certified Records Manager examination.

The six parts of the CRM examination are as follows:

Part I: Management Principles and the Records Management Program

Part II: Records Creation and Use

Part III: Records Systems, Storage, and Retrieval

Part IV: Records Appraisal, Retention, Protection, and Disposition

Part V: Equipment, Supplies, and Technology

Part VI: Case Studies

Parts I thru V include multiple choice questions as well as short answer essay questions. Part VI, Case Studies, tests the candidate's ability to analyze a problem and write a clear solution to the problem. Since the case studies are comprehensive, the candidate is given a total of four hours to complete the three case problems.

The designation CRM is as important to the records manager as CPA is to an accountant. These titles indicate a high degree of professionalism and competency in an individual area. A prospective candidate may write to the ICRM

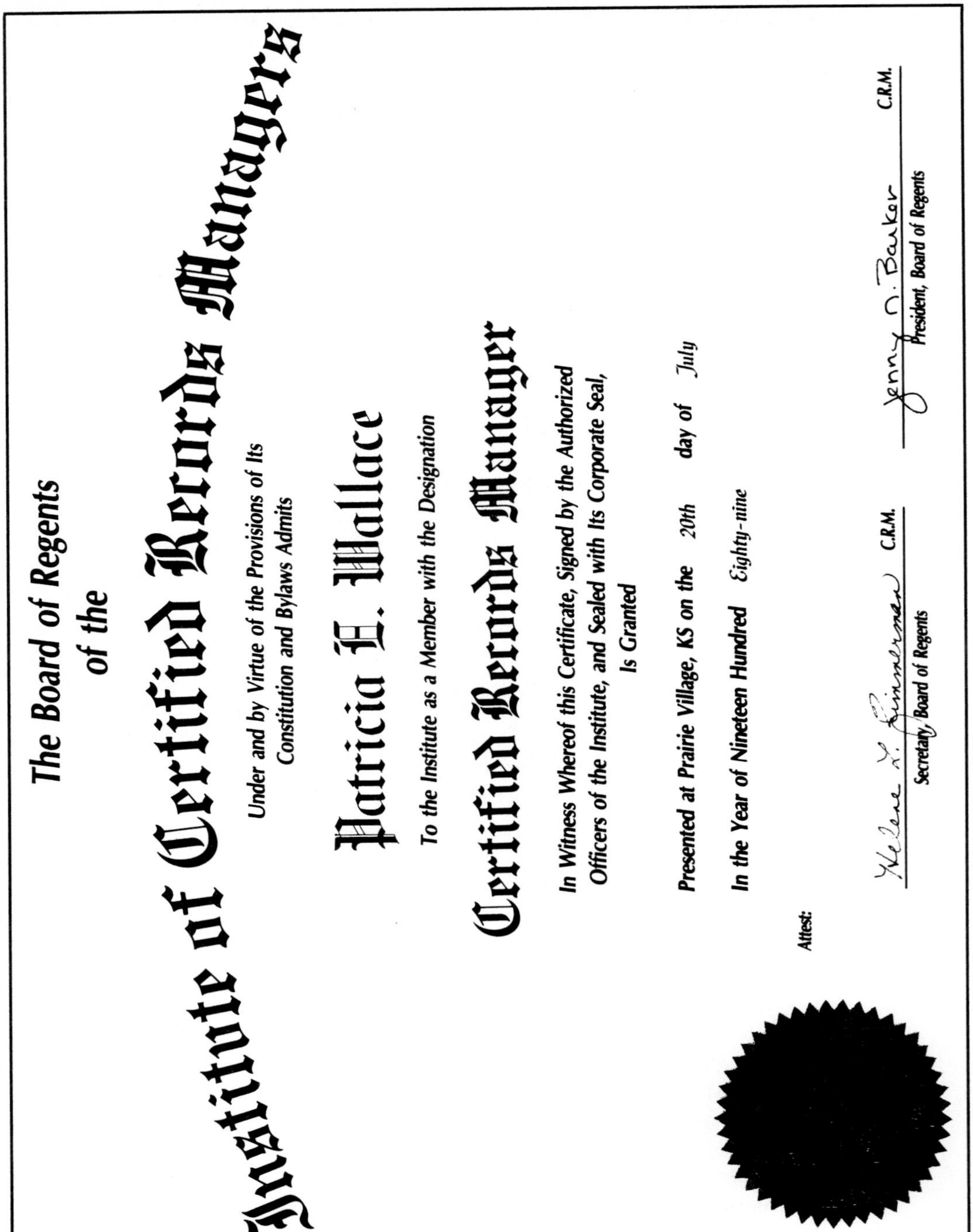

The Board of Regents
of the

Institute of Certified Records Managers

Under and by Virtue of the Provisions of Its
Constitution and Bylaws Admits

Patricia E. Wallace

To the Institute as a Member with the Designation

Certified Records Manager

In Witness Whereof this Certificate, Signed by the Authorized
Officers of the Institute, and Sealed with Its Corporate Seal,
Is Granted

Presented at Prairie Village, KS on the *20th* day of *July*

In the Year of Nineteen Hundred *Eighty-nine*

Attest:

C.R.M.
Secretary, Board of Regents

C.R.M.
President, Board of Regents

FIGURE 1-10

for a handbook titled, "Preparing for the CRM Examination." This book contains sample examination questions, a study guide, bibliography, and other instructions and guidelines. Details may be obtained from the following address:

Institute of Certified Records Managers
P.O. Box 8188, Prairie Village, KS 66208

See Appendix B for additional information on the CRM examination.

The Association of Records Managers and Administrators (ARMA) Started in 1955 as the American Records Management Association, ARMA has emerged as the most prominent records and information management association in the world. Now—in the decade of the 90s—ARMA has over 10,000 members worldwide including chapters in the United States, Canada, Puerto Rico, New Zealand, and Japan. ARMA's objectives are as follows:

1. To promote and advance the improvement of records and information management and related fields through study, education, and research
2. To advance professional knowledge and techniques by sharing and exchanging experiences and information related to the field of records and information management
3. To develop and advance standards of professional competence in the field of records and information management[1]

ARMA International's continued commitment to excellence is exemplified in its membership benefits and professional publications. ARMA members benefit through continuing education at professional conferences, technical publications, and networking opportunities. For more information regarding ARMA International, see Appendix A.

The Association of Information and Image Management (AIIM) Founded in 1943, the Association for Information and Image Management (AIIM) provides a forum which contributes to the effective development and application of information and image management systems. Serving both corporate and individual members, AIIM provides solutions to the most important challenge facing organizations today—the management of document-based images. The information and image management industry now represents 5 percent of information storage.[2]

AIIM provides members with information on the storage, transfer and retrieval of document-based information. AIIM members are concerned with

[1]ARMA, *Records and Information Management* (Prairie Village, KS: Association of Records Managers and Administrators).

[2]AIIM, *Your Access to Information and Image Management Solutions.* (Silver Springs, MD, February, 1990).

electronic imaging, micrographics, optical disks, image transmission, and document digitization, to name just a few topics. AIIM members benefit through professional publications, equipment buying guides, a resource center, and regional as well as national seminars.

International Records Management Council Founded in 1971, the International Records Management Council (IRMC) is comprised of members from over 40 countries around the world. The IRMC was organized by the American Records Management Association now ARMA, the South African Records Management Association, and the Records Management Association of Australia. This international professional association seeks to advance the records management profession through professional conferences, research, publications, and membership growth.

History of Records Management

Definition of Records Management

Records management is the planning and controlling of records from the time of their creation until their final disposition. This disposition may be either permanent retention or destruction after the documents have fulfilled their purpose.

A more comprehensive definition was drafted by the U.S. Postal Service and the Civil Service Committee in H.R. 14935 and was introduced by the Honorable Richard C. White in the Ninety-third Congress, Second Session, on May 21, 1974. The bill defines records management as follows:

> . . . the planning, controlling, directing, organizing, training, promoting, and other managerial activities involved with respect to records creation, records maintenance and use, and records disposition, including the management of correspondence, forms, directives, reports, machine-readable records, microforms, information retrieval, files, mail, vital records, records equipment and supplies, word processing and source data automation techniques, records preservation, records disposal, and records centers or other storage facilities.[3]

Records Management Events and Legislation (1930s–1950s)

The Hoover Studies President Harry Truman recognized the need for a well-planned records management program in order to control the volumes of records generated by World War II. He issued an executive order on September 25, 1946, requiring all agencies of the executive branch of the

[3]The Honorable Richard C. White, *Records Management Journal,* Vol. 12, No. 2 (Summer 1974), p. 16.

federal government to implement programs that would provide not only for the management of their records, but also for the proper disposition of records. The following year, President Truman approved the Lodge-Brown Act, which established the Commission on Organization of the Executive Branch of the Government. President Truman appointed former President Herbert Hoover to chair the commission. In 1948, the commission studied the operation, organization, and policies of the government in broad areas of governmental functions. Emmett J. Leahy chaired the Task Force on Paperwork Management, whose conclusions and recommendations were reviewed by the commission in reaching its conclusions.

General Recommendations of the First Hoover Commission The commission recommended the following:

1. Create a Records Management Bureau in the Office of General Services to include the National Archives.
2. Enact a new Federal Records Act to provide for the more effective creation, preservation, management, and disposition of U.S. government records.
3. Establish an adequate records management program in each department and agency of the federal government.

Legislation Resulting from the First Hoover Commission Two laws were passed following the recommendations of the first Hoover Commission. The first, the Federal Property and Administrative Services Act of 1949, established the General Services Administration and authorized the transfer of the National Archives to the General Services Administration. Also, the administrator of the General Services Administration was authorized to survey government records and to promote improved practices and controls in the area of records management.

The second law passed after the Hoover Commission recommendations was the Federal Records Act of 1950. Proper control and improvement of procedures in creating records was outlined as a responsibility of the GSA administrator. The administrator was also given the responsibility for disposing of outdated records.

The Second Hoover Commission On July 10, 1953, President Eisenhower approved Public Law 108, the Brown-Ferguson Act, which provided for a second Commission on Organization of the Executive Branch of the Government. In 1954, former President Hoover headed the commission and again he asked Emmett J. Leahy to serve as chairperson of the Task Force on Paperwork Management. The task force reported that $15 million worth of useless paperwork costs to companies and government agencies were eliminated as a result of its study.

The task force study uncovered the following:

1. A large number of reports were required of industry by a government agency, although the information was already on hand in another bureau down the hall.
2. Great quantities of records submitted by industry were not used and, in one case, not even filed by the government.
3. Nearly a million reports were submitted reporting that there was nothing to report.
4. Reports or pages of reports were deliberately omitted by industry but never missed by the government.[4]

As a result of the findings of the task force, the second Hoover Commission made two major recommendations to Congress. The first recommendation included three proposals:

1. The president shall establish a government-wide paperwork management program.
2. The GSA shall be given responsibility for supervision over all phases of paperwork management throughout the executive branch of the government.
3. The National Archives and Records Service paperwork management shall be consolidated in the General Services Administration.

The second major recommendation of the commission was that one official in each governmental agency shall be responsible for reducing the volume of paperwork in that agency.

The General Services Administration now recognized the need for guidelines in the retention time of records. As a result, the GSA published the *Guide to Records Retention Requirements* in 1955 and a second edition the following year. The *Guide to Records Retention Requirements* is published annually and may be obtained from the Superintendent of Documents, U.S. Government Printing Office, Washington, D. C. 20402.

A summary of the major events affecting records management history from the 1930s through the 1950s, including important legislation, is detailed in Table 1-2.

Current Records Management Events and Legislation (1960s–1990s)

Freedom of Information Act During the past few decades, records management has been affected greatly by several key pieces of legislation. Passed in 1966, the Freedom of Information Act permits individuals to obtain information on the operation of federal agencies. Meeting the demands of this

[4]"Report on Paperwork Management, Part II," prepared for the Commission on Organization of the Executive Branch of the Government, June 1955, p. 1.

TABLE 1-2 SUMMARY OF RECORDS MANAGEMENT HISTORY AND LEGISLATION (1930s–1950s)

Year	*Event*
1934	United States National Archives established
1943	Records Disposal Act—authorized use of the records disposal schedule developed by the national Archives
1948	First Hoover Commission—task force created to study the records management problems of the federal government
1949	General Services Administration established; National Archives transferred to GSA
1950	Federal Records Act—defined records management and directed federal agencies to establish and maintain effective records management programs
1952	Nine federal records centers established throughout the country
1954	Federal agencies reported that 95 percent of their records were covered by records retention schedules
1954	Second Hoover Commission established the Task force on Paperwork Management
1955	The first *Guide to Records Retention Requirements* published by the GSA

legislation greatly increased the importance of records management programs. The amendments to the Freedom of Information Act, passed in 1974, were set forth in three subsections as follows:

*Each Federal agency is required to make information available to the public regarding agency rules, opinions, orders, records, and proceedings.

*Withholding of information by the Federal government is permissible, but must be justified by one of nine specific exemptions included in the Act.

*Federal agencies can withhold only materials "specifically stated" in the Act but cannot withhold such information from Congress.[5]

Privacy Act Also passed in 1974, the Privacy Act safeguards individuals from the wrongful use of personal records held by federal agencies. This act proclaims the rights of individuals to have access to records held by the government, to obtain copies of those records, and to make corrections to records held by government agencies. In addition, it specifies that consent must be given before one's personal records are reviewed by others and permits individuals to determine who has reviewed their records. Specifically, the Privacy Act:

*Limits the disclosure of personal information to authorized persons and agencies;

[5]*Source:* Electronic Recordkeeping, U.S. General Services Administration, July, 1989.

*Requires the maintenance of accurate, relevant, timely, and complete records; and

*Requires the use of administrative, technical, and physical safeguards to ensure the security and integrity of records.[6]

Fair Credit Reporting Act While the above two pieces of legislation pertain to the public sector, the Fair Credit Reporting Act of 1970 applies to the private sector. This legislation allows individuals the opportunity to correct false credit reports held by private agencies, which may affect an individual's ability to obtain mortgages, loans, credit cards, and other forms of credit. An individual has the right to correct any false or misleading information held in such files.

Buckley Amendments Another important even in the records management field was the passage of the Buckley Amendments of 1974, which proclaim the right of parents and young adults (18 years and older) to review records held by schools. Obviously, passage of this legislation greatly increased the records management responsibilities of both public and private educational institutions.

Records Management Amendments Passed to update and supplement the Federal Records Act of 1950, the Federal Records Management Amendments of 1977 stress the "life cycle" concept of records in defining records management. This amendment also emphasizes the importance of paperwork reduction in the government as well as the need to maintain adequate program documentation.

Paperwork Reduction Act The Paperwork Reduction Act of 1980 was an important landmark in the effort to establish consistent federal information policies. The bill created a central office, called the Office of Information Resources Management, which is responsible for setting government-wide information policies and providing control of information management activities. The chairman of the Federal Paperwork Commission, Congressman Frank Horton, stated, "Information is a resource, not a free good. Like all resources, information is an asset to be managed, allocated efficiently, used wisely, and disposed of when it no longer serves a useful purpose."[7] Thus information is recognized by the federal government as a resource that needs to be controlled and managed.

[6]*Source:* Electronic Recordkeeping, U.S. General Services Administration, July, 1989.

[7]Frances E. Fuller, "Records Management in Government: The Paperwork Reduction Act," *Records Management Quarterly*, Vol. 14, No. 2 (April 1980), p. 48.

Table 1-3 STATE COURT SYSTEMS USING LETTER-SIZE PAPER (IN WHOLE OR IN PART)

Alabama	Georgia	New York	Wisconsin
Arizona	Illinois	Oregon	Wyoming
California	Kentucky	Pennsylvania	
Colorado	Minnesota	Utah	
Connecticut	New Jersey	Washington	

Source: Association of Records Managers and Administrators, *Project ELF* (Eliminate Legal Files), Prairie Village, Kansas

Eliminate Legal Files (ELF) Owing to the lobbying efforts of ARMA, the Judicial Conference of the United States decided in 1981 to eliminate the use of legal-size paper in all federal courts. The effective date for conversion to the 8 1/2-by-11-inch standard was January 1, 1983, but many law firms and individuals who deal with the courts converted immediately to lower the cost of paper, storage, and postage and to conserve paper. Many states have since passed similar legislation or made administrative decisions to eliminate the use of legal-size paper in state court systems. Table 1-3 shows the states whose court systems have wholly or partially eliminated the use of legal-size paper.

Electronic Communications Privacy Act The intent of the 1986 Electronic Communications Privacy Act is to establish penalties for the intentional interception of electronically transmitted information. Since the use of electronics for transmitting information has escalated, this Act defines electronic communications and describes prohibited activities.

According to this Act, "Electronic communications" means any transfer of signs, signals, writing images, sounds, data, or intelligence of any nature transmitted in whole or in part by a wire, radio, electromagnetic, photoelectronic, or photo-optical system that affects interstate of foreign commerce. Prohibited activities under this Act include the attempted or actual interception, use, or disclosure of wire, oral, or electronic communications to which access is not authorized. According to this Act, such unauthorized access must be intentional and, therefore, is subject to penalties.[8]

A summary of records management events and legislation from the 1960s to the present time is depicted in Table 1-4.

[8]*Source:* Electronic Recordkeeping, U.S. General Services Administration, Washington, D. C., July, 1989.

TABLE 1-4 RECORDS MANAGEMENT EVENTS AND LEGISLATION (1960s to PRESENT)

Year	*Event*
1966	Freedom of Information Act—permits individuals to obtain information on the operation of federal agencies
1970	Fair Credit Report Act—allows individuals to view credit reports and correct false statements
1974	Buckley Amendments—permits parents and young adults to review school records
1974	Freedom of Information Act Amendments—permits individuals to obtain copies of their personal records from federal agencies
1974	Privacy Act—protects individuals from the misuse of personal records held by the federal government
1976	Federal Records Management Amendments—clarify and update the provisions of the Federal Records Act of 1950
1980	Paperwork Reduction Act—emphasizes the need to manage information as a resource
1983	*Report of the Proceedings of the Judicial Conference of the United States*—included an administrative decision to eliminate the use of legal-size paper in federal courts
1986	Electronic Communications Privacy Act—establishes penalties for the intentional interception of electronically transmitted information.

CHAPTER HIGHLIGHTS

- Records management is the planning and controlling of records from the time of their creation until their final disposition.
- Records—recorded information—can be in paper-based, microform-based, or electronic-based form.
- Records management's overall goal is to provide the right information, at the right time, in the right order, to the right person, at the lowest possible cost.
- The designation CRM (Certified Records Manager) indicates a high degree of professionalism and competency in records management.
- Outstanding professional trade organizations, such as ARMA and AIIM, are available for membership by records management personnel.
- The National Archives and Records Service is responsible for developing and maintaining retention schedules, storing records, referencing inactive records, and controlling all records of continuing value for the federal government.
- Developing a comprehensive records management system requires an organized approach to the management of recorded information.
- The records manager must be knowledgeable about the ever-evolving tech-

nological advancements in equipment and systems and about new government regulations.

- Records managers must be able to integrate all forms of records storage into their records management systems and be willing to incorporate the use of automated office technologies into their programs.

QUESTIONS FOR REVIEW

1. Define records management and the various types of recorded information that should be included in a records management program.
2. Describe the life cycle of a business record.
3. Identify the overall objective of records management and list at least three secondary objectives of records management.
4. What is a records management system?
5. Name and describe at least four subsystems or components of records management.
6. Describe Project ELF and its impact on the federal court system.
7. Indicate how records management fits into the administrative services structure of an organization.
8. What is ICRM and how does one attain CRM designation?
9. Describe two professional associations in records management and the advantages of joining such organizations.
10. List at least three recent records management legislation (or events) that occurred in the 1980's.

THE DECISION MAKER

Case Studies

1. Top management at Sunshine Products, a Fortune 500 corporation, is concerned about the company's fragmented approach to managing information throughout the organization. Currently, each department handles its own records, regardless of their form. For example, the accounting department uses many business forms in its daily operations; they create or procure the forms on their own. In the personnel department, which handles all employee records, the staff lack an awareness of current retention requirements. The purchasing department is running out of files storage space, because the manager refuses to discard any records. The administrative services director is alarmed by the increasing amount of paperwork that comes through his department. What actions should Sunshine Products take in order to remedy the problems of the accounting, personnel, purchasing, and administrative services departments?

2. For the past ten years, the office manager of Burton Legal Associates has been managing the law firm's paper records. In the last few years, however, the firm has begun using records in digital form as well as microforms. The manager of the word processing center has been storing the digital-based records, while an administrative assistant has been charged with the management of the micrographic records. While attending an ARMA seminar, the office manager realizes that this approach needs to be corrected. What remedy can you suggest for this law firm? How can the office manager tactfully inform those charged with digital-based and micrographic records that a change is needed?

ORGANIZATION AND STAFFING OF RECORDS MANAGEMENT SYSTEMS

OBJECTIVES

Upon completion of this chapter, the student should be able to:

1. Describe the records system.
2. Explain how to conduct a feasibility study for a records management system.
3. Identify the educational needs of records management personnel.
4. Describe the advantages and disadvantages of using internal vs. external personnel in planning records systems.
5. Identify the career opportunities and duties of records management personnel.
6. Explain how to implement a training program for all employees.
7. Describe effective ways of supervising and evaluating employees.

Records Management is both a business function and a profession. Today's records managers play a significant role in contributing to an organization's efficiency and effectiveness. All organizations, regardless of their size, have records. The same care must be taken in smaller organizations as in larger organizations to maintain and preserve the records. The smaller organization will, no doubt, have fewer records than the larger organization, but this does not mean that those records are of any lesser importance. The successful operation of a business organization is highly dependent on the effectiveness of its records management program.

Planning the Records System

A system is an array of components that when functioning together form a unified whole. The components of a records system include the people, procedures, budget, equipment, and facilities that are necessary to control the records of an organization. The records systems may be quite sophisticated comprising electronic files, imaging, micrographics, and off-site storage; or it may be quite simple, including just a few filing cabinets with one person in control. Regardless of size, the records management system needs to interact effectively with each of its components as well as the larger organization system of which it is a part. Figure 2.1 below illustrates the components of the records systems in relation to the total organization system in which it operates.

Steps in planning the records system include determining:

*Organizational placement
*Goals and objectives
*Functions and responsibilities
*Staffing and training needs

Organizational Placement of Records Management

Often the records manager occupies a middle-management position, on the same level as the office administrator. On a triangle marking the different levels of management, the records manager position in many organizations would be right in the middle (see Figure 2-2).

Top management, in many organizations, is the policy-making and decision-making level. Middle management is also a decision-making level and acts as the go-between for upper and lower management. The lower level of management supervises employees and is responsible for achieving production goals.

An **organization chart** shows the line of authority and the span of control in a firm. Figure 2-3 portrays the line of authority and the span of control for the

FIGURE 2.1
The Organization System and Subsystems

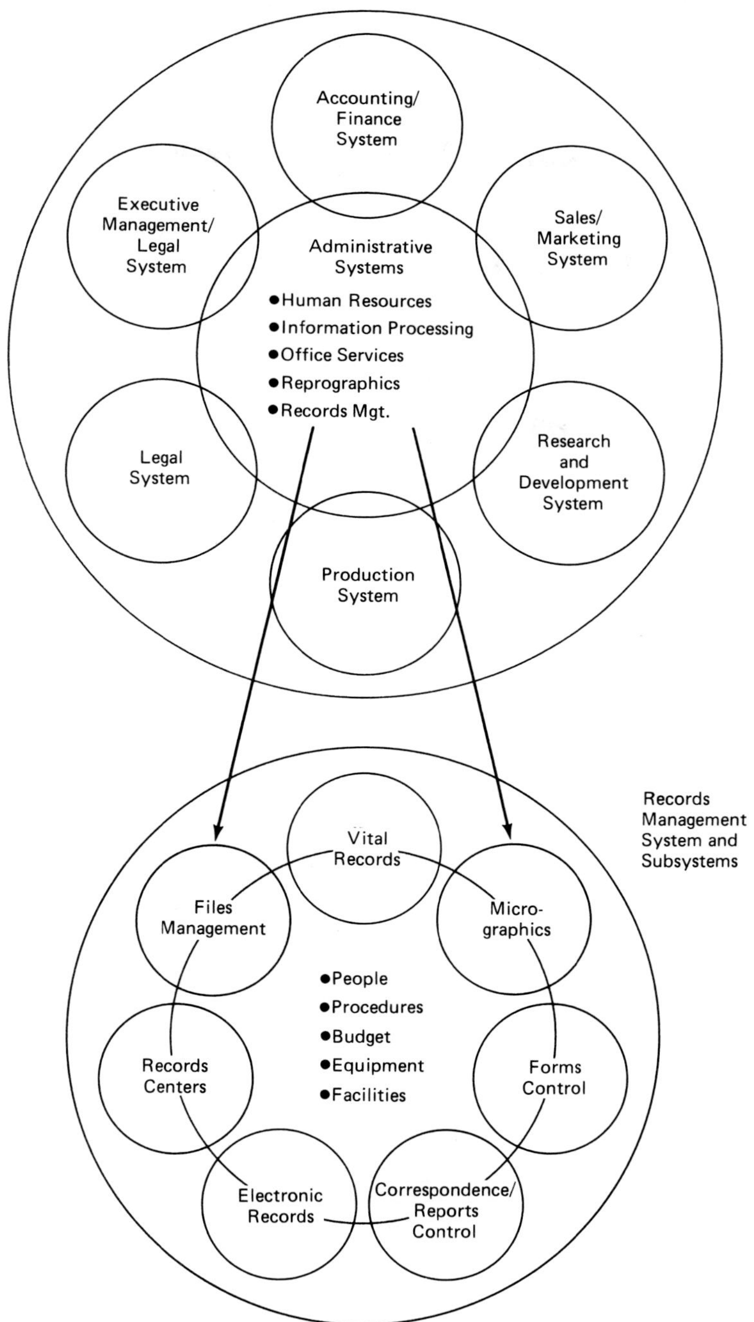
Accounting/
Finance
System
Executive
Management/
Legal
System
Sales/
Marketing
System
Administrative
Systems
●Human Resources
●Information Processing
●Office Services
●Reprographics
●Records Mgt.
Legal
System
Research
and
Development
System
Production
System
Records
Management
System and
Subsystems
Vital
Records
Files
Management
Micro-
graphics
●People
●Procedures
●Budget
●Equipment
●Facilities
Records
Centers
Forms
Control
Electronic
Records
Correspondence/
Reports
Control

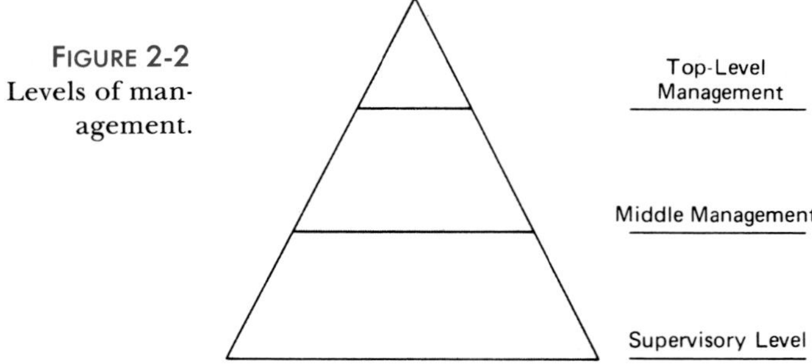

FIGURE 2-2
Levels of management.

records manager of Tenneco Inc. The chart depicts the records manager and those individuals who are under his or her supervision.

Within an organization, records management is considered part of the information service function that generally falls under administrative services. Thus, on a typical organization chart, records management is placed on the same level as other related services. Figure 2-4 is an organization chart that shows the records manager on the same middle-management level as the managers of Information Processing (IP), Administrative Systems, and Office Services. In this type of arrangement, the Director of Administrative Services, usually a vice president or similar top-level management position, would have

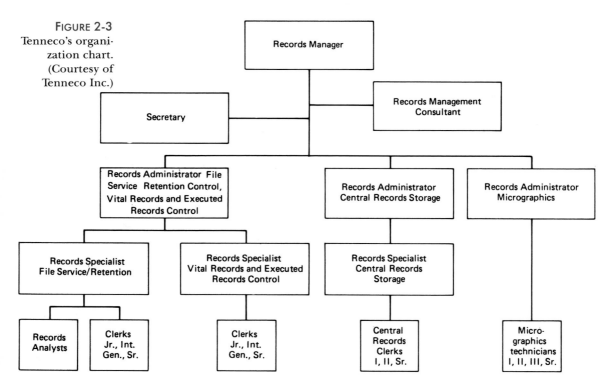

FIGURE 2-3
Tenneco's organization chart. (Courtesy of Tenneco Inc.)

Records Manager

Secretary

Records Management Consultant

Records Administrator File Service Retention Control, Vital Records and Executed Records Control

Records Administrator Central Records Storage

Records Administrator Micrographics

Records Specialist File Service/Retention

Records Specialist Vital Records and Executed Records Control

Records Specialist Central Records Storage

Records Analysts

Clerks Jr., Int. Gen., Sr.

Clerks Jr., Int. Gen., Sr.

Central Records Clerks I, II, Sr.

Micro-graphics technicians I, II, III, Sr.

FIGURE 2-4 Typical administrative services organization chart.

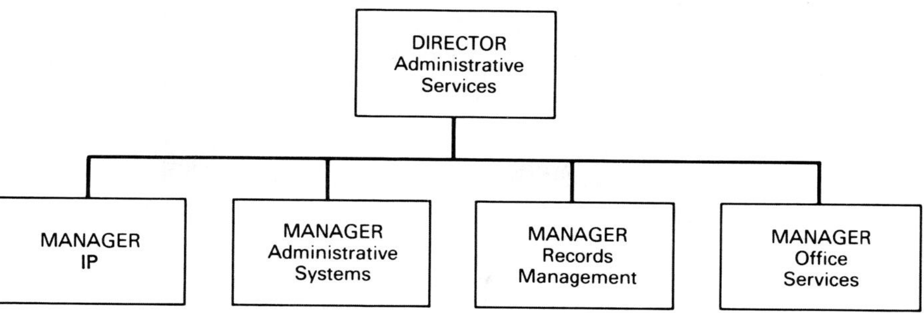

control of all the various information service functions. The records manager would be responsible for achieving the records management program objectives, which would vary depending on the goals of the organization. A 1987 study by Hay Management Consultants for ARMA International notes that records managers report to the head of Administrative Services in 35 percent of the organizations surveyed. Other functional reporting relationships are noted in Figure 2.5 below. Conversely, the same study reported that in many instances the Records Manager has other functions reporting to him or her as noted below.

FIGURE 2-5 Records Management Reporting Relationships In Percentages

Functional Area	*RM Reports to*	*Functions Reporting to RM*
Administrative Services	35	10
Data Processing	11	3
Facilities Management	24	5
Library	16	11
Mail Services	35	14
Purchasing	17	3
Telecommunications	16	3
Word Processing	24	6

Source: Compensation and Benefits Survey of Records Management Positions, ARMA International, 1987.

Size is also an important determinant of organizational structure. In a small company, the degree of specialization may not be found and the office manager may be in charge of all the information service functions depicted in Figure 2-4.

Goals and Objectives in Records Management

The mission or overall goal of an organization is usually directed toward its prime reason for existence, i.e., to produce goods or to provide services. For example, a transportation company would have as its mission to provide superior transportation services to their customers while an automobile manufacturer would endeavor to produce high-quality automobiles to its consumers. Since the records management department needs to obtain management support for its continued existence, records managers need to be aware of corporate goals and objectives to survive and flourish. While goals are stated in general terms, objectives are specific and measurable. Some specific records management objectives are as follows:

1. Reduce records misfiles to 3 percent.
2. Decrease paper records storage by 20 percent.
3. Provide retrieval time of 5 minutes for records requests.
4. Increase micrographic storage by 10 percent.

Conducting the Systems Study

Establishing a new records management system or revitalizing an existing one requires a systems study to determine if the proposed system or proposed changes will be cost-effective, improve productivity, and satisfy user requirements. Before the records management program can be implemented, a system study must be undertaken to ascertain the appropriate course of action. The objective of a systems study is to assess the current situation to determine what changes are necessitated. Next, the design of the new system or program is arrived at to modify the existing deficiency. The third step is to implement the modifications arrived at during the design stage. Evaluation is the fourth and final step of the study to determine if the new system or modifications had a significant impact on the problem. Figure 2.6 illustrates the systems study process.

A popular systems study tool available to records personnel is the feasibility study. A feasibility study is a survey of all functions performed by both management and support staff in the records management department. The goal of the study is to determine if the proposed changes are necessary or desirable. The results also provide management with direction in carrying out the proposed changes. The records manager should involve his or her staff, administrators, and key office personnel in planning the feasibility study. A liaison person may be appointed in each department to communicate with the feasibility study committee. The liaison person will keep the planning committee informed as to work flow, revisions of procedures, updated materials, and problems experienced in records management. Figure 2.7 shows the steps in conducting a feasibility study.

FIGURE 2.6
Systems Study Process

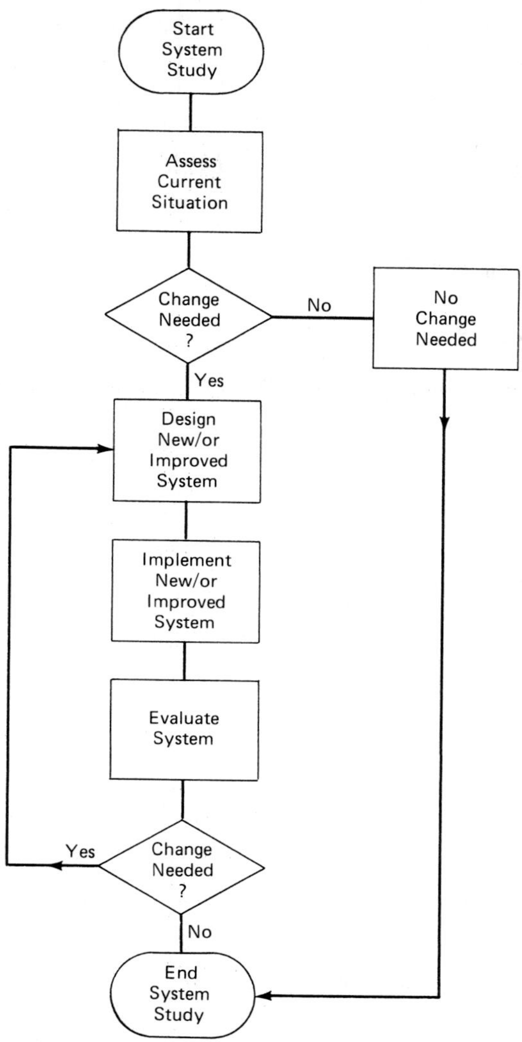

For most feasibility studies, the following steps are recommended:

1. Tour the facility, giving particular attention to the area or unit being studied.
2. Conduct orientation sessions with management personnel.
3. Conduct orientation sessions with all support staff who will be involved in the study.
4. Conduct personal interviews with support staff and management.
5. Collect and coordinate information pertaining to the existing organizational structure, including work samples and statistical data.

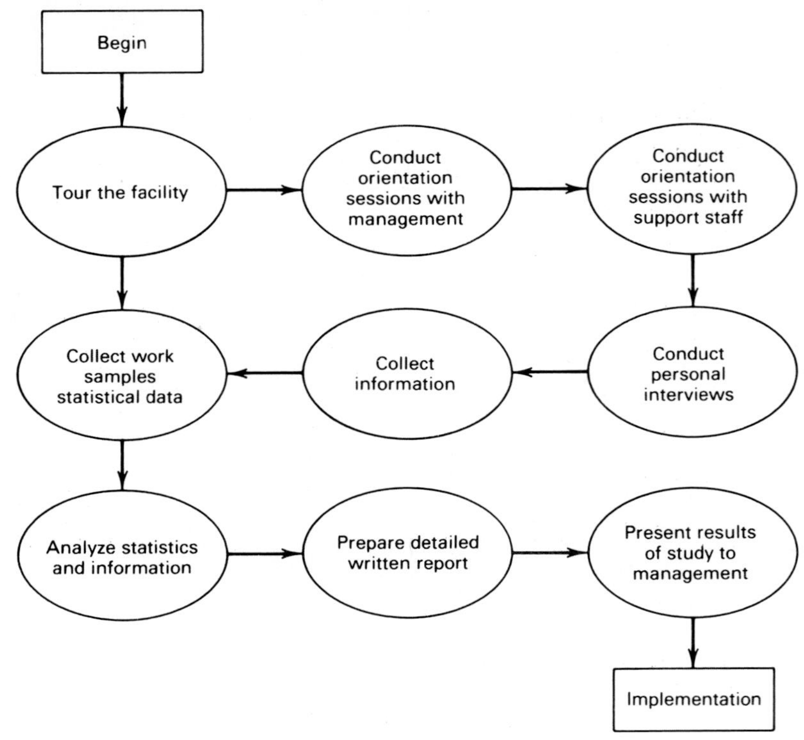

FIGURE 2-7 Conducting a feasibility study. *Source:* Mary M. Ruprecht and Kathleen P. Wagoner, *Managing Office Automation* (New York: John Wiley & Sons, Inc., copyright © 1984), p. 309.

6. Analyze all the statistics and information and verify the results with the management of each department.
7. Prepare a detailed written report.
8. Present the results of the study to management decision makers.[1]

This approach to organizing or modifying an existing records management program ensures that the proposed changes will be based on a detailed analysis of information collected, together with the informed opinions of those directly involved with the current records management system.

Brainstorming, staff meetings, seminars, speakers, equipment vendors, and field trips to other organizations and libraries will provide invaluable assistance in the decision-making process.

Once a tentative plan for the records system has been approved by administration, the third step is a trial run to work out the flaws that may not have been encountered during the decision-making process. An **office layout**

[1]Mary M. Ruprecht and Kathleen P. Wagoner, *Managing Office Automation* (New York: John Wiley & Sons, Inc., copyright © 1984), pp. 308–309.

should be drawn in detail to give personnel an opportunity to evaluate the proposed change. New **job descriptions** should be written to reflect the new duties for each position that may evolve from the change. Work flow and communication patterns must be given consideration to ensure a cost-effective operation.

Using Internal or External Personnel

Before conducting a feasibility study, the study team must be selected. Management must decide whether to use internal personnel from the records management department or to hire external consultants to proceed with the study. The choice between the two depends on several important considerations, such as:

1. Do internal personnel have the necessary experience to conduct the feasibility study?
2. Do internal personnel have both the time and the desire to conduct the feasibility study?
3. Will external personnel be more effective in collecting and interpreting data in an objective fashion?
4. Will the hiring of external personnel place unnecessary constraints on the budget?
5. Which personnel—internal or external—will be more cost-effective?
6. Which personnel—internal or external—will complete the study in the shorter period of time?
7. Will internal personnel accept the results of hired consultants and be willing to implement them?
8. Will company employees accept and implement the results of the study if it is conducted by internal personnel?

Such questions need to be considered seriously before the selection of a study team.

Before deciding whether to use a consultant from inside or outside the organization, there are advantages and disadvantages to be considered.

Advantages of using an internal consultant are:

1. The internal consultant already has an understanding of the office and its operations.
2. The cost is usually less than for an outside consultant.
3. The work flow of the office should proceed normally, since the internal consultant probably can perform the work during the normal hours of the day without too much disruption of workers' activities.
4. The internal consultant will be available to work on problems that may develop in the future.

Disadvantages of using an internal consultant are:

1. The employee may not be knowledgeable in all phases of records management.
2. Co-workers may not be willing to share information or documents that they consider to be confidential in their sections.
3. The internal consultant may look on the project as just another task to be completed and lack enthusiasm.

Advantages of using an outside consultant are:

1. The outside consultant will be knowledgeable about new equipment, systems that have proved successful, and personnel required to manage any new system.
2. The outside consultant will devote full time to the work and thus will probably formulate recommendations much sooner than the internal consultant who has to attend to routine duties while also acting as a consultant to the business firm.
3. The outside consultant is more apt to be objective in proposing recommendations.
4. The outside consultant may be more successful in overcoming resistance to change by other employees.

Disadvantages of using an outside consultant include:

1. The cost is much greater, naturally, than if an employee acts as a consultant to the firm.
2. The outside consultant may make quick decisions without delving deeply enough into the cause of an organization's records management difficulties.
3. The consultant's recommendations may not offer enough detail to implement them effectively.
4. The outside consultant may not be available to address problems or concerns after the feasibility study is completed.

Once the decision has been made to hire a consultant, top management should give wholeheartedly of their support and work closely with the records manager in implementing the records management system. Consultants should be encouraged to work closely with internal personnel to involve them as much as possible with the data collection, analysis, and final report recommendations. Office personnel should be apprised of the plans early in the process, and key personnel should assist in revamping the records system. Each department should be represented by a person who is knowledgeable about the operations of the department and who has an appreciation for the importance of the task.

Importance of Communication

Lateral and vertical lines of communication must be open for all office personnel, and especially so during the period of changing procedures. Top-level management must be accessible to middle-management employees, such as the records manager. In turn, the records manager must communicate with the lower-level supervisory employees, including the liaison person from each department. The records manager, as the middle-management employee, is the go-between for top-level management and lower-level management.

Control of Records

The control of records is a responsibility of the entire records staff, including the records manager. The number of staff members in an organization will depend on the size of the office, the type of business, and the records system. The records program includes the control of records from the time of their creation until their final disposition or permanent retention.

The formal records program encompasses the records manual, which outlines the procedures in detail; the retention and disposition schedule; the inventory; the equipment; and job descriptions for the records staff who keep the system operating effectively and efficiently.

THE ROLE OF THE RECORDS/INFORMATION MANAGER

The records manager cannot be successful in directing a records management program if top management is indifferent or unsupportive of the program. The first requirement, then, for the successful implementation of a records management program is active support by top administrators. Once this is assured, the records manager can proceed with confidence.

The records manager faces a Herculean task in becoming knowledgeable about the many possibilities of records control in the 1990s. In addition to the ever-evolving technological advancement in equipment and systems, new regulations—federal, state, and local—constantly come into being. These new regulations often affect the control of records.

Records Control

Regardless of the size of the office in which records are created, the life cycle of all records is the same. A **record's life cycle** spans the time from its origination until its final disposition, whether that disposition is permanent retention or destruction. Records must be controlled throughout their life cycle in order to be handled efficiently. This control must begin with the creation of the records. Records control also includes responsibility for the records' justification and maintenance, for use of the records according to established procedures, and, finally, for disposition of the records. Control of the records should be under the management of a person who understands their importance to the life of the business. Only a well-qualified records manager can perform the essential duties in an effective manner.

Records management has been developing over the centuries from a simple method of records security to the present-day sophisticated control methods. Records managers have many options available for selecting a system of records control. These systems of control are presented throughout this textbook. Selecting the most effective records control system for a business is one of the responsibilities of the records manager.

Qualifications of the Records Manager

For a records manager to fulfill his or her duties effectively, certain qualifications are needed. Qualifications needed for effectively directing a records program are acquired through academic preparation as well as through experience in the business world. Experience in areas of records management as well as in all phases of office work is certainly beneficial to the records manager. Office experience, regardless of the type of work, gives the manager an awareness of the flow and pattern of work and the purpose of documents. A person who cannot tell the difference between an invoice and a statement is apt to go astray in establishing guidelines for their retention or destruction. Do you know which is the invoice in Figure 2-8? A greater confidence in knowing the purpose of documents generated in an office will aid the records manager in fulfilling the duties and responsibilities of the position.

Academic preparation for a career as a records manager should include courses in office administration as well as other business courses, such as economics, accounting, management, communication, and information processing. In addition, history courses are excellent in providing an awareness of the historical value of documents for preservation in an archives. A degree in office administration, information management, or business administration is highly desirable.

In addition to academic preparation and experience in business, a top priority in preparing for a career in records management is the art of communication. This skill, whether used in written or oral communication, should not

FIGURE 2-8
An invoice and a statement, for comparison.

Quantity	Description	Price	Total

			Balance
Date	Purchases	Payments	Balance Due

be underestimated by business persons, and especially not by the records manager. Understanding the principles of effective written communication enables the records manager to write and update records manuals, to write instructions and guidelines that are clear and concise, and to communicate with top management through well-written reports and proposals. The ability to communicate orally is equally important in supervising personnel. An articulate person will give clear, correct, and complete instructions to supervisees.

Duties of the Records Manager

The *Dictionary of Occupational Titles,* which is published by the U.S. Department of Labor, lists several titles for the records manager. Among the titles listed are records management director, management analyst, forms analysis manager, records analysis manager, reports analysis manager, forms analyst, records management analyst, and reports analyst. These positions would not all necessarily cover the entire scope of records management, but the titles do indicate positions with administrative duties. The duties given by the *Dictionary of Occupational Titles* for the records management director are:

> Plans, develops, and administers records management policies designed to facilitate effective and efficient handling of business records and other information. Plans development and implementation of records management policies intended to standardize filing, protecting, and retrieving records, reports, and other information contained on paper, microfilm, computer program, or other media. Coordinates and directs, through subordinate managers, activities of departments involved with records management analysis, reports analysis, and supporting technical, clerical, micrographics, and printing services. Evaluates staff reports, utilizing knowledge of principles of records and information management, administrative processes and systems, cost control, governmental recordkeeping requirements, and organizational objectives. Confers with other administrators to assure compliance with policies, procedures, and practices of records management program.[2]

Records managers must be thoroughly skilled in the techniques and principles of records management if they expect to take full responsibility as qualified administrators. They need to be acquainted with computerized records and computer-based systems, word processing, effective personnel supervision, updated systems of records management, and administrative procedures in business organizations.

In comparing the duties given in the *Canadian Classification and Dictionary of Occupations* for records manager, one finds that the duties are similar for Cana-

[2]*Dictionary of Occupational Titles*, 4th ed. (Washington, DC: U.S. Department of Labor, 1977), pp. 93–94.

dian records managers. See Figure 2-9 for the position description of the records manager at Tenneco Inc.

TENNECO

POSITION DESCRIPTION

I. Position Title Corporate Records Manager — Date January, 1982

Reports To Director (Title) — Department Office Services

Director ~~Supervisor~~ Reports To V.P.; AIS (Title) — Location Corporate Records Management

II. PURPOSE AND DUTIES: Directs and evaluates internal department operating procedures, standards and controls for activities involved in the File Service, Retention Control, Central Records Storage, Microfilm, Vital Records and Executed Records Control operations. Recommends and consults with all officers and department heads with reference to requirements for records retention and systems. Interviews and employs Records Management personnel. Interviews and recommends for employment of records personnel for other departments upon request. Evaluates personnel performance and recommends changes of employee status concerning selection, promotion, transfer, salary administration, training and development and termination. Responsible for company-wide consulting regarding Records Management programs and compliance.

III. EDUCATIONAL BACKGROUND:

Minimum of Bachelor's degree or intensive experience (5-10 years) in records management and 10 years of directly related company supervisory experience.

IV. WORK EXPERIENCE:

Five to 10 years of records management experience in advanced phase with major corporation.

V. COMPLEXITY:

Independent judgement and action required. Creative, problem solving and planning required. Ability to "sell", communicate and present the advantages of records management to officers, etc., to the Tenneco family of companies. Travel required. Represents company at industry meetings, seminars and professional associations concerning activities of records management applications.

VI. SCOPE: 1. Employees Directly Supervised

Title	Number
Records Management Consultant	1
Records Administrators	3

Total Number of Employees Directly and Indirectly Supervised 46

2. Measurement (for exempt positions only)

Annual Budget-$1,500,000

Cu. Ft. of Records Stored-63,000

FIGURE 2-9 Position description of the records manager. (Courtesy of Tenneco Inc.)

FIGURE 2-10 Task Specifications for Advanced Records Management Positions

Level of Educational Training:	Four-Year College/University
Advanced Jobs Available:	Records Manager, Records Management Analyst, Records Management Coordinator, Archivist

Minimum Tasks by Duty Category

A. Records Organization and Evaluation Procedures
   1. Plan and organize new records programs or systems
   2. Implement new records programs or systems
   3. Establish records retention schedules
   4. Obtain and review federal and state legal requirements for records retention
   5. Evaluate the effectiveness of the records management program
   6. Determine administrative retention period for records
   7. Determine the effectiveness of existing filing systems
   8. Develop and analyze the organizational structure of the records management program
   9. Identify categories for vital records
   10. Maintain records retention schedules
   11. Determine and establish "best ways" of protecting records against natural hazards
   12. Establish criteria to be used in designating records as vital, important, or useful
   13. Supervise the establishment and installation of new records series
   14. Develop and maintain a follow-up program of records management activities
   15. Prepare a physical inventory of all records accumulations
   16. Maintain up-to-date records inventories
   17. Identify archival company records for permanent storage

B. Active Records
   1. Recommend equipment and supplies for filing
   2. Review the need for new filing equipment
   3. Select storage equipment and supplies
   4. Determine the "best" filing system
   5. Establish filing methods for active records
   6. Formulate and establish filing procedures
   7. Simplify filing procedures
   8. Determine the arrangement of office area and equipment
   9. Write a filing procedures manual

C. Forms Control
   1. Design a new form
   2. Recommend that a new form design be implemented
   3. Recommend that a form be eliminated

Minimum Tasks by Duty Category
D. Inactive Records Control
1. Determine a schedule for destruction of records
2. Determine methods of disposition of records
3. Establish and maintain a central storage area for inactive records
4. Select equipment for inactive records storage
5. Distribute written procedures for records storage
6. Locate and design a records center for inactive records
7. Supervise the destruction of records
E. Micrographics and Reproduction
1. Prepare studies to determine the feasibility of microfilming
2. Determine which records should be microfilmed
3. Authorize the microfilming of records
F. Records Management—General
1. Educate personnel in other departments regarding the records management program
2. Sell new records-related programs to top management
3. Hire records management personnel
4. Prepare records management manuals
5. Sell new records programs or systems to operating personnel
6. Write specifications
7. Orient new employees to the total records management program

FIGURE 2-10 (continued)

Patricia Wallace surveyed the Association of Records Managers and Administrators (ARMA) in the United States and Canada. Three hundred questionnaires were classified as usable responses. Findings revealed that training for four positions in records management could be completed at the four-year college level: records manager, records management analyst, records management coordinator, and archivist. See Figure 2-10 for the tasks that are performed by records managers as revealed by the Wallace study.[3]

Keeping updated on technological developments, such as laser-beam data retention and electronic mail delivery via satellite beam, is an important responsibility of the records manager. Periodicals that will help keep one updated include the *Records Management Quarterly, Information Management, The Office, Administrative Management, Modern Office Technology,* and *Infosystems.* Of the periodicals listed here, the *Records Management Quarterly* will probably prove most helpful to personnel in charge of records, because the authors of the

[3]Patricia Erwin Wallace, "A Study to Identify Career-Ladder Positions, Records Management Tasks, and Educational Curricula for Entry-Level, Intermediate, and Advanced Records Management Positions," Temple University, 1980, pp. 89–91.

articles are considered authorities in the area of records management. See Appendix D for addresses of the periodicals listed here.

In addition, the **Federal Register** should be reviewed regularly to keep updated on federal legislation pertaining to the control of records.

The *Federal Register,* published daily, updates the **Code of Federal Regulations.** Both publications must be read by the records manager to keep updated on federal legislation.

The Superintendent of Documents, U.S. Government Printing Office, Washington, D. C. 20402, is in charge of mailing the *Federal Register*, which will be sent for a nominal charge to anyone requesting a copy.

The records manager's duties will vary, depending on the size of the office. In a small office, one person may be the office administrator as well as the records manager. In this case, the individual might work with personnel performing daily tasks while supervising the office as well. On the other hand, a large office will have, no doubt, a records manager whose duties center completely around the records of the office.

Staffing of Records Management Systems

In addition to the generic job titles shown in Figure 1-9 (Chapter 1) and the job descriptions presented in Appendix A, there are specific records/information management career paths in active records control, inactive records control (the records center), forms control, micrographics control, and correspondence/reports control. The following sections will discuss job titles and descriptions specific to each of these subsystems of records management.

Active Records Control

Active records are those that are used frequently in the daily operations of the business. Such records include both conventional hard-copy records and nonconventional records, such as photographs, magnetic disks, and microforms. Employees in active records control are involved with procedures for the collection, use, and dissemination of stored information.

Figure 2-11 describes the available positions for individuals wishing to specialize in active records control. Note that the entry-level position, records clerk, requires a high school education with some training in records management, while the highest position, records analyst, requires a four-year college degree.

Inactive Records Control

When records are referred to less than once per month per file drawer, they are considered inactive. Such records are transferred to low-cost storage areas known as record centers. Employee job titles for **inactive records** control are indicated in Figure 2-12. Note that the career ladder is very similar to the one

FIGURE 2-11 Careers in active records control. (Courtesy of ARMA, 4200 Somerset Drive, Suite 215, Prairie Village, KS 66208.)

Records Analyst

surveys, analyzes, recommends department filing systems, procedures, equipment for economic and efficient procedures & utilization
reviews, evaluates, recommends changes of retention schedules
conducts periodic department inventories
participates in training personnel

ED—minimum of Bachelor's Degree or intensive course work in areas related to records management
EXP—2 years experience as junior records analyst or records center clerk
SALARY (Average) $33,000

Records Supervisor

organizes and maintains active records systems throughout the organization selects and supervises support staff
designs efficient methods of records control and maintenance

ED—minimum 2 years of college or vocational training in business

EXP—2-5 years in records operations

SALARY (Average) $26,000

Records Technician

operate, control, maintain technical files center of a reasonably complex nature
organizes & maintains file in conformance with system & standards developed by corporate records management
oversees disposal of unneeded records at the proper time

ED—high school diploma and advanced work in office procedures
EXP—2-5 years file or records experience in difficult records area
NOT AN ENTRY-LEVEL POSITION
SALARY (Average) $19,000

Records Clerk

sorts, indexes, files, and retrieves all types of records
may enter data on records
may search & investigate information in files
classifies materials & records
transfers records & disposes of records according to retention schedule

ED—high school where some training in records management, filing, and office procedures received
ENTRY-LEVEL POSITIONS
SALARY (Average) $16,000

for active records control. Thus mobility in records management positions can be accomplished both laterally (between departments) and vertically (within the same department).

Forms Control

Employees involved in forms control work in various areas of forms analysis, design, construction, and management of forms. Positions include entry level

FIGURE 2-12 Careers in inactive records control. (Courtesy of ARMA, 4200 Somerset Drive, Suite 215, Prairie Village, KS 66208.)

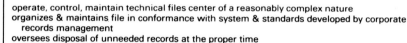

Records Analyst

surveys, analyzes, recommends department filing systems, procedures, equipment for economic and efficient procedures & utilization
reviews, evaluates, recommends changes of retention schedules
conducts periodic department inventories
participates in training personnel

ED—minimum of Bachelor's Degree or intensive course work in areas related to records management
EXP—2 years experience as junior records analyst or records center clerk
SALARY (Average) $33,000

Records Center Supervisor

operates and maintains a corporate records center
selects & supervises records center clerks and support staff
responsible for vital records protection, storage, disposal

ED—minimum 2 years of college or vocational training in business or related areas
EXP—2-5 years in records center operation
SALARY (Average) $27,000

Records Technician

operate, control, maintain technical files center of a reasonably complex nature
organizes & maintains file in conformance with system & standards developed by corporate records management
oversees disposal of unneeded records at the proper time

ED—high school diploma and advanced work in office procedures
EXP—2-5 years file or records experience in difficult records area
NOT AN ENTRY-LEVEL POSITION
SALARY (Average) $19,000

Records Center Clerk

assists in accessioning, reference, retrieval, & disposal activities of center
assists with vital records
searches, sorts, & files records as requested by users

ED—high school where some training in records management and office procedures received
May be an ENTRY-LEVEL POSITION
SALARY (Average) $16,000

through advanced levels; for the higher-level positions, experience in graphic arts and knowledge of forms design are required. Figure 2-13 depicts the career path for individuals interested in working with forms.

Micrographics Control

Organizations that operate in-house micrographics departments require individuals specially trained to work with the various microforms, equipment, and

FIGURE 2-13
Careers in forms control. (Courtesy of ARMA, 4200 Somerset Drive, Suite 215, Prairie Village, KS 66208.)

Forms Manager

plans, implements, coordinates forms control program throughout company
provides technical assistance regarding design, use, specifications, cost, procurement of forms
prepares & maintains control records for company standardized forms

ED—college graduate
EXP—5 years experience, preferably as forms analyst in forms control section of a systems administration or industrial engineering organization

SALARY (Average) $34,000

Forms Analyst

investigates and analyzes forms requirements
designs, drafts, & prepares finished art work masters
analyzes, revises & consolidates existing forms
maintains records required to document and control all company forms

ED—minimum 2 years of college
EXP—5 years experience, preferably in general business functions & management methods, graphic arts, duplicating, or other related fields

SALARY (Average) $26,000

Forms Clerk

updates records and inventories all company forms
determines reorder points for forms
stores and distributes company forms
ED—High school diploma with training in office procedures and records managements
May be an ENTRY-LEVEL POSITION

SALARY (Average) $15,000

retrieval systems involved in a well-managed micrographics program.

Typical positions in micrographics include micrographics clerk (entry level); micrographics technician (intermediate level); and micrographics services supervisor (advanced level). Emphasis in training is on the technical aspects of working with micrographics systems. Figure 2-14 illustrates the career ladder in micrographics control.

Correspondence/Reports Control

Managing correspondence (letters and memorandums) and reports is an important skill for businesses that want to control paperwork costs. While only the largest companies have separate correspondence/reports departments, many organizations maintain the position of reports analyst to manage an

FIGURE 2-14
Careers in Micrographics control. (Courtesy of ARMA, 4200 Somerset Drive, Suite 215, Prairie Village, KS 66208.)

Micrographics Supervisor

operates a central micrographics program
works closely with records analyst & other corporate members in development of micrographic applications trains micrographics technicians

ED—high school plus additional training in micrographics
EXP—high school plus additional training in micrographics
EXP—3 years experience as micrographics technician (may substitute vocational training for experience)

SALARY (Average) $30,000

Micrographics Technician

operates various types of cameras
operates film processor
tests developed film for overall quality
operates microform preparation equipment
conforms to production standards

ED—high school plus technical training in microfilming
EXP—previous records experience helpful but not necessary

SALARY (Average) $20,000

Micrographics Clerk

Prepares documents for microfilming
indexes and codes documents
files and retrieves microforms

ED—High school diploma with training in records management and office procedures

Entry-Level Position

SALARY (Average) $15,000

organization's correspondence, directives, and reports. Figure 2-15 describes the positions of reports clerk, reports analyst, and reports manager.

Among the specific job titles in records management shown in Figures 2-11 through 2-15, the most common positions are records clerk and records supervisor. These are discussed in detail in the following sections.

Job Description of a Records Clerk

Depending upon the size of the organization and the type of records system, a typical job description for a **records clerk** will include the primary function, requirements for the job, skills needed, and specific duties. The primary function of the records clerk is to perform routine duties under supervision, such as sorting and filing correspondence and other records. One of the job re-

FIGURE 2-15 Careers in correspondence/reports control. (Courtesy of ARMA, 4200 Somerset Drive, Suite 215, Prairie Village, KS 66208.)

Reports Manager

responsible for development & implementation of all company reports management policies and practices
develop & implement efficient techniques to assist department and line management in identifying, reviewing, & establishing controls on reports

ED—college graduate
EXP—5 years of experience, preferably in paperwork management & work simplification
SALARY (Average) $34,000

Reports Analyst

provides on company-wide basis, most efficient methods of reports creation, improvement & control through review of reports procedures & systems
designs and formats reports to obtain maximum information required at minimum cost
participates in training personnel

ED—minimum 2 years of college
EXP—3 years experience as report writer, preferably in one of the functional departments of a company
SALARY (Average) $26,000

Reports Clerk

maintains and retrieves all company reports
inventories reports
classifies reports by function
ED—high school diploma with training in records management and office procedures
May be an Entry-Level Position
SALARY (Average) $15,000

quirements may be an ability to communicate both in oral and written form. Other requirements may be the ability to establish coding systems, to set up filing systems, and to abstract data from reports. Skills needed for the records clerk position may be minimal; however, a good knowledge of the filing procedures for numeric or alphabetic filing may be required.

Jo Ann Lee found in her analysis of the tasks performed by clerical workers in selected businesses in southern California that filing activities are performed between 70 and 100 percent of the time by the records clerk. She further states, "Between 10 and 39 percent of the job time is devoted to filing activities performed by the secretary, clerk typist, accounting clerk, and stenographer."[4] From this study one may conclude that many office workers find that some phase of their jobs pertain to records control, regardless of their job titles.

Specific duties of the records clerk, as outlined in the job description, may include any or all of the following:

1. Performs routine duties, such as sorting and filing correspondence and other records in alphabetic or numeric order or according to subject matter.
2. Maintains charge-out records of documents removed from the files.
3. Retrieves records upon request.
4. Prepares index and cross-reference aids.
5. Classifies material for filing, disposes of outdated files within established procedures and policies. This duty may be the responsibility of higher-level personnel, however.
6. Performs other miscellaneous duties as required.

The records clerk job is an entry-level position, and a high school graduate with training in office procedures and filing should be able to perform the duties capably. See Figure 2-16 for careers in records management that are attainable according to one's educational level.

Qualifications of the Records Supervisor

Probably one of the best qualifications of a **records supervisor** is that he or she relates well to people. The records supervisor supervises any number of records clerks and reports directly to the records manager. The records supervisor should be highly qualified and have at least two or more years' experience in general business operations, including the records area. In addition, the supervisor should have a minimum of two years of college, including such courses as office procedures, office administration, and personnel management. The supervisor must be able to supervise staff effectively; coordinate available resources; establish priorities; communicate well, both in writing and orally; make decisions; and plan, organize, and control the records system. The supervisor should cooperate with the records manager in implementing changes that may be needed. He or she will assist the records manager in setting up an ongoing training program for all of the employees. Evaluating employees on a regular basis and sharing the results of that evaluation in interviews with the employees are also the supervisor's duties.

[4]Jo Ann Lee, "An Analysis of the Tasks and Responsibilities Related to Filing Activities Performed by Clerical Workers in Selected Businesses in California in Relation to Instruction in Filing Skills and Knowledges in Selected California Schools and Colleges," California State University, Los Angeles, October 1976, p. 241.

FIGURE 2-16 Careers in Records Management

Position Level	*Level of Academic Attainment*	*Job Title*
Managerial	College or university	Records and Information Manager Records Management Analyst Records Management Coordinator Reports Manager Forms Manager
Supervisory	Junior or community college	Records Center Supervisor Records Supervisor Reports Analyst Micrographics Services Supervisor Forms Analyst
Operating	High school	Records Technician Micrographics Technician Records Center Clerk Records Clerk

The supervisor should assist the records manager in selecting and orienting new employees. Job descriptions should be updated regularly to reflect any changes in duties and requirements of the job. The supervisor is in a position to make sure that individuals filling these positions do indeed keep the job descriptions updated.

Specific Duties of the Records Supervisor Specific duties of the records supervisor may include any or all of the following:

1. Determines classification of all documents to be filed
2. Ensures that documents are filed according to established policies and procedures
3. Provides documents and information to authorized personnel
4. Develops, revises, and implements, with the approval of the records manager, policies and procedures for the records section
5. Recommends filing equipment and supplies
6. Reviews the list of charge-out files to see that files are returned within a prescribed time period. Takes follow-up action on files that are overdue
7. Prepares activity reports as directed by the records manager
8. Attends meetings to expand professional expertise

Supervising, Training, and Evaluating Employees

Supervision of Employees

The supervisor who will be most successful in supervising staff is the one who demonstrates good interpersonal relations with all levels of personnel and uses flexible methods of supervising. At times, an autocratic style, in which directives are given with the expectation of compliance, is the only choice. Certainly, the supervisor will follow the policies and procedures of the organization in an autocratic style of supervising. On the other hand, a democratic style of leadership and supervision may be most effective when the supervisor and the supervisees plan and implement activities in the records area. The atmosphere among the employees must be pleasant in order to foster harmonious relationships. A disgruntled employee can be a negative force in any office. High morale will be achieved among the employees who have confidence in their supervisor and who feel that they are a part of the organization. For a more detailed discussion on leadership styles, consult a current office administration textbook.

Specific rules for managing people, unfortunately, will not work for all supervisors. There are many thousands of different personalities in the world; and each person is influenced by his or her childhood experiences, academic preparation, peer groups, and work experiences. A supervisor, then, cannot categorize people or situations and decide that certain methods of supervising will always be effective. The effective supervisor will empathize with supervisees and view each situation in its context and environment. Wholesale disciplining performed on a large scale without individual distinctions is rarely acceptable. When an employee has violated a procedure and disciplining seems to be in order, the supervisor should do so in an interview in which the offending employee may discuss the situation with the supervisor. The supervisor should listen to the employee to determine what is being said. The supervisor who does all of the talking in such an interview has missed the whole point of the interview.

Development of a Training Program

An important element of the staffing function in the records management program is the development of a training program so that present employees can maintain a high level of effectiveness and new employees will become quickly oriented to their positions.

In the study mentioned earlier in this chapter, Lee found that there are certain weaknesses in the performance of beginning clerical and secretarial employees. She states that "... the ability to establish coding systems is a weakness; also, the ability to set up filing system(s) and the ability to abstract data from reports, forms, and files."[5] Other weaknesses may surface in individual

[5]Ibid., p. 263.

offices, and these areas should be identified and targeted as prime topics for a training program.

Training for the New Employee Whereas the training program should be designed for the entire records staff, there are certain activities for the new employee on the first day on the job.

The supervisor will probably introduce the new employee to others in the records department and in other departments with related work functions. A brief history of the company should be given to the new employee, as well as a tour of the offices, especially those offices that communicate with the records area. The employee needs to become familiar with the personnel and the layout of departments that have interrelated duties.

Next, the new employee should read the job description for his or her job and then become familiar with the records manual. The employee will become more quickly familiar with policies and procedures if some time is set aside for assimilation of the manual.

The supervisor may assign the new employee to another worker for on-the-job training, or the supervisor may undertake this task. On-the-job training is highly successful in offices, and especially successful in the records management program.

This early training of the new employee is very important in improving productivity and lessening errors. Moreover, the task of supervising a new employee is less difficult after a sound introductory training program.

Training for All Employees The best training program for an organization is an ongoing process, and even the very new employee will derive much benefit from participating in the activities. The records supervisor will assist the records manager in identifying the needs of the employees and then in developing a program that is designed to benefit the employees as well as the organization. The supervisees also may be in on the early planning stages. Their input will broaden the perception of the supervisor in establishing the needs to be met through the training program.

The following steps are necessary in setting up an effective training program:

1. Identify the short- and long-term objectives of the records program. These objectives should be reviewed and revised periodically in order to keep the objectives in line with the broader goals of the organization.
2. Identify the needs of the employees in order to help them attain the objectives of the records program.
3. Determine the training that will benefit the employee's needs as well as the needs of the organization.
4. Implement the program with periodic evaluations along the way to determine the adequacy of the program.

Implementing a Training Program

Flexibility is a keyword in implementing a training program—not only for the personnel, but also for the program itself. The flexible program is one that encourages creativity in personnel and motivates them to offer suggestions for improvement. In order to prevent boredom, the program must be stimulating and fresh in the methods used in the training process.

Various types of training programs can be considered: in-house training by internal personnel; seminars conducted by professional associations; consulting services offered by private agencies; and institutional training programs/courses offered by colleges and universities.

Here are a few suggestions for making training sessions effective.

1. Cross-train employees so that they understand the activities of jobs other than their own.
2. Hold brainstorming sessions for all employees. These sessions may provide the records manager with some new insights toward solving problems.
3. Enlist guest speakers from equipment suppliers, a college, or a public office.
4. Provide an incentive for employees to take relevant courses at an institution of higher learning. Partial reimbursement of the tuition may provide incentive enough for the employee to take advantage of the formal training. Courses that would be helpful include business report writing, personnel management, business English, accounting, data processing, word processing, office systems and procedures, and office management. Other courses may be helpful, and the supervisor should be able to counsel employees in selecting courses that would provide the greatest benefit.
5. Provide "hands-on" learning experiences with microcomputers to acquaint all employees with computer applications related to records management. Use computer games and simulations to attract employees who may be fearful of computers. See Appendix E for a listing of records management software.

Designing Training Sessions

When training sessions are held in-house, it is important to present them as professionally as possible. Although a straight lecture may communicate to employees the information we wish them to acquire, it is a known fact that most of us actually learn only about 13 percent of what we hear. Thus we need to use our other senses, most notably our eyesight, to increase our learning capacity. Presenting information via various audiovisual aids can increase trainees' learning capacity by 75 percent. In other words, by using both the senses of hearing and eyesight, we can often increase trainees' learning capacity to 88 percent. Figure 2-17 presents a variety of training aids that bring both

	Tools	Advantages	Limitations
Slides		Require only filming, with processing and mounting by film laboratory. Result in colorful, realistic reproductions of original subjects. Easily revised and updated. Easily handled, stored, and rearranged for various uses. Increased usefulness with tray storage and automatic projection. Can be combined with taped narration for greater effectiveness. May be adapted to group or individual use.	Can get out of sequence, be turned upside down, and be projected incorrectly if slides are handled individually. Best in a darkened room, which limits note taking.
Films		May consist of complete films or short film clips. Are particularly useful in describing motion, showing relationships, and giving impact to topic. Are useful with groups of all sizes and with individuals. Ensure a consistency in presentation of material.	May be expensive to prepare in terms of time, equipment, materials, and services. Best in darkened room, which limits note taking. Require careful planning and some production skills.
Videotapes Videodisks		Require some planning and production skills commensurate with quality desired. Permit showing of action, relationships, and otherwise unavailable scenes. Almost immediately available after production. Playback capability of video recording permits analysis of on-the-spot action.	Sound and action must be planned to occur effectively at the same time. Space must allow technical requirements of production and showing. Require relatively expensive equipment
Cassettes		Easy to prepare with regular tape recorders. Can provide applications in most subject areas. Equipment for use is compact, portable, easy to operate. Flexible and adaptable as either individual method of training or in conjunction with slides and other programmed materials. Duplication is easy and economical.	Subject to a tendency to overuse. Fixed rate of information flow.
Manuals: Operations Procedures		Easy to prepare with the use of copying machines. Step-by-step sequence can be provided for operations or procedures. Can be carried around for use anywhere, including study at home. Act of putting in print often brings care and clarity.	Require user to be a good reader. Can be overused.
Overhead transparencies		Can present information in systematic, developmental, or step-by-step sequence. Uses simple-to-operate projector with presentation rate controlled by instructor. Require only limited planning. Can be prepared easily by variety of simple, inexpensive methods. Particularly useful with large groups.	Require special equipment, facilities, and skills for more advanced. preparation methods. Type must be large enough to be read. Are large and can present storage problem.

Source: Mary M. Ruprecht and Kathleen P. Wagoner, *Managing Office Automation* (New York: John Wiley & Sons, Inc., 1984), p. 484.

FIGURE 2-17
Training Tools.

sight and sound to the learning process. In addition, we can add another 6 percent to trainees' learning capacity by having them actually become involved in applications and hands-on exercises during the training sessions. Figure 2.18 illustrates the importance of our senses during the learning process.

Finally, follow-up sessions and exercises should be designed, since learning that is not put to use is forgotten quickly. For example, the Research Institute of America states that one day after a training session we typically retain only one-third of what we had learned, forgetting two-thirds of what we had acquired only the previous day![6] Obviously, follow-up sessions that focus on reviewing previously learned material are important to ensure higher retention rates from training sessions.

Performance Reviews

There is more to the performance review of an employee than formally filling out an evaluation form. The effective supervisor will establish open communication with each employee and discuss how well the employee is doing and areas where improvement is needed. The time to discuss a problem with a subordinate is when the problem surfaces, rather than to wait for the formal appraisal. Written notes should be kept of the problems discussed and the resolution of those problems. If no improvement is evident at the time of the performance review, this will be noted on the evaluation form.

The performance criteria must be *objective* rather than *subjective.* If the performance standards are measurable, they are objective. The number of documents coded and filed per hour is a measurable performance standard. The enthusiasm of the worker is not a measurable performance standard; this type of subjective evaluation should not be used. Some organizations use a self-appraisal sheet that the employees fill out. The self-appraisal sheet then becomes the basis for the performance review. During the interview with the subordinate, the supervisor will discuss the department's short-term goals and objectives for the coming year as well as long-term goals. In light of these goals, the job description may require updating.

Supervisors will encourage their subordinates to set their goals and objectives to fit those of the organization. **Management by objectives** (MBO) is a tool used by management to encourage employees to establish goals and to formulate objectives that are practical in attaining those goals. As a motivational device, MBO is highly successful in many organizations, whether large or small.

[6]Mary M. Ruprecht and Kathleen P. Wagoner, *Managing Office Automation* (New York: John Wiley & Sons, 1984), pp. 485–486.

FIGURE 2-18 Learning Via Our "Senses"

	% of Learning
Hearing	 13%
Eyesight	 75%
Hearing & Eyesight	 88%
Hearing, Eyesight & Touch	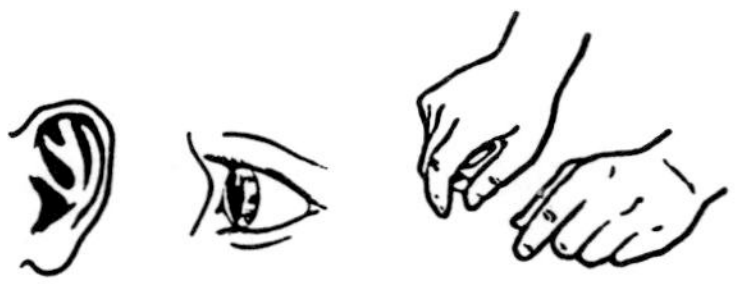 94%

Employee Concerns

While a good training program is essential for employee productivity, managers need to be aware of other issues which concern their employees. A recent study by a Human Resources Management consulting firm reported that employees are generally satisfied with their work but are concerned about the stability of their company and their jobs. This study reported that 91 percent of employees rated their relations with their immediate boss as good; 89 percent believe their work is important; 87 percent expressed cooperative relations with coworkers; and 80 percent expressed company pride.

Issues that concerned employees in this study were job security, 92 percent; productivity lags due to work pressures, 68 percent; receiving adequate compensation, 62 percent; and being informed about company plans, 56 percent.

Source: "Employees are Happy, But Worried," *Modern Office Technology*, May, 1990, page 92.

CHAPTER HIGHLIGHTS

- The records system comprises the equipment, materials, and staff necessary to maintain effective and efficient control and management of the records of an organization.
- Establishing a new records management system or revitalizing an existing one requires a feasibility study to determine if the proposed system changes will be cost-effective, improve productivity, and satisfy user requirements.
- Management must decide whether to use internal or external personnel to conduct the feasibility study, based on a review of the advantages and the disadvantages of both options.
- Specific career paths in records management are available in the areas of active records control, inactive records control, forms control, micrographics control, and correspondence/reports control.
- Position mobility can be accomplished both laterally and vertically in the records management profession.
- An important element of the staffing function in records management is the development of a training program so that present employees can maintain a high level of effectiveness and new employees will become more quickly oriented to their positions.
- The best training program for an organization is an ongoing process with participation by all of the employees.
- Performance reviews of employees must be objective rather than subjective.
- Supervisors should encourage their subordinates to set goals and objectives to fit those of the organization.

QUESTIONS FOR REVIEW

1. Identify the parts of a records system.
2. Indicate the steps that are involved in planning a records system.
3. Define the term *feasibility study* and indicate the overall goal of a feasibility study.
4. List one significant advantage and one disadvantage of using internal personnel in developing records systems.
5. List one significant advantage and one disadvantage of using external consultants in developing records systems.
6. Describe several comprehensive duties of records managers.
7. Trace the career path that is available to records personnel interested in specializing in micrographics systems.
8. How does the job description of a records clerk differ from that of a records supervisor?

9. Indicate the types of audiovisual aids that are most effective in training sessions.
10. Give an example of both an objective and a subjective performance criteria for evaluating records personnel.

THE DECISION MAKER

Case Studies

1. Anne Smith is resigning from her job as records manager of the Tri-Delta Insurance Company. Several persons have applied for the position, which involves many duties and responsibilities. Anne has been asked to assist her superior in selecting the person to carry on as records manager. Below is a description of the three individuals from whom Anne will choose. Select the one individual best qualified for the job, and give the reasons the other two candidates were not selected for the job.

	Fred Blair	*Scott Smith*	*Mary Brown*
Academic preparation	Bachelor's degree, major in history	Bachelor's degree, major in liberal arts	Business school—2 years of accounting and finance
Business experience	2 years, State Archives; 3 years, State Museum	15 years County Offices: filing, accounting, office supervision	10 years, owner and operator of a secretarial services firm
Other information	Member, Rotary Club; Chairperson, United Fund Campaign, Member, Speakers' Organization; Member, AIIM	Member, ARMA; Member, ICRM	Member, ARMA; Member, Administrative Management Society, serving as secretary of the local chapter

2. As the records manager of the Standard Paper Corporation, you need to hire a records analyst to assist you in various areas of active records control. Develop a job description for this new position, and indicate the objective performance criteria upon which this individual will be evaluated.

ESTABLISHING A RECORDS MANAGEMENT PROGRAM

OBJECTIVES

Upon completion of this chapter, the student should be able to:

1. Outline the objectives of a records management program.
2. Explain the rationale for implementing a records management program.
3. Discuss each of the three benefits of an effective records management program.
4. Describe the seven management principles used in establishing a records management program.
5. Identify why, what, for how long, and where records should be retained.
6. Compare the features of centralized records storage, decentralized records storage, and combination storage.
7. Define the concept of electronic recordkeeping and its relationship to the overall records management program.

Records management, as defined earlier, deals with the management and control of records from the time of their creation or origination to their storage, use, transfer, and disposition or destruction. Records may be paper-based documents (such as correspondence and reports, cards, business forms, and photographs); microforms (such as rolls, fiche, and computer-output microfilm); or electronic records (information stored on such magnetic media as disks, tapes, and optical disks).

Maintaining and controlling the records in any organization is itself a costly operation because of the large expenditures for personnel, equipment, supplies, and maintenance. To enable this operation to be effective and efficient in providing essential information to users, a company must establish a systematic method of managing and controlling all its records.

OBJECTIVES OF A RECORDS MANAGEMENT PROGRAM

As part of an organization's comprehensive records management system, a program for the management of records should have as its objectives the following:

1. To ensure continuity of business operations in case of disaster where there is a potential for loss or destruction of records.
2. To provide for effective and economical procedures, systems, personnel, and equipment to protect records and to standardize the processing and control of these systems.
3. To establish guidelines for the maintenance, use, and control of active, inactive, and vital records.
4. To identify and classify the various types of records to be retained; establish their location within the company; and account for specific records, systems, equipment, and procedures.
5. To designate responsibility for and authority over the total records management program within a business to a records manager and a specially trained staff of records personnel.
6. To integrate the records management function into the total organizational structure and operations.

RATIONALE FOR A RECORDS MANAGEMENT PROGRAM

According to David Barcomb, once paper records are stored, 35 percent are never again accessed; 60 percent are accessed only during the first year of storage; and only 5 percent are accessed after the first year.[1] Thus, although a small percent of all records in an organization are active, a records management program must be directed toward a records *retention* program that defines the following:[2]

1. The period of time during which records have operational, legal, fiscal, or historical value (see Chapter 4).
2. The period of time records are considered active and must be maintained in the primary filing area (see Chapter 8).
3. The point in time when records can reasonably be transferred to a secondary storage facility (see Chapter 11).
4. The methods of records disposal (see Chapter 5).
5. The procedures for operating and ensuring compliance with the retention program (see Chapters 5 and 17).
6. The relationship between records retention and other aspects of the records management program, such as microfilming (see Chapter 16), filing (see Chapter 7), and data processing (see Chapter 9).

An effective records retention program provides benefits to the organization in terms of economic factors, operational efficiency, and legal protection or safeguards.

Economic benefits. The cost of storing records having little or no value is reduced when the amount of records storage space itself is decreased. The savings is measured in terms of cost per square foot of storage space. Following a sound records retention program, the company can transfer inactive records to less costly storage areas and eventually destroy or dispose of those records when appropriate.

With prime records storage space allocated to current and active and valuable records, there are cost savings in the amount—and perhaps the types—of equipment and supplies used to house inactive or valueless records.

Operational efficiency. Active records are more accessible if separated from the inactive records. Records personnel are more efficient workers when they can devote their time and energies to maintaining current, active records.

Having a records retention program helps ensure that procedures, schedules, and overall management of records are consistent and that both records retention and records disposition are done systematically following established guidelines.

Legal safeguards. Certain types of records must be retained for certain periods of time, and some must be retained indefinitely to meet statutory require-

[1]David Barcomb, *Office Automation: A Survey of Tools and Techniques* (Bedford, MA: Digital Press, 1981).

[2]*Developing and Operating a Records Retention Program* (Prairie Village, Kansas: Association of Records Managers and Administrators, 1989), p. 6.

ments. A records retention program outlines when and which records must be retained for a minimum period, which records must be retained permanently, and which records can be destroyed or disposed of and when. Following such schedules allows a company to operate consistently and enables it to provide the necessary documents to anticipate or support litigation and to support its rationale for destroying or disposing of certain records.

DEVELOPMENT OF A RECORDS MANAGEMENT PROGRAM

The process of developing a records management program includes the basic seven management principles: planning, budgeting, controlling, decision-making, documenting, communicating, and evaluating.

Before any of these activities are undertaken, however, the approval and support of senior management must be obtained. The planning and the development of an effective program require the time, efforts, and resources of all levels of personnel. Without support and approval of these endeavors by top-level management, neither the preliminary planning nor the program itself—if ultimately implemented—will succeed. As stated by Bradford M. Burch, "Understanding the need for information, its completeness, its integrity, and its time factors is critical in making a judgment on a new system deployed to improve productivity."[3]

Senior management can be motivated to become involved in the planning and development of a records management program if made aware that the eventual standardization and integration of systems, operations, and personnel will achieve greater productivity and increased cost-effectiveness.

Planning

Planning is the most crucial activity in developing an effective records management program. Planning activities focus on the total organization; its existing policies, practices, staffing, and facilities; and its future requirements.

The records management program encompasses both active and inactive records. *Active records* are those that are referred to frequently and generally consist of current correspondence, reports, forms, etc.; *inactive records* are those that are referred to less than once a month per file drawer. A records management program should focus on the maintenance, use, and control of its active records, although as mentioned previously active records comprise only 25 percent of a company's records; it is the active records that are currently generating business for the company.

The maintenance and control of inactive records, however, is also important; such documents represent correspondence and agreements from past

[3]Bradford M. Burch, "Are We Automating the Problem or the Process?" *Information Management*, Vol. 18, No. 12 (December 1984), pp. 1, 10–11.

business operations and transactions. As such, they serve a useful purpose and should be retained as necessary—although apart from the active records. The maintenance, use, and control of inactive records is discussed in Chapter 8.

The following questions should be considered in the development of an effective records management program:

Why should records be retained?

What records should be retained?

Where should records be stored?

How long should records be retained?

How should records be classified?

Who should manage and control records?

Why Should Records Be Kept? The purposes for storing records are as follows:

1. To provide for future reference, a record of business transactions between individual individuals and companies. Examples of such records include invoices and purchase orders, contracts for services, general correspondence, and loan agreements.
2. To prove the lawful existence and operation of a company under various city, state, and/or federal regulations. Examples of such records are organizational charters, incorporation documents or partnership agreements, and stockholder information.
3. To meet government and other regulatory standards regarding the length of time certain records must be retained by a company. For example, the Internal Revenue Service requires that tax records and supporting documents be retained permanently. Other records requiring retention for specific periods include financial records, personnel data, legal contracts, and stockholder records.
4. To substantiate management decisions and financial operations that are presented or distributed to other businesses, government agencies, and the public in general. Such information includes general announcements concerning new products or services, new processes or technologies, shareholder earning reports, and research and development data.
5. To protect the company from—and to defend against—legal claims and litigation in tort and contract actions. For example, all materials related to patents, trademarks, and copyrights must be retained permanently.

What Records Should Be Retained? The use of computers and other electronic technologies has in turn created both a "paperwork explosion" and an "information revolution." These terms refer not only to the proliferation of data, correspondence, forms, and reports in paper or hard-copy form but also duplication of documents and other records that are stored in image and/or digital form—hard-copy records stored also on microforms and/or on computer tapes or disks. Just as paper records can be retained indefinitely regardless of their need or value, documents stored in image or digital forms can also be retained without regard for storage space, need, time requirements, or value. The fact that microforms and computer tapes or disks occupy less storage space in relation to the amount of data or information stored on them is irrelevant; time, effort, and personnel are still required to store, retrieve, and maintain records so stored.

According to Bradford Burch, "... although information is needed, perhaps for years after its creation, it is not always clear exactly what piece is needed."[4] While information management research shows that "demand for information falls mostly within the first year, "the need for newly created information peaks out after two weeks."[5] Burch further states that beyond the first year in the life of recorded information, "only 2-5 percent ... is actually needed for decision making or historical research purposes—but we do not know which 2-5 percent." The dilemma is, "Do we keep everything to make sure we can get at it if its [*sic*] needed?[6]

A company must analyze the value of various documents created and received by it and how these records are used and by whom. A criterion for deciding which records are to be kept and which are not is the extent to which the company would be able to function if certain records were lost or destroyed in a disaster. A **disaster** is a flood, fire, earthquake, hurricane, or other such acts of God or nature where there is destruction of property.

Documents may be categorized as vital, essential, useful, or nonessential to a company's operations and existence (see Chapter 10).

Where Should Records Be Stored? After determining what records need to be retained, a company must consider the best location for the storage of records. This decision is based on the space available for records storage, the personnel who will use and maintain the records, the use for the various records, and the growth potential of the business.

Three methods of storing records are (1) centralized, (2) decentralized, and (3) combination.

In a **centralized records storage system,** records for the entire business are gathered and stored in one location within the company. This type of system is most effective for large companies that must maintain large volumes of records. Responsibility for the maintenance and control of records rests with a records manager and specially trained full-time records personnel. Other features of a centralized storage system are as follows:

[4]Burch, p. 10.

[5]P. Kalthoff and L. Lee, *Productivity and Records Automation* (Englewood Cliffs, NJ: Prentice-Hall, Inc., 1981), p. 34.

[6]Burch, p. 10.

1. Records referred to by several people or departments are more accurately maintained and controlled because access to the files is limited to records personnel.
2. Duplication of office personnel, records storage equipment and supplies, and time and effort is eliminated.
3. Office floor space devoted to records storage can be used more cost-effectively because such space—in relation to the total office floor space—has been allocated specifically for this use.
4. Records management procedures can be standardized to provide better use of records personnel and their time, storage facilities, and space.
5. Better protection, control, and security of records can be provided, because responsibility has been assigned to specific persons for the efficient operation of the systems, procedures, and personnel.

When records are maintained within their respective departments in a company, a **decentralized records storage system** is used. This type of system allows each department to maintain and control its own records to suit its own requirements. Such records are seldom referred to by others outside the department where these records are created or received. A decentralized system has the following features:

1. Records pertaining to only one or a few departments can be maintained and controlled more accurately because of the personnel's familiarity with such records.
2. Records that need to be referenced frequently or quickly can be accessed more conveniently and economically because they are stored near their most frequent point of use.

Because each department has its own records storage system, however, there is lack of uniformity within the entire company. Also, in a decentralized system, duplicate records are frequently created or photocopied and stored, requiring additional storage space, equipment, and perhaps personnel.

In a **combination records storage system,** features of both the centralized and the decentralized storage systems are combined within the same company. This kind of system allows individual departments and personnel immediate access to records while at the same time offering some standardization of procedures and personnel found in a centralized system. Advantages of the combination records storage system are as follows:

1. A records manager establishes standardized records storage and control procedures for all departments and for the centralized records storage area.
2. Although the duplication of records storage equipment, supplies, and personnel is not altogether eliminated, there is a reduction in costs because of

the centralized control of the combination systems.

3. Records pertaining to only a few departments doing similar work can be decentralized and made available nearest their points of use; other records can be accessed from the centralized storage area conveniently and economically on an as-needed basis.

How Long Should Records Be Kept? As mentioned previously, the ultimate use of records and their value in the operation of a business dictate what records need to be retained and for how long. There are over 1,000 federal and state regulations that dictate how long a company must retain certain records.

For example, the Fair Labor Standards Act requires that businesses retain payroll checks, vouchers, and earnings and payroll registers for a specified number of years. Records such as accounts payable ledgers, check registers, certified financial statements, contracts and specifications, and litigation records must be retained permanently.

A detailed discussion of records retention schedules is presented in Chapter 5.

How Should Records Be Classified? Should records be filed alphabetically or by number? Should a geographic or a subject method be used? How records are classified is based on their value and how they will be referenced, or called for. For example, an automobile manufacturer may maintain its inventory of automobile parts either by their names (alphabetically) or by part or stock number (numerically). A marketing organization may classify its sales personnel by regional sales areas (geographically), while a retailer may classify its merchandise by type of goods (subject).

The types of records to be stored—paper, microforms, and/or magnetic media—also determine how they should be classified. Within a word processing center, for example, floppy disks containing correspondence and reports (called *text files*) could be classified alphabetically by originators' names or departments, chronologically by date of origination, or numerically by assigning a number to each disk in order of use.

Some additional factors to consider in the selection of a **records classification system** are how frequently and by whom records must be referenced, the amount of records storage space available, the anticipated growth of the company and its records storage needs, and the organization or **work flow** within the office or company.

It is likely that no one system will be found feasible for an entire company's use. For example, the personnel department of a company may determine that some of its records would be frequently referenced according to such subjects as job/position announcements, employee benefits, state and federal employment guidelines, insurance programs; some of its records would be frequently referenced alphabetically by employee name or department; some of its records would be referenced by date according to employees' ages or date of employment. In the same company, the sales or marketing department may refer to its records by invoice number or customer number, while the accounting department would refer to its records by customer name or account number. Thus in any one company, it is not uncommon to find more than one classification system in use for its various records.

Records classification systems, filing rules, and components and procedures are presented in Chapter 7.

Who Should Manage and Control the Records? As mentioned in Chapter 1, the records management function requires a management-level person who has expertise in all aspects of records control and in all phases of office work and who has a broad knowledge of the business or organization's operations and objectives. The **records manager** must not only plan, develop, and administer the company's records management policies but must also coordinate these efforts with other personnel, equipment, and systems. The records manager interacts with every department within a company and as such must be thoroughly familiar with the structure, operations, and work flow of the company.

Whether a centralized or decentralized records storage system is used, the records manager should be given responsibility for implementing and administering the company's total program: inventorying and classifying records; establishing the records retention schedule; ensuring that schedules meet legal, fiscal, and management criteria; providing adequate notices for the transfer, destruction, or disposition of records according to schedules; serving as liaison between upper management and department and staff personnel; and coordinating the records retention program with all other aspects of the total records management program.

Once these planning questions and elements have been addressed and the position and the role of the records manager determined, the company must examine its existing policies and practices by conducting a records inventory. This inventory provides information about all currently stored records—what and how much there is, where, how and by whom they are used—and about records storage equipment and systems in use. The records inventory is discussed in Chapter 4.

Budgeting

In records management, budgeting involves determining the current costs of managing records and information and projecting future cost requirements. Budgets must reflect not only the costs of creating records but also the costs of storing, retrieving, and disposing of them. An alternative budget should also be prepared if the company anticipates any changes that will affect records storage and retrieval.

The budget will include costs for personnel; office floor space allocated for records storage and retrieval; equipment and supplies; systems hardware and software; and maintenance of the facilities, equipment, and systems hardware.

Controlling

During the initial planning stage, the records manager was identified as the individual who will be responsible for planning, developing, and administering records management policies. If this function is recognized and accepted by top-level management, the records manager must assume overall control of the records operation.

Decision Making

The quantitative data collected during the records inventory and the subsequent analysis of those data will provide management with sufficient information on which to base decisions about present and future records management operations. If existing policies, practices, staffing, and records storage equipment and systems need to be modified, the changes can be charted based on preliminary budget figures. The company can then compare the cost of continuing present practices with the cost of using alternative methods.

Documenting

Once decisions have been made and necessary approvals have been obtained, the records manager should develop written procedures for each phase of the records program. These procedures formalize the whole records operation; designate lines of authority and areas of responsibility; and make personnel, procedures, and systems accountable for the smooth functioning of the records process.

Records retention and disposition schedules should be developed so personnel know what records need to be retained and for what periods of time (see Chapter 5). Procedures relating to the maintenance, use, and control of active and inactive records can be documented (see Chapter 8). Procedures for correspondence and reports control and for operations manuals (Chapters 13 and 17) and for forms design and control (Chapter 14) can also be developed so that standardized practices and guidelines for all records management functions are identified.

Communicating

All the planning, budgeting, decision-making, and documenting will be to no avail unless the resulting policies and procedures are communicated throughout the organization. Relevant documents, including procedures and operations manuals, should be distributed to appropriate personnel and discussed with them so they will understand their function, role, and responsibilities. As the person responsible for the control of all aspects of the records operation, the records manager must maintain proper channels of communication with top management as well as among all levels of personnel.

Communication includes informing all records personnel of the rationale behind the program and the importance of a records retention schedule; training in the use of systems and equipment, in filing tasks and procedures, in proper charge-out and follow-up policies and procedures; and incorporating appropriate handing, care, and protection or security procedures of all records. Personnel need to know as much as possible about the policies and the rationale behind them in order that they may contribute to the overall effectiveness of the records operation.

Evaluating

Once in operation, each phase of the records management program should be continuously evaluated by asking "Is it doing what we planned it would do?" and "Are users' needs for timely information being met?" Based on this ongoing evaluation by *all* records personnel and users, the program—or certain aspects of it—can be updated and revised to ensure that it is meeting the company's records storage and retrieval needs.

A records management audit (discussed in Chapter 17) should also be completed to compare the cost-effectiveness of the new operation with that of the previous operation. Cost-benefit analyses can be determined phase by phase or during other interim periods, or after a specified period upon implementation of the full records management program.

CHAPTER HIGHLIGHTS

- A records management program encompasses the management and control of all records—paper records, microforms, and electronic records.
- In any organization, records management requires a large expenditure for personnel, equipment, supplies, operation, and maintenance. A systematic records management program can reduce operating costs and improve productivity throughout an organization.
- Ensuring the continuity of business operations; providing for the effective and economical procedures, systems, personnel, and equipment; and establishing guidelines for the maintenance, use, and control of records are three major objectives of a records management program.
- The rationale for a records management program includes accessibility to records in a timely manner; reduction of retrieval or search times in locating records; and appropriate retention of records to meet legal, fiscal, and administrative needs.
- Top-level management must understand and acknowledge the need for accurate information as a basis for decision making and for improving productivity.
- The steps in developing a records management program are planning,

budgeting, controlling, decision making, documenting, communicating, and evaluating.

- Factors to consider in planning a program are why, what, where, and how long records should be retained; how records should be classified; and who should manage and control records.
- In determining what records should be retained, a company must consider the importance of various kinds of records and the extent to which it would hinder the operation of the business if they were lost or destroyed in a disaster.
- Whether to use a centralized or decentralized records storage system depends on who needs access to the records and how frequently; whether duplication of personnel, storage equipment, and supplies can be justified or avoided; where and how much office floor space can be allocated for records storage; and the need for protection, control, and security of stored records.
- Two factors to consider in the budget phase are the cost of creating records and the cost of storing, retrieving, and disposing of them.
- The records manager will be responsible for planning, developing, and administering the records management policies. The overall control of the records operation rests with this individual.
- To aid in decision making, a records inventory and an analysis of existing records, records storage equipment, and practices should be completed.
- Documenting procedures helps formalize the records operation; designate lines of authority and areas of responsibility; and make personnel, procedures, and systems accountable for their existence.
- The records management program—or certain aspects of it—should be continuously evaluated, updated, and revised to ensure that it meets the company's records storage and retrieval needs.

QUESTIONS FOR REVIEW

Refer to the listening of objectives of a records management program at the beginning of this chapter. Provide a rationale for each of the objectives.

What are the seven management functions related to the development of a records management program?

What information should be identified during the planning stages of a records management program?

Why should businesses retain records?

How does a business determine which records should be retained and the length of time for their retention?

6. What are some advantages and disadvantages of centralized records storage for a small business? For a large business?
7. What are some advantages and disadvantages of decentralized records storage for a small business? For a large business?
8. In what ways can a records manager communicate information, policies, and procedures to records personnel?
9. Why must an organization evaluate its records management program periodically? What should such an evaluation consist of?

THE DECISION MAKER

Case Studies

1. From a preliminary study of the types of records kept in your company's files, the following records have been listed: paid invoices, original blueprints, deeds and leases, lists of corporate officers, purchase orders, bank reconciliation statements, customer mailing lists, general ledgers, minutes of meetings, canceled checks, insurance policies, personnel records (general), audit statements, employee time cards, merchandise price lists, magnetic tapes, customer order letters, copies of miscellaneous correspondence, sample business forms, and word processing floppy disks. Based on your knowledge of the records management program at this point, give reasons why each type of record listed should or should not be retained.

You have been hired as a records manager for a large metropolitan school district. When a teacher submits an application for a teaching position, the district office duplicates several copies of the application and supporting records (transcripts, letters of recommendation, student teaching records, fingerprint card, and so on). These copies are then distributed to the personnel division, certification division, fingerprint control division, and accounting/payroll division. When a job applicant calls to determine the status of an application, the district personnel are often not able to respond quickly to the inquiry. What recommendations would you make for more efficient and economical operation of the district office?

RECORDS INVENTORY AND ANALYSIS

OBJECTIVES

Upon completion of this chapter, the student should be able to:

1. State the objectives of, and the rationale for, conducting a records inventory.
2. Describe the procedures for conducting a physical inventory of records and records storage equipment.
3. List the pertinent information included on a records inventory form and on a records storage equipment inventory form.
4. Identify the personnel and other resources involved in conducting both a physical inventory and a questionnaire survey.
5. Describe the elements required in conducting a records analysis.
6. Identify the qualitative and the quantitative criteria for an efficient records storage operation.

Chapter 3 presented the rationale and some general guidelines for establishing a records management program. Such general guidelines help to determine what types of records should be retained, for how long, and in what type(s) of classification systems; and who should oversee the program.

Once these general guidelines have been established—whether for a new business or an existing one—the company can begin a systematic examination and analysis of both records and equipment.

The Records Inventory

An important preliminary step before developing a records management program is to determine the extent and nature of the company's present system. A **records inventory** is conducted to examine and analyze the records presently stored, as well as the types of storage equipment presently used. The following are the major objectives of a records inventory:

1. To identify the types and quantities of records stored and the records storage equipment used. Records would be categorized as correspondence, business forms, reports, books, cards, media, and so forth. Records storage equipment would be categorized as standard- or legal-size; metal or wooden; cabinets or drawers; automated or electronic; correspondence, card, forms, or media files.
2. To provide information on the types of business activities conducted by the company now as well as in the past. Based on the types and quantities of records stored, one could determine the nature of the activities conducted either on a company-wide basis or on a departmental basis. The function of each department—as well as the individuals in the department—may help clarify the structure of the entire organization and lines of responsibility or authority.
3. To ascertain the value of records currently stored. Records and the equipment in which they are stored can be further categorized as vital, essential, important, or nonessential, as discussed in Chapter 10. Determining the value of records would provide guidelines for their proper storage in equipment and in specific classification systems. Identifying the location of vital and essential records is crucial if proper security measures for safeguarding such records have not been previously established.
4. To identify the location of, and need for, stored records within the company. A records inventory reveals not only where records are currently stored but also whether such locations are cost-effective in terms of floor-space utilization; whether storage facilities are accessible to their nearest points of use; and whether proper storage equipment is used in decentralized and/or centralized records storage locations.

5. To provide the basis for establishing records destruction and retention schedules on a company-wide basis. An examination and analysis of the types of records stored will reveal whether records are active or inactive. This would enable management to establish schedules and other guidelines to indicate how long records should be kept before they are transferred to inactive storage areas, destroyed, or otherwise disposed of.

Rationale for a Records Inventory

Records management encompasses all phases in the life cycle of a record. The life cycle begins with the creation or receipt of a record and extends through its storage and retrieval and use to its ultimate disposal or disposition. Even though an organization does not impose or determine a life cycle for specific records, Joan Boyle states:

> Records are created or collected and live on whether... they are organized... or whether... they are stored as part of a records system. In organizations without records programs, records are created or collected, filed or boxed, perhaps stored indefinitely, and may be destroyed without regard for their value to the organization.[1]

Boyle continues that, without a planned records management program, there will appear:

> ... the conflicting claims for ownership of the records, the overlapping and duplicate information in records in different media or different storage locations, the non-record material, the growth in volume, the dissatisfaction, the cavalier attitude of records custodians, the gaps and losses.[2]

Thus before establishing a records management program, a company must conduct a thorough examination of existing records and records storage equipment and then analyze those results. The outcome of such an examination and analysis will yield answers to the following questions:

1. How will records be requested and located—by name, subject, or number?
2. What is the volume of records to be filed, measured in filing inches?
3. How much filing and retrieval activity is anticipated?
4. Are the records active or inactive; vital or historical?
5. Are there peak periods of filing and retrieval activity? When?

[1]Joan Boyle, "Managing the Records Life Cycle," *Information Management*, Vol. 18, No. 11 (November 1984), p. 25.
[2]Ibid.

6. How many people have access to the records? What people? What filed information do they require?
7. What methods of charge-out and follow-up will be used?
8. What types of and how much equipment is available?
9. How much space is available? How much additional space will be needed for projected growth and expansion?
10. How do the records flow through the organization?[3]

Such a survey may be accomplished by a physical inventory of records, a personal interview of individual departments and/or users, or a questionnaire. Using a combination of methods provides more accurate information because a more comprehensive survey would be accomplished and more users would be involved.

The Inventory

The **records inventory** is an inventory taken of all records and their supporting data, classified according to categories of documents. Such an inventory provides a consistent and objective evaluation of the functions of the records stored as well as the business activities reflected by the stored records. The need to conduct a records inventory usually becomes apparent when the volume of records increases beyond the existing storage capacity.

The records inventory provides management with a sound foundation upon which to base its entire records management program, especially its records retention and destruction schedules (discussed in Chapter 5). Based on both qualitative and quantitative information, management can also make long-range plans for implementing phases of the program. Appropriate personnel and fiscal resources can then be allocated for the overall operation of the program, and relevant policies for managing and controlling records can be established as follows:

1. Organize and develop a central system to increase efficiency and reduce costs.
2. Accurately estimate growth and provide adequate space and allow for expansion.
3. Select equipment that is flexible enough to accommodate different types, sizes, and styles of media stored.
4. Improve security for the entire records system.
5. Develop a filing system within each record series to access any specific file.

[3]*ARMA International Guideline for Records and Information Management: Numeric Filing* (Prairie Village, Kansas: Association of Records Managers and Administrators, Inc., 1989), p. 1.

6. Develop a records control system for documents that are charged out of the system[4].

The inventory involves collecting information about all records according to their types, functions, and value and then identifying them by record series. A *record series* is a group of identical or related records that are normally used and filed as a unit. Correspondence in hard-copy form is an example of a record series, since such records are stored together in standard file-drawer cabinets or shelves, or in drawers. Other examples of record series include microfilm, microfiche, or aperture cards stored in file drawers; 16mm films or computer tapes stored in open-shelf units; and computer floppy disks or microfiche stored in desk-top rotary file units.

Each record series, then, consists of individual *files* or *file groups*, which are groups of related documents. For example, within a correspondence file there could be separate folders or files for each correspondent or customer, each topic, or each geographic location.

In addition to accounting for all active records, the inventory also includes collecting information on the flow of these records through the organization—to determine how and where records are used and by whom, what their chronological span is, and what their final disposition is.[5]

The records inventory involves completing some type of records inventory form for each record series, with the inventory to include the contents of all records storage equipment—file cabinets, drawers, and shelves; file boxes, trays, and bins; desktops and countertops; and desk drawers. All forms of records must be included in the inventory—paper records, microforms, and electronic records. A comprehensive inventory will yield an accurate picture of the company's total records collection, maintenance, and use.

Physical Inventory

To take a **physical inventory,** selected individuals conduct a physical search of all records, records storage equipment, and facilities. A thorough accounting of all records stored with the company makes possible an objective analysis—item by item—of their types, quantities, and locations.

Factors to be considered in conducting a physical inventory are personnel needs, the scope of the inventory, and the survey instruments to be used for inventorying both records and equipment.

Personnel Needs The individuals who conduct the records inventory must be aware of the objectives and methods for conducting such an inventory. Because of the amount of time, effort, and expense that goes into such an

[4]Susan L. Cisco, "The Records Manager and a Total Systems Approach," *The Office*, Vol. 100, No. 4 (October 1984), pp. 188, 196.

[5]Jean Ciura, "Establishing Criteria for Information Appraisal," *Information Management*, Vol. 18, No. 12 (December 1984), pp. 14–15.

undertaking, the people selected must be able to work together toward the stated goals; to communicate effectively with one another, with management, and with their co-workers; and to perform a thorough, accurate, and objective inventory.

In establishing a records management program, a company may require that 50–60 percent of the planning time be allocated solely to the physical inventory. This percentage of time, and the commitment of management to perform this inventory, indicates the importance of an inventory preliminary to developing a sound records management program.

Management personnel will either appoint a committee of company employees to conduct the inventory (in-house committee) or hire an outside consulting firm. The number of people required to conduct the inventory will depend on the size of the company, the time allotted for the inventory, and the volume of records to be inventoried.

According to Leahy and Cameron, an average of 150 cubic feet of records can be inventoried per day by a well-trained, experienced records analyst.[6]

An in-house committee may comprise management-level people, such as the records manager, financial officer, an office manager, and perhaps a legal officer. These individuals are familiar with the activities of the business; they are known to other employees of the company; and they can have access to records without difficulty or interference. These advantages of using an in-house committee are, however, offset by the following disadvantages:

1. The individuals must be adequately trained to conduct a comprehensive inventory. This training must cover not only the role of the inventory to the total records management program, but also the procedures for categorizing records and the equipment. Such individuals must also know how to record data on the inventory forms and how to follow the procedures to conduct the inventory efficiently. Such training would involve additional preparation time prior to the actual inventory.
2. In-house personnel may tend to overlook certain areas of stored records because of their familiarity with the company, the individual departments, and/or the nature of the records themselves. These individuals may assume many facts about the records and bypass a thorough and objective inventory.
3. Not being professional records analysts, company personnel may tend to take more time to complete the inventory satisfactorily. This will increase the cost of the inventory, and time is taken away from the employees' jobs. In addition, there is the possibility of overtime pay and/or the hiring of outside temporary help to maintain the employees' work loads during the inventory.

[6]Emmett Leahy and Christopher A. Cameron, *Modern Records Management* (New York: McGraw-Hill Book Company, 1965), p. 30.

4. Because employees are taken away from their regular jobs, the inventory may be considered by the employees as an additional chore for which no extra compensation is offered. Thus the inventory may not be taken as seriously as it should, or it will be completed hurriedly so the employees—and the company—can resume their normal operations.

Outside consulting firms provide specially trained individuals to conduct records inventories and analyses. They understand the importance of the inventory in the development of a records management program. They can also be objective in their approach to the inventory. They know what practices other comparable businesses follow and can make recommendations based on such comparative data.

A written proposal should be obtained from several consultants to determine the scope of work to be done, the costs, the estimated time for completing the inventory, and references from companies for whom inventories were previously conducted. Even after a careful investigation, some disadvantages will still exist:

1. Consultants are not as knowledgeable about the company or its operations as its employees. Therefore, consultants see only fragments of the total operations and procedures.
2. These individuals usually perform only one phase of the records analysis—the physical inventory—and may not be on hand to follow through with the complete analysis. For the consultants to participate in the analysis stage, additional costs could be incurred.
3. Because they are outsiders to the company, outside consultants may not gain the confidence of company employees. Also, there exists the possibility of altered work loads for employees resulting from the completed inventory and analysis.
4. In spite of their training and knowledge, consultants may not be able to produce a workable plan for implementing needed changes, partly based on factors 1 and 2 above. Additional time may be warranted to allow the consultants to implement their recommendations and to guide the company during the transition into an operational records management program.

Scope of the Inventory One of the major objectives of the records inventory is to identify the types and quantities of records and records storage equipment located within the company. Included within the scope of such an inventory are factors such as where to begin, what time schedule should be followed, and what is to be inventoried.

Where to Begin. Before starting the actual inventory, floor plans of each department or unit should be drawn to identify the locations of all existing records storage areas and equipment. This can greatly expedite inventory taking because individuals can be assigned specific areas. Such floor plans would be required eventually as part of the records analysis phase to determine the appropriateness of existing storage locations. All storage areas should be identified by location, using number codes to identify both the location and number of each piece of equipment (see Figure 4-1).

The currency and the accessibility of active records would make it easy to inventory the active records storage area before the inactive records. However, because inactive records are not being used frequently, these storage areas can be inventoried without interfering with personnel and normal business operations. Also, by inventorying inactive records first, personnel are able to establish and refine inventory-taking procedures before inventorying the active records.

Inventory Schedule. As mentioned previously, between 50 and 60 percent of the planning of a records management program can be devoted to the physical inventory itself. A schedule must be developed and coordinated with those who will be conducting the inventory as well as with all departments and employees. Ideally, the inventory should be approached on a department-by-department basis, with approximate dates set up and a sequence of inventory sites established. Following a timetable will ensure that all areas of the company are covered and that the individuals conducting the inventory can plan for their respective assignments. A schedule will also prevent fewer disruptions of the normal operations of the company, especially during peak work loads.

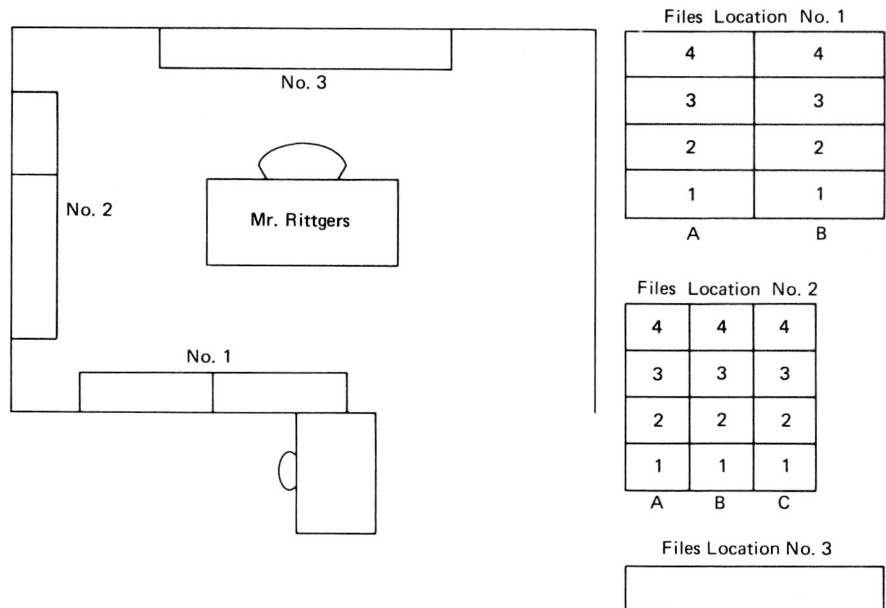

FIGURE 4–1 Identification of records storage areas by location and number.

What to inventory. If an inventory is to be thorough and comprehensive, all records must be accounted for: correspondence, business forms, reports, books and catalogs, maps, photographs, media, cards, microforms, and so on. Since records are inventoried and accounted for by types of categories, each should be assigned a predetermined code number so it can be readily identified and tallied by the inventory personnel.

The inventory should encompass not only those records stored in file cabinets, drawers, and shelves, but also those housed in employees' desk drawers or credenzas, those stored on top of desks or counters, and those housed in metal or wooden card file boxes, trays, wheels, or tubs.

Both active and inactive records should be inventoried. Inactive records are no longer referred to on a regular basis and should be stored separately from the active, or frequently referenced, records. By including inactive records in the inventory, management will be able to develop records maintenance, retention, transfer, and destruction schedules appropriate for these records and for subsequent inactive records. Since inactive records provide historical data about the company and its operations, there should be a category for them in the inventory (also based on types of records) and in the records management program when it is implemented.

Identifying and accounting for records storage equipment is also part of the records inventory. Such information would reveal whether the types and number of equipment are appropriate for the kinds and quantities of records presently stored. Distinctions should be made, for example, among letter- or standard-size file drawers and cabinets and legal-size drawers and cabinets; two-, three-, and four-drawer cabinets; correspondence and card or forms files; microforms files; floppy disk, magnetic card or tape, and optical disk files; wooden and steel storage equipment; and so on. A predetermined coding system, such as that used for various types of records, should be developed to allow the inventory personnel to record the existence and location of each type of equipment (see Figure 4-2).

Records Inventory Form A **records inventory form** should be developed for each record series identified in the company. In order to account for all records properly, the following information should be obtained from each department during the inventory:

1. Name of the department or unit
2. Titles of all record series stored and their content
3. Physical descriptions, such as size and color
4. Type of record stored—paper, image, or digital
5. Function or use of each record or record series
6. Filing classification system(s) used
7. Time periods of storage
8. Frequency with which records are used

9. Quantity of records stored (in linear measurement)
10. Records storage equipment used—type and number
11. Location of records storage equipment
12. Suggested retention/disposition of records
13. General comments and recommendations

Figure 4-3 shows two samples of records inventory forms. Neither form requires that much writing be done by the inventory personnel; yet both forms would provide the necessary data for both the inventory and the subsequent analysis of records.

Equipment Inventory During the physical inventory of stored records, records storage and retrieval equipment can also be inventoried. The equipment should provide the following information:

1. Types of equipment used
2. Kinds or forms of records stored in the equipment
3. Location of all equipment
4. Condition of each piece of equipment
5. Recommendations for retention/disposition or use
6. Comments or recommendations

A separate equipment inventory form can be designed for this purpose, although such information will generally be incorporated in the records inventory form itself.

A physical inventory involves a great deal of effort from the company personnel or outside consultants. It takes time to complete a physical inventory thoroughly and correctly. In addition, an understanding of the role the inventory will play in the establishment of the total records management program is important.

The second method of conducting an inventory of company records and records storage equipment is the questionnaire.

Questionnaire Inventory

The **questionnaire** method seeks to obtain the same information about records and records storage equipment as the physical inventory. The questionnaire is developed and distributed to key departmental personnel for completion. The questionnaire form should contain questions similar to the items included on the records inventory form shown in Figure 4-3 so that identical types of information can be gathered.

One advantage of using a questionnaire is that fewer records management employees are required to participate in the inventory, since completing the questionnaire becomes a part of each department manager's responsibilities.

INVENTORY EQUIPMENT CODE

Code

Code		
L	-	Legal metal transfer case
l	-	Letter metal transfer case
L_5	-	Standard 5 drawer, legal size, metal cabinet (L_4 - 4 drawer, L_3 - 3 drawer, L_2 - 2 drawer)
l_5	-	Standard 5 drawer letter size, metal cabinet (l_4 - 4 drawer, l_3 - 3 drawer, l_2 - 2 drawer)
P	-	Packages or bundles of any kind
V	-	Volumes (Books of Account, Tab Reports)
SS	-	Steel Shelving
SC	-	Supply Cabinets metal
S	-	Safe - metal
T	-	Tabulating Card Boxes (Standard metal or wood)
D	-	Desk or tub files - metal
C	-	Card Files - metal - C^3 - 3 x 5, C^4 - 4 x 6, C^5 - 5 x 8
W	-	Wooden Equipment lW_5 - 5 Drawer, letter size wodden cabinet lW - Wooden transfer case, letter size LW_4 - 4 Drawer, legal size wooden cabinet WS - Wood shelving
F	-	Cardboard or fibre equipment lF - Fibre transfer case - letter size

Examples: (In inventory, equipment is expressed in terms of drawers.)

- 3 l_5 - 3 Drawer - letter size in 5 drawer cabinet
- 10 lW_5 - 10 Letter size wooden transfer cases
- 6 CW - 6 Wooden 5" x 8" card files

Volume: 1 - 1.50 cubic feet - L - 2.00 cubic feet

Coding system for inventorying equipment. (Courtesy of William Benedon.)

Because the questionnaire reflects the records storage systems and equipment in individual departments, a quicker classification of records and equipment may be obtained. The questionnaire method has all the same disadvantages as using in-house personnel to conduct a physical inventory. The following additional disadvantages may also apply:

1. The questionnaire must be carefully constructed and worked by knowledgeable management personnel (or perhaps by records management consultants) to cover specific aspects of the particular company. Department personnel responding to the questionnaire must be able to understand the instructions, the terminology, the coding system, the purpose for the survey, and its importance. Questions must be clearly written so that individuals report the required data properly.
2. The questionnaire cannot provide as thorough an inventory or accounting of records and storage equipment as a physical inventory. It can only cover the surface of records storage systems and equipment, and such a picture is based on only one person's interpretation or knowledge. Thus while it does reveal how records are classified, in what types of equipment they are stored, and where the equipment is located, it may not give a very accurate representation of the actual value of records stored or their functions.
3. A questionnaire does not reveal the duplication of records in other departments. Thus the accuracy of such a survey is questionable. Coordinating efforts to cross-check possible duplication of records and equipment is costly and time-consuming. Thus the attempt to obtain a thorough inventory may be defeated.
4. There is usually no interaction or communication among departments unless all participants are eventually involved in the analysis of the questionnaire results. At that point, any questions or comments may be discussed and some coordination of efforts may be needed to complete additional phases of the records inventory.

Whether a physical inventory or a questionnaire is used, the end result is the same—the identification of the kinds of records that are kept, how many, and where. An intermediate result of a records inventory is the knowledge of which inactive records can be discarded or destroyed immediately, which records can be moved to other storage equipment or facilities, and which records (active) should be included in the records maintenance program in the future.

Electronic Media Inventory

Just as paper records and microforms stored in file drawers, cabinets, and shelves must be accounted for in a records inventory, so must computer software—programs and data disks. **Programs** refer to either commercial programs created for such specific purposes as word processing, database man-

Years	Description	Location	Equipment	Footage

Department	Division	Section	Unit	O C D

Record Title	Form No.	Report No.

RECORDS INVENTORY WORK SHEET

RECORDS INVENTORY WORK SHEET

Years	Range	Area	Location	Equipment	Cu. Ft.	Action

Description	
	Off. C. F.
	Stor. C. F.
	Vault C. F.
Records Title	Organization

FIGURE 4-3 Sample records inventory forms. (Courtesy of William Benedon.)

agement, graphics and spreadsheets, or project management (off-the-shelf programs), or proprietary programs created by programmers to meet specific functions within an organization. **Data disks** are magnetic floppy disks on which information or data are stored for later retrieval, manipulation, and retention. Floppy disks are available either in the 5-1/4 inch format or the 3-1/2 inch format.

The records inventory must include a comprehensive inventory of all computer software, whether commercial software or proprietary—whether stored on hard disk systems, floppy disks, or other storage source. (It should be noted that whether commercial programs or in-house proprietary programs are used, the original programs are stored separate from any legally-authorized working copies.)

A software inventory can be created and maintained on a computer using a commercialized database management program such as **dBASE** by Ashton-Tate, or similar applications software designed for maintaining collections of data files. Such **database programs** allow information to be entered and stored in random sequence, accessed sequentially or randomly according to predefined characteristics, sorted by particular characteristics, and printed in various formats.

The characteristics, objectives, and various media and procedures related to the creation and maintenance of electronic records are discussed in Chapter 9.

The Association of Records Managers and Administrators, Inc., suggests that the following types of information be maintained for each copy of each software program:[6]

Name of software
Vendor
Type of software
Brief description (user and function)
Software version and copyright date
Owner/user/department name
Owner/user/department manager name
Location of software
Date of purchase
Serial number
Language(s) used, if applicable
Hardware requirement
System memory requirement
Special requirements: computer or operating system specifications; type of monitor or printer
Security considerations

Each descriptive piece of information listed above is called a *field*, referring to a single statement. A *record* would consist of all information—all fields about any one software program. The entire collection or grouping of records

[6]*Electronic Recordkeeping* (Prairie Village, Kansas: Association of Records Mangers and Administrators, 1989), p. 4.

related to one type of general information is called a *file* or a *database* of all such related information.

Once all software programs have been accounted for—listed or entered in the database program—specific records are retrieved or accessed by keyboarding the particular identifying characteristics desired, such as the following:

Type(s) of programs available (word processing, database management, accounting, graphics, spreadsheets, etc.)

Type(s) of programs available for specific systems (IBM or IBM-compatible environment or the Macintosh environment)

Software programs in use within certain departments

Software programs in use by function of use

Databases for other types of records can be created in the same way, based on the type of database program or database management system available. The general purpose is to account for equipment (hardware) as well as the software (programs).

Dedicated or specialized **database management programs** (DBMS) are discussed in Chapter 9.

Records Analysis

Once an inventory of existing records and storage equipment has been completed, all data from the various departments or units can be combined for the **records analysis.** From these data, an organization can proceed to analyze its total records management operations by assigning values to records, documenting current operations, analyzing functions and tasks, establishing standards, and identifying needed changes or improvements.

Assigning Values to Records

Having identified through the inventory the types of records stored, an organization can assign a value to each series of records. These values will then be used to determine the retention period or disposition schedule for each record series. Records are categorized into four levels according to their value or function in the operation of the business: administrative, fiscal, legal, or historical.

A record having **administrative value** is one that relates to the organizational structure, operations, or function of the company. Examples of such records are organizational charts, procedures or operations manuals, policies, and personnel or product development information. **Fiscal value** is assigned to records that provide evidence of a company's financial condition, data used to prepare annual reports or tax returns, and documents used to support purchases and sales. Examples of such records are accounts receivables and accounts payables, earnings records, and purchase and sales invoices.

Records that have **legal value** could include incorporation, ownership, or acquisition/merger documents; shareholder information; contracts and legal agreements; or documents required by government agencies. The **historical value** of a record relates to "the usefulness of records for documenting an organization's policies, key personnel, major transactions, processes, trademarks and events. Typically, about 5 percent of total records have historical value."[7] Examples of records with historical value include minutes of directors' meetings, marketing and advertising materials, and other items that may be of interest to the company or the public in the future. These types of records are generally considered irreplaceable and should be earmarked for storage in a vital records, archival records, or other protective storage environment.

Documenting Current Operations

Based on a company-wide inventory of records and records storage equipment, an organization can identify the existing functions and operations of each department; the flow of work among personnel and work stations; and the use made of records, equipment, and personnel. The analysis will also yield information about the location and use of records storage equipment and how efficiently such systems are being used.

Analyzing Functions and Tasks

Once current operations, job functions, and work flow are identified, each can be analyzed further in terms of its effectiveness, cost, and productivity. Although the critical question to be answered is, "Are records accessible when needed by individuals?" other questions should also be asked:

1. Who uses the records?
2. How often are records referenced?
3. How are records used?
4. Where are records stored in relation to those who must use them?
5. When is a record considered inactive?
6. Who is responsible for the stored records?

Establishing Standards

Records management functions should be established, maintained, and evaluated in terms of their overall effectiveness in meeting predetermined standards. A *standard* is a measure of quality and quantity. The results of various

[7]Katherine Aschner, ed., *Taking Control of Your Office Records: A Manager's Guide* (White Plains, NY: Knowledge Industry Publications, Inc. 1983), p. 247.

work measurement studies should be consulted to obtain data that can be used to establish standards relevant to a company's needs.

The following benefits can be derived by using standards for measuring records management activities:

1. The cost of performing specific tasks or work can be determined.
2. Personnel costs, equipment costs, and floor space costs can be allocated according to each cost center—department or section.
3. More effective control of work, personnel schedules, equipment, and systems can be maintained.
4. Employees can be held accountable for their work, which should be based on predetermined goals or objectives.
5. Each department or unit can also be held accountable for its productivity and its contribution to the overall effectiveness of the organization.
6. Guidelines can be established against which to measure future operations, personnel, equipment, and systems.

Qualitative standards for records management relate simply to how effective or ineffective an operation is in providing information to users when needed. Factors include the quality and number of trained personnel to perform the necessary work; comfort and safety of the work environment; efficient arrangement of workers, equipment, and systems; efficient flow of work from one work station to another; clearly defined and understandable procedures and tasks; and effective supervision.

The quantitative standards established include work standards for the manual sorting and filing of records, filing efficiency, and records retrieval efficiency. Quantitative standards are generally measured in terms of quantity of documents sorted and filed per hour. The sorting standard is based on the time required to sort documents such as invoices and vouchers and other number-coded records into numeric sequence. The filing standard is based on the time required to file paper records and cards in alphabetic sequence, by subject sequence, and so forth. The Administrative Management Society, Willow Grove, Pennsylvania, publishes a *Reference Guide* outlining standards of work per hour for these tasks.

The efficiency of a filing operation is measured by the amount of time required to place a record in its proper storage place in a file drawer or on a shelf. The efficiency of a records retrieval operation is measured by the speed with which stored records can be located and removed from their storage places. The following are factors that influence the efficiency of the filing and retrieval processes:

Records classification system(s) (used—alphabetic, numeric, alphanumeric)

The volume of records

The forms of records (paper, microimages, digital)

The types of records storage equipment and systems used

The amount of cross-referencing required and the components used for cross-referencing

Ease of use of records storage equipment

Johnson and Kallaus cite the following statistics concerning the ability of a records storage system to provide information when needed:

1. A typical office struggles along with about 3 percent of its paper physically misfiled. However, this fact is not known until a record is accidentally discovered to be filed in the wrong location.
2. One filing authority suggests that even a 1-percent failure to find requested items would be excessive.
3. In subject files, it is estimated that 20 percent of the search time is spent in looking several places before the desired document is found. Normally, no more than two to three minutes should be required to locate any item requested.[8]

Identifying Needed Changes

The records analysis can now proceed to comparing the existing operations and functions with those that are recommended as a result of the inventory and analysis. If standards have previously been defined, they should be the basis against which current operations, personnel, and procedures are evaluated.

According to George C. Cunningham, "The analysis of current operations in the office often means... a redefinition of responsibilities and redistribution of functions."[9] Changes that may result from the analysis include developing more effective operating procedures or guidelines; reallocating space for records storage equipment and systems; reorganizing personnel or job responsibilities to create a smoother work flow; redefining job specifications; and automating records operations. However, anyone who thinks that an automated system is the cure for any problem identified in the records inventory and analysis should heed this warning from Cunningham:

> In pursuit of the desire to "automate the office," one of the most frequent mistakes is the automating of the status quo. The result, when dealing with a system or approach that has been unchanged and uncontrolled for

[8]Mina M. Johnson and Norman F. Kallaus, *Records Management* (Cincinnati: South-Western Publishing Co., 1982), p. 350.

[9]George C. Cunningham, "Preparation and Planning for Technology in Records Management," *Information Management*, Vol. 18, No. 3 (March 1984), p. 24.

years, can be the disastrous automating of a poor, inefficient and archaic operation.[10]

The records inventory and analysis should provide the following information, which can be incorporated into the planning for the records management program:

1. Recommendations for a company-wide records management program (discussed in Chapter 3)
2. Development of records retention/destruction schedules (discussed in Chapter 5)
3. Determination of filing classification system(s) for various departments or units or for certain types of records (discussed in Chapter 7)
4. Identification of types, quantities, and locations of vital records within the company (discussed in Chapter 9)
5. Recommendations for controlling correspondence and reports (discussed in Chapter 11)
6. Development of records management procedures manuals for all departments and company personnel (discussed in Chapter 12)
7. Recommendations for controlling the design and use of forms (discussed in Chapter 13)
8. Determination of the need for micrographic applications (discussed in Chapter 15)

CHAPTER HIGHLIGHTS

- A records inventory is an examination and analysis of the records presently stored in an organization. Completing an inventory is the first step in developing a records management program.
- The objectives of a records inventory are to identify the types and quantities of records and records storage equipment; to provide information about the types of business activities conducted; to determine the value of stored records; to identify the location of stored records; and to provide the basis for establishing records retention and destruction schedules.
- The business activities conducted by an organization or a department can be revealed by analyzing the function and flow of information.
- A physical inventory requires that selected individuals conduct a physical search of all records, records storage equipment, and facilities.
- Without a records inventory and analysis, a company is not able to account

[10]Ibid.

for costs of its overall operations, personnel effectiveness, document creation and retention patterns, or the usefulness of stored records.

- The outcome of a records inventory provides the basis for management decisions concerning projected growth and adequate allocation of space to house records and equipment, selection of equipment to accommodate the various types of records stored, development of filing system(s) to aid in accessing information, and development of a records control system for charged-out documents.
- A record series is a group of identical or related records generally used, filed, and disposed of as a unit. Files or file groups are groups of related documents within a series of records.
- The personnel who conduct the inventory—whether in-house or outside consultants—need to be familiar with its objectives, methods and procedures, and importance.
- Individuals within an organization who may participate in the inventory may include the records manager, a financial officer, a legal officer, and an office manager.
- Disadvantages of having in-house personnel conduct the physical inventory are that they would require training in both the role of the inventory and the procedures involved in categorizing records and equipment; that they are so familiar with the company, its operations, and the nature of records that they may overlook certain areas of stored records; that they may take more time to complete the inventory; that they would be taken away from their regular jobs, so they may not take the inventory work as seriously or may complete it hurriedly.
- Employing outside consultants to conduct the records inventory has the advantage of having specially trained individuals who know what practices comparable businesses are following.
- Outside consultants do not have first-hand knowledge of the company or its operations, and they do not generally participate in the follow-up inventory analysis. Thus consultants may not perform as comprehensive a survey as in-house personnel.
- An inventory of all records storage equipment would include identification of the types of equipment used, the kinds or forms of records stored in them, and the location and the condition of each piece of equipment.
- The records inventory questionnaire seeks to obtain the same information about records and equipment as the physical inventory; however, the duplication of records cannot be identified through the questionnaire.
- Key departmental personnel complete the questionnaire as part of their responsibilities. These individuals are familiar with their own records, equipment, and records use, so they can provide a quicker and more accurate classification.
- The questionnaire must be carefully constructed so individuals responding

to it can understand the instructions, the terminology, and how to complete it.

- A records analysis, the examination of the results of the records inventory, provides information that can be used to assign values to records, to document current operations, to analyze functions and tasks, to establish standards, and to identify changes or improvements needed in the records management operations.
- Records can be categorized according to their administrative, fiscal, legal, or historical value to the organization.
- Documenting current operations—existing functions and operations of each department; the work flow among personnel and work stations; and the use made of records, equipment and personnel—provides the basis for a comparison of functions and tasks.
- Qualitative and quantitative standards are used to measure the efficiency and effectiveness of the current operations and systems. Qualitative standards relate to how accessible information is to users when needed. Quantitative standards relate to the amount of time required to place or replace a record in its storage place and the amount of time required to access and retrieve stored records.
- The results of a records analysis should provide information for establishing the records management program: developing records retention/destruction schedules; determining what filing classification system(s) to use; identifying types, quantities, and locations of vital records; developing procedures manuals; controlling correspondence, reports, and forms; and determining the feasibility of micrographics applications.

QUESTIONS FOR REVIEW

1. What is the purpose of a records inventory? What role does it have in the total records management program?
2. What types of information about records and records storage equipment can be determined by a records inventory?
3. What is the difference between a physical inventory and a questionnaire inventory? What are the advantages and disadvantages of each?
4. In determining the scope of a record inventory, what factors should be considered?
5. What types of information should be included on a records inventory form and on a records equipment inventory form?
6. What are the five elements of a records analysis? Describe each briefly.
7. What are the four values that can be assigned to records, based on their function in a company?
8. What are some of the benefits that can be derived by having predetermined standards for tasks and personnel?

In what quantitative ways can the efficiency of a filing operation be measured or determined?

How can a company use the results of the records inventory and the analysis in establishing or implementing a records management program?

THE DECISION MAKER

Case Studies

1. The records manager of a local college has asked that a records inventory be made using a survey questionnaire. The questionnaire will be submitted to the president of the college, three vice presidents (personnel, instruction, and student activities), and eight department heads. Develop an appropriate questionnaire that can be used by the college's administrative staff.
2. Based on Case Study 1, what types of records and records storage equipment might you expect to find within the offices of the college's administrative staff? Prepare a listing of the possible types of records to be listed on the survey questionnaire. After the results of the inventory are collected and analyzed, what would be the next step taken by the college in establishing a records management program? Outline those steps for the president.

Retention and Disposition of Records

OBJECTIVES

Upon completion of this chapter, the student should be able to:

1. Discuss the importance of a records retention program.
2. Explain the different values a record may have.
3. Cite the purposes of the *Code of Federal Regulations* and the *Federal Register.*
4. Explain the steps for transferring records.
5. Describe the importance of a records disposal program.

It has been estimated that the typical company doubles its volume of records every 10 years. This rapid growth emphasizes the need for an efficient records handling plan, founded on a solid understanding of the life cycle of a record. (Chapter 1 included a discussion of the life cycle of a record.) For a records system to function smoothly, records must move through the various phases of the life cycle on a predetermined schedule.

Records Retention

Following the records inventory discussed in Chapter 4, the records manager can begin developing the retention and disposition program. In general, records retention programs are developed to retain and protect a company's vital records and to dispose of the records that no longer serve a useful purpose. The most important document in any retention and disposition program is the retention schedule.

Records Retention Schedule

A **records retention schedule** is a documented agreement among the records creator, the records user, and the records manager as to the retention and disposition of a record. In effect, the schedule specifies how long each type of active record is to be held for reference, the length of time it is to be held in storage for semiactive reference, and when the record may be destroyed.

What Is a Record?

Documents may be records or nonrecords. In simple terms, a **record** is any document valuable enough to be retained. The record can take the form of motion pictures, microfilm, maps, charts, drawings, correspondence, photographs, magnetic tapes, and so on. In most organizations the majority of records are paper documents.

Since retention programs also deal with nonrecords, it is crucial to recognize them. **Nonrecords** are documents made for the convenience of the organization that are disposed of after use. Nonrecords may include routing slips, transmittal sheets, temporary copies of correspondence, reading-file copies of correspondence, duplicate copies of all documents in the same file, superseded manuals, and notes. When developing retention schedules, one must remember this vital difference between records and nonrecords. If nonrecords are allowed to become mixed with records, many hours of valuable time and floor space will be wasted.

As discussed earlier, records can be active or inactive. Active records are those used in the normal everyday operation of an organization. Inactive records are not used in the normal everyday operation of an organization and have therefore been transferred to an inactive storage area.

RECORDS APPRAISAL

The beginning phase of the process is to appraise the records. The *appraisal* determines the value of the records to an organization. There are two basic appraisal categories: (1) records of a permanent nature to be preserved by the organization; and (2) records that are disposable, either immediately or at some later date. To determine in which category a record belongs, the records manager appraises the function and use of the record.

Value of Records

When the value and purposes of a record are assessed, every record will fall into at least one of six subcategories. These six subcategories are administrative, evidential, fiscal, informational, legal, and scientific. The National Archives and Records Service (NARS) of the U.S. government describes the primary and secondary values of records, based on their uses. These values and uses are:

Primary Value	Secondary Value
1. Administrative	5. Evidential
2. Legal	6. Informational
3. Fiscal	
4. Scientific	

The **primary** or **active value** of records is of interest to the organization only for current operations and includes the administrative, fiscal, legal, and scientific uses. Records have an **administrative value** if they help an organization perform its current work, whether short- or long-term work. Therefore, routine requisitions have short-term value, while certain directives, policies, and regulations have long-term value. Records have a **legal value** if they contain evidence of the legal rights and obligations of an organization. Documents having legal value may consist of leases, titles, contracts, legal decisions and opinions, and agreements. Recrods having **fiscal value** are generally those relating to all financial transactions and are accumulated for fiscal or year-end use. Records with fiscal value may include budget documents, vouchers, accounting records, tax statements, and licenses. Records with **scientific** or **research value** are ones that consist of technical data gathered as a result of scientific research. These records may also be used for organizational studies or in legal investigations.

The **secondary** or **inactive value** of records pertains to those that may have a historic or archival use. The NARS categorizes these records as evidential and informational. Records with evidentiary value deal with an organization's origins, policies, and procedures. These records may include directives, manuals, organizational charts, directories, articles of incorporation, and handbooks. Records with informational value deal with information generated by the organization, in which the data relates to persons, places, things, and phenomena. Records having informational value could include lists of boards of directors, a document signed by a well-known person, patent documents, building blueprints, field-survey notebooks, aerial photographs, maps, or documents dealing with an election or some catastrophe like a fire or flood.

One can readily see that after reviewing all the values of records that some records may have more than one value. They may also have different values at different times. Therefore, it is incumbent upon the records management personnel to make the proper classification of a record.

Federal, State, and Local Legal Aspects

The legal implications of records retention must also be considered. As one might expect, the various legal requirements affecting records retention are staggering. According to Records Control, Inc., there are more than 240 federal regulations pertaining to business in general. There are well over 900 federal regulations pertaining to records retention, as well as more than 430 state regulations that pertain only to the retention and/or microfilming of business records.[1] There are also many county and municipal regulations. Depending upon the kind of organization, regulations from one or more sectors may apply to records retention. Records personnel, with assistance from the organization's legal department, must keep abreast of all regulations pertaining to records retention. In addition to regulations regarding retention, the records manager should maintain a file of regulations pertaining to all aspects of the records management program.

According to ELECTRONIC RECORDKEEPING, "While an approved records schedule for a record requested in a court proceeding does not guarantee the court's acceptance of it, the fact that a record is scheduled definitely helps to meet the requirement given in federal government regulations of a submitted record being created as a "regular practice" of the agency. Federal courts accept the defense that records have been disposed of under an approved records disposition schedule."

Source: ELECTRONIC RECORDKEEPING, U. S. General Services Administration, July, 1989, p. 20.

[1]*The Retention Book—Retention and Preservation of Records with Destruction Schedules,* 10th ed. (Chicago, IL: Record Controls, Inc., 1981).

National Archives and Records Service

In 1934, Congress founded the National Archives, which put controls on the growth of federal records. The Records Disposal Act of 1943 is the basis for today's records disposal programs, which became mandatory for federal agencies in 1950 through the Federal Records Act and was updated by the Federal Records Amendment of 1976. In 1980, the Paperwork Reduction Act addressed the need to manage information as a resource.

Among its many activities, the **National Archives and Records Service (NARS)** publishes the **Code of Federal Regulations**, which is a guide to federal regulations. This publication is the codification of rules and regulations issued by the various agencies of the federal government. Figure 5-1 shows a section from the *Code of Federal Regulations.* The code is separated into 50 titles representing broad subject areas, such as agriculture and commerce. Every title or subject area is further divided into chapters that normally bear the name of the issuing agency. Within each chapter the material is sub-divided into parts containing specific agency regulations. The *Code of Federal Regulations* is updated daily by the **Federal Register.** Each year in January the code is revised from the year's *Federal Register.* To find the latest applicable federal regulations, both publications must be consulted.

FIGURE 5-1 A section from the *Code of Federal Regulations.* (Courtesy of Records Controls, Inc.)

CODE OF FEDERAL REGULATIONS
UNITED STATES GOVERNMENT DEPARTMENTS AND THEIR DIVISIONS

AGRICULTURE DEPARTMENT

Agricultural Marketing Service

Licensed Cottonseed chemists, must retain certain records at least 1 year after date of analysis. 7 CFR 61.15

Fruits, nuts, and vegetables handlers must retain certain records 2 years. Fruits 7 CFR 906.51, 911.60, 916.60, 928.60–993.174. Nuts 7 CFR 981.70, vegetables. 7 CFR 946.70–966.80.

Commission merchants, dealers, and brokers of fruits and vegetables subject to the Perishable Agricultural Commodities Act of 1930 must keep records disclosing all business transactions for 2 years. 7 CFR 46.14–46.32, and 17 CFR 1.20–1.31. Records disclosing ownership and management of business must be kept 4 years. 7 CFR 46.14.

Milk handlers must keep pertinent records 3 years. This period may be extended by market administrators. 7 CFR 1000.5.

Licensed agricultural products warehousemen must retain records 6 years. 7 CFR 101.36, 103.41, 111,44.

Records Retention Publications

In addition to the Code of Federal Regulations, a handful of records retention publications are available to assist the records manager in determining legal requirements. One such publication, the ENCYCLOPEDIA OF RECORDS RETENTION, contains specific retention periods based on operating, research, historical, audit, tax, and legal requirements for over 4,000 records. The Encyclopedia's author, Jesse L. Clark, president of The Records Management Group states:

> "American businesses are creating over a billion documents a year, and the rate of document production is increasing 8 percent annually. About 70 percent of those documents are paper, with the balance on computer media and microfilm. Half of a typical company's data, Clark says, is duplicate or valueless; 40 percent of most organizations' records can be safely destroyed provided it is known which records are of no further value. He estimates that about 87 percent of all computer output should be printed on microfilm instead of paper, for a savings of six cents per page or image. When you factor in the other costs of excess or obsolete business information—in floor space, manpower, inefficiency, and even morale—it's easy to see how good records management practices can drop straight to an organization's bottom line."

Figure 5-2 illustrates a retention schedule from the Encyclopedia of Records Retention by Clark. The illustration shows suggested retention requirements for Accounting, Finance, Insurance, and Taxes.

After carefully considering all the legal ramifications pertaining to records, the records manager may wish to be cautious and retain records longer than required by law. This decision should not be made lightly. Before actually retaining records longer than required, the records manager should carefully review the records value and volume as well as the facilities and resources available.

Development of the Retention Schedule and Form

The records manager should use the records inventory sheets to determine the retention period for each record series. Frequently, the records manager will need assistance in determining the records retention periods. Depending upon organizational structure and operating procedures, a committee may be formed to perform the task. This permits departmental personnel to participate in the decision making. The committee should consist of employees from various parts of the organization who use, store, route, and dispose of the records; it should also include someone from the firm's legal department to advise on the legal aspects of retaining records. Many records managers obtain

FIGURE 5-2 Records Retention Schedule

RC PREFIX 20	FUNCTIONAL CLASSIFICATION ACCOUNTING, FINANCE, INSURANCE, AND TAXES	ISSUE DATE 1990		PAGE 20-1	
RECORD CODE NUMBER	TITLE OR DESCRIPTION OF RECORD	VITAL RECORD	MICRO-FILM	RETENTION PERIOD YEARS	CODE
20-1	Account cards and ledgers except those pertaining to structures			3	06
20-2	Account ledgers—code, date, name and location of subcriber, renewal one year, renewal two years, sales tax and postage, invoice amount, date paid or debited, balance due, voucher number		X	6	04
20-3	Accounting statements showing client positions	X	X	6	
20-4	Accounting workpapers—daily record of department proofs			6	
20-5	Accounts payable index files reflecting voucher numbers pertinent to expenditure of funds			6	
20-6	Accounts payable invoice and paid check files		X	6	04
20-7	Accounts payable ledgers—date, explanation of payment, amount, date paid, voucher, invoice number; serves as a book of original entry recording all payments made by department	X	X	6	04
20-8	Accounts receivable accounting controls/reports (government)		X	6	
20-9	Accounts receivable customer open-item statements			1	
20-10	Accounts receivable details		X	6	
20-11	Accounts receivable details (government)		X	6	
20-12	Accounts receivable invoices and invoice registers, including pertinent credit memoranda	X	X	6	04
20-13	Accounts receivable invoices on uncollectible accounts	X	X	6	04
20-14	Accounts receivable ledgers (government)		X	6	
20-15	Accounts receivable ledgers showing name, personnel number, account, department, floor, subdivision, description, debit, credit, date, new and old balance		X	6	06
20-16	Accounts receivable statements of wages, rents, taxes, miscellaneous income, summaries and lists of disbursements and income		X	6	04
20-17	Accounts receivable tickets—debit and credit tickets which are created for special purposes under management's authorization			6	
20-18	Accrual distribution account records			4	
20-19	Accrued expense files—accrual and reversal memos, workpapers, and accrual vouchers; used for comparative analysis			3	04
20-20	Administrative reports of check-cashing activities prepared weekly showing reconciliation of funds			2	

Source: Courtesy of the Records Management Group, Northfield, IL

two or three levels of approval for the retention schedule.

The actual retention period can be based on company experience, on what other like firms are doing, on other published schedules, or on a combination of all three factors. Figure 5-3 on pp. 102–3 shows a sample records retention schedule. Similar retention schedules are published by many equipment, supplies, and services vendors; they are generally available for the asking. One must remember, however, that these retention schedules should be used not as a final authority but only as a guide in developing a company's retention schedule.

If so desired, the form used for the records inventory can be designed to serve also as the retention schedule form. Regardless of form design, certain specific information must be gathered. Figure 5-4 shows approvals and finalized retention periods listed along with other valuable information.

Principles for Making Valid Retention Decisions

David O. Stephens, CRM and past President of ARMA International, cites five principles for making "good" or "valid" records retention decisions. These principles of retention decision-making are:

PRINCIPLE NUMBER 1: Avoid the "every conceivable contingency syndrome." A records retention program cannot and should not be designed to accommodate every conceivable need for information at any future time, however remote the probability of the need might be.

PRINCIPLE NUMBER 2: Information should be retained if there is a reasonable probability that it will be needed at some future time to support some legitimate legal or business objective and the consequences of its absence would be substantial.

PRINCIPLE NUMBER 3: Records retention policies should generally be conservative in the sense that they do not expose the organization to an inordinate degree of risk. If the only benefit of a short retention period is savings in space, a substantial degree of risk is usually not justified to attain this reward.

PRINCIPLE NUMBER 4: Retention decision-makers must be mindful of the fact that the presence or absence of information can be either helpful or harmful to an organization, depending on specific legal or business contingencies that may arise at any time in the life of the business. It is difficult to predict the occurrence of these contingencies with any certainty. Therefore, the best way to minimize the risks associated with document retention is to provide their systematic disposal immediately after the expiration of their value for legal and business purposes.

PRINCIPLE NUMBER 5: A retention period is most likely to be valid if it is based on a professional consensus of the opinions of persons most knowl-

Suggested Retention Schedule for Business Records

The Retention Schedule shown below was determined by a nationwide survey of record retention schedules recommended by leading authorities on records storage and by the practices of businesses with established procedures. This schedule reflects current business thinking.

A word of caution: Although much study has gone into the preparation of this schedule, the retention periods shown are not offered as final authority, but as guideposts against which to check your company needs. Statutes of limitations for your State, as well as regulations of government agencies pertaining to your business must be considered. Because state retention statutes vary widely on tax, unemployment, and worker's compensation records, check with your regional tax authorities for details. A final precautionary step is to have your CPA or attorney approve your records retention timetable in its final form. Also, there may be very good reasons to keep records longer than legally required, for historical reference purposes.

To be sure that you establish retention periods that are both legal and practical for your own company, follow the procedure outlined on pages 8 to 11 of this Handbook.

For retention requirements established by Federal laws and regulations, see the current "Guide to Record Retention Requirements" published annually in the Federal Register which can be obtained at nominal cost from the Superintendent of Documents, U.S. Government Printing Office, Washington, D.C. 20402.

KEY:
"P" means Permanently, "O" stands for Optional, otherwise the figures represent the suggested number of years for retaining the records.

Accounting and Fiscal

Accounts, charged off	7
Accounts payable ledger	P
Accounts receivable	10
Accounts receivable ledger	10
Balance sheets	5
Bank deposit record	6
Bank reconcilement papers	8
Bank statements	8
Bills collectible	7
Bills of sale of registered bonds	3
Bill stubs	7
Bonds cancelled	3
Bonds registered	P
Bonds, sales or transfer	15
Budget work sheets	3
Building permits	20
Capital stock bills of sales	P
Capital stock certificates	P
Capital stock ledger	P
Capital stock transfer records	P
Cash books	25
Cash receipts & disbursement records	10
Cash sales slips	3
Cash slips	3
Charge slips	10
Check records	7
Check register	10
Checks, dividend	10
Checks, expense	10
Checks, paid & cancelled	9
Checks, payroll	7
Checks, voucher	6
Checks, warrants	P
Correspondence, accounting	5
Correspondence, credit & collection	7
Cost account records	7
Customer ledger	P
Donations	7
Drafts paid	8
Earnings register	3
Entertainment, gifts & gratuities	3
Estimates, projections	7
Expense reports, departmental	5
Expense reports, employees	5
Financial statements, certified	P
Financial statements, periodic	P
Fixed capital records	P
General cash book	25
General journal	10
General journal supporting papers	P
General ledger	P
Notes, cancelled	10
Note ledgers	P
Payroll register	7
Petty cash records	3
Plant ledger	P
Profit and loss statements	P
Property asset summary	10
Royalty ledger	P
Salesman commission reports	3
Stock ledger	P
Tabulating cards & magnetic tape	1
Traveling auditor reports	15
Trial balance, accounts receivable	3
Trial balance sheets	P
Uncollectible accounts	7
Work papers, rough	2

Administrative

Audit reports, internal	10
Audit reports, public & government	P
Audit work papers, internal	6
Classified documents: control, inventories, reports	5
Correspondence, accounting	5
Correspondence, advertising	3
Correspondence, credit & collection	7
Correspondence, engineering & technical	10
Correspondence, general	3
Correspondence, personal	6
Correspondence, production	2
Correspondence, purchase	5
Correspondence, sales & service	3
Correspondence, tax	20
Correspondence, traffic	6

FIGURE 5-3
Records retention schedule. (Copyright © 1986 by Bankers Box/Fellowes Manufacturing Co., Itasca, IL.)

Record	Retention
Forms control	5
Inventory cards	3
Inventory, plant records	P
Organized charts	P
Requisitions	3
Research reports	20
System & procedure records	P
Telegram & cable copies	3
Telephone records	P
Advertising	
Activity reports, media schedules	5
Contracts	10
Contracts, advertising	7
Correspondence	5
Drawings & artwork	P
Estimates	2
House organs	P
Market data & surveys	5
Samples, displays, labels, etc.	P
Tear sheets	3
Corporate	
Annual reports	P
Authority to issue securities	P
Authorization & appropriations for expenditures	3
Bonds, surety	10
Capital stock certificates	P
Capital stock ledger	P
Capital stock transfer records	P
Charters, constitution, bylaws & amendments	P
Contracts, employee	P
Contracts, government	P
Contracts, labor union	P
Contract, vendor	10
Dividend checks	10
Dividend register	P
Easements	P
Election ballots	20
Election records, corporate	10
General cashbooks, treasurers' and auditors'	25
Incorporation records & certificates	P
Licenses, federal, state, local	P
Permits to do business	P
Records of mergers, consoliations, acquisitions, dissoluions & reorganizations	P
Reports to Securities & Exchange Commission	P
Securities: documents of issuance, listing, & registration	P
Stock applications for issuance	P
Stock certificates, cancelled	10
Stock, stock transfer & stockholders records	P
Stockholder minute books, resolutions	P
Stockholder proxies	10
Stockholder reports	P
Voter proxies	15
Executive	
Correspondence	2
Policy statements, directives	P
Projects, ideas, notes	P
Research reports	20
Speeches, publications	10
Insurance	
Accident reports	11
Appraisals	P
Claims, automobile	10
Claims, group life & hospital	4
Claims, loss or damage in transit	7
Claims, plant	P
Claims, workmen's compensation	10
Expired policy, accident	7
Expired policy, fidelity	7
Expired policy, fire	6
Expired policy, group	6
Expired policy, hospital	6
Expired policy, inspection certificates	7
Expired policy, liability	7
Expired policy, life	7
Expired policy, marine	7
Expired policy, property	8
Expired policy, surety	10
Expired policy, workmen's compensation	10
Legal	
Affidavits	10
Charters	P
Claims & litigation of torts & breach of contract	P
Copyrights	P
Mortgages	5
Patents & related data	P
Trademarks	P
Manufacturing	
Authorities for sale of scrap	3
Bills of material	5
Blueprints	30
Correspondence, engineering & technical	10
Correpondence, production	2
Credit memoranda	5
Credit ratings & classifications	2
Drafting records	8
Drawings & tracings, original	P
Inspection records	5
Inventory records	16
Invoice copies	5
Invoices, received	7
Job records	10
Journals	10
Ledgers	P
Operating reports	10
Order register	6
Production reports	6
Quality control reports	5
Receipts, delivery	3
Reliability records	P
Specifications, customer	P
Stores issue records	3
Time & motion studies	P
Tool control	5
Work orders	5
Personnel	
Accident reports, injury claims, settlements	11
Applications, changes, terminations	3
Attendance records	6
Clock records	4
Correspondence	6
Daily time reports	5

Source: Courtesy of Fellowes Manufacturing Company

edgeable about the value of the information and the costs, risks and benefits of its disposal after varying time periods.

Source: David O. Stephens, CRM, "Making Records Retention Decisions: Practical and Theoretical Considerations," ARMA Quarterly, January, 1988, p. 7. Courtesy of ARMA International.

Nonpaper Records

With the spread of automation, nonpaper records have become more numerous. Optical disks and various types of magnetic media (computer tapes, disks, diskettes, tape cassettes, belts, videotapes, and magnetic cards) have joined microfilm, motion pictures, and conventional paper records in retention programs.

Microfilm, which is discussed separately in Chapter 15, is an important records retention medium. By its very nature, microfilm is an excellent method of storing thousands more records in the same amount of space as conventional paper documents. When a record is required from a microfilm medium, the originator may receive a paper hard copy, a duplicate of the microfilm, or even the original microfilm, depending upon need. Roll microfilm and motion pictures are generally stored in plastic or metal storage containers; microfiche and microfilm jackets are stored in specially made boxes or cabinets.

Magnetic media are volatile, because they tend to lose their magnetic characteristics over time and thus become unusable. Many experts consider ten years the limit that magnetic media can be stored safely. To reduce the possibility of losing information, some records managers organize their retention

RECORD TITLE
CORRESPONDENCE, SALES & MARKETING

INVENTORY

DEPARTMENT
MARKETING

RECORD COPY	[X]	DUPLICATE COPY	[ ]

VOLUME

INCLUSIVE DATES	LOCATION	QUANTITY
1/1/86-12/31/86	OFFICE	42 CU. FT.
1/1/83 - 12/31/85	STORAGE	120 CU. FT.

REMARKS
Duplicate copy in regional sales office

COUNTED BY P.R. Wimsley DATE 2/1/87

RETENTION

APPROVALS	YEARS
RECOMMENDED (SPECIFY SOURCE) COMPANY AGREEMENT & MARKETING JOURNAL (1985)	3
ADMINISTRATIVE BY Ron Le Moyen, Mgr. DATE 1/20/86	4
LEGAL COUNSEL BY Marylnn Jones DATE 2/16/86	3
EXECUTIVE BY O. H. Summner, Ex. VP. DATE 2/24/86	3

FINALIZED SCHEDULE

IN OFFICE	IN STORAGE	DESTROY
1 YEAR	3 YEARS	AFTER 4 YEARS

BY G.W. Wallace, R.M. DATE 3/16/86

SPECIAL INSTRUCTIONS
Note activity in storage - Possible reduction of time in storage may be appropriate.

RECORDS INVENTORY AND RETENTION CONTROL CARD

FELLOWES MANUFACTURING CO.

FORM 4797

FIGURE 5-4 Records inventory and retention control card. (Copyright © 1986 by Bankers Box/Fellowes Manufacturing Co., Itasca, IL.)

schedules to allow for magnetic media to be rotated. A magnetic tape can be rerecorded, for example, and the new copy of the tape can be rotated into storage, while the previously stored tape is returned to the originator or destroyed. This rotation of media can be scheduled for predetermined intervals (monthly, quarterly, or yearly, for example). If magnetic media are to be retained permanently, a good practice is to place the data on computer-output microfilm. Once the media are no longer needed for records retention, they can be erased and the blank media returned to the originator or destroyed.

Videotape, even though magnetic, has different archival characteristics than other types of magnetic media. Experts estimate that videotape's performance does not begin to degrade until after the tape has been read or written on about 100 times. If the tape is stored in a protective cover or cassette, videotape can be expected to be usable almost indefinitely.

Optical disk, a relatively new storage medium, does not record information magnetically, so its retention properties are greater. In general, however, all records should be kept in a controlled environment to prevent damage by extreme temperatures, dust, or other environmental factors.

Master Retention Schedule

Once the records have been appraised and the retention schedule set, a few more steps must be completed before the retention program can be implemented. First, a **master retention schedule,** an alphabetical listing of all records with specific retention and disposition data, is developed (see Figure 5-5 on p. 106). The schedule is then reviewed for errors, corrections are made, and the document is issued to the appropriate staff members. The schedule will be extremely useful for rapid reference, for determining employee work loads, for estimating space requirements, for ordering supplies, and so on.

As the retention program moves through a few cycles, the records manager will probably find that the retention schedule needs to be updated. Therefore, a periodic review and revision process should be developed. Changes in government regulations, company policies, the rate of record references, and so on, are a few of the many reasons a review and revision procedure is needed.

According to Ken Hayes, Consultant and Contributing Editor of RECORDS MANAGEMENT QUARTERLY: "If your organization is large enough to require a records retention schedule at all, it is probably also large enough to require a microcomputer or word processor. If this is the case, developing and maintaining your records retention schedule on this equipment is a perfect application, will save time and money, ensure accuracy in each revision, and may well justify the equipment on that single application."[1]

[1]Kenneth V. Hayes, "Using a Microcomputer for Retention Schedule Maintenance," RECORDS MANAGEMENT QUARTERLY, April, 1985, p. 22.

MASTER RECORDS RETENTION SCHEDULE

	Record Description	Department	Retention of original record in yrs			Microfilm		Comment
			in Dept.	in Storage	Tot. Yrs.	Orig. Rcd.	Ret. Period	
1	Advertising contracts	Public Relations	3	-	3	No	-	*
2	Applications, empl.	Personnel	1	5	6	No	-	
3	Audit, annual	Comptroller	1	9	10	Yes	20	
4	Bank deposits	Comptroller	1	3	4	No	-	
5	Bonds	Comptroller	P	-	P	No	-	
6	Cash receipts	Comptroller	2	7	9	No	-	
7	Check register	Comptroller	-	P	P	No	-	
8	Checks, payroll	Comptroller	1	2	3	No	-	
9	Contracts	Legal	20	-	20	No	-	*
10	Contracts, Purchasing	Purchasing	3	-	3	No	-	*
11	Correspondence	Executive	-	P	P	Yes	P	
12	Correspondence	Sales	1	4	5	No	-	
13	Depreciation schedules	Physical plant	-	P	P	Yes	P	
14	Empl. clearance list	Security	1	-	1	No	-	#
15	Financial statements	Comptroller	2	P	P	Yes	P	
16	Internal publications	Executive	1	P	P	No	-	1 copy
17	Legal codes	Legal	1	-	1	No	-	#
18	Memos, production	Production	1	-	1	No	-	+
19	Price lists, catalogs	Sales	1	-	1	No	-	=
20	Tech. Pubs., charts	Production	1	-	1	No	-	=

LEGEND: * - Dispose of after termination
- Dispose of when superseded
+ - Dispose of after completion of job or contract
= - Dispose of when obsolete

GL-RM-08

Sample master records retention schedule.

The retention schedules and the related policies and procedures should be gathered together to create a reference manual. Generally the manual becomes a part of the organization's records management manual (see Chapter 12). This permits all relevant records management policies, procedures, guidelines, and so on, to be centralized in one publication for the organization's employees.

A flow chart depicting the records retention through disposition process is shown in Figure 5-6.

RECORDS TRANSFER

Records transfer is the physical movement of records from the office to the records center. It is also the transfer of records from high-cost office space to low-cost, high-density storage space. In general, records may be transferred at any time, even though some specific transfer methods have been developed.

Transfer Methods

The **continuing** or **perpetual method** of transferring records is used most effectively where unit or job files are maintained. Records such as legal cases, student records, or any files closed by an event or date can be transferred.

In the **periodic-transfer method,** all files for a given time period are transferred, usually annually or semiannually. New files for the coming period are then established.

Under the **double-file** or **duplicate equipment method** of transferring records, the previous period's or year's files are retained in file cabinets next to the current period's or year's files. At the end of the period, the previous period's files are transferred to the records center and the current period's records then become the previous period's records.

Regardless of when records are transferred, there is generally an overlap during which records from the current period and the previous period are both on hand. Therefore, it is better to keep both sets of records in the file until the previous period's records are moved. Many companies keep both periods of records in the same file cabinet.

Conversion Table

Records being sent to the records center should be sent in standard-size, records center transfer cartons. Since the volume of records is expressed in cubic feet, it is important for the personnel transferring records to know how many records will fill a box. The following conversion table might be helpful:

1. One cubic foot of records equals about 3,000 sheets of paper. A standard-size records carton holds about 3,000 sheets of paper.

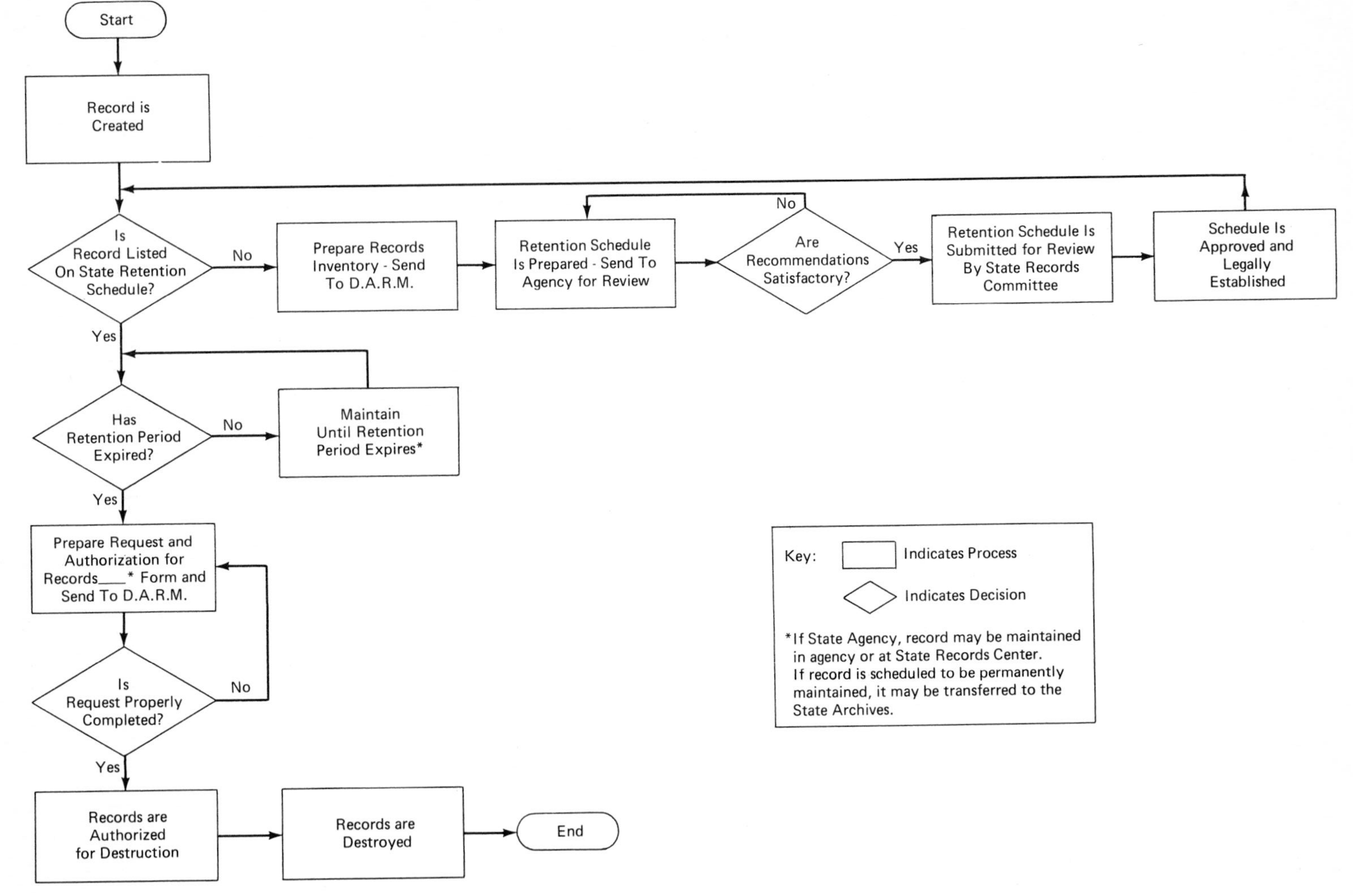

FIGURE 5-6
BASIC RECORDS MANAGEMENT PROCESS DEPARTMENT OF STATE - DIVISION OF ARCHIVES AND RECORDS MANAGEMENT (D.A.R.M.) Courtesy of New Jersey State, Division of Archives and Records Management.

2. One letter-size file drawer will hold 1 1/2 cubic feet of records.
3. One legal-size file drawer will hold 2 cubic feet of records.
4. One standard-size records center carton will hold 10,000 computer punch cards.
5. One standard-size records center carton will hold one hundred 100-foot, 16mm microfilm reels.
6. One standard-size records center carton will hold fifty 100-foot, 35mm microfilm reels.

Records Transfer Procedure and Documents

In addition to the conversion table, a records manager should also develop some transfer procedures for the departmental personnel who ship records. A comprehensive procedure will provide for the systematic and organized transfer of records. Seven basic steps for records transfer follow:

1. Decide when records are to be transferred.
2. Identify the records to be transferred.
3. Use only transfer cartons provided by the records center.
4. Pack cartons properly so that files can be easily retrieved and refiled should the need arise.
5. Mark the cartons only in the required location with specific predetermined data.
6. Complete a records transfer document and send it to the center with the records.
7. Contact the records center for specific shipping instructions. Records center personnel normally pick up the records and transfer them to the center.

A **records transfer document** should accompany the records from the office to the records center. The purpose of this form is to record the transfer of specific records for storage. Since both the departmental personnel shipping the records and the records center personnel sign off on the form, an audit trail is maintained. Figure 5-7 shows a sample transfer document. It is generally a two-part document so that both shipper and receiver will have a record of the transaction.

As records are received at the records center, a storage and destruction control card is completed. Records center personnel actually assign the storage location for the records and enter that location on the control card. As can be seen in Figure 5-8, the control card contains all necessary information for storing and retrieving records.

RECORDS TRANSFER LIST

FORM 3308

BANKERS BOX records storage systems
Division of Fellowes Manufacturing Company
1789 Norwood Avenue Itasca Illinois 60143 • (312) 893-1600

Print or type in triplicate. Keep third copy. Send original and second copy along with your boxed records to the Records Storage Area. Second copy will be returned to you showing the permanent Record Storage Box No. assigned. When second copy is received destroy your third copy.

TO: RECORDS STORAGE AREA	FROM: Marketing Department
DATE RECEIVED: 1/20/83	
BY: B. Wilson	BY: Debby Jones

TEMPORARY BOX NO.	RECORD TITLE OR DESCRIPTION	CONTENTS ALPHABETIC / NUMERIC FROM	TO	DATES FROM	TO	RECORD STORAGE FILE NO.
6	Correspondence, Sales & Marketing	A	C	1/1/82	12/31/82	361
7	" " "	D	Ka	"	"	362
8	" " "	Ke	Q	"	"	363
9	" " "	R	St	"	"	364
10	" " "	Su	Z	"	"	365

FIGURE 5-7
Records transfer list. (Copyright © 1986 by Bankers Box/Fellowes Manufacturing Co., Itasca, IL.)

Records Request Document

A department will frequently need information in records stored at the records center. The retrieval service may be handled in many different ways. One of the most convenient is to develop a departmental request card. Any authorized person in the office may visit the records center in person, call on the telephone, or mail the form to the center. This procedure provides a measure of security over access to the records and also provides a mechanism for assessing the effectiveness of retention periods. Figure 5-9 on p. 112 shows a sample request form. A careful perusal of the form reveals the type of information necessary for retrieving a file. The form should be prepared in three copies, one for each area in which a record of the transaction should be maintained. These forms should be reviewed at the end of each year to determine the amount of use for each type of record. A high amount of reference might indicate that the office should retain the records longer before storage. On the other hand, a low amount of reference over a predetermined period might indicate a need to revise the retention period.

RECORD TITLE
CORRESPONDENCE, SALES & MARKETING

RECEIVED FROM
MARKETING DEPT.

DATE RECEIVED	FILE OR BOX NO.	CONTENTS: ALPHABETIC / NUMERIC		CONTENTS: DATE		LOCATION			DATE TO DESTROY	DATE DES-TROYED	CERTIFIED BY
		FROM	TO	FROM	TO	BLDG. OR ROOM	AISLE	SECTION			
1/20/87	361	A	C	1/1/86	12/31/86	2ND Level	14	7	1992		
"	362	D	KA	"	"	"	"	"	"		
"	363	KE	Q	"	"	"	"	"	"		
"	364	R	ST	"	"	"	"	8	"		
"	365	SU	Z	"	"	"	"	"	"		

FORM 1607 RECORDS STORAGE INDEX AND DESTRUCTION CONTROL CARD BANKERS BOX records storage systems Division of Fellowes Manufacturing Company

FIGURE 5-8
Records storage index and destruction control card. (Copyright © 1986 by Bankers Box/Fellowes Manufacturing Co., Itasca, IL.)

REFERENCE REQUEST CARD — BANKERS BOX records storage systems, Division of Fellowes Manufacturing Company

FORM 3007

DEPARTMENT	REQUESTED BY	
Marketing	Ronald Le Moyen, Mgr.	
RECORD TITLE	DATE OF RECORD	R.C. BOX NO.
Correspondence, Sales & Marketing	about 11/20/82	363
RECORD DETAIL		
Sale of 3500 radios to Kellog + Potter Co.		
INFORMATION INSTRUCTION	TIME REQUIRED	
Send photocopy	2 days	

REQUESTED BY	SERVICED BY			
(Phone) Visit	Phone Visit	Messenger	Record	(Photo copy)

SEARCHED BY	REFILED BY	RETURN DATE	
B. Wilson	B. Wilson	4/12/84	1. Return Tickler File 2. On record 3. On out card

Print or type in TRIPLICATE. Send all copies to the Records Center. FIRST copy will be put in Records Center tickler file, SECOND copy on the record itself, THIRD copy on the out card in the file.

FIGURE 5-9
Reference request card. (Copyright © 1986 by Bankers Box/Fellowes Manufacturing Co., Itasca, IL.)

Tickler File

Tickler files should be maintained in the various operational and administrative sections of the records center. Whenever files have been removed from the center, a record of the removal should be kept in a tickler file. Tickler files may also be developed for the review and destruction of records.

RECORDS DISPOSITION

Records disposition is the final phase of a record's life cycle. In this phase, records with specific retention periods are normally destroyed. Records that are to be retained permanently are considered vital records; they are not normally stored with records that are to be destroyed. Therefore, records with permanent retention periods are not included in this discussion.

At some point, at least two weeks before actually destroying the records, records center personnel should contact the office concerned to inform them of the impending destruction of some of their records. This early warning gives the department time to decide if the records should be retained for a specific additional time period. This two-way communication between departments and the records center may be facilitated by some type of review document. Another method might be simply to make a copy of the storage and destruction control card and send it with instructions to the department concerned. Here again the procedure is notification, review, and retention or destruction.

Destruction Control Form

Once the decision is reached to proceed with destruction, the records can be taken from their storage location and moved to the disposal area. After the records have actually been disposed of, the storage and destruction control card for each record series is completed. The person who destroyed the records or who witnessed the records destruction signs off on the form. Some organizations may wish a more formalized document for destruction. This type of form is normally a two-part form, one for the records center file and one for the office that sent the records to the center for storage.

Records Security

Many organizations have records that contain confidential information that must remain secure even during the destruction process. Therefore, it is important to ensure that the destruction process used does, in fact, destroy the records, thereby preventing reassembly. When Iranian terrorists occupied the American embassy in Teheran in 1979, the terrorists were able to use rug weavers to reconstruct a large percentage of the shredded documents they found in the embassy. The federal government has since changed its destruction specifications to prevent such reconstruction.

According to ELECTRONIC RECORDKEEPING, Magnetic media—disks, diskettes, and tapes—that contain sensitive or classified electronic records should not be discarded in regular waste containers. Destruction should be by shredding or burning. This publication cautions that using PC "erase commands" do not actually remove the file. These commands perform a logical erase by blanking out or voiding the file name and by zeroing sector pointers in the file allocation table. The electronic records remain unchanged until that portion of the disk is reused. Such "erased" records files can be recovered by using commercially available utility programs.

Records Disposal

Before any record is destroyed by the records center, the records manager should have conducted research to determine the proper destruction method for the organization. Records can be disposed of in many different ways. Paper documents and photographs can be sold intact as scrap or shredded, pulver-

Source: ELECTRONIC RECORDKEEPING, U.S. General Services Administration, July, 1989, p. 21.

ized or incinerated. Microfilm and magnetic media can be burned, shredded, or pulverized. When deciding upon a method of destruction and the equipment to use, a records manager should consider the following:

1. What are the volume, frequency, and size of the documents to be destroyed?
2. What are the local and state restrictions concerning burning or any other type of disposal?
3. Is there a reliable salvage company available that would satisfy organizational requirements?
4. Does the organization wish to set up an in-house destruction operation?
5. Are in-house facilities and personnel, such as power, space, water, waste storage, and trained operators, available?
6. What problems might be encountered in handling confidential records?
7. What are the cost benefits to the organization of disposal compared to selling the records as scrap?

Selling records as scrap can be a very viable alternative. This type of disposal can generate income, as well as saving the costs of setting up an in-house disposal operation. In many areas, it may be possible to have competitive bidding by vendors for the scrap material.

One of the most common methods of disposal in use today is shredding. Cummins-Allison Corporation manufactures shredders in all sizes—from a small personal shredder to one that can shred a full 3" binder. In addition to size, shredders vary according to the type of shred they produce. Figure 5-10 illustrates a strip-cut shred while Figure 5-11 shows a crosscut shred. Finally, Figure 5-12 depicts a top security cut shred that is recommended for confidential documents. Thus, shredders may be obtained in many sizes and capacities to meet a company's requirements (see Figure 5-13).

Figure 5-14 illustrates the Model 96 high capacity crosscut shredder by Cummins-Allison Corporation. This machine is able to shred 55 sheets in a single pass as well as handle flat, crumpled, and continuous form paper. Medium to large shredders can shred paper, paper clips, credit cards, microfilm staples, and some fasteners. Shredders can be portable, semifixed, or fixed. Baling attachments can also be purchased with shredders. These units can compact shredded paper and bale it with heavy wire. Medium- to heavy-duty machines can shred from 750 to 1000 pounds of paper per hour. Large high-volume units can shred material almost as fast as the operator can feed the machine.

Pulverizers or *disintegrators* are generally found where there is a high volume of records to be destroyed and complete destruction is required. The U.S. government uses disintegrators for records destruction. In many areas the resulting dust or pulp is used for fertilizer. The units can destroy paper, microfilm reels, paper clips, plastic cards, binders, and fasteners. Depending upon

FIGURE 5-10
Courtesy of Cummins-Allison Corporation.

FIGURE 5-11
Courtesy of Cummins-Allison Corporation.

FIGURE 5-12
Courtesy of Cummins-Allison Corporation.

FIGURE 5-13
Courtesy of Cummins-Allison Corporation.

FIGURE 5-14
Courtesy of Cummins-Allison Corporation.

size, these devices can destroy a few hundred pounds to a few thousand pounds per hour (see Figure 5-15).

Burning records in **incinerators** was a very popular method of records destruction prior to the Federal Clean Air Act. Even though strict regulations now apply, incinerating records can still be a viable alternative. Certain classified government documents, military scrip, and old paper money are burned in accordance with federal regulations. Personnel are also present to certify that all records are, in fact, destroyed.

The destruction of confidential records is one aspect of records destruction that requires a great deal of care. Here the records manager must ensure that the records are properly destroyed. This may be accomplished by having either the records manager or a deputy present during the destruction of the records to certify that the records were in fact destroyed. A certificate of destruction is completed and retained.

CHAPTER HIGHLIGHTS

- The primary purpose of records retention and records disposition programs is to retain, protect, and dispose of a company's records.
- The steps in developing the records retention and disposition process include the records inventory, appraisal of the records, development of the retention schedule, transferring records, and finally, disposal of records.
- Records appraisal determines the value of records, which may be administrative, evidential, fiscal, informational, legal, and scientific.

FIGURE 5-15 Security Engineered Machinery model 1012 disintegrator. (Courtesy of Security Engineered Machinery.)

By far the most numerous constraints on records retention stem from legal requirements, both federal and state.

After considering the legal aspects, the records manager can begin developing the actual retention periods.

The retention periods can be developed by the records manager alone or through the group consensus of a committee.

Once the records retention schedule is completed, the actual transfer of records can commence.

Proper transfer documents must accompany properly packed and labeled shipping cartons.

Records can be retrieved from, and returned to, storage through the use of an effective reference system.

When records reach the end of their retention period, destructing may be done by shredding, burning, pulverising, or sale as scrap.

Once records have been destroyed, the proper disposition should be recorded and the record of disposition should be maintained for future use.

QUESTIONS FOR REVIEW

1. Distinguish among the values a record may have.
2. Identify the four phases of a record's life cycle.
3. What purposes do records retention programs serve?
4. Discuss records appraisal.
5. Why should a records manager be concerned about legal constraints in a retention and disposition program?
6. What is the purpose of a records transfer form?
7. Identify three important considerations when deciding what equipment and method to use in destroying records.
8. What is a record?
9. When would a records manager consider selling records as scrap rather than obtaining a shredder to destroy the records?
10. Discuss the committee approach to developing records retention periods.

THE DECISION MAKER

Case Studies

You are the assistant records center officer responsible for the daily coordination and operation of the GWW Manufacturing Company's record center. Ron Johnston, your records destruction clerk, has been complaining to you for about six months that the company's shredder is unable to handle the volume of records that need to be destroyed. The machine has been used for about eight years and breaks down about every three weeks. You decide it is time to see your supervisor, the chief records officer, about the shredding-machine problem. Mr. Wallace, your supervisor, tells you to survey the equipment available, look at the various methods of destroying records, and prepare a recommendation with supporting evidence for him. The company destroys about 1500 pounds of records each week. All the electrical and water utilities that might be required are available. The recommendation should not include a machine that costs over $5000.

Records Storage and Retrieval Systems

OBJECTIVES

Upon completion of this chapter, the student should be able to:

1. Identify what types of records are commonly stored in businesses and how information is referenced in the files.
2. Describe the criteria for selecting records storage and retrieval systems.
3. Identify the six types of records storage equipment and systems.
4. Explain how to select and evaluate records storage equipment and systems for storing paper records and microforms.
5. Identify the components of effective records storage equipment, how they are used, and their advantages and disadvantages.

The management of records in both small and large organizations involves large investments in office equipment and supplies, personnel, and office floor space. These investments affect both operating costs and productivity. Therefore, an integrated systems approach must be used to plan for the storage, maintenance, and protection of records and to determine the types of records storage and retrieval systems that will best suit a particular company's needs.

DEFINITION OF RECORDS STORAGE AND RETRIEVAL

Records storage refers to the equipment and systems used to file records during their useful lifetime in an organization. A determination must be made, then, as to which records should be retained in a company's files and for what period of time and which records should not be retained. For those documents that are worth keeping, a systematic records storage system should be developed, so that records can be safely stored and properly maintained.

Records retrieval refers to the removal of records from storage for referencing or updating information in the files. Documents must be stored in such a way that they can be located quickly when needed. Retrieval systems encompass not only the way in which records are stored—such as by alphabetic, numeric, or alphanumeric classifications—but also the types of equipment used to store them.

A **system** refers to a series of interrelated tasks or procedures followed to perform a major activity. The components of a system include the equipment, personnel, and the step-by-step tasks or procedures used to carry out the particular objectives of the system.

Various records storage and retrieval equipment and systems for the three types of records—paper-, electronic-, and microform-based—will be discussed.

The term **paper-based records** refers to information generated and stored on paper or paper card stock. Paper-based records, also called hard-copy records, include business correspondence, such as letters, memorandums, and reports; business forms, such as invoices, purchase orders, vouchers, and computer printouts; and cards, such as index cards, account ledger cards, and punched cards. (Examples of paper-based records are shown in Chapter 1.)

In addition to original correspondence, business forms, and cards, paper records also include the copies of records that are created by photocopying or other means of reproduction or that are generated or converted electronically from an image or magnetic medium. For example, when information stored on a computer floppy disk is printed or when an image from microfiche is produced by a microfilm reader-printer, a paper record is created. Also included as paper-based records, because of their standardized sizes, are checks, X rays, blueprints, maps and charts, and other drawings.

Electronic-based records encompass information or data recorded in digital form on a magnetic medium, such as computer tape, floppy disk, magnetic card, hard disk, or optical (laser) disk. Data or information is stored in digital form and retrieved by a word processor, a computer, or a computer-assisted retrieval system. (Examples of digital-based records are shown in Chapter 1, Figure 1-4.)

Microform-based records are data or documents whose images have been photographed in highly reduced form and stored on a microform. Examples of microimages include microfilm rolls, microfiche, aperture cards, jackets, and ultrafiche. (Image-based records are shown in Chapter 1, Figure 1-3)

Rationale

With the records inventory and its analysis completed, a company can proceed to identify its records storage and retrieval needs, based on its existing records and on anticipated records storage needs in the future.

Records storage and retrieval equipment and systems require a large investment for any organization, both to develop and to maintain the system. Salaries of clerical employees and supervisory personnel make up approximately 70 percent of the cost of a filing operation. The rising cost of office floor space for records storage amounts to about 15 percent of the total cost; this percentage includes both the cost of constructing or renting floor space for records storage area(s) and such overhead expenses as lighting, heating, security, and maintenance. The cost of records storage equipment (file cabinets, drawers, or shelves) constitutes another 10 percent of the cost; and supplies (file folders, guides, and so on) make up the remaining 5 percent of the overall cost of a records storage and retrieval system.

Criteria for Selecting Records Storage and Retrieval Systems

Records storage and retrieval equipment is available in a variety of sizes, shapes, price ranges, and configurations. Before an organization can select any equipment or system, it must consider the following factors to ensure that its specific records storage needs are met:

1. What needs to be filed?
2. Should the current method of filing be retained (e.g., alphabetic, terminal digit, numeric, color-coded, alphanumeric, side/top tab, hanging trays for fiche)?
3. What files can be moved to off-site storage or destroyed?
4. Will files be consolidated or expanded?
5. How many lateral inches will be needed?
6. What, if any, special size considerations will be involved?

7. How much accessibility to the files will be required?
8. What are the peak periods of filing activity?
9. Who needs access to the files?
10. Is controlled access desirable?
11. Where will the files be stored?
12. What are the space's dimensions?
13. What load will the floor accept?[1]

Forms of Records Stored

In what forms are records currently stored? Even with the increasing uses of computers and electronic technologies, a large number of records are still being generated and stored in paper form. Do these paper-based records include correspondence, reports, business forms, maps, catalogs, or cards? Are magnetic media used to store records? Are microforms currently used for records storage? Does the company anticipate greater use of magnetic media and/or microforms for records storage?

The forms in which records are created or processed generally dictate how they will be stored, how they are used, and by whom. From this determination, an organization can select the most appropriate types of equipment to suit the types of records it houses.

Wright Line, Inc., groups various forms of information into six categories and refers to each as a form of "information media," as shown in Table 6-1.

Use of Stored Records

How are records used? Distinctions should be made between reference filing and transaction filing. In **reference filing and retrieval,** entire files must be located and removed from the records storage area periodically for review, editing, or updating. Records may or may not need to be added to existing files with each reference, but ease of retrieving files is an important consideration.

Transaction filing involves active files that require records to be removed, added, or refiled regularly as transactions occur. In such cases, entire files need not be removed form the records storage area; however, accessibility to individual records in the files is essential.

Frequency of Use

How often are records referenced? The frequency of use is related to employee productivity for those who must use the equipment and the system. The

[1]"Records Management: Making the Right Choices," MODERN OFFICE TECHNOLOGY, (April 1990) p. 38.

frequency of use is also a cost factor for management to be aware of; the frequency of use—and more important, infrequency of use—have a bearing on personnel, floor space, and overall maintenance cost of records storage.

How often records are referenced will determine the eventual location of records storage equipment and operations within a department or organization. The organization's need to expand or modify a system to meet changing requirements is another factor related to activity levels of stored records, also called reference ratios. To determine the reference ratios of a group of records, use the following formula:

$$\text{Reference Ratio} = \frac{\text{Total Number of Records Referenced}}{\text{Number of Records Stored}}$$

TABLE 6-1 SIX CATEGORIES OF INFORMATION MEDIA

Category	*Examples*
Magnetic Media	Computer tape
	Disk packs or modules
	Data cartridges
	Optical digital discs
Micrographic Media	Roll film
	Microfiche
	Computer-output microfilm (COM)
Paper Media	Documents
	Computer printout reports
	Manuals
	Books
	Periodicals
Audiovisual Media	Photographic sheet film/prints
	35mm slides
	Motion picture film
	Videotape or cassettes
	Videodiscs
	Audiotape or cassettes
Display Media	Data processing terminals
	Word processing terminals
	Personal computers
	Micrographic readers
Audiovisual Display Media	Overhead projectors
	Slide projectors
	Film projectors
	Video players
	Audio players
	Teleconferencing equipment
	Screens

Source: Gary J. Bellanca, *Managing Information Media in the Automated Office* (Worcester, MA: Wright Line, Inc., 1983), p. 31.

Supreme Equipment & Systems Corporation reports that most records storage equipment is referenced between 25 and 40 times per hour. Thus these figures could be used as a guide in determining the actual reference ratio—depending on the type of equipment used, the file capacity, filing system and components used, and available floor space.[2]

The higher the reference ratio, the more active the records. A low reference ratio—generally between 5 and 10 percent—is an indication that records should be moved from the active storage area to an inactive records storage area.

Personnel

Who must use the records storage equipment? Who else must have access to stored records? As cited earlier, personnel costs amount to approximately 70 percent of the cost of a records storage operation. The efficiency and the cost-effectiveness of the system should be evaluated both quantitatively and qualitatively, by examining the following factors:

Quantitative Factors
Volume of records stored
Volume of records retrieved
Frequency of use (reference ratio)
Overall floor space
Time required to store and retrieve records

Qualitative Factors
Types of records stored (image, paper, media)
Types of information stored and their arrangement
Filing classification system(s) used
Types of records storage equipment used
Location of stored records in proximity to users
Accuracy in storing and retrieving records
Anticipated growth needs

Space Requirements or Limitations

How much space is available? How much will it cost? No more space than is absolutely necessary should be allocated for records storage. The volume of records currently housed, as well as anticipated volumes in the future, should be used to determine how much space should be allocated and the costs of

[2]*Office Productivity: The Strategies of Filing* (Brooklyn: Supreme Equipment & Systems Corporation, 1986), p. 14.

staffing and maintaining the area. Space requirements can be determined either by calculating storage capacity per square foot of floor of space or by determining the total volume of records in cubic measures.

Two important considerations in allocating floor space are aisle space and air space. In addition to the height, width, and depth of the records storage equipment, aisle space requirements must also be included in the space calculation. *Aisle space* refers to the amount of space (usually measured in inches) required for a file worker to gain working access to stored records and for an adequate walking aisle between pieces of equipment.

Air space refers to the space above eye level, up to the ceiling, that can be used for records storage equipment. Generally, the more air space that can be used, the more cost-effective the use of floor space.

File capacity—measured in terms of storage capacity per square foot of floor space—depends on the type of equipment and folders used and how densely records are stored in drawers, cabinets, or shelves. To determine file capacity requirements, use the following formula:

$$\text{File Capacity (records per square foot)} = \frac{\text{Number of records stored}}{\text{Total square footage}}$$

Consider anticipated growth of the organization and its accompanying growth in records storage needs. Average annual growth allowances range from 10 to 20 percent, depending on the type of business or industry.

Another method of calculating records storage needs uses cubic measures, usually cubic feet, to determine the total volume of records stored in existing equipment.[3] The storage capacity of common records storage equipment is estimated as follows:

1 letter-size file drawer	1.5 cu ft
1 legal-size file drawer	2.0 cu ft
15 linear inches of letter-size files	2.0 cu ft
12 linear inches of legal-size files	1.0 cu ft
12 linear inches of computer printouts	1.5 cu ft
1 desk drawer file	2.0 cu ft

Protection and Security

Will records be adequately protected? If records are of a confidential or security nature, locks or other security devices must be provided to safeguard contents and to ensure privacy. Other security considerations include protection against human elements, prevention of wear and tear owing to the nature of the records or their use, and protection from natural disasters.

[3]Katherine Aschner, "How To Do a Files Inventory," *Taking Control of Your Office Records: A Manager's Guide* (White Plains, NY: Knowledge Industry Publications, 1986), p. 22.

The human elements include theft, accidental loss or destruction of records, and damage to records that render them useless. In addition, preventing unauthorized use or access is critical to maintaining the integrity of confidential, secure, or other restricted records.

The nature of records—their form, manner and frequency of use, and environmental requirements—and the equipment, supplies, and personnel procedures also affect the safekeeping of records. Magnetic media, such as computer tapes and disks, may be damaged by extremes in temperature and humidity and also by dust and pollutants. Static electricity from carpeting and furniture can destroy information stored on magnetic media.

Wear and tear occurs each time a paper record is filed or refiled; the higher the frequency of use and the greater the density of records stored in drawers, shelves, or cabinets, the more quickly the document will deteriorate. In computerized systems, program or equipment malfunctions can cause not only delays in storing and retrieving information but also potential loss or destruction of records.

Natural disasters include fire, floods, earthquakes, and lightning. Any of these disasters could cause damage and destruction of property that could also affect stored records. The majority of records lost in fires are damaged by water and smoke.

The following guidelines will contribute to an adequate protection system for records:

1. Make backup copies of important records, and store the backups in different locations than the originals.
2. Use fireproof storage equipment, and install appropriate fire and smoke detection devices and sprinkler systems.
3. Identify areas that are prone to flooding, and keep records out of those areas.
4. Protect computerized systems against power failures or surges.
5. Maintain appropriate environmental controls in all records storage areas.
6. Keep vital records in a secure area that is not accessible to unauthorized personnel.
7. Select records storage equipment and systems that provide reliable and efficient service and that meet all the requirements of the organization's records storage and retrieval needs.[4]

[4]Harold T. Smith, et al., *Automated Office Systems Management* (New York: John Wiley & Sons, Inc., 1985), pp. 230–232.

Length of Storage Time

For what period of time must records be retained before their destruction or disposition? Following the established records retention schedule, an organization can select equipment, estimate the period of use for specific types of records, and match the value of records with their retention requirements.

Summary

The selection of an appropriate records storage and retrieval system is based on the interrelationship of the seven factors discussed above and two common elements—cost and productivity. What is suitable for a company can only be determined by an objective and comprehensive analysis of all these factors. The final decisions should allow the organization to select equipment that fits into an integrated records storage and retrieval system rather than having to select a system that is determined by the equipment.

Records Storage and Retrieval Systems and Equipment

Table 6-2 shows a chronology of records storage systems. The chronology illustrates three trends in the evolution of filing systems: (1) the progression from manual records storage systems to mechanical systems and then to electronic systems; (2) the emergence in each decade of faster and higher-density records storage and retrieval equipment and systems; and (3) the continued traditional use—in spite of the new technologies—of conventional records storage systems for paper-based records, as well as for the newer electronic- and microform-based records.

There are six basic types of records storage and retrieval systems:

1. Standard vertical file-drawer cabinets (paper-based)
2. Lateral file-drawer cabinets (paper-based)
3. Open-shelf file units (paper-, electronic-, and microform-based)
4. High-density file units (paper-, electronic-, and microform-based)
5. Automated or power filing units (paper- and microform-based)
6. Electronic systems, both computerized and computer-assisted (electronic-based)

Figure 6-1 illustrates the storage capacity of four of these systems and compares the space requirements in terms of air space.

According to Supreme Equipment & Systems Corporation, the selection of equipment is based partly on the activity or reference rates of stored records. The company provides a comparison of activity rates for five types of records storage equipment, shown in Table 6-3.

TABLE 6-2 A CHRONOLOGY OF RECORDS STORAGE SYSTEMS

Date	Development
1900s	Verticle files
1940s	Lateral file cabinets
	Hanging or suspended files
1950s	Lateral shelf files
	Side-tab file folders
	Alphanumeric indexing methods
1960s	Mechanical filing systems
	Color-coded indexing methods
	Micrographics for active records storage
1970s	Computer-assisted retrieval systems
1980s	Videomicrographics systems (a hybrid of computer-assisted retrieval systems)
1990s	Optical disk systems
	Electronic imaging systems

Source: Hank De Cillia, "The Evolution of Document-Based Filing Systems," *Information Management,* Vol. 17, No. 4 (April 1983), p. 36.

TABLE 6-3 ACTIVITY RATES OF RECORDS STORAGE EQUIPMENT

Equipment	*References per Hour*	*File Actions per Day per Employee*
Verticle files	25–35	280
Lateral files	30–40	320
Open-shelf files	30–40	320
Mobile file units	25–35	280
Automated units	50–60 per console	960 for two consoles

Source: Supreme Equipment & Systems, *Office Productivity: The Strategies of Filing* (Brooklyn, 1986), p. 14.

MANUAL SYSTEMS

Systems that store and retrieve records without the use of mechanical or automated devices are known as **manual storage and retrieval systems.** A manual system can be simply the storing or removing of a file folder from a four-drawer file cabinet or an open-shelf file. Although the trend is toward mechanical and computerized systems, manual systems will remain an integral part of the office environment because of their ease of use and relatively low cost.

Standard Vertical File-Drawer Cabinets

Conventional upright steel-constructed file-drawer cabinets have the capacity to store between 60 and 70 pounds of letter-size records per drawer. These cabinets are available with from two to six drawers, in both letter size (8 1/2 by

FIGURE 6-1 Comparison of floor space and capacity of various records storage systems. (Courtesy of Supreme Equipment & Systems Corp., Brooklyn, NY.)

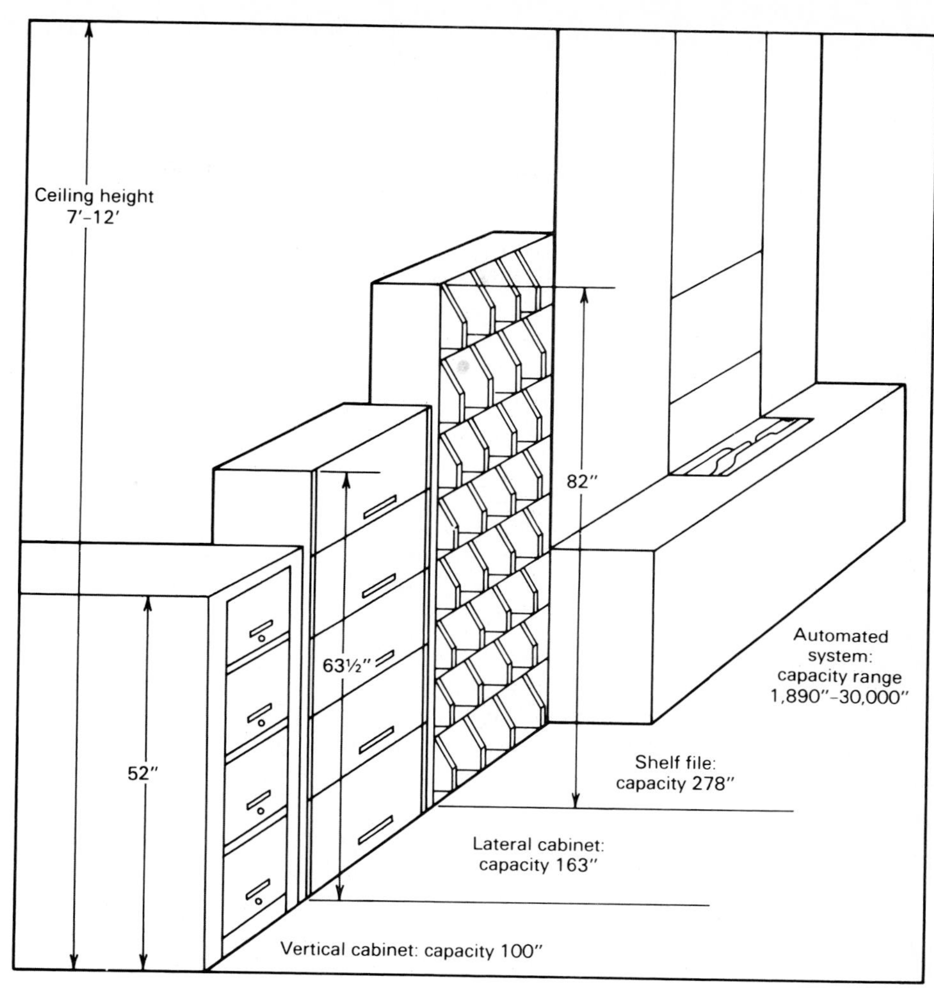

11 inches) and legal size (8 1/2 by 13 or 14 inches), and in 24-, 26-, and 28-inch depths.

The most efficient model for active records storage is the five-drawer letter-size cabinet, which provides easy access to records, because its floor height allows office personnel to use all the drawers without ladders or stepstools. The five-drawer letter-size cabinet also has approximately 25 percent more storage capacity than the more commonly used four-drawer model, and it provides better space utilization than the two-, three-, or four-drawer models. These latter three models are not commonly used because they do not use available air space or floor space efficiently. However, two-drawer units may be used for desk- or tabletop storage; three-drawer units may be used alongside desks to provide convenient and accessible records storage and retrieval for frequently referenced information.

Six-drawer units require the use of ladders or stepstools for office personnel to gain access to the top drawer. Their height thus hinders ease of accessibility to records. For inactive records, however, the six-drawer model provides cost-effective storage.

The standard vertical file-drawer cabinets are most commonly used to store various paper-based records—correspondence, reports, business forms, and cards. Correspondence files make up a large part of the transaction filing and retrieval operations in organizations. All the drawers in the vertical cabinet may be used to store correspondence; or the top drawer(s) may be designated for storing special paper records such as cards, checks, or standardized business forms. Regardless of the sizes of the paper records, letter-size file cabinets are the most popular. They offer many advantages over comparable legal-size equipment, including the following:

1. Generally only a small portion of a company's records consist of legal-size documents, and many states have mandated conversion of all court documents to letter size. Even law offices store letter-size correspondence and business forms, as well as their legal-size court documents. When different sizes of records are stored in legal-size folders in legal-size storage cabinets, the folders and the records become unwieldy to manipulate, store, and retrieve.
2. The cost of using legal-size cabinets or drawers is between 5 and 25 percent higher than that for letter-size equipment. This range depends on the grade of equipment and accessory components purchased, as well as the difference in costs of floor space, personnel, and maintenance.

A 26-inch-deep file drawer can hold approximately 3,500–5,000 sheets of paper in addition to guides and file folders, or approximately 150 sheets of paper per inch of depth. Vertical file units are ideal when records are referenced only when they need to be filed or refiled, and when only a few people must use or have access to stored records. In other words, vertical file cabinets provide speed and ease of records storage because records are merely dropped into their appropriate folders within the drawer, as shown in Figure 6-2, without having to remove the folders from their positions in the drawer.

The major disadvantage of vertical file-drawer units—regardless of the number of drawers—is the amount of floor space required in the records storage area. The depth of file-drawer cabinets, as well as the length of a drawer when it is fully opened—usually 28 inches—must be provided for, as well as space for an aisle. Maintenance costs are also higher, because there is more open floor space to be cleaned.

Another disadvantage of the vertical file-drawer cabinet is that only one file worker can gain access to the files at a time. In an active records storage area or where transaction filing occurs, this limited accessibility to records can create a bottleneck if several people must obtain information from the files at the same time and when records are being updated by filing or refiling.

FIGURE 6-2
Ease in filing and retrieving records.

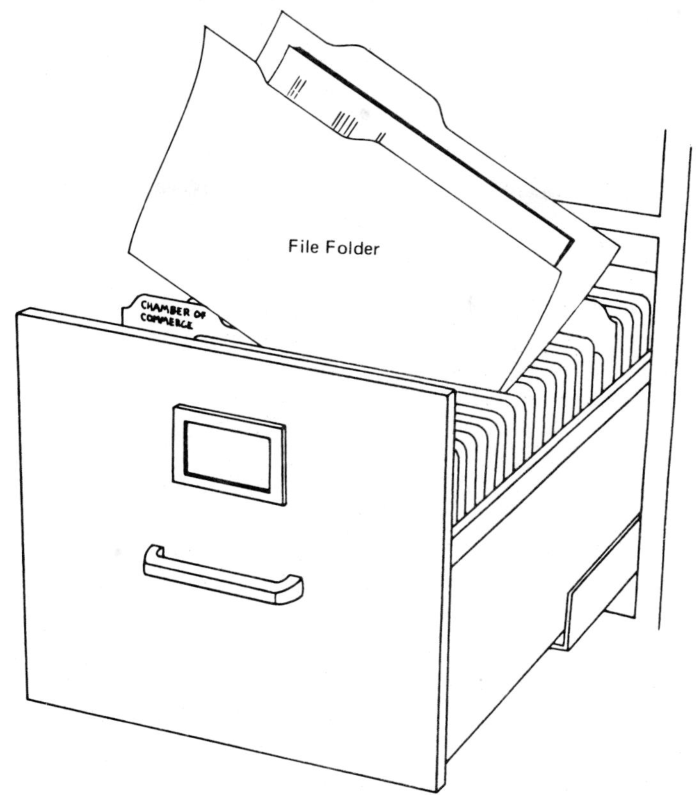

The quality of records storage cabinets affects the efficiency of the system. Equipment is graded by manufacturers to distinguish various levels of quality among the many styles and models. Features of high-quality storage cabinets or drawers include the following:

Sturdy frame bracing: Reinforces the sides and back of the entire cabinet to support the 60–70 pounds of records per drawer

Compressors or follower blocks: Slide forward and backward in the drawer to support records upright and to compress folders when the drawer is partially filled

Telescoping slides on ball-bearing rollers: Allow drawers to be opened and closed smoothly and evenly and provide support when drawers are fully extended

Guide rods: Insert through holes at the bottoms of permanent guides to secure guides in their positions in the drawer; prevent guides from being lifted out when folders are removed

Lateral File Cabinets

Lateral file cabinets are lengthwise units whose drawers or shelves are opened broadside (see Figure 6-3). Available with two to six drawers or shelves, lateral file cabinets may be 26, 30, or 42 inches wide. They provide quick and easy access to records, because all records are visible when a drawer is opened or a shelf pulled out from the cabinet. Because lateral file drawers are shallow, less effort is expended by records personnel in opening drawers and accessing records.

Records in a lateral unit can be stored lengthwise, facing one side of the drawer or shelf; or the drawer or shelf may be divided into sections and records stored horizontally, facing the front. Some lateral files are not entirely closed or protected, as are the standard vertical file-drawer cabinets. Open-shelf lateral units may have retractable drop-lid doors to protect records from dust and fire when not in use.

A six-drawer or six-shelf lateral file requires 40 percent less floor space than a standard four-drawer vertical cabinet. In addition, lateral file units require only 6 inches of aisle space.

The storage capacity in the six-drawer lateral file is approximately 192 inches; the capacity in a four-drawer vertical cabinet is approximately 100 inches. Thus lateral file units provide economical and efficient records storage and retrieval.

With the various sizes of lateral file units, additional flexibility is provided because records of different sizes and forms may be stored in the same unit.

Open-Shelf File Units

Records may be stored in bookshelf fashion on lateral open shelves so they are exposed for ease in referencing. Ideal for high-volume filing, **open-shelf units** provide easy access to records. Because all records are visible and there are no drawers to be opened. These units allow approximately 20–40 percent faster filing and refiling and retrieval of records than file drawer cabinets. (See Figure 6-4.) Open-shelf units may also be enclosed with a rocking or drop-lid door for protection.

Open-shelf file units occupy approximately 50 percent less floor space than traditional file-drawer cabinets. Thus, in terms of maintenance cost per square foot, they are less expensive than cabinets. Open-shelf files can be expanded by stacking as many as eight additional tiers of storage units on top of an existing unit. Less aisle space is required for working within the files—approximately 6 inches, compared with 28 inches for vertical file-drawer cabinets. The compactness of open-shelf units allows lateral or sideways arrangements of the 30-, 36-, or 42-inch-wide storage units. The smaller amount of floor space means that records personnel do not have to move around as much, thus minimizing fatigue.

FIGURE 6-3
Lateral file cabinets.
(Courtesy of Essette Pendaflex Corporation.)

FIGURE 6-4 Automated open-shelf file units. (Courtesy of White Office Systems.)

One disadvantage of open-shelf units, however, is that individual file folders must be removed from the shelves for referencing or when records need to be placed in the folders. Also, depending on the height of the shelving units, ladders or stepstools may be required to reach the higher shelves. Security and the difficulty of preventing unauthorized access to stored records are additional disadvantages of open-shelf units.

Open-shelf filing units are best suited for companies where records are referenced frequently, where individual documents are stored in individual folders, and where the system must allow for expansion without adding new equipment. The records may be paper-based (folders containing correspondence or business forms, books, and pamphlets); electronic-based (magnetic media such as computer tapes or trays of floppy disks); microform-based (microfilm reels or trays of microfiche); or a combination of forms.

Open-shelf filing has been used effectively to store medical records, mortgage loan records and other credit documents, insurance policies, catalogs and brochures, court and police records, and other information that is filed by account or customer numbers, case numbers, or policy numbers.

High-Density Storage Units

High-density storage refers to equipment and systems used to store large volumes of highly active records. A large number of records must be compactly and efficiently stored in a particular location, perhaps in a relatively centralized area within a company or department, to provide quick and easy access to stored records. Two systems discussed here are the open-shelf lateral units and mobile storage units.

Open-shelf lateral file units, discussed previously, lend themselves to high-volume, highly active storage and retrieval of all types and forms of records. The open-shelf units shown in Figure 6-5, for example, provide movable files in double depths and make efficient use of both air space and floor space. A typical double-depth lateral file unit occupies the same amount of floor space as a standard vertical file-drawer unit—29 to 30 inches, but it holds twice as much. The inner row of lateral files consists of either suspended pull-out cradles or fixed shelving, while the cradles in the outer section move from side to side on suspension rails. Open-shelf lateral units provide flexible records storage and retrieval for correspondence files, microfiche, microfilm, computer tapes, and X rays. In addition, existing records storage can easily be converted to a double-depth lateral file system, which accommodates either top- or side-tab folders as well as suspension folders.

Mobile storage files are another type of high-density storage. These movable units require the installation of permanent tracks in the floor, on which several rows of separate open-shelf lateral file units can be rolled. The separate lateral file units are moved back to back against one another, thus eliminating multiple aisles and conserving valuable floor space. To access records from a specific row of files, the file worker moves the individual units to create an aisle that allows access to the desired set of records, as shown in Figure 6-6. Rather than providing a permanent aisle between sets of file units, a "moving aisle" is created, providing 100 percent more records storage capacity in the same floor area.

FIGURE 6-5 High-density open-shelf movable lateral shelving system. (Courtesy of Acme Visible Records.)

FIGURE 6-6

TABLE 6-4 FLOOR SPACE NEEDED FOR 1000 FILING INCHES

Storage System	*Storage Equivalent*	*Net Filing Capacity (Square Feet Total Area)*
Spacesaver	1	19.5
8-Tier Open Shelf	4	27.0
4-Drawer	10	69.3
4-Drawer Lateral	6	73.5

Source: The Spacesaver Corporation, Fort Atkinson, WS, 1988

Table 6-4 compares the space required by a high-density mobile storage unit (manufactured by the Spacesaver Corporation) with the space required by some other types of records storage systems discussed previously.

Automated Systems

Automated records storage and retrieval systems use some type of mechanical or electrical assist in storing and retrieving records. These devices generally decrease storage and retrieval time, lessen employee fatigue, and provide a measure of security. The types of equipment generally found in this category of storage equipment include power files, mobile track files, and conveyor files.

In most automated systems, trays of records are brought to the operator. The easy access to records eliminates the need to reach for records, so worker fatigue is minimized. The records stored in such systems are generally standardized; that is, records are all of one type—cards or correspondence or microforms, for example. Two commonly used automated systems are mechanical mobile storage units and the conveyor or elevator-type units.

The mobile storage units described earlier are also available as electrically operated units. By pressing a control button at the end of each storage unit, a file worker can move the storage unit sideways along the track to create an aisle in front of the unit that contains the desired records (see Figure 6-7).

Conveyor or **elevator-type files** are motorized storage units that rotate, bringing the desired set of records to the worker. Such units are available for index or ledger cards, punched cards, microfiche, or correspondence. Some conveyor systems, such as that shown in Figure 6-8, provide metal or heavy plastic card trays that fit inside the larger storage unit. These portable trays can slide in and out of the conveyor unit so records can be referenced or updated by individual workers.

A large volume of records stored in a centralized location within a company may be housed in a large built-in compartment that encloses all records. The records are not externally visible, so security is provided and records are protected. Records are stored on trays inside the unit; they are retrieved by using a keypad on the console to call up the desired record. The internal elevator mechanism locates and retrieves the tray on which the desired records are stored; records are then brought out and placed in front of the worker.

Conveyor, or elevator-type, file units can store several kinds of records. In a lateral shelf filing configuration, letter- and legal-size correspondence files and folders can be accommodated. When pull-out trays are stored within the units, microfilm, microfiche, cards, and check files can be accommodated.

FIGURE 6-7 Electronic mobile shelving system. (Courtesy of Acme Visible Records.)

FIGURE 6-8 Conveyor-type open-shelf unit for correspondence. (Courtesy of White Office Systems.)

MICROFORM STORAGE AND RETRIEVAL SYSTEMS

Records storage and retrieval systems are available for the various types of microforms—microfilm rolls and cartridges, microfiche, aperture cards, jackets, and ultrafiche. Microforms may also be used with computer-assisted retrieval (CAR) systems and computer-output microfilm (COM) systems, which are described in Chapters 16 and 18.

Microforms The field of **micrographics** encompasses the filming, storage, and retrieval of information, data, or records in miniaturized form. Microforms are images of documents that have been photographed in highly reduced form—with a reduction ratio of from 24:1 to 48:1. Special cameras are used to capture the images on film, and special readers and printers are used to view the microimages or to print a hard copy. Micrographics is discussed in Chapter 16.

The following are advantages provided by micrographics for records storage and retrieval:

1. Because records have been so highly reduced on film, less storage space is required (see Figure 6-10). Between 95 and 98 percent of records storage space can be saved with micrographics.
2. Since less space is required to house microfilmed records, the company's overall records are reduced. More microfilmed records can be stored in an area previously occupied by paper-based records storage equipment.
3. Microforms are economical to maintain because of the smaller area required for their storage and use.
4. Documents can be accessed and retrieved quickly, regardless of the form of microform used. Even rolls of microfilm can be scanned quickly to locate a particular record.

FIGURE 6-9
Optical character recognition moves information from paper to computer in seconds. (Courtesy of CompuScan, Inc.)

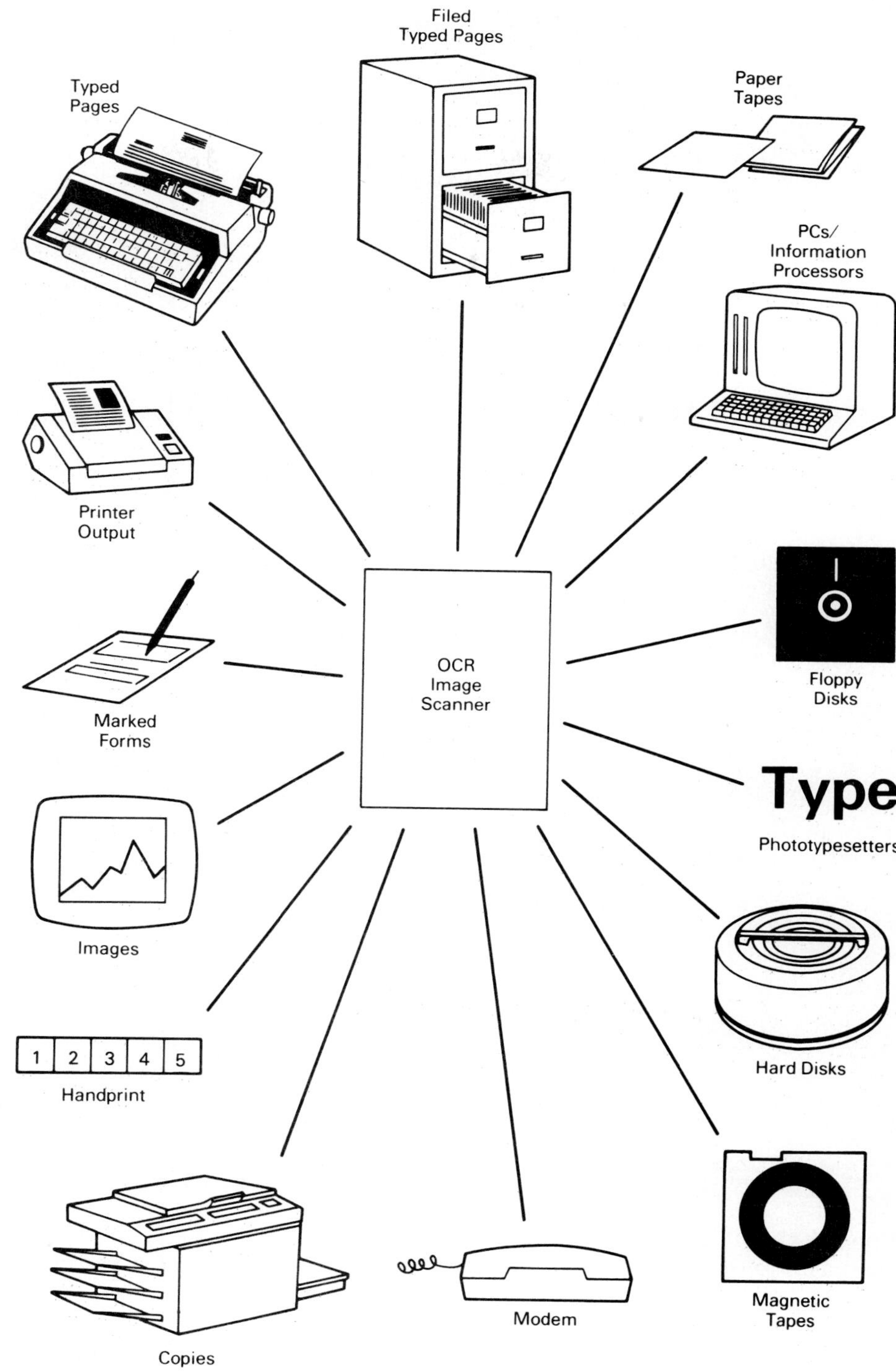

FIGURE 6-10
Storage cabinets for microforms. (Courtesy of Business Efficiency Aids, Inc.)

FIGURE 6-11
Optical disk technology: CD-ROM, Rewritable Optical Disk Cartridge, and Videodisk. (Courtesy of 3M Optical Recording.)

Specialized Storage and Retrieval Equipment

The records storage and retrieval equipment and systems discussed up to this point are general in purpose, suitable for various forms of ordinary records. However, plans, drawings, blueprints, maps, photographs, and other large records require specialized storage equipment, because they do not lend themselves to storage in conventional file-drawer cabinets or shelves. Another type of specialized records is audiovisual media.

Three systems for storing these special types of records are: (1) oversized file-drawer cabinets, (2) suspension files in open-shelf or lateral units, and (3) rolled-plan files.

Oversized File-Drawer Cabinets These special cabinets are similar to those used for correspondence and business forms, but they are much larger units and can extend from floor to ceiling. Figure 6-12 shows two- and three-drawer lateral file cabinets designed to house oversized paper-based records. File-drawer cabinets are also available with a large number of wide, shallow drawers so that records like drawings, maps, photographs, and plans can be stored face up and flat. Cabinets like the one shown in Figure 6-13 hold large documents vertically and take up as much as 60 percent less space than flat-drawer filing equipment. An index of the records stored in the file unit can be affixed to the inside of the lid of the file unit.

FIGURE 6-12
Oversized lateral file cabinets. (Courtesy of Plan Hold.)

FIGURE 6-13
Cabinet to hold oversized documents vertically. (Courtesy of Plan Hold.)

Suspension Files Suspension files consist of wall-hung or free-standing units of either open shelving or cabinets, in which documents within folders or entire notebooks are suspended from rods that extend along the width of the shelf or cabinet. For records other than correspondence, each record is attached to a hook or clip that is hung from the shelf; the hook or clip itself serves as the tab for identifying the stored record. Large and bulky documents, such as maps, photographs, drawings, books, newspapers, and catalogs, can be stored in suspension files. These files are best suited for records that are referenced frequently by many people.

The storage unit shown in Figure 6-14 includes suspension files on the top for loose prints and charts; a set of flat drawers in the middle section; and on the bottom, "box folders" for reference materials, artwork, and general files, as well as transparent envelopes.

FIGURE 6-14
Storage unit that combines suspension files, flat drawers, and "box folders." (Courtesy of Plan Hold.)

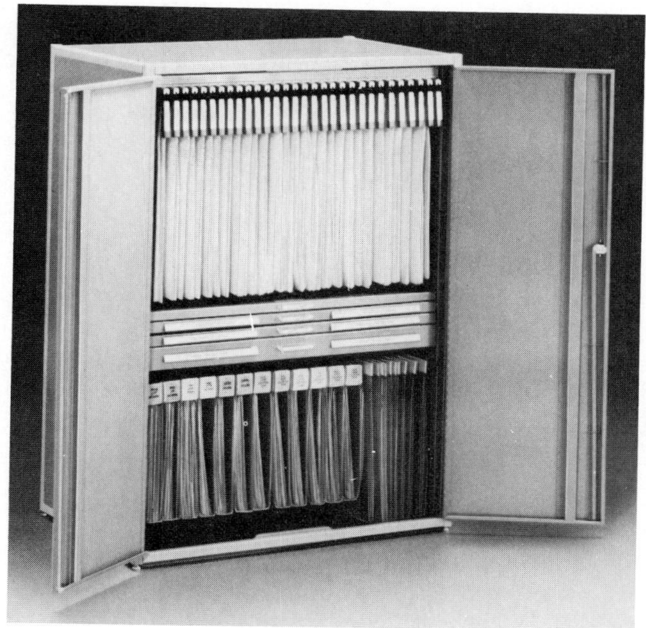

In data processing centers, computer disks and cartridges, as well as bound volumes of computer printouts, are generally stored in open suspension file units, as was illustrated in Figure 6-14.

To store correspondence, suspension folder systems are used in conventional file-drawer cabinets, in open-shelf or lateral units, or in specially manufactured suspension file-drawer cabinets. Figure 6-15 illustrates such a unit. Files containing preprinted forms that are used many times each day, like those often found in government offices, are best maintained in suspension-file drawers or open-shelf units. For correspondence and business forms, special suspension folders hang from the sides of a steel frame inserted into a standard file-drawer cabinet or from the sides of a regular suspension cabinet. Each folder has metal hooks extending from either end that hang on the sides of the steel frame. Because each folder is supported by the steel frame, all records stand upright; folders do not sag to the bottom of the drawer or shelf as they tend to do in standard file-drawer cabinets. Suspension folders are made of sturdier material than ordinary file folders and are intended to withstand a higher frequency of use. The tabs on suspension folders are made of heavy plastic, so they can be handled more often without replacement.

Rolled-Plan Files Rolled-plan files provide convenient and relatively compact storage for large document-like plans, drawings, and maps. The plans or maps can be rolled and then placed in "pigeonhole" storage cubicles or shelves; the

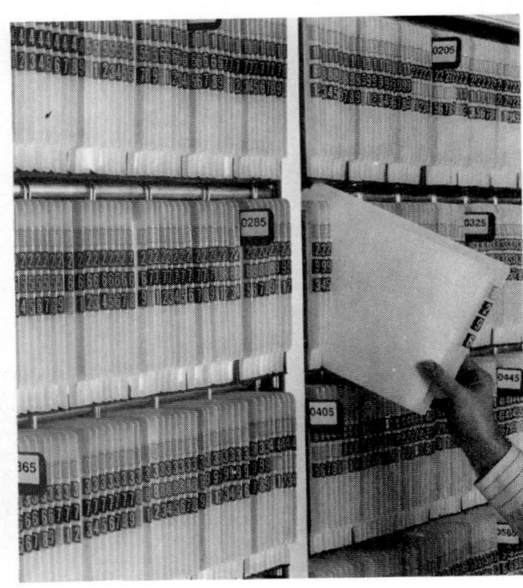

FIGURE 6-15 Suspension systems for alphabetic and numeric systems. (Courtesy of Oblique by Gillotte Co.)

contents can be identified by a label on the edge of the tube. Figure 6-16 shows a rolled-plan file cabinet in which forty-eight files can be stored. An index on the cabinet door identifies the document stored in each cubicle. One disadvantage of using rolled-plan files is that the unrolling and curling of plans can make them difficult to read. A second disadvantage is that records are easily torn or creased if they must be rolled and unrolled frequently. Third, plans and other large documents are available in too many sizes to standardize cabinets or shelving. Finally, rolled documents are difficult to transport easily.

Audiovisual Media Cassette tapes and such other media as filmstrips, slides, and sound recordings also require special storage and retrieval equipment. The three-drawer vertical file cabinet shown in Figure 6-17 stores slides, cassette tapes, and filmstrips. The contents of each cassette tape can be typed on a label and affixed to the cassette directly. If plastic cassette cases are used, a more complete listing of the contents can be inserted in each case. Each slide or set of slides can be identified by writing the information directly on the slide mounts or by providing an alphabetic/numeric index, so individual frames can be accessed quickly. Filmstrips are generally stored in plastic or metal containers; a label can be prepared and affixed to the outside of the container.

Storage units for audiovisual media can be stacked on top of one another, as shown in Figure 6-18, to provide a flexible storage configuration that can hold several different types of media in one central storage location.

COMPONENTS OF CORRESPONDENCE SYSTEMS

Certain components are needed to aid in the efficient use of stored records. Components used to store correspondence, business forms, cards, and other

FIGURE 6-16 Rolled-plan file cabinet. (Courtesy of Plan Hold.)

paper-based records include such signposts as guides, file folders, tabs, and labels.

Guides

Guides are the key components to an efficient system. As their name indicates, guides lead an individual to specific sections of a file drawer or shelf and thus serve as dividers for groups of records (see Figure 6-19). In addition, guides support the individual folders to prevent their sagging or sliding to the bottom. Every five to ten folders in the system should be preceded by a guide. Having fewer than five folders behind a guide is unnecessary and expensive; however, having too many folders behind a guide creates cluttered files, provides inadequate support, and prevents quick referencing of records.

Guides are made of heavy pressboard, fiber, or manila stock and are often reinforced with metal or steel for durability and added strength. Each guide has an extended *tab* at the top or side that is positioned in widths of one-fifth, one-third, or one-half "cuts" across the guide as illustrated in Figure 6-21.

Primary Guides A set of **primary guides** highlights the major divisions and subdivisions of records contained in each drawer or on each shelf. In an alphabetic classification system, for example, records may be separated into 26 major divisions—one for each letter of the alphabet. When a larger volume of records must be maintained, additional primary guides can be added to divide each letter group into smaller groupings. For example, the letter *A* may be

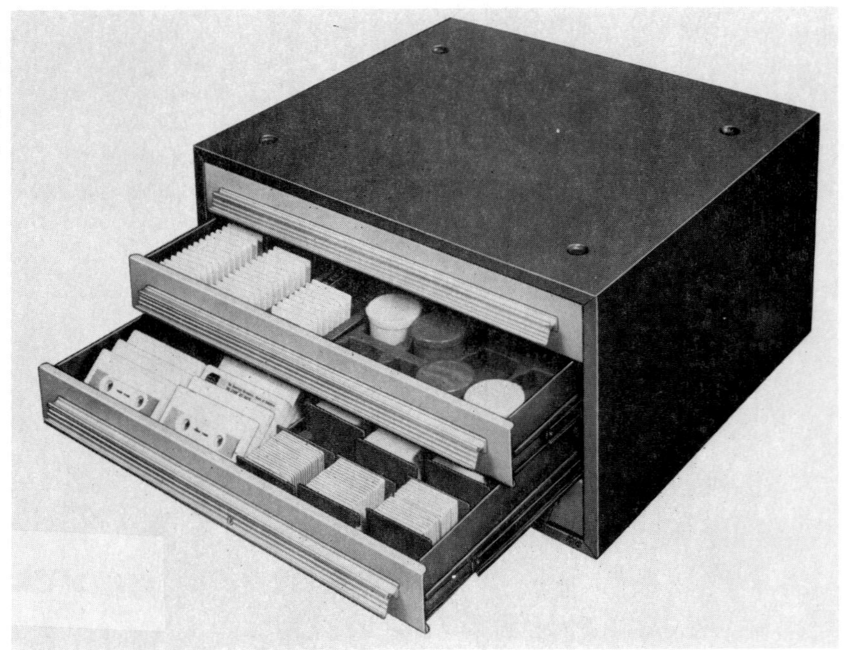

FIGURE 6-17 Media storage cabinet. (Courtesy of Luxor Corp.)

FIGURE 6-18 Stackable media storage cabinets. (Courtesy of Luxor Corp.)

FIGURE 6-18
(continued)

FIGURE 6-19 File drawer arrangement for correspondence files.

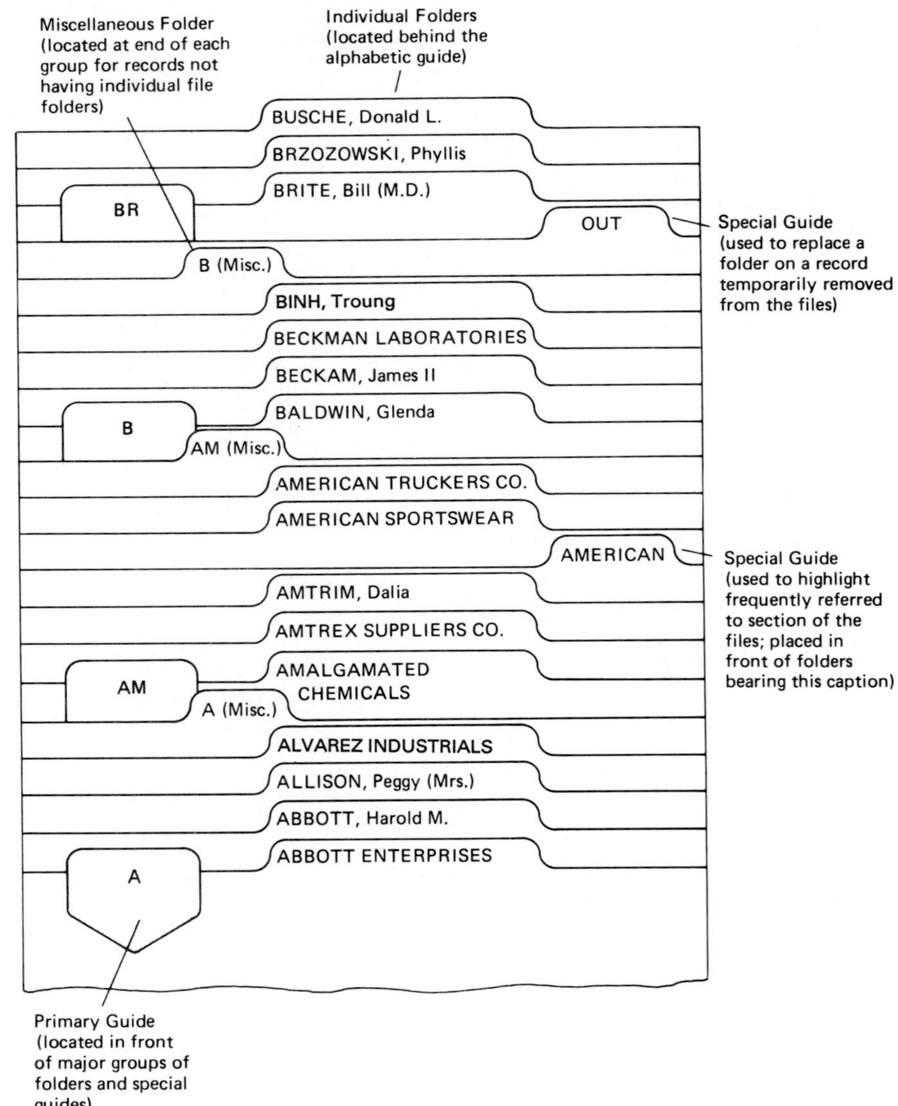

further divided as follows: *Ag, Am,* and *As.*

The tabs on primary guides are printed with the standard divisions for the most common groupings of records, as follows:

Alphabetic, A, B, C, D, and so on.

Days. Numbers 1 through 31 for each day of the month.

Months. January through December.

Other time periods. January–March, April–June, and so on.
Geographic. California, Washington, New York, and so on.

Guides are also available with blank tabs so that records personnel can insert appropriate division and subdivision captions to meet their individual needs. Primary guides are placed in a file drawer in what is generally called "first position"; that is, so the tab on each guide is positioned at the extreme left of the drawer. For open-shelf or lateral units, the tabs on the primary guides are positioned toward the top of each shelf.

Secondary or Auxiliary Guides In large records storage systems, **secondary guides** are used in addition to primary guides. These special guides may be used to highlight frequently referenced sections of records, such as those for customers with active accounts or correspondence files; special topical sections, such as "Taxes," "Personnel," or "Forms"; or where customer or correspondent names begin with common similar words or prefixes, such as American, United States, United, General, Mac, Mc, or Smith.

Secondary guides are generally labeled in a different color from the primary guides and are placed in a straight line or in a staggered position of their own behind their respective primary guides.

Out Guides An **out guide** is a special guide that is substituted for a folder or for a record within a folder that has been temporarily removed from the drawer or shelf (see Figure 6-20). The guide notifies other people that a particular record has not been lost or misplaced but is out on loan. The guides may be printed to include space for writing such information as the name of the borrower of the file and the date the record was borrowed.

Out guides are placed in file drawers or on open shelves of that their tabs are prominent and can be distinguished from the tabs on the primary and secondary guides and the file folders. Out guides are used in charging out and in following up records, which are discussed in detail in Chapter 7.

File Folders

Individual **file folders** are used to store records pertaining to one correspondent or customer, one account or case, one subject or topic, or one geographic region, depending on the filing classification system used. A separate folder is generally created when five or more pieces of correspondence have been accumulated for one correspondent or customer. Individual company procedures will vary, however, as to when new file folders are created and added to the system.

File folders are available in kraft, manila, and plastic, as well as the heavier pressboard that should be used for bulky reports or other materials. Folders should be selected for their durability and strength, since they must withstand heavy use, hold up to 100 records, and resist wear and tear from frequent use.

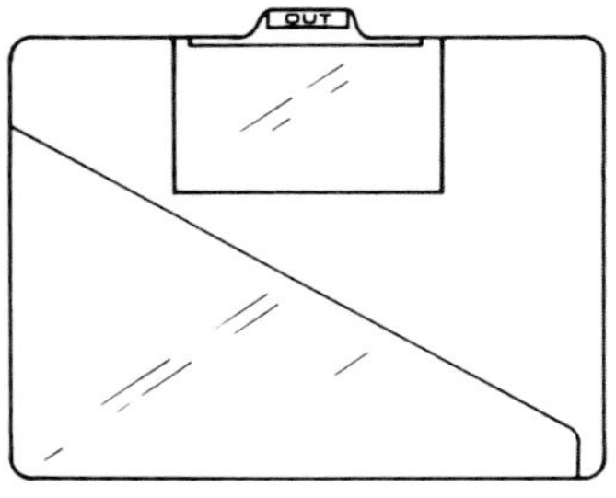

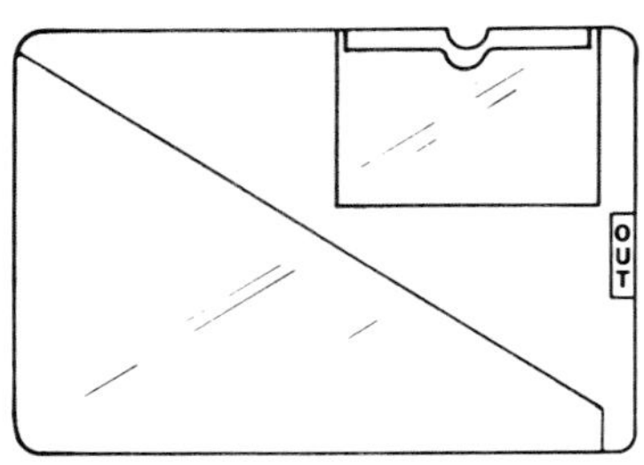

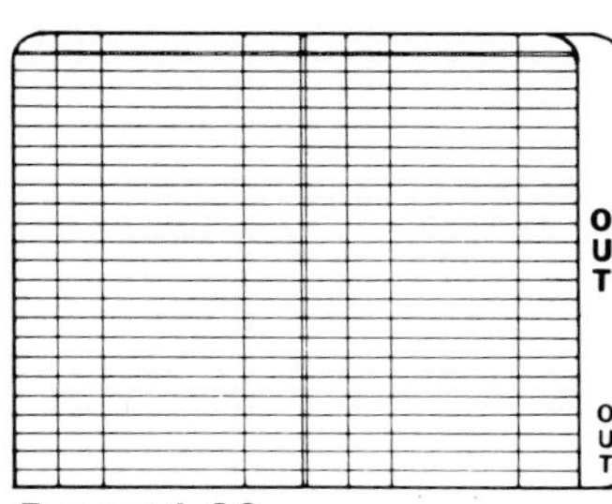

FILE NAME/NUMBER ____________

DATE OUT ____________ DATE TO RETURN ____________

NAME (PRINT) ____________ DEPT

SIGNATURE ____________

INSERT THIS CHARGE-OUT FORM INTO THE POCKET ON THE OUT-GUIDE AND REPLACE CHARGED-OUT FOLDER WITH OUT-GUIDE NOTE DUPLICATE CHARGE-OUT FORMS CAN BE USED FOR FOLLOW-UP PURPOSES IN "FILE NAME/NUMBER" ORDER OR "DATE TO RETURN" ORDER

TABBIES STOCK NO 74559

FIGURE 6-20
Out guides and out folders. (Courtesy of Tabbies, Division of Xertex International, Inc.)

Each folder has a one-half inch protruding **tab** in one-fifth, one-third, one-half, or "full-cut" position (see Figure 6-21). Rather than type a customer's name or account directly on the tab of a folder, information is first typed on file-folder labels. Labels are available in different colors and widths to be coordinated with the file folders; labels come in rolls or strips with self-adhesive or gummed backings.

File-folder labels should include only the identifying information needed to store and retrieve records quickly and easily. For example, if records are stored by customer name, each label should contain only the customer's complete name, typed or printed as the record would be referenced by individuals using the file.

When new file folders are prepared, the position of the tabs and placement of the folders within the drawer or shelf should be identical to folders already stored—either in a straight-line position, where folder tabs are placed one behind the other, or staggered from left to right (see Figure 6-22).

The individual folders, once properly labeled and arranged in sequence in the drawer or on the shelf according to the appropriate filing classification system, are placed behind their respective primary and/or secondary guides.

Near the folded edge of each folder are "score" lines that provide expansion capacity for the folder as more records are added (see Figure 6-23). Up to 25 sheets of paper can be stored in a folder before "breaking" the first score;

FIGURE 6-21 Folders and guides for open-shelf units. (Courtesy of Tab Products Co.)

when the first score is broken, an additional 25 sheets of paper can be placed in the folder. Each folder, then, can hold approximately 100 pieces of paper. If a score is broken too soon, the papers will curl and sag toward the bottom of the folder; if a score is not broken when it should be, papers will protrude over the edge of the folder and cover the tab, creating not only an unsightly file but also a cluttered file drawer or shelf.

Color-coding files for open-shelf units provide greater accuracy in storing records and faster retrieval of records. Identification guides in color-coded systems consist of combinations of folder and tabs, index strips, and other visual signals that form blocks of color. The blocks of color aid in identifying series of records when filing and refiling and help prevent misfilings. By using thirteen different color bars on folders, all twenty-six letters of the alphabet can be represented in an alphabetic filing classification system. In a numeric filing classification system, only ten colors are required to represent the primary indexing digits 0–9.

FIGURE 6-22
Files with staggered and straight-line tab arrangements.

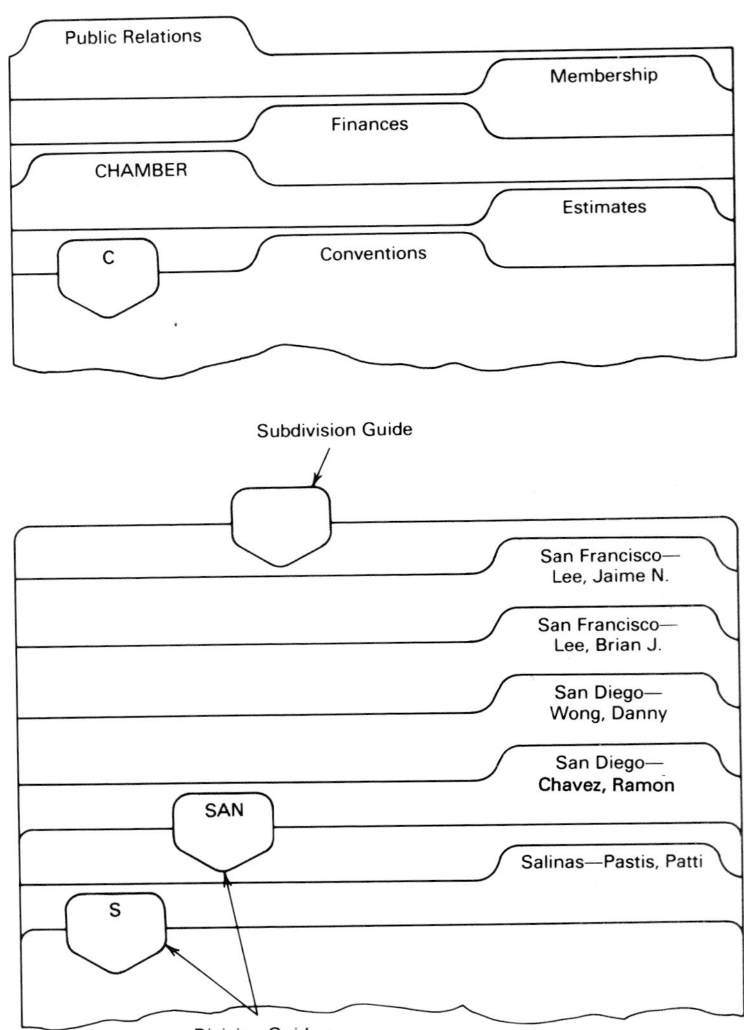

Card-Storage Systems

Storage and retrieval systems for cards include **vertical files** and **visible card files.** Both types of card files can hold index cards that may contain such information as names and addresses of correspondents, customers, suppliers, or personnel; account or credit records for accounts receivable or accounts payable; and cross-references or indexes to other files or information within the company.

Card files may also hold punched cards used in data processing; these cards may contain inventory data such as stock numbers, quantities, style numbers,

FIGURE 6-23
File folder scores for expansion capability.

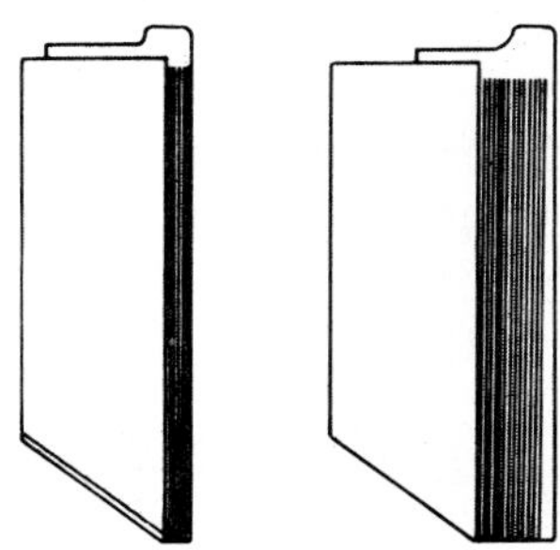

and prices; employment data such as wage and salary information and job classifications; or data on customers and suppliers.

Each card generally contains a record of a single business transaction. Cards may be used to organize or summarize data recorded elsewhere within the system, or they may serve as an index to other records within the system. Perhaps the most commonly used card files are the card catalogs in libraries, where each card contains the relevant information about a published work stored in the library. Each card serves as an index to a work stored within the library system, so it serves as a guide in helping a reader locate the work by using an alphabetic or numeric code. The card contains a summary of the contents of that work; it serves as a record of a business transaction as well—namely, the acquisition of the work—and it is used as an inventory control card for periodic checking of the library's holdings.

Card files are used to store information of either a temporary or a permanent nature. Standard sizes of index cards are 5 by 3 inches, 6 by 4 inches, and 8 by 6 inches. Punched cards are 7 3/8 by 3 1/4 inches. These dimensions refer to both the direction in which information is printed, typed, or written on the card and the direction in which the card is stored.

Because of the uniformity of sizes, cards are compact and take up little storage space. Card files can be updated easily by making appropriate notations on the card or by preparing a new card and destroying the old one. Card files can easily be expanded by adding new cards to the system as required. Also, depending on the nature of information contained on cards and how the information is used, the cards can easily be arranged and rearranged in different sequences.

There are some distinct disadvantages of using card files, however. Some of these are as follows:

1. Cards are easier to lose, misplace, and misfile than other records.
2. If information is copied from a source document (an original letter, contract, or business form), time is spent in transferring information onto a card. The copying can also result in transpositions of figures or mistyped information and other types of errors.
3. If stacks of cards are removed from the files at one time, it is too easy to get the cards out of sequence, for example, they might be shuffled on a desk top or simply dropped.
4. Unless the cards have been carefully designed according to what information is to be included and where specific pieces of information are to be written, individuals having to refer to information on the cards can waste a great deal of time reading the cards to obtain specific information.

Vertical and visible card-filing systems are discussed in this chapter. As with the correspondence storage systems, each card-filing system has a separate set of components to aid in its efficient use.

Vertical Card Files Cards are stored upright — in vertical position — in card-filing equipment. Because cards are of heavier weight than correspondence, and because each card contains essentially one item of information, cards are filed directly into file drawers, boxes, or trays, without file folders.

Card-storage systems for vertical card files include drawers, cabinets, boxes, trays, wheels, and rotary systems. The features of high-quality storage cabinets and drawers for correspondence storage listed on page 131 apply also to vertical card files.

Standard file-drawer cabinets are made for cards of various sizes. Since card files are often used in conjunction with other records, businesses will often use a combination file-drawer cabinet that provides separate drawers for storing cards in one section, with the remainder of the drawers used for storing correspondence or business forms. For example, a standard letter- or legal-size file cabinet may have two correspondence drawers, with two smaller drawers on top divided into two compartments to store 6-by-4 inch or 5-by-3-inch cards.

Card file boxes are available for all standard card sizes and may be used for temporary or permanent storage of card files (see Figure 6-24). These boxes are available in plastic, wood, or metal for durability, strength, convenience, and appearance. Such file boxes are best suited to situations in which a small volume of cards must be maintained, several people must reference the cards frequently, or the records must be moved from one work station to another.

Punched cards are often stored in boxes specially made for punched cards because of the ease and speed with which the cards can be retrieved for use on

FIGURE 6-24 Card file box. (Courtesy of Business Efficiency Aids, Inc.)

data processing equipment. An entire set of cards for a particular data processing program can conveniently be stored in one or more boxes.

Card file boxes are especially suitable for cross-referencing purposes where notations can be made on the cards to refer individuals to specific sources of records for more detailed information.

When more permanent card-storage equipment is required for card files, metal or heavy plastic card trays, as shown in Figure 6-25, can be used. These portable trays can slide in and out of specially equipped desks or file equipment, or trays can be stored in a desk drawer or on top of a desk or cabinet.

Another type of card file is the wheel file, which is used primarily to store cards needed for quick reference (see Figure 6-26). These files are generally small desk-top revolving wheels on which 3 1/2-by-2-inch business calling cards or 5-by-3-inch index cards are placed. These wheels operate on the "Ferris wheel" idea, where the stack of cards on the wheel is turned until the desired card is located.

Such files are popular because they provide quick access to customer names and addresses, personnel telephone numbers, or other commonly used items of information. These wheel files take up little space on a desk top or counter top, are easy to update and expand, and are used to store only one piece of information per card.

A more elaborate system for maintaining card files is the **rotary card file.** These large motorized storage units revolve, bringing the desired set of records to the operator. This equipment stores 6-by-4-inch cards or 8-by-5-inch cards. Rotary card files offer advantages similar to those of automated conveyor units used for correspondence: They can store thousands of card records within one compact unit, and information can be retrieved very quickly.

Rotary card-storage equipment, depending on size and on the types of information stored on the cards, is advantageous when several people need to reference the files simultaneously. Punched cards are often stored in such units in engineering and utility companies, where each card contains information concerning one project or one customer.

FIGURE 6-25 Card tray files. (Courtesy of Kardex Systems, Inc.)

FIGURE 6-26 Rotary wheel card files. (Courtesy of Rolodex Corp.)

Components Although cards are not stored in individual file folders as is correspondence, guides are still required in all forms of vertical card files. The guides serve as signposts for referencing, storing, and retrieving information. Guides are available in all sizes to correspond with the various sizes of cards used in the system. These guides are compatible with file-drawer cabinets, boxes, trays, and wheel or rotary equipment (see Figure 6-27).

A common practice is to precede every 25–50 cards in a drawer with a guide, whether in an alphabetic, numeric, or alphanumeric classification system and regardless of the size of the cards stored. It should be noted, however, that all similar types of data should be recorded on the same size card. It is common, though, within a company or office to have more than one size of card file on which different kinds of information are recorded.

As with correspondence systems, the tabs on the guides contain identifying information for the records stored behind the guides. Also, the guides may be positioned in either a straight-line or staggered arrangement.

Visible Card Files **Visible card files** are those in which information printed on the protruding edge of a card can be referred to without having to handle the card or remove it from its position in a card file. Cards are arranged either horizontally or vertically in staggered positions within the drawer, tray, or panel to allow essential information on the top or bottom of the card to be read easily. Information can be printed on both front and back of a card so that each card serves as an independent source of information by itself. Other advantages of such files are their speed and ease of referencing and compactness of storage space (see Figure 6-28).

Visible card files are suitable for use where records need to be easily accessible for updating or posting of information on a regular basis. Customer accounts, library subscription acquisition data, medical or dental patient examination records, audiovisual equipment checkout requests, and cumulative student attendance or scholastic records are examples of information that can be stored effectively in visible card systems.

The cards created for use in visible card storage systems must be designed

FIGURE 6-27 Verticle card file cabinet. (Courtesy of Tabbies, Division of Xertrex International, Inc.

FIGURE 6-28 Visible file desk stand with frame. (Courtesy of Kardex Sytems, Inc.)

so that commonly referenced information may be printed on either the top or bottom margin of the card, 5/16–5/8 of an inch from the edge of the card.

Visible Card Cabinets The most popular type of equipment to house visible cards is a cabinet with shallow pull-out trays or drawers. In this type of equipment, cards overlap one another horizontally, so the top or bottom edge of each card protrudes and only one or two lines of information are visible.

In a pocket-type visible card file, individual cards are inserted into clear plastic or transparent holders that are attached to the tray or drawer. Where the card file serves as a quick-reference source only, the entire card may be enclosed in a protective plastic holder. If the file must be updated or postings made periodically, the cards are inserted into holders so that only the bottom or top edge is covered by the protective plastic. To obtain specific information from a card, the individual flips the preceding layers of cards upward to expose the entire card on which the desired information appears, as shown in Figure 6-29.

Unlike the vertical card systems, in which cards are filed loosely in drawers, visible cards are attached to the drawer or tray via the holders and are less likely to be lost, misplaced, misfiled, or shuffled out of sequence. An entire tray or drawer can be pulled out and removed from the cabinet if necessary for updating large numbers of records.

Although vertical card files can be stored in the same file-drawer cabinet with correspondence, visible card files are stored in self-contained, table- or desk-top cabinets or floor-model units.

Similar to visible cards, visible strip records are made of card stock and are used for quick-reference files only. They are available in strips as narrow as 1/2 inch, on which only one line of information can be typed. They are commonly used in libraries to store information on certain books and periodicals; in hospitals and hotels for directories of personnel; by the telephone company for customer listings; and by other businesses for customer listings, inventory records, stock control numbers, or membership rosters.

Visible strips may be placed on vertical rotary racks, on vertical or horizontal panels or frames, or on trays. Because of the width of strips, each end of the strip has a set of sprocket holes used to attach the strip to corresponding pegs on the rack, panel, or tray.

Although visible card systems do not require guides to divide their major divisions or subdivisions, these systems do use other types of signposts: colored card stock for certain types of records, notched-edged cards, color-coded strips inserted in the visible edge of the card holders, or color-coded card holders. The color coding of cards or their visible edge enables quick identification of information on specific types of records.

Microform Files

The various microforms can be stored in standard file drawer cabinets, shelves, and trays, which can house any combination of roll film, microfiche, and aperture cards.

Roll film and cartridges can easily be housed in a carousel system such as that shown in Figure 6-35.

Because microfiche are the same sizes as various card files, the same storage and retrieval equipment can easily be adapted for microfiche.

In addition, since each microfiche contains identifying information on its edge, these microforms can also be stored in visible files or trays similar to those shown in Figure 6-30 for magnetic media. Microfiche can also be inserted into envelopes or sleeves attached to rotary desktop units similar to that shown in Figure 6-32.

FIGURE 6-29
Visible card files.
(Courtesy of Kardex Systems, Inc.)

FIGURE 6-30
Diskette trays for 3 1/2 inch diskettes. (Courtesy of Ring King Visibles, Division of HON Industries.)

FIGURE 6-31
Mini-diskette tray cabinet and file trays. (Courtesy of Ring King Visibles, Division of HON Industries.)

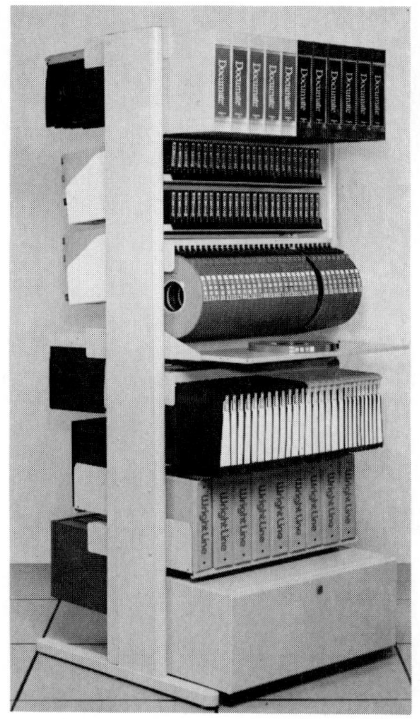

FIGURE 6-32 Optimedia back-to-back tape library storage unit. (Courtesy of Wright Line, Inc., Worcester, MA.)

FIGURE 6-33 Computer printout storage cabinet. (Courtesy of Fellowes Manufacturing Co.)

FIGURE 6-34 Open-shelf suspension cabinet for computer printouts. (Courtesy of Wright Line, Inc., Worcester, MA.)

FIGURE 6-35 Carousel storage system for microfilm. (Courtesy of Information Design Products, Inc.)

CHAPTER HIGHLIGHTS

- An integrated systems approach must be developed and used for the storage, maintenance, and protection of records. A system is a series of interrelated tasks or procedures used to perform a major activity and includes efficient use of personnel and equipment.
- Records storage refers to the equipment and systems used to file records during their useful lifetime in an organization.
- The retrieval of records refers to the removal of records from storage for referencing or updating of information.
- Records storage and retrieval systems must include equipment and the components to accommodate paper-based, electronic-based, and microform-based records.
- The costs of records storage and retrieval include the salaries of personnel who maintain the filing operation; the floor space allocated for records storage equipment and personnel; the cost of equipment and supplies; and such operating expenses as lighting, heating and air conditioning, maintenance, and security.
- When selecting records storage and retrieval systems one must consider the forms of records stored, how records are used, how frequently records are used and by whom, space requirements or limitations, protection and security, and the required length of storage.
- The six basic types of records storage and retrieval equipment are (1) the standard vertical file-drawer cabinets, (2) lateral file-drawer cabinets, (3) open-shelf file units, (4) high-density file units, (5) automated (power) filing units, and (6) electronic (computer-based) systems.
- The costliest system is the standard vertical file-drawer cabinet, because of the large amount of floor space required to house the cabinets, the cost of maintaining and protecting the large area, and the personnel costs.
- Open-shelf file units are considered the most efficient in terms of cost and productivity. They provide easy access to stored records, occupy 50 percent less storage space than standard vertical file-drawer cabinets, and can be expanded easily.
- High-density storage units include open-shelf lateral file units and mobile storage files. Both are effective for high-volume, highly active records storage and retrieval for all types of general records.
- Automated, or power, systems are also ideal for high-volume, highly active records storage and retrieval, especially when used for centralized records storage.
- Electronic records storage and retrieval systems use the video display terminals of word processors, computers, or computer-assisted retrieval systems to store information and data electronically on magnetic media.

- Magnetic media include 3 1/2-, 5 1/4-, and 8-inch floppy disks or diskettes used on microcomputers and reels of computer tapes stored in disk packs or cartridges. Information stored on magnetic media can be accessed quickly and requires less office floor space because of the media's high-density storage capacity.
- Optical character recognition (OCR) is a method whereby printed text, photographs, and other images in hard-copy format can be scanned electronically and stored in digital form on a computer storage medium. OCR eliminates the need to rekey or re-create information already produced in printed form.
- Microforms may be stored in standard file drawer cabinets or in trays or bins for desk-top use. Special equipment is required to read and to print a hard copy of an image stored on microform.
- Optical disk systems use lasers to store and read both data and images at high speed. A system used for restoring and retrieving records consists of a disk, a scanner-printer, a high-resolution video display terminal, and a microcomputer. Optical disks offer the potential for permanent, high-density, random-access storage and retrieval of vast quantities of records.
- Audiovisual media include cassette tapes, filmstrips, slides, and sound recordings. Special storage and retrieval equipment is used to store these types of records.
- Three systems used to store large, odd-sized, or bulky records are oversized file-drawer cabinets, suspension files in open shelfing or in cabinets, and rolled-plan files. Special records storage components are used to identify these records so they can be stored and retrieved as easily as the more conventional types of records.
- In suspension files, documents are suspended from hooks or clips hung from rods along the shelf or cabinet. Correspondence and forms files are stored in suspension folders and placed in standard file-drawer cabinets, open-shelf or lateral units, or specially designed suspension file-drawer units.
- Components of efficient correspondence systems include guides, file folders, tabs, and labels. Guides lead an individual to specific sections of a file drawer or shelf and divide groups of records; primary guides are used to highlight major divisions and subdivisions of records. Secondary or auxiliary guides are used to highlight special sections of records or those frequently referenced. Out guides are substituted for a folder or a record that has been temporarily removed from the drawer or shelf.
- File folders are used to store correspondence and business forms related to one correspondent, account or case, subject or topic, or geographic region. A separate file folder is generally created when five or more pieces of correspondence or forms have been accumulated for one correspondent or customer.

- Card files generally contain records of single business transactions and can be easily updated. Standard sizes of cards are 5 by 3 inches, 6 by 4 inches, and 8 by 6 inches. Because of their uniformity in size, cards take up little storage space.
- Card systems include vertical and visible card files. Cards in vertical card files are stored upright; primary and secondary guides are used to separate divisions and subdivisions of records. Cards may also be stored in file boxes or trays for point-of-use access and retrieval.
- Visible card files are those in which information printed on the protruding edge of a card can be referred to without having to handle the card or remove it from its position in the card file. Visible cards are housed in cabinets with shallow pull-out trays or drawers, where cards overlap one another so the top or bottom edge of each card protrudes and only one or two lines of information are visible.
- Media storage systems for floppy disks and diskettes consist of file-drawer units or trays or bins that are kept in open-shelf or lateral file units. These media are generally used at word processing or computer work stations, so information or data can be stored, accessed, and retrieved at the point of use. Computer tapes and cartridges are generally stored in open-shelf suspension-file units.

QUESTIONS FOR REVIEW

1. What seven criteria should be considered in the selection of records storage equipment and systems? Describe features of each.
2. What are the six basic types of records storage and retrieval systems? Describe the features of each.
3. What are some advantages and disadvantages of electronic records storage and retrieval systems for digital-based records?
4. What purpose do guides, folders, and tabs serve in correspondence storage systems?
5. In what ways do visible storage systems, equipment, and components differ from vertical card storage systems, equipment, and components?
6. Why would the records storage facility's physical conditions, such as sanitary and health facilities, lighting, and heating, be important in the selection and use of records storage equipment?
7. The cost of records storage and retrieval equipment is a major consideration for any organization. Compare the costs of acquiring, using, and maintaining (a) traditional file-drawer cabinets, (b) open-shelf or lateral units, and (c) mobile storage units.
8. What factors should be considered when a business is determining the quality and price of such records storage supplies as file folders, guides, and file-folder labels?

9. For what types of information and in what types of businesses would visible card records be advantageous?
10. For each type of record listed in the table below, indicate which records storage system(s) would be most appropriate. Be prepared to justify your selections.

	Records Storage Systems				
	Open-Shelf Files	Lateral Files	File Drawers	Visible Files	Suspension Files
Blueprints					
Optical discs					
Customer business cards					
Catalogs and brochures					
Employee payroll information					
Accounts receivable or payable information					
Medical and dental charts					
Canceled checks					
Prospective customer listings					
Computer tapes					
Preprinted business forms					
Computer printouts					
Punched cards					
Library acquisitions and catalog information					
Audiovisual media catalog and requisition data					
Magnetic floppy disks and diskettes					
General correspondence					
Microfilm rolls and cartridges					

THE DECISION MAKER

Case Studies

1. You have just been employed as a consultant to a newly established medical-dental clinic incorporated by 12 physicians and dentists, each with his or her own office. Each office will maintain its own set of records, which will include patient records, insurance documents, insurance claims forms, hospital records, X rays, billing information, personnel listings, general correspondence, journals and periodicals, and so on. Your recommendation is that all offices purchase the same types of records storage

equipment. List the types of equipment and systems that you believe would best meet the needs of this corporation. Present an itemized list of the types of records that would be stored in each type of equipment or system. Include a list of auxiliary equipment and supplies needed for each system.

2. As more and more correspondence and other records in your company are created on microcomputers, more of the records will be stored on floppy disks or diskettes. Before operations get too big, you need to develop a system to accommodate records stored on these media. The system needs to fit into the company's overall records storage and retrieval plans for other types of records. Prepare a proposal for the records manager that includes: (1) suggested equipment, systems, and auxiliary supplies to store the floppy disks or diskettes; (2) recommended methods or systems to identify records stored on disks; and (3) recommended methods to retrieve or access information on disks.

Records Classification Systems

OBJECTIVES

Upon completion of this chapter, the student should be able to:

1. Describe the factors to be considered when selecting a records classification system.
2. List the features of both the direct-access system and the indirect-access classification systems.
3. Know the advantages and disadvantages of the three basic records classification systems: alphabetic, numeric, and alphanumeric.
4. Apply the alphabetic records classification rules for indexing and coding personal names, business and organization names, government agency names, and institution names.
5. Apply the alphabetic records classification rules for indexing and coding records by subject and by geographic location.
6. Identify the features of the consecutive, middle-digit, terminal-digit, and decimal numeric records classification systems.

With the increasing usage of automated and electronic records storage and retrieval systems, one function remains common to all records maintenance programs: selecting an appropriate records classification system. The three basic records classification systems are *alphabetic* (by name, subject, or geographic location); *numeric* (by consecutive or straight-numeric sequence, middle-digit, terminal-digit, or decimal-numeric sequence); and *alphanumeric* (a combination of alphabetic and numeric systems). Within each of these records classification systems, records are then filed *chronologically* (by date), with the most recently dated record on top or in front of others.

SELECTING A CLASSIFICATION SYSTEM

Because each system has certain advantages and disadvantages, each company must select a filing classification system based on the size of the company and its volume of records, type(s) of records stored, how and by whom records are used, and how quickly records need to be accessed.

1. *SIZE OF THE COMPANY* — The size of the company dictates the number of individuals responsible for the actual filing of records, as well as those who are authorized to have access to stored records. The larger the company, the greater the number of people who will process or use the records.
2. *VOLUME OF RECORDS* — In a small company, where a small volume of records is to be maintained, an alphabetic records system is generally adequate. However, in a larger organization, where greater volumes and a larger variety of records must be maintained and where more people and equipment are involved, a numeric or alphanumeric system should be considered.
3. *TYPES OF RECORDS* — Although paper records are still the predominant type of records stored, more and more records are being stored on various types of magnetic media—floppy disks and hard disk drives—for use on computerized systems—as well as on various types of microforms. Classification systems should consider all types and forms of records to be stored and retrieved.
4. *HOW RECORDS ARE USED* — The nature of the records and how records will be called for from the files determine the most appropriate classification system to use. Customer account records are generally processed by number; therefore, a numeric filing system would be appropriate. Sales data may be best classified geographically by various sales territories. Inventory merchandise records may be categorized in an alphabetic system by subject according to a company's line of products.

5. *WHO USES RECORDS* — Whether an executive uses records frequently or exclusively and whether other personnel handle records also determine the best classification system to use. A subject system may best serve the executive's need to categorize special information that only the executive needs to refer to. When a number of employees need access to records, an alphabetic or numeric system may be appropriate.
6. *HOW EASILY RECORDS NEED TO BE RETRIEVED* — The ease of records retrieval dictates whether a direct-access system or an indirect-access system is selected. A **direct-access system** is one in which a person can locate a particular record by going directly to the files and looking under the coded name of the record. The alphabetic classification system is referred to as a direct-access system. An **indirect-access system** is one in which an index must first be consulted in order to determine the special code assigned to a particular record. Numerical classification systems and the alphabetic subject system are known as indirect-access systems. Table 7-1 lists some of the features of both types of access systems.

The three basic records classification systems described in this chapter relate to all types of records: paper records, microforms, and electronic records. The criteria for selecting records storage and retrieval equipment and systems, discussed in Chapter 6, must also be considered when deciding whether records will be classified alphabetically, numerically, or alphanumerically.

ALPHABETIC CLASSIFICATION SYSTEMS

An **alphabetic classification** is used to file records by names of individuals, businesses, institutions, government agencies, subjects, or geographic locations—all according to the sequence of letters of the alphabet. With the exception of the alphabetic subject classification system, the other alphabetic systems are direct-access systems.

Each record that is released for filing must be indexed and coded to expedite the eventual filing of records in their appropriate storage places. The rules for **indexing** (determining the caption under which a record is to be filed) and **coding** (marking the filing caption on the record) for filing by name, subject, and geographic location are discussed below.

The rules presented here, based on those developed by the Association of Records Managers and Administrators (ARMA), serve as guidelines for the standardization of alphabetic filing. These rules are based on filing names on a **unit-by-unit** basis; that is, each part of the name is a separate unit. The individual filing units of each name must be compared letter by letter in order to place the names in proper alphabetic sequence.

Robert C. *Browning*

John B. *Browne*

In the above example, the individuals' last names are the primary **indexing** or **filing units.** The first five letters of the last names are identical. The sixth letter in each name reveals the difference—the *e* in *Browne* appears in the alphabet before the letter *i* in *Browning.* Thus these two names need to be reversed to appear in correct alphabetic sequence.

The combination of individual units that comprise a name is called a *filing segment.* One entire name, subject or topic title, geographic location, or number is a filing segment. In the above example, *John B. Browne* is one filing segment; *Robert C. Browning* is another.

TABLE 7-1 FEATURES OF DIRECT- AND INDIRECT-ACCESS SYSTEMS

Direct-Access Systems	*Indirect-Access Systems*
* Records can be located by going directly to the files and referring to the name of the particular file. * Time is saved in both filing and retrieving records. * Guides that show names commonly referred to can lend speed in filing and retrieving records. * The system is cumbersome to use when large volumes of records are stored. * Specific rules for filing must be strictly followed by all personnel. * Frequent confusion and congestion exist when dealing with files with common, similar, or identical names. * Duplication of records is a common problem; there is no index or other control to show whether a file already exists under a particular name.	* Filing and retrieval of records require a two-step process. * Use of an index is required to obtain the code assigned to a record; the index must be consulted before one can locate a filed record. * Records having identical or similar file names can be misfiled in a numeric system unless both the alphabetic index and the accession book provide for special identifying comments about such records or files. * Security is provided for all records; individuals unfamiliar with the coding system cannot gain access to specific records. * The system is most efficient when large volumes of records are stored. * Duplication of records is avoided because each code can be used only once. * Greater accuracy in filing and retrieving is generally provided; out-of-sequence records are easier to spot. * Several different sets of files and indexes are necessary to maintain control over the entire system. * Misfiled records are difficult to locate. * Since only file numbers or other codes appear on file folder labels, one cannot scan or browse through the files to locate a specific file.

Identifying elements are additional units of information placed as the last unit of the name and considered as indexing units only when needed to distinguish identical names. An identifying element can consist of titles, degrees, or city or state names.

Filing by Personal Names

Personal Names The first set of indexing and coding rules are for personal names—names of individual people. All personal names should be transposed so that the individual's last name (**surname**) is the primary indexing unit, the first name (**given name**) is the second unit, and the middle name or initial is the third unit.

If the primary units—the surnames—are identical, the second units—the given names—must be compared. Should the second units also be identical, then the third units—the middle names or initials—are used to determine the proper alphabetic filing sequence.

FIGURE 7-1

	Names As Indexed				
Names as Written	*First Unit*	*Second Unit*	*Third Unit*	*Fourth Unit*	*Fifth Unit*
Sabrina Le	Lee	Sabrina			
Brian J. Lee	Lee	Brian	J		
Brian T. Lee	Lee	Brian	T		
Christopher S. Lee	Lee	Christopher	S		
Jaime N. Lee	Lee	Jaime	N		
Stephanie M. Lee	Lee	Stephanie	M		

Initials An initial in a name is indexed and coded so that it appears before a name that begins with the same letter. This principle is commonly referred to an "Nothing comes before something."

FIGURE 7-2

	Names As Indexed				
Names as Written	*First Unit*	*Second Unit*	*Third Unit*	*Fourth Unit*	*Fifth Unit*
D. L. Busche	Busche	D	L		
Don L. Busche	Busche	Don	L		
Donald L. Busche	Busche	Donald	L		

Abbreviated Personal Names Abbreviated personal names such as *Ed.* for *Edward* or *Edwin, Geo.* for *George, Thos.* for *Thomas, Chas.* for *Charles, Robt.* for *Robert,* and *Wm.* for *William* are indexed as if they were spelled out.

FIGURE 7-3

	Names As Indexed				
Names as Written	*First Unit*	*Second Unit*	*Third Unit*	*Fourth Unit*	*Fifth Unit*
Chas. Harrington	Harrington	Charles			
Charles J. Harrington	Harrington	Charles	J		
Geoffrey Hom	Hom	Geoffrey			
Geo. Y. Hom	Hom	George	Y		

Married Women Index the names of married women according to their legal names. A married woman's legal name consists of her given name; her middle name, maiden name, or initial; and her husband's surname. A married woman may also use her professional name. A cross-reference notation should be made under the alternative name under which a record could be found if appropriate.

FIGURE 7-4

	Names As Indexed				
Names as Written	*First Unit*	*Second Unit*	*Third Unit*	*Fourth Unit*	*Fifth Unit*
Mrs. Robert Swinney	Swinney	Robert	Mrs.		
	(SEE Ms. Sandra L. Whitcomb) OR (SEE Ms. Sandra L. Whitcomb-Swinney)				
Ms. Sandra L. Whitcomb	Whitcomb	Sandra	L	Ms.	
Ms. Sandra L. Whitcomb-Swinney	Whitcomb Swinney	Sandra	L	Ms.	

Identical Names If all indexing units of two or more persons' names are identical, use as **identifying elements** the individuals' city, state, and street names, in that order, to place the names in alphabetic sequence.

FIGURE 7-5

	Names As Indexed				
Names as Written	*First Unit*	*Second Unit*	*Third Unit*	*Fourth Unit*	*Fifth Unit*
L. Theresa Peebles, Palo Alto, California	Peebles	L	Theresa	Palo Alto	
L. Theresa Peebles, Pasadena, California	Peebles	L	Theresa	Pasadena	

If the city names, state names, and street names are all identical, then the house or building numbers should be used (with the lowest number filed first) to place the names in sequence. Street names containing compass directions and numbered streets are indexed and filed before alphabetic names.

FIGURE 7-6

		Names As Indexed					
Names as Written	*First Unit*	*Second Unit*	*Third Unit*	*Fourth Unit*	*Fifth Unit*	*Sixth Unit*	*Seventh Unit*
Raymond Gibbs	Gibbs	Raymond					
Raymond L. Gibbs 9919 Aspen Circle Kansas City, Missouri	Gibbs	Raymond	L	Missouri	Kansas City	Aspen Circle	
Raymond L. Gibbs 2931 Mission Avenue Kansas City, Missouri	Gibbs	Raymond	L	Missouri	Kansas City	Mission Avenue	2931
Raymond L. Gibbs 3647 Mission Avenue Kansas City, Missouri	Gibbs	Raymond	L	Missouri	Kansas City	Mission Avenue	3647

Names with Prefixes Prefixed surnames are indexed and coded as one filing unit, disregarding any punctuation marks or spacing within the name. Examples of surname prefixes are *de, de la, Des, Du, Fitz, La, Mac, Mc, O', Saint, San, St., Van, Vander,* and *Von.*

FIGURE 7-7

	Names As Indexed				
Names as Written	*First Unit*	*Second Unit*	*Third Unit*	*Fourth Unit*	*Fifth Unit*
Amedee La Croix	LaCroix	Amedee			
Randall R. MacRae	MacRae	Randall	R		
Thomas A. McDannold	McDannold	Thomas	A		
Thomas McDonough	McDonough	Thomas			

A separate section of the file drawer or cabinet can be designated for such common prefixes as *Mac, Mc,* or *Van* if a large volume of records warrants it. In such cases, the separate group would precede the other files for that letter of the alphabet.

Hyphenated Names Names that are hyphenated are considered one indexing unit; disregard the hyphen between the names. Be sure that a surname is indeed hyphenated and not a middle name-surname combination, which is indexed differently.

FIGURE 7-8

	Names As Indexed				
Names as Written	*First Unit*	*Second Unit*	*Third Unit*	*Fourth Unit*	*Fifth Unit*
Nancy Patricia Lee	Lee	Nancy	Patricia		
Nancy-Patricia Lee	Lee	NancyPatricia			
Lin McNulty	McNulty	Lin			
Lin McNulty-Robbins	McNultyRobbins	Lin			
Gladys Robbins	Robbins	Gladys			
Mary Jane Wilson	Wilson	Mary	Jane		
Mary-Jean Wilson	Wilson	MaryJean			
MaryJean Wilson R.	Wilson	MaryJean	R		

Personal Titles Personal titles, such as *Miss, Mr., Mrs.,* and *Ms.,* when followed by a complete name are disregarded as indexing units unless needed as an identifying element; in such a case, the title is the last indexing unit.

FIGURE 7-9

	Names As Indexed				
Names as Written	*First Unit*	*Second Unit*	*Third Unit*	*Fourth Unit*	*Fifth Unit*
Ms. Joan Lauricella	Lauricella	Joan	Ms		
Joan B. Laurick	Laurick	Joan	B		
Ms. Marion E. Graff	Graff	Marion	E	Ms	
Mr. Marion Griffith	Griffith	Marion	Mr		

Professional Titles, Degrees, and Designations Professional titles (such as *Prof.* or *Professor, Rev.* or *Reverend,* and *Captain*), academic degrees (such as *Ed.D., M.D., Ph.D., J.D.,* and *D.D.S.*), and professional designations (such as *CPA* and *CRM*), when followed by a complete name are disregarded as indexing units unless needed as an identifying element; in such a case, the title or degree is the last indexing unit. Disregard any punctuation.

FIGURE 7-10

	Names As Indexed				
Names as Written	*First Unit*	*Second Unit*	*Third Unit*	*Fourth Unit*	*Fifth Unit*
Ray Imatani, M.D.	Imatani	Ray	MD		
Mayor Raymond Imes	Imes	Raymond	Mayor		
Donald L. Reynoso	Reynoso	Donald	L		
Reverend Donald L. Reynoso	Reynoso	Donald	L	Reverend	
Darlene Wills, CPA	Wills	Darlene	CPA		
Darlene Wills, J.D.	Wills	Darlene	JD		

Pseudonyms and Royal and Religious Titles Pseudonyms—fictitious names or pen names—are indexed as written. Names that begin with a royal title or religious title followed by only one name are indexed as written—with each word a separate indexing unit.

FIGURE 7-11

	Names As Indexed				
Names as Written	*First Unit*	*Second Unit*	*Third Unit*	*Fourth Unit*	*Fifth Unit*
Dr. Seuss	Dr.	Suess			
Duchess of Windsor	Duchess	of	Windsor		
Mister Rogers	Mister	Rogers			
Mother Theresa	Mother	Theresa			
Pope John Paul, V	Pope	John	Paul	V	
Pope John Paul, VI	Pope	John	Paul	VI	

Seniority Titles and Suffixes Seniority titles used to indicate birth order, such as *Jr., Sr., 2nd, 3d, II, III,* etc., are disregarded as indexing units unless needed as identifying elements. The titles *Jr.* and *Sr.* are filed alphabetically as written; numeric designations are filed numerically in ascending order, with Arabic numerals preceding Roman numerals.

FIGURE 7-12

	Names As Indexed				
Names as Written	*First Unit*	*Second Unit*	*Third Unit*	*Fourth Unit*	*Fifth Unit*
John S. Wong, 3d	Wong	John	S	3	
John S. Wong, II	Wong	John	S	II	
John S. Wong, Jr.	Wong	John	S	Jr	
John S. Wong, Sr.	Wong	John	S	Sr	

Foreign Names Index foreign personal names as any other personal name. When foreign surnames and given names cannot be distinguished, use the last name as the first indexing unit; provide cross references where necessary under other possible indexing units.

FIGURE 7-13

	Names As Indexed				
Names as Written	*First Unit*	*Second Unit*	*Third Unit*	*Fourth Unit*	*Fifth Unit*
Thuy Diep	Diep	Thuy			
Zarin Khan	Khan	Zarin			
Yabedjian Khatounik	Khatounik	Yabedjian			
	(SEE YABEDJIAN, Khatounik)				
Vi The Lieu	Lieu	Vi	The		
Tran Van Nguyen	Nguyen	Tran	Van		
	(SEE TRAN, Nguyen Van)				
Alfa Sahibzada	Sahibzada	Alfa			
Nguyen Van Tran	Tran	Nguyen	Van		

Filing Business and Organization Names

In general, index business and organization names as written, using the business or organization letterhead stationery or trademark as a guide. Include as indexing units prepositions (such as *at, of, in,* and *by*), conjunctions (*and* and the ampersand *&*), and articles (*a* and *an*). If *The* appears as the first unit in a name, use it as the last indexing unit; disregard *the* if it appears elsewhere in the filing segment. Spell out such symbols as *&* (an ampersand representing *and*), *$* (for dollar), and *#* (for number or pound(s)). Disregard such punctuation marks as commas, periods, and apostrophes. Index hyphenated words as one unit.

FIGURE 7-14

Names as Written	Names As Indexed First Unit	Second Unit	Third Unit	Fourth Unit	Fifth Unit
Agencia Guadalajara	Agencia	Guadalajara			
Agency Publications, Ltd.	Agency	Publications	Ltd		
Childs' Photography, Canton	Childs	Photography	Canton		
Child's Photography, Lima	Childs	Photography	Lima		
Info-Data Inc.	InfoData	Inc			
Information Works	Information	Works			
Rittgers' ArithMatics	Rittgers	ArithMatics			
Rittgers, Woods & Paxton	Rittgers	Woods	and	Paxton	
Rittman Office Temps	Rittman	Office	Temps		

Personal Names in Business Names When the full name of an individual is incorporated into a business name, index the personal name first by transposing it; then index the other words as written, following the appropriate rules.

FIGURE 7-15

Names as Written	Names As Indexed First Unit	Second Unit	Third Unit	Fourth Unit	Fifth Unit
Jason P. McDonald	McDonald	Jason	P		
McDonald-Lopez Enterprises	McDonaldLopez	Enterprises			
Carlos E. Yadao Law Corp.	Yadao	Carlos	E	Law	Corp
Yadao-Yadalian Imports	YadaoYadalian	Imports			

Titles in Business Names When a title appears within a business name, followed by only one name, file the business name as written.

FIGURE 7-16

Names as Written	First Unit	Second Unit	Third Unit	Fourth Unit	Fifth Unit
		Names As Indexed			
Dr. Well's Health Spa	Dr	Wells	Health	Spa	
Madam Leong's	Madam	Leongs			
Mr. Jack's Gourmet Shoppe	Mr	Jacks	Gourmet	Shoppe	
Mr. Green Thumb's Nursery	Mr	Green	Thumbs	Nursery	
Princess Shara Designs	Princess	Shara	Designs		

Abbreviations and Acronyms Business abbreviations such as *Co, Corp., Inc., Ltd., Mfg., Genl.,* and *U.S.* (when not related to an agency of the federal government) are indexed as written. Abbreviated names and acronyms and abbreviations are indexed as one unit cross-referencing where necessary to the complete name.

FIGURE 7-17

Names as Written	First Unit	Second Unit	Third Unit	Fourth Unit	Fifth Unit
		Names As Indexed			
A & F Lumber Mills	A	and	F	Lumber	Mills
AFL-CIO	AFL-CIO				
American Food Products Corp.	American	Food	Products	Corporation	
Americo's Ristorante	Americos	Ristorante			
CBS	CBS (SEE Columbia Broadcasting System)				
Columbia Broadcasting System	Columbia	Broadcasting	System		
Ft. DeRussy Limo Service	Ft. DeRussy	Limo	Service		
IBM	IBM (SEE International Business Machines)				
International Business Machines	International	Business	Machines		
Kiyo's Kitchen Kreations, Ltd.	Kiyos	Kitchen	Kreations	Limited	
KKGO Radio Station	KKGO	Radio	Station		
Women at Work, Inc.	Women	at	Work	Incorporated	
Women's Healthcare Network	Womens	Healthcare	Network		

Hyphenated Business Names A hyphenated business name may be the last names of the individual owners, or it may be a hyphenated surname. In either case, index the hyphenated name as a single unit, disregarding the hyphen.

FIGURE 7-18

	Names As Indexed				
Names as Written	*First Unit*	*Second Unit*	*Third Unit*	*Fourth Unit*	*Fifth Unit*
Louis C. Nanassy	Nanassy	Louis	C		
Nanassy-Selden Publications	Nanassy	Selden	Publications		
William Selden	Selden	William			
Maxine K. Wilson	Wilson	Maxine	K		
Wilson-Robbins Computers Ltd.	Wilson	Robbins	Computers	Limited	

Geographic Names Names of cities or other municipalities or street names included within business and organization names are generally indexed as written. Names containing foreign prefixes such as *La, Las, Los, San,* and *Santa* are indexed as one unit.

FIGURE 7-19

	Names As Indexed				
Names as Written	*First Unit*	*Second Unit*	*Third Unit*	*Fourth Unit*	*Fifth Unit*
El Dorado Springs Medical Center	ElDorado	Springs	Medical	Center	
Elk River Resorts International	Elk	River	Resorts	International	
Los Angeles Metropolitan Water District	LosAngeles	Metropolitan	Water	District	
Los Angeles Sports Arena	LosAngeles	Sports	Arena		
Saint Dominick Convalescent Home	Saint	Dominick	Convalescent	Home	
The San Marino Tribune	SanMarino	Tribune	(The)		
San Mateo Power Company	SanMateo	Power	Company		
Shanghai Importers, Inc.	Shanghai	Importers	Inc		

Compass Terms Compass terms within business and organization names may be written as separate words or as hyphenated words. Index hyphenated words as one unit; index other terms as written.

FIGURE 7-20

Names as Written	*Names As Indexed*				
	First Unit	*Second Unit*	*Third Unit*	*Fourth Unit*	*Fifth Unit*
East Lansing Billiards	East	Lansing	Billiards		
Eastern Billboard Mfg. Co.	Eastern	Billboard	Manufacturing	Company	
North West Acupuncturist	North	West	Acupuncturist		
North-West Academy	NorthWest	Academy			
Northwest Airlines	Northwest	Airlines			

Possessives For indexing purposes, disregard the apostrophes; and index and file business and organization names as written.

FIGURE 7-21

Names as Written	*Names As Indexed*				
	First Unit	*Second Unit*	*Third Unit*	*Fourth Unit*	*Fifth Unit*
It's a Pizza Palace	Its	a	Pizza	Palace	
Sebastian's on the Pier	Sebastians	on	the	Pier	
Sebastians' Winery	Sebastians	Winery			
Sebastian's Wingate West	Sebastians	Wingate	West		

Subsidiaries and Divisions In general, index names of subsidiary companies, affiliates, and divisions under their own names as shown on their organization letterhead stationery or other business forms. Provide a cross-reference to the parent company if necessary. (Refer to Poor's *Register of Directors & Executives* and Moody's *Industrial Manual* as guides for determining the interrelationships within or among companies.)

FIGURE 7-22

Names as Written	Names As Indexed First Unit	Second Unit	Third Unit	Fourth Unit	Fifth Unit
Pillsbury Commodity Services (Subsidiary of The Pillsbury Co.)	Pillsbury	Commodity	Services		
The Pillsbury Co. (Subsidiary of Gramet Holdings Corp.)	Pillsbury	Company	The		
Security Pacific Asian Banking Co. (Subsidiary of Security Pacific Corp.)	Security	Pacific	Asian	Banking	Co.
Security Pacific Business Finance (Subsidiary of Security Pacific Corp.)	Security	Pacific	Business	Finance	
Security Pacific Equipment Leasing (Subsidiary of Security Pacific National Bank)	Security	Pacific	Equipment	Leasing	
Security Pacific National Bank (Subsidiary of Security Pacific Corp.)	Security	Pacific	National	Bank	

Numbers in Names Names beginning with numerals are indexed in numeric sequence, with the smaller numbers arranged before the larger ones. Names beginning with Arabic numerals are filed before names with Roman numerals. Such records are filed as a separate section in the drawer or cabinet preceding the alphabetically arranged names. If the numbers appearing at the beginning of the name are spelled out, such names are indexed and filed according to the alphabetic rules; the entire number, when spelled out, is considered *one* indexing unit.

FIGURE 7-23

Names as Written	Names As Indexed First Unit	Second Unit	Third Unit	Fourth Unit	Fifth Unit
6th Lane Bowling	6(th)	Lane	Bowling		
1570 University Building	1570	University	Building		
2400 Reprographics Center	2400	Reprographics	Center		
Four Hundred Corp.	FourHundred	Corporation			
Three-Sixty Degree Club	ThreeSixty	Degree	Club		
Two-by-Four Builders	Two	by	Four	Builders	

Names with numerals appearing other than at the beginning are filed preceding the first similar name without a numeral.

FIGURE 7-24

		Names As Indexed			
Names as Written	*First Unit*	*Second Unit*	*Third Unit*	*Fourth Unit*	*Fifth Unit*
Barrett's 600 Inn	Barretts	600	Inn		
Barrett's Tax Service	Barretts	Tax	Service		
Borden's 350 Desktop Publishing Inc.	Bordens	350	Desktop	Publishing	Inc
Bordens' Three-Hundred Security Co.	Bordens	ThreeHundred	Security	Company	

Coined Words and Trade Names Coined names are phonetic spellings, prefixes or suffixes, or other special combinations of letters or words that make up a business or organization name. Index such names as one indexing unit, disregarding any punctuation within the name.

FIGURE 7-25

		Names As Indexed			
Names as Written	*First Unit*	*Second Unit*	*Third Unit*	*Fourth Unit*	*Fifth Unit*
Date-A-Mate Studios	DateAMate	Studios			
NuLawn Gardening Center	NuLawn	Gardening	Center		
Ship-to-Shore Freight Lines	ShiptoShore	Freight	Lines		
Tea-for-Two Cafe	TeaforTwo	Cafe			

Filing Government Names

Government agencies include the various levels of governmental and political divisions—federal, state, county, city; and their subdivisions—offices, bureaus, departments, commissions, agencies; and so on.

The general rule is to index by the distinctive name of the governmental unit. If all indexing units are identical in the names, use as identifying elements the city, state, street name, and/or building number, in that order. Include the word *of* as an indexing unit.

Federal Government When indexing names of departments or agencies of the federal government, use the words *United States Government* as the first three indexing units. Then index by the department name, followed by the office or bureau designation. Military installations—bases, camps, stations, etc.—are so indexed and filed.

A separate section of the file drawer or cabinet can be designated for the *United States Government* if a large volume of files involve federal government departments or agencies. (Refer to the *United States Government Manual* as a guide for determining the structure of federal government departments and agencies.)

FIGURE 7-26

Names as Written	*Sequencing for Indexing*
Department of Housing and Urban Development, Office of Economic Affairs	United States Government Housing (and) Urban Development Department (of) Economic Affairs Office (of)
Division of Environmental Planning, Tennessee Valley Authority	United States Government Tennessee Valley Authority Environmental Planning Division (of)
Department of Interior, Bureau of Indian Affairs	United States Government Interior Department (of) Indian Affairs Office (of)

State and Local Governments State and local governmental units include states, counties, cities, towns, and townships. Index by the geographic name, followed by its designation as county, state, city, and so on. Then index by the name of the department or agency.

FIGURE 7-27

		Names As Indexed			
Names as Written	*First Unit*	*Second Unit*	*Third Unit*	*Fourth Unit*	*Fifth Unit*
Fulton County Health Department, Atlanta, Georgia	Fulton	County	Health	Department	
Fulton County Juvenile Court, Atlanta	Fulton	County	Juvenile	Court	
Massachusetts Registry of Motor Vehicles	Massachusetts	State	Motor	Vehicles	Registry (of)
Bureau of Employment Services, Ohio	Ohio	State	Employment	Services	Bureau (of)
Pittsburgh Chamber of Commerce	Pittsburgh	City	Chamber (of)	Commerce	

Foreign Governments Index names of foreign governments by their distinctive name and then by their particular designation.

FIGURE 7-28

	Names As Indexed				
Names as Written	*First Unit*	*Second Unit*	*Third Unit*	*Fourth Unit*	*Fifth Unit*
Commonwealth of Australia	Australia	Commonwealth	of		
Ministry of Education, People's Republic of China	China	People's	Republic (of)	Education Ministry (of)	
Socialist Republic of Czechoslovakia	Czechoslovakia	Socialistic	Republic (of)		
Socialist Republic of Czechoslovakia, National Committee	Czechoslovakia	Socialistic	Republic (of)	National	Committee
Parliament of the Kingdom of Norway	Norway	Kingdom (of)	Parliament		

Filing Institution Names

Institutions include schools, colleges and universities, churches, hospitals, financial institutions, and libraries. The general rule is to index according to the distinctive word in each name.

Schools Index names of elementary and secondary schools first by their distinctive names, then by their cities, and then by their states. Note that when an individual's complete name appears in the school name, the personal name is transposed for indexing purposes.

FIGURE 7-29

Names as Written	Sequence for Indexing
John F. Kennedy High School, Pasadena, California	Kennedy, John F., High School Pasadena California
John F. Kennedy High School, Pasadena, Texas	Kennedy, John F., High School Pasadena Texas
Thomas Starr King Junior High School, Los Angeles, California	King, Thomas Starr, Junior High School Los Angeles California
Madison Park Elementary School, Shreveport, Louisiana	Madison Park Elementary School Shreveport Louisiana
McCormack School, Boston, Massachusetts	McCormack School Boston Massachusetts

Colleges and Universities Index college and university names as written. If necessary to distinguish multiple-campus institutions, include the city and state name as the last indexing unit(s).

FIGURE 7-30

Names as Written	Sequence for Indexing
University of California at Santa Barbara, California	California, University (of) Santa Barbara California
University of California at Santa Cruz, California	California, University (of) Santa Cruz California
Michigan State University	Michigan State University
University of Michigan, Ann Arbor	Michigan, University (of) Ann Arbor
U.S. International University, San Diego, California	United States International University San Diego California
George Washington University Medical School, Washington, D.C.	Washington, George, University Medical School Washington District of Columbia

Religious Institutions Churches and such other religious institutions as synagogues, temples, and cathedrals are indexed as written, followed by the city and state names.

FIGURE 7-31

Names as Written	*Sequence for Indexing*
Temple Beth Torah, Alhambra, California	Beth Torah Temple Alhambra California
Chinese Baptist Church of Yuma, Arizona	Chinese Baptist Church (of) Yuma Yuma Arizona
Church of Jesus Christ of Latter Day Saints	Jesus Christ (of) Latter Day Saints Church (of)
Saint Barnabas Episcopal Church	Saint Barnabas Episcopal Church

Hospitals Names of hospitals, sanitariums, and convalescent homes are indexed as written, followed by the city and state names.

FIGURE 7-32

Names as Written	*Sequence for Indexing*
National Children's Cardiac Hospital	National Children('s) Cardiac Hospital
Saint Joseph's Hospital, Asheville, North Carolina	Saint Joseph('s) Hospital Asheville North Carolina
Saint Joseph's Hospital, Durham, North Carolina	Saint Joseph('s) Hospital Durham North Carolina
Veterans Hospital, Cincinnati, Ohio	Veterans Hospital Cincinatti Ohio
Veterans Hospital, Cuyahoga Falls	Veterans Hospital Cuyahoga Falls

Financial Institutions Financial institutions include banks, savings and loan associations, credit unions, thrifts, trust companies, and insurance companies. Index under the distinctive names of the institutions, followed by the city and state names. If other geographic information such as branch name or location is necessary, index each word as an additional indexing unit.

FIGURE 7-33

Names as Written	*Sequence for Indexing*
Saratoga Savings and Loan Association, Lafayette Branch, New Orleans	Saratoga Savings (and) Loan Association Lafayette Branch New Orleans
Saratoga Savings and Loan Association, Loyola Avenue Branch, New Orleans	Saratoga Savings (and) Loan Association Loyola Avenue Branch New Orleans
Security Mortgage Corp.	Security Mortgage Corp.
Security Pacific National Bank, Lake and Colorado Branch, Pasadena, California	Security Pacific National Bank Lake (and) Colorado Branch Pasadena California
Security Pacific National Bank, Pasadena Office, Pasadena, California	Security Pacific National Bank Pasadena Office Pasadena California

Subject Classification Systems

A second method of alphabetic filing is the **subject classification system,** which is the arrangement of records by names of topics or categories rather than by personal or business or organization names. The two methods of filing records by subject are the **dictionary system** and the **encyclopedic system.** In a dictionary system, records are filed in alphabetic sequence similar to the way words are listed in a dictionary—with no grouping of related topics. This system lends itself to storing a small volume of records—records consisting of no more than two drawers of a filing cabinet or 3 cubic feet of storage space. Such a system is found in an executive's office where special records are used primarily by the individual executive. See Figure 7-34 for an example of subject filing using the dictionary arrangement. Larger volumes of records filed in the dictionary subject system become unwieldy to manage because of the general diversity of topics. Cross-referencing and a general index of topics is not used in such a system.

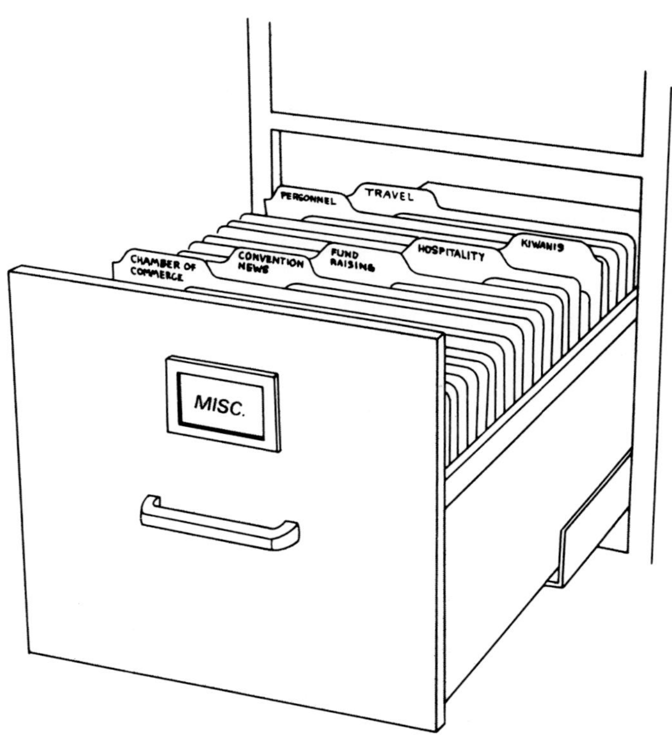

FIGURE 7-34 Dictionary arrangement for subject files.

When larger volumes of records must be stored by subject, the encyclopedic system should be used. In addition to having records filed under the major or broad topic names, subheadings of related subjects are provided for each of the major topics (see Figure 7-35).

A subject records classification system is an indirect-access system requiring the use of a **relative index.** This index lists in alphabetic order all the topic names that are used in the system (see Figures 7-36 and 7-37). Before a particular record can be indexed and coded, the file worker must refer to the relative index to find out under what topic name the record will be filed. In order to retrieve a particular record from the files, the file worker must again know to which topic name to refer. Thus those who are involved in the filing process must read each record carefully to determine the most appropriate caption. Using such an indirect-access system, then, a person cannot file or retrieve a record by going directly to the files and looking under a correspondent's name as is done in a direct-access system.

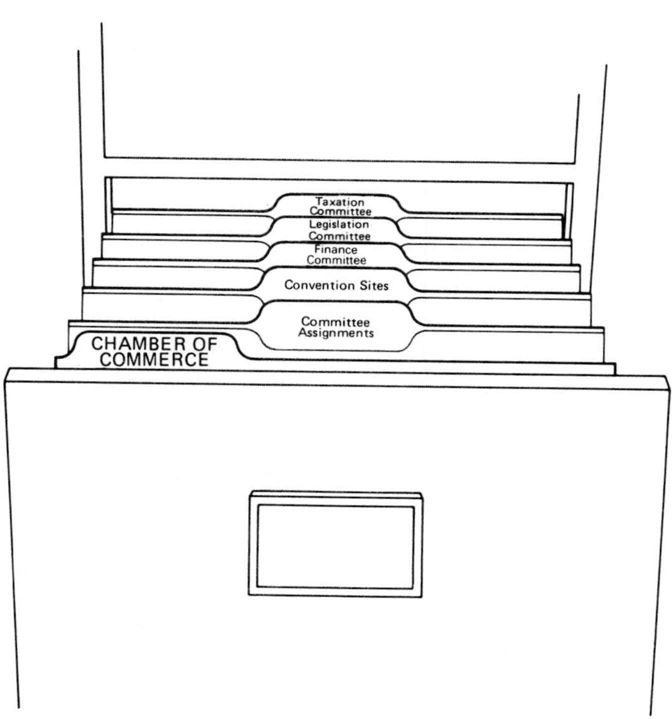

FIGURE 7-35 Encyclopedia arrangement for subject files.

Indexing and Coding The topic names or categories are arranged in alphabetic sequence according to the major or broad topic names. Each topic is indexed as written, with each important word considered a separate indexing unit. Many of the rules for filing business and organization names can be used as guidelines for filing names of topics alphabetically.

FIGURE 7-36 Alphabetic subject index.

Travel

Client Visitation Reports
Domestic Travel
  Local Representatives
  Lodgings
International Travel
  American Embassies
  Local Representatives Abroad
  Lodgings
  Interpreters—Pacific Rim
  Interpreters—European Countries
  Interpreters—Middle East
  Interpreters—Others
  Passport Requirements
  State Department Guidelines
  Visa Requirements
Transportation
  Air Travel
    Domestic Travel
    International Travel
  Automobile Travel
    Local Travel
    Mileage Reimbursement
    Out-of-State Travel
  Oceanic Travel
  Rail Travel—International
Travel Allowances
  Client Conferences
  Entertainment
  Family Travel Plan
  Meal Allowances
  Per Diem Allowances

FIGURE 7-37 Relative index for alphabetic subject file.

Subject	*Refer to*
Air Travel	Transportation
American Embassies	International Travel
Automobile Transportation	Transportation—Auto
Client Conferences	Travel Allowances
Client Visitation Reports	Client Visitation Reports
Domestic Air Travel	Transportation—Air Travel
Domestic Travel	Domestic Travel
Entertainment	Travel Allowances
Family Travel Plan	Travel Allowances
International Travel	International Travel
Interpreters—Pacific Rim	International Travel
Interpreters—European Countries	International Travel
Interpreters—Middle East	International Travel
Interpreters—Others	International Travel
Local Representatives	Domestic Travel
Local Representatives Abroad	International Travel
Local Travel—Automobile	Transportation—Auto
Lodgings—Domestic	Domestic Travel
Lodgings—International	International Travel
Meal Allowances	Travel Allowances
Mileage Reimbursement	Transportation—Auto
Oceanic Travel	Transportation
Out-of-State Travel	Transportation—Auto
Passport Requirements	International Travel
Per Diem Allowances	Travel Allowances
Rail Travel—International	Transportation
State Department Guidelines	International Travel
Travel Allowances	Travel Allowances
Transportation	Transportation
Visa Requirements	International Travel

Structured-Functional Subject System

A more specific subject classification system is the **structured-functional system,** based on the six basic organizational functions—finance, manufacturing, marketing, information systems, human resources, and engineering—or other suitable functions. As with the encyclopedic subject system, broad topic or function headings are used. Major divisions and related subdivisions are categorized under each major topic, as shown below:

HMR HUMAN RESOURCES
- Attendance and Leave
  - Jury duty
  - Military leave
  - Personal leave
  - Sick leave
  - Vacation time
- Employee Benefits
  - Insurance
    - Dental
    - Life
    - Medical
    - Other
  - Pensions
  - Other
- Employee Records
- Health and Safety
- Job/Position Descriptions
- Laws and Regulations
- Recruitment
- Training and Career Development
  - Career Counseling
  - Education Programs
  - Seminars/Workshops
  - Tuition Reimbursement

GEOGRAPHIC CLASSIFICATION SYSTEM

The **geographic classification** system involves arranging records alphabetically according to the names of geographic locations—street names, towns or townships, cities, counties, states, and countries. As in a subject system, records in a geographic system can be classified either in a dictionary arrangement or in an encyclopedic arrangement (see Figures 7-38 and 7-39). The specific number of geographic divisions used is based on the volume of records, the size of the geographic boundaries, and the number of subdivisions required.

FIGURE 7-38
Dictionary and encyclopedia arrangement for geographic files.

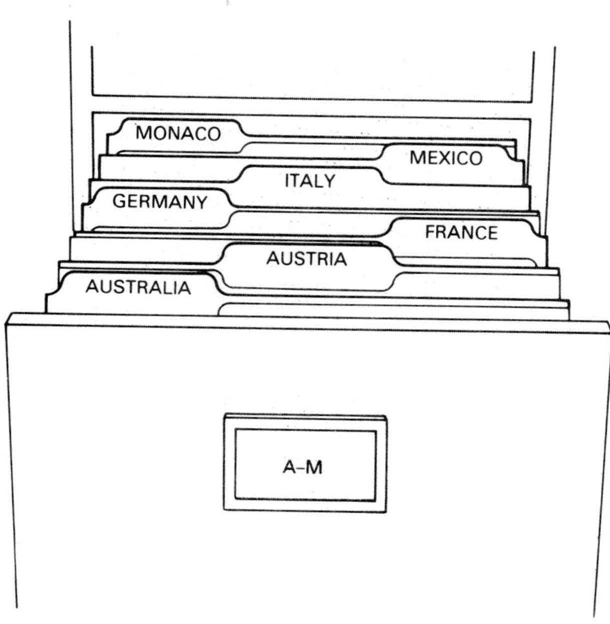

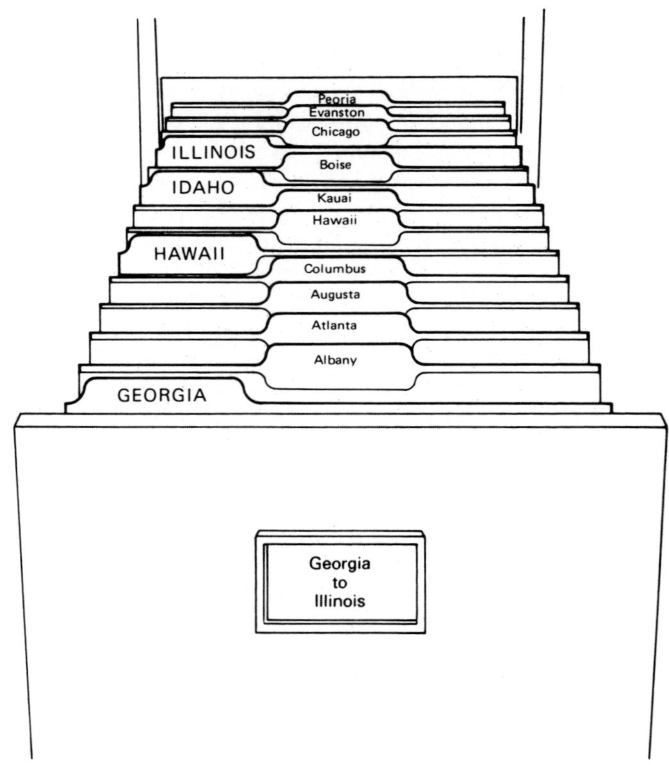

FIGURE 7-39 Enclopedia arrangement for geographic files.

A business or organization that operates throughout the United States may divide its records first by state, then by county, then by cities or towns, and then by the names of businesses, organizations, or individuals. A single-city business may require a geographic system that is divided by districts within the city and then by street names. A multinational business might use names of countries for the major geographic divisions, followed by the names of states, then by cities or towns, and then by the names of businesses or individuals. Figure 7-40 shows geographic files organized by country and then by state and city.

FIGURE 7-40
Arrangement of files in geographic system by states and cities (*top*) and by countries and cities (*bottom*).

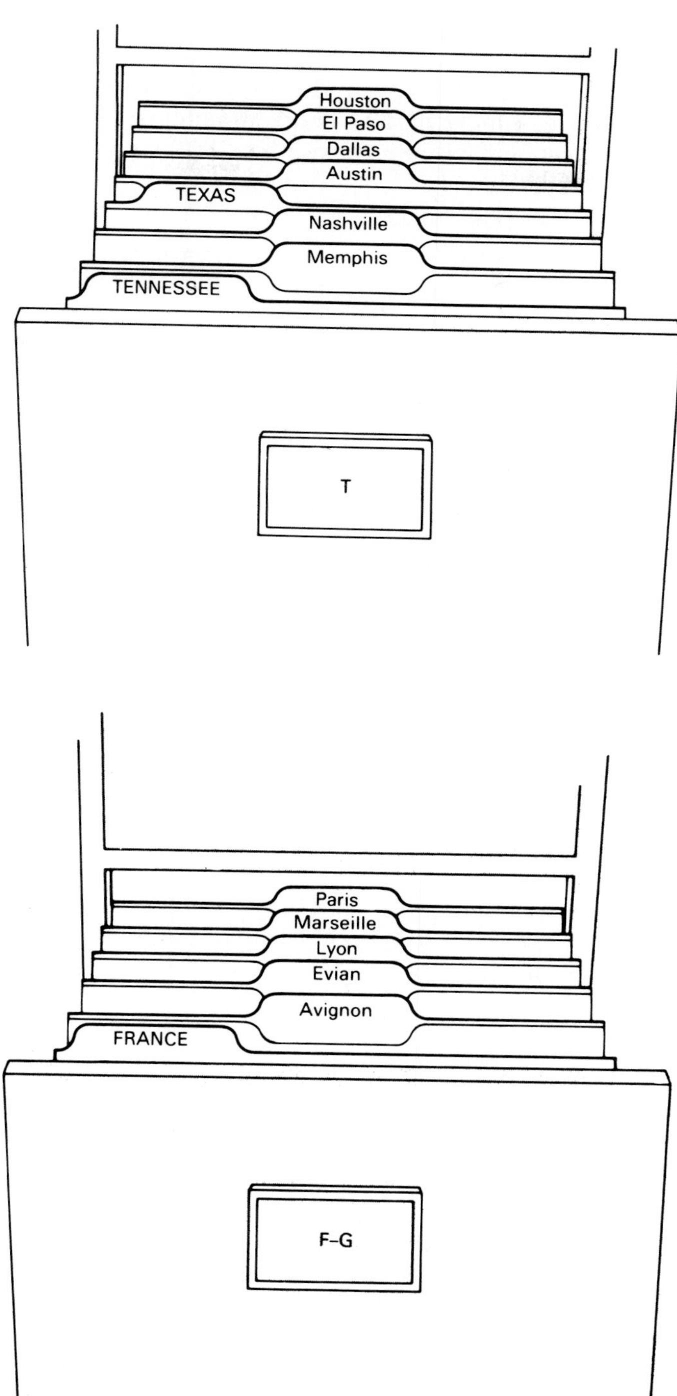

Within each geographic file, records are arranged alphabetically by correspondents' names. Multiple records for the same correspondent are arranged in **chronological sequence,** with the most recent record on top (see Figure 7-41). When five or more pieces of correspondence for the same correspondent have been accumulated in a geographic file, a separate file is created for that correspondent, as shown in Figure 7-42.

FIGURE 7-41
Alphabetic and chronological arrangement of records in geographic files. Records are arranged alphabetically by correspondents' names.

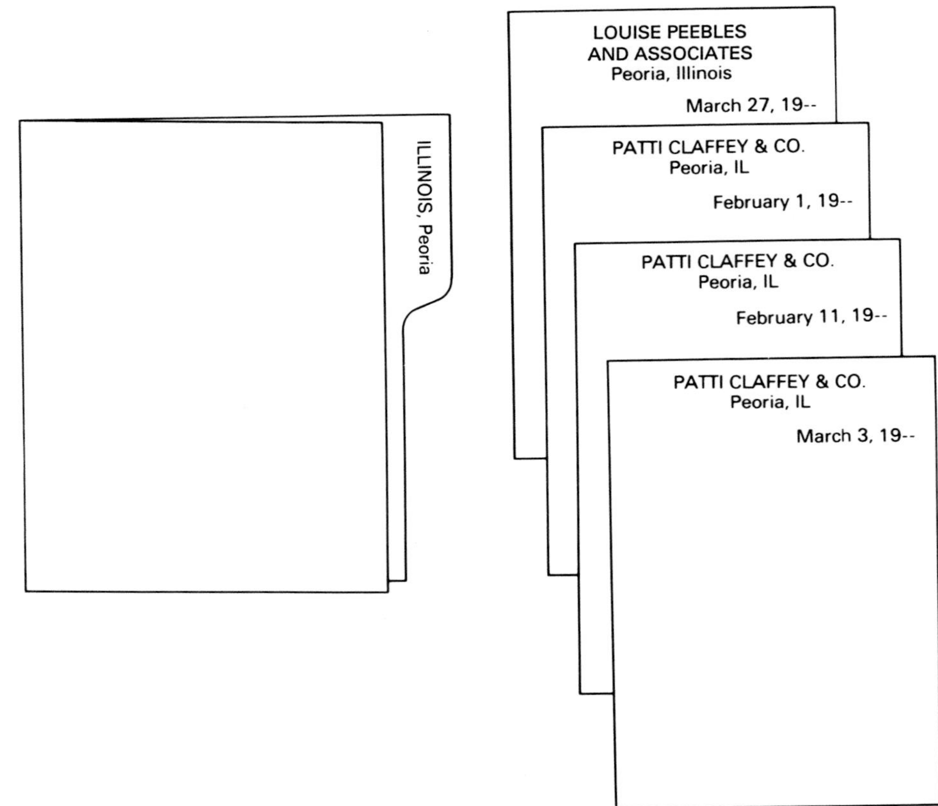

FIGURE 7-42
A separate file has been created for a correspondent for whom five or more pieces of correspondence have been accumulated.

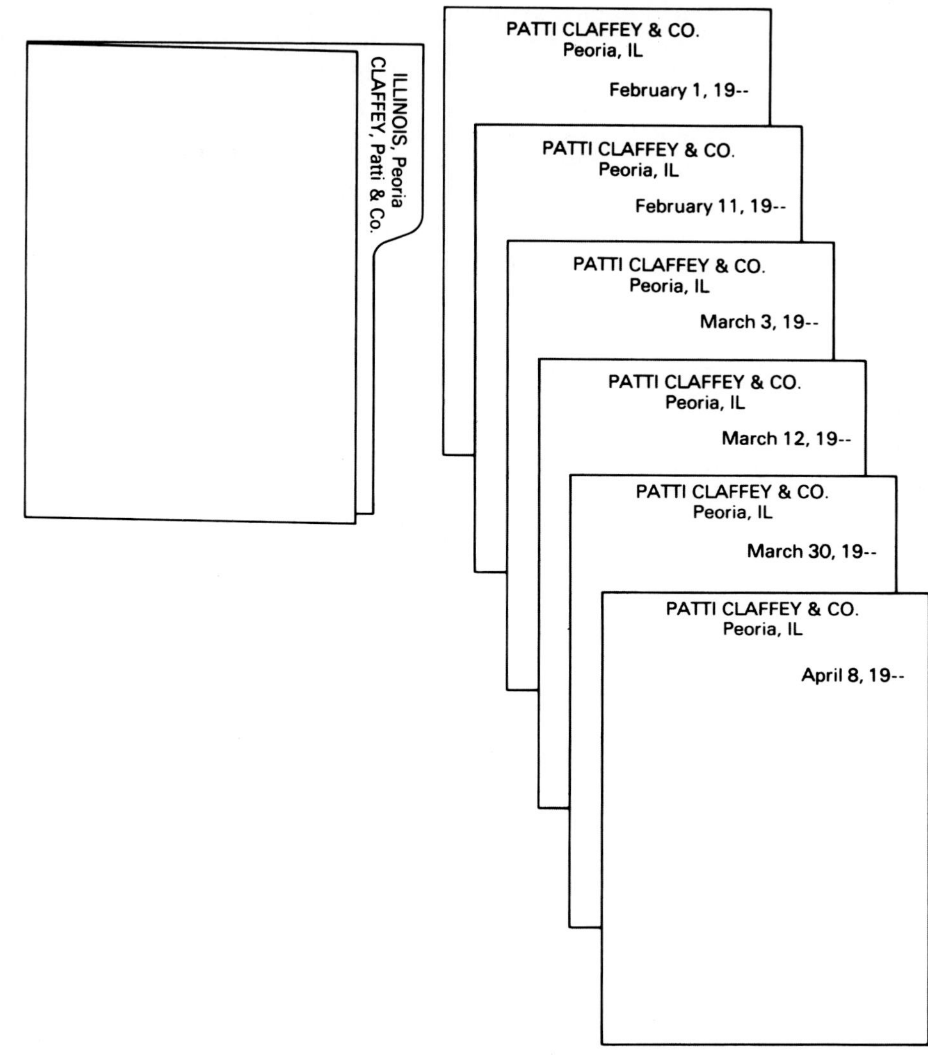

Indexing and Coding The primary geographic name is the basis for storing records in alphabetic sequence. Each word in the name is considered an indexing unit. The state or country name is the first indexing unit, followed by each geographic subdivision, as shown in Figure 7-43. When the geographic names and correspondents' names are identical in all indexing units, the street addresses are used as identifying elements to determine the filing sequence (see Figure 7-44).

FIGURE 7-43

Names as Written	*Sequence for Indexing*
Hayes & Hayes Law Corporation 3340 Yexir Road Boston, Massachusetts	Massachusetts, Boston Hayes & Hayes Law Corporation 3340 Yexir Road
Hayes & Hayes Law Corporation 11440 York Boulevard Boston, Massachusetts	Massachusetts, Boston Hayes & Hayes Law Corporation 11440 York Boulevard
Boston IronWorks Co. Chicopee, Massachusetts	Massachusetts, Chicopee Boston Iron Works Co.
LaFever Enterprises Chicopee, Massachusetts	Massachusetts, Chicopee LaFever Enterprises

NUMERIC CLASSIFICATION SYSTEMS

The **numeric classification system** is an indirect-access system that relies on the use of code numbers assigned to businesses and organizations, individuals, or subjects. The numbers used as indexing units within the numeric system may be preprinted on a set of documents (such as invoice numbers or check numbers; or assigned to documents (such as on insurance policies, drivers licenses, or medical, criminal or court case records, Social Security numbers, etc.). Using numbers as indexing units is convenient because each is unique and significant in identifying a particular correspondent, customer, or subject.

Records can also be filed by assigning numbers consecutively and chronologically according to a pre-arranged listing of code numbers contained in an accession book. An **accession book** or **log** is maintained to keep track of the dates on which files were created and to ensure that no more than one correspondent or subject has been assigned the same number. When a new file is to be created, the file worker refers to the accession book to obtain the next number in sequence (see Figure 7-44).

The numeric classification system is an indirect-access system because an index to the numbered files must be used. The index is an alphabetic card file or index, which contains the names and addresses of all correspondents or

FIGURE 7-44
Accession book numbering.

File No.	NAME OF CORRESPONDENT	DATE
99	Nadia Straghalis	2/22
100	June Barrett, CPA	2/26
101	Angelus Mfg. Co.	2/28
102	Pereppa Kirk	2/28
103		
104		
105		
106		
107		
108		
109		
110		
111		

names of subjects. Each card shows the code number assigned to that correspondent or subject, as shown in Figure 7-45.

Once the code number has been determined from the index, the file worker can file or retrieve the desired record. Any needed cross-referencing can be done within the alphabetic index without creating additional paperwork in the numeric files.

In addition to the disadvantages of indirect-access filing systems shown in Table 7-1, numeric systems have these specific disadvantages:

1. There is a greater chance of errors in both filing and refiling when numbers can easily be transposed, either in coding or when reading numbers on records. Errors are likely to occur more frequently as the sequence of numbers in the system becomes larger and the volume of files increases.

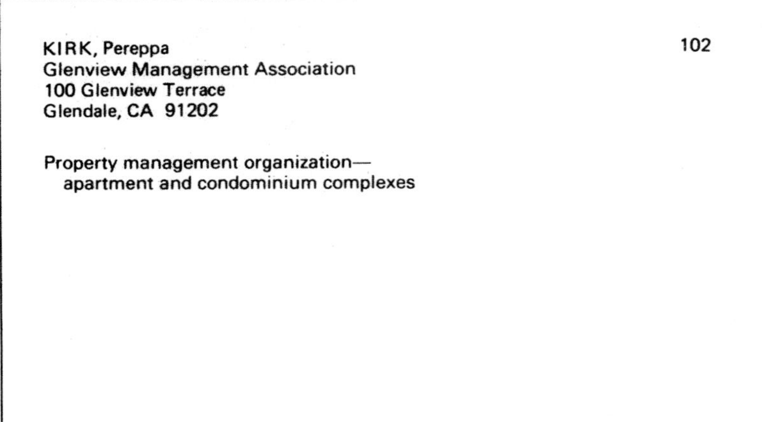

KIRK, Pereppa
Glenview Management Association
100 Glenview Terrace
Glendale, CA 91202

102

Property management organization—
apartment and condominium complexes

FIGURE 7-45 Alphabetic card index for numeric filing system.

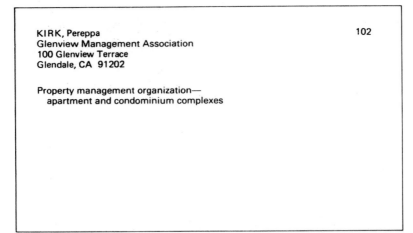

2. Two sets of files must be maintained—the main numeric files and a separate alphabetic file to hold records for miscellaneous correspondence or records.
3. Miscellaneous records for any one correspondent or subject—those that do not yet warrant separate folders—must be maintained in a separate alphabetic file until a sufficient number of records have been accumulated to create a separate file under an assigned number.

Numeric classification systems include the **straight-numeric** or **consecutive, middle-digit, terminal-digit, duplex-numeric,** and **decimal** filing systems.

Straight-Numeric (Consecutive) System

The **straight-numeric system** is a system in which files are arranged consecutively in **ascending order**—from the lowest number to the highest number. As shown in Table 7-1, an indirect-access system has many advantages. The straight-numeric system, although the most commonly used, is not without one distinctive disadvantage: Active records—those referred to often—are the ones filed toward the end of the number sequence. With active records confined to a particular section of the drawer or cabinet or to a particular records storage area, congestion may arise when several people need access to the same section of the files at the same time.

Indexing and Coding In a straight-numeric system, *each digit* in a number is an indexing unit. The primary units—the first digits—of a group of numbers are compared to determine the proper numeric sequence for filing. Only when the primary units are identical are the second or subsequent units compared to determine the sequence in which numbers should be placed.

	First Unit	Second Unit	Third Unit	Fourth Unit
File No. 1654	1	6	5	4
File No. 1658	1	6	5	8
File No. 1667	1	6	6	7
File No. 1701	1	7	0	1

Middle-Digit Numeric System

A **middle-digit system** is one in which records are first divided into three groups of two or three digits. Records are then filed according to the **middle digits**, considered the primary indexing unit; then according to the digits on the left, considered the secondary unit; and finally by the digits on the right. For example, File No. 246810 would be divided into indexing units as follows:

24	68	10
Secondary Unit	Primary Unit	Final Unit

Instead of being filed in a drawer or section labeled *24* as in the straight-numeric system, File number 24-68-20 would be filed in a drawer or section labeled *68*. The particular record would be filed as follows:

Drawer/Shelf	68
Guide	24
Folder	20

Only when the primary units—the middle digits in this system—are identical are the second or subsequent units compared to determine the sequence in which numbers should be placed.

	Primary Unit	Second Unit	Third Unit
File No. 24*68*35	68	24	35
File No. 25*68*35	68	25	35
File No. 33*68*35	68	33	35

File numbers in the accession book or log are still listed in consecutive numeric sequence, and those numbers are written on records and the file folders; but the numbers on files and records are read, filed, and retrieved according to their middle digits.

Advantages of the middle-digit numeric system are as follows:

1. Equal distribution of records throughout the records storage area
2. Assignment of one file worker responsible for one section of the files
3. Security over records stored from those individuals unfamiliar with the number coding and filing systems

The main disadvantage of the middle-digit system is that its effectiveness decreases when file numbers extend beyond six digits. For example, file number 2,614,108 would be interpreted as follows:

261	41	08
Secondary Unit	Primary Unit	Final Unit

This record would be filed as follows:

Drawer/Shelf	41
Guide	261
Folder	08

In this case, the primary unit (41) remains as two digits while the secondary unit (261) is extended to three figures. The filing process in handling large numbers would then involve an additional sorting step to accommodate the three-digit secondary units.

Indexing and Coding The primary indexing unit is the middle digit. Depending on the number of digits in the file numbers assigned—and the volume of records—the middle digit may consist of one digit (14-8-6), two digits (14-86-20), or more.

Terminal-Digit Numeric System

The most efficient numeric system is the **terminal-digit classification system.** Records are also divided into three groups of two or three digits, as in the middle-digit system. However, numbers are read from right to left, with the final digits the primary unit; the middle digits, the secondary units; and the digits on the left, the final unit. File number 24-68-10 would be divided as follows:

24	68	10
Final Unit	Secondary Unit	Primary Unit

The filing arrangement for this record would be as follows:

Drawer/Shelf	10
Guide	68
Folder	24

The terminal-digit system can accommodate large volumes of records because the numbers can be divided into groups of two, three, or four digits and still be manageable. File number 2,614,108, for example, would be read and filed as follows:

26	14	108
Final Unit	Secondary Unit	Primary Unit

Drawer/Shelf	108
Guide	14
Folder	26

The number of digits used in each group depends on the ultimate capacity of the file system developed. File numbers in the accession book are listed consecutively, but the numbers are read and records filed and retrieved according to the terminal digit (or group of digits) (see Figure 7-46).

Additional advantages of this numeric system are as follows:

1. Equal distribution of records throughout the records storage area
2. Greater efficiency and control of records
3. Assignment of records clerks to certain sections of the files
4. Security over records stored from those unfamiliar with the number coding system
5. Greater accuracy in filing and retrieving since there is less chance of transposing numbers since numbers are divided into small groups

Indexing and Coding The last digits—the terminal digits—are the primary indexing units in the terminal-digit numeric system. File numbers are written in their normal consecutive sequence as shown in the accession book; it is during the filing and retrieval processes that records are arranged, stored, and retrieved according to their terminal digits.

Decimal Classification System

The most commonly used and most widely known numeric classification system is the **decimal classification system.** Developed primarily for library use in

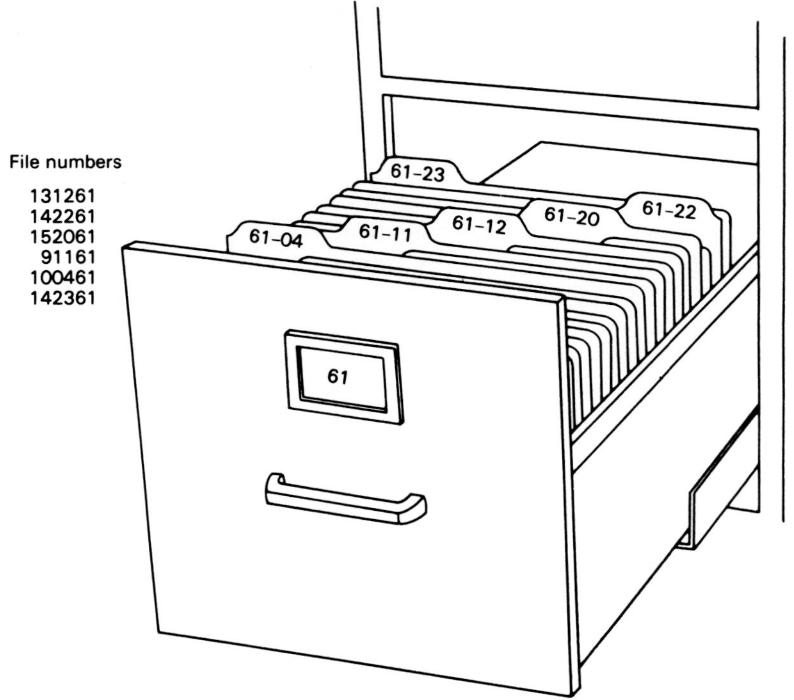

FIGURE 7-46
Terminal-digit numeric arrangement.

1873, the decimal system is based on ten general categories of subjects, as follows:

000 General Works
100 Philosophy
200 Religion
300 Social Science
400 Philology
500 Pure science
600 Applied Science or Useful Arts
700 Arts Recreation
800 Literature
900 History

Each of the major numeric groupings is divided into ten parts, which are then further divided into ten subdivisions, as illustrated below:

500 Pure Science
- 510 Mathematics
- 520 Astronomy
- 530 Physics
- 540 Chemistry
  - 540.1 Philosophy and Theory
  - 540.11 Ancient and Medieval Theory
  - 540.112 Alchemy

The advantages of the decimal classification system are as follows:

It allows unlimited expansion of files because of the fine divisions within each of the major three-digit codes for each general category.

Records can be retrieved more quickly because of the simplicity of the decimal system as opposed to the use of names or even other numeric systems.

All related records are grouped together, making referencing and retrieval convenient and easy.

The decimal filing system is ideal for when records must be classified by subject or by geographic location and when large numbers of records, subdivided into smaller groupings, need to be stored. With a decimal system, files can be divided into nine general or main categories of subjects or geographic locations; then subjects or locations can be arranged from general to specific divisions. Each division in turn is divided into nine or fewer subdivisions.

The major disadvantage of the decimal system is that only 10 major categories of subjects or geographic locations and only 9 divisions within each major category can be used.

Indexing and Coding A relative index lists the subjects or geographic locations in alphabetical sequence, followed by the major decimal number categories assigned to each subject or geographic location and then the subdivisions. The file worker refers to the index to determine the decimal numeric code to be assigned for each file for a new correspondent.

A relative index for the Chamber of Commerce illustration in Figure 7-34 would contain the following categories of topics within a decimal filing system.

500 Chamber of Commerce
- 510 Committee Assignments
  - 510.1 Membership
  - 510.2 Scholarship
- 520 Convention Sites
- 530 Finance Committee
- 540 Legislation Committee
  - 540.1 Senate Bills
  - 540.2 Assembly Bills
- 550 Taxation Committee
  - 550.1 Federal
  - 550.2 Local
  - 550.3 Multinational
  - 550.4 Foreign Tax Credits

Duplex Numeric System

In a **duplex-numeric classification system,** the records are divided according to the way numbers are written or separated by dashes, spaces, or periods. Code numbers generally have been preassigned (such as Social Security or drivers license numbers) or preprinted on records (such as invoice numbers), so records can be filed consecutively by the first set of numbers—the primary units—and then sequentially by the second set of numbers, and so forth.

The two major advantages of this system are as follows:

1. The ease in reading file numbers because of the way they are written in groups
2. The ease in filing record numbers because of the groupings of numbers and their separation by dashes, spaces, or other marks

The duplex-numeric system lends itself to the subject and geographic systems that use the encyclopedia arrangement with subdivisions of each major category of names. The subject system shown in Figure 7-35 can be converted to a duplex-numeric system as follows:

Chamber of Commerce	12
Committee Assignments	12-10
Membership	12-10-1
Scholarship	12-10-1
Convention Sites	12-11
Finance Committee	12-12
Legislation Committee	12-13
Senate Bills	12-13-1
Assembly Bills	12-13-2

Taxation Committee	12-14
Federal	12-14-1
Local	12-14-2

Indexing and Coding A relative index must first be developed for the duplex-numeric system. The major categories of information—subject listings or geographic locations and subdivisions for each—must be determined and primary numbers assigned to the various categories and subdivisions.

Alphanumeric Classification Systems

An **alphanumeric classification system** may use a combination of personal or business names and numbers or, most commonly, subject names and numbers.

Once the alphabetic divisions or topic headings have been determined, together with their appropriate subdivisions, number categories can be assigned in groups of 10s or 100s as follows, depending on the size of the files:

10	A	100	A
20	B	200	B
30	C	300	C
40	D	400	D

The previous illustration of indexing and coding a file for the Chamber of Commerce can be used to develop an alphanumeric system as follows:

300 Chamber of Commerce
- 310 Committee Assignments
  - 310.1 Membership
  - 310.2 Scholarship
- 311 Convention Sites
- 312 Finance Committee
- 313 Legislation Committee
  - 313.1 Senate Bills
  - 313.2 Assembly Bills
- 314 Taxation Committee
  - 314.1 Federal
  - 314.2 Local

If larger quantities of records are to be stored within the system, smaller divisions within each letter of the alphabetic can be used, as shown by the following 30-division arrangement:

A	1	H	11	P-Q	21
B	2	Ho	12	R	22
Bl	3	I-J	13	S	23
Br	4	K	14	Si	24
C	5	L	15	St	25
Co	6	M	16	T	26
D	7	Me	17	U-V	27
E	8	Mo	18	W	28
F	9	N	19	Wi	29
G	10	O	20	XYZ	30

Indexing and Coding A relative index lists the number codes assigned to each letter of the alphabet or to its divisions. The file worker refers to the index to determine the primary classification digit to be assigned to a file for a new correspondent.

CHAPTER HIGHLIGHTS

- The selection of a filing classification system is based on the size of the company, the nature and volume of records, how and by whom records are used, and how readily records need to be retrieved.
- The basic filing classification systems are alphabetic (by personal name, business name, subject, or geographic location); numeric (straight, duplex, terminal-digit, middle-digit, and decimal); and alphanumeric.
- The straight alphabetic and the geographic filing classification systems are direct-access systems because an individual can go directly to the files to locate a particular record by name or geographic location.
- The subject filing classification system and all numeric classification systems are indirect-access systems because an index must first be consulted to determine the code number assigned a particular record or correspondent.
- Indexing and coding refer to the process of determining the name, subject, geographic location, or number of the filing caption under which a record will be filed.
- Personal names are generally indexed and coded with the surname (last name) of the individual as the first indexing unit.
- Business names are generally indexed and coded as the names are written, with each important word considered a separate indexing unit.
- Government agency names are generally indexed and coded by the distinctive name of the governmental unit, followed by such identifying elements as city, state, street name, and/or building number.

- Departments and agencies of the federal government are indexed with the words *United States Government* as the first three indexing units.
- Names of elementary and secondary schools and of colleges and universities are indexed and coded by their distinctive names and then by their cities and states.
- Names of religious institutions, financial institutions, and hospitals are generally indexed and coded as written, followed by the city and state names.
- Records filed in subject and geographic alphabetic systems may be arranged in either a dictionary arrangement or an encyclopedia arrangement. Records are arranged in the folder alphabetically by topic or correspondent name and then chronologically, with the most recent item on top.
- Of the various numeric filing classification systems, the terminal-digit system is the most efficient. Because records can be distributed equally throughout the records storage area, file workers can be assigned to certain sections, security of records is provided, and the system can be expanded easily.
- The most commonly used numeric filing classification system is decimal filing, used primarily in libraries to categorize records in major numeric groupings according to ten major divisions and ten subdivisions.
- Alphabetic filing systems are best suited for small volumes of records and where records are filed by subject; numeric systems, particularly terminal-digit and decimal-numeric systems, are ideal for storing large volumes of records and for providing unlimited expansion capabilities.

QUESTIONS FOR REVIEW

1. What factors should be considered in selecting an appropriate filing classification system?
2. What are the advantages and disadvantages of direct-access and indirect-access filing systems?
3. What are the two methods of organizing subject and geographic files? What are the advantages and disadvantages of each method?
4. What are the characteristics of each of the numeric filing classification systems?
5. What would be the feasibility of deciding which filing classification system(s) to use at the time a company is establishing a records management program?
6. What would be the feasibility of deciding which filing classification system(s) to use at the time a company is planning the organization and staffing of the records management system?

7. In what sequence would the following names be listed in a straight alphabetic filing system? Prepare a complete alphabetical listing of the names.

1 2

Eugene Pinchuk (Pinchuk, Eugene)
Mrs. Byron Peebles (Theresa Louise)
R. L. Gibb
Hoa Tran
Donald Paxton
Dr. E. Pinchuk
R. L. Gibbs
Lupe Trillo
Phuong Ha
Captain R. Gibbson
Raymond L. Gibbs
Phuong Truong
Captain Gibbs
Amanda Trujillo
Khanh N. Tran
Capra Gibbson, Jr.
Chau L. Tsui
Prof. Louise Peebles

8. In what sequence would the following business names be listed in a straight alphabetic filing system? Prepare a complete alphabetical listing of the names.

1 2 3

RCM Office Supplies (RCM Office Supplies)
1500 Avery Building
Armours' 280 Diner
ABC Nursery School
Riverton Memorial High School, Springfield, Mo.
Brian J. Lee Enterprises, Inc.
Armours Delicatessen
Riverside Cleaners
Riverton Animal Hospital
Armours' 250 Club
Alfred Riverton
Armours' Dental Clinic

Riverton-Angus, Inc.
ABC Nurseries
B. J. Lee Engineering Corp.
R. & C Maintenance Co.
2600 Auto Sales
Ling-Tsang Gardens
Riverton Memorial High School, Springfield, Ill.
Lington Trust Co., Southgate, Miss.
Lington Trust Co., South Gate, Calif.

9. The following are names of four federal government departments and commissions.

Housing and Urban Development
Federal Aviation Administration
Federal Trade Commission
Federal Communications Commission

The following names are those of agencies belonging to the departments and commissions listed above. Categorize the agencies in alphabetic sequence under the appropriate departments or commissions.

Historic Preservation
Airspace and Air Traffic Management
Research and Development
Community Development Training Programs
Truth in Lending
Radio Operators
Urban Design
Common Carrier Communications
Civil Aviation Abroad
Cable Television
Model Cities
Textile and Fur Labeling
Air Navigation Facilities
Urban Studies Fellowship Program
Safety Regulations
Broadcast
Compliance Activities

Airport Planning and Development Programs
Fair Credit Reporting Act
Aviation Board

10. Which of the four filing classification systems would be most appropriate to meet each of the 12 requirements listed below? Place an *x* in the appropriate column(s).

	Straight Alphabetic	Subject	Geographic	Numeric
1. Records related to one company or individual must be grouped together.				
2. Records will be referenced by topics or categories of information.				
3. There is a need to classify records by city, state, county, or other region.				
4. Security is essential in maintaining records.				
5. The classification system must be easy to use.				
6. An index or cross-reference is necessary or desirable.				
7. Several people will be referring to or maintaining stored records.				
8. Maintenance and labor costs are important considerations.				
9. There must be provision for expansion of files within the system.				
10. Records must be stored in certain ways or in certain areas to be compatible with the work flow, space limitations, or personnel needs.				
11. There are various sizes or shapes of records to be stored.				
12. There is currently a large volume of records.				

THE DECISION MAKER

Case Studies

1. Your company, the Ambassador Employment Agency in Washington, D.C., maintains an extensive card file of full-time, part-time, and temporary positions for various types of clerical workers. The government offices in both Washington, D.C., and Baltimore, Maryland, use your company's services frequently; your office also fills business positions in the greater Baltimore area.

   At present, your job records are filed in a straight alphabetic sequence by job titles, such as accounting clerk, data entry clerk, data processing operator, and steno-clerk. Your manager has suggested that a different filing classification system be developed to eliminate the following problems:

   1. Jobs in both Washington, D.C., and Baltimore, Maryland, are mixed together.
   2. Similar types of jobs are scattered throughout the files.
   3. Full-time, part-time, and temporary positions are also mixed together in the files.
   4. Employees are not always familiar with the exact job titles used to classify various positions.

   Explain to your manager the probable causes for each of the four problems listed.

2. Based on the information given in Case Study 1 and any reasonable assumptions you wish to make, prepare a proposal for developing a new filing classification system to store the approximately 1000 cards for the Ambassador Employment Agency.

Records Maintenance and Control

OBJECTIVES

Upon completion of this chapter, the student should be able to:

1. Distinguish the various ways in which records are categorized within a records maintenance program.
2. Apply the procedures for gathering, preparing, sorting, and storing records.
3. Explain the rationale and the procedures for charging out and following up records.
4. List the sequence of steps to follow in locating records missing from the files.
5. Identify possible solutions to common files maintenance problems.
6. Compare the differences between active and inactive records storage systems and their objectives.
7. Identify the four steps to consider when implementing a records storage program for electronic records.

Records maintenance and control includes categorizing records according to their nature and use; gathering, preparing, sorting, and storing records; charging out records; following up records; and locating lost or misplaced records. All these procedures are related to the collection, use, and distribution of stored information.

The procedures for maintaining and controlling records that are discussed in this chapter apply to all forms of records—paper-based, electronic-based, and microform-based. Although emphasis is placed on the maintenance and control of active records, the discussion is equally relevant to the maintenance and control of **inactive records**.

ACTIVE RECORDS MAINTENANCE

Active records were defined previously as those records that are referenced frequently in the daily operations of the business. Since these records are used to generate business or to follow up on current business transactions, every company needs to develop a systematic method of maintaining active records. If active records are maintained effectively, the company should have immediate access to stored records and immediate retrieval of information.

Regardless of the size of a company, it is essential that records flow smoothly through the records cycle—from creation or receipt of the record, to retention and use, to transfer or disposal.

Categorizing Records

Besides being classified according to their value or importance (as discussed in Chapter 5) and by type (as discussed in Chapter 6), records also need to be classified by their nature and use.

Paper-based records may be categorized as correspondence, business, forms, legal resources, graphics or technical documents, reference sources, and cards. Examples of records included in each category are as follows:

Business forms: Checks, credit memos, invoices, purchase orders, requisitions, sales slips, vouchers, computer printouts

Cards: Index cards (5 by 3, 6 by 4, 8 by 5 inches), ledger cards, punched cards

Correspondence: Letters, memorandums, reports, telegrams

Graphics or technical documents: Charts, maps, survey records, architectural renderings or drawings, blueprints, photographs, plans

Legal resources: Journals and periodicals, government publications, regulations, codes

Reference sources: Equipment or supply catalogs, operational manuals, procedures manuals, technical manuals or handbooks, sales catalogs

Microform-based records are categorized by the form of the microimage: roll film, microfiche, aperture cards, jackets, or ultrafiche. Other image-based records include negatives, prints, 35mm slides, 16mm films, filmstrips, transparencies, and X rays.

Electronic-based records are categorized by the medium on which data information is stored:

Magnetic media: Computer tapes, cartridges, or disk packs; floppy diskettes (3 1/2 and 5 1/4); cards; audiocassettes and audiotapes; videocassettes and videotapes

Optical media: Optical disks; video disks

Clearly, the various groups of records are categorized mainly by the types of records storage equipment used. The decisions to store records in one continuous, integrated file arrangement; in separate groups by nature or size of records; or in some other arrangement depends on the volume of records, their use, and the number of people who need access to the records. For example, a small volume of business forms may not warrant using separate records storage equipment; incorporating these records in a continuous correspondence file would provide a more complete file for each correspondent or customer. A large number of floppy diskettes used by a few individuals could best be stored centrally at the point of use. However, if many people needed access to the records on these diskettes, the files might be better arranged by the nature of the records and type of use.

Records are also categorized by their use or function. Such categories are based on the organizational structure of the firm. The main record functions are administrative, financial, legal, operational, personnel, and public relations. Other functions may include sales/marketing, manufacturing, and research and development, depending on the nature of the business.

Filing Procedures

Routine activities performed by file clerks, secretaries, and other office personnel consist of gathering all records to be filed, preparing the records for filing, and actually storing the records. Figure 8-1 illustrates the path of records from the time they are created until they are finally stored in their appropriate places.

Gathering the Records Each section within a department will generally accumulate records of various kinds during its daily operations. Crucial to the maintenance program is the gathering of all documents that are ready to be filed. The records clerk should establish a system, which includes a timetable, whereby records ready to be filed can be collected from each section regularly each day. The amount of paperwork generated by each section or department will determine the number of collections made each day.

FIGURE 8-1
Path of a record from creation or origination to final storage.

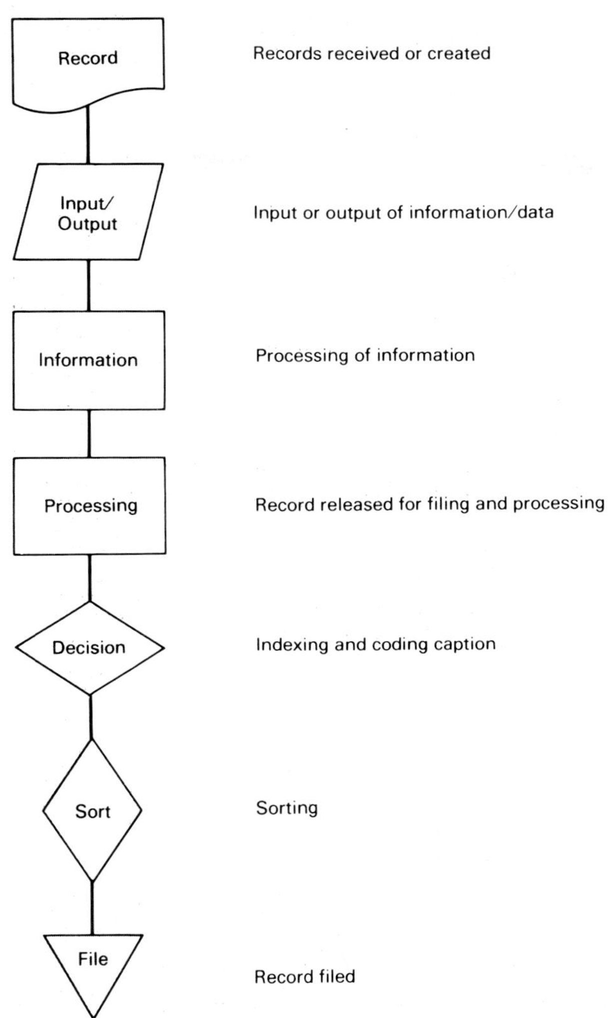

The orderly collection of records and the placing of these records in an established **holding file** are important for both the security of the records and the accessibility for use during the interim. It is at this point in the processing of records that they may become misplaced or lost. Misplaced or lost documents can mean not only inconvenience and wasted time spent looking for them, but also the possibility of lost business transactions.

A separate holding file should be used to store each type of record that is to be filed. For example, a file box or tray or a specially marked folder may be used to gather correspondence, reports, business forms, and similar types of paper-based records; a card file box or tray should be used to gather index cards; a media storage box or tray should be used to gather magnetic cards and disks. Separate holding files keep similar types of records together until they can be filed; they also ensure that records can be easily located and retrieved by individuals who need to refer to them. The type of equipment used to house records temporarily depends on the volume of records gathered and the frequency with which the records are processed and filed.

Preparing the Records Preparing the records for filing consists of inspecting, indexing, coding, and sorting. Regardless of the form or type of record to be stored, each step of the filing process is important in maintaining a standardized routine.

The **inspection task** involves checking each item of correspondence, report, business form, or other such record to be sure it has been released for filing. The release, noted by the person who last handled the document, may take the form of a check mark, an initial, or a stamp (see Figure 8-2). During the inspection process, the records clerk also checks to see that any papers attached by paper clips, clamps, or pins actually belong in the same file. Any clips, clamps, or pins should be removed and all related documents stapled together to prevent other papers from accidentally becoming attached.

As the records clerk inspects each record, he or she should also note how each is to be **indexed** and **coded.** These tasks refer to determining the name or number under which a record should be filed (indexing) and actually writing or otherwise marking that name or number on the record (coding). In an alphabetic filing system, for example, records may be indexed by the name of the person or company that originated the correspondence, the topic about which the document is written, or the city or state of the originating document. Coding can be done by circling or underlining the caption or by writing the caption name or number on the record.

If there is a possibility that a record might be referred to by another name, the record should be cross-referenced. **Cross-referencing** means coding a record with a second filing caption and creating a special cross-reference sheet under the second caption. In this way, both filing captions appear in the files; a person who looks for a record under a name other than the main file caption will locate the cross-reference sheet, which will refer him or her to the appropriate file. Figure 8-3 illustrates a letter that is being cross-referenced and a typical cross-reference sheet.

Some companies, instead of using a cross-reference system, photocopy records and place the photocopies in the file under their own captions. This practice, however, should be discouraged because it creates additional paper and additional work in both filing and maintaining the duplicate records.

Coding each record is important not only when a new file is created for a new correspondent or customer but also saves time and reduces errors later when records are refiled after they have been temporarily removed from the files.

The task that expedites the actual filing of records is sorting. **Sorting** is the process of arranging documents into some sequence before filing them. In an

FIGURE 8-2
Circled filing caption; release mark on correspondence ready for filing.

October 3, 19--

O.K.
aj
10-6

Jennings Co.
23 Sierra Madre Boulevard
Mission Viejo, CA 92726

Ladies and Gentlemen:

Thank you for your recent order of 10 dozen women's sweaters, Stock No. 7345. Your order is being shipped by United Parcel Express and should reach you within a week.

Your selection of these sweaters is an excellent choice. Other retailers in your city have remarked on the fine quality of these sweaters, the attractive choice of colors available, the washability of these goods, and the reasonable selling price. We know you will soon be reordering this item because this line of sweaters has sold exceptionally well this season.

A letter is being sent to Ms. Jaime Lee today to thank her for referring your company to us. Her Fashion Fields Shop has done very well over the years with a variety of specialty items for women.

Best wishes to you for continued success in your new business venture.

Sincerely,

FELICITAS SPORTSWEAR

Maxine K. Wilson

Maxine K. Wilson

iti

alphabetic filing system, for example, records may be sorted into predetermined alphabetic groups, as follows:

A–F	6 divisions
G–L	6 divisions
M–S	7 divisions
T–Z	7 divisions

FIGURE 8-3
Cross-referencing correspondence for the files (*right*). Cross-reference sheet (*below*).

Felicitas
SPORTSWEAR

October 3, 19--

O.K.
aj
10-6

Jennings Co.
23 Sierra Madre Boulevard
Mission Viejo, CA 92726

Ladies and Gentlemen:

Thank you for your recent order of 10 dozen women's sweaters, Stock No. 7345. Your order is being shipped by United Parcel Express and should reach you within a week.

Your selection of these sweaters is an excellent choice. Other retailers in your city have remarked on the fine quality of these sweaters, the attractive choice of colors available, the washability of these goods, and the reasonable selling price. We know you will soon be reordering this item because this line of sweaters has sold exceptionally well this season.

A letter is being sent to Ms. Jaime Lee today to thank her for referring your company to us. Her Fashion Fields Shop has done very well over the years with a variety of specialty items for women. X-ref.

Best wishes to you for continued success in your new business venture.

Sincerely,

FELICITAS SPORTSWEAR

Maxine K. Wilson

CROSS-REFERENCE SHEET

Jaime Lee
Name of Subject

October 3, 19–
Date of Record

Regarding:
New customer referral

REFER TO: Jennings Co.

Date: October 3, 19–

These groupings are only suggested ones that might be used; the actual divisions of the alphabet would depend on the volume of records that need to be sorted at any one time.

In a numeric filing system, records may be sorted into several numeric groups, as follows:

10, 20, 30, 40, 50, and so on
100, 200, 300, 400, 500, and so on

Again, the number of groupings would depend on the volume of records as well as the number sequence used within the system.

The first sorting task performed is called **rough sorting** because records are sorted only into large categories of alphabetic or numeric groups. Two or more additional sorting steps must be completed in order to place all records into proper sequential alphabetic or numeric order prior to filing. When records are further sorted from the large categories of alphabetic or numeric groups into smaller groups, the task is known as **fine sorting.** Although these various sorting steps may seem an extra effort and time-consuming, sorting is considered the key to the quick and easy filing of records.

Various commercial sorting devices are available to increase speed in sorting. Sorters are available with various divisions, such as 26 alphabetic groupings, various numeric groupings, 7 groupings for days of the week, or 31 groupings for the days of the month. Thus sorters can be selected to conform to the filing system(s) used.

The sorting task can be performed periodically during the day even if the records clerk is not able to file the records immediately. If a secretary, for example, is responsible for filing records for a particular section or department, he or she can sort the preindexed, precoded records as soon as the documents are released for filing.

Storing the Records Placing records in their appropriate file drawers or cabinets is called **filing;** the term **records storage** may also be used. Once records have been properly coded and sorted, they can be filed quickly. Having presorted the records, the file clerk can file documents in sequence in one drawer, cabinet, or shelf at a time. The clerk can proceed from front to back of one drawer, proceed to the next drawer, and so on, to accomplish the filing task in an efficient manner. Without presorting, the clerk would be opening and closing several drawers or cabinets; moving back and forth, up and down to store records; and wasting time, motion, and energy. With presorted records, the filing task can be distributed among several file clerks, each assigned to a different section of the records storage area(s).

Besides filing recently received or generated records into their respective files, filing also involves **refiling**—or returning—records that have been temporarily removed from the files.

The captions on the primary guides in the file drawer or cabinet are used to help the clerk find the location of the desired folder. Records are filed within their folders with the heading to the left. In most filing classification systems, records are filed in **chronological sequence** in the folder, with the most recently dated item in front. File folders for individual correspondents are generally created only when five or more pieces of correspondence have been accumulated. Until this time, correspondence is stored in a miscellaneous file, arranged in alphabetic sequence by correspondents' names. The chronological sequence of filing is maintained for each correspondent.

Accessing Records The efficiency of any records storage system is determined by how quickly and easily a record can be located and retrieved from the files. A records storage and retrieval system, as previously mentioned, includes the personnel, the equipment and supplies, and the step-by-step tasks and procedures used to maintain and control the records. Personnel who work with the files must know the operation of the system and how records are categorized in order to obtain information quickly when needed.

Efficient access to records also depends on the records classification system used, as was discussed in Chapter 7. The alphabetic classification system, which includes subject and geographic methods, is a direct-access system. An individual can retrieve a record by going directly to the files and locating the record by its name, topic, or location. The numeric classification systems, however, are indirect-access methods because an individual must first refer to an alphabetic index to determine the file number assigned to a name, subject, or geographic location.

Maintenance and Care of Records

All forms of records maintained within a company should be properly maintained and handled so they can serve their useful function in the operation of the business. With the various types of records stored—paper, electronic, and microforms—greater care must be taken in not only who has access to records but also how they are maintained and used.

Charging Out Records

Since by definition active records are those referred to frequently, such records will be removed from the files often by various authorized personnel. Thus, a system must be developed for keeping track of records—or complete files—that have been temporarily removed from their places. Such a system is called a *charge-out system.*

In maintaining an effective charge-out system, the records clerk will know:

1. Who has borrowed a record or complete file
2. In which department the person is located
3. When the item was borrowed
4. The probable return date of the item

Effective charge-out procedures are important for maintaining control over all stored records; in addition, when a particular document or file is requested by someone else, the clerk will know the probable date he or she will receive it.

Charging out—or borrowing—a record generally begins by the authorized employee's completing a **charge-out request form** similar to that illustrated in Figure 8-4. Such a request form is usually prepared in duplicate. The original is substituted for the borrowed record, and the copy is retained by the file clerk for follow-up purposes.

Although some companies prefer to make photocopies of requested documents rather than remove the actual document from the files, this practice should be controlled carefully. In addition to generating more paper, confusion can be created later as to whether the copy should be filed or destroyed. Perhaps the borrower's purpose for requesting the record should be determined—whether it will be used for informational purposes (in which case the actual document should be charged out) or whether it will be used as a working copy (in which case a photocopy should be made).

Figure 8-5 shows **out guides** that are used to replace individual records that have been removed from a file folder. When an entire file is removed, an **out folder,** also shown in Figure 8-5, is substituted for the borrowed file and is used to house any incoming records that subsequently need to be placed in the file. The original charge-out request form is placed in the transparent pocket on the outside of the out folder.

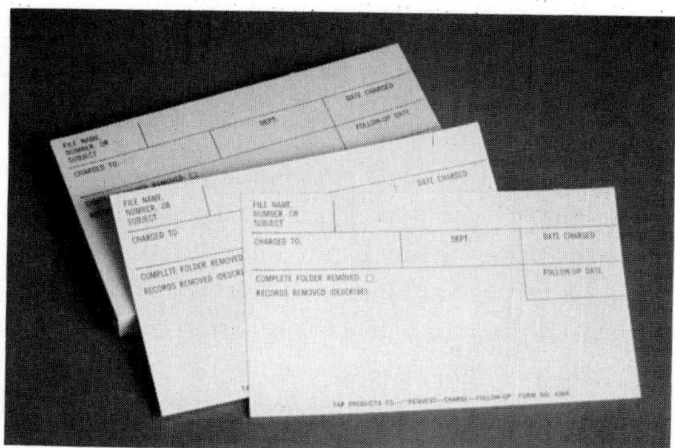

FIGURE 8-4
Charge-out request form.

FIGURE 8-5 Out guide and out folder. (Courtesy of Tabbies, Division of Xertrex International, Inc.)

When a borrowed record is returned to the folder, the out guide is removed from the folder and the borrower's name is removed from the guide. When a file folder is returned, the out folder is removed and any papers in it are interfiled within the original file; the borrower's name is removed from the folder.

A well-organized charge-out system enables files personnel to maintain an accurate accounting of where each stored record or file is at all times.

Following Up Records

When charged-out records have not been returned to the files by the due date indicated by either the records clerk or the borrower, the records must be followed up. Each company will establish the length of time a record can be removed from the files.

Following up on charged-out records is usually done via the charge-out request form. Since the form contains the borrower's name and department and the date on which the record was charged out, follow-up is relatively easy. The records clerk must take care to follow up on all borrowed records according to their due dates.

The duplicate charge-out request forms are filed in a special card file box or drawer, or information can be taken from the forms and noted in a notebook or calendar to indicate when borrowed records are due. Such a chronological reminder system is called a **tickler file,** a file that is referred to regularly as a reminder about items that need attention on specific dates. Figures 8-6 illustrates the kind of card file box or drawer often used as a tickler file.

The card tickler file contains guides for each month. Behind the guide for the current month are individual guides for each day of the month. The fact that there is only one set of guides for the days reveals that records are charged

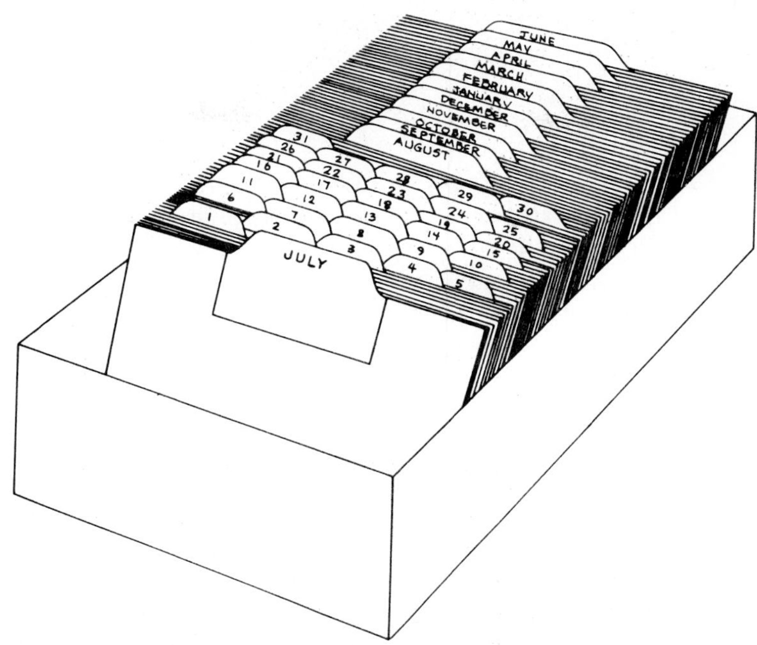

FIGURE 8-6
Card file for tickler file.

out for periods of less than one month. At the end of the current month, the guide for the next month is moved to the front. Each day the records clerk checks behind the guide for that day for any items that need follow-up.

The follow-up is usually done by telephone to determine if the borrower has finished with the borrowed record or if he or she will need the record longer. Generally speaking, the longer a record or a file folder is out of the files, the greater the chance of its being misplaced or lost. There is also potential for damage to magnetic media or microforms if these records are not used or maintained properly while out of their storage places. During the follow-up, should it be determined that the borrower no longer has the charged-out records and does not know their location, a search can be started immediately. The longer the wait to begin the search, the longer it will take to locate lost or misplaced records.

If a record or file should be needed beyond the due date, the borrower should charge the records out again. All authorized personnel should be requested to return charged-out records to the files as soon as the records have served their purpose. Therefore, the follow-up process is the control part of the records maintenance and use program.

Locating Missing Files

Even with a well-controlled and systematic records maintenance program, records can be misplaced or lost. Therefore, a systematic process for searching for lost records must also be developed and followed.

If it is known who handled the record most recently before its loss was noticed, the person conducting the search should:

1. Look on the desk tops and the desk trays of those who last handled the record.
2. Search the file clerk's (or secretary's) desk top or desk tray.
3. Look in the records clerk's (or secretary's) holding file of records to be filed or refiled.
4. If more than one roll of microfilm was referenced at the same time, check that each was returned to its proper box.
5. If a floppy diskette, aperture card, fiche, jacket, or optical disc is missing, look through the stacks of papers and books on desk tops, in drawers, and on shelves.
6. Look in the disk drives of word processors, computers, and computer-assisted retrieval equipment for missing diskettes.
7. Look in micrographics readers and printers for missing microforms.
8. Look in audiovisual equipment (projectors, film canisters, tape players, and so on) for missing items.

If no one recalls the particular record, reference to the file drawer, cabinet, or shelf should be made and these steps followed:

1. Look through the files to see if the record has been filed out of sequence.
2. Look through the folders, jackets, or other containers in front of and behind the one for the missing record.
3. Look in the spaces in front of and behind the folder as well as underneath the folders.
4. Look through files bearing similar names or numbers (such as *Hawkins* for *Hawkin;* 167111 for 176111).
5. Look in the miscellaneous files to see if the record has been inadvertently misfiled.
6. Look under other possible filing captions, such as cross-references, other topics or geographic locations, and so on.

If after these systematic searches the record is not found, the likelihood is that it has become attached to other records; it may have been filed with other records; or it may have been disposed of accidentally. In such cases, the record can be considered lost and further efforts to locate it will probably be a waste of time. Only by chance it might reappear later when other records are processed in the normal operations of the company.

It should be evident that the time spent following the established procedures for charging out and following up records is less than the time required to locate a missing record. Table 8-1 details some common file maintenance problems and several possible solutions for them.

INACTIVE RECORDS MAINTENANCE

When stored records are no longer referred to on a regular basis as part of the business's daily operations, they become *inactive.* It is often difficult to determine exactly when an active record becomes inactive. While some records are semiactive (referred to occasionally) for a short time and then become inactive, other records may remain semiactive for a longer period. Attempting to identify inactive records is difficult because of the frequently overlapping use of certain records by various departments and also because of a lack of definite guidelines for the retention and use of records.

TABLE 8-1 COMMON FILE MAINTENANCE PROBLEMS

Problem	*Possible Solutions*
Too many people doing the filing	Assign responsibility or authority to one individual; limit access to certain personnel
Duplication of records; too many filing places for similar records	Centralize records maintenance; maintain specialized records at points of origin or frequent use
Records difficult to locate	Determine proper nature or use of records; redesign filing classification system used; eliminate some cross-referencing; change indexing or coding of captions on records
Related records filed in separate places	Provide for continuous filing of all related records; use the cross-referencing system
File folders or card files difficult to locate within drawer or cabinet	Use more file drawer guides—provide one guide for every 8–10 folders or every 20–30 cards
Captions and file folder tabs hidden	Break a score on the file folder for every 25 sheets in the folder
File folders buckle in the drawer	Tighten the compressor or follower block in the drawer or cabinet; do not break scores on folders too soon; investigate use of the suspension filing system
Frequently misplaced or lost records	Provide centralized collection of records to be filed; file more often; use out guides and out folders for charged-out records; increase controls in charging out records by limiting persons authorized to charge out records; provide earlier follow-up of charged-out records; train personnel in using filing classification system(s) and filing procedures

TABLE 8-1 *(continued)*

Problem	*Possible Solutions*
Costs for files personnel and records maintenance increasing	Retrain personnel in efficient filing and records maintenance procedures; reclassify records according to their nature and use; rearrange records storage equipment; inventory active and inactive records; cut down on correspondence and reports generation
Records and files not available when needed	File more often; increase controls in charging out records; provide earlier follow-up of charged-out records
Slow access to, and retrieval of, stored records	Retrain personnel in records maintenance and filing procedures; determine proper nature of use of records; change configuration of records storage and retrieval system or equipment; evaluate records staff workload; centralize records storage and retrieval function or staff
Miscellaneous folders filed with too many papers	Create separate files whenever five or more items have accumulated for a correspondent; use smaller divisions for each miscellaneous folder
Inconsistency of filing, retrieving, charging-out, or following-up records	Train or retrain personnel in proper procedures to be followed; adhere to records management manual

Of the ten problem areas of office operations cited by James C. Bennett, four areas are related to records maintenance:

1. The human nature to hoard is carried over into records operations.
2. High retention costs of useless records are not understood.
3. No distinction is made between active and inactive records.
4. Records are not being used in helping to plan the future development of a company.[1]

When it cannot be easily decided whether a record is active or inactive, the tendency is to continue to retain it in the active files "in case someone needs to refer to it later." If the record is no longer referred to frequently, the company is incurring higher records maintenance costs, for the following reasons:

1. Storing questionable active or inactive records makes it difficult for files personnel to locate needed records easily and quickly among the cumbersome files.

[1]James C. Bennett, "Records Management," *The Changing Office Environment,* National Business Education Yearbook, No. 18 (Reston, VA: National Business Education Association, 1980), p. 96.

2. Maintaining too many records creates higher labor costs because of the additional time and effort required to file and retrieve records.
3. Retaining records that should be classified as inactive produces higher maintenance costs for equipment and supplies.

According to Bennett, inactive records "are not necessarily *dead records* . . ." and thus they must still be available when needed.[2] Inactive records, as well as some less frequently used active records, should be transferred from the active file drawers, cabinets, or shelves to less costly records storage facilities either within the company or at a central records center.

The periodic transfer and disposition of records helps purge the files of unused records to provide for more efficient maintenance and use of the remaining active records. Which records are to be transferred and the length of time they are to be retained before final disposition or destruction are discussed in Chapter 5.

Care must be exercised in identifying inactive records. If records are deemed inactive and are transferred out of the active records storage area(s) too soon, other problems may arise:

1. Important records will no longer be available when needed; and the records maintenance operations will no longer efficiently serve the needs of the individuals who need information upon which to base decisions.
2. Operations and personnel costs will be high because of the time and effort spent in attempting to locate needed records.

One criterion, then, for deciding whether a record should be active or inactive is its retrieval time from the inactive records storage facility. If a central records storage facility, whether in-house or outside the company, is used for all inactive records storage, access time for a record ranges from 4 to 24 hours.[3]

To cut down on the retrieval time, companies will often designate part of their active records storage areas to house some of the recently dated inactive records. For example, the bottom one or two drawers of several active records storage cabinets can be used for inactive records. In this way, all inactive records for a recent period can be within easy reach when needed; the remainder of the inactive records can be transferred elsewhere without hindering the smooth operation of normal business activities.

[2]Ibid., p. 99.

[3]Ibid.

Records Retention Schedule

The procedures for handling active and inactive records will vary among companies. Varying procedures highlight the need for developing and adhering to a **records retention schedule.** This schedule outlines specific periods set by government regulations and company policies as to how long records should be retained and when certain records can be disposed of.

The establishment of a records retention schedule is discussed in Chapter 5.

CHAPTER HIGHLIGHTS

- All forms of records—paper-based, electronic-based, and microform-based—must be properly maintained and controlled.
- The effective maintenance and control of active records—those referred to frequently in daily operations—provides for immediate access to and retrieval of stored records.
- Paper-based records may be categorized as cards, correspondence, business forms, graphics or technical documents, legal resources, and reference sources.
- Image-based records may be categorized by the forms of microimages: roll film, microfiche, aperture cards, jackets, or ultrafiche. Other image-based records include negatives, prints, slides, films, and filmstrips; X rays; and transparencies.
- Digital-based records may be categorized by types of magnetic media (computer tape, cartridge, disk pack; floppy diskette; card; audiocassettes and audiotapes, videocassettes and videotapes); and optical media (optical disc and video disc).
- The filing procedures consist of gathering in one place all records that are to be stored; inspecting for an appropriate release mark; indexing and coding of a file caption; sorting into groups; and storing.
- Indexing a record is the mental process of determining the filing caption under which a record will be filed; coding is the process of writing, circling, or underlining the file caption on the record.
- Cross-referencing refers to coding a record with a second filing caption under which the record could be referenced.
- Rough sorting of records is done by sorting a group of records into large alphabetic or numeric groupings. Fine sorting is done by sorting each large group of records into smaller groups.
- Filing refers to placing recently received or generated records into their respective files; refiling refers to returning to the files those records that have been temporarily removed.

- A charge-out system is one that keeps track of records or complete files that have been temporarily removed from their storage places.
- The objective of a charge-out system is to determine who has borrowed records or files, in which department the borrower is located, when the item was borrowed, and the probable date of return. A charge-out request form serves as the basis for the charge-out and follow-up system.
- An out guide is used to replace an individual record that has been removed from a file folder; an out folder is substituted for the entire borrowed folder and is used to store any incoming records in the interim.
- A follow-up system is a reminder system used to follow up on all borrowed records according to their probable return dates.
- A tickler file is a chronological file referred to periodically as a reminder of items that need attention on specific dates.
- To locate missing files, look first on the desk(s) of the individual(s) who last handled the record. Look in areas of the cabinet, drawer, or shelf in proximity to the missing record; look in disk drives of word processors and computers, in micrographics readers and printers, and in audiovisual projection and playback equipment.
- Common files maintenance problems include the following: too many people are doing filing, individuals are not familiar with efficient filing and records maintenance procedures; records are duplicated, difficult to locate, or frequently misplaced or lost; file folders or cards are difficult to locate, file folder tabs are hidden, or folders are inadequately supported; and increased costs for personnel and records maintenance.
- The difficulty of determining when an active record becomes inactive is due to frequently overlapping use of certain records by several departments and to lack of a definite records retention process.
- Maintaining too many active records creates higher labor and maintenance costs and results in inefficient records storage and retrieval operations because of overcrowding.

QUESTIONS FOR REVIEW

1. What procedures are involved in the maintenance and control of records?
2. What is the advantage of categorizing records according to the types of records storage equipment used?
3. Describe each task in the preparation of records for filing.
4. What are the objectives of an effective records charge-out system, and what is the importance of such a system?
5. Describe the components of an effective charge-out system.
6. Outline the steps followed in attempting to locate a missing record.

7. What types of records maintenance problems can arise if either too few or too many records are stored among the active records?
8. For each group of records illustrated below, indicate how many times the records would need to be *sorted* to be placed in proper sequence for filing.

A. 106
134
218
460
253
110
227
229
281
148

B. 4321
2860
2348
4320
4006
4810
3113
4729
4323
4819

C. J. C. Feeney Corporation
United Refrigeration Corp.
R & R Electronics
Swing-Shift Music Co.
Frank's Tax Service
Shop 'n Save Home Center
Union Finance Co.
United Airway
Reliable Equipment Co.
Ray D. Franklin

D. Nancy P. Lee
Phyllis Brzozowski
Lisa Sugimoto
Joseph G. Muha
Eugene Pinchuk
Amedee LaCroix
Judy M. Meredith
Joan Pinchuk
J. G. Muha
Brian G. Wilson
Carolyn Laeser
Sherwood S. Lee
L. Norman Rittgers
Maxine K. Wilson
Glenda Baldwin

THE DECISION MAKER

Case Studies

1. A charge-out system for a centralized file maintenance program required the personnel borrowing records to complete the appropriate information on a standard charge-out request form. Files personnel were well trained in the operations of this charge-out system. Therefore, it was decided that a follow-up system was not necessary, since all employees were informed of the proper charge-out procedures. Do you agree with the elimination of the follow-up system? Why or why not?
2. The CAP Company, distributors of imported clothing and accessories, has been integrating its files of correspondence, business forms, and reports; catalogs and brochures; computer diskettes of form letters, customer billings, inventory accounting; and photographs and 35mm slides used for sales presentations. Although presently a medium-sized firm, the company expects to grow steadily over the next three to five years.

Incorporating information from the previous chapters (particularly Chapters 6 and 7), suggest appropriate records classification systems and records storage equipment for this company.

ELECTRONIC RECORDS STORAGE AND RETRIEVAL

OBJECTIVES

Upon completion of this chapter, the student should be able to:

1. Describe the characteristics of electronic records storage and retrieval systems.
2. Explain the need for a storage and retrieval system for electronic records.
3. List the four factors to consider when implementing an electronic records storage program.
4. Describe the life cycle of electronic records, comparing and contrasting each phase with other types of records.
5. Distinguish the three types of computers by their sizes and characteristics.
6. Identify records storage media and their features, advantages, and disadvantages.
7. Discuss the importance of maintaining and caring for electronic records.

Information is a valuable resource that must be accessible on demand to users in any part of the organization. Electronic records storage and retrieval systems involve the use of a computer to create, store, access or retrieve, edit or update, and delete records. Rapid storage and retrieval is the cornerstone of a computerized—or electronic—system.

Objectives of Electronic Records Storage and Retrieval Systems

Electronic files generally consist of any collection of information that is recorded in a code that can be read and stored by a computer and stored on some medium for retrieval, viewing, and use. According to the Information Resources Management Service of the United States General Services Administration:

> "Electronic records are records just as much as paper documents, and their creation, maintenance and use, and disposition must be managed accordingly. Electronically created information in electronic mail systems, business graphics systems, digitized voice mail systems, office electronic message and calendaring systems, management information systems, and decision support systems must be reviewed and analyzed."[1]

Records maintained on electronic records storage systems are more susceptible to alteration, loss, and unauthorized access and disclosure of information than records stored in other forms. Thus a specific set of procedures to ensure the security, accuracy, and accessibility of records or information stored on electronic media must be incorporated in the overall records management program.

In many small businesses and organizations, individuals often select their own computer hardware and software systems based on personal preferences and needs. Such individuals are generally also allowed to determine what, how, when, why, where, and for how long records are to be stored. The nonstandardized systems and methods may not adversely affect a small business; however, if such individual choices and practices are allowed in large organizations, it would cause not only inefficient operation of the total business due to the lack of controls and accountability of all equipment, systems, and records, but also possibly chaos because of the inherent potential for loss, destruction, and inaccessibility of information.

Electronic files can be one of two types:

1. information that is created on a computer using applications software for

[1]*Electronic Recordkeeping,* Information Resources Management Services (Washington, D.C.: U.S. Government Printing Office, July 1989), p. 6.

such functions as word processing, spreadsheets, graphics, accounting, desktop publishing, or project management
2. a database of information maintained and managed by a database manager

A **database** is a collection of related information (usually information that has never existed in any particular document format). Such information is stored on the computer and is retrievable for referencing, updating, sorting, and printing in various report forms. The local telephone directory is an example of a database. The entire directory for a city or a particular telephone service area is a *database.* Each entry listed in the directory consisting of a subscriber's name, address, city, area code, and telephone number represents a *record*; each piece of information within the entry or record is a *field.*

Whichever viewpoint is adopted, data or information is recorded in digitized codes; is stored on computer disks, magnetic tape, or optical disks; and retrieved by a computer.[2]

Characteristics of Electronic Records Storage and Retrieval Systems

The primary purpose of any storage and retrieval system is to allow the user to store and retrieve records accurately and efficiently when needed. Computer-based or computer-assisted retrieval systems use the power, speed, and flexibility of a computer to help maintain records.

According to John Dykeman, the different technologies available—from desk-sized standalone units to sophisticated integrated systems—have the following characteristics:

a computer as the heart of the system

an automated means of entering documents into the system, such as scanners or other communications devices

a high capacity storage system, such as optical disk (WORM [sic]) for secure and archival files, and erasable or rewritable disk for temporary files. In the mini and mainframe environment, hybrid systems access a variety of media (including magnetic tape, magnetic disk, micrographics, and optical disk)

a screen capable of displaying a high resolution image of a stored document

an output device such as laser printer

networking for multiuser systems

[2]Charles Ray, Janet Palmer, and Amy Wohl. *Office Automation: A Systems Approach* (Cincinnati: South-Western Publishing Co., 1991), p. 203.

specialized software for image enhancement, database, and operating systems."[3]

Advantages and Disadvantages of Electronic Records Storage: The following are advantages of electronic records storage:

faster and direct access to information
simultaneous access and use by multiple users
centralized storage of information
greater accuracy in storage
ability to share data with many users

The following are disadvantages of electronic records storage:

initial cost of equipment and the system
continued costs in upgrades to the equipment and system
need for specialized, knowledgeable personnel to create, maintain, and manage the system
existence of duplicate records in paper forms and/or microforms that must still be maintained

Thus, because an electronic records management system utilizes storage and retrieval devices, it is important to understand the impact of electronics and computers on records systems.

CREATING AND MAINTAINING AN ELECTRONIC RECORDS STORAGE SYSTEM

With the use of computers to create, store, and retrieve data and information, records managers must also consider the nature of electronic records and how such records are to be used, maintained, and stored. Electronic recordkeeping is defined as:

> "the operation of records systems in which a computer is required for the user to create, work with, or delete records. Examples of electronic records are those residing on magnetic tapes, disks and drums, on video files, and on optical disks."[4]

[3]John Dykeman, "Technology Advances on All Fronts," *Modern Office Technology* (January 1990), p. 50.

[4]*Electronic Recordkeeping,* ibid., p. 1.

Developing Electronic Records Storage Systems Electronic records storage, (also referred to as *electronic filing* or *electronic recordkeeping*) refers to the storage and retrieval of information or data in digital form in such a way or using such language that the computer can understand. Electronic filing encompasses three types of files: text files, data files, and databases.

1. *Text files* are documents such as correspondence, reports, and statistical data that are created, edited, stored, retrieved, and printed using a word processing system or word processing systems software (such as **WordPerfect**, **WordStar**, **Microsoft Word**, or **DisplayWrite**); spreadsheet programs (such as **Lotus 1-2-3** or **Excel**); or accounting programs (such as **BPI Peachtree**, or **DacEasy**).
2. *Data files* are collections of information generally created, maintained, organized, and used for specific and limited applications. Examples of data files would be personnel or payroll information, name and address files used to generate mailing lists, and merchandise inventory.
3. *Databases* are collections of all data files that are combined into one large storage area for use in a variety of ways by multiple users.

Determining Electronic Records Storage Requirements There are four steps to consider when implementing a records storage program for electronic records:

1. *IDENTIFY THOSE WHO CREATE AND USE THE INFORMATION OR DATA* — One department may create for its own use certain types of records; or such records may also be shared with other users. The same set of records or information may then serve different purposes and may be used—manipulated—in different ways based on the nature of the records, their content, and who created it.
2. *DIFFERENTIATE BETWEEN WORKING COPIES OF DOCUMENTS OR RECORDS AND FINAL RECORDS* — Until a document has been finalized, previous versions are drafts or working copies. There may be several drafts or versions of the same document, especially if it is a long or complex and technical one. In addition, back-up copies of all work must necessarily be made to protect against inadvertent destruction, alteration, or loss. A procedure needs to be established for identifying final documents and for maintaining control over the various edited or working versions and their back-up copies.
3. *DETERMINE THE LIFESPAN OF RECORDS* — The lifespan—or life cycle—of electronic records should be identical to that of the same type of record stored in paper form or on microforms. The periods of retention, as well as the "transfer," destruction, and disposition, should follow those guidelines discussed in Chapter 5.
4. *ANALYZE THE TYPES OF DOCUMENTS CREATED AND STORED* — Records and data stored electronically can be analyzed on a document-by-

document basis or by record series or groupings in the same manner as other records (see Chapter 4).

The Life Cycle of Electronic Records

The **life cycle** of records, as mentioned earlier, consists of creation, storage/retrieval, manipulation, distribution, and final disposition. As with paper-based and microforms systems, each of the stages in the life of an electronic record also involves specific systems, procedures, terminology, hardware, and issues.[5]

Creation or Input The creation stage of a record is called the *input* stage in electronic records storage. Text files are created from an idea in the mind of the originator who transforms the idea into some form of business record or communication such as a letter, memorandum, report, graphic, or image. Text can be keyed directly into a word processor or into the system by computer-aided transcription (**CAT**). Existing text, documents, or images can be incorporated into the system by **optical character recognition** (OCR or OCR scanner).

Optical character recognition (OCR) is a method whereby printed text, photographs, and other images in hard-copy (paper) format can be scanned electronically and stored on a computer storage medium—disk or tape.

Information or data thus stored can be accessed by compatible word processing or data processing equipment and updated or edited in the usual manner for that type of record. According to Pamela M. Bond:

> By recognizing the input data with a detector that analyzes the light reflection of characters on the surrounding white field, the OCR's recognition unit interprets characters. The characters are distinguished by their topology—loops, lines, directions, positions and shape variations.[6]

Advantages of an optical character recognition system are as follows:

1. An existing hard-copy document can be stored on a system-compatible medium without the need to re-create or rekey the information. Word processors and computers are freed so that other information and data not already in hard-copy form can be entered in conventional ways. This process allows for greater efficiency of personnel and more productive use of a variety of equipment.

[5] Ray, Palmer, and Wohl, ibid., pp. 186–187.

[6] Pamela M. Bond, "OCR: Examining the Benefits of Page Readers," *Words,* Vol. 14, No. 4 (December-January 1985), pp. 34–35.

2. Graphics, artwork, photographs, and signatures can be captured in the scanning process, thus allowing storage of varying sizes, types, and shapes of characters; layout for format; and spacing.
3. Information or data can be scanned and converted into digital form faster than by an operator's direct keyboarding on a word processor or computer.[7]

A major disadvantage of optical character readers is that the scanning-reading process depends on high-quality input. The documents to be scanned and read must be clear; the characters and images must be distinct; the page must be clean and free of dirt or stray marks; and the page must be free of wrinkles and tears. Additional requirements for an effective OCR system are that the OCR unit be compatible with the typestyles or fonts used with word processing equipment; that word processing operators or others who keyboard or input data or information understand how to format documents that will later be scanned; and that the OCR function be compatible with, and complementary to, the total records storage and retrieval system within the organization.

An example of an OCR system is the Kurzweil 5200 by Xerox, which scans mixed typefaces, italics, underscore, bold, text on shaded backgrounds, draft dot matrix, and facsimile copies. This system recognizes English as well as Danish, Dutch, Finnish, French, Italian, Spanish, German, and other languages.

Data files are created by developing a specific data file of related records about individuals, organizations, customers, merchandise, etc., using such database management software as **dBase III Plus** or other applications software.

Databases are created by combining all data files into one large storage area, from which authorized users can access any specific data file and any records contained in it.

Storage and Retrieval As with other forms of records, the media on which electronic records are stored should be classified and processed for storing and made easily accessible to those who need them for administrative and operational purposes.

Manipulation Manipulation or processing is the step in the life cycle during which stored information may be edited by adding or deleting or otherwise updating information, reformatting, or rearrange. Manipulation, therefore, involves making a change in the record so that the record is in a usable form.

Distribution Information is a valuable resource that must be accessible on demand. With much of an organization's information created and stored in computers, it is necessary to have a means of transferring or disseminating information from one part of the organization to another. Electronic mail, voice

[7]Bond, Ibid.

mail, local area networks, and wide area networks serve such a need.

Electronic mail. Electronic mail involves the use of a computer as a mailbox to allow messages to be sent from the sender's terminal to the recipient/addressee's terminal. Messages can be composed at the keyboard, edited, distributed, and filed/stored until the recipient retrieves them, after which the messages can be stored, answered, or deleted.

Voice mail. As an alternative to electronic mail, which provides a written message on the screen, **voice mail** allows the sender to relay messages as though he or she were talking on the telephone; messages are relayed to all recipients. Messages can be stored in memory until retrieved and can also be delivered at a specific time or on a future date.

Networks. Two types of networks are local area and wide-area. A **local area network,** or LAN, is a group of interconnected processing devices distributed throughout a given geographic area. Microcomputers, minicomputers, mainframe computers, printers, plotters, and intelligent copiers are some of the devices that can be networked in a building or group of buildings. The communications function of a LAN system handles digital, video, and voice data to provide a typical office with simultaneous electronic mail, word processing, video conferencing, voice communications, and data processing applications. Local area networks are now being used with some CAR microfilm systems, as discussed in Chapter 18.

The Xerox Corporation's Ethernet System (see Figure 9-1) links equipment such as word processing work stations, printers, and disk drives by a coaxial cable to allow information to be exchanged with each other. A document composed at one work station can be transmitted and displayed on the terminal of another work station or printed at a third location via the network.

Wide area networks, or WANS, are nationwide networks that use telephone lines, microwave relays, and satellites to communicate to users over long distances. Thus the larger geographical range allowed by WANs is the primary difference between the two network systems.

Both network systems offer the following benefits:

They make it easier for employees to communicate via computer.

They save time by cutting down on meetings and enabling several employees to concentrate on the same problem at their respective work locations.

They make it easier to digest larger amounts of information, letting a company react faster and generally be more competitive.

They improve the return on investment in computers by combining the use of the machines in new ways to solve problems.

They can cut software costs by eliminating duplicate purchases of programs.[8]

[8]"The Personal Computer Finds Its Missing Link," *Business Week,* Industrial/Technology Edition (June 5, 1989), p. 120.

Xerox Ethernet System. (Courtesy of Xerox Corporation.)

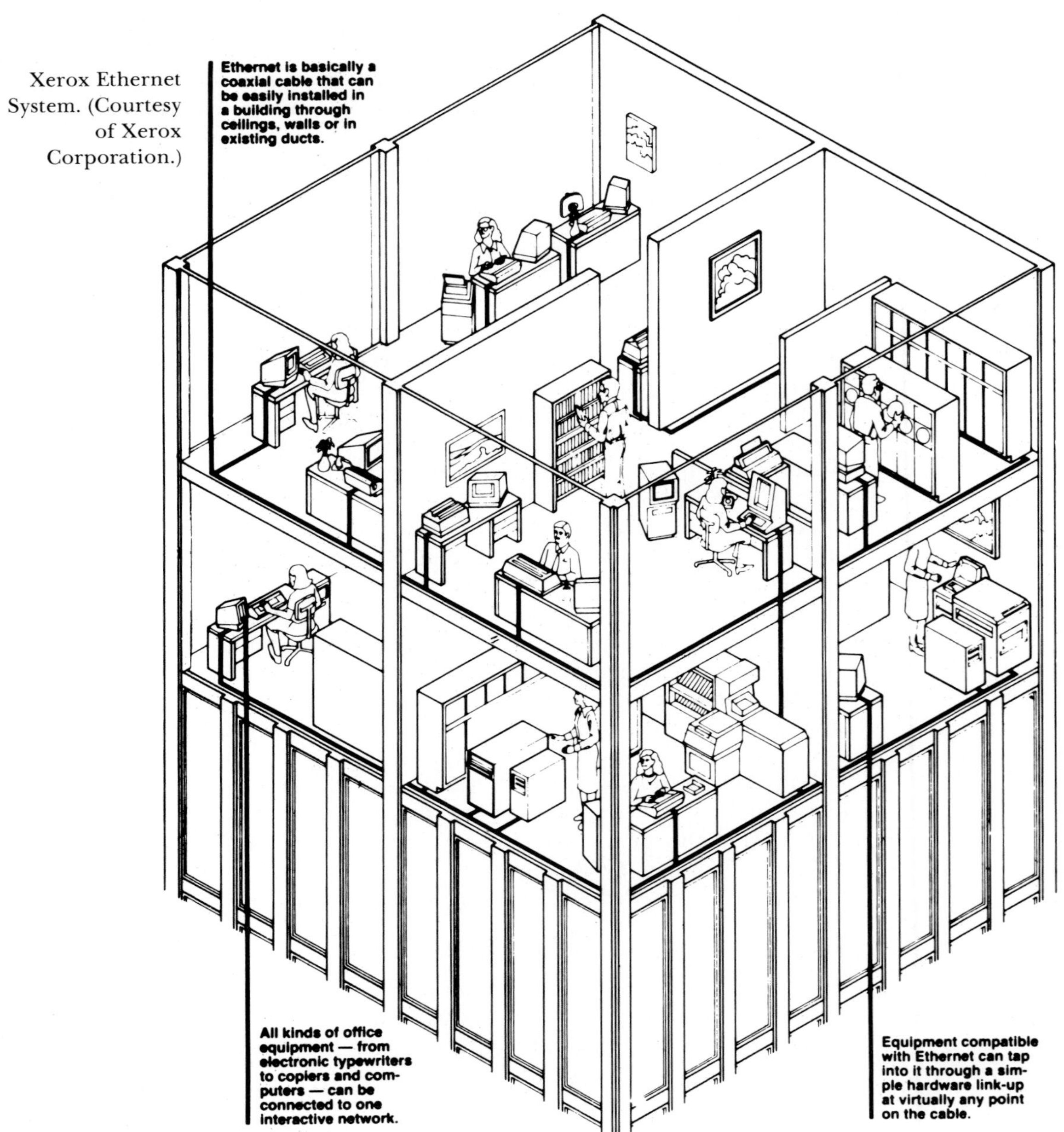

Ethernet is basically a coaxial cable that can be easily installed in a building through ceilings, walls or in existing ducts.
All kinds of office equipment — from electronic typewriters to copiers and computers — can be connected to one interactive network.
Equipment compatible with Ethernet can tap into it through a simple hardware link-up at virtually any point on the cable.

Retention As with other forms of records, a retention schedule for electronic records—individual documents and data files and the various media themselves—should also be developed. Such a schedule should be incorporated in the overall records retention scheme of the organization.

Disposition When electronic records, whether stored temporarily in the computer's memory or on a disk, are no longer useful, they should be purged to prevent unnecessary burdens upon equipment.

COMPUTERS AND ELECTRONIC RECORDS STORAGE AND RETRIEVAL

Electronic storage and retrieval systems store, retrieve, and control records with the aid of a computer. A **computer** "is a system of interconnected components that electronically processes (calculates, correlates, selects, and compiles) information according to a set of instructions and has a capacity for storage of information."[9]

Components of Computer Systems The operations of a computer are performed through a **central processing unit** (or **microprocessor**) that coordinates the operations or functions with the five components of the system.

1. **Input devices:** allow the system to receive information by way of, for example, keyboarded information and commands, optically-scanned text or images, and voice-activated words and speech patterns.
2. **Processing unit:** the central processing unit (or microprocessor) that processes or manipulates information according to the instructions, commands, and codes of the disk operating system for the particular computer system and those of the particular computer **program** or **applications software.**
3. **Internal memory units:** store both the programs and the data or information being processed.
4. **Storage devices:** allow processed information to be recorded and stored for future use. Such storage devices can be internal (hard disk) or external (floppy disks, magnetic tape, etc.) (See **Selecting Records Storage Media**)
5. **Output devices:** allow information or data to be displayed (on the video display terminal), stored (on disks or tapes), printed (in paper form or on microforms), or transmitted (via modem).

Types of Computers Computers are classified by size as microcomputers, minicomputers, mainframe computers, or supercomputers.

A **microcomputer,** also called a personal computer (or **PC**), is a small (desktop or laptop), low-cost computer system that may sell for less than $1,000, depending on the hardware and software options and systems configuration (see Figure 9-2). Microcomputers generally include between 640 kilobytes to one megabyte of random access memory (**RAM**), a hard disk and one or

[9]Ray, Palmer, and Wohl, Ibid., p. 87.

Microcomputer (personal computer). (Courtesy of NCR Corporation.)

two external floppy disk drives. Such computers can be used as standalone units or as multi-user applications and may be connected to a central mainframe or a minicomputer. Microcomputers are found in simple control systems such as security alarm systems, vending machines, automobiles, and household appliances.

A **minicomputer** is a small, fully functioning general-purpose computer, programmable to permit the user to do many of the tasks that larger general-purpose computers can perform. Often selling for less than $20,000, these systems can process data for such complex functions as payroll, inventory, accounting, and shipping and receiving functions, among others. Figures 9-3 and 9-4 show a family of minicomputers.

A **mainframe computer** is used to handle large multi-function tasks at tremendous speeds and serves as the "brains" of an information system or network in an organization, whether within a local site or around the world. Millions of characters of data or information can be accessed and sent around the office or around the world.

Supercomputers, similar to the one shown in Figure 9-5 and costing several million dollars, are the most powerful category of computers. These systems have the ability to process hundreds of millions of instructions per second and are used for such technically sophisticated applications as weather forecasting, space exploration, and other jobs requiring long, complex calculations.[10]

[10]Gary B. Shelly, Thomas J. Cashman, Gloria A. Waggoner, *Computer Concepts* (Livermore, CA; South-Western Publishing Co., 1990), p. 1.9.

FIGURE 9-3 Microcomputer system. (Courtesy of NCR Corporation.)

Computer Applications The routine in transactions that occur daily and the tasks that are performed with or by computers have become commonplace and taken for granted. Gas stations use computers to measure input and output at the pumps, track sales, and maintain records of transactions. Airlines use computers to book seat reservations, schedule aircraft maintenance, handle food planning and distribution, and provide weather and navigation information. Automobiles are equipped with self-contained computer systems that

FIGURE 9-4 NCR Corporation's Tower Family of minicomputers. (Courtesy of NCR Corporation.)

FIGURE 9-5 Cray Y-MP/832 Supercomputer—contains 8 central processors and 32 million 64-bit words of memory. (Courtesy of Cray Research, Inc.)

control the ignition and temperature and climate; microprocessors monitor and control engine performance.

Medicine has become dependent on computers. Doctors' offices use computer technology to schedule patient visits, maintain accounts, and prepare and mail billings. Hospitals perform not only administrative functions with computer technology, but also patient diagnosis and treatment. Patients' medical files are updated, medication is dispensed and accounted for, and staff work schedules and payroll accounts are maintained. Computer-assisted diagnostic devices are used to examine patients, collect test data, and evaluate the results.

Banks and other financial institutions use computers to maintain up-to-the-minute customer account information. Computers provide current account balances, electronic funds transfers (EFT), and automated teller machine (ATM) transactions to accept deposits and payments and to dispense money. The Federal Reserve System uses a computer network to transfer billions of dollars between member banks and local clearinghouses. The Social Security Administration uses computers for direct deposits of Social Security payments to recipients.

Certain aspects of the records management functions can be computerized to save not only hours of manual or even mechanical labor, but also to provide for more accurate, up-to-the minute information with greater security. Computers can be combined with micrographic equipment to create computer-assisted retrieval systems (CAR) (see Chapter 18). Records inventory lists and reports can be produced simply and quickly. Forms creation, generation, and management can also be easily handled via computer.

SELECTING RECORDS STORAGE MEDIA

A records manager is faced with a variety of choices of not only computer systems and programs and configurations, but also of electronic storage media. The records manager often may not be the person who determines the electronic media on which data are created or stored. Thus, problems may arise in coordinating or integrating what may be separate operations and areas of responsibility; for example, data on disk files may be created or stored on a system that is not compatible with another system; information from outside the office or organization must be input by scanning or by rekeyboarding into the internal system; and paper documents may need to be converted to electronic media.

In selecting the media for storing electronic records, the records manager must be familiar with the appropriate types of media and must select them in combinations that will build an effective system that meshes with the total records management program and its overall objectives. Magnetic media offer the following advantages:

1. They can store vast amounts of information—from 160 kilobytes to 1.44 megabytes of information.
2. Less office floor space is required both for the system equipment (computer, word processor, or other electronic retrieval system) and for the storage media themselves.
3. Information stored on magnetic media can be retrieved quickly, depending on the access time and capabilities of the equipment. *Access time* is the time it takes a user to log on to the particular system and obtain the specific set of stored records or information.
4. The storage media can be used on any other compatible equipment within the organization. This capability increases the efficiency and the productivity of the system and the personnel.
5. The storage media are easily transportable, allowing information to be shared by several individuals in different departments, offices, or regional locations.
6. The media can be duplicated and copies distributed to individuals in other locations if necessary. Also, individual records or documents can be transmitted over network systems.

Figure 9-6 illustrates how easily records stored on disks can be transported. Figure 9-7 shows individual disks stored in a rotary storage wheel.

Electronic records pose three challenges for users, according to Bonnie Canning:

1. Preserving record integrity, because data on electronic media are easy to manipulate.

FIGURE 9-6 Looseleaf diskette pockets for floppy disks. (Courtesy of Ring King Visibles, Division of HON Industries.)

2. Prolonging the life of the record, because electronic media are not archival.
3. Managing data created on incompatible systems.[11]

Electronic media include floppy or flexible disks (or diskettes), hard disks, magnetic tape, and optical digital disks. Magnetic media discussed here relate to *types* of media used for records storage and retrieval rather than the systems themselves. Data or information can be retained on various forms of media for future referencing, editing, or updating. In computerized systems, magnetic media—such as 3-1/2 inch disks, 5-1/4 inch disks, and optical disks—are components used to store data or information outside the computer. Other forms of magnetic media include computer tapes, cassettes, and removable hard disk cartridges.

Floppy or Flexible Disks The two popular formats of floppy or flexible disks used on microcomputers are the 5-1/4 inch and the 3-1/2 inch. The 5-1/4 inch magnetic disks are a thin, flat circle of mylar plastic, coated with magnetic material that allows for storage of information as a sequence of magnetic pulses. The disk is encased in a protective vinyl jacket to prevent dust, dirt, and grease from contacting the magnetic material.

The 3-1/2 inch disks are encased in a heavy plastic protective unit and can store 740 kilobytes to 1.44 megabytes of data.

Table 9-1 shows the sizes and capacities of floppy disks. The size of a disk refers to its diameter. The capacity of a disk refers to the number of **bytes** (a byte represents a character or a symbol) that can be stored on a medium;

[11]Bonnie Canning, "Options in Electronic Records Management," *Office Administration and Automation*, Vol. 45, No. 1 (January 1984), pp. 48–50, 52.

FIGURE 9-7 Storage container for 5 1/4 inch diskettes. (Courtesy of Ring King Visibles, Division of HON Industries.)

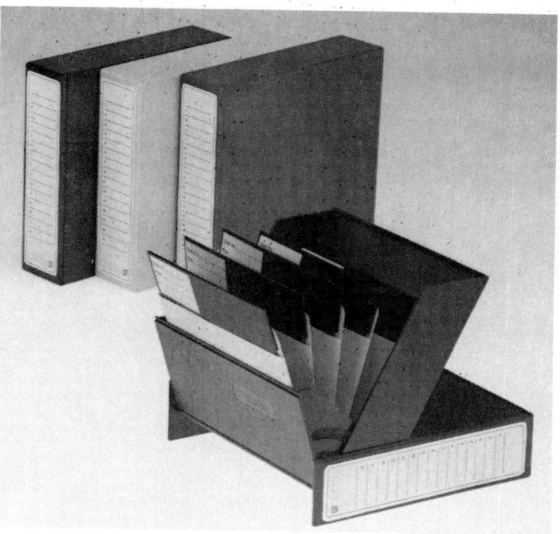

capacity also refers to **density**—how compactly or densely data or information can be stored on a disk.

Hard disks During processing, data or information is stored internally in the computer's random access memory (RAM), but only temporarily for a limited time—during the current working session or until the system is turned off—and in limited amounts—based on the system's RAM capacity. In addition to the disk operating system and the computer programs that direct the operation of the system, data or information can also be stored on a **hard disk** housed within the computer, as shown in Figure 9-8. The hard disk retains data indefinitely until they are erased or moved to an external storage medium, such as floppy or flexible disk.

Hard disks are flat circular plates that spin at high speed, permitting extremely rapid reading and writing of information. As with floppy disks, information on hard disks is stored as a sequence of magnetic pulses. Hard disks come in various types—internal, external, and hard card—and can store vast amounts of information. For example, a 20-megabyte hard disk can store the

TABLE 9-1

Size	*Media*	*Capacity**
5 1/4″	Single-sided disk	160/180KB
5 1/4″	Double-sided disk	320/360KB
5 1/4″	High-capacity disk	1.2MB
3 1/2″	Double-sided disk	720KB
3 1/2″	High-capacity disk	1.44MB

*One kilobyte (K or KB) is equivalent to approximately 1000 bytes; one megabyte (MB or M-byte) represents 1 million bytes

FIGURE 9-8. Computer hard disk mechanism. (Courtesy of Hewlett Packard.)

same amount of information as 56 double-sided floppy disks. (Data or information stored on the internal hard disk should also be stored—backed up—on some external storage medium on a regular basis (daily) in case the third disk "crashes" and data are irretrievable.)

Hard disks offer the advantages over floppy disks of providing greater speed in retrieving data, greater storage capacity, and minimal data handling because of increased convenience and efficiency in accessing data. A major disadvantage of hard disks is that because of the vast amount of memory, users must consider carefully how files are organized to enable greater efficiency both in storing and retrieving files.

While a hard disk is non-removable, removable hard disk cartridges can be interchanged, removed, and locked securely into a computer; they offer the versatility of a floppy disk and the storage capacity of a hard disk.

Hard disks placed in a stack as several platters are referred to as **disk packs,** which are used on minicomputers and mainframes.

Optical Digital Disks Optical disk technology was introduced in the 1980s and offered potential for high density random access storage and retrieval applications. Optical digital disks record "digital data in the form of microscopic pits etched in a spiral on a plastic surface. A laser beam just 1 micron wide is scattered by the pits and reflected by the flat 'lands' between them, enabling the encoded information to be read."[12] Optical disks are either glass or plastic disks available in 5-1/2-inch, 12-inch, and 14-inch formats. A 12-inch disk can store approximately one billion bytes (one gigabyte) of information per side—

[12]Jeffrey Baristow, "CD-ROM: Mass Storage for the Mass Market," *High Technology,* October 1986, p. 44.

the equivalent of 20,000 standard 8-1/2 by 11 inch documents. Data, text, graphics, and scanned images can be permanently recorded—etched—on the medium.[13] Plastic optical disks allow data to be erased from the disks; as such, these disks are reusable, rewritable disks.

Optical disks are housed in devices similar to the way phonograph records were housed in jukeboxes; in fact, the storage device for optical disks is called a **jukebox** or a **disk library** from which disks can be selected, retrieved and inserted into the disk drive, and the desired data displayed. Individual workstations within an integrated environment, as well as individual video display terminals, can access and retrieve and print data from the optical disk.

An **optical disk system** used for records storage and retrieval consists of a disk, a scanner-printer, a high-resolution video display terminal, and a microcomputer. Individual records are located on the disk and displayed on the terminal. Using database management software, the microcomputer controls the interactions of the whole system.

There are three main types of optical disks used to store information. The **read-only memory (ROM),** used for recording and distributing high-density encoded information, is a prerecorded, nonerasable medium. Memory is programmed at the time of manufacture; therefore, the user cannot alter its contents. Read-only disks are suitable for materials that do not require input by the user; for example, training and educational materials and reference works.[14]

The user-writable disk, known as **write-once read many (WORM)**, is a one-time use disk where the user, rather than the manufacturer, writes (stores) information on the disk. Once information is stored, additional information cannot be written on it; and currently stored information cannot be edited or altered. Thus, the write-once disk is suitable for archival storage and transaction recordings.[15]

The third type of optical disk is the **compact disk read-only memory (CD-ROM)** unit. The CD-ROM has tremendous storage capabilities and is used to store general-purpose digital data for personal computers. One compact disk is capable of holding 543 megabytes of information on one side, the equivalent of 1,500 5-1/4 inch floppy disks.[16] Each CD-ROM can store the equivalent of a 25-volume set of encyclopedias, as shown in Figure 9-9.

[13]Ray, Palmer, and Wohl, Ibid., p. 206.

[14]Elshami, Ahmed M., *CD-ROM Technology for Information Managers* (Chicago, 1990), p. 5–22.

[15]Ibid.

[16]Ibid.

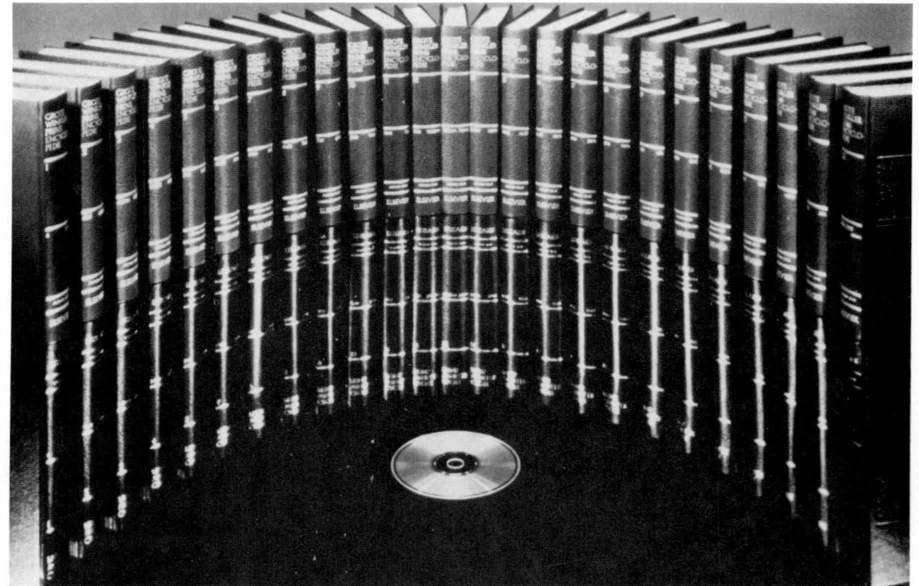

FIGURE 9-9. CD ROM disk and disk drive (*top*). A single CD ROM disk can store the contents of a 25-volume encyclopedia (*bottom*). (Courtesy of North American Philips Corporation and 3M Company.)

MAINTAINING, ACCESSING, AND RETRIEVING STORED DATA

Once the types of magnetic media for records storage have been selected, decisions about how records stored on those media will be identified, accessed, and retrieved must be determined. With regard to data stored on floppy disks, the Association of Records Managers and Administrators

(ARMA) identifies the following issues that should be addressed early in the decision-making process:

1. How can records and nonrecords be distinguished from one another?
2. What subject captions and codes are to be used?
3. How can color coding be used to improve efficiency?
4. How should program disks be distinguished from data disks and how can each group of disks be managed effectively?[17]

Electronic records are accessed through the video display terminal of the word processor, computer, or computer-assisted retrieval system. Each disk, tape, or card includes an index or a directory of its contents, which allows an individual to access and retrieve the desired records.

Identifying Magnetic Records As with other forms of records, information stored on magnetic media must be easy to access. Proper identification of records for storage and retrieval is the key to an efficient electronic system. Documents stored on disk can be identified by document name, author name, type of document, and/or date of creation, whichever indexing method provides for quick and accurate access to and retrieval of records by users. The following guidelines for developing and maintaining electronic files are offered by Sheldon H. Jaffee:

1. Establish a standard format for naming documents, such as using a key word (or words) from the beginning document title.
2. Use logical code names related to the type of document to enable other people to recall the names.
3. Have users agree to an accepted set of standard abbreviations or other codes based on the needs of the organization.
4. Number or date successive drafts, updates, or revisions of documents so each can be readily identifiable, especially for retention purposes.
5. Create a retention schedule for individual records. Determine which records on disk need to be retained permanently and the dates on which others should be deleted or reviewed.
6. Use floppy disks to back up on-line work periodically, to prevent slowdowns and failures of the system and loss of records.[18]

Jaffee also suggests maintaining a document library (or database)—an index of all documents created—listing each document by number, name, type,

[17]*Filing Procedures, ARMA International Guideline For Records and Information Management* (Prairie Village, KS: Association of Records Managers and Administrators, 1989), p. 5.

[18]Sheldon H. Jaffee, "PC/WP Storage: Finding the Files," *Today's Office,* Vol. 101, No. 2 (February 1985), pp. 32–33.

author or operator, retention date, and disk name or number. In addition to allowing users to access specific information quickly by calling up any one piece of known information about a record, such an index or database serves as a cross-reference to all information stored within the system.

Labeling Magnetic Media A standardized labeling format should be followed to ensure uniformity in how magnetic media are prepared, maintained, identified, filed, and retrieved.

Proper labeling of disks is critical since they can store so much information — each disk can hold between 100 and 300 pages of information, the equivalent of one to two file folders of paper records. Floppy disks can be labeled by affixing an identifying label on the outside of the disk itself (**external label**); or the disk can be labeled as part of the formatting process (**internal label**). Adhering to predetermined labeling guidelines is important if the entire records storage and retrieval system is to function effectively. Each label should contain enough identifying information as to the contents of the disk to enable individuals to locate the appropriate disk and desired files easily and quickly.

External labeling of disks. Floppy disks can be identified by placing adhesive labels on the disks themselves. (Since the disks can become separated from their sleeves or envelopes, labels should not be affixed only to the disk sleeves.) As with paper-based records, disks can be labeled, classified, and stored according to the same records classifications as other records of those types: alphabetically (by department or division, project name, subject or geographic area, originator, function, etc.); numerically (by sequence of disks in use within a department or division, by department or cost center numbers, etc.); chronologically (by day, week, or month; by date of document creation or origination, etc.). Number codes provide security and confidentiality, and disks may be stored according to the consecutive, terminal-digit, middle-digit, or Dewey-decimal classification systems (see Chapter 7). Numeric coding also allows unlimited expansion in the number of disks to be stored in the system.

ALPHABETICAL LABELING—BY SUBJECT:

BOARD OF DIRECTORS Minutes January through March 19__

NUMERIC LABELING:

Department 12-45 Week of November 12, 19__	Disk # _____

CHRONOLOGICAL LABELING:

Year: _____ (February-	Disk # _____

Color-coding devices can also be used to identify or distinguish disks. The adhesive labels are available in different colors and with different color markings, so each department or cost center or user can be assigned a particular color of label to use on its floppy disks. Both the 5-1/4 inch or 3-1/2 inch disks themselves are available in a variety of colors. All program disks, for example, can be coded in one color and be distinguishable from data disks, which can be coded in another color, and so forth. The use of color labels or disks not only identifies the source of the media, but also aids in their storage and retrieval.

Internal labeling of disks. Floppy disks can also be labeled internally as part of the disk **formatting** process—that is, the procedure used to initialize or prepare a blank disk for use on a particular computer system and with a particular **disk operating system** (DOS). This procedure is known as formatting a disk with a **volume label.** The following screen prompts and messages will be displayed during the formatting process:

For floppy disk systems:

A>FORMAT B:/V [ENTER]

Formatting . . . Format complete

Volume label (11 characters, enter for none)? __

For hard disk systems:

C>FORMAT A:/V [ENTER]

Formatting . . . Format complete

Volume label (11 characters, enter for none)? __

At the > prompt, the name to be assigned that disk would be keyed—based on the predetermined alphabetic, numeric, chronologic, etc., naming conventions. A label can consist of up to 11 characters. The internal label would generally also appear on the external label.

Labeling hard disk files. The same document-naming conventions used to store individual documents or records on floppy disks would be used when such records are stored directly on the hard disk. File names can consist of up to eight characters followed by a three-character extension (FILENAME.EXT). As documents or records are created and stored on the disk, they will be stored under or within specific directories or subdirectories, depending on the organization of the hard disk.

In general, a hard disk directory (referred to as the *root directory*) is likened to main entries of topics in an encyclopedia; each subdirectory within the directory is a branch or a separate category within the main topic or record. (Refer to the Disk Operating System Manual accompanying computer systems for guidelines on organizing directories and sub-directories on hard disks.)

Accessing and Retrieving Electronic Records Information is stored—and thus retrieved—either sequentially or in random order, depending on the media used. Indexing or accessing data, then, varies also depending on the media used. Magnetic computer tape, which is similar to audio cassette and video cassette tapes, is typically available in 1,200 to 2,400 feet reels. Information on magnetic tape is written to (stored) sequentially or serially; that is, records are stored one record at a time in sequence. Likewise, when information must be referenced or accessed, it must be done by viewing or accessing one series of records at a time in sequence until the desired information is located. Thus magnetic tapes provide **sequential storage and retrieval/access** of information, a time-consuming and generally inefficient process when information must be referenced and/or updated frequently. Because of these disadvantages, magnetic tapes are generally used for backup and archival storage purposes for mainframe and minicomputers.

Information stored on the 5-1/4 inch and 3-1/2 inch disks, as well as optical disks, can be randomly stored, indexed, and accessed or retrieved. **Random access** means that any record on the disk, in whatever sequence it was stored, can be accessed directly—in random sequence—when needed. As with hard disks, information is stored as a sequence of magnetic pulses. Removable hard disk cartridges, which can be inserted and removed from a personal computer offer the versatility of a floppy disk and the storage capacity of a hard disk.

Media Storage Systems

Media files include magnetic tapes or cartridges used with minicomputers; floppy disks and diskettes used with word processors and microcomputers; and cassette tapes used with dictation-transcription equipment, word processors, microcomputers, and audiovisual equipment.

The standard sizes of each of these media enable companies to use standard vertical records storage equipment similar to that used for paper-based records, with some modification. The large amount of information that can be stored on magnetic media makes for compact and economical storage.

Disk and Diskette Storage Magnetic media, such as floppy disks and diskettes, are often stored in special desk-top trays or rotary stands. These storage devices provide easy access at the point of use for individuals who must use or retrieve data stored on the media. The storage tray shown in Figure 9-10 holds up to seventy 5-1/4-inch diskettes in a durable shell with a security lock. Figure 9-11 shows similar diskette storage trays that can be used at a word processing or computer work station. Adjustable index dividers or guides allow the user to organize a suitable indexing system for storage and retrieval of the diskettes.

The rotary stand shown in Figure 9-12 holds 150 diskettes back to back in vinyl files. The titles of the disks are visible on the vertical tabs as well as on the diskette labels. Rotary stands and special binders with vinyl pockets for individual diskettes are also available for storing smaller numbers of diskettes.

Figure 9-13 shows an enclosed cabinet that houses two tiers of eight individual trays of diskettes. The slide-out drawers may be removed to a computer or word processing station, allowing easy access to the media when needed for processing. Diskettes may also be kept in letter- and legal-size folders, and stored in conventional file-drawer cabinets. In such cases, a hard copy of the record, an index, or other related documentation is usually stored with the diskette.

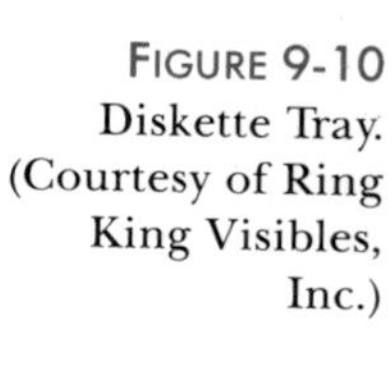

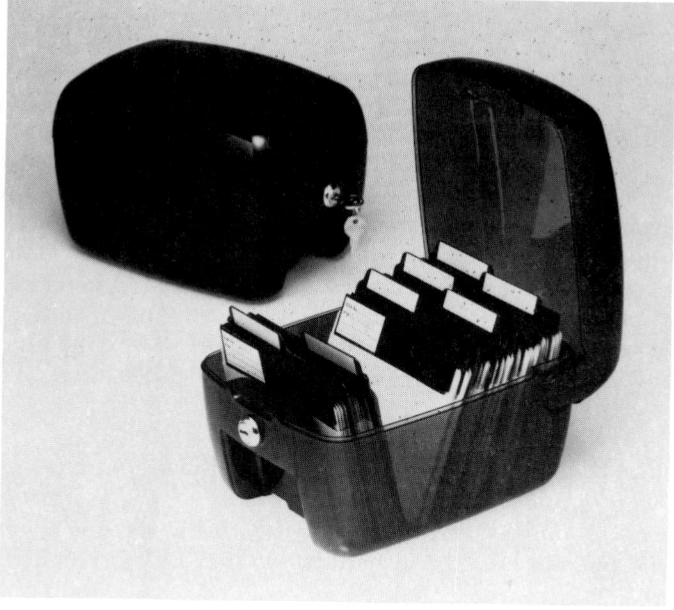

FIGURE 9-10 Diskette Tray. (Courtesy of Ring King Visibles, Inc.)

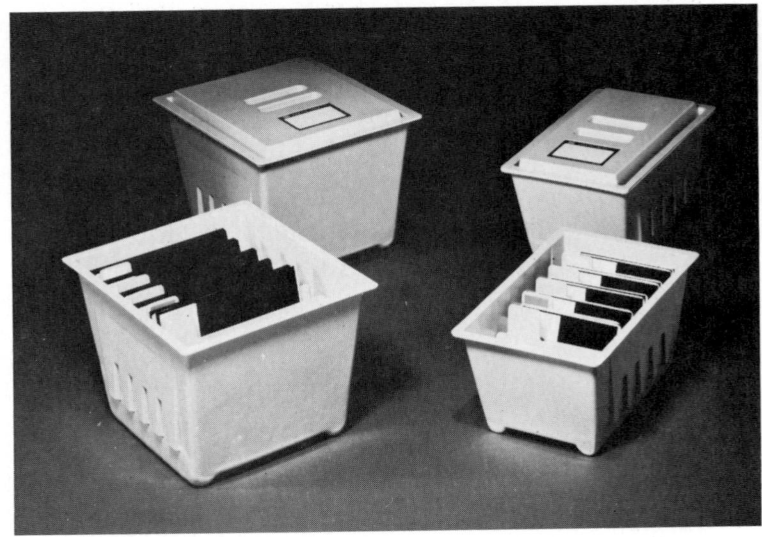

FIGURE 9-11 Diskette trays for 5-1/4-inch diskettes. (Courtesy of Acco International.)

Computer Tapes Reels of computer tape, tapes in canisters or cartridges, and magnetic disks in disk packs are other forms of magnetic media. These media require special storage equipment, such as open suspension-type cabinets or cabinets with slots to hold each reel, cartridge, or canister. (See Figure 9-14).

The hard-copy printouts generated by computers and word processors also need to be stored and retrieved. An open-shelf printout organizer can be used to house bound and unbound computer reports. Such a unit has 16 compartments, which accommodate a total of 20,000 printout sheets, or 60 inches, in 3 square feet of floor space. According to *Information Management,* "Rather than reducing or eliminating paper, electronics, computers and word processors have increased the amount of paper (printout) being generated, distributed, and filed in the office."[19]

Disk File Guides. Whether disks are stored in trays, bins, or file drawers, disk file guides (similar to those used to store paper records and microforms) are required for floppy disks. Disk file guides separate sections of disks and serve also to hold them upright in the tray, bin, or drawer. Guides can be used as signposts to separate and distinguish types of disks (data disks, program disks, or applications software disks), categories of data or information, or originating departments, etc. Captions affixed to the tabs of the file guides identify the appropriate nature or range of disks filed behind them.

PROTECTION AND CARE OF ELECTRONIC RECORDS

As with all other forms of records, electronic records kept within a company should be maintained and handled so they can serve their useful function in

[19]*Information Management,* Vol. 18, No. 3 (March 1984), pp. 16–17.

FIGURE 9-12
Diskette rotary stand. (Courtesy of Ring King Visibles, Inc.)

the operation of the business. Frank Tetz indicates that a company must consider the following five basic steps for maintaining security of all records, especially employee personnel records:

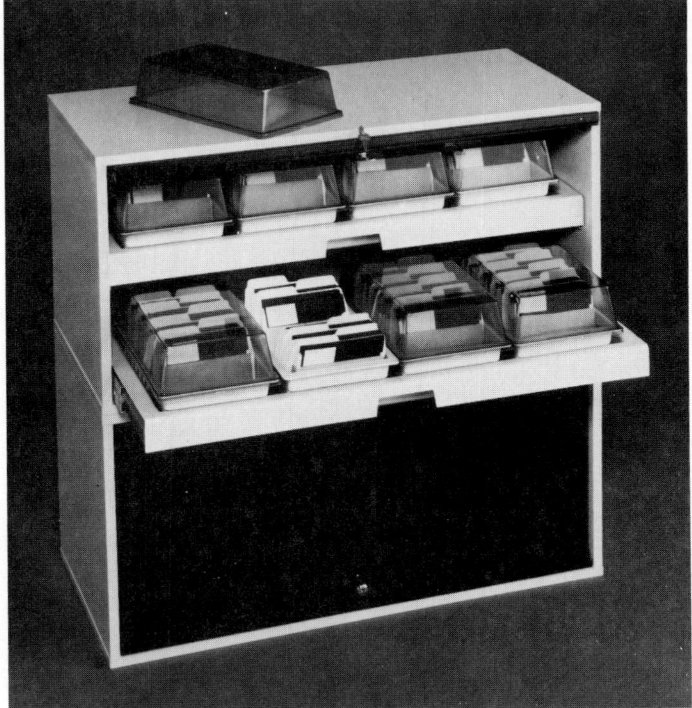

FIGURE 9-13
Mini-diskette tray cabinet and file trays. (Courtesy of Ring King Visibles, Inc.)

FIGURE 9-14 Optimedia back-to-back tape library unit. (Courtesy of Wright Line, Inc., Worcester, MA.)

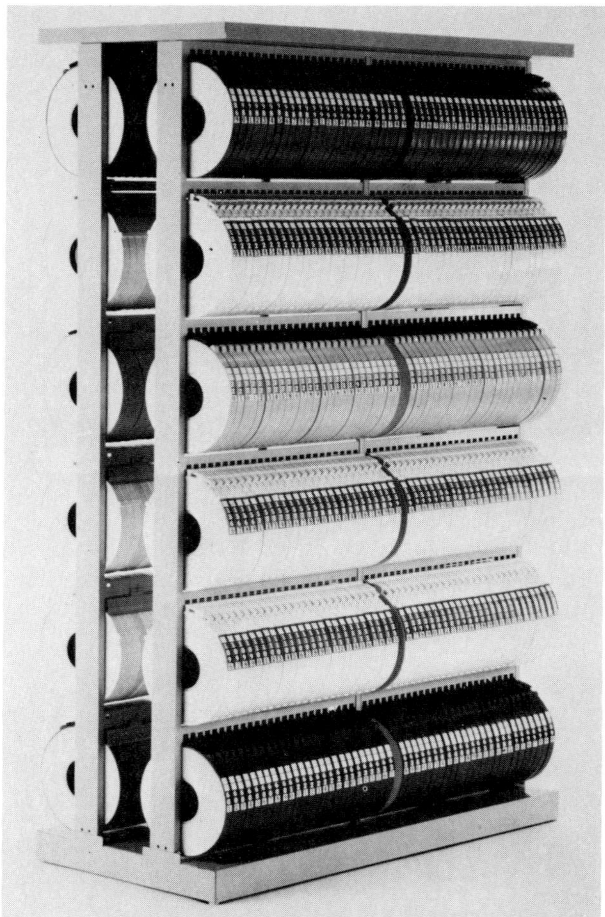

1. Store only information that is necessary.
2. Eliminate unnecessary duplication, both paper and electronic.
3. Select the best hardware for the type of information you require and the way that it will be used.
4. Design security into the system from the very beginning.
5. Establish privacy policies; tell your staff the kind of information you are recording, why you have it, and who has access to it.[20]

James A. Colwell had predicted that by 1989, there would be 500 million floppy disks used as records storage and retrieval media, compared with 79

[20]Frank Tetz, "Computers Can Make Office Records More Private," *Office Administration and Automation*, Vol. 46, No. 3 (March 1985), pp. 30–32, 80.

million disks in use in the early 1980s.[21] Based on current usage and trends, Colwell makes the following recommendations for storing magnetic media:

1. Since the loss of information on magnetic media generally occurs when there is a separation between medium and the read/write head [of the disk drive], cleanliness is vital.
2. Fingerprints and cigarette smoke, in particular, attract dust and other contaminants.
3. Storage should be at temperatures between 50° and 125°F and between 8 percent and 80 percent humidity, lest the medium become warped or brittle and not move freely in the disk drive.
4. Do not pile disks on top of one another, since the static electricity which will build when they are rubbed against each other will erase stored data.
5. Do not expose magnetic media to extraneous magnetic fields which can "wipe" all the data.
6. Do not scratch a disk by writing on an identification label which is already affixed to the disk.[22]

Since hard disks store such vast amounts of information, special procedures should be established for the protection and integrity of those records. ARMA suggests the following:

1. The data should be backed up weekly to assure information security. This can be done with a mechanical device attached to the PC, a special software package, or by using DOS instructions.
2. Documents may be transferred to inactive flexible disks when there is a very low probability of revising or re-using the document. Similar documents may be batched on one flexible disk.
3. If a document is a record which requires some official retention, it should be retained in hard copy or on a microform. Correspondence stored in electronic devices does not carry signatures.[23]

Optical disks are able to withstand considerable handling without fear of damaging the disks or the data or information stored on them. Unlike magnetic media, optical disks are not affected by normal heat or humidity or by magnetic force fields, all of which can ruin magnetic media.

Protection of Electronic Records With the ever-increasing roles of the computer in the management and operation of an organization, managers

[21]James A. Colwell, "The Fourth 'Great Lie'," *Information Management,* Vol. 19, No. 4 (April 1985), p. 22.

[22]Colwell, Ibid.

[23]*Filing Procedures,* Ibid., p. 8.

must control and protect computer data as other valuable company resources are controlled and protected. As data or information is being incorporated or transferred, file integrity must be maintained to ensure both the accuracy and, where appropriate, the confidentiality of information. Payroll files on magnetic tape or disks, for example, must be protected from unauthorized access and use, as well as from accidental destruction. These magnetic media must be environmentally protected from humidity, magnetic influences, water, and dust. Some magnetic media must be recopied onto new media at regular intervals to prevent the media from becoming demagnetized and thus losing data.

Dr. Arlene Motz, CRM, points out the need for organizations to formalize a policy for protection of magnetic media and identifies four principles in managing magnetic media.

Principle I. To apply the management principles of planning, organizing, and controlling to magnetic media.

Principle II. To establish policies for the backing up of files as well as the retention and disposition of magnetic media.

Principle III. To protect the privacy, confidentiality, and security of the files stored on magnetic media.

Principle IV. To identify and protect vital records and to archive those permanent-type files.[24]

To protect and control any type of magnetic media, company management must take an active role in developing, implementing, and adhering to its policy regarding magnetic media.

Using Database Management Systems (DBMS)

Management requires accurate and up-to-date information in order to make sound decisions. Typically, an organization will have computer equipment and data stored in various locations or departments. It is often impossible to combine data from various locations in order to generate the desired reports. This unstructured approach can lead to missed deadlines; incomplete, inaccurate, and inconsistent reporting; and inefficient use of company resources. To eliminate these and other problems, many organizations today are using the database concept for managing computer-generated data.

A *database* refers to "a collection of related information (as opposed to a collection of documents)."[25] There are two types, internal and external:

[24]Arlene Motz, "Applying Records Management Principles to Magnetic Media," *Records Management Quarterly*, Vol. 20, No. 2 (April 1986), pp. 22–26.

[25]Ray, Palmer, and Wohl, Ibid., p. 201.

1. Internal databases are housed within the organization's own computer system. Internal databases contain records that have been created, edited or updated, manipulated, sorted, and stored for use by individuals within the organization. At the California Institute of Technology in Pasadena, California, for example, a database containing records on local and global seismic activity is maintained.
2. External databases are housed in computer systems outside the organization and are accessed for a fee. Examples of companies that supply information to users for a fee are Dow Jones News Retrieval Service and CompuServe Information Service Co.[26]

A **database management system (DBMS)** is specific-purpose or customized computer software that "directs the creation of records, addition of data to the records, calculations, sorting and combining data from the database, and production of reports containing data from the database."[27] A database management system is a file organization concept. Database management software uses a structured approach to organize data, which may never have existed in document form, into one large file without duplication. For example, data from the Personnel Department records and those from the Payroll Department would contain certain identical elements. If those two sets of data were merged into a single database, duplicate information from both files would be omitted to avoid redundance. Figure 9-15 shows the structure of the database file for the Personnel Department.

Data are entered in a record format (see Figure 9-16). Either the Payroll or the Personnel Department could access the database for such information as an employee's name, address, and Social Security/employee number. When there is a change in an employee's personnel record, for example, the change is made only once—in the master database.

The characteristics of a well-designed database are the following:

1. It is an organized, integrated collection of data.
2. It can be referred to by all relevant applications with relative ease and with no (or limited) duplication of data.
3. It is a model of the natural relationship of the data in the user's real-world environment.[28]

Since both the management procedures and the records are stored in a database management system, hardware and software requirements are determined by the size and use of the records in the database. While a quantity of 5,000 records is beyond the capabilities of a microcomputer, this quantity

[26]Ibid., p. 201.

[27]Ibid., pp. 201–202.

[28]Marilyn Bohl, *Essentials of Information Processing* (Chicago: Science Research Associates, Inc., 1986), p. 309.

FIGURE 9-15 Structure of a database.

```
Structure for database: A:PERSNL.dbf
Number of data records:          5
Date of last update    : 01/30/91
Field  Field Name   Type        Width      Dec
    1  EMPNO        Numeric         4
    2  LNAME        Character      14
    3  FNAME        Character      10
    4  B_DAY        Date            8
    5  DEPT         Character      10
    6  SALARY       Numeric         6        2
    7  PEN          Logical         1
    8  SOC_SEC      Character      11
** Total **                        65
```

FIGURE 9-16 Record format.

```
Record #     EMPNO     LNAME         FNAME       B_DAY     DEPT        PEN  SOC_SEC
       1      1230     BLASZCAYNSKI  CAROL       02/05/60  PERSONNEL   .T.  534-86-9360
       2      1232     EDWARDS       BARTON      10/08/61  GRAPHICS    .T.  510-08-7657
       3      1216     ELY           ROBERT      11/18/60  SALES       .T.  589-23-3620
       4      1234     STABLER       AMY         03/11/65  PUBLIC REL  .F.  543-34-7602
       5      1211     WEILER        ROWENA      05/26/55  ACCOUNTING  .T.  401-70-4061
```

would not be a limitation for hardware used in a database management system, which should have at least 640 kilobytes of random access memory and a 20-30 megabyte hard disk—the upper limits of a microcomputer.[29]

As mentioned, database management systems for use on mainframe computers may be complex and expensive; however, relatively inexpensive database management systems software, such as **dBase III Plus** by Ashton-Tate, can be used quite effectively on microcomputers. The management aspect of both types of databases includes "adding new information, sorting, searching, printing reports, editing, and deleting data."[30]

[29]Terry D. Lundgren and Carol A. Lundgren, *Records Management in the Computer Age* (PWS-Kent, 1989), p. 252.

[30]Alan Simpson, *Understanding DBase III PLUS* (Alameda, CA: Sybex, Inc., 1986), p. 6.

CHAPTER HIGHLIGHTS

- Electronic records storage and retrieval systems involve the use of a computer to create, store, access or retrieve, edit or update, and delete records.
- Computer-based or computer-assisted retrieval systems use the power, speed, and flexibility of computer systems to maintain records so they can be retrieved accurately and quickly when needed.
- Electronic files consist of collections of information recorded in a code that can be read and stored by a computer.
- Because records maintained on electronic records storage systems are more susceptible to alteration, loss, and unauthorized access and disclosure of information than other forms of stored records, specific procedures for protecting such records are required.
- Electronic records consist of data or information recorded in digitized code on computer disks, magnetic tape, or optical disks.
- Electronic files consist of (1) information created on a computer using applications software (such as word processing, spreadsheets, graphics, accounting, and desktop publishing) and (2) a database of information maintained and managed by a database manager.
- A database is a collection of related information.
- Electronic records storage provide the following advantages: faster and direct access to information, simultaneous access and use by multiple users, centralized storage of information, greater accuracy in storage, and the ability to share data with many users.
- Electronic records have the following disadvantages: initial cost of equipment and the system; continued costs to upgrade both equipment and systems; need for specialized personnel to create, maintain, and manage the system; and the continued maintenance of duplicate records in paper forms and/or microforms.
- There are three types of files involved in electronic filing: text files, data files, and databases.
- Text files include documents such as correspondence, reports, and statistical data created, edited, stored, retrieved, and printed using a word processing system or word processing systems software.
- Data files are collections of information generally created, maintained, organized, and used for specific and limited applications.
- Databases are collections of all datafiles combined into one large storage area for use in a variety of ways by multiple users.
- The four steps in implementing an electronic records storage and retrieval system are: (1) identify those individuals or departments that create and use the information or data; (2) differentiate between working copies of documents or records and final records; (3) determine the lifespan of records; and (4) analyze the types of electronic documents created and stored.

- The life cycle of electronic records consists of those same phases that exist for other forms of records: creation or input, storage/retrieval, manipulation or use, distribution, and final disposition.
- Optical character recognition (OCR) is a method of inputting existing text, photographs, and other images into a computer system for manipulation and storage on a magnetic medium.
- The distribution phase of the cycle can be accomplished via electronic mail, voice mail, local area networks, and wide area networks.
- Electronic mail uses the computer as a mailbox to allow messages to be sent to and from one terminal to another.
- Voice mail allows a sender to relay messages through a telephone system where messages can be stored in memory until retrieved.
- Networks consist of groups of interconnected processing devices—such as microcomputer, minicomputers, mainframe computers, printers, plotters, and intelligent copies—distributed throughout a given geographic area.
- A local area network (LAN) handles digital, video, and voice data communications functions.
- Wide area networks (WANs) are nationwide networks that use telephone lines, microwave relays, and satellites to communicate between users over long distances.
- The central processing unit of a computer coordinates the operations or functions of its five components: input devices, processing unit, internal memory units, storage devices, and output devices.
- The four types of computers, distinguished by their sizes and capabilities for storing and processing information, are the microcomputer, the minicomputer, the mainframe, and the supercomputer.
- Magnetic media used as storage devices offer the following advantages: they can store vast amounts of information; less storage space in terms of office floor space is required to house magnetic media; information stored on magnetic media can be retrieved quickly; the media can be used on any compatible system; and the media are transportable and easily duplicated and distributed.
- Magnetic media used for records storage include the 3-1/2 inch and the 5-1/2 inch floppy disks, hard disks, removable hard disk, and optical digital disks.
- Optical disk systems are available as read-only memory (ROM), write-once read many (WORM), and compact disk read-only memory (CD-ROM).
- Information or data recorded/stored on magnetic records need to be identified so their contents are easily accessible; standard formats for naming documents, labeling the various forms of media, and retention schedules should be established.
- The magnetic media themselves can be labeled internally such as using the system's disk operating system (DOS) "formatting with a volume label" feature.

- Magnetic media should be protected from environmental contaminants, such as dust, dirt, and smoke; extreme hot and cold temperatures; and magnetic fields.
- A database management system (DBMS) is specific-purpose or customized computer software that uses a structured approach to organize data; DBMS directs the creation, addition, deletion, calculation, sorting, and combining of data from the various datafiles stored.
- The characteristics of a DBMS are that it is an organized, integrated collection of data that can be accessed for a variety of applications; duplication of data are eliminated or limited.

QUESTIONS FOR REVIEW

1. What are the characteristics or features of an electronic records storage and retrieval system?
2. What is the importance of a records storage and retrieval system for electronic files?
3. What four factors must be considered in implementing an electronic records storage program?
4. What advantages does an electronic records storage system offer an organization? What disadvantages are there?
5. How do the five phases in the life cycle of records relate to electronic records?
6. What benefits are provided by optical character recognition (OCR) systems? What are the limitations of an OCR system?
7. What are the various methods by which information or data can be distributed within an organization?
8. Compare and contrast the four types of computers and their possible applications in records storage and retrieval.
9. Discuss the various types of magnetic media used to store data or information; compare and contrast their advantages and any disadvantages.
10. What guidelines should be followed for the protection and care of electronic records and the magnetic media on which records are stored?

THE DECISION MAKER

Case Study

You work for Gibbs Public Enterprises, which has created and stored all its documents on microcomputers using commercial word processing, database management, and accounting applications software. The company's records include correspondence, reports, meeting agendas and minutes, employee handbooks and procedures manuals, budget and other financial statements, payroll and personnel records, names and addresses of clients and area government agencies, and current and old government reports, and advertising brochures. The company has thus far accumulated all its records on floppy disks.

Part 1: Assist the Gibbs company in the following:

1. suggest ways in which the various types of information or data can be input efficiently;
2. suggest ways in which the different types of data or information stored on magnetic media can be identified/labeled;
3. suggest appropriate guidelines for using and charging out magnetic media;
4. determine the length of time various types of records should be retained;
5. suggest methods for protecting the records.

Part 2: Suggest appropriate records classification systems for the various types of records that must be stored by the Gibbs company (see Chapter 7). Create a chart outlining the appropriate systems selected. Prepare a memorandum justifying your choice of classification system(s) for the various types of records.

MANAGING VITAL RECORDS AND DISASTER RECOVERY

OBJECTIVES

Upon completion of this chapter, the student should be able to:

1. Identify the vital records of an organization.
2. Plan a vital records program.
3. Select the proper method of vital data storage.
4. Write a vital records manual.
5. Determine the procedure for evaluating a vital records program.
6. Identify factors to consider in disaster prevention planning.
7. List the key resources needed for effective disaster recovery.

"Earthquake Strikes San Francisco"
"Fire Destroys Research and Development Lab"
"Tornado Rips through Midwest"
"Flooding Causes Local Damage to Office Buildings"

Try to imagine some of the problems that a business organization might encounter because of the above headlines. Over the course of one year, the U.S. government declared parts of 15 states as federal disaster areas due to both natural and manmade catastrophes. What percentage of businesses recover and survive such disasters? According to the National Fire Protection Association, 40 percent of all corporations that lose their records due to fire, fail to survive the next business year. In a Texas survey, 43 percent of companies involved in a disaster never reopened and 29 percent closed within two years. In addition, only 15 percent of U.S. companies have workable disaster recovery plans and only 10–15 percent more are addressing this problem.[1]

Identification of Vital Records

If an office were destroyed by a natural or a human-caused disaster, which records would one consider absolutely essential for rebuilding the business? That question deserves serious thought. The records that are essential for the continuous operation of a business firm are identified as the **vital records.**

Among the vital records of an organization are the copyrights, leases, accounts receivable, tax returns, legal documents, formulas, bylaws, franchises, personnel records, licenses, and insurance policies. This list is by no means a complete listing of the vital records that are found in most organizations.

In addition to vital records, other records in an organization may be categorized as follows:

1. Important records
2. Useful records
3. Nonessential records

Important records, such as data banks on computer tapes, may take months to replace. Important records contribute to the smooth operation of a company and can be replaced or duplicated if lost or destroyed in a disaster. These records include documents that might be needed to support or prevent legal action on behalf of business; reports to be submitted to the government; financial statements such as audits, tax records, and general ledgers; microforms; and punched cards or magnetic tapes or disks.

[1]Annie Hoffman and Bryan Baumann, "Disaster Recovery—A Prevention Plan for NWNL," RECORDS MANAGEMENT QUARTERLY, April, 1986, pp. 40–44.

If these original records were lost or destroyed, chances are that copies of these records—or data that could be obtained to reconstruct these records—would be available. Although the loss or destruction of these essential records would create a temporary disruption in the company's operations, it would not affect its existence or create legal difficulties in its business dealings with the public or government agencies. Important records should be given the same protection as vital records, namely, fire-resistant vaults or fireproof cabinets.

Useful records are records that can be easily replaced; their loss would not prevent the organization from resuming business. Such records are not considered essential because the data can be obtained or verified from other sources, either within or outside the company. Requests for materials and the register of sales orders are examples of useful records.

Nonessential records are records that are not essential to the restoration of business and should be destroyed once their purpose has been fulfilled. Memorandums, correspondence, customer inquiries, mailing lists, order letters, dated books, brochures, and catalogs are examples of nonessential records. The loss or destruction of these records would pose no inconvenience to the company in case of a disaster.

Another more direct approach is to divide records into two basic categories: vital and non-vital. This method simplifies the decision making involved in differentiating between the four categories discussed above: vital, important, useful, and nonessential records. The use of the vital and non-vital groupings would place vital and important records into the former group while useful and nonessential records would be placed into the latter.

Potential Business Disasters

The need to protect records against potential business disasters makes it essential to maintain a viable records management program. The most obvious disasters that occur as so-called "acts of God" are depicted in Figure 10-1. Records need to be protected against floods, tornadoes, earthquakes, fires, and nuclear threats.

Records can also be threatened by such man-made hazards as theft, security leaks, and simple loss of records due to misplacement. Other everyday hazards that need to be guarded against include water, insects, rodents, mold, mildew, hazardous chemicals, light, dust, and improper temperature and humidity controls.

Need for Vital Records Protection

As indicated by the various categories of potential disasters that can befall records, vital records protection is obviously an everyday need. Such protection will enable an organization to resume operations quickly should a natural or man-made disaster occur.

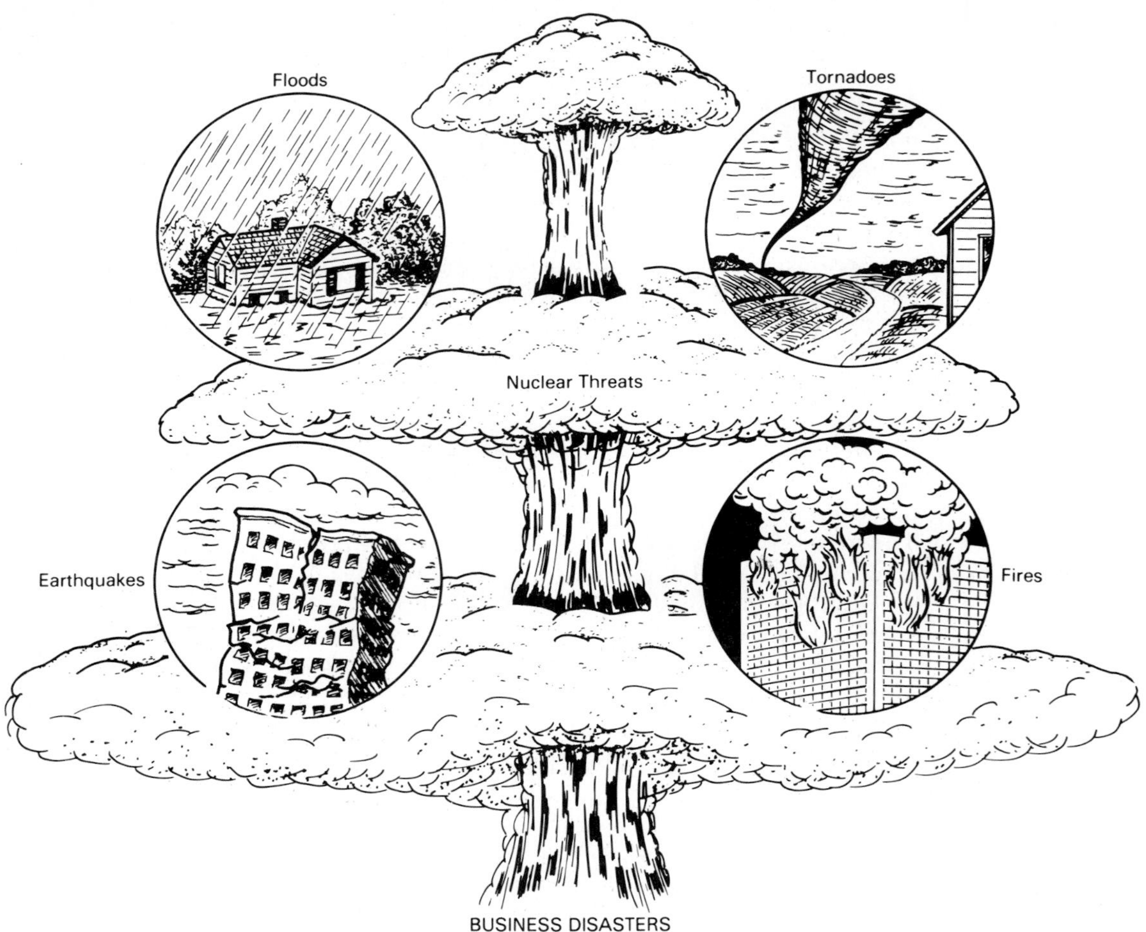

FIGURE 10-1
Potential business disasters. (Courtesy of ARMA, 4200 Somerset Drive, Suite 215, Prairie Village, KS 66208.)

Important reasons for vital records protection are as follows:

1. To resume operations of a business as expeditiously as possible
2. To reestablish the financial and legal status of a business
3. To fulfill obligations to employees, customers, stockholders, government agencies, and others

The need for such protection makes it necessary for management to establish a comprehensive plan for a vital records protection program.

Planning the Vital Records Program

Steps in Planning the Vital Records Program

The following steps are recommended in planning the vital records program:

1. Secure the approval and support of top management. The records manager should involve top management in all proposed changes or new programs. A top-level manager is more apt to support those changes in procedures that he or she has been apprised of. This support by top management is especially important when the records manager needs additional budget to implement changes in the records program.
2. Select one person from each department to be responsible for identifying the vital records generated by that department.
3. Determine the location for storing the vital records. Vital records may be stored in the active files area or in an off-site location. If off-site storage is to be used, careful consideration must be given to the selection of the facility and the location that will be adequate for the business organization.
4. Decide on the method of storing the data.

Once the decision is made on the method for storing the data, the vital records program can be implemented. The on-going system used for managing the active records may continue to be used for the control of the vital records. A document that is classified as vital does not need a different system from the active records unless confidentiality is a consideration. Secret coding may be used to protect certain vital records, such as blueprints, formulas, and personnel records.

The Vital Records Retention Schedule

The vital records of an organization should be described and recorded on a form like the vital records retention schedule shown in Figure 10-2. Note that this form is quite comprehensive and requests the following information:

1. Vital records code
2. Vital records title
3. Purpose of the vital record
4. Distribution of the vital record
5. Protection method or instructions for vital record
6. Frequency of submission of vital record
7. Retention period of vital record

VITAL RECORDS RETENTION SCHEDULE

DIVISION		DEPARTMENT			LOCATION	
V.R. CODE	VITAL RECORDS TITLE	PURPOSE	DISTRIBUTION	PROTECTION METHOD / INSTRUCTIONS	V. R. CENTER	
					SUBMIT	RETENTION

D = Daily W = Weekly BW = Every two weeks M = Monthly Q = Quarterly SA = Semiannually A = Annually C/R = Computer Report

DEPARTMENT CODE: ______

PAGE ____ OF ____

EFFECTIVE DATE: ______

FIGURE 10-2
Vital records retention schedule

The Vital Records Manual

Chapter 17 emphasizes the importance of the records manual for every organization. Whether an organization is large or small, the vital records manual is an important management tool. The **vital records manual** will identify the documents that are classified as vital. Also included in the vital records manual is the following information:

1. Method of data storage for different types of documents
2. Instructions for filling out the vital record deposit schedule
3. Location of vital records
4. Instructions for destruction of the vital records

Evaluation of the Vital Records Program

Just as schools conduct fire drills and the military simulates the battleground, so should records managers test their vital records programs to assess their effectiveness in case of an emergency. Simulated problems may be posed and answered with the personnel, equipment, and records that would be available at the time of an actual emergency. Any problems that are not solved satisfactorily should be analyzed to determine the cause. If the cause is the inability of the person to find the records, either the person needs further training or the system needs revision. The critical point is that the reason for the confusion or the unsolved problems must be determined and analyzed. Measures to correct the situation should be given top priority.

PLANNED PRESERVATION OF VITAL RECORDS

Protection Methods

Those records that are vital should be classified as such at the time of their creation, and special care must be taken to ensure that these records will be available in the event of a disaster. Since vital records may be active or inactive, vital records planning necessarily involves the availability of duplicate records.

Figure 10-3 illustrates the six basic forms of vital records protection. These protection methods are used in vital records planning and include:

1. *EXISTING DISPERSAL* — Dispersal is the practice of duplicating copies and storing them in another location. Built-in or existing dispersal occurs as a result of normal business operations. That is, vital record copies are stored in another location as a matter of procedure. Copies of a document that originates in a branch office, for example, are often stored in the home office.

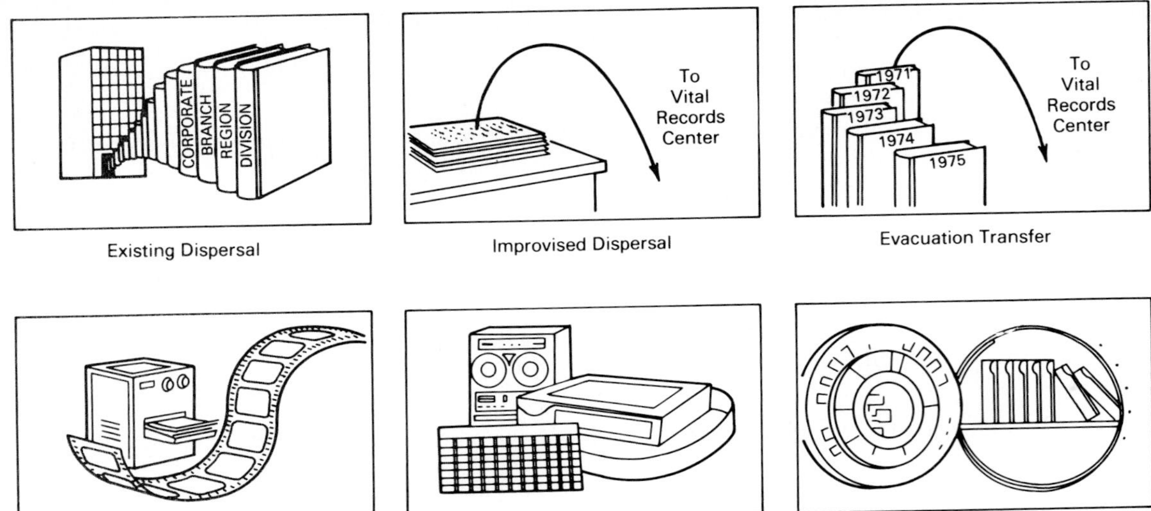

FIGURE 10-3
Preventive maintenance—methods of protection for vital records. (Courtesy of ARMA, 4200 Somerset Drive, Suite 215, Prairie Village, KS 66208.)

2. *IMPROVISED DISPERSAL* — This type of dispersal occurs by making an extra copy of a document for vital records protection. Thus, the duplication of an extra copy for storage in a second location is improvised dispersal. An example of this is the photocopying of formulas to be stored in an off-site location such as the Vital Records Center.
3. *EVACUATION TRANSFER* — The original source document of a vital record is transferred to the Vital Records Center for storage and protection in evacuation transfer. Thus, this protection method is for vital records that are referred to infrequently, but still considered vital. The original copy is evacuated to the vital records depository, and if limited reference is needed, no duplication is required.
4. *DUPLICATION* — This protection method for vital records simply insures that a second copy of a vital record is made. Such duplication may be made by electronic tape, floppy disk, microform, optical disk, or photocopy. The back-up is stored in the Vital Records Center.
5. *COM* — Another popular method of protection is computer-output microfil (COM), which permits information to go directly from computer tape to microfiche and requires limited storage space.
6. *VAULTING* — This method uses a heavy-duty combination lock vault to store vital records on site. Placing documents in a fire-resistant vault protects vital records from possible hazards.

TABLE 10-1 PROTECTION METHODS AGAINST NATURAL AND MAN-MADE HAZARDS

Hazard	*Recommended Protection*
Theft	Use security systems
Misplacement	Restrict or bar access to original record; use charge-out systems
Security leaks	Require individual identification; have authorized user access list
Water	Do not store vital records in basement areas; check for leaks in floors, walls, and ceilings
Insects, rodents	Maintain exterminator services; check for visible signs of damage
Mildew, mold, excessive humidity	Provide proper temperature range of 65–75° F; keep humidity in the 40–50 percent range
Dust	Use electric air cleaners to minimize dust damage; keep records securely enclosed
Light	Limit the number of windows and doors in the vital records center; use window covers that filter out bright sunlight.
Hazardous chemicals	Use only duplicates of vital records when working with such chemicals

Table 10-1 summarizes the recommended methods for protecting vital records from damage by either natural or man-made hazards.

Methods of Recording Data

In addition to the availability of records, another consideration in storing vital records is the method of recording data on one or more of several media, such as paper, magnetic tape, film, or floppy disks. Of these media, only paper has been available for more than a few decades, so paper is the only medium for which there is definite proof of longevity. Experts have estimated that a good quality of bond paper has a life expectancy of 200–300 years. For other media, however, extra precautions must be taken to protect the data from deterioration. According to the National Bureau of Standards, tapes that are stored from 1 to 7 years can be expected to show varying degrees of error. Tapes can be severely damaged by high temperatures and high humidity, and may also be damaged by storing them near electrical fixtures. Because tapes are so vulnerable, it is risky to have vital information preserved exclusively on tapes. A precautionary measure is to have a **back-up copy** of vital information in readable language also, preferably on microforms. A **microform** is a form that contains microimages, such as microfiche, roll film, or an aperture card. Chapter 15 explains the various microforms in detail.

Microforms as a Back-Up Source

A microform has several advantages as a back-up source of vital data. Microforms, one of the best media for long-term retention of vital data, require minimum storage space. Because of this factor, microform copies may be stored easily in different locations. In one instance, bank personnel were unaware of the danger of storing duplicate microform copies of vital records in the same room with the original documents. A fire, earthquake, bomb, or flood could wipe out all traces of the vital records when stored in such proximity. The bank personnel were advised to move the back-up copies to an off-site location for greater security. Duplicate copies of microforms may be made simultaneously at a fraction of the cost of the original microform.

Protection of EDP Files

Protection of electronic data processing vital files and tapes is important not only for the information they contain, but also for the time involved in getting the data processing applications on-line again. A time lapse ranging from 3 months to 11 months may be necessary to reconstruct vital EDP files from raw data, depending on the size and type of the organization. In a very active organization, catching up might prove difficult, if not impossible, because of new data generated daily.

An article titled, "Avoiding Electronic Media Disasters," in the RECORDS MANAGEMENT QUARTERLY, stresses the importance of storing magnetic media in fireproof data safes. The author cites fire protection as the primary data safe benefit, since such data are vulnerable to heat and flame. According to the author, diskettes become distorted and unreadable at 125 degrees, tapes at 130 while paper doesn't smolder until the temperature reaches 350 degrees. Such data safes allow you to keep magnetic media close at hand yet protected from disasters.[2]

Equipment for Housing Vital Records

According to experts, only about 2 percent of an organization's records are vital. In a small organization, the vital records may occupy a small percentage of office space and might be housed in the active file area. Even so, care must be taken to protect these records from the hazards mentioned earlier. The ordinary steel file cabinet will not provide adequate protection. Insulated files with seamless steel exteriors will help to protect irreplaceable records from fire. See Figure 10-4 for an example of the type of insulated file cabinet that is available in 4-, 3-, and 2-drawer models, with either letter- or legal-size capacity. Notice the insulation between the drawers of the cabinet.

[2]Van G. Carlisle, "Avoiding Electronic Media Disasters," *Records Management Quarterly*, January, 1986, pp. 42–43.

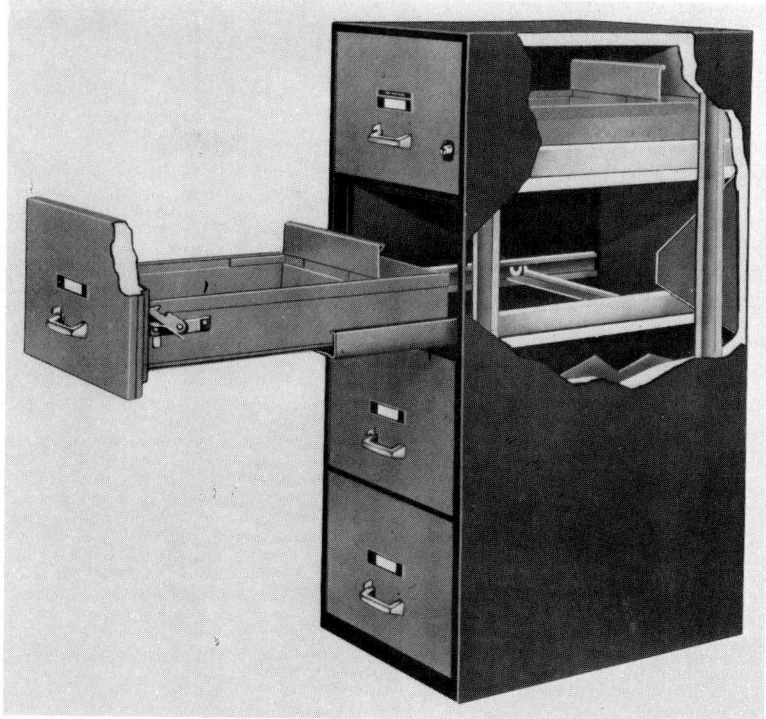

FIGURE 10-4 Insulated file cabinet. (Courtesy of Diebold Incorporated.)

The file room that houses vital records must be kept free of combustible materials. Insulated file cabinets should be used for vital record storage, since standard steel file cabinets do not provide fire protection. In fact, the metal conducts heat rapidly to paper records inside, which char at about 350°F (162°C). Figure 10-5 shows an insulated lateral file cabinet. These insulated file cabinets pass the Underwriters' Laboratories test with the temperature carried to the one-hour 1700°F (912°C) point. In this test, the file remains in the closed furnace until cool. The file cabinet passes the test if the interior temperature remains below 350° F (162° C) and papers inside the file can be handled without breaking and are not charred. An important point to remember after a fire is to leave file drawers closed until the contents have cooled. A file drawer that is opened before the contents have cooled may burst into flames.

Location of Vital Records Storage

On-Site Storage Vital records may be stored on-site in the organization's file rooms or in vaults. A small organization with few vital records may find that a **safe deposit vault** affords adequate storage. An organization with a large volume of records may store its vital records in a **record vault** that has been constructed with fireproof materials.

FIGURE 10-5 Insulated lateral file cabinet. (Courtesy of Diebold Incorporated.)

Underground storage of vital records is becoming popular because of greater security provided the documents. Figure 10-6 shows an underground vault that is carved out of rock. Microfilm is housed in the underground facility shown in Figure 10-7.

Off-Site Storage Off-site storage for vital records offers the following advantages:

1. The location is often in a lower-rent area than the office.
2. The security of the records is usually much greater in off-site storage facilities.
3. The responsibility for the maintenance and control of the vital records will be more clearly assigned to an individual.

Careful consideration should be given to selecting the most appropriate site because of the importance of vital records in reorganizing an organization's operations after a disaster.

FIGURE 10-6 Underground vault. (Courtesy of National Underground Storage.)

FIGURE 10-7 Microfilm vault. (Courtesy of National Underground Storage.)

Disaster Prevention Planning

Webster's Dictionary defines a "disaster" as an unforeseen mischance bringing with it destruction of life or property or utter defeat.[3] Another publication defines a disaster as a "sudden or great misfortune" or simply "any unfortunate event." To be more precise, a disaster is "an event whose timing is unexpected and whose consequences are seriously destructive."[4]

Disaster planning goes beyond vital records identification and scheduling; it details a workable plan that protects and/or reconstructs vital company records. Such a plan insures that an organization will survive a disastrous event and resume or continue operations as quickly as possible following a disaster.

Disaster Types. As indicated in Table 10-1 and Figure 10-1, disasters can be categorized into "Acts of God" and "Natural or Man-Made Hazards." An ARMA publication on DISASTER PREVENTION AND RECOVERY divides disasters into the following categories:[5]

Acts of God—Hurricanes, volcanic eruptions, earthquakes, tornadoes, heavy storms, snow, lightning, hail, cyclones, and erratic weather patterns.

Building/equipment failure or malfunction—refer to the causes of fire and flooding: leaky roofs, broken pipes, defective wiring or switches, faulty machinery or equipment, broken heating or cooling systems, electrical outages and malfunctions.

Acts of deliberate destructiveness—theft, espionage, vandalism, terrorism, and war. Theft is a common problem that most organizations need to address. Most of these acts can be significantly reduced by effective security measures.

Human error or carelessness—smoldering cigarettes, unattended stoves, open windows, unlocked doors, negligent storage of flammable materials, and careless computer errors.

Disaster Team. The formation of a disaster prevention/recovery team is recommended to insure the plan's successful operation. The committee members may include the following: Records/Information Manager, Corporate Attorneys, Vice-President of Administration, and Functional Department Heads. The team members are given specific responsibilities and the appropriate authority to activate their portion of the plan. Team members should be identified by job title rather than name to eliminate plan revisions when individuals leave the company due to resignations, terminations, or retirement.

[3]Webster's Dictionary.

[4]Hilda Bohem, DISASTER PREVENTION AND DISASTER PREPAREDNESS (Berkeley: University of California, 1978), p. 1.

[5]Susan L. Bulawicz and Charles E. Nolan, DISASTER PREVENTION AND RECOVERY: A PLANNED APPROACH. ARMA: 1988, pp. 4–21. Courtesy of ARMA International.

Disaster Planning Elements. According to CRMs Bulgawicz and Nolan, the key elements of the disaster prevention plan include:

1. Clear policy statement establishing the plan and its authority;
2. Clear activation authority: WHO is in charge of implementing the disaster prevention plan;
3. Task organization (organization of disaster prevention team);
4. Establishment of information distribution procedures;
5. Monitoring of destructive forces (initial and periodic review of local disasters).
6. Provisions for employee training;
7. Provisions for ongoing review and revision.[6]

Disaster Recovery Planning

Like disaster prevention planning, disaster recovery planning results in a detailed set of procedures that can be put into effect immediately after a disaster occurs. Such a plan is an insurance policy that one hopes never has to be used. According to Balon and Gardner, two records managers who survived several disasters, the key to such a plan is the resource list. Such lists should include:

Insurance agent contacts
Freeze-drying/vacuum-drying facilities
Transportation companies
Salvage equipment
Experts—both in-house and external
Department contacts—both home and work numbers
Floor plans of the records buildings[7]

The overall objective of the Disaster Recovery Plan is the resumption of business as soon as possible. For this to occur, reconstruction and salvage operations following a disaster must commence immediately. Thus, the time for planning for disaster recovery is before the disaster occurs—not after. The old saying, "an ounce of prevention is worth a pound of cure" is certainly applicable to disaster and recovery planning.

[6]Susan L. Bulawicz and Charles E. Nolan, DISASTER PREVENTION AND RECOVERY: A PLANNED APPROACH. ARMA: 1988, pp. 4–21. Courtesy of ARMA International.

[7]Brett J. Balon and H. Wayne Gardner, "Disaster Contingency Planning: The Basic Elements," RECORDS MANAGEMENT QUARTERLY, January, 1987, pp. 14–16.

Disaster Recovery Elements Disaster experts recommend certain key components be included in the disaster plan if disaster recovery is going to be successful. Such elements include:[8]

A current inventory of all company records, including vital records.

Designation of alternative operating locations.

A current inventory of all information processing and communications equipment.

Priority list for restoration of essential functions.

Contracts and agreements with disaster support agencies.

A list of disaster salvage equipment and supplies.

Document Restoration Restoration companies offer a full range of services to companies in need. Such services vary from company to company but the following services are generally available: reproduction, deodorization, fumigation, damage assessement, inventory, packing, blast freezing, shipping, and freeze-drying.

BMS CAT, a document restoration company, offers all of the above services on a 24 hour a day basis, nationwide. This company recommends both blast freezing and freeze-drying to prevent damage from mold and mildew due to water damage. Blast freezing minimizes the size of ice particles in documents. Freeze-drying removes frozen water before it can return to the liquid state. Freeze-drying is considered the safest procedure because the liquid state of water is the most damaging state.[9]

Restoration companies offer freeze-drying chambers to restore water-damaged documents. Such a chamber is shown in Figure 10-8. In addition, freeze-drying prevents ink from running and photos from sticking together.

Freezing will prevent mold from growing and further deterioration from water. Once frozen, books can be stored in a freezer for as long as ten years and then thawed and air-dried with no extensive damage. Since freezing is an intermediate stage, air-drying is the next step in the document restoration process. Air-drying is an extensive process which varies depending on the degree of wetness and the type of documents being dried. Air-drying should only be done in a stable environment where the temperature is 50–60 degrees to inhibit the growth of fungi. Again, salvage and/or restoration companies provide this service for damaged files, books, and documents.

[8]Susan L. Bulgawicz and Charles E. Nolan, "DISASTER PREVENTION AND RECOVERY: A PLANNED APPROACH, ARMA, 1988. Courtesy of ARMA International.

[9]BMS Catastrophe, Fort Worth, Texas.

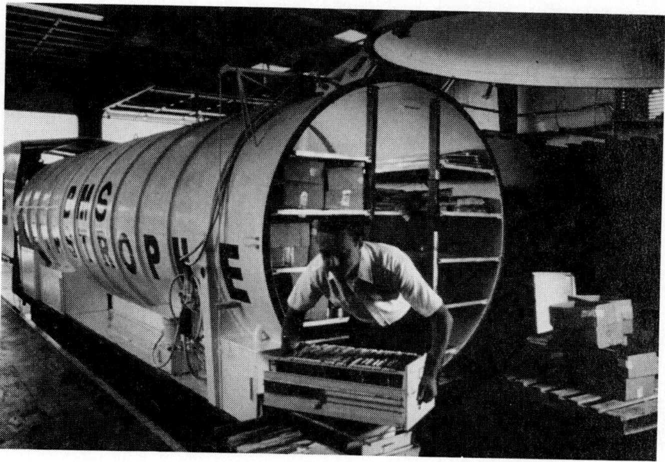

FIGURE 10-8 (Courtesy of BMS Catastrophe, Fort Worth, Texas.)

CHAPTER HIGHLIGHTS

- Vital records are the records that are essential for the continuous operation of a business in the event of a disaster; other categories of records include important, useful, and nonessential records.
- Vital records may be active or inactive, and it is essential that duplicate copies be made available to users of the vital records.
- Microforms are good media for long-term retention of vital data, and they require very little storage space.
- All the vital records of an organization should be listed and described, including protection requirements, on the vital records retention schedule.
- The vital records program should be evaluated annually to ensure its effectiveness in case of an emergency.
- Vital records need to be protected against "Acts of God" as well as man-made hazards and natural hazards.
- Protection methods for vital records include existing dispersal, improvised dispersal, evacuation transfer, duplication, COM, and vaulting.
- Disaster prevention planning details a workable plan that protects and/or reconstructs vital company records in the event of a disastrous event.
- Disaster recovery planning details a workable plan that facilitates the resumption of business operations as soon as possible following a disaster.
- Disaster restoration companies offer services such as reproduction, deodorization, fumigation, damage assessment, inventory, packing, blast freezing, shipping, and freeze-drying.

QUESTIONS FOR REVIEW

1. Define the term *vital records* and identify specific vital records that are found in most business organizations.
2. Discuss the four classes of records and the fire protection requirements for each class.
3. Besides "acts of God," what human-caused hazards must records be protected from?
4. What steps are recommended in planning the vital records program?
5. Describe the various protection methods that can be used in a vital records program.
6. Describe the vital records retention schedule including the types of information that should be recorded on it.
7. Define the term "disaster" and describe what is included in disaster prevention planning.
8. List the key elements of disaster prevention planning.
9. Identify disaster recovery planning including a typical resource list.
10. Describe the difference between blast freezing and freeze drying.

THE DECISION MAKER

Case Studies

1. Turner's Travel Agency, in business since 1951, has no vital records protection plan. The second-generation owner and manager is Devon Turner, the daughter of founder Thomas Turner. Devon is a good manager and "people person"; however, she is lacking in records management "know-how." She hires your consulting agency to set up a vital records protection plan for Turner Travel. Prepare a report of your recommendations for Devon including recommended protection methods and location of vital records storage.
2. College professors at a leading New England University have been involved in a ten-year longitudinal research project on twins since the early 1980s. Recently, the Education Building was damaged by fire. Many professors lost valuable research documents and notes. In hindsight, what disaster prevention and recovery procedures could you recommend to overcome a similar disaster in the future?

PLANNING AND MANAGING THE RECORDS CENTER

OBJECTIVES

Upon completion of this chapter, the student should be able to:

1. Identify factors to consider in selecting a records center.
2. Describe both the stack and nonstack areas of a records center.
3. Explain records transfer procedures.
4. List various space numbering systems that can be utilized in a records center.
5. Justify the computerization of inactive records.
6. Detail the services offered by commercial records centers.

The storage of inactive records in records centers appears to be a growing trend in both the public and private sectors of business. A 1985 national study of records managers reported that 72 percent had included records center operations in their records management responsibilities. Why have records centers grown in popularity? Answer: simple cost savings. When records are stored in a well-run records center, the cost savings can literally add up to thousands of dollars per year.

By 1994, our nation's files and storage facilities will contain over 46 trillion documents—over 90 percent of it on paper. In addition, federal, state, and local governments alone spend nearly $600 million a year to create, store, retrieve and manage their records.[1]

The Records Center

A **records center** is a low-cost storage facility for housing the inactive and semi-active records of an organization. Some companies also house their vital records and/or archives in the records center. Records centers may be in-house, either on-premises or off-premises, or in commercial storage. Figure 11-1 shows the various types of records centers available to business organizations. Obviously, there are records centers with different purposes and in different locations.

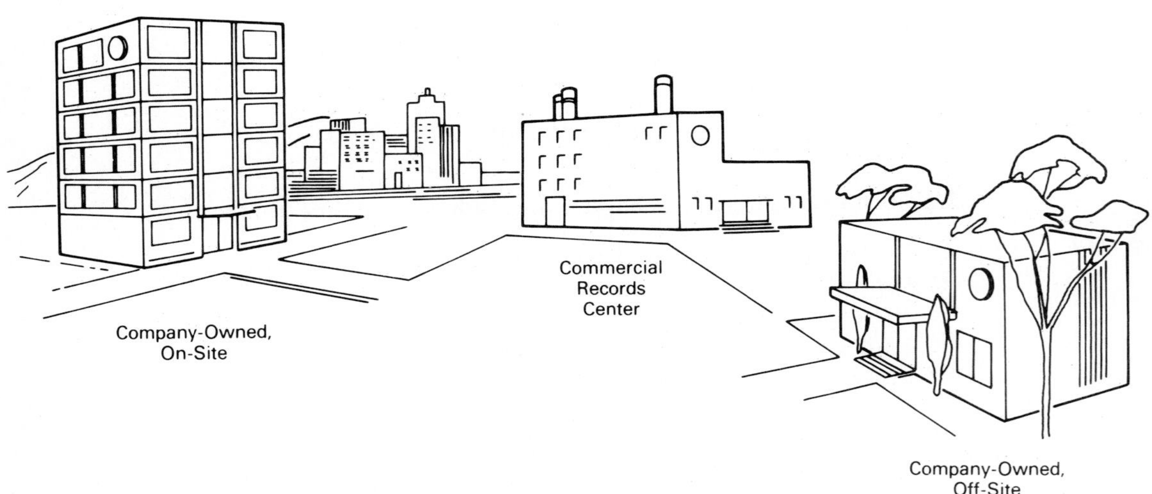

FIGURE 11-1
Types of record centers. (Courtesy of ARMA, 4200 Somerset Drive, Suite 215, Prairie Village, KS 66208.)

[1]Borroughs Manufacturing Corporation, 1990.

Regardless of the type or location of the records center, its main purpose is to provide low-cost storage of inactive records to protect the legal and financial integrity of an organization and to maintain its operating flexibility.

Table 11-1 illustrates the cost savings from transferring eight storage cartons to inactive storage for a period of one year. The yearly savings for these cartons is $168.36.

Company-Owned Records Centers

Two main purposes for creating a *company-owned records center* are:

1. To reduce the amount of records held in high-rent office space
2. To reduce the amount of equipment needed to store records in offices

Other purposes for creating records centers are: (1) to have an effective storage and retrieval system, and (2) to set up a comprehensive records transfer and storage program with destruction schedules.

An in-house records center is often found in the basement or storage area of an office or in a warehouse adjacent to the office area. One of the greatest advantages of the in-house records center is the convenience of the location. However, other factors are as important as accessibility: security of the records, proper lighting, and proper ventilation.

If an off-site company-owned records center is desired, the location should be convenient for parts of the organization that send personnel to store and retrieve documents. Moving records from offices to the center and retrieving them again both involve considerable transportation and personnel costs. The associated costs, as well as the location itself, should be considered when selecting the site.

TABLE 11-1 COST COMPARISON OF ACTIVE VS. INACTIVE RECORDS STORAGE FOR ONE YEAR

Active Storage		*Inactive Storage*	
Equipment Costs:		Equipment Costs:	
Five-drawer file cabinet ($250 depreciated at $25 per year)	$ 25.00	1/8 of steel shelf to hold storage cartons ($175 shelf depreciated at $17.50 per year)	$ 2.19
		8 storage cartons	20.00
Floor Space and Overhead Cost:		Floor Space and Overhead Cost:	
5 3/4 square feet of floor space at $33 per square foot plus overhead expense	189.75	2 2/10 square feet of floor space at $11 per square foot plus overhead expense	24.20
Total Cost	$214.75		$46.39

Yearly Difference: $168.36 ($214.75–$46.39)

Source: Eleanor Hollis Tedesco and Robert B. Mitchell, *Administrative Office Management: The Electronic Office* (New York: John Wiley & Sons, Inc., 1984), p. 469.

Planning the Records Center

A well-thought-out plan is needed in order for the records center to accomplish its purpose. The purpose and scope of the center should be defined and the responsibilities of the personnel established. Included in the planning stage is the physical inventory of all records. The inventory identifies the location of the records as well as the type and volume.

After the inventory is completed, the records identified as inactive can be transferred to the company records center, following the procedures outlined in the records management manual. Detailed instructions must be given in the manual to ensure the uniformity of procedures for all departments of an organization.

The Storage Facility

A facility selected for the storage of records must provide security. Records must be protected from moisture, rodents, dust, fire, heat, humidity, and, of course, unauthorized access. Smoke alarms, fire doors, fire alarms, fire extinguishers, and automatic sprinkler systems afford a measure of protection for the records. Infrared heat sensors and silent alarms are used by some centers as further safeguards.

Adequate lighting and ventilation are required for a records center. Proper lighting helps to prevent accidents, does away with dark corners, and helps to keep filing mistakes to a minimum. Good ventilation, of course, aids both employee working conditions and proper records protection by helping to reduce moisture. Heat and moisture promote the growth of fungi. Air conditioning systems provide temperature and humidity control, where needed. An ideal temperature of 65° to 75°F (3° to 8°C) with a humidity range of 30 to 60 percent is easily controlled in an air-conditioned facility. Any electrically operated equipment in the center should have back-up battery power. In addition, ventilation should include a manual switch to outside air that could be used for smoke removal in the event of a fire.

The records center should be constructed of concrete block and functional in arrangement. The site should be easily accessible by motor vehicle and large enough to include parking space. Storage areas should be partitioned off from other areas of the structure by four-hour fire-resistive walls. Other factors to consider in selecting an off-site storage center will depend largely on the varying needs of the organization. There may be need for a proper storage area for disposal of records, telephone service, duplicating services, and microfilming services.

Physical Layout of the Records Center

A records center consists of two major areas: the stack area and the nonstack areas. The stack area is the place where the inactive records are actually stored. Nonstack areas are primarily administrative and processing areas designed to facilitate the efficient and economical storage of inactive records.

Although many variations occur in company-owned records centers, the following nonstack areas are recommended for a well-equipped records center:

1. *ADMINISTRATIVE AREA* — Office space must be provided to enable records center personnel to perform the tasks required of them. As a rule of thumb, approximately 100 square feet per person should be adequate office space. The offices should be equipped with desks, chairs, telephones, filing cabinets, and indexing devices that facilitate the maintenance of records in the center. In addition, many companies install personal computers in employees' offices, so they can maintain computerized indexes of records stored in the center.
2. *RECEIVING/PROCESSING AREA* — Situated near the loading dock, the receiving area provides temporary storage for records as they are brought into the records center. Owing to work schedules and other limitations, many records will not be shelved immediately. Thus, many centers use the term *processing area* to refer to the area where records are accounted for and assigned a permanent address for placement in the stack area. Some companies have separate receiving and processing areas if sufficient space is available in the records center.
3. *STAGING AREA* — Some companies have an intermediate storage area, called a staging area, where boxes are stored after being accounted for in the receiving/processing area. This area can also be used as a preparation area particularly when large deliveries have been received and additional temporary storage space is needed. The staging area should be adjacent to the receiving area.
4. *REFERENCE AREA* — Once records are located in the stack areas, space must be provided for reference to inactive records. A reference area provides users with a mini-library, with tables, chairs, copiers, and microfilm readers/printers for reviewing inactive records.
5. *DESTRUCTION/DISPOSITION AREA* — Another necessity in a records center is a separate destruction/disposition area for records that have reached the end of their life cycles, according to the records retention schedule. Some companies opt to destroy records on-site; in these firms, a shredder and bailer would be situated in this area. Other companies prefer to contract out to scrap-paper dealers and others who provide destruction of records. The ideal location for this area is adjacent to the loading dock.

The layout of the records center is a key factor in using space efficiently. Floor space and ceiling heights should be used to their fullest extent. When records are stored in active office areas, one square foot of floor space is required for each cubic foot of records stored. Ideally, when records are stored

TABLE 11-2 RATIO OF CUBIC FEET OF STORED RECORD TO SQUARE FEET OF FLOOR SPACE

Stack Height	*Ratio*
Typical office file cabinet	1.0 to 1
8-foot stacks	2.7 to 1
10-foot stacks	3.3 to 1
12-foot stacks	3.9 to 1
14-foot stacks	4.5 to 1

in a records center, the ratio of cubic feet to square feet is increased to provide additional storage capacity.

Table 11-2 shows the ratio of cubic feet of records stored to square feet of floor space. As ceiling heights and stack heights increase, a corresponding increase in storage space occurs, while the actual floor space required to store records decreases. As stack heights increase, floor strength must be considered. A typical filled records center carton weighs 30–50 pounds; an engineer's appraisal may be required before stacks as high as 14 feet are permitted. Figure 11-2 shows a well-designed records center.

Records Center Equipment

In the stack area of a records center, steel shelving is normally used to hold the storage boxes in a functional manner (see Figure 11-2). The steel shelves of each unit usually measure 30 or 32 inches in depth and 42 inches in length and accommodate six single-stacked or 12 double-stacked cartons per shelf. Shelving units are normally arranged back to back in duplex arrangement. Although the size of the records center dictates the length of the rows of steel shelving, care should be taken to avoid excessively long rows. Shorter rows allow more efficient movement and improve traffic patterns. Side aisles between rows of shelving should be approximately 30–36 inches wide and main aisles, which need to accommodate movable carts and trucks, should be 5–7 feet wide.

Storage containers should be stacked no higher than 72 inches unless the proper types of ladders are available. If a platform-type safety ladder is used, boxes may be stacked higher if a suitable structure supports the boxes. Before stacking records, the floor should be tested to determine its load-bearing capacity. Some centers have developed the mezzanine approach to solve their height problem. With this concept, walk space and stairs are built up at 6-foot intervals, providing safe working conditions. Others have built their storage areas as high as 50–75 feet, with operators riding electrically operated lifts, moving between rows to store and retrieve boxes.

In determining the type of container to use in storing a company's valuable records, the records manager should look at the protection factors for each alternative. Steel file cabinets provide excellent security, but are not fireproof. Although the cabinet does not burn, it acts as an oven; and at 350°F (162°C)

FIGURE 11-2
Records center. (Courtesy of National Underground Storage.)

the contents of the file cabinet will catch on fire and burn. Metal file cabinets, however, are the best protection against dust and rodents.

Corrugated fiberboard boxes or transfer files have been known to provide a certain amount of protection against fire, water, and dust. Metal file cabinets are more costly than transfer file boxes and cannot be moved or transferred as easily. Metal file cabinets are usually considered relatively permanent.

A distinct advantage of the fiberboard boxes is that when the destruction date arrives, the entire contents, together with the container, can be disposed of at once. Much of the material can be sold to a salvage company, if the contents are not confidential. Storage boxes like those shown in Figure 11-3 are available in both letter and legal size. The boxes shown are called the Ecologic series from Bankers Box and are made from recycled materials—an important trend in the storage field.

RECORDS CENTER PROCEDURES

Records Transfer

Records that are ready for transfer to the records center are packed in either standard or nonstandard containers, depending on their size and shape (see Figure 11-4).

ECOLOGIC 772
ECOLOGIC 771

FIGURE 11-3
Ecological series storage boxes. (Courtesy of Bankers Box.)

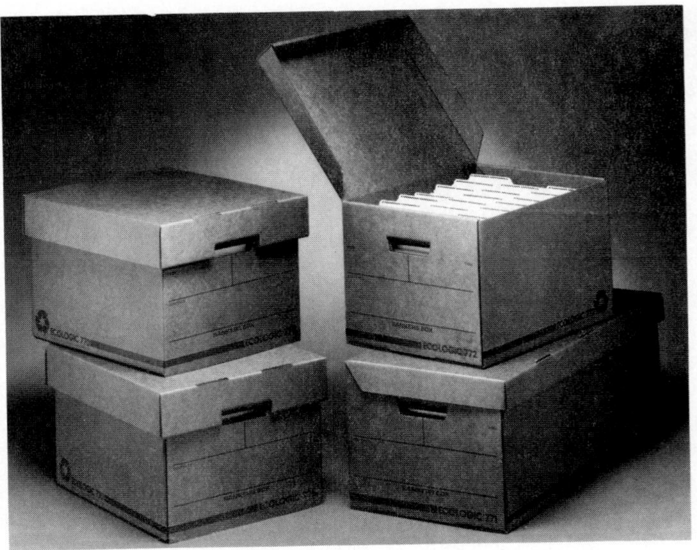

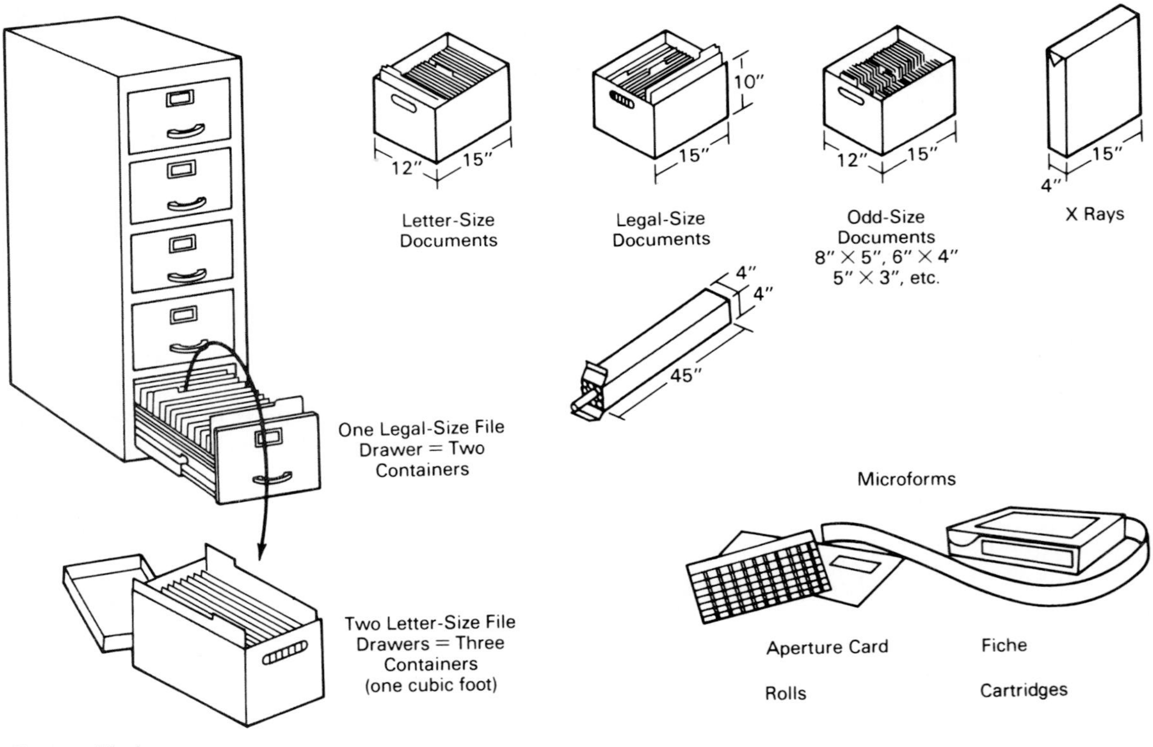

12″
15″
Letter-Size Documents
10″
15″
Legal-Size Documents
12″
15″
Odd-Size Documents 8″ × 5″, 6″ × 4″ 5″ × 3″, etc.
4″
15″
X Rays
4″
4″
45″
One Legal-Size File Drawer = Two Containers
Two Letter-Size File Drawers = Three Containers (one cubic foot)
Microforms
Aperture Card
Fiche
Rolls
Cartridges

FIGURE 11-4
Transferring records using standard containers. (Courtesy of ARMA, 4200 Somerset Drive, Suite 215, Prairie Village, KS 66208.)

The New Jersey State Records Center issues the following packing guidelines to its state agencies regarding the proper packing of records into records storage boxes:[2]

1. Records should be packed in the same order as they are filed in the agency.
2. All records in each box should belong to the same record series.
3. All records in each box must have the same retention period.
4. About one inch of space should be left in each box to facilitate referencing.
5. Records should not be placed on top of other records in the box.
6. The weight of each box should not exceed 35 pounds.
7. Records should face the long (15 inch) side of the box; letter size records may face the short (12 inch) end of the box to make use of available space in the back of the box. See Figure 11-5.

After the records are packed in the records storage containers, a transfer list must be prepared by the office that is transferring the records. A Records Transfer Request Form is shown in Figure 11-6. The transfer list will show the name of the office or department, the title of the records series, the records description, the inclusive dates, access restrictions, personnel contacts, and disposition dates. A records center may provide pickup service; if not, transmitting the records to the center may be the responsibility of the mail department. In either case, the cartons are coded at the center and assigned a space that bears the same code. This code is generally noted on the Records Transfer List as shown in Item 16, Figure 11-6. A copy of this form is retained by the issuing department or agency.

Some records centers establish criteria such as the following for accepting records in an inactive storage facility:

The Records Storage Center will accept only those records which:

1. appear on an approved Records Retention Schedule.
2. are scheduled for temporary storage in the Records Storage Center for at least one year.
3. are properly identified and documented for transfer and reference.
4. are properly packed in standard Records Storage Center boxes.
5. have a specific date (month/year) when disposition may take place.

Space Numbering

In order to control records housed in the center, a space-numbering system must be developed. Each unit that is accessioned should be assigned a space number for easy retrieval. Each row of shelving is identified by a number or a

[2]New Jersey State Records Center

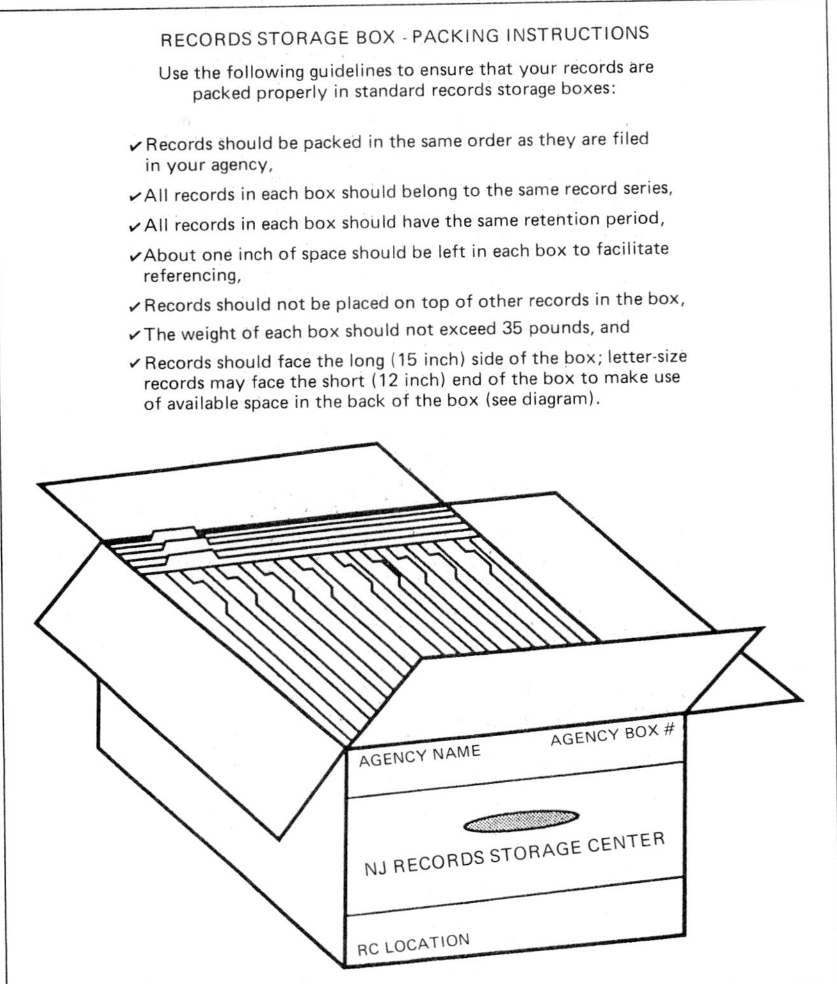
RECORDS STORAGE BOX - PACKING INSTRUCTIONS

Use the following guidelines to ensure that your records are packed properly in standard records storage boxes:

- ✓ Records should be packed in the same order as they are filed in your agency,
- ✓ All records in each box should belong to the same record series,
- ✓ All records in each box should have the same retention period,
- ✓ About one inch of space should be left in each box to facilitate referencing,
- ✓ Records should not be placed on top of other records in the box,
- ✓ The weight of each box should not exceed 35 pounds, and
- ✓ Records should face the long (15 inch) side of the box; letter-size records may face the short (12 inch) end of the box to make use of available space in the back of the box (see diagram).

FIGURE 11-5 Records storage box. (Courtesy of New Jersey State, Division of Archives and Records Management.)

letter and a number combination. This code is posted on the end of the row so that it can be easily identified. Spaces within the row are also numbered and, as a result, proper coding enables personnel to file and retrieve efficiently.

The following space-numbering systems may be used:

1. Row/space numbering
2. Row/shelf/space numbering
3. Row/unit/shelf/space numbering
4. Continuous or sequential numbering

Page _____ of _____

RECORDS TRANSFER REQUEST

1. **Agency Number**	2. **Schedule Number**	3. Record Series No.	4. Record Series Title	5. Date Completed

6. Department	7. Division	8. Bureau	DISPOSITION CODES
9. Person To Contact	10. Title	11. (Area Code) Telephone No.	R - Recycle S - Shred A - Archives D - Destroy
12. Location of Records	13. Access Restriction	14. Statutory Authority	

17. Agency Box Number	18. Description of Box Contents (Year, Range)	15. Disposition: Date (Month/Year)	15. Disposition: Code	**16. Records Center Location Number**

19. **Received By**	20. **Title**	21. **Date Received**	22. **Remarks**

CR-AA-0010-XX-(1/84) DEPARTMENT OF STATE, DIVISION OF ARCHIVES AND RECORDS MANAGEMENT

FIGURE 11-6

Figure 11-7 illustrates the various numbering systems that can be used to assign an "address" to each records storage box that enters the records center.

Charge-Out Procedures

One of the hard-and-fast rules concerning records is never to remove documents without recording the name of the borrower and the due date of the records. This is an equally important rule in a records center where the personnel are responsible for huge volumes of records.

The charge-out form is prepared in triplicate. The first copy is placed in the file as a substitute for the original record; the second copy is attached to the document to remind the borrower of the due date; and the third copy is kept in a suspense file for follow-up purposes.

Instead of sending the actual document from the container or the file, the center personnel may send a microimage or a duplicate copy to the borrower. In that case, no charge-out form is needed. This is especially effective when a vital record is requested. The integrity of the files and the records center are preserved through careful policing of the records and their containers. If for some reason duplicate vital records cannot be given to a borrower, a time limit of 24 hours should be placed on the use of the document. As mentioned earlier in this chapter, vital documents should have duplicate copies on file. Even

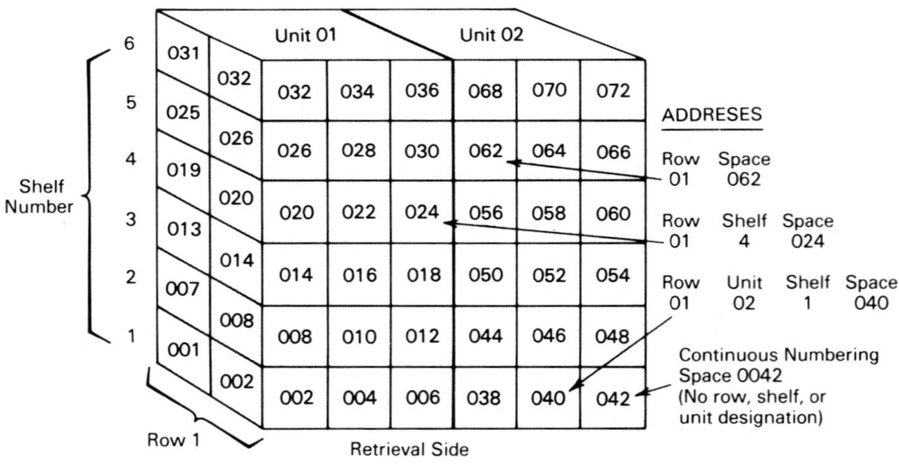

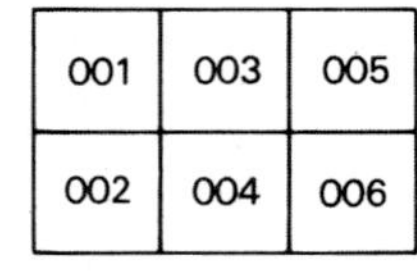

FIGURE 11-7 Space numbering systems.

so, the importance of the security of the duplicate copies cannot be overstressed.

A reference service request form used by the State of New Jersey is shown in Figure 11-8. Note that the request does not have to be made in person but can be phoned or mailed into the center.

Refiling and Interfiling

The **refiling** process is the same in the records center as in the office files. After a borrower is finished with a document, it is returned to the records center to be restored to the place from which it was removed. **Interfiling,** on the other hand, is the procedure of placing records within containers that have previously been accessioned. This process is difficult, especially if space in the container is limited. Ideally, of course, units will be complete upon the accessioning and no interfiling will be necessary.

AUTOMATED RECORDS CENTERS

A records center is an ideal application for computerization of records. Such automation provides records managers with a cost-effective way to track inactive records. The essential ingredient to successful automation of any records center is selecting the correct hardware and software. Corporate standards may dictate the type of equipment allocated for departmental use; this does make the selection process easier. Microcomputers or personal computers with fixed disk storage are generally recommended.

Selecting software for the records center computerization is usually a more time-consuming task. Various computer software packages should be reviewed, and specific criteria for adoption should be established. Such criteria might include:

1. Ease of Learning. Does the software provide help screens or on-screen menus?
2. Ease of Use. Will extensive operator training be necessary? Are user manuals easy to understand?
3. Vendor Support. Is on-site training included? Is an 800 number available?

Sophisticated PC based records management software is available for purchase for inactive records centers. Appendix E lists records management software that is currently available for many records management applications. In addition, general purpose applications software, specifically database software, can be utilized for records centers. This software is designed to simplify data collection tasks. Once a database is established, reports can be generated as needed.

FIGURE 11-8
Reference service request. (Courtesy of Division of Archives and Records Management, Department of State, State of New Jersey.)

707-20(Rev.2/83) No. 1900 Form 2 (1/83)

BUREAU OF RECORDS MANAGEMENT SERVICES
RECORDS STORAGE CENTER
CN 502, 2300 STUYVESANT AVE
TRENTON, N.J. 08625
(609) 633-7373, 633-7370

REFERENCE SERVICE REQUEST

AGENCY NAME AND ADDRESS		AGENCY NO.
REQUESTED BY		
AUTHORIZATION NO.	DATE REQUESTED	TELEPHONE NO.
RECORD SERIES TITLE		
DESCRIPTION OF REQUESTED FILE, DOCUMENT, ETC.		
RECORD CENTER LOCATION NO.		
RECEIVED BY (SIGNATURE)		
AUTHORIZATION NO.	DATE RECEIVED	TELEPHONE NO.

TYPE OF REQUEST
- ☐ VISIT
- ☐ MAIL
- ☐ TELEPHONE

RECORD STATUS
- ☐ INVALID DATA
- ☐ MISSING
- ☐ NOT IN CENTER
- ☐ CHARGED OUT TO

TYPE OF SERVICE
- ☐ TEMPORARY WITHDRAWAL
- ☐ PHOTOCOPY
- ☐ PERMANENT WITHDRAWAL

ACTION TAKEN
- ☐ DELIVERED BY DRIVER
- ☐ TELEPHONE REPLY
- ☐ SENT BY MAIL
- ☐ REVIEWED IN REFERENCE ROOM
- ☐ AGENCY PICK-UP

Bureau of Records Management Services, Records Center

Consultant Peter J. Oliva recommends database software to generate the following records center reports:[3]

1. Available Space Report: indicates the spaces available for empty boxes in the center.
2. Receipts Report—Monthly: indicates all the records received during the last month.
3. Out of File Records—Aging Report: lists records removed for 30, 60, 90, or more days.
4. Departmental Inventory List: indicates what each department has stored in the Records Center.
5. Reference Activity Report by Department: indicates the activity of specific users.
6. Client Usage Report: Similar to the previous report except that it can be generated by percentage of space.
7. Destruction List—Year End: lists all records due for destruction at the end of the year.

Commercial Records Centers

There are several types of **commercial records centers** across the country. Many large cities have such centers, which are becoming widely accepted and used by many business people. There are above-ground and below-ground facilities offering a variety of special services. Magnetic tapes are stored in the underground vault shown in Figure 11-9. Some of the services offered by commercial records centers include 24-hour service, duplicating capabilities, facsimile transmission, and microfilming services. One of the advantages of using a commercial records center is that the services are performed by professionally trained personnel who are bonded. The confidentiality of secret documents is almost guaranteed.

To maintain security, many commercial records centers require client companies to complete a records center access authorization form to inform them of individuals who are permitted to view the company's stored records (see Figure 11-10.

The Association of Commercial Records Centers (ACRC) consists of Professionals that are specialists in records center storage. ACRC recommends the use of off-site storage for these following reasons:

[3]Peter J. Oliva, "So You Want to Automate Your Records Center," ARMA International Conference, Baltimore, Maryland, October, 1988.

WHY USE OFF-SITE RECORDS CENTERS

- Secured protection of information.
- Controlled but easy access.
- Additional services are available.
- More staff time available.
- Chance to accomplish other objectives.
- Realistic costs for inactive records.
- Cost control opportunities.

Source: Association of Commercial Records Centers, 1988.

Before deciding if a commercial records center will meet the company's needs, the records manager may want to inspect the facility and interview key personnel at the center. Another good source to turn to for information concerning a center's reputation is a person who has used the center's services. Such experience is invaluable in determining the effectiveness of the center and its services.

A few selected commercial records centers will be mentioned in order to give the reader an appreciation for the many services offered by these facilities.

The Inland Vital Records Center is a maximum-security, atomic-blast-proof records center for the storage of magnetic tapes, microfilm, microfiche, and paper documents. Inland is located 175 feet underground, outside of Kansas City, Kansas, and is easily accessible to any part of the country. Constant archi-

FIGURE 11-9 Magnetic tape storage. (Courtesy of Underground Vaults and Storage, Inc.)

NO 1300 FORM 1 (11/82)

RECORDS CENTER ACCESS AUTHORIZATION

INSTRUCTIONS
1. Please type the information requested below
2. Do not type in the shaded areas.
3. Return this form to Supervisor, Records Storage

DEPARTMENT	DIVISION		BUREAU, SECTION	AGENCY NUMBER
PERSON AUTHORIZED	TITLE	TELEPHONE NUMBER	ACCESS RESTRICTION	AUTHORIZATION NUMBER

I hereby authorize the personnel listed above to request and receive records of this agency which are stored at the New Jersey Records Storage Center

AGENCY HEAD OR OFFICIAL SIGNATURE	TITLE	DATE

BUREAU OF RECORDS MANAGEMENT SERVICES RECORDS CENTER

FIGURE 11-10

Records center access authorization. (Courtesy of Division of Archives and Records Management, Department of State, State of New Jersey.)

val record storage conditions are maintained with a temperature of 70°F (7°C), relative humidity at 35 percent, and electronically filtered clean air. This facility has microfilm service, 24-hour record retrieval service, and bonded personnel who perform all of the services in connection with record security storage.

The Southern Vital Records Center is another large center that is designed for maximum security from natural and human-made disaster or intrusion. Sixty-one underground vaults are stationed across 600 acres of rolling hills in Flora, Mississippi. Constant security and surveillance are maintained by guards, guard dogs, closed-circuit TV, electronic alarm devices, and a six-foot chain-link fence. In the event of emergency, the center is served by its own water system and an auxiliary electrical generating system. Each vault is air-conditioned with temperature and humidity controls. The center has one of the largest and most technically complete underground processing and duplicating laboratories in the United States.

The Detroit Record Services Center is a 100,000-square-foot facility with 500 private vaults. Its services include retrieval and refiling, pickup and delivery, destruction of documents, and transfer boxes.

The Metro is the largest exclusive off-site business records storage company in southern California. Among the services that it offers are secured, confidential storage; quick and dependable low-cost retrieval; and a destruction service that can be used by its customers as well as the general public.

The Mohawk Business Record Storage located in Minneapolis, Minnesota, is a modern fireproof facility. Mohawk also provides many services to its customers, including climate-controlled vaults for computer tape, microfilm, and microfiche storage.

The underground storage vault under the Catskill Mountains in New York was formerly a limestone mine. Known as IMAR (Iron Mountain at Rosendale), this records storage center is one of the busiest in the country. Even though there is neither heating nor air conditioning, the temperature and humidity are ideal for storing microfilm. IMAR has an auxiliary computer room for clients whose systems are wiped out. Another computer can be brought in by the client that plugs into the back-up tapes, and within a few hours the client can be back in business.

Increasingly, business firms are taking advantage of underground storage facilities that offer more security, ideal temperature and humidity conditions, and a measure of protection from earthquakes.

CHAPTER HIGHLIGHTS

- A records center is a low-cost facility for housing an organization's inactive and semiactive records; records centers may be in-house, either on-premises or off-premises, or in commercial storage.
- The physical layout of the records center includes both stack and nonstack areas; floor space and ceiling heights should be used to their fullest extent.
- Before records are sent to a records center for storage, a transfer list must be prepared by the office transmitting the records. When records arrive at the center, they receive an "address" according to the space numbering system the record center is utilizing.
- Commercial records centers include both above-ground and below-ground facilities offering a variety of special services such as 24-hour security, duplicating, vaulting, microfilming, and facsimile transmission.
- Automated records centers are a cost-effective way to track inactive records; selection of computer hardware and software is an essential ingredient for successful automation.
- Database software simplifies data collection in records centers and generates usage and productivity reports which management requires.

QUESTIONS FOR REVIEW

1. Identify the various types of records centers in existence today.
2. Describe the physical layout of a records center, including both stack and nonstack areas.
3. Differentiate between the terms *refiling* and *interfiling.*
4. In terms of assigning addresses to boxes in the records center, discuss the difference between the row/unit/shelf/space system and the sequential numbering system.
5. Discuss the services available from commercial records centers.
6. Identify the records center equipment which is essential for operating efficiency.
7. List the information that should be included in a Records Transfer Request.
8. What criteria should be established for accepting records in inactive storage?
9. Differentiate between a reference service request and an access authorization form.
10. What types of reports can be generated by a records center that is computerized?

THE DECISION MAKER

Case Studies

1. You have recently been hired by the Crown Corporation for the new position of records center supervisor. There is no existing inactive records storage center, and records are being warehoused haphazardly in closets and out-of-the-way areas throughout the corporate offices.

   Your task is to establish an on-site records center. Fortunately, space has been made available by a recent expansion. As the records center supervisor, you must present to management a plan for the physical layout and organization of the center: Prepare the plan, including the following details:

   1. Establish a floor plan (a rough estimate) that includes aisle arrangements in the stack area.
   2. Determine what nonstack areas will be essential in the new center.
   3. Discuss equipment and supplies requirements for the new center.

2. The Jade Corporation established a records center last year, but the numbering system now being used does not seem adequate. To date, each record carton has been assigned a sequential number from the accessions register. The first space assigned was carton number 000001. Records personnel claim it is difficult to retrieve cartons quickly because of the lack of detail in the present addressing system. Describe several alternatives to the system now being used by the Jade Corporation.

Managing the Archives

OBJECTIVES

Upon completion of this chapter, the student should be able to:

1. Explain the importance of an archive.
2. Select and preserve historical documents.
3. Select the proper storage facilities for an archive.
4. Describe the procedures for maintaining the company archives.
5. Explain the importance of planning for security of the archives.

Over two centuries ago, an important document was signed, which is now preserved in the federal archives in Washington, D.C. This original document, the Declaration of Independence, is sealed in a protective airtight enclosure filled with gas. Even though 100 percent rag paper may have a life expectancy of several hundred years, this important historical document must be carefully preserved according to strict regulations on storage procedures in order to maintain its archival permanence. Thus, archival management is concerned with the selection, preservation, and storage of archival documents, in both the public and private sectors.

THE EVOLUTION OF ARCHIVAL RECORDS MANAGEMENT

From the time records were preserved on the walls of caves and on earthenware jars to today's preservation and control of computerized records, there is an intervening period of tremendous progress and unbelievable delay. Most of the innovative records management systems have been introduced in the last half of the twentieth century. Until that time, progress was slow.

No one can say for sure who was responsible for the first formal records management program. The first national archive was established in 1790 by France, whose revolutionary government proclaimed the right of access to public records. About 50 years later, in 1838, a central archival institution was established in England.

As the need for records control was recognized, creative methods were implemented. The discovery of America in 1492 by Columbus, for instance, led to brisk trading between the Old World and the New World. Merchants became aware of the need to control their records as the volume of business increased. The popular filing method at that time was to pierce the papers on a long spike, known as a *spindle file,* which is shown in Figure 12-1. As business increased, merchants found two spindles a better arrangement for records control. One spindle held the unpaid bills and the other, the paid bills.

For nearly four centuries, few innovative techniques came along to take care of the paperwork that increased dramatically during the last half of the nineteenth century. One of the reasons for the burgeoning paperwork during the 1860s was the invention of the typewriter. Figure 12-2 is a chronological listing of the records storage methods used from the Middle Ages to the 1990s.

Figure 12-3 shows the *flat file* that was used in the 1860s to file papers flat in drawers. Each letter was assigned a drawer, but this was not very satisfactory. Some drawers filled more quickly than others. After all, how many documents would the *X* or *Z* drawer contain?

Another disadvantage of the flat file was that the papers were loose in the drawer, whereas when they were pierced on the spindle file they were held securely. The *Shannon file,* similar in principle to a clipboard, held papers securely and provided business people with a sense of security.

FIGURE 12-1
Spindle file.

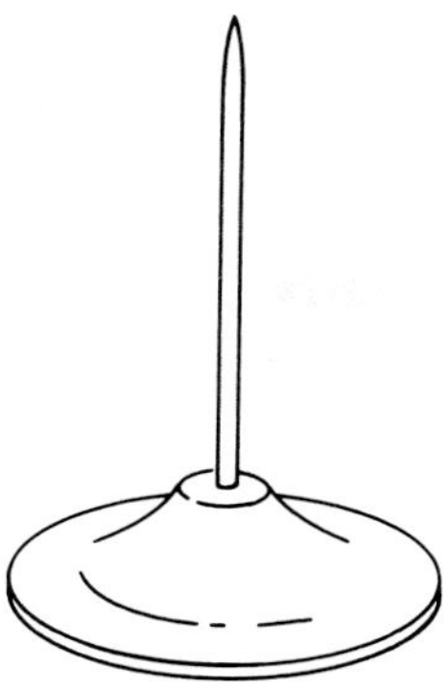

FIGURE 12-2 Chronology of records storage methods

Period or Year	Method	Comments
Middle Ages	Spindle file: one at first, two later (one for paid bills, one for unpaid bills)	Increased business
19th Century		
1860s	Flat file and drawer file: papers laid flat	Influenced by invention of the typewriter
1880	Shannon file: similar to a clip-board	People felt more secure
1892	Vertical file	Dr. Nathaniel S. Rosenau's discovery
20th Century		
1914	New York School of Filing	J.M. McCord, Remington Rand representative
1930s	First commercial use of micro-graphics	George McCarthy, bank clerk
1945	Digital computer	World War II, paperwork greatly increased
1950s	Computers with punched cards	Stored large amounts of data
1960s	Increased computerization and use of microforms	Primary use was inactive records storage
1970s	Integration of computers and micrographics	COM, CAR—active records storage
1980s	Microcomputers	Floppy disk storage
1990s	Electronic Imaging Systems	Optical disk storage

Dr. Nathaniel S. Rosenau, a secretary of a charity organization in Buffalo, New York, filed numerous index cards in the course of his work. He reasoned that papers could be filed in the same manner as cards; that is, standing on end. It was a big step for offices to change from flat filing to **vertical filing,**

FIGURE 12-3
Flat file.

since people were as averse to change in the 1890s as they are today. However, vertical filing became popular in the early twentieth century, and filing schools appeared in the larger cities to train office workers in filing techniques.

The first commercial use of **micrographics,** producing microimages on film, occurred in the 1930s when George McCarthy, a blank clerk in New York, hit upon the idea to photograph customers' checks before they were returned to the customer. McCarthy's invention was crude, but Eastman Kodak saw its possibilities and bought it from him.

Vannevar Bush first proposed the use of the digital computer for information systems in 1945 in the United States. In the early 1950s, the first commercially available computers used punched cards for storing large amounts of data outside the computer and small magnetic drums for storing relatively small amounts of data and instructions inside the computer.

The 1960s brought more sophisticated computerized methods of records control and micrographic usage for inactive record storage. During the 1970s, greater usage of micrographics appeared in both large and small offices. More sophisticated equipment and more reasonable costs helped to popularize the use of microforms, such as roll film, microfiche, and the aperture card.

Both the micrographics and the computer systems revolutionized the management of records, because of the form of the data to be stored and retrieved. Micrographics reduced hard copy to a fraction of its original size, and the computer enabled data to be retrieved in a fraction of the time needed for retrieval of hard copy. In the 1970s, micrographics and computer systems were combined to produce computer-output and computer-input micrographic systems.

In the 1980s, microcomputer use skyrocketed as managers used this computer technology to store records in electronic or magnetic form (floppy disk) rather than on paper. In the 1990s, image systems that utilize optical disk technology to store documents are gaining in popularity. Coupled with computer systems that distribute information and database software that organizes it, optical disk storage offers high volume data backup for archival records. Thus, archival records management has moved into the 1990s with electronic image management systems for long-term storage of data and more rapid access to records than micrographics can provide.

THE NATIONAL ARCHIVES

Although billions of records have been created since the signing of the Declaration of Independence, the United States was by no means the first modern nation to establish a national archives. France led the way in creating a national archives almost 150 years before the United States. England and Canada also established national archive before the United States. England preceded the United States by a century, and the Public Archives of Canada was founded in 1872. Along with the historical records of Canada, business records were then recognized as having research value. In 1934, during the presidency of Franklin Delano Roosevelt, a national archives was created in the United States.

In 1984 the National Archives and Records Service celebrated its fiftieth anniversary. In honor of the event, the United States Postal Service issued the commemorative stamp, shown in Figure 12-4. The stamp shows the profiles of two famous presidents, Lincoln and Washington, and the notation, "What Is Past Is Prologue." This saying refers to the importance of understanding the past before we proceed into the future of our existence as a nation.

The National Archives was established with a threefold mission: (1) to select, (2) to preserve, and (3) to service the archives of the federal government. Upon its establishment, the National Archives received many of the older records of the government, some dating back to colonial times. Because the records had been neglected for many decades, a large portion of the records were received in damaged condition. Thousands of records are withdrawn from use each year because of deterioration. Many records received in good condition in 1934 or later have deteriorated over the years because of chemical changes related to age or because of wear and tear on the original documents.

Archival holdings in the National Archives include still pictures, motion picture films, sound records, video recordings, machine-readable items, maps,

FIGURE 12-4 National Archives commemorative stamp. (Courtesy of U.S. Postal Service.)

charts, architectural and engineering plans, aerial photos, and numerous artifacts. They are stored at the National Archives Building and at two other sites in the Washington, D.C., metropolitan area; at the various presidential libraries; and at National Archives regional branches throughout the country.

In order to avoid further deterioration problems, data processing tapes are preserved by reproducing them onto other stable media. Textual records are supposed to be fumigated upon accessioning, and where necessary, deacidified and laminated.

Archivists of various countries have set chronological datelines for retention of archival records. In Germany, all records created before 1700 are kept. In England the date is 1750; in France, 1830; and in Italy, 1861. The Italian date coincides with the date adopted by the National Archives of the United States, where surviving records created before the Civil War, which began in 1861, are also being preserved.

Ronald Reagan is the first president of the United States to be governed by a law that became effective in 1981 mandating that the records generated by the White House automatically belong to the government.

THE ARCHIVAL PROFESSION

An **archivist** selects, appraises, and preserves those documents of an institution or organization that are deemed to have historical value. If the materials to be preserved are damaged in any manner, the archivist chooses an appropriate method for repair. The archivist also arranges and describes documents so that potential users have a clear understanding of their purpose and historical background.

Thus the records manager controls the creation and the use of documents, while the archivist preserves, and organizes the classification of, documents that have permanent value. The archivist who has both an academic background in history and a strong business preparation will have an appreciation for the value of a business organization's records. With the assistance of a competent records manager, the archivist will retain only those records that are worthy of permanent preservation.

Staff Functions

Many activities are associated with the archivist's duties. The number of staff members needed in the archives will depend on its size, nature, and scope. Personnel may be needed for referencing, cataloging, indexing, duplicating, and microfilming documents. In a small organization, the archivist may perform all of the activities with no additional staff. In very small organizations, one person, such as a records manager, may oversee active records, inactive records, and archival documents.

Archival Careers

For individuals interested in the archival profession, career opportunities exist in academic institutions and research libraries, government agencies (both federal and state), private business and labor archives, churches, fraternal associations, political clubs, and ethnic organizations. It should be noted that the federal government's National Archives and Records Service is the largest employer of archivists in the United States.

Individuals interested in archival careers should become members of the Society of American Archivists, a professional association of individuals and institutions that was founded in 1936. The Society of American Archivists (SAA) serves the profession in various ways. SAA promotes communication and exchange among archivists and archival institutions, as well as advancing professional education and training in the profession. SAA offers placement services, publications, and workshops; the organization also supports research dealing with archival problems. Appendix C provides additional information on the Society of American Archivists.

ARCHIVIST FUNCTION IN BUSINESS

An archive is different from the records center in the purpose for which it is established. The records center houses inactive records that are retained for their legal, administrative, or fiscal purposes. An **archive** is a facility that houses records that are retained for historical or research value after their main purpose has been fulfilled. In some business firms, the records center and archives may be combined in one facility.

Justification of an Archive

Before establishing a business archive, it may be necessary to demonstrate to top management the potential value the archives has to the organization. The records manager or business historian who approaches management with a plan to establish an archive must produce justification for undertaking such a project.

Some important reasons for establishing a business archive are:

1. To preserve the company history for posterity
2. To heighten the public image of a company by permitting public use of its archives
3. To maintain relevant information for legal, administrative, or fiscal purposes
4. To use archival material for public relations purposes during company anniversaries

5. To review techniques used in the past for such activities as new product development or marketing, for possible reuse or to avoid repeating costly mistakes.

For example, Walt Disney Productions Archivist David R. Smith identified three types of records—business, creative, and product. Included in the business category are all of the traditional paper records. In creative are all of the many types of materials generated in planning and producing films and in planning and constructing Disneyland and Disney World. Among the product records are films, books, comic books, phonograph records, press clippings, still photographs, insignia, character merchandise, employee publications, audio-animatronics, props and costumes, and Walt Disney memorabilia.[1]

Planned Preservation of a Company's History

There are two types of archives:

1. Public archives that may be accessed by the general public
2. Private archives that may be referred to by the company

Determining what should be preserved in a company's private archives is known as appraising the records. The **appraisal** is the responsibility of the archivist, but the records manager usually works with the archivist in making these decisions.

Figure 12-5 illustrates the life-cycle flowchart of a document. Notice the decisions needed from the time of the creation of the document until its final resting place in the archives.

Records that are housed in the archives may not necessarily follow all of the steps in the life-cycle flowchart. Many records go through the complete cycle, but other documents may skip from active file status directly to the archives. The flowchart simply identifies the many decisions that could be made concerning the disposition of a record from its creation to its final housing in the archives. These decisions are critical in assessing the value of documents for inclusion in the archives.

Selecting Archival Documents

No prescribed formula exists for selecting materials for archival preservation. The background and common sense of the archivist are the two most helpful skills in appraising documents.

[1]Charles R. Schultz, "Archives in Business and Industry: Identification, Preservation, and Use," *Records Management Quarterly*, Vol. 16, No. 1 (January 1981), pp. 5–8, 29.

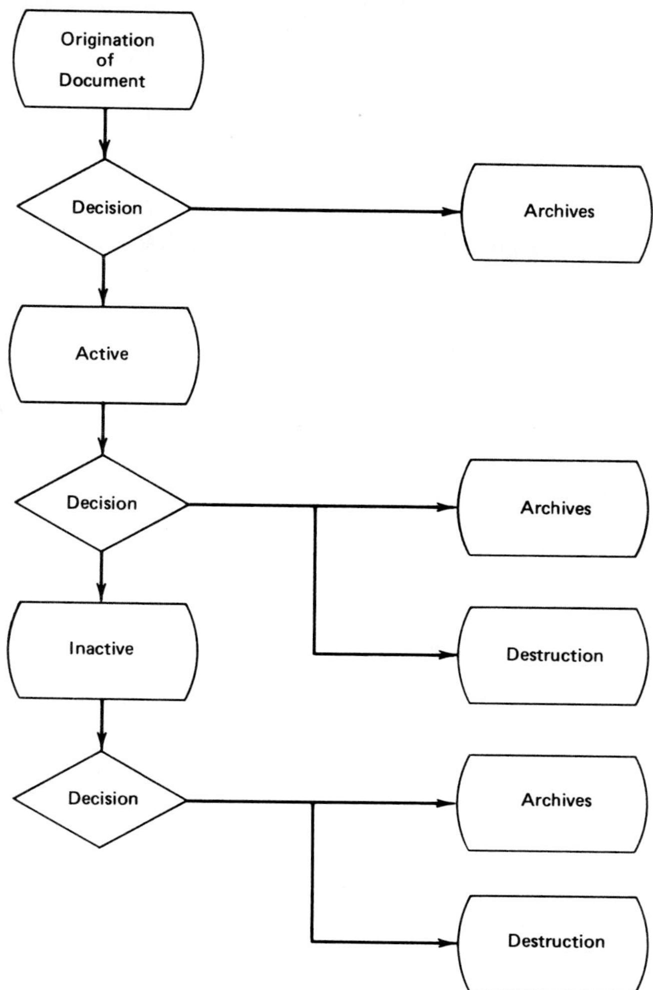

FIGURE 12-5
The life cycle of a document.

The decision to retain a document for a company business archive may be based upon any of the following characteristics:

1. The "uniqueness" of the information contained in the record
2. The importance of the record in documenting company history
3. The information the record yields regarding a company's operations and past actions

Additional guidelines for selecting archival documents for company business archives are shown in Figure 12-6. Note that the following record categories are suggested as sources for documenting a company's history: ownership, management, financial, production, research and development, marketing,

FIGURE 12-6 Guidelines for selecting archival documents.

SUMMARY OUTLINE OF SOURCES USEFUL IN WRITING A COMPANY HISTORY

I. Company Records

A. Ownership
1. Charter
2. Stock Ledger
3. Stockholder Minute Books

B. Management
1. Minutes, Reports, and Correspondence
   a. Board of Directors and Officers
   b. Standing and/or Special Committees
   c. Department Heads
   d. Special Reports by Consulting Agencies, etc.
2. Manuals
   a. Procedure
   b. Job Description
   c. Job Training
3. Biographical Summaries of Executives

C. Financial
1. Annual Budget
2. Annual Statement and Balance Sheets
3. Accounting Records and Manual
4. Stock Issuance Prospectus
5. Tax Statement—Federal, State, and Local
6. Outside Appraisals/Audits

D. Production
1. Annual Reports by Dollar Value and Physical Number (More often if necessary to show seasonal or other trends)
2. Annual Inventories
   a. Finished Goods
   b. Semi-Finished Goods
   c. Raw Materials
3. Plant
   a. Lay-out (Blueprints and Photos)
   b. Location
   c. Capacity
   d. Machinery
      (1) Drawings
      (2) Specifications
      (3) Supplier
      (4) Cost
   e. Processes
      (1) Flow Charts
      (2) Time Schedules
      (3) Patented Operations
   f. Raw Material
      (1) Source
      (2) Cost
      (3) Quantity
   g. Labor
      (1) Recruitment Procedure
      (2) Application Forms
      (3) Testing Programs
      (4) Job Descriptions
      (5) Training Manuals
      (6) Number of Employees
      (7) Personnel Records
      (8) Employee Turnover
      (9) Union Relationships
      (10) Supervision Methods
      (11) Promotional Procedure

E. Research and Development
1. Types of Products
   a. Engineering Reports
   b. Catalogs
2. Product Development and Design
   a. Lab Notes
   b. Lab Reports
   c. Patent Application

F. Marketing
1. Sales Manuals
2. Sales Reports
3. Price Lists
4. Sale Contracts
5. Organizational Charts
6. Market Reports
   a. Demand Studies
   b. Forecasting Reports
   c. Product Choice Analysis
7. Transportation Contracts

G. Trade or Manufacturing Association Activities
1. Correspondence
2. Assessments
3. Committee Work

H. Governmental Relations
1. Aid Secured from Agencies
2. Investigations of Agencies
3. Activities to Secure or Prevent Passage of Legislation

I. Community Relations
1. Participation in Local Fund-raising campaigns
2. Chamber of Commerce, PTA, etc.
3. Visitor Program

II. Sources Which Supplement Company Records

A. Records of Government, Competitors, Associations, etc.

B. Newspapers and Magazines

C. Pictorial Sources

D. Oral History Interviews and Written Commentaries

E. Labor Union Files

F. Bank Records

G. Court Actions

Note: All correspondence, memos, reports, etc. should be carefully screened by someone trained in historical methods before it is disposed of. The establishment of retention schedules for all paper created would aid in carrying out this task.

Source: Thomas W. Riley and John G. Adorjan, "Company History—A By-Product of Good Records Management," *Records Management Quarterly,* Vol. 15, No. 4 (October 1981), p. 8.

trade or manufacturing association activities, government relations, and community relations. Figure 12-6 also details sources that should be consulted for collecting such records.

Values of the Documents

The values of records were discussed in Chapter 5; this chapter considers the archival value of records. The values that are inherent in records are of two kinds: (1) **primary values** for the originator of the documents, and (2) **secondary values** for researchers or private users. Records are created to accomplish administrative, fiscal, legal, and operating purposes. These uses are of primary importance. Records are preserved in an archival institution because they have values that will exist long after they cease to be of current use to the originator. Because the records' values will be for others, rather than for the current users, this value is called secondary. This secondary value may be further classified as evidential value or informational value.

The values that attach to records because of the evidence they contain about company organization and function are called **evidential** values. Incorporation records and annual reports are examples of records with evidential value. Records having evidential value should be preserved regardless of whether there is an immediate or even a forseeable specific use for them. An archivist will assuredly preserve documents that contain evidence on how a firm was organized and how it functioned. The values that attach to records because of the information they contain are called **informational values**. These values derive from the information contained in the records about particular persons, situations, events, conditions, or problems. The memoirs of the company president would be considered records with informational value.

Records that have evidential value are arranged either in provenance order or original order. **Provenance order** means that records are arranged in groups that pertain to their initial use. **Original order** means that records are not rearranged but are left in their original order. Records that have informational value are usually arranged by subject category in order to facilitate the work of the researcher.

Clearly, a record may have archival value for various reasons. The archivist must know the significance of particular groups of records produced in different departments or sections in relation to the entire operation of the organization. The archivist is the person who is responsible for the careful selection and preservation of the documents that are to be included in an archive. Some who are knowledgeable about the preservation of documents recommend that only 1 percent of an organization's records have archival value.

Documents To Be Preserved

Certain documents lend themselves naturally to the status of archival records. These documents are found in all sizes of organizations; they have equal value regardless of the organization's size. Documents that have archival value include annual reports, certificates of incorporation, deeds, land records, organization charts, partnership records, and patents. Naturally, there are many more documents of archival value and the number of such documents varies with the size and type of the organization.

For instance, The Coca-Cola Company in Atlanta, Georgia, has one of the finest archives in the United States. The archivist is knowledgeable about the business operations and the history of the company. This is a qualification of any archivist. The holdings of The Coca-Cola Company archives include such items as the fountain trays advertising Coca-Cola, the various shapes of the Coke bottle, a multimillion-dollar art collection, scrapbooks of all advertising and other items too numerous to mention. Those who wish to use The Coca-Cola Company's archives for research purposes file an application and make appointments in advance to use the documents.

In contrast to The Coca-Cola Company's vast archives, a company opening its doors for the first time may find that a single storage carton will hold all of its archival documents for the first year or two. Nevertheless, the managerial team should be aware that history is being made and documents should be kept for posterity through a careful selection program.

Preserving Documents

For many decades, archivists have been responsible for the preservation of paper documents. In more recent years, the computer has generated new media for data storage. Archivists must decide which documents are to be stored and how they shall be preserved. For example, posters are sometimes microfilmed and stored on roll film; they may also be copied on 35mm slides. Both methods save wear and tear on the original posters by avoiding handling.

Another method of preservation is **lamination.** The process of laminating documents was developed in the 1930s as a means of protecting old newspapers from aging. Documents to be laminated are placed between two layers of plastic and run through a press, which seals the plastic to the documents through heat and pressure. Lamination can present problems, however. In many instances, maps have been burned by the laminating process. Furthermore, lamination can leave air bubbles or produce sharp corners; in some cases, the laminated pocket has even separated.

Two alternatives to lamination are polyester encapsulation and leaf-casting. **Encapsulation** is used in the Public Archives of Canada as well as in the Library of Congress. Encapsulation is a relatively simple process in which a document is placed between two sheets of plastic that are then fastened together with adhesive on both sides. This process differs from lamination in that neither heat nor pressure is used. An encapsulated document may still suffer damage from a chemical reaction with the plastic or the adhesive. Documents needing repair must be mended before encapsulation.

Leaf-casting is the process of restoring paper documents that have deteriorated. A leaf-casting machine repairs documents by bonding fibers to the document, reinforcing the worn areas.

Storage Facility

Selecting the location for the archives is an important decision, especially if the archives is to be off-site. The archives may be housed in the records center of an organization, in an area within the premises of the organization, or in a separate facility removed from the organization's day-to-day operations.

The building that houses the archives should be fire-resistant and of sturdy construction. Temperature and humidity should be controlled to provide the best possible environment for paper documents as well as for various microforms.

Protection from Other Elements

In addition to proper environmental controls, the archives' documents must be protected from other elements that cause paper deterioration. Specific causes of paper deterioration include heat, humidity, light, dust, vermin, fungi, and air pollution.

Documents should be fumigated upon accession, as fumigation is one of the best methods to control vermin and fungi. The National Archives's documents are fumigated upon accession. Because sunlight bleaches paper documents and the ultraviolet rays of the sun destroy paper, there are no windows in the National Archives in Washington.

The relative humidity is important in the storage of archival documents. Parchment and paper absorb or give up moisture according to the rise or fall in the relative humidity. When the humidity is too low, parchment shrinks and paper becomes brittle. When the humidity is too high, mold and bacteria grow. Ventilation helps to fight mold. The amount of moisture the atmosphere can hold varies with its temperature. A temperature range of 68° to 70° F (6° to 7° C) and 50 percent relative humidity are ideal for the preservation of paper. Microforms, on the other hand, are best stored at 10 percent less relative humidity than that recommended for paper storage. Relative humidity of 40 percent is considered ideal for microform storage, with a temperature range of 65° to 75° F (4° to 9° C).

Filing cabinets should not be used to house the archives because documents may curl. Also, filing and retrieving will cause folders to wear out. The archives' documents should be stored in acid-free fiber boxes. Folders and storage cartons must be acid-free in order to protect the documents from contamination. Even acid-free paper will become brittle through contamination if stored in an acidic file folder. The acid in paper, folders, and storage cartons causes an increased rate of deterioration. In addition, all paper clips, staples, and rubber bands should be removed before filing.

Two types of storage cartons are popular with archivists. One is the gray fiberboard box, known as the **Hollinger carton.** Several sizes and shapes are available for different types of material. The other type of storage carton that is popular is the corrugated box with fitted lid, commonly known as a records center carton. This carton was originally designed for the federal records center and is less expensive than the Hollinger carton (see Figure 12-7).

Shelving the boxes makes maximum use of available space. Small organizations, as well as large ones, find that shelves are space-efficient and accessibility is relatively easy. Figure 12-8 shows records shelved in boxes.

Natural Disasters

Archival documents, must be protected from such natural disasters as fire, earthquake, and flood. A well-built structure will provide a measure of security from these disasters. A large structure that houses archives should have fire walls that are capable of protecting the documents for a period of three hours. A floating foundation may be considered as protection from an earthquake.

An enterprising merchant in Mexico City devised a method to protect his records from earthquake, fire, theft, and flood. Each night the room that housed the documents was lowered into a cave that had been hollowed out of solid rock. The suspended room was raised to normal height in the morning for activity as usual. During the hours that the firm was closed, the records were safe from destruction.

Minor floods may be avoided by carefully selecting the site for the archives. Lowland and old riverbeds are not desirable sites for records storage. Major floods can cause irreparable damage to archival documents. Documents that have been water-soaked need immediate and careful attention. Several options are available for drying documents that have been damaged by water. Some of the possibilities for drying documents include the following methods:

1. Spread the documents around a hot room with air fans circulating. Turn the documents frequently until dry.
2. Hang the document around a warm room that is well ventilated.
3. Run the water-soaked documents through a blueprint or photographic dryer.
4. Vacuum dry the documents in a chamber that has been emptied of air and refilled with hot dry air.
5. Freeze the documents and slowly dry them out.

The freeze-drying method was effective in restoring water-soaked books at the Stanford University Library in the late 1970s. An outside groundwater main burst and flooded the basement of the library. Forty thousand books were soaked. The Lockheed Missiles and Space Company came to the rescue with its vacuum chamber. After the water-soaked books were taken to an ice and storage company for freezing, Lockheed dried out the books. Next the books were stored for several weeks at normal room temperature and humidity. Six months after the event, most of the books were ready for use on the library shelves.

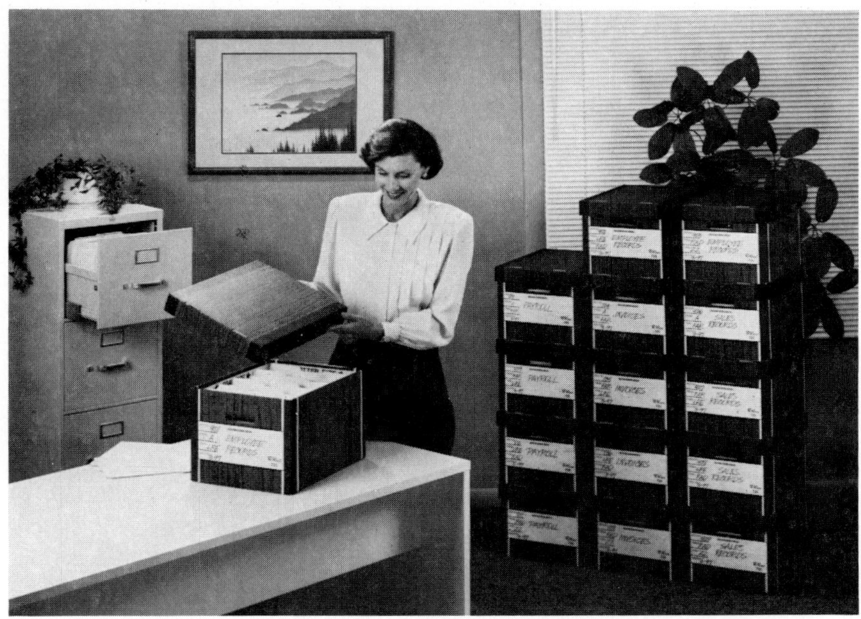

FIGURE 12-7
(Courtesy of Fellowes Manufacturing Company/Bankers Box Storage Systems.)

Vandalism

Vandalism is a growing problem in the United States. One can observe the destruction or defacement of documents in a public library as an example of this problem. Pages are torn out, scribbling appears throughout books and periodicals, and in many instances, complete magazines and books are stolen. Acts such as these must be curbed or prohibited in both public and private archives.

It must be remembered that, in many instances, archival documents are the original historical documents of an organization. Yet whether they are originals or copies, the fact that they have been accessioned into the archives stands as silent testimony to their importance. These documents must be protected from vandalism.

Guidelines for Protecting Against Vandalism A few guidelines may be helpful in protecting against vandalism:

1. Structures should have few or no windows.
2. Facilities should have controlled access rather than unlimited access.
3. Building should be protected by burglar alarms.
4. Archives should be placed in charge of a trusted employee.
5. Only copies of documents should be provided for the public's use.

FIGURE 12-8
Records housed in shelved boxes.
(Courtesy of Fellowes Manufacturing Company/Bankers Box Storage Systems.)

The Accessions Register

Specific information is needed to identify records, and this information should be kept in the **accessions register.** The archivist will find that this register is indispensable in controlling the accessioning and the retrieval of documents. In addition, duplication of records can be avoided through reference to the accessions register, thereby eliminating the use of space for unnecessary documents.

The minimum information to be included in an accessions register is the following:

1. Accession number
2. Date received
3. Source
4. Description (including covering dates)
5. Quantity (number of boxes, files)
6. Location or classification

Figure 12-9 shows an accessions register that includes spaces for all of the pertinent information. A responsibility of the archivist is to design and/or revise the accessions register form as the need becomes apparent.

Accession Number	Date Received	Source	Description	Covering Dates	Location
Form No. AR 8201					

FIGURE 12-9
Accession register.

CHAPTER HIGHLIGHTS

- Billions of records have been created since the signing of the Declaration of Independence; however, many of the records from colonial days are lost forever because of deterioration.
- Documents must be prepared carefully if they are to withstand deterioration from natural and artificial causes.
- An archive is different from a records center in that the archive houses records that are retained for historical or research purposes, whereas a records center houses inactive records.
- The archivist appraises records, with the help of the records manager, for inclusion in the business archives.
- Records are preserved in an archival institution because they have values that will exist long after they cease to be of current use to the originator.
- Certain documents have archival value, including annual reports, certificates of incorporation, deeds, land records, organization charts, partnership records, and patents.

- Paper documents may be preserved by lamination, encapsulation, or leaf-casting.
- Companies are now experimenting with film to determine its usefulness as an archival medium.
- An off-site storage facility for the archives should be sturdy and fire-resistant; the temperature and humidity must be controlled to combat deterioration.
- Other causes of paper deterioration include light, dust, vermin, fungi, and air pollution.
- Two types of storage cartons are popular with archivists: the Hollinger fiberboard carton and a corrugated box with a fitted lid.
- Archival documents must be protected from fire, earthquake, flood, and vandalism.
- The accessions register is indispensable in controlling the accessioning and retrieval of documents.

QUESTIONS FOR REVIEW

1. What is the difference between an archive and a records center?
2. Discuss the duties and responsibilities of an archivist.
3. Identify three reasons a records manager may use to justify the establishment of a business archive.
4. Describe the difference between a public archive and a private archive.
5. At what point during the life cycle of a document can records be designated as archival?
6. List three criteria for selecting documents to be included in the business archive.
7. Differentiate between the terms *evidential value* and *informational value.*
8. Describe the two methods of arranging documents with evidential value in an archive.
9. Define the three methods of preserving documents: lamination, encapsulation, and leaf-casting.
10. How should documents be stored in an archive to prevent decay and contamination?

THE DECISION MAKER

Case Studies

1. The International Machines Corporation, a Fortune 500 Corporation, is planning to start a business archives. As the records manager, you have been asked to identify records that you feel have archival qualities. Write a brief memorandum to management detailing the types of records that IMC (a manufacturer of typewriters, word processors, and office computers) should include in its archives. Include in your memo possible sources for collecting such documents.
2. Ted Brown Manufacturing Company, after 20 years in business, has decided to set up an archives for preservation of its important documents. The company now employs a records supervisor and three records clerks. None has had courses in history or law. To be sure that documents that have archival value are preserved, the records staff has decided to retain a copy of each document that is 10 years or older. Would you agree, under the circumstances, with their decision? What alternatives would be available to the company? What steps would you suggest the company take in this situation?

CORRESPONDENCE AND REPORTS CONTROL

OBJECTIVES

Upon completion of this chapter, the student should be able to:

1. Describe the need for correspondence control.
2. Design form letters.
3. Identify the guidelines for controlling correspondence.
4. Explain the need for reports control.
5. Describe the role of electronic records storage and retrieval.
6. Explain the problems of distribution of written communications.

Every office, whether large or small, must control correspondence and reports in order to be cost-efficient. A recent study by a large consulting organization revealed that white-collar professionals spent approximately 29 percent of their time in "thought work." Almost half of this time—13 percent—was spent in document creation; 8 percent in analyzing; and 8 percent in reading. Thus, white-collar workers are spending a significant portion of their workday creating, analyzing, and reading correspondence.[1]

Correspondence Management and Reports Control

Correspondence Control Objectives

An effective correspondence control program requires top-management support for implementation. Such support can be documented through a directive identifying the major objectives of a correspondence control program. Objectives of such a program include:

Improve the readability and tone of correspondence;

Increase the response time to routine correspondence;

Encourage the use of personal computers and word processors to produce correspondence;

Ensure the use of correct company format, letterhead, and style;

Encourage the use of dictation equipment as an inputting method;

Suggest the use of guide letters and form letters for routine inquiries;

Improve mail distribution of incoming and outgoing correspondence.

Need for Correspondence Control

Correspondence includes letters, memorandums, and directives. The control of correspondence begins with its creation. Through effective planning, organizing, and controlling, much of the decision making involved in creating correspondence can be eliminated. By establishing company-wide standards for correspondence creation, letter styles, formats, and paper use can be standardized. A significant aspect of correspondence control is controlling the cost of paperwork. A general guideline for controlling the creation of correspondence is to use the least expensive form of communication. For example, when written confirmation is not required, a telephone call is often less time-consuming and less costly than composing and writing a letter.

[1]Gerald Tellefsen, "No Requiem for Records Management," *Modern Office Technology*, Vol. 29, No. 10 (October 1984), p. 67.

Correspondence Surveys

A correspondence survey consists of a sampling of a department's routine correspondence over a specific period of time to determine if the correspondence adheres to company policy. Such a study can answer the following questions:

1. Was the correspondence produced by a personal computer or word processor?
2. In what format—machine or shorthand dictation, longhand, rough draft—was the correspondence submitted to the secretary?
3. Does the correspondence conform to company format and style?
4. Was correct company stationery utilized?
5. How many copies were made of the correspondence?
6. Was distribution of the correspondence appropriate?
7. How many revisions were made before final correspondence was produced?
8. Would a guide letter or a form letter be appropriate for this correspondence?
9. Could the letter have been authored by a lower-ranking employee?
10. Was the appearance, tone, and fog index appropriate for the reader?

The answers to the above ten questions will determine if a department is following company policy in the area of correspondence control. Such a periodic review on a department-by-department basis will insure the production of timely, effective, and quality correspondence.

Letter Design and Use

Correspondence Costs The cost of written communication has increased many times in the recent past along with other office expenses. In fact, one of the major reasons that the cost of letters has increased so much is that salaries, office rent, and other operating costs are considerably higher than a decade ago. Half a century ago, the cost of a business letter was approximately $.50, according to the Dartnell Corporation. In the 1980s, the cost went from $6 to $10 depending on the length of the letter and the method used in dictating and transcribing the letter. The cost to produce a business letter in 1990 was $10.85, according to Dartnell Institute of Business Research (see Figure 13-1).

The average cost of a business letter will vary greatly, depending on several factors. One factor is the time involved in dictating the letter and the dictator's salary. The dictator who receives a salary of $25,000 a year contributes $1.50 to $2.00 to the cost of the letter if 7–10 minutes are required for dictation. The dictator whose salary is twice as much, or $50,000, will double the dictating cost of the dictation, depending on the length of the letter and whether the

FIGURE 13-1 The cost of producing a business letter. (Courtesy of Dartnell Corporation, 1990.)

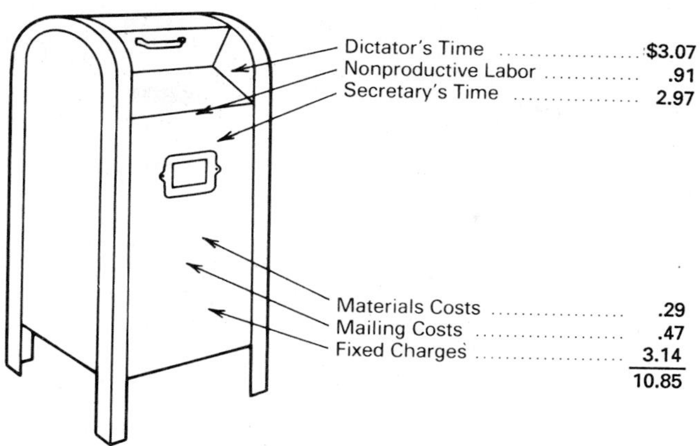

dictation is given directly to a secretary or whether dictation equipment is used. While machine dictation does not affect the cost for the dictator, the savings is in the secretary's time, since the secretary is not present for machine dictation.

Offices that have voluminous correspondence should consider using dictation equipment rather than face-to-face dictation, since the saving is approximately 22 percent for machine-dictated letters.

Geographic location of an office also contributes to the letter cost, since salaries and office rent are higher on the East and West Coasts than in the South. Other contributing factors figured in the cost of a letter, in addition to the dictator's salary and the wages of the transcriber, are the fixed charges, such as overhead, depreciation, maintenance, light, and heat, as well as materials costs, such as stationery, envelopes, and other supplies. Mailing costs and filing costs also must be included and will vary according to the other cost factors.

Figure 13-2 is the Dartnell Corporation's report on correspondence production costs. In order to determine the current cost in a particular office, a study could be made to determine the length of time required by the persons involved in creating the letter. Using their salary base and current costs for the materials, fixed charges, and mailing, a realistic cost figure could be determined. Such a study may support the need for updating the method of dictating letters and perhaps the need for up-to-date equipment in the mailroom.

Originating Correspondence

There are three basic ways of originating correspondence in a business organization: longhand, shorthand, and machine dictation. Figure 13-3 highlights the advantages and disadvantages of each method. In addition to the points enu-

FIGURE 13-2 Determining the cost of one letter

Cost Factor	Average Cost	Your Cost	Determining Cost
Dictator's Time . . . For this cost, it was established that the executive received an average weekly salary of $920 and takes approximately 8 minutes to dictate a single business letter.	$3.07		Based on a 40-hour week, this cost is determined by calculating an executive's salary for 8 minutes. ($920 ÷ 40 hrs. = $23.00 per hour) ($23.00 ÷ 60 min. = 38.3¢ per min.) (38.3¢ × 8 min. = $3.06 per letter)
Secretarial Time . . . Based on a salary of $331 for the secretary, this figure includes all the time involved from dictation through filing of the letter.	$2.97		This cost is obtained in the same manner as the dictator's cost, using 18 minutes for all time involved.
Nonproductive Labor . . . This is the time consumed by both dictator and secretary that is not directly productive when a letter is being prepared. It has been set at 15% of labor costs for both.	.91		This cost is arrived at from the use of previous studies. It is especially aimed at interruptions during dictation or transcription and time lost when participants are involved in producing a letter.
Fixed Charges . . . A catchall charge that wraps up the share of overhead, depreciation, taxes, heating, etc. given to the letter. It also includes the fringe benefits share for the time consumed by letter preparers. Set at 52% of total labor costs.	$3.14		This is a hard cost to pinpoint but it is necessary to cover those regularly running or recurring costs of doing business. It is the letter's share (18 minutes of time for a secretary and 8 minutes of manager's time).
Materials Costs . . . Stationery, envelopes, carbon paper, copy machine paper, typewriter ribbons and cartridges and other supplies needed to get out a letter.	.29		This cost is easily arrived at if you maintain records covering your supplies and basic equipment expenses. Multiple copies cost extra money.
Mailing Cost . . . First class postage (22¢) added to cost of labor for gathering, sealing, stamping, sorting done by personnel other than the secretary.	.47		If you are using more express mail for your correspondence, this cost could go much higher. Otherwise it is easy to determine.
	TOTAL COST $10.85	YOUR COST	

Source: Copyright © 1990, The Dartnell Corporation.

Note: It should be pointed out that the figures presented here are based on a formula to determine the cost of a single, traditional boss-secretary type of letter dictated face to face with the secretary completing the transcribing and connected filing. Communications with repetitive copy, lengthy reports, and/or bids are not represented in this survey.

FIGURE 13-3 Origination methods: Advantages and disadvantages.

MACHINE DICTATION

Advantages	*Disadvantages*
1. Machine dictation is a faster method than longhand. It is also an acquired skill. With a little practice, an originator can increase the dictation rate and thus increase office productivity.	1. The initial cost of equipment may discourage many employers from using it.
2. A secretary doesn't need to be present to take notes. The originator is not affected if the secretary is absent, away from the desk, or occupied with other important matters.	2. Dictation is a skill that must be learned. The originator must be trained to dictate properly.
3. Anyone in the office can transcribe the originator's notes. The message is not a jumble of symbols readable by only a few.	3. If the company does not replace its outdated machine dictation units, it might be using older units, which are sometimes inferior.
4. The transcriptionist no longer has to decipher written symbols. Instead, the transcriptionist listens to spoken words and types.	
5. The transcriptionist can transcribe faster from the spoken words than from any other means.	
6. Some equipment even permits the secretary to transcribe while the originator is dictating.	
7. Electronic note taking is possible. The originator can leave messages for the secretary that aren't intended to be transcribed.	

Source: Marly Bergerud and Jean Gonzalez, *Word/Information Processing* (New York: John Wiley & Sons, Inc., 1984), p. 43.

merated in Figure 13-3, the time element in creating correspondence by these various methods should be considered.

When creating documents by longhand, the executive uses his or her own handwriting to put ideas down on paper. Correspondence can be created at an average of 15 words per minute. If the same executive were to switch to short-

FIGURE 13-3 *(continued)*

LONGHAND

Advantages	*Disadvantages*
1. Only one person is involved. 2. No special skill such as shorthand is required. 3. Only a pad of paper and a pen or pencil are needed.	1. This method is a slower means of transmitting ideas than shorthand or machine dictation. 2. Transcribing from written notes can be tedious and time-consuming.

SHORTHAND

Advantages	*Disadvantages*
1. This method is faster than longhand. 2. The transcriptionist transcribes from own notes, not from the originator's. 3. The secretary can assist the originator in dictation by supplying the right word.	1. Much time is wasted during the dictation process because the originator is often interrupted. 2. The secretary must be present while the originator is dictating. 3. The transcriptionist must know some form of shorthand. 4. The person who takes the notes or someone who knows the same system of shorthand must transcribe the notes. 5. The secretary must transcribe from written symbols. Therefore, the transcription rate often decreases when symbols are illegible or after long periods of time have elapsed between dictation and transcription.

hand as a means of originating correspondence, secretarial personnel would be involved, but the rate would increase to 30 words per minute. Finally, the same executive, using machine dictation, could generate correspondence four times faster than by longhand or twice as fast as by shorthand.

Thus, using machine dictation generates documents at an average of 60 words per minute and is the fastest means of originating correspondence. The use of machine dictation for creating correspondence has many other advantages; the best advantage is that machine dictation is the most compatible method for those companies that use word processing centers to produce correspondence. Word processing systems are an integral part of the total information system of many offices. The use of dictation equipment also lowers the cost of the typical business letter, as computed by the Dartnell Institute in Figure 13-4.

Using Form and Guide Letters

Messages of a similar nature are produced quickly and efficiently by using information processing equipment and composing **form letters** in advance. Form-letter paragraphs can be stored easily and cheaply in a word processing system, to be used subsequently in letters. Customers who receive form letters will not be offended if the letters are free of stereotyped expressions and positive in approach. Organizations that use repetitive letters find that a form letter that has been typed on an automatic typewriter has the appearance of an individually typed letter.

Advantages of using form letters are:

1. Better use of the executive's time
2. Better use of the typist's time
3. Error-free letters
4. Cost savings

Standardized Designs for Form Letters Four standard designs for form letters are:

1. *PLAIN* — Letters are completely printed and do not require any fill-ins. This type of form letter might be used in announcing the opening of a branch store.
2. *FILL-IN* — Letters have spaces for fill-ins, such as names, dates, and amounts. This type of form letter is often used to remind a customer of an unpaid bill.

FIGURE 13-4 Cost of a business letter dictated via machine

Here is the current cost of an average business letter dictated via machine:

$3.07	Dictator's time, cost based on 8 minutes and a salary of $920 a week.
1.65	Secretarial time, cost based on 10 minutes and a salary of $396 a week.
.47	Nonproductive labor cost based on 10 percent of total labor costs
2.44	Fixed charges based on labor costs
.31	Material costs, including tapes, disks, belts, supplies, maintenance
.47	Mailing costs, including new increase in salaries
$8.41	Total Cost (originating on dictating machine)

Source: Courtesy of Dartnell Corporation, 1990.

3. *CHECKLIST* — Optional statements are preceded or followed by a box or space for checking before mailing. The checklist form letter may be used to notify an applicant that his or her request for credit has been denied.
4. *REFERENCE NUMBER* — Optional statements are referred to by number.

Guide Letters and Paragraphs Office personnel are often able to answer routine correspondence by using letters that have been previously written for specific purposes. Several standard paragraphs may be available; personnel then select the paragraphs that are the most appropriate under any given circumstance.

Paragraphs should be updated from time to time and new paragraphs added as necessary. A good source of new paragraphs is incoming letters. A well-written letter may contain a paragraph or two that would be effective in outgoing correspondence at some future date.

Word choice is of utmost importance in guide letters. The letters should be free of trite phrases and sentences such as, "If we can be of further service, please do not hesitate to contact us." The language and tone should be fresh and positive in order to achieve the purpose of the letter, namely, to communicate. Similarly, negative words and statements are barriers to communication. Negative words often cause the reader to feel guilty and, as a result, the import of the message is lost. For instance, instead of the negative statement, "You failed to pay for your last order," why not say, "May we have your payment within 10 days."

Guide letters should be written with effective letter-writing principles in mind. As in other types of correspondence, the form letter should be "you-oriented" and should be clear, concise, and correct. Sentences should be neither overly long nor short and choppy. A variety of sentence lengths contributes to the ease of reading.

Personalized Correspondence

Personalized letters do not always need the attention of top executives. Letters should be written by the lowest-level employee who has the expertise needed for the task. The greatest cost factor in writing letters is the salary involved in the dictator's time. This cost can be measurably reduced by having correspondence produced by employees of lower rank.

Every business letter should build goodwill, except in those instances where the organization for one reason or another may not wish any further communication with the reader. Goodwill statements in the form letter add a personal touch, and the sender has the satisfaction of knowing that a conscious effort has been made to retain the reader's loyalty.

Letter Styles

There are three common letter styles: block, modified-block, and AMS simplified style. Letter style is a matter of preference in an organization, but usually one style is used in any given department. Personnel should refer to the correspondence manual to determine the letter style used in the office. Another source to check to determine the preferred style of letters is the correspondence file. Figure 13-5 shows the **block letter style.** Notice that each line begins at the left margin.

Figure 13-6 is the **modified-block style.** The only difference between this style and the block style is the position of the date and the closing. These letter parts begin at the center in the modified-block style. The position of the dateline varies according to the length of the letter. Most letters are average length, that is, between 100 and 200 words in the body of the letter. The inside address is placed four lines below the date, and the complimentary closing is a double space below the body of the letter. There should be three blank lines left for

FIGURE 13-5
Block letter style.

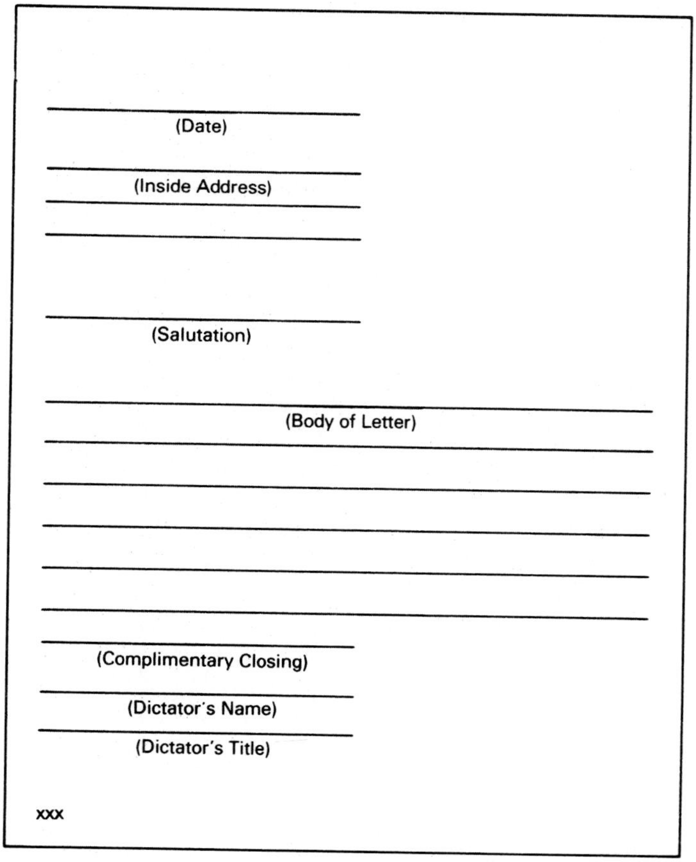

(Date)

(Inside Address)

(Salutation)

(Body of Letter)

(Complimentary Closing)

(Dictator's Name)

(Dictator's Title)

xxx

FIGURE 13-6
Modified-block letter style.

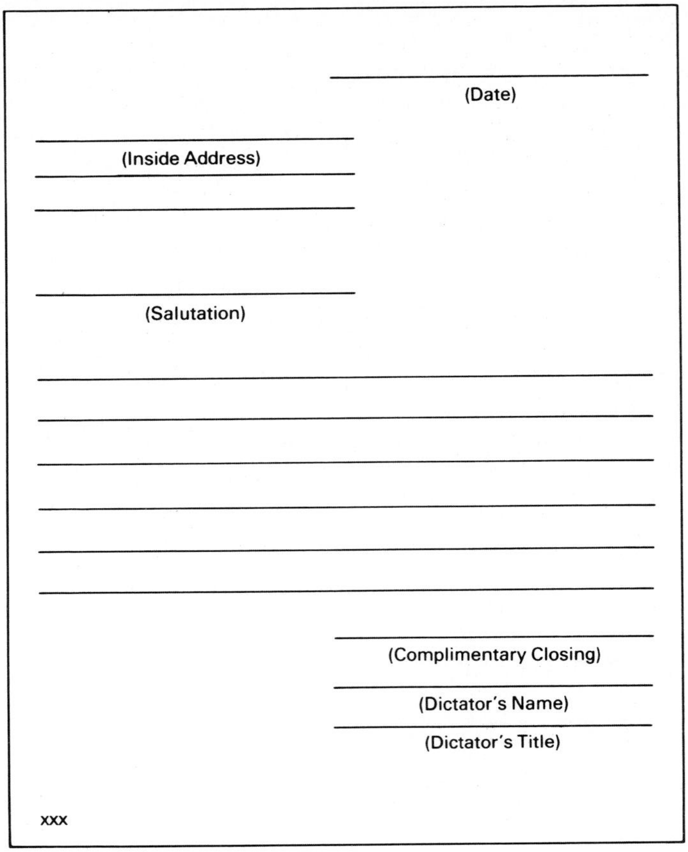

(Date)

(Inside Address)

(Salutation)

(Complimentary Closing)

(Dictator's Name)

(Dictator's Title)

xxx

the signature. The placement of the letter is important so that the letter will be pleasing to the eye. A letter that is typed too high or too low on the page is most unattractive. A short letter (fewer than 100 words in the body) or a long letter (over 200 words in the body) should be adjusted slightly in line length and vertical placement. The salutation and the closing should be in consonance with the tone of the letter. If the message is a stern request prompted by a long-overdue payment, a closing such as "Cordially yours" is inappropriate. It would be far better to use "Sincerely yours" or "Very truly yours."

The **AMS simplified letter style** is endorsed by the Administrative Management Society and is the most efficient letter style; however, many office personnel prefer the block or modified-block style. The salutation and the closing are omitted in the simplified style to give the letter a "let's get down to business" tone. The Administrative Management Society considers the salutation and closing nonessential parts of a business letter. In addition, omitting the salutation solves an often-encountered dilemma: how to address a woman in business when we are unsure of her marital status—Miss, Mrs., or Ms. See Figure 13-7 for the AMS simplified letter style.

FIGURE 13-7
AMS simplified letter style.

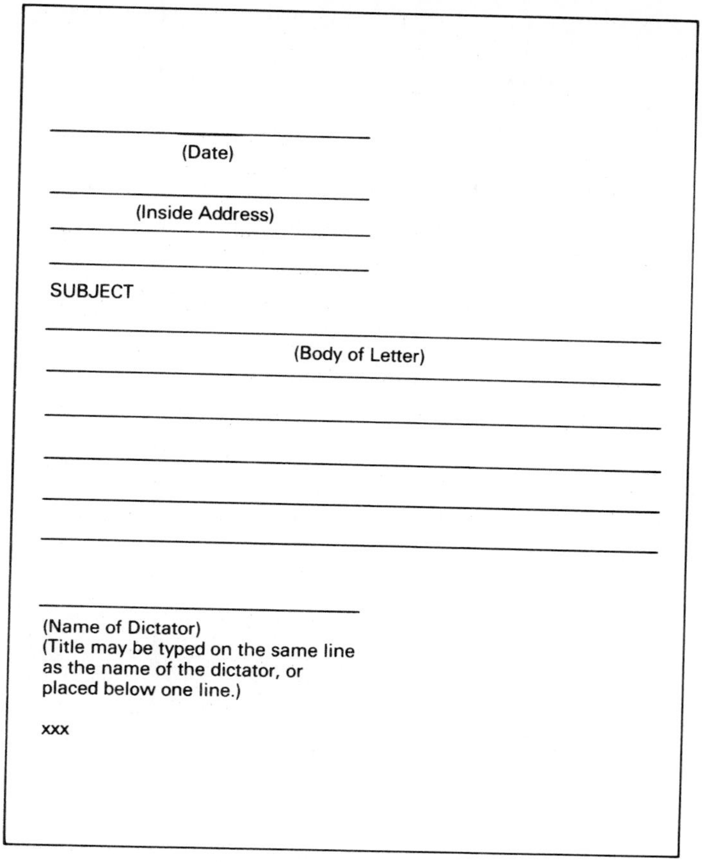

(Date)

(Inside Address)

SUBJECT

(Body of Letter)

(Name of Dictator)
(Title may be typed on the same line as the name of the dictator, or placed below one line.)

xxx

Memorandums

Memorandums are generally short, informal messages used to communicate to employees within an organization. Memorandums should be used only for internal correspondence. An acceptable format for memorandums is shown in Figure 13-8. It is particularly important that the subject line be descriptive enough so that records clerks have no problem identifying how the memo should be filed. Usually an office will have printed memorandum forms that are less formal than the letterhead stationery. Offices that do not have printed memorandum forms may print their own by typing the headings on a full sheet or a half sheet of plain paper and reproducing the form. For memorandums to be cost-effective, the same letter-writing principles should be followed as when creating letters.

FIGURE 13-8 Memorandum style.

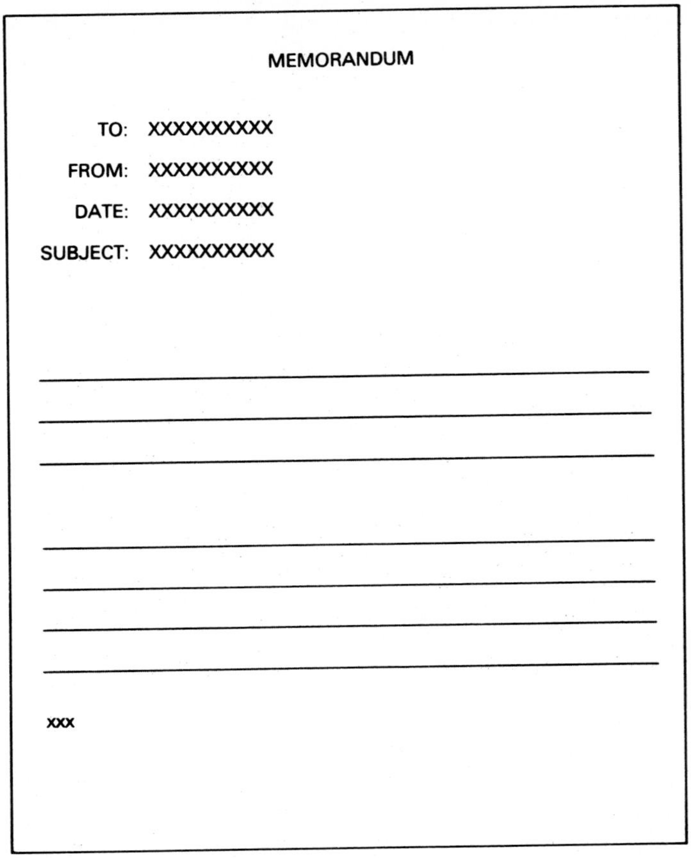

MEMORANDUM

TO: XXXXXXXXXX

FROM: XXXXXXXXXX

DATE: XXXXXXXXXX

SUBJECT: XXXXXXXXXX

XXX

Maintaining Correspondence Files

Much of the correspondence that is filed could be destroyed 30 days after it is written. Files are cluttered unnecessarily by useless correspondence, more than one copy filed, and correspondence that has passed its destruction date.

Methods of Filing Correspondence There are two methods of filing correspondence manually:

1. *SUBJECT MATTER* — Correspondence is filed with other documents pertaining to the same topic or case.
2. *ALPHABETIC METHODS* — Correspondence is filed alphabetically according to the sender's name or according to a topic that identifies the sender.

Another method adopted by some offices is to keep an extra copy of each piece of outgoing correspondence in chronological filing order so that reference may be made easily to recent correspondence. This method proves helpful in finding the name of a correspondent that is unfamiliar to office personnel. The approximate date that the outgoing letter was written helps locate the individual's name and address.

Controlling Correspondence Correspondence is time-consuming and costly to an organization. Purging the files of unneeded correspondence will free filing space for active records. In addition to purging, however, careful planning in the creation of correspondence enables the office personnel to control the volume of correspondence.

Notes taken in the form of telephone messages are not categorized as correspondence and should not be kept once the required action has been taken. Memorandums, too, are usually disposed of after they have been acted upon.

An attractive and well-placed bulletin board may be used to convey messages. One individual in an organization should be in charge of approving directives and materials for bulletin boards. Directives should be coded and logged in record form in order to control the number and the content of the directive.

Correspondence Manuals The correspondence manual is a guide for all personnel who are responsible for the creation and control of correspondence. The content of the manual will depend on the size of the office and the volume of correspondence. A typical correspondence manual will include sections on policies and procedures governing correspondence and dictation and provide illustrations of letter styles and envelopes used in the organization, as well as instructions on maintaining correspondence files. Form letters should also be included, together with an explanation of when to use each form letter.

Negative words and phrases as well as stereotyped expressions and clichés should be listed with recommendations for revision. Terms or technical words that may be unusual or unique to an organization, together with their definitions, should be included. Listing these words introduces the new personnel to the spelling and meaning of words that may otherwise cause problems in taking dictation and transcribing messages.

The correspondence manual will also contain guidelines for the creation and control of reports and directives. Other topics may be included in the correspondence manual according to the needs of the organization.

Everyone who is involved in the creation, control, or disposition of the correspondence of an organization should be asked to contribute ideas to the manual. The correspondence manual may be a section within the records management manual or a separate manual by itself. In either case, it should be in loose-leaf form for ease in updating. One person should be responsible for keeping the correspondence manual updated.

Directives

A **directive** is a communication from management that instructs, informs, or guides employees in performing their work responsibilities. A directives control program, as part of correspondence control, helps to regulate the issuance, format, and distribution of directives to employees. The objectives of directives control are enumerated below:

1. To serve as a vehicle for communications from management to employees on company-related issues
2. To instruct employees on new procedures, policies, guidelines, and regulations
3. To keep employees informed of possible changes in organizational plans
4. To eliminate repetitive judgments on routine situations
5. To encourage cooperation by establishing work responsibilities and reporting relationships

For such a program to be effective, top management must assign program responsibility to an individual. In addition, some organizations appoint directives coordinators in each department to assist in issuing directives related to their organizational units. Directives should be issued in a standardized, distinctive format that makes them stand out to employees as important communications from management. To prevent overlapping, an inventory of current directives should be undertaken to ensure that duplicate or conflicting directives have not been issued. Finally, directives should be stored in a looseleaf binder for ease of additions, deletions, and revisions. The binder should have sections for the subject categories that are identified on the directives. Many corporations use a combination of subject and numeric classifications for ease of identifying various directives in each category.

REPORTS MANAGEMENT AND CONTROL

Need for Reports Control

Many office personnel will agree that far too many reports are expected and demanded of them, whether by the government or top management. Reports are time-consuming and costly to prepare; therefore, only the reports that are needed to fulfill a purpose should be made. The major function of a report is to help management make sound business decisions. Other obvious purposes of a report are (1) to communicate to persons within the organization, and (2) to satisfy legal requirements.

Classification of Reports

Reports are classified as formal or informal. The formal report is longer—generally 10 pages or more—than the informal report. Certain sections that may comprise the formal report include:

1. *SUMMARY* — A summarization of important points placed at the beginning of a long report enables the busy executive to scan the key points without reading the entire report.
2. *INTRODUCTION* — This section explains the purpose of the report and identifies the scope of the problem.
3. *BODY OF THE REPORT* — This section of the formal report includes the method used in the research and the findings.
4. *CONCLUSION* — This section of the report states logical conclusions that are reached from the findings stated in the body.
5. *RECOMMENDATIONS* — The recommendations are based on the conclusions, and they are logical outcomes and not personal recommendations.

The formal report is purely a statement of facts, devoid of personal opinion or slanted statements.

Informal reports may be oral or written. In many cases, the oral informal report at staff meetings is sufficient to fulfill one of its purposes: communication within the organization.

The written informal report is often in memorandum form, because it is intended for internal communication. Written informal reports that are not in memorandum form will be shorter than formal reports. All of the sections may be included or the summary and other sections may be omitted, such as the findings and conclusions. An informal report may include only a simple statement of the problem and the recommendations.

Reports Design and Use

Communication Costs Owing to the time required for research and writing, reports are considered the most expensive form of communication to create. The cost of a written report will depend on several factors:

1. Length of the report
2. Research required
3. Salary level of the report writer
4. Fixed costs, such as overhead expenses, heating, lighting, and fringe benefits
5. Typist's wages

Management is always concerned with controlling costs. One factor that will help to reduce the cost of report writing, as in correspondence writing, is to use the lowest-level employee who has the expertise to write effective reports. In some instances, it may be most cost-effective to have one person do the research and another employee with writing skills do the writing.

Standardized Formats Reports that are routine will be written more easily if a sample report is provided in the correspondence manual, together with clear instructions for its use and completion. Here again, with proper supervision, an employee of lower-level status may be given the responsibility for preparing routine reports.

Computer-Generated Reports Care must be taken to control the number of reports generated by the computer. Even though the cost of a computer-generated report is much less than the cost of the personally prepared report, an additional cost is incurred in maintaining computer-generated reports. Computer output can be difficult to house even though special binders are available. Ideally, the computerized data will be maintained on microfilm in order to save space.

Maintaining Reports Files

Reports are usually filed in an area set aside for them, only because of their size. Hard-copy reports are easily filed and retrieved on shelves. The exception, of course, is the memorandum form or short report. Very often, there is no need to file the memorandum form once the required action has been taken. Reports, like all records, are subject to a retention schedule. When the destruction date is reached, reports should be disposed of promptly. The originator of the report should be consulted about the date of the destruction at the time the report is written. Later, when the destruction date arrives, the report writer should confirm that the report is no longer needed.

Reports Functional File

The **reports functional file** contains a copy of each type of report generated in an office. Reports should be grouped by function or purpose, and this in turn reveals possible duplication of information. Reports should be numbered according to function so that all reports pertaining to a particular function will have the same prefix number and will be in proximity in the file. All reports should be listed by subject and number on a reports inventory form.

Evaluation of Correspondence and Reports Control Programs

The correspondence and reports control programs will not be effective without a continuous evaluation. Those personnel who are involved in correspondence and/or reports creation and maintenance should be alert to improving the quality while keeping in check the quantity of letters, memorandums, and reports. Whereas input (by all individuals) should be encouraged, one person should be assigned the responsibility of overseeing a particular phase of the program.

Silverman proposes the use of an Optimum Legibility Formula that serves as an editing method for rearranging and consolidating content in order of priority. The Optimum Legibility Formula also restricts the use of verbs to one per sentence, written in the active voice and adjacent to its subject.[2] This formula, shown in Figure 13-9, can be applied to any type of writing—letter, memorandum, directive, or report. It uses seven steps to make correspondence as clear, concise, and concrete as possible. As writers, we must strive to "express not to impress" our readers.

Evaluating Reports

Since reports are considered the most expensive means of written correspondence, the reports control program should include a vehicle for evaluating reports. One consultant recommends the use of the Recurring Report Evaluation Form that is shown in Figure 13-10.

This form should be sent to recipients of reports that are distributed on a regular basis—weekly, monthly, semiannually, and so on. These reports are costly to an organization and their effectiveness needs to be monitored. Suggestions for improvements, additions, or deletions, can be gathered from the input of the recipients.

CHAPTER HIGHLIGHTS

- Correspondence control includes letters, memorandums, directives, and reports.
- The control of correspondence begins with its creation.
- Company-wide standards should be establlished for correspondence creation, including letter styles, formats, and paper use.
- A general guideline for controlling the creation of correspondence is to use the least expensive form of communication.
- The cost of creating a typical business letter varies based on both the dictator's and the secretary's salaries, the method of origination, the location of the office, and the fixed charges of the business.

[2]Buddy Robert Silverman, "On Writing," *Records Management Quarterly,* Vol. 17, No. 2 (April 1983), pp. 38–39.

FIGURE 13-9 (Courtesy of ARMA, 4200 Somerset Drive, Suite 215, Prairie Village, KS 66208.)

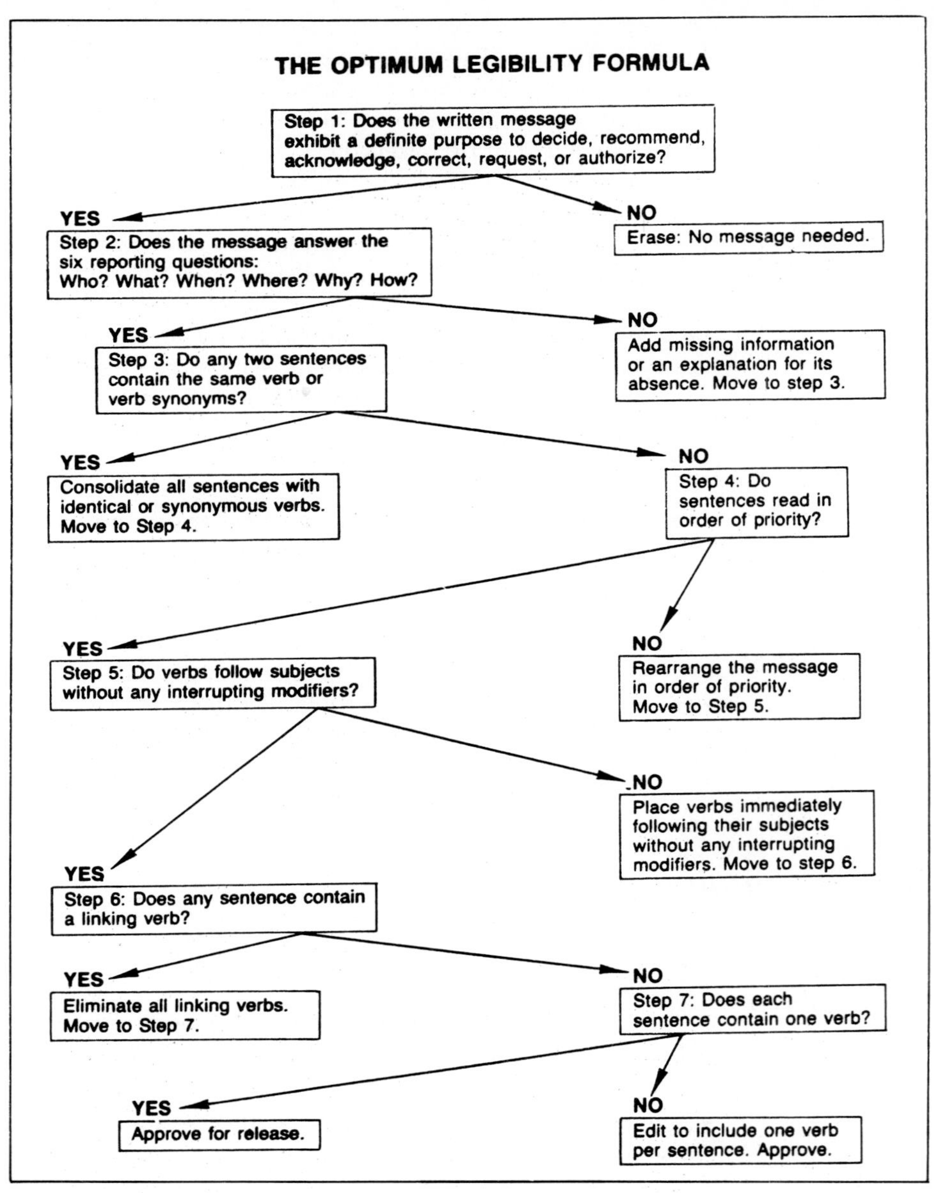

THE OPTIMUM LEGIBILITY FORMULA
Step 1: Does the written message exhibit a definite purpose to decide, recommend, acknowledge, correct, request, or authorize?
YES
NO
Erase: No message needed.
Step 2: Does the message answer the six reporting questions: Who? What? When? Where? Why? How?
YES
NO
Add missing information or an explanation for its absence. Move to step 3.
Step 3: Do any two sentences contain the same verb or verb synonyms?
YES
Consolidate all sentences with identical or synonymous verbs. Move to Step 4.
NO
Step 4: Do sentences read in order of priority?
YES
NO
Rearrange the message in order of priority. Move to Step 5.
Step 5: Do verbs follow subjects without any interrupting modifiers?
NO
Place verbs immediately following their subjects without any interrupting modifiers. Move to step 6.
YES
Step 6: Does any sentence contain a linking verb?
YES
Eliminate all linking verbs. Move to Step 7.
NO
Step 7: Does each sentence contain one verb?
YES
Approve for release.
NO
Edit to include one verb per sentence. Approve.

Source: Buddy Robert Silverman, "On Writing," *Records Management Quarterly,* Vol. 17, No. 2 (April 1983), pp. 38–39.

FIGURE 13-10 Recurring report evaluation form. (Courtesy of ARMA, 4200 Somerset Drive, Suite 215, Prairie Village, KS 66208.)

RECURRING REPORT EVALUATION FORM

To be completed by persons receiving a report

I. Title or Brief Description of Report ______________________ Form or Report No. (if any) ________

____

II. Why is this report prepared? ______________________

____

____

III. Think about how this report relates to your management duties and needs for information, and answer the following questions. Explain any "NO" answers in the remarks section provided, as well as any additional comments or amplifications on your answer that you care to make.

QUESTION		*Yes*	*No*
1.	Does report include only essential information?		
1a.	Too much information. ☐ Explain.		
1b.	Too little information. ☐ Explain.		
2.	Does it provide appropriate data for your level of management?		
3.	Is report arranged by organizational unit so those responsible can be held accountable?		
3a.	Too finely divided. ☐ Explain.		
3b.	Not finely enough divided. ☐ Explain.		
4.	Was report designed with you in mind?		
5.	Is the terminology used understandable?		
6.	Is a comparison with some yardstick provided?		
6a.	If no, would one be useful? Explain which one.		
7.	Does the report accent out-of-line performance?		
8.	Does the report show trends or tendencies?		
8a.	By the time you see the report, are the trends and tendencies too late to change?		
9.	Are controllable and non-controllable items segregated?		
10.	Are reports issued promptly, regularly, and at appropriate intervals?		
11.	Are they in neat, logical order and easy to handle?		
12.	Do they provide accurate information?		
12a.	If no, are corrections easily made and acted upon by the issuer?		
13.	Do you need all the detail you are getting?		
13a.	If no, do you need ☐ more, explain. ☐ less, explain.		
13b.	If less, would a summary do as well?		
14.	Do you get enough assistance when you have a question about the data in this report?		
14a.	Who do you ask? ______________________		
15.	When you need a breakdown of the data in the report, is such a breakdown available?		
15a.	Is it easy to get?		
15b.	Is it received in a timely manner?		
15c.	Does the breakdown serve the purpose you need?		
16.	Are the number of copies produced being kept to a minimum?		

Source: Kenneth V. Hayes, "Procedures for Analyzing Reports; Part II—the Qualitative Approach," *Records Management Quarterly*, Vol. 17, No. 4 (October 1983), pp. 24–26, 28–31.

FIGURE 13-10
(continued)

REMARKS FROM SECTION III QUESTIONS

Question No. *Remarks*

IV.

1. When was the last survey of users made to determine their satisfaction? ___________

1a. By whom was survey made? ___________
2. Referring to the information contained in the report:
2a. What information is missing from report that you need to have? ___________

2b. How do you now get this information? ___________

2c. What information now on the report is not needed? ___________

3. How do you use this report? (Check as many as applicable.)
   - ☐ This report is needed to meet a specific one-time need. (Explain on back.)
   - ☐ This report is needed to meet a specific recurring need. (Explain on back.)
   - ☐ I use this report to manage my immediate operation and take action based upon its information.
   - ☐ I use this report to answer questions of others about my operation. Who:
     - ☐ District Supervisor(s)/Superintendent(s)
     - ☐ District Manager(s)
     - ☐ Division Manager
     - ☐ General Office Functional Department
     - ☐ Other General Office Department
     - ☐ General Office Executive Management
     - ☐ Customers/Suppliers
     - ☐ Other Outside Company
     - ☐ Other ___________
4. Do you need this report:
   - ☐ Not at all. Why? ___________
   - ☐ I do not need this report but would like to review it if it continues to be prepared. Why? ___________
   - ☐ Yes. (If checked, answer the following.) Why? ___________

     What particular information in the report do you use and for what purpose? ___________

     What suggestions do you have for improving the report's usefulness to you? ___________

General Comments

Prepared by: ___________ Department: ___________
Location: ___________ Date: ___________

- There are three basic ways of originating correspondence in a business organization: longhand, shorthand, and machine dictation.
- Form letters, guide letters, and guide paragraphs can be used to answer correspondence of a recurring nature and, in addition, to lower the cost of creating letters.
- The three common letter styles are block, modified-block, and AMS simplified; companies should specify which style to use to control correspondence costs.
- Memorandums are short, informal messages used to communicate to employees within an organization. Directives are communications from management that instruct, inform, and/or guide employees in performing their work responsibilities.
- Reports are classified as formal or informal; the formal report is usually organized into several sections, while the informal report is often in memorandum form.

QUESTIONS FOR REVIEW

1. Should a company adopt a uniform style for producing letters? Why or why not?
2. Based on the data from the Dartnell Corporation, what is the most expensive factor in creating correspondence? How does this vary for different parts of the country?
3. Which method of originating correspondence is recommended?
4. Differentiate between a form letter and a guide letter.
5. What are the three common letter styles? How do they differ?
6. What topics should be included in a correspondence manual?
7. List three basic objectives of directives control.
8. How does an informal report differ from a formal report?
9. Describe the Optimum Legibility Formula.
10. When storing correspondence on magnetic tape, what controls need to be applied?

THE DECISION MAKER

Case Studies

1. As the reports manager for the WINCO Company, you have noticed that although the cost of creating both letters and reports has been increasing, the quality of correspondence produced by employees of WINCO has

been decreasing. Specifically, you have noticed the following areas of concern:

1. Run-on sentences
2. Use of the passive voice
3. Incorrect letter format
4. Wordiness in reports
5. Increase in use of longhand drafts
6. Grammar and punctuation errors

Obviously, these problems must be remedied. However, you are unsure what approach to take since a large portion of the staff are professional employees with college degrees, who should have acceptable writing skills. Indicate your plan of action for addressing the areas of concern.

2. The Vice President of Administrative Services has directed you to lower the cost of correspondence for your organization, a law firm. As office manager, you have been concerned with the increasing cost of both letters and reports.

Currently, correspondence is originated by both rough draft (longhand) and face-to-face dictation (shorthand). Also, various letter styles and report formats are used by the secretarial staff. Changes must take place in procedures used by both the legal staff and the clerical staff.

Outline the changes that you feel would reduce the cost of correspondence for the law firm. Be prepared to present your proposal to the Vice President of Administrative Services and to indicate how both attorneys and clerical support staff will be affected.

FORMS DESIGN, CONTROL, AND MANAGEMENT

OBJECTIVES

Upon completion of this chapter, the student should be able to:

1. Describe the rationale behind a forms design, control, and management program.
2. Discuss the important differences between well-designed and poorly designed forms.
3. Cite the important aspects or techniques of good forms design.
4. Explain the importance of forms procurement and inventory control to the overall success of a program.

The majority of all business records today are in paper form. Paper records are the one transaction medium common to businesses around the world. The basic types of paper documents are preprinted business forms, correspondence, and computer-generated forms or material. Often there is a fine line between these types of documents. Computer-generated data, for example, can be printed on business forms, on regular computer printout paper, or on special paper so that it resembles correspondence. Of the basic types of paper documents, an organization's primary means of communicating with its customers, employees, suppliers, government agencies, and other firms is by way of such business forms as payroll checks, insurance forms, customer billing, purchase orders, employment applications, and shipping and receiving documents.

According to FORMS AND SYSTEMS PROFESSIONAL, the cost of handling forms is skyrocketing. Some interesting "Facts about Forms" are noted below:

33% of all documents in business are forms.

U.S. companies spend upwards of $6 billion every year to purchase preprinted forms.

Companies spend $100 billion annually using preprinted forms.

$94–120 billion is spent to distribute, store, and process forms.

Companies waste or destroy $2 billion a year in preprinted forms.

The hidden cost of forms is 40 times their purchase price.

Millions are spent collecting information twice. That is, first someone handwrites information on a form and then someone else reads it off the form and enters it into a computer (often in error).[1]

To the user this means that more forms are being produced at higher costs. Therefore, organizations must be concerned with the design, production, and inventory of forms. Many small operations with five or fewer employees use personalized, preprinted sales receipts, order forms, and so on. For that reason it is important to remember that the size of the organization is not a prerequisite for the use of business forms. Company size does dictate to some degree when a formalized forms design, control, and management program is instituted. In small firms the owner is generally responsible for designing, ordering, and stocking forms.

[1]"Hidden Costs," FORMS AND SYSTEMS PROFESSIONAL, Winter, 1989.

Forms Analysis and Design

Since the design of a form may dictate the flow of work and manner of processing a task, careful consideration must be given to designing a form. Forms design is the number one responsibility of forms professionals as noted in a recent national survey. As one might expect, poorly designed forms and/or the uncontrolled production of forms by various departments within an organization can lead to the following problems:

1. The use of inefficient and ineffective forms
2. The use of many forms with similar functions and design
3. The maintenance of unrealistic inventory stock levels
4. The collection of unnecessary information
5. Loss of time and money resulting from the use of inefficient forms

For these reasons alone, management should consider developing an efficient forms design, control, and management program. Such programs can promote the efficient processing of forms, better customer relations, reduced forms costs, and realistic inventory levels.

What Is a Forms Program?

If on the first day of business every company had an efficient forms program in operation, many of the areas to be discussed in this chapter would not be everyday problems. However, it is more often the case that businesses need to develop the proper procedures and organizational structure to facilitate an effective forms program.

Management must be sold on the need for an effective, centralized, functional forms program. According to a national consultant, "Forms are to managers what spreadsheets are to accountants."[2] Management's approval and backing across departmental or divisional lines must be obtained to develop a program. A good program should include forms analysis, design, construction, control, and management. Each part is interrelated and contributes to the success of the entire program.

Forms Analysis **Forms analysis** is the process of learning how a new form is to be used or how a form to be revised is currently being used. Generally, this is a cooperative effort between the forms analyst and the forms user. The basic steps used by any forms analyst to solve problems related to forms include (1) identifying the problem, (2) dissecting the problem into its parts, and (3) analyzing each part to determine the flow of information.

[2]Michael J. McCoy, *Forms & Label Purchasing*, March, 1990.

1990 Census Creates Challenge

The 1990 bicentennial census created unique printing demands for the U.S. forms division of Moore Business Forms—the $2.6 billion printing company awarded the government contract. Each form had to be personalized with name and mailing information and individual bar codes—for the government to analyze responses.

The 1990 census is divided into two forms—a short form with 14 questions and a long form with 59 questions. Each mailing piece consists of five parts: a mailing envelope with a window; a return envelope with two windows; a three-fold instruction guide; a one-part motivational piece; and a questionnaire, which prints two colors—blue and black. Plus, each questionnaire has its own bar code.

Responsible for printing the short form, Moore's presses ran at two separate plants—one in Logan, Utah and another in Thurmont, Maryland. Each plant has similar equipment to print both fixed and variable information, fold, cut, and insert the forms into envelopes. Finally, the forms were zip coded and carrier sorted. A third plant in Buckhannon, West Virginia, was responsible for printing the instructions and the motivational pieces.

The contract called for approximately 100 million forms; the $20 million printing job is the largest single-run order in the company's 108-year history. It is also the largest single contract in printing ever cut by the federal government.

Source: Forms and Label Purchasing, March, 1990.

During the problem-identification phase of the forms analysis, the analyst needs to pay particular attention to how paperwork is prepared or created, and how the paperwork is processed. In addition, the analyst needs to be aware of any necessary design details. Breaking the problem down into its parts allows the analyst to learn how the form actually functions. Here the analyst looks at the "what, where, when, who, and how" of the form. These questions can identify the strengths as well as the weaknesses of a form.

Analyzing each part to determine information flow will aid in proper forms design and construction. Information such as how new forms will be prepared, processed, distributed, and filed is developed and retained during the analysis phase for use during the design and construction phase. In effect, forms analysis is a process that is used to determine if an entire form can be eliminated, combined with another form, or expanded. After the entire form has been reviewed, each item on the form, as well as the number of copies, is put to the same test. In this manner only necessary items or forms are retained and used.

Forms Design and Layout **Forms design** is the process of designing a form that meets the requirements learned during the analysis phase. The forms designer takes all the information gathered and uses it to produce the required form. Many liken this process to that of an architect designing a building or a ship. Both the forms designer and architect use the tools of their trade to produce a cost-effective product.

Before actually designing the form, the designer needs information learned during the analysis phase; for example:

1. How the form will be prepared—typewritten, handwritten, and so on
2. How many copies of the form will be prepared, and how and by whom each is to be read
3. How the form will be filled out physically—hand-held, on a clipboard, on a desk, and so on

Using this information the designer can begin a rough sketch of the form. The size of the form, item arrangement, spacing, word or caption clarity, line form, and margins are important items for design layout.

One of the more important elements of good forms design is the selection of the proper size. Once a rough sketch of the form is completed, the approximate size of the form can be determined. Since paper comes from the mill in standard sizes, the designer needs to remember that forms designed to fit on standard-size paper are less expensive than odd-size forms. Other factors bearing upon the size of a form are (1) filing considerations, (2) the throat size of the machine the form will be used in, (3) the need to mail the form, and (4) the amount of blank space that can be omitted to reduce the form size.

Forms that are to be filed must be the proper size to fit such devices as posting trays, binders, file cabinets, or other filing media. Forms are also designed to be used with machines like time clocks or cash registers. Therefore, one must ensure that the form is the proper size to fit into the devices. Frequently, a form or a copy of a form must be mailed. This means the form must be designed with this purpose in mind, since postal regulations can affect envelope design and size. Blank or unused space can often be reduced, allowing the form to be redesigned so that it will fit on standard-size paper, thereby allowing a standard-size envelope to be used. Figure 14-1 shows the number of business forms of various sizes that can be cut from standard-size sheets of paper.

Item arrangement is the proper placement of items on the form. Here the important point to remember is that all items or groups of items must be arranged in the proper sequence on the form. The designer must take into consideration the source of the information, how the data are collected, and

FIGURE 14-1
The number of standard-size business forms that can be cut from standard sheets of paper.

Size of Cut Form*	Number of Forms Cut from Sheets					
$2\frac{3}{4} \times 4\frac{1}{4}$	8	32	40†		64	80†
$2\frac{3}{4} \times 8\frac{1}{2}$	4	16	20†		32	40†
$3\frac{1}{2} \times 4\frac{1}{4}$	6†	24†	32		48†	64
$3\frac{1}{2} \times 8\frac{1}{2}$	3†	12†	16		24†	32
$4\frac{1}{4} \times 5\frac{1}{2}$	4	16			32	
$4\frac{1}{4} \times 7$			16		24†	32
$4\frac{1}{4} \times 11$	2	8			16	
$4\frac{1}{4} \times 14$			8			16
$5\frac{1}{2} \times 8\frac{1}{2}$	2	8	10†		16	20†
$5\frac{1}{2} \times 17$		4	5†		8	10†
6×9				8†		
$7 \times 8\frac{1}{2}$		6	8		12†	16
7×17		3†	4		6†	8
$8\frac{1}{2} \times 11$		4			8	
$8\frac{1}{2} \times 14$			4			8
$8\frac{1}{2} \times 22$		2			4	
11×17		2			4	
12×19				2		
14×17			2			4
17×22		1				
	$8\frac{1}{2} \times 11$	17×22	17×28	19×24	22×34	28×34

Note. Sizes of paper sheets:
, all sizes in inches; †, with a small amount of waste.

the way in which the user will process the data. For example, if the form is to be completed outside on a loading dock, then more space should be allowed for entering amounts, signatures, and so on by hand. If the form is to be filed, the designer must ensure that the data used to retrieve the form are properly located, given the type of storage equipment used.

Many forms designers use a design technique that arranges forms into five basic sections: (1) title or name and number, (2) instructions and routing information, (3) introduction, (4) body, and (5) closing or conclusion. Figure 14-2 shows the five basic sections.

The **form title or name and number** are necessary for the proper use of any form and should be located in the upper-left section of the form. The form title should be clear, meaningful, and easily understood by those who use the

INSTRUCTIONS – PREPARE IN INK

ACCIDENT REPORT
WJ–P–13

ROUTING: COPY 1 – SAFETY
COPY 2 – OSHA
COPY 3 – INJURED

Name of Injured			Injury Date
Date of Birth	Social Security No.	Sex	Time of Injury ☐ A.M. ☐ P.M.
☐ Employee ☐ Visitor ☐ Other ______	Department	Injured's Title or Occupation	
Address of Injured			
Injured's Statement			
Injured's Signature		Date	
This Portion to be Completed by Reporting Individual			
Was First Aid Rendered at Scene? ______	First Aid Rendered By Whom?		
Was Injured Moved To Hospital? ______	If Yes, What Hospital?		
Nature of Injury			
Witnesses			
Where Did Accident Occur?			
How Did Accident Occur?			
Identify Conditions and Possible Causes that Led to Accident			
Measures Taken to Prevent Similar Accidents			
Reporting Individual's Signature		Date	

COPY I

FIGURE 14-2
The five parts of a form.

form. The purpose of the form should be reflected in the title, such as "Travel Expense Voucher," "Application for Employment," or "Change of Schedule." A good practice is not to include the word *form* in the title.

Form numbers allow for ease of controlling forms as well as providing other selected pieces of information. The number is generally controlled from a **forms register,** which is simply an index of all forms in numerical order. The register should, at a minimum, contain the form number and title. A register may also contain any other information the author wishes to keep. The form number could be made up of an organizational prefix, a departmental or divisional designator, the number itself, and revision data. The number GWW-Per-146-Rev-4 is the fourth revision of form number 146 belonging to the personnel department of the GWW Company. The number could be reduced to "GWW146-4." Keep in mind that long numbers tend to be error-prone; therefore, the number should be simple and as short as possible.

The **instructions and routing information** should be located at the top center or top right of the form. The user of the form must be able to find and read the instructions quickly and easily before completing the form. These instructions should include the proper use of pencil, pen, typewriter, or any other specific user information. If the instructions are long and detailed, they may be placed on the back of the form or on a separate instruction sheet. Routing information for the proper separation and dissemination of the form must be included. If the top of the form is too crowded for the routing information, the bottom portion of the form should be used.

The next section of the form, the *introduction,* is limited to specific information concerning the department or division completing the report, date of the report, subject of the report, and other related items. This section can be described as the "who, what, when, and where" of the form. The section should follow directly below the title, number, instructions, and routing portions of the form and in front of the body.

The **body** of the form is the section where information relative to the subject of the form is placed. Information such as statistics, production data, monetary figures, and medical terms, to name a few, are contained in this section. A crucial point to remember about the body is that information should be grouped into logical, common categories.

The last section is the **closing,** or **conclusion,** portion of the form. In this area the designer includes such items as signature or approval blocks, date blocks, summary data, and closing statements. Since not all forms have all five basic sections, designers need to take care not to complicate the forms. Some forms may be so simple that instructions are not necessary. Other forms may not require signatures or approvals.

Providing the right amount of space on the form for entering information is particularly important. Too little or too much space may cause people to enter incorrect responses. Since many forms may be either handwritten or typewritten, a good rule to follow for spacing is to allow 1/3-inch vertical spacing and 1/8-to 1/4-inch horizontal spacing per number or letter. Some forms designers recommend that 1 inch of horizontal space be used for every five handwritten characters. For forms that are always handwritten, the 1/3-inch vertical spacing and 1/8- to 1/4-inch horizontal spacing rule still applies. Typewriter forms spacing allows 1/6 inch for a single vertical space and 1/3 inch for a double vertical space. Horizontal typewriter spacing should accommodate both elite type, which allows 12 characters per inch, and pica type, which provides 10 characters per inch.

The forms designer should use care in selecting captions so that *word clarity* is achieved. The form must be specific. For example, when asking for an address, one should be specific about requiring "Street or P.O. Box Number, City, State, and Zip Code." If the question is not properly worded, the desired response may not be provided.

The proper arrangement of the captions also helps with clarity. Most forms designers recommend the use of **upper-left captions** (ULC), also called the box design, in designing forms. In Figure 14-3, one would have difficulty entering information. The upper-left captions in Figure 14-4 make it much easier for the user to enter data. Advantages of using upper-left captions follow: (1) more space is available for entering data; (2) typewriter tab stops are easier to set; (3) captions are visible while the form is being typed; and (4) the form does not have a cluttered, jammed-together look.

Check boxes are an excellent method of gathering information, as can be seen in Figure 14-5. When gathering handwritten data with more than one answer, the boxes should be placed vertically, one below the other, in front of the answers. If the data are to be typed and there is more than one answer, the

FIGURE 14-3
Poor caption design.

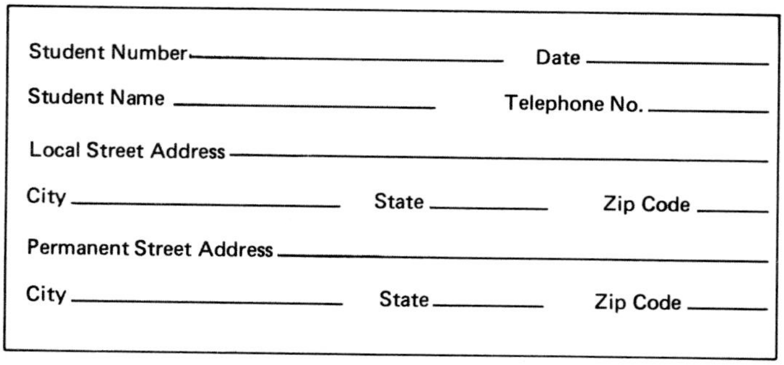

Student Number ____________ Date ________
Student Name ____________ Telephone No. ________
Local Street Address ____________
City ________ State ________ Zip Code ________
Permanent Street Address ____________
City ________ State ________ Zip Code ________

FIGURE 14-4
Upper-left caption design.

Student Name	Date
Local Street Address	Student No.
City, State, Zip Code	Telephone No.
Permanent Street Address	
City, State, Zip Code	Telephone No.

FIGURE 14-5 Check box design.

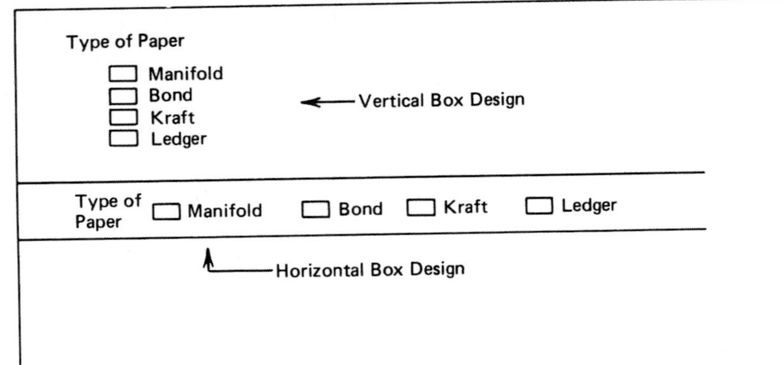

boxes should be spaced horizontally on one line with the appropriate typewriter spacing.

Another way to add clarity and function to a form is through the use of **screening** and other visual aids. Screens are normally used to highlight areas, offset captions from blank fill-in spaces, and in general separate areas of the form. Arrows, stars, asterisks, and the like are good visual aids to draw attention or point out items. Notice in Figure 14-6 how effective screening can be.

Line form and margins are two areas of forms design where the designer can make a good form better. Lines are drawn on a form to separate items, guide the eyes, and draw attention to items. A thin line (hairline) is used to draw most writing lines, subdivide writing lines, construct boxes, and separate columns. The double line (parallel hairline) is used at the beginning or top of the form, at the end or conclusion of the form, and to separate major areas of the form. A dotted line is used to separate dollars and cents in money amounts. A heavy line is used to underscore column headings, separate major vertical columns, and subdivide major sections of the form. Last, combination lines are composed of a heavy line and a hairline. Both lines are used together to separate major sections of the form and sections of the form that are to be filled in at a later time. Figure 14-7 shows how various lines are used.

Providing a proper margin on a form is necessary from the printer's point of view as well as from the user's. First, printing presses require a "lockup" or "gripper" space. This area is set aside on the press to hold the printing plate stationary. Therefore, a good rule of thumb is to allow at least a 3/8- to 5/8-inch margin around the form during the design phase. The margin could be larger should the particular use of a form require it. Often forms are retained in binders or on clipboards or attached to some other device. Wider margins of up to an inch or more may be required for holes and lockdown areas.

Before reading the discussion of forms construction, note the poorly designed form in Figure 14-8, paying particular attention to such things as arrangement, spacing, and word clarity along with other good design principles.

REORDER DATE | SALES AREA ☐ MIDWEST-0 ☐ EAST-2 ☐ SOUTH-3 ☐ WEST-4 | DATE OF ORDER | S'REP CODE | ORDER NO. | YEAR - PLANT

NEED BY | SPECIAL PROMISE NUMBER | DO NOT SHIP B/4 | SPECIAL SHIPPING INSTRUCTIONS PLANT OPTION ☐ OR VIA | PACKING LIST REQUIRED | ORDER COD

PRINTED FOR IF OTHER THAN SOLD TO | COMBINATION RUN ORDER NUMBERS | REPEAT ORDER NUMBER/PREVIOUS SUPPLIER | SPECS EX RPT Y N | COPY EX RPT Y N

PRODUCT NAME BASIC SPECIAL STD. CUST. S/S CONT. BOOK F/P S/PLY S/MAILER S/FORM S/SEAL S/WEB T/CARD CUT SINGLE C/R | PRICE BOOK CLASS/SEC. | SALES REPRESENTATIVE | LOC. CODE | MOORE-COM (OR DIRECT DIAL)

SOLD TO NAME | SHIP TO (SAME AS LAST UNLESS INDICATED: ☐ SOLD TO, ☐ BILL TO, ☐ BASE, ☐ SEE LIST.)

ATTN. OF | ATTN. OF

USE IMPRINTER PLATE

STREET | STREET

CITY STATE ZIP REG/DIST. | CITY STATE ZIP

ACCOUNT NUMBER | NEW ACCT | ORDER NEW 1 RPT 2 COMP 3 REG'D 4 | AUTH DEALER | ACCOUNT NUMBER

XXXX COLLECT 1 | IN-PRICE | CHARGE | INSIDE DELIVERY COLLECT 1 IN-PRICE 2 CHARGE 3 | PALLETS YES NO | BILL ☐ ON COMP — 2 ☐ AS SHIP — 1 | WAREHOUSE CHARGES IN-PRICE CHARGE | NO. MOS. STD | NO. RELS. | NUMERICAL CONTROL Y N | QTY. TO WHSE.

CUSTOMER PURCHASE ORDER NUMBER | RELEASE/REQUISITION NUMBER | CONTRACT/AGREEMENT NUMBER | F M P | ND/FM ACCOUNT NUMBER | CATALOG NUMBER

ESTIMATE NUMBER | CUSTOMER FORM NUMBER | CUSTOMER FORM NAME | CUSTOMER COST CENTER NUMBER

BILL TO: (IF OTHER THAN SOLD TO ABOVE) | TAX EXEMPT Y N | SAMPLES | NO. INV. COPIES | Y | LOCATION CODE

ATTN. OF | CHANGE PRICE Y N | SPECIAL BILLING INSTRUCTIONS

STREET

CITY STATE ZIP | COMM AGENT ☐ — 1 OR DSD NAME ☐ — 1

ACCOUNT NUMBER | DSC SALES CODE | COMPUTER SYSTEM MAKE & MODEL

ADDITIONAL INSTRUCTIONS | 30 | F R T. | ROUTE TO DIST. CTR. | LOC. CODE | IN-PRICE | CHG. | ROUTE TO CUST. | COLL. | IN-PRICE | CHG.

IF WHSE OR FMP ONLY ONE FORM PER ORDER	CPO LOOK ALIKE	PRODUCT CODE	QUANTITY	NO. PARTS	SETS PER BOOK	WIDTH	LENGTH	DESCRIPTION / MISC. STOCK NUMBER	PRESET NUMBER	UNIT PRICE	AMOUNT

NUMBERS | COMPLETE NUMBER SPECS BELOW | CUSTOMER SIGNATURE X | TOTAL

CLEAR THRU | ALL RED | SPECIAL COLOR | SORT & LIST | NO MISS. NOS. | CONSEC. INCL. PREFIX/SUFFIX LAST & UP ☐ | MICR. CONSEC. INC. PREFIX/SUFFIX LAST & UP ☐ | BOOK & CHECK | CHECK ONLY

THIS ORDER IS SUBJECT TO THE TERMS & CONDITIONS PRINTED ON THE BACK HEREOF WHICH ARE HEREBY AGREED TO AND MADE A PART OF THE OREDER TERMS NET 30 DAYS

MOORE®

MOORE BUSINESS FORMS

Moore Business Forms, Inc.

GENERAL PURPOSE SALES CONTRACT

N001 (REV. 12/83)

CUSTOMER

FIGURE 14-6
Screening design. (Courtesy of Moore Business Forms and Systems Division.)

TRAVEL AUTHORIZATION
AU-P-24-2

COMPLETE IN INK OR PENCIL
ROUTING: COPY 1 – TRAVEL
COPY 2 – ACCOUNTING
COPY 3 – EMPLOYEE

Employee Name	Employee No.	Department

Reason for Trip

Itinerary
From ______ To ______ Date ______
From ______ To ______ Date ______
From ______ To ______ Date ______

Mode of Travel ☐ Air ☐ Auto ☐ Bus ☐ Train Other ______

Department Approval	Employee's Supervisor	Dept. Head	Date

If you claim travel expenses, complete this section	Transportation		Amount $
	Room, Board + Misc.		$
Received ☐ Cash ☐ Check	Received by	Cashier	Total $
If you require a travel advance, complete this section	Transportation		$
	Room, Board + Misc.		$
Received ☐ Cash ☐ Check	Received by	Cashier	Total $

Travel Dept. Approval	Date	Comptroller	Date

HAIRLINE
DOUBLE LINE
HEAVY LINE
DOTTED LINE

FIGURE 14-7
Line design.

Forms Construction Before the forms design can be completed, the form must pass through the construction phase. This is the point at which decisions are made regarding (1) the type and weight of paper to be used for the form, (2) the type of carbon paper or carbonless paper that will be used, (3) the type of binding required, (4) the type of paper needed for continuous-paper forms, and (5) the type and size of envelopes to be used.

Most forms are designed to be printed on bond paper. The proper weight of paper for any form is determined by the use and construction of the form. In general, 16-pound bond paper is used for single-sheet, one-sided printed forms. Two-sided, single-sheet forms are normally printed on 20-pound bond paper. Paper weights for multiple-part forms are determined by the number of copies and how the form is to be completed. The key to determining the number of copies is the legibility of the copies. If forms are to be completed on an electric typewriter, for example, then the forms may contain up to four or five parts. Hand-completed forms generally have fewer parts. This is because people normally do not press hard enough to make all the copies legible. Generally, the top copy of a multiple-part form may be 16-pound paper, with all the other copies being printed on 12-pound paper. The uses of various types and weights of paper are shown in Figure 14-9.

In developing multiple-part forms, a great deal of consideration must be given to the type of carbon paper or carbonless paper to be used. **Carbon paper** used in multiple-part forms is referred to as "one-time" carbon paper, since it is discarded after use. This type of carbon paper comes in many colors, with blue and black the most common. Blue carbon is typically used for hand completed forms, while black carbon is used in sets completed on machines.

FULL NAME ______ LAST ______ FIRST ______ M.I. ______ JR. OR SR. ______ DATE OF BIRTH ______ SOCIAL SECURITY NO. ______

SPOUSE'S NAME ______ JR. OR SR. ______ SOCIAL SECURITY NO. ______ MARITAL STATUS ☐ MARRIED ☐ UN-MARRIED ☐ SEPA-RATED | NO. OF DEPENDENTS ______

HOME ADDRESS ______ APT. OR SPACE # ______ CITY ______ STATE & ZIP ______ HOME PHONE NO. ______

MAILING ADDRESS ______ CITY ______ STATE & ZIP ______ HOW LONG AT RESIDENCE ______ YEARS — ______ MONTHS

PREVIOUS ADDRESS (If home address is less than five years)

______ CITY ______ STATE & ZIP ______ HOW LONG THERE ______ YEARS — ______ MONTHS

NEAREST RELATIVE ______ ADDRESS ______ RELATIONSHIP ______ PHONE NO. ______

SPOUSE'S NEAREST RELATIVE ______ ADDRESS ______ RELATIONSHIP ______ PHONE NO. ______

*Income from alimony, child support, or maintenance payments need not be revealed if you do not choose to disclose such income in applying for credit. As a creditor, we may inquire whether any income stated in an application is derived from such a source.

PRESENT EMPLOYER ______ POSITION ______ HOW LONG ______ YEARS — ______ MONTHS ______ BUSINESS PHONE ______

ADDRESS ______ CITY ______ STATE & ZIP ______ UNION & LOCAL NO. ______ MONTHLY TAKE HOME PAY $ ______

SPOUSE'S EMPLOYER ______ POSITION ______ HOW LONG ______ YEARS — ______ MONTHS BUSINESS PHONE ______ TAKE HOME PAY $ ______

PREVIOUS EMPLOYER'S NAME & ADDRESS ______ HOW LONG ______ YEARS OTHER INCOME* (DESCRIBE) ______ *OTHER INCOME $ ______

NAME OF YOUR BANK ______ BRANCH ______ TOTAL INCOME $ ______

CHECKING ACCOUNT NO. ______ AVERAGE BALANCE ______ DATE OPEN ______ SAVINGS ACCOUNT NO. ______ AVERAGE BALANCE ______ DATE OPEN ______

FIGURE 14-8
A poorly designed form.

FIGURE 14-9 Business forms selection chart.

Type of Paper	Weight of Paper (Pounds)	Recommended Use	Estimated Lifetime of Paper with Average Use (Years)	Paper Content	Handling Quality
Manifold (onion skin)	8–11	Carbon paper, multipart forms	15	Wood	Minimum
Bond	12–24	Letterhead, memos, business forms, continuous forms, legal documents, envelopes	15–20	Wood/Rag	Normal
Manila	16–32	Envelopes, file folders, filing jackets	15–20	Wood	Normal
Ledger	28–40	Permanent and semipermanent records–ledgers	25–50	Wood/Rag	Heavy
Offset	40–70	Labels, announcements, booklets, leaflets, maps	50–75	Wood/Rag	Normal
Tab card	99	Computer punch cards	75–100	Wood/Rag	Heavy
Index	70–150	Card forms, calendars, file folders, manual covers, time cards, posters	Permanent	Wood	Heavy

If there are data on the top copy of the form that the user does not want printed on the additional copies, the carbon paper can be manufactured with uncoated areas. This paper is referred to as **spot carbon.** Using spot carbon paper is an excellent method of selective information distribution. The user of any particular copy receives only the data required for that function.

Initially more expensive to purchase but more convenient and easier to use than carbon paper, **carbonless paper** is used more and more in offices today. Carbonless paper is often referred to as "NCR" paper, which means "no carbon required." Three types of carbonless paper are available. The most widely used type is chemical carbonless paper: bond paper coated with two chemicals—one on the front of each sheet of paper in the form and another on the back of each sheet. When the copies of the form are joined and pressure is applied to the top copy, an image appears on the bottom copies. The reaction of the chemical from the back of one copy with the chemical from the front of the copy under it creates the image.

After the forms are printed, the binding process takes place. If necessary, the forms are cut to the right size; holes are punched or drilled; perforations and scoring are done; and windows are die-cut. The forms are collated before being interleaved with carbon paper, if used, and glued together. Before the forms are delivered to the user, the forms are padded, if required, and packaged. Many users today require forms to be packaged in groups of 100, 250, or 500 for ease of storing, inventory control, and issuing.

Many times a form must be designed for use in a continuous-flow process. This means that the forms are joined in one continuous scroll, attached head to foot. These forms can be used in computer printers, typewriters, and various types of writing machines and registers. The forms are printed on a roll of paper and perforated between the individual forms.

Envelopes are designed to carry documents, primarily through the mail. Therefore, many envelopes today are designed with a window that allows the name and address of the recipient to show through. As can be seen in Figure 14-10, standard window envelopes come in many sizes, with the window placed

FIGURE 14-10 Standard envelope sizes, including window dimensions.

Envelope Size Number	Envelope Dimensions	Window Size				Type*
		$1\frac{1}{8} \times 4\frac{1}{2}$	$1 \times 3\frac{3}{4}$	$1\frac{1}{4} \times 3\frac{3}{4}$	1×4	
$2\frac{1}{2}$	$4\frac{1}{2} \times 5\frac{7}{8}$					B
3	$4\frac{3}{4} \times 6\frac{1}{2}$					B
5	$5\frac{1}{2} \times 8\frac{1}{8}$					B
6	$5\frac{3}{4} \times 8\frac{7}{8}$					B
$6\frac{1}{4}$	$3\frac{1}{2} \times 6$	x				C
$6\frac{1}{2}$	6×9					B
$6\frac{3}{4}$	$3\frac{5}{8} \times 6\frac{1}{2}$	x				C
7	$6\frac{1}{4} \times 9\frac{5}{8}$					B
7	$3\frac{3}{4} \times 6\frac{3}{4}$	x				C
$7\frac{1}{2}$	$7\frac{1}{2} \times 10\frac{1}{2}$					B
$7\frac{3}{4}$	$3\frac{7}{8} \times 7\frac{1}{2}$	x				C
$8\frac{5}{8}$	$3\frac{5}{8} \times 8\frac{5}{8}$	x	x	x	x	C
9	$3\frac{7}{8} \times 8\frac{7}{8}$	x				C
9	$8\frac{3}{4} \times 11\frac{1}{2}$					B
$9\frac{1}{2}$	9×12					B
10	$4\frac{1}{8} \times 9\frac{1}{2}$	x				C
10	$9\frac{1}{2} \times 12\frac{5}{8}$					B
11	$4\frac{1}{2} \times 10\frac{3}{8}$	x				C
12	$4\frac{3}{4} \times 11$	x				C
14	$5 \times 11\frac{1}{2}$	x				C

Note. *B, Booklet envelope; C, commercial envelope.

in different locations. If a standard size cannot be used, a special one can be designed. Envelope manufacturers should be consulted before designing and ordering special envelopes, since costs may be prohibitive. When designing an envelope, some basic minimum requirements must be followed. The transparent window panel must run parallel to, and a minimum of 3/8 inch from, the bottom edge of the envelope. The left edge of the transparent window can be no closer than 3/8 inch to the left end of the envelope. The top of the transparent window may be no closer than 1-3/8 inch from the top edge of the envelope.

Some forms manufacturers provide, at no cost to the user, many forms design aids. One of the design aids provided is the forms design layout sheet. These sheets are used by designers to draw up forms. Figure 14-11 shows a forms design layout sheet with a sample form. Note such items as screening, line form, word clarity, and spacing.

Business Forms Design Checklist

As an aid to effective forms analysis and design, the serious student should develop a checklist of important items to review when preparing a form. The

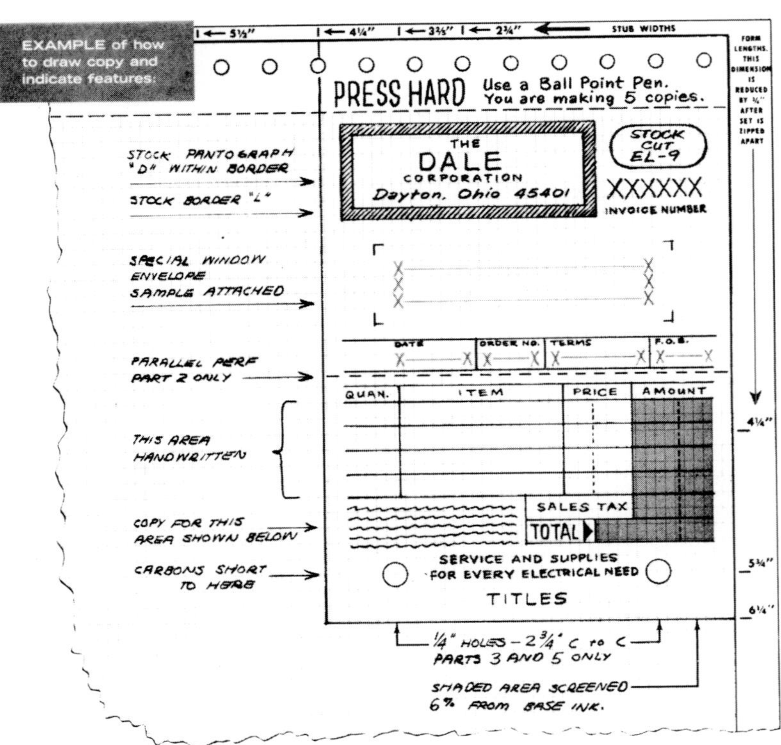

FIGURE 14-11 Forms design layout sheet. (Courtesy of The Standard Register Company, Dayton, OH.)

following checklist can be used as a basic working document that one can alter as necessary:

1. Has the problem-identification process been completed?
2. Was the "what, where, when, who, and how" procedure used?
3. Can the form be designed to fit on standard-size paper?
4. Will the form be used in posting trays, binders, file cabinets, typewriters, registers, and other equipment?
5. Has blank or unused space been reduced on the form?
6. Has the design technique that arranges forms into five basic sections been used?
7. Are the form title, name, and number clear and meaningful?
8. Do the instructions and routing information provide the user with adequate instruction?
9. If the form is to be completed by typewriter, have the horizontal and vertical spacing been set for proper tab stops and carriage returns?
10. Has the upper-left-caption arrangement been used?
11. Has word clarity been achieved by structuring the questions in such a way as to receive the desired responses?
12. Have check boxes been used in the proper horizontal and vertical configurations?
13. Can screening and/or visual aids be used to separate, highlight, and identify portions of the form?
14. Has proper line form been used to achieve good form design?
15. Since presses require a "lockup" or "gripper" space, has at least a 3/8- to 5/8-inch margin been left around the form?
16. If holes or a lockdown area are required, has a wider margin of 1 inch or more been left on the form?
17. Was the use and construction of the form considered in determining the proper weight of paper used?
18. If the form is to be multiple-part, was consideration given to the type of carbon paper or carbonless paper used?
19. Have all the appropriate holes, perforations, scoring, padding, packaging, and so on been determined prior to sending the form to the printer?
20. What window envelope construction been considered for a form designed to be mailed in a window envelope?

Computer Forms Design

Forms designed specifically for computer use have some characteristics that apply only to data processing forms. Line and tab spacing are different for computer forms than for standard business forms. Computer forms must also have pin-feed holes along the sides for feeding through a computer printer. The form shown in Figure 14-12 is specially designed to be printed by computer.

Computer forms are also printed in plies or copies. This means that two, three, four, five, or six copies can be printed at one time to make the most efficient use of a computer's printer. In general, it is not a good practice to print a report with five or six copies. The fifth and sixth copies are often of such poor quality as to be unusable.

Computer forms are referred to as *continuous,* which means the forms are printed on long rolls of paper. Each page is perforated at the top and bottom, and the pages are fan-folded. Once a multiple-copy form or report has been printed, it must be *decollated.* This process separates the copies and removes the carbon paper. The form or report can be left fan-folded and bound in covers to form a book. Should the user wish to use the pages separately, the report can be run through a *burster*, a device that breaks or tears the pages apart along the perforations between pages.

Forms Control and Management

Forms control and management have been practiced by government and businesses for years. This function has as its primary objective the monitoring and controlling of all the forms used by an organization. The control and management function can be divided into the development of forms-control files, calculating forms, costs the development of procurement procedures, the management of inventory control, the disposal of obsolete forms, and the management of personnel.

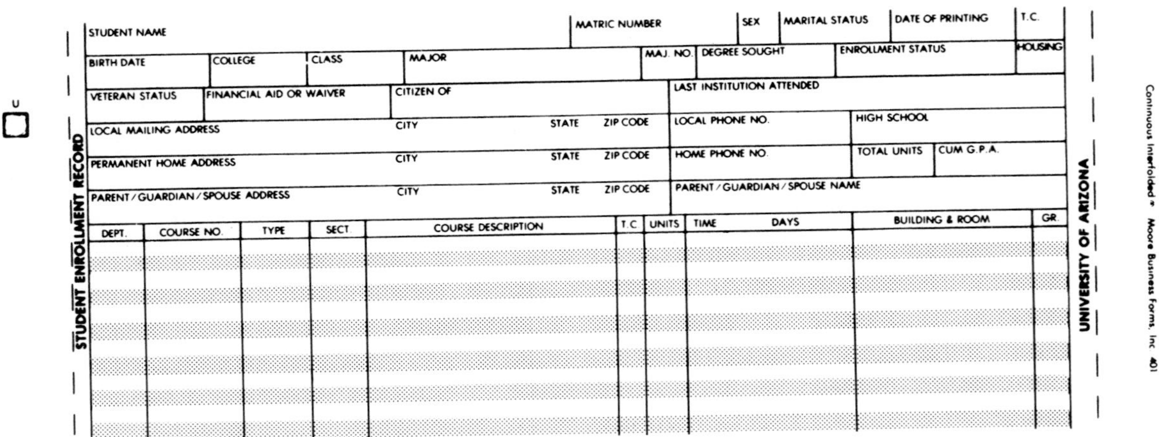

STUDENT ENROLLMENT RECORD

STUDENT NAME	MATRIC NUMBER	SEX	MARITAL STATUS	DATE OF PRINTING	T.C.

BIRTH DATE	COLLEGE	CLASS	MAJOR	MAJ. NO.	DEGREE SOUGHT	ENROLLMENT STATUS	HOUSING

VETERAN STATUS	FINANCIAL AID OR WAIVER	CITIZEN OF	LAST INSTITUTION ATTENDED

LOCAL MAILING ADDRESS	CITY	STATE	ZIP CODE	LOCAL PHONE NO.	HIGH SCHOOL	
PERMANENT HOME ADDRESS	CITY	STATE	ZIP CODE	HOME PHONE NO.	TOTAL UNITS	CUM G.P.A.
PARENT / GUARDIAN / SPOUSE ADDRESS	CITY	STATE	ZIP CODE	PARENT / GUARDIAN / SPOUSE NAME		

DEPT.	COURSE NO.	TYPE	SECT.	COURSE DESCRIPTION	T.C.	UNITS	TIME	DAYS	BUILDING & ROOM	GR.

UNIVERSITY OF ARIZONA

Continuous Interfolded ® Moore Business Forms, Inc. 401

U

FIGURE 14-12
Form designed to be printed by computer. (Courtesy of Moore Business Forms, Inc.)

Forms-Control Files

An integral part of any forms program is the development and maintenance of forms-control files. These files are inventories of all the forms used in an organization. There are two basic types of control files: numeric and classification. The *numeric control file* is in numeric order by form number (see Figure 14-13). The primary purpose of this file is to show the history of each form from its creation to its present status. A simple method of setting up a numeric control file is to use one file folder for each of the different forms in the active inventory. The folder should contain a copy of the latest revision of the form, all data relating to changes or revisions, authorizations, and specific design or printing requirements. As forms become obsolete, the folders are removed from the active file and moved to an obsolete file.

A *classification control file* is one in which forms for related functions or uses are grouped together (see Figure 14-14). For example, under the classification

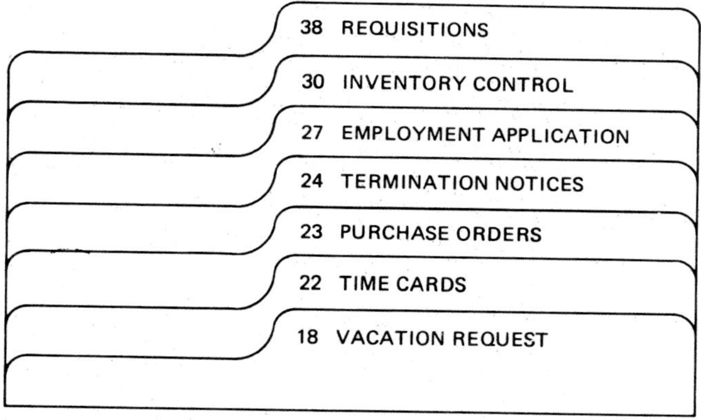

FIGURE 14-13 Numeric control file.

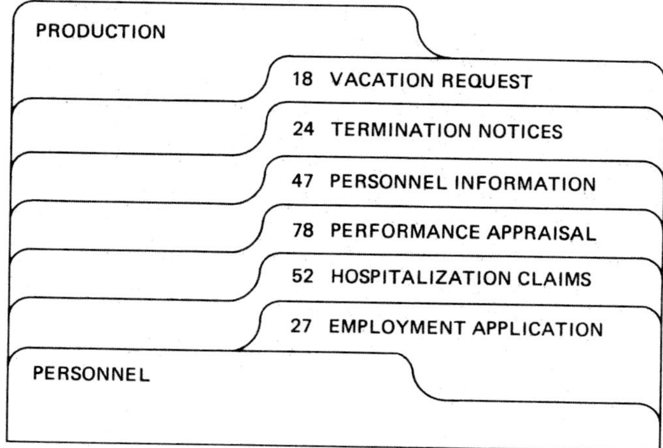

FIGURE 14-4 Classification control file.

"Personnel" one might find employment applications, termination notices, personnel information, and performance-appraisal forms. Each folder should contain at least one copy of the form. This type of file permits forms administrators to detect forms that can be eliminated or combined with other forms, to avoid designing new forms when similar forms exist, and to locate and standardize company-wide forms.

Another file that can be extremely useful is a ready-reference control file, maintained by form number or form title on 3-by-5-inch cards. A ready-reference file card should contain the form number, title, number of copies, and size of the form, using department(s), vendor, and any other useful data. This type of file can be a rapid reference for certain types of information. More detailed data should be kept in the control file.

In many organizations, forms administrators have developed a forms catalog or manual. The forms catalog can be compared in some respects to the forms control file, with the exception that all information is in a single book or binder. Generally, these catalogs contain the same information about every form, while the control files vary according to the number of revisions of a form, age of the form, and so on. Along with forms-related information, catalogs may also contain inventory-related information. Since catalogs duplicate much of the information available in other sources, management may feel that a catalog is unnecessary. A catalog would be an optional item rather than a requirement.

CALCULATING FORMS COSTS

The actual cost of acquiring a form is very slight—4.4 percent—compared to the cost of clerical processing—a whopping 84.4 percent—and the cost of maintaining forms in files, 11.2 percent. However, according to Mark Langemo, CRM, and Daniel Brathal in MANAGING BUSINESS FORMS, "cost" and "price" should not be considered synonymous. The price of the form is the amount of money paid for the forms, i.e., $36 for a thousand forms. The true cost of a business form is calculated by the following formula[3]:

Step 1: Determine Physical Cost to Acquire a Form:

Multiply Cost Per Thousand × the Number in Thousands Used Each Year.

Example: $36 × 2 = $72 (Cost of 2,000 Forms)

[3]Mark Langemo, CRM, and Daniel A. Brathal, MANAGING BUSINESS FORMS, ARMA International, 1988. Courtesy of ARMA International.

Step 2: Determine the Annual Labor Cost to Use the Form:

Multiply the Number of Minutes Required to Complete a Form × Salary Per Minute of the Personnel × Number of Forms Used Each Year

> Example: 25 minutes × .24 per minute (Based on $30,000) × 2,000 = $12,000.

Step 3: Combine Physical Cost to Acquire the Form plus Annual Labor Cost to Use the Form = The Total Annual Forms Cost

> Example: $72. (Step 1) plus $12,000 (Step 2) = $12,072 (Step 3)

Note: An average of 25 minutes is spent completing, reviewing, routing and filing each form and the average form is used in quantities of two thousand per year.[4]

Procurement

Whether procuring forms for a large organization or a small firm, one must be acutely aware of all procurement options available. Some knowledge of printing and forms design is important in the operation of an effective procurement program. By carefully using ordering techniques and other information that may be available, a purchasing agent or forms administrator can achieve significant cost savings. Such ordering techniques as centralized purchasing, combination ordering, blanket ordering, and in-house printing will be discussed.

Centralized Purchasing **Centralized purchasing** of forms by large organizations on a company-wide basis can show very good cost savings. In this type of purchasing, all divisions of an organization combine their forms requirements into one large volume order for each form. Normally, the purchasing department then asks for bids from vendors on the yearly requirement of forms, selects the most advantageous bid, and negotiates a contract with one or more of the vendors. Under most circumstances, a vendor is awarded a contract for the lowest price per item. A vendor may be awarded a contract for the lowest overall prices for a group of forms. For example, there may be different types and designs of forms, with varying quantities and prices; yet the total package might cost less through one vendor.

[4]Michael J. McCoy, "Corporate Profitability and Good Forms," FORMS AND LABEL PURCHASING, March, 1990

Blanket Ordering In recent years many companies have used the **blanket ordering** technique for procuring forms. Using this process, forms that are not subject to frequent revision, such as letterhead paper, interoffice memo paper, standard worksheets, envelopes, routing pads, and other special forms, are ordered for a specific period of time from a single vendor. This type of purchasing is good for both the vendor and the user. The user has a certain supply over the contract period for a set price. The printer knows there will be no forms revisions over the period and can schedule the work accordingly.

Combination Ordering Another possibility not to be overlooked when procuring forms is **combination ordering.** Forms that are of different design but have the same basic construction can often be printed together in a combination run. For example, it would be possible to have two different forms, each containing four parts, requiring the same color paper and the same size. The printer is able to position the forms copy on the same large printing plate and can print both forms during one press run.

In-House Printing Organizations that have in-house printing capability are indeed fortunate. The key to a successful in-house printing operation is selective printing—printing in-house only those forms that can be economically justified. The printing equipment should be used to the maximum of its design capabilities. For printing jobs in excess of machine limits, outside printing can be justified by economies of scale.

When deciding to order a form, one of the first considerations must be to determine if the job is to be printed in-house or sent to a vendor. In addition to considering the volume, the user must also consider the form's costs, convenience, and security.

In many cases small-volume orders of forms are more economically printed in-house, since vendors must charge for extras, such as shipping, handling, and billing. In-house operations, on the whole, do not generate these kinds of charges. The cost factors must be established for each operation of the in-house printing facility to determine the actual in-house cost of a form. These factors may include labor, materials, waste, light, water, and so on. If all factors are established, analyzed, and kept current, a realistic comparison can be made between the two printing options. Forms or printed reports are often needed quickly. Here, the convenience of an in-house printing facility becomes apparent. Work can be produced without the long delays usually encountered by outside procurement.

Another advantage of in-house printing is security. The ability to have confidential and/or controlled forms or documents printed or copied in-house is desirable and important. In some cases federal security regulations may be in effect when military or other governmental contracts are involved.

Inventory Control

An efficient and effectively run **inventory control** program can help make or break any forms program. A well-run inventory system will provide the user with the following important information:

1. The amount or number of each form on hand.
2. The point at which a particular item must be reordered.
3. Daily, weekly, or monthly usage trends.
4. A detailed history of all forms, covering the amount of required safety stock, the amount of lead time needed to order stock, backorder statistics, and data on obsolete forms. Safety stock is the amount of extra stock on hand for emergencies when an order of stock does not arrive on time.

Several inventory control methods can be used to maintain a forms inventory. Even though this discussion focuses on the perpetual inventory method, the user should develop and use the method that best meets organizational needs and operational considerations.

Considered by many to be the most flexible inventory system of all, **perpetual inventory** control is an extremely simple system to use. Under this system, changes in stock level are recorded on an inventory control card as stock is received or issued (see Figure 14-15). An up-to-the-minute record of the stock level is maintained. When the reorder point (a minimum predetermined stock level) is reached, and before the form is reordered, the form's user should be queried as to the projected use of the form.

FIGURE 14-15 Perpetual inventory control card.

Item No. P24-1 — INVENTORY STOCK CONTROL RECORD — R-90

Item Name: Employee performance evaluation form — RO 2500

Comment: Issue in packages of 250 only — LOC A-17 — QPP 250

DATE	QUANTITY ORDERED	QUANTITY RECEIVED	QUANTITY ISSUED	BALANCE ON HAND
6-14-90	10,000			2500
7-14-90		10,000		12500
7-30-90			2500	10000
6-17-91			3000	7000
7-3-91			4500	2500
7-10-91	10,000			2500
8-20-91		10,000		12500
6-30-92			3000	9500
7-7-92			2750	6750

Possibly the most crucial aspect of the perpetual inventory system or any other inventory system is the stock reorder point or RO. The reorder point is the minimum stock level at which an organization can function until new stock is received. Factors to be considered in developing reorder points are (1) the time necessary to design or revise a form; (2) the time required to purchase or place an order; (3) the time required to print, ship, and receive the form; (4) the amount of safety stock required to have on hand; and (5) the amount or quantities to order. Generally, a reorder point of 2 1/2 months' stock should be maintained when ordering in-house forms. A 3 month stock-on-hand reorder point can be used for reordering forms purchased from outside vendors.

The specific quantity of forms to be purchased is generally controlled by the price discount given for various quantities, the rate at which the stock is consumed, and the cost of reordering stock versus storing large quantities of stock. Many records or forms managers believe that when in doubt as to the amount of stock to order, it is better to "order smaller quantities because the loss is less."

Any decision as to whether the organization should stock a form or not should be the responsibility of the forms-control section. In cases where forms are used by many different departments, the forms should be stocked by central supply so that forms can always be available for all users. In some organizations forms will be used by only one department or at a single site. When this occurs, a good practice is to allow the users to maintain their own stock. In this situation, the user must accept the responsibility for ordering the forms and maintaining control over them. There may be a time when a form is not stocked and is ordered as it is needed. Typically, this is not an effective way to operate, but circumstances might dictate otherwise.

Disposition of Obsolete Forms

One aspect of forms control and management most often ignored is the deletion and disposition of obsolete forms. Many times obsolete forms are not removed from inventory until after the forms have been used and problems have arisen. Any forms operation should remove all obsolete or unusable forms on a regular basis.

Normally, forms become obsolete when the form's content has changed or been revised; at the end of a specific time period, as with IRS forms; or when a specific function supported by a particular form has ended. With proper revision data available, one can easily determine when a form has been revised or has become obsolete. One can also easily recognize and dispose of forms that have become obsolete at the end of specific time periods. On the other hand, it is almost impossible to know that a form has become obsolete if the reason is that a function has ended or the data collected is no longer needed. Therefore, the personnel responsible for handling obsolete forms must keep abreast of all organizational changes on a daily or weekly basis.

Another method of determining obsolescence is to contact the form's user to determine the form's status. Here the inventory control personnel could flag all forms that have not been issued to the user during a specific period of time. For example, if stock for form number DRS-133-7 had not been issued to the user in six months or even one year, this could be a good indicator of the form's obsolescence. On the other hand, the user may just have a large supply of the form on hand. The forms personnel must determine the form's status before disposing of the forms.

Once a form has been found obsolete, all the forms for that number and revision should be destroyed. The printer who printed the forms should be notified of the form's obsolescence so the printing plates and other related material can be destroyed. This prevents obsolete forms from being printed by mistake.

Forms Management Personnel

According to a recent survey in FORMS AND SYSTEMS PROFESSIONAL, 30 percent of forms professionals indicated they are responsible for a forms budget of $100,000 to $500,000 per year while 26 percent handle a budget of over $1 million. These data are presented in Figure 14-6.

This survey also revealed that 25 percent of Forms Managers had 3 to 6 employees reporting to them while an additional 25 percent had 7 or more employees under them. More than half of the forms professionals responding to this survey had either Data Processing or Systems Analyst experience and managed forms at more than one location.[5]

FIGURE 14-16
Forms Budgets

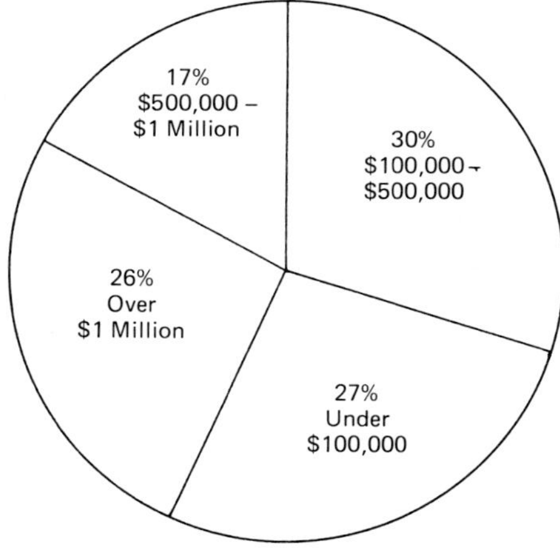

[5]"How Do You Compare?," FORMS AND SYSTEMS PROFESSIONAL, Winter, 1989.

Regardless of the size of an organization, certain forms-related tasks must be performed. Although all functions may be performed by one person in a small firm, the discussion here deals with the company large enough to maintain a forms administration department with full-time employees. The positions in a typical firm might be (1) the forms department manager, (2) a forms analyst, (3) a forms designer, and (4) a stockroom supervisor or forms clerk.

The forms department manager directs and controls the organization's forms administration program. More specifically, the manager supervises personnel, interacts with other company management and department heads on areas of common concern, and formulates the department's forms-related policies.

The forms analyst assists other departments with their forms-design requirements. Specific tasks may include developing paperwork systems, designing forms, assisting with employee supervision, and helping to develop forms-related policy.

The forms designer may assist the forms analyst, design forms, order forms, follow up on forms-related problems, and assist where necessary.

Last, the stockroom supervisor or forms clerk is responsible for all stockroom activities, which may include receiving, storing, and issuing stock; checking for obsolete stock; maintaining up-to-date records; notifying the forms designer of stock to be ordered; and supervising employees, if any.

BFMA (Business Forms Management Association) is a professional association for forms and information resource management professionals. BFMA offers technical educational programs, an annual Symposium, publications, and networking opportunities to its members. BFMA is international in scope with members chapters throughout the United States and Canada and members-at-large in eight countries. For more information on BFMA, see Appendix C.

Technological Change

Over the past 20 years technological change has greatly affected the forms industry. New printing presses, phototypesetting devices, and improved camera equipment, to name a few, have been the instruments of growth and change in the industry. These devices now permit better artwork, improved forms construction, and increased production rates. For example, phototypesetting allows (1) the copy to be tighter (more characters per page), neater, and more readable; (2) the copy to have a more aesthetic appearance; and (3) a wide variety of type styles to be used, from fine to bold. These new type styles have increased the legibility of forms and have improved the appearance and design techniques. The development of new types of paper for specific job applications has increased special forms production. In effect, the production side of the forms industry has experienced phenomenal growth.

Forms analysis and design have been changed dramatically by the use of computers to aid in designing forms. With the computer's ability to store and recall a form's image, alterations can be made rapidly without redrawing the form. By using the computer's vast storage capability, the forms analyst can rapidly analyze forms by looking at the various aspects of a form's history, use, and so on.

Typesetting is moving out of the print shop and into the modern office with the use of computer phototypesetting or photocomposition. The three major reasons for using photocomposition are (1) the appearance of the copy, (2) ease of reading, and (3) reduced costs from compacting the typeset copy.

The future of the printing industry seems just as bright today as it did 10 years ago. With computers leading the way, there will be more innovations in the various processes used in the print shop. There will be significant changes in the inputting and creating of documents as well as the formatting and transmitting of the document to the end user. Since images are electronic and stored in the computer memory, it is simple to change, move or delete any part of a document. Computer programs that permit an operator to design page elements for appearance, by placing the type and illustrations where it is desired, has helped solve the page layout problem. Now with the work in the computer memory, a customer's information data bank can be available through a telephone modem. This ensures that the latest information is always available for printing.

CHAPTER HIGHLIGHTS

- The basic types of documents in an office environment are preprinted business forms, correspondence, and computer-printed data.
- The preprinted business form is the company's primary means of communicating with customers, suppliers, employees, and governmental agencies.
- A forms program is divided into analysis, design, construction, control, and management.
- A forms analyst looks at all the circumstances surrounding a form's current or projected use to determine if a new form is needed, if an old from can be revised, or if two forms can be combined.
- Information found in the analysis phase is used during the design and layout process to draw up the actual form.
- Aspects of good forms design are item arrangement, spacing, word clarity, line form, and margins.
- Other considerations, such as filing and mailing, intended use in machines, and the form's construction, must also be considered in the design phase.
- Forms control and management are concerned with the monitoring and controlling of forms used by a company.

- The control and management function can be divided into the procurement of forms, development of control files, inventory control, disposal of obsolete forms, and staffing or personnel requirements.
- Forms procurement deals with the many processes used to purchase forms. By using the techniques of centralized purchasing, combination ordering, in-house printing, and blanket ordering, a company can realize significant cost savings for forms.
- There are two basic types of forms-control files. The numeric control file and the classification control file are used to provide history on forms and to reveal forms that can be combined or eliminated altogether.
- Many consider the perpetual method of inventory control to be the best of all inventory systems.
- Obsolete forms must be removed from the inventory system as soon as they become obsolete.
- The four primary positions in a forms administrative program are the forms manager, forms analyst, forms designer, and stockroom supervisor or clerk.

QUESTIONS FOR REVIEW

1. What are the various parts of a forms program?
2. Define forms analysis.
3. What are the five parts of a form?
4. Why is word clarity important in forms design?
5. Discuss carbonless paper.
6. Why is it important to consider envelope design when designing a form?
7. Discuss the two primary types of forms-control files.
8. What are four considerations when procuring forms?
9. Why is it crucial to remove obsolete forms from the forms inventory?
10. What are the four most common staff positions in a forms administration program?
11. Discuss the pros and cons of printing all of an organization's forms in-house.

THE DECISION MAKER

Case Study

As a recently hired forms designer for a major auto manufacturer, you have been assigned your first forms design task by the forms analyst. You are to take the data provided by the forms analyst and make a rough sketch of an employee job application form for a recently acquired subsidiary company. The job applicant needs to supply the following information on the form: the person's name; address; date of birth; social security number; date of the application; home and message telephone numbers; position applied for; minimum acceptable salary; availability for work full-or part-time, days, evenings, weekends, and nights; military service; education and training; professional and technical license data; medical questions concerning worker's compensation; clerical skills and machines operated by the applicant; work experience, including company name, address, supervisor's title and name, pay rate, job title and duties, dates of employment, and reason for leaving; statement concerning truthfulness of facts; and the applicant's signature and date. The name of the form is "Job Application." The form number is POP181-3 and there will be no routing. Leave a block for the interviewer's notes. You may look at other job application forms for ideas and assistance.

REPROGRAPHICS MANAGEMENT AND CONTROL

OBJECTIVES

Upon completion of this chapter, the student should be able to:

1. Describe the current status of the copier industry.
2. Differentiate between the various categories of copiers.
3. List and describe copier features.
4. Explain the photocopying process.
5. Describe recent improvements in copier technology.
6. Describe the growth and future of facsimile terminals.
7. Distinguish between centralized and convenience copying arrangements.
8. Identify the components of the CPC calculation.
9. Provide suggestions for controlling copier abuse.

REPROGRAPHICS MANAGEMENT AND CONTROL

The office of the 1990s, using modern technology, can produce a volume of work that would have been thought impossible in the 1950s. Today's offices contain sophisticated communication equipment, computer systems, micrographics equipment and reprographic machines. Within this constantly changing office environment, the records manager must be alert, well-informed, and knowledgeable to do an effective job. An area of prime concern for the records manager is reprographics. **Reprographics** is the facsimile reproduction of graphic material. In the records management field, reprographics includes the control and management of copying machines, practices, and procedures.

According to a 1990 issue of MODERN OFFICE TECHNOLOGY, 400 billion images a year are produced by the copier industry. Apparently, the paperwork explosion and the "make an extra copy" mentality are in full swing. While some analysts are predicting a slower growth rate in copier purchases through the 90s, revenues for copiers exceeded $18 billion in 1989. The latest technology—full-color copying—is now available and affordable. Industry experts predict 1992 revenues from color copiers alone to be $860 million. Thus, this mature industry, is addressing the needs of all sectors of business. Copiers are available in selections ranging from "plain vanilla" to a virtual smorgasbord of features. The records manager needs to tame the "paperwork tiger" and, at the same time, deliver copying services with the features and services required by the organization.

COPIER GROWTH

The 1990s will, no doubt, continue the growth experienced in the 1980s by the copier industry. The "Buyer's Reference Guide to Office Copiers" in the July, 1990 issue of MODERN OFFICE TECHNOLOGY magazine, listed 22 companies selling a variety of "regular" copiers and 9 companies selling "color" copiers.

To better understand the copier environment, one must categorize the equipment. One effective way to do this is by the number of copies delivered per minute by a copier. Using a copies-per-minute (CPM) delivery rate, the following categories are noted by industry experts:

Personal Copiers: 1 to 10 CPM = low volume

Convenience Copiers: 11 to 45 CPM = medium volume

Copier Center Machines: 46 or more CPM = high volume

To show the emphasis of the marketplace in 1990, convenience copiers held 71 percent of the market share of the copier industry. Convenience copiers are those copiers making 11 to 45 CPMs or 1,500 to 20,000 copies per month.

These copiers are equipped with basic features, such as zoom, enlargement, reduction, and collating, and retail from $3,000 to $9,500.

However, the fastest growing segment of the copier industry is the personal copier, making 10 CPM or 500 copies per month. These are reliable copiers offering minimal features and available for about $1,200. The high-volume end of this industry belongs to copier center machines that offer many features and are used for volume copying. These machines, loaded with memory, editing, and job-management features typically start at $10,000 and up depending on level of sophistication and features. Super-high volume copiers may retail in the $50,000 range producing close to 500,000 copies per month at speeds of 90 CPM.

Copier Features

Records managers need to keep up to date on equipment features that could save money and/or increase productivity. Generally, one or two improvements are not justification for acquiring a new copier. All capabilities of a copier must be weighed and evaluated to determine the best copier for a given task or procedure. Features such as color copying, enlargement and reduction, automatic exposure control, automatic feeders, key counters, collator or bin sorters, and duplexing will be discussed in the following sections.

Color Copying

One-pass, full-color copying is now available in copier machines for approximately $8,000. The Cycolor Division of the Mead Corporation (Dayton, Ohio) has recently marketed Cycolor ®, a color-imaging technique that makes affordable color copies with good speed at a reasonable cost. Figure 15-1 shows the Brother CC5500 full-color copier that utilizes the Cycolor® technology. Since the color is in the paper, there are no toners, ribbons, or chemicals to change. As noted previously, at least 9 companies currently offer color copiers with additional companies entering this market daily.

According to industry analysts, this market is "hot" and will continue to grow. Why? Because we are starting to realize the value that color adds to documents, particularly graphics. According to a U.S. Testing Research Company, there is an 82 percent higher attention span in presentations that use color. Thus, a major advantage to using color copying is not only a higher attention span, but also higher retention after a meeting is over.

Enlargement and Reduction

A number of equipment manufacturers are marketing copiers with **enlargement** and/or **reduction** features. The enlargement mode permits an original image to be copied in a larger size. The image on the copy might be, for example, 154 percent of the image on the original document. Conversely, the reduc-

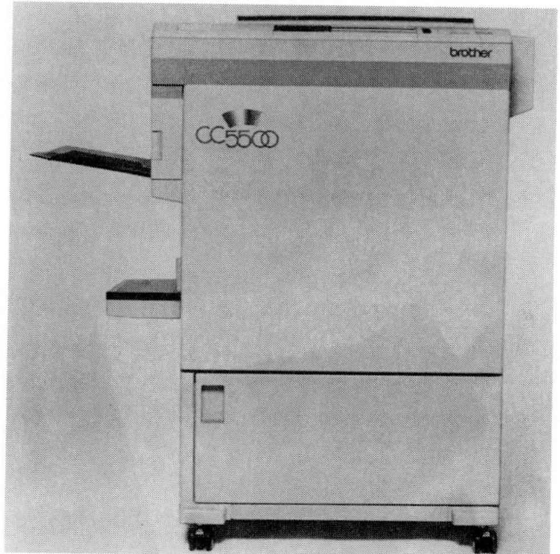

FIGURE 15-1 Brother CC5500 copier.

tion mode permits the image on a copy to be reduced to a fraction of the size of the original document. Some common reduction percentages found today are 65 percent, 79 percent, and 98 percent. Many copiers may have one or both modes. The zoom process provides a continuous range of reduction enlargement ratios between, for instance, 154 percent and 65 percent.

Automatic Exposure Control

A recent development in the copying industry is **automatic exposure control.** A copier with this feature uses a microprocessor to monitor the original document and adjust the amount of light and toner to ensure a high-quality copy.

Automatic Feeder

Automatic-feeder options, found on many copiers and shown in Figure 15-2, allow the operator to feed individual originals. In some vendors' machines, up to 100 originals can be stacked in the feeder at one time for automatic feeding and copying. This option, in whatever form the vendor provides on the equipment, allows the operator to handle other tasks while copies are being produced.

Key Counter

Within a company or office many different departments or sections may use the same copier. This can cause security and cost-allocation problems, such as the unauthorized use of copiers by employees or an inability to charge client accounts on an individual job basis. Additionally, management may find it difficult to determine the number of copies generated by each section of an

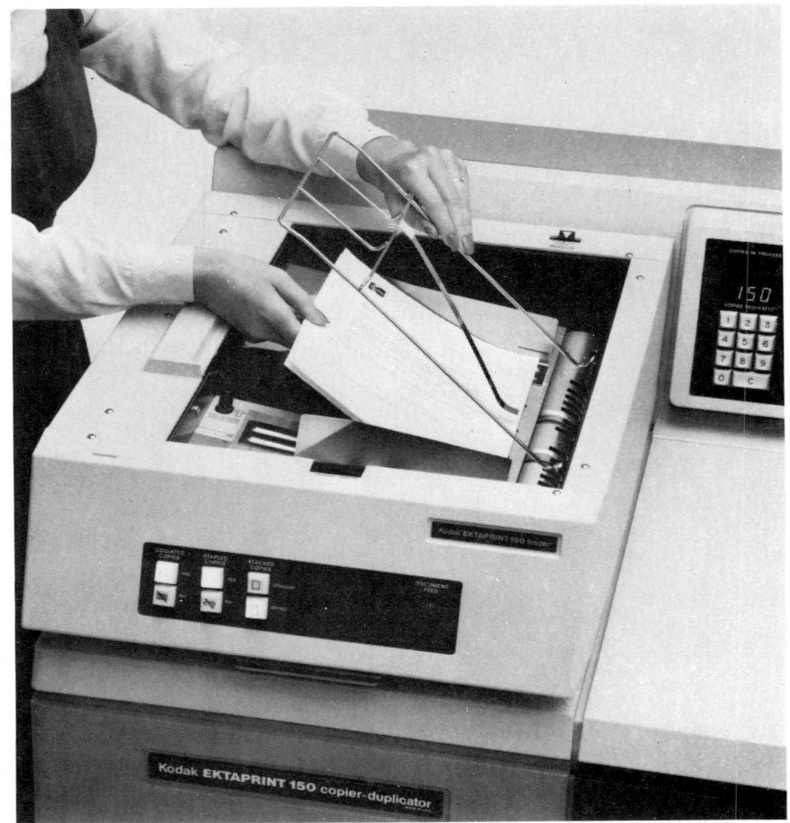

FIGURE 15-2
Kodak Ektaprint 150 feeder. (Courtesy of Eastman Kodak Company.)

office over a specific period of time. All of these problems can be addressed with the **key counter,** which is shown in Figure 15-3. A key counter is simply a device for counting the number of copies produced by a copier. When inserted into a copier, the device activates the machine and keeps count of the copies made. A more sophisticated innovation on the market uses an employee-coded identification card to record the employee's number and number of copies made. These devices can be added to many vendors' machines.

Collator or Bin Sorter

A piece of equipment that can be extremely useful in many offices is the **collator** or **bin sorter,** shown in Figure 15-4. This option, when attached to a copier, can save literally hundreds of hours of a secretary's or clerk's time by collating copy sets. Some vendors provide a finisher option that, in effect, collates and staples the copies into sets. In an environment where sets are frequently produced, this feature would be invaluable.

FIGURE 15-3
Key counter.

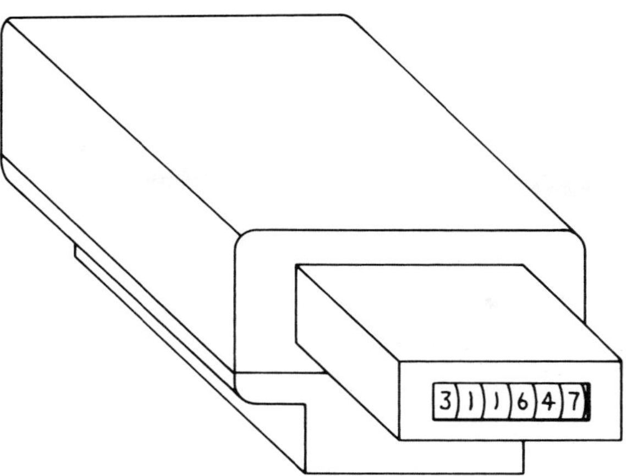

Duplexing

Automatic **duplexing** is a feature that can be useful in certain office applications. With this option both sides of a sheet of copy paper can be imaged without having the paper leave the machine between cycles. The use of this feature has shown some savings in paper costs. Many may question whether the savings are enough to justify the added cost of the feature. This must be answered on an individual basis. Some copiers turn out an excellent two-sided copy that may be justification enough for many users. Many copiers have a sheet bypass feature that allows the user to manually duplex copies.

FIGURE 15-4
IBM Copier III Model 20 with collator. (Courtesy of IBM Office Products Division.)

The Copying Process

Of all the equipment found in the office, the copier is rapidly becoming the most indispensable. Since the copier's early days, it has helped to speed up office communication. Memorandums, charts, forms, drawings, and pictures can be rapidly copied and sent on to the recipient. Copiers are now found in almost every type of office, helping to produce various kinds of work. Business offices use copying machines to make copies of purchase orders, customer billings, payroll documents, and shipping and receiving manifests. Hospitals use copiers to duplicate doctors' reports, insurance billing forms, patient billings, and cafeteria menus. In all areas, the speed and convenience of copiers is increasing the amount of work an office is able to produce.

The copier uses photographic techniques and principles to produce copies. Often referred to as photocopying, the process is classified by the type of chemical or physical process used to produce copies. The processes are referred to as "wet" and "dry." The wet process includes dye transfer, diazo, and diffusion transfer. Dry-process copiers, now used for office copying, include thermal, dual spectrum, and electrostatic.

Dry Copiers The dry-process copiers used today in most offices use heat and/or light to reproduce copy. The thermal or **thermographic process** may be more commonly known as Thermofax or heat transfer. The operating principle is that images absorb more heat than do areas without images. This process is often used for the production of overhead-projector transparencies and for low-volume copying. It may also be used for making spirit-duplication masters or stencil-duplication masters. In recent years the thermal copier has moved from the copier market into the audiovisual market. The advantages of this method of reproduction are (1) low equipment costs, (2) relatively fast production of copies, (3) simplicity of operation, and (4) little or no maintenance.

The **dual-spectrum process** (see Figure 15-5) was developed because of the inability of the thermal process to reproduce certain shades from originals. Heat and light are instrumental in reproducing copies by this method. This type of process is used primarily in the home and small office environment. Over-head-projection transparencies can also be produced with this method. The advantages of this type of machine are (1) the inexpensive equipment costs, (2) the fact that color can be copied, and (3) the permanence of the copies.

The **electrostatic process** is composed of two separate copying processes. The first is called transfer and is more commonly known as *xerography* (see Figure 15-6). Here light is reflected for the original copy through lenses to a charged photoconductive drum. Wherever light strikes the drum from the nonimaged areas of the original document, that part of the drum loses its charge. The drum then passes a toner-dispenser station where a powdered toner clings to the charged or imaged areas. A sheet of plain copy paper comes

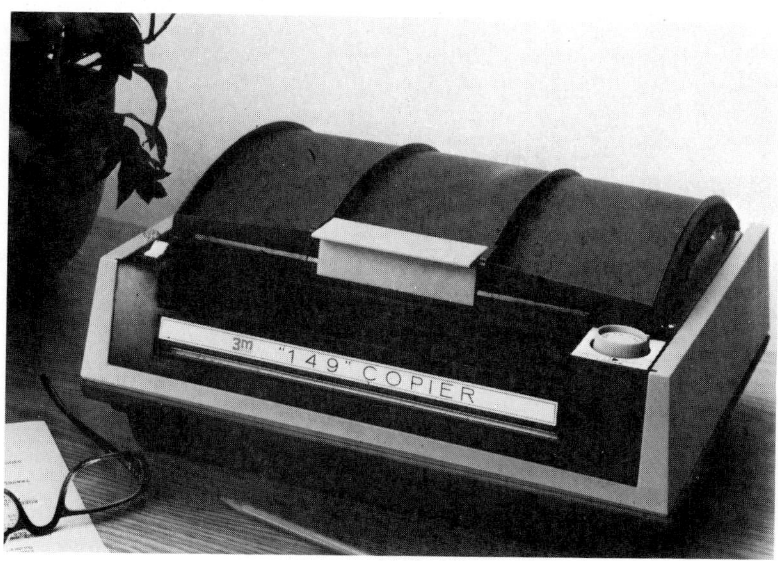

FIGURE 15-5
Dual spectrum copier. (Courtesy of 3M Company.)

in contact with the drum and the image is transferred to the paper. The toner is fused to the paper by heat or pressure.

Advantages of this process are (1) ease of operation, (2) relatively fast speed, (3) clean and dry copies, (4) capability of copying most colors, (5) reduction capability, and (6) the permanence of the copies. The process may be used to copy documents, drawings, transparencies, labels, and books. The quality of the process permits copying onto letterhead, colored paper, and many other types of material. If the copiers are rented, the cost per copy can be less than 4 cents when large numbers of copies are made. Most vendors' pricing plans have lower charges per copy after the monthly minimum number of copies has been made. In situations where the copier is owned by the user, the per copy cost is computed on supplies and maintenance charges. Therefore, the more copies generated, the lower the per copy cost becomes until a bottom cost is reached.

In the direct process, which is the second electrostatic process, the image is projected directly onto specially treated copy paper. The image does not have to be transferred through lenses as with the transfer process. Light is reflected from the original to the electrically charged copy paper. The charge dissipates from the area where there is not an image, leaving a latent image on the paper. Toner is sprayed or brushed onto the charged area. The image is affixed by pressure, heat, or air. Most direct-process copiers use liquid toner, although some do use dry toner and copy onto roll or cut sheet paper.

The advantages of this process are (1) it is clean and simple, (2) it generally produces grey tones more accurately, (3) it copies most tones or shades, (4) it makes copies fairly rapidly, and (5) the equipment is easy to operate. The process may be used to copy most documents, offset master plates, books, and

FIGURE 15-6
Xerographic transfer process. (Courtesy of Xerox Corporation.)

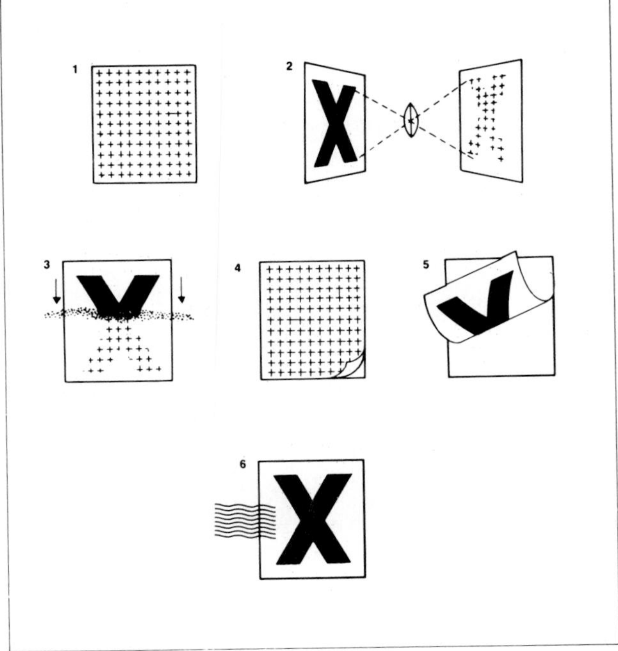

Basic Xerography

(1) A photoconductive surface is given a positive electrical charge (+).

(2) The image of a document is exposed on the surface. This causes the charge to drain away from the surface in all but the image area, which remains unexposed and charged.

(3) Negatively charged powder is cascaded over the surface. It electrostatically adheres to the positively charged image area making a visible image.

(4) A piece of plain paper is placed over the surface and given a positive charge.

(5) The negatively charged powder image on the surface is electrostatically attracted to the positively charged paper.

(6) The powder image is fused to the paper by heat.

After the photoconductive surface is cleaned, the process can be repeated.

labels. Like the transfer method, the direct method of copying can produce copies for less than 4 cents per copy with volume copying. Today the majority of all copiers utilize the transfer process to produce copies.

COPIER TECHNOLOGY

Microprocessors

The modern copier is a marvel of microminiaturization and engineering technology. The **microprocessor,** a small computer, is the heart of today's copier. It permits the copier to be smaller, more reliable, and simple to operate. The microprocessor monitors many machine functions. The operator is kept informed as to the machine's operational status through visual display codes or messages. The interrupt function found on many copiers is an extremely useful function of the microprocessor. An operator can interrupt a job to permit another job with a higher priority to be run. The microprocessor stops the original job and stores the number of copies produced. The counter is set to zero and the higher-priority job is run. When the second job is completed, the counter is reset to the correct number of copies and the original job is restarted.

A microprocessor also permits a copier to be self-diagnostic. The copier can display a coded message on the operator console to inform a maintenance person of copy status or malfunctions within the machine, thus helping to reduce repair time. A simulation function also found on some copiers helps a repair person to simulate or perform various tests that can lead to decreased repair time and increased reliability of the machine.

Fiber Optics

Fiber optics in copiers was introduced by the Minolta Corporation in 1978. This innovation holds great promise for the future as well as the present. In a copier, **fiber optics** replaces the conventional lenses and mirrors used to transmit images. This mechanism is formed from extremely small light-transmitting tubes or pipes. A flexible light path is formed when the tubes are grouped together. This allows very little light to be lost during transmission. This technical advancement has gained acceptance because it has fewer moving parts, can become extremely cost-effective, uses less energy, and requires less maintenance. Wang's Image Printer, shown in Figure 15-7, was designed to operate with Wang computer and word processing equipment. This printer uses fiber optics to transmit light to the photoconductor. The photoconductor in turn images paper through the electrostatic process.

Intelligent Copiers

An **intelligent copier** is a device combining technologies from data processing, photocopying and phototypesetting. The equipment can be used as a printing unit for a data or word processing system. It can also function as a text processor, communicate with other office equipment, and serve as a convenience copier. These copiers receive coded data, translate them, and form a line of characters that is scanned. The data are then transmitted to a photosensitive device, where an image is formed and transferred to paper. Intelligent copiers print so rapidly that their speed is measured in pages per minute instead of characters per second.

The Xerox Corporation Model 9700 Electronic Printing System was originally designed to function as a printer for a computer. The system has evolved into a veritable publishing center (see Figure 15-8). Featuring a laser printer,

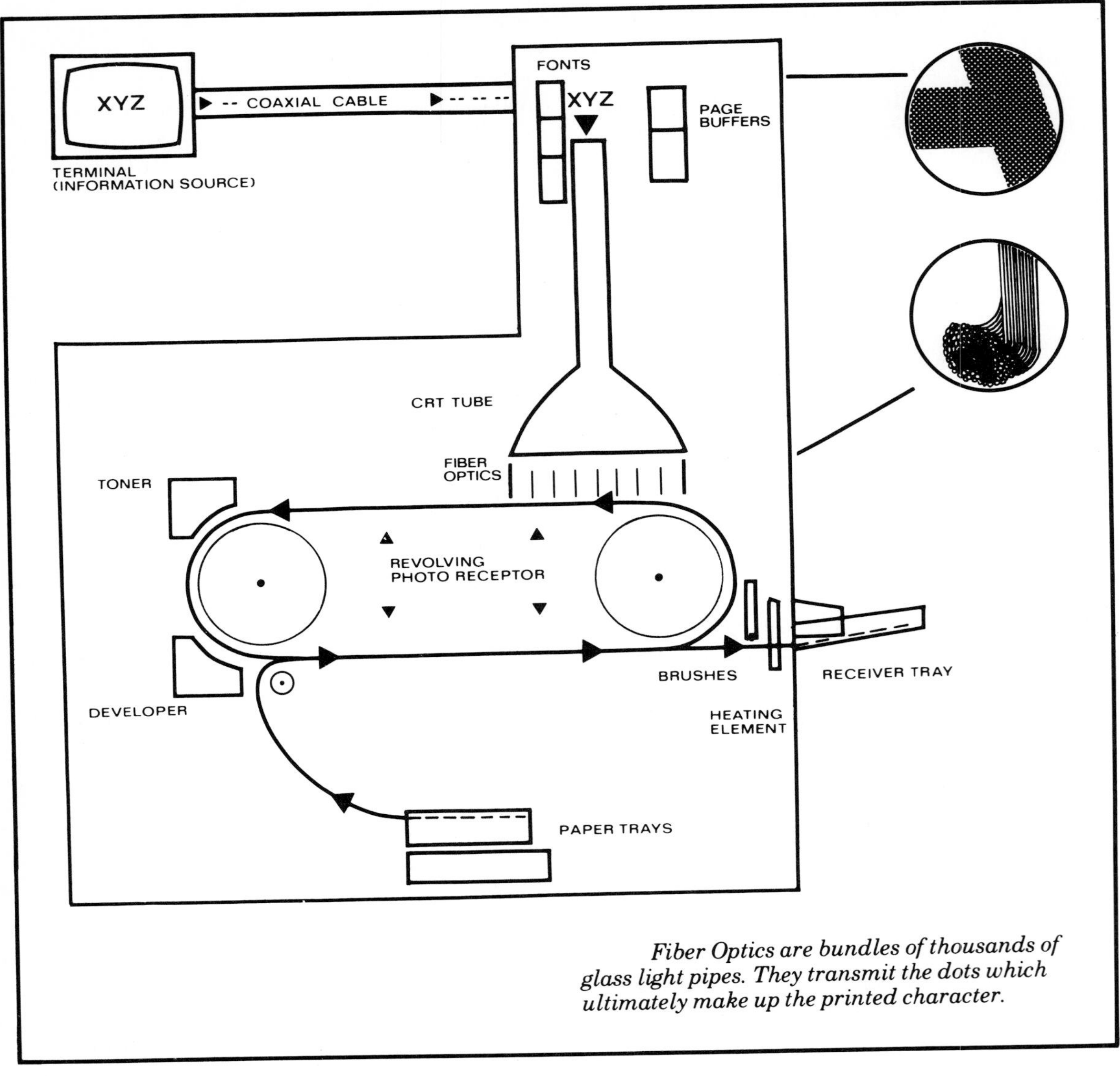

FIGURE 15-7
Sketch of Wang's image printer. (Courtesy of Wang Laboratories, Inc.)

the system receives text in digital form from a computer, converts the data into characters or graphics, and prints out high-quality images. The system permits form layouts to be designed, logos and signatures to be reproduced, and multiple fonts (print styles) to be generated with relative ease.

The laser imaging module directs a beam of light to strike a photoconductive medium. The pattern generated by the laser is data in alphabetic, nu-

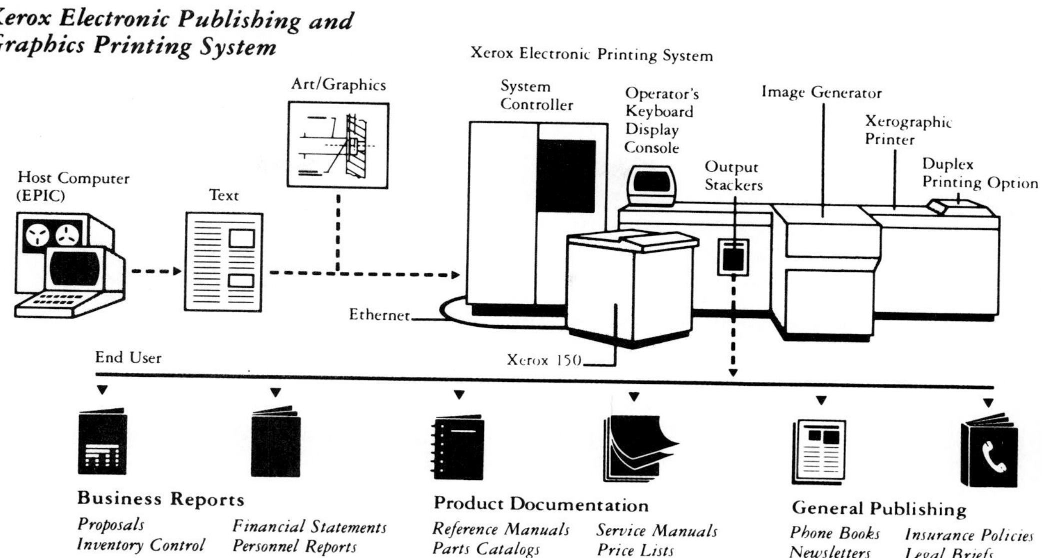

FIGURE 15-8
Xerox 9700 electronic printing system. (Courtesy of Xerox Corporation.)

meric, or special character form. Next, the image on the photoconductor is transferred to paper through the electrostatic process at a rate of 120 pages per minute. Owing to the sophistication and cost of the system, it is recommended for use by companies that make 500,000 to 2,000,000 copies per month.

FACSIMILE

According to recent estimates, in 1988 there were 1.2 million fax machines in the United States with 10 million people using them. Since facsimile machines are reliable, speedy, and inexpensive to operate, they may be considered an upgraded photocopier machine. According to CRM Robert Sanders, the average time required to send a page on a fax has been reduced to under 10 seconds (with a four second-per-page rate available on the latest machines).[1] Thus, facsimile systems have become standard equipment in most businesses. Sanders cites the following advantages of fax machines.

1. Fax machines are able to deliver an entire message, whether or not the intended recipient is available to receive it at the time it is sent.

[1]Robert L. Sanders, CRM, "Faxing From Memory: The Promise, The Problem, The Procedure," RECORDS MANAGEMENT QUARTERLY, January, 1990. Courtesy of ARMA International.

2. Fax machines produce a hard copy of the message for documentation which is an advantage over voice message systems.
3. Fax machines can send messages 24 hours a day—when both the originator and recipient are asleep—and when telephone rates are at their lowest.
4. Fax machines—unlike the telephone—can confirm an agreement with a legally binding signature immediately.

FAX in the Nineties Facsimile machines in the 1990s will be more affordable and offer increased features. Plain-paper faxes continue to be the most popular with 92,000 units sold in a year according to Dataquest, a market research organization. Plain-paper faxes are available for under $5,000 and offer transmission speeds of mere seconds. In addition, fax distribution/network services offered by companies such as AT & T, MCI, and Western Union will grow in the 90s. These services will provide more efficient utilization of fax machines. They will allow users to send documents from their fax or PC into their service and then transmit the message to thousands of locations simultaneously at a lower cost than the subscribers would pay individually.[2]

Facsimile Technology

Facsimile terminals, shown in Figure 15-9, are devices that transmit document images over telephone lines. This machine uses a beam of light to scan the face of the document to be copied. The beam of light moves across the document in a series of extremely fine lines. As the light beam passes over letters and spaces, light is reflected at varying intensities. These differing intensity light waves are converted into electrical signals. Telephone lines, microwave relay stations, and satellites move the transmissions to the receiving units. At the receiving station the electrical impulses are converted into the original form. These electrical signals activate a printing mechanism to create a paper copy of the original.

There are two types of facsimile devices, *analog* and *digital. Analog* is the older and slower of the two processes. Earlier analog units scanned the entire page or image, transmitting both blank spaces and printed material. Newer analog devices skip over the white space between lines, which allows the printed material to be compacted and sent at higher speeds. The *digital* process is the faster transmission and reception technique. The encoding process used by the digital-facsimile process is similar to the digital process used by computers. Many facsimile units are full duplex machines, which means they can send and receive documents simultaneously.

[2]"Fax in The Nineties: The Story Continues," by Sherli Evans, MODERN OFFICE TECHNOLOGY, September, 1990, p. 58.

FIGURE 15-9

Many facsimile devices have automated document feed and can receive messages without operator assistance. Some units are designed to monitor the telephone line and answer all incoming calls. When a call is received, the message is decoded and printed and then the call is disconnected.

Often referred to as electronic mail, facsimile is reaching its potential due to its increased use and compatibility standards. The Consultative Committee for International Telephone and Telegraph (CCITT), a part of the International Telecommunications Union, has revised its transmission standards into three compatibility groups. With these compatibility standards in place, facsimile devices of differing types, models, and manufacture are better able to communicate. In an electronic mail-routing system, the facsimile unit would transmit all messages, for example, to an information processing unit. The information processing unit would then route the messages to an intelligent copier, or another computer.

MANAGEMENT CONSIDERATIONS

The reprographics marketplace always has something new. Trade publications, vendor pamphlets, trade shows, and seminars are a few of the ways vendors supply the marketplace with equipment performance data. Through this sea of informative, but often confusing, data the user needs to steer a safe course.

Whether it is a team's or one individual's responsibility to select equipment, there is generally a great deal of information to evaluate. Many times the person making the selection has only a passing acquaintance with the reprographics environment. Since the records managers are the persons ultimately responsible for managing and storing a great deal of the paper generated, they should have some input into the selection process. In many cases, the records manager is in a better position than, for example, the company comptroller, to make an effective and knowledgeable decision. Because of their position in the company structure, records managers may be more attuned to management philosophy and goals.

Evaluating Needs

Before the first piece of equipment is installed and the first copy produced, someone must conduct research to determine what equipment will best serve the company's needs. In many cases it is the records manager who conducts this study. To do the job effectively, the records manager should (1) review copiers and/or duplicators based upon specific selection criteria, (2) evaluate the need for a convenience or centralized duplicating arrangement, (3) determine and evaluate equipment and supply costs, and (4) make recommendations to management.

Selection Criteria

There are many factors to consider in selecting the best copying process and the particular equipment to meet one's needs. Items to consider are as follows:

1. The largest size of originals to be copied must first be determined. Then the copiers under consideration must be checked to ensure that the largest originals can be accommodated.
2. The type of paper on which the originals are printed is an important factor. For example, if all documents to be copied were from a normal office environment, then an electrostatic-process copier would be satisfactory. On the other hand, if only one-sided translucent documents are to be copied, then a diazo copier would serve the purpose.
3. The acceptable copy quality must be determined. If only the best-quality copy will meet a company's requirement, then one could probably rule out all but the electrostatic process.
4. An important consideration is whether the reduction and/or enlargement feature is needed on a copier. Even though this option adds to the price of a copier, the feature can show some savings in supplies.
5. An extremely crucial factor is the volume of copies produced. Machines today are built to handle varying volumes of work. In general, a low-volume copier is expected to produce only a few thousand copies per month.

High-volume models are designed to provide many thousands of copies per month. Therefore, it is important to keep in mind the type and volume of the work to be done.

6. Other optional machine features must also be considered. Automatic document feed, key counter, and collators are desirable features designed to accomplish specific tasks. These features may add to the overall cost of equipment and should only be considered where there is a need for them.
7. The cost of the machine in terms of capital investment and vendors' pricing plans are important considerations. Would a lease/purchase arrangement be better than just a lease or outright purchase? In some cases company policy will dictate which plan to use. Therefore, it is important to review all the options closely before reaching a decision.

After reviewing the selection criteria, there are usually two further things to determine before selecting a machine. First, a selection of some samples of the work that would be copied should be run through the machines under consideration. A good look at the copies should determine which machine delivered the best copies. Finally, one should contact persons who are currently using a copier that is under consideration and obtain their opinion of the quality and quantity of copies produced, ease of use, and maintenance problems.

The factors involved in choosing a duplicator are similar to those in choosing a copier. As mentioned before, duplicating is the process in which copies are produced from some form of fluid master or stencil. Items to consider are:

1. The size and weight of paper to be used must be checked against equipment specifications to ensure that the duplicator will meet the stated needs.
2. Color printing requirements should not be overlooked, since color copiers are now affordably priced.
3. The capital investment in equipment, cost of supplies, and employee training should be computed and evaluated with the other factors.

As with copiers, it might be useful to try out a vendor's product prior to committing oneself to a particular piece of equipment. Also, contacting others who use the equipment under consideration is important. From these references, one should learn if the machine is performing satisfactorily in its intended role.

Convenience Copying Versus Centralized Arrangements

Convenience copying is the placing of copying equipment at the site where it is needed by the user. On the other hand, a *centralized-copying arrangement* is one in which a copying service is provided from a single site or a few central locations. The average person would think that having a copier at the point of need (a convenience copier) is the best option. Clearly, time and effort would be saved by not having work taken to, or collected from, a centralized site.

Advantages of Convenience Copying Point-of-need copying advantages are:

1. The user is able to obtain a copy when it is needed. All employees tend to be more cost-efficient for management if point-of-need copying is available.
2. Generally, low-volume, less-expensive copying equipment is used for convenience copying. It may be difficult to justify expensive high-volume equipment for convenience copying.

Advantages of Centralized Copying The advantages of having a centralized site might not be as clear. However, there are advantages that need to be considered:

1. Centralized copying can provide a more closely controlled reprographics operation. Under these conditions, it is easier to supervise personnel, monitor machine usage, and generally be aware of problems.
2. The unauthorized use of equipment and waste of materials can be more closely controlled. Normally, a centralized operation has permanently assigned personnel who are responsible for operating the equipment and performing maintenance. This prevents employees or others from misusing the equipment.
3. Personnel can be used more efficiently. Employees need not spend time learning how to operate and maintain a copier. The fewer people operating the equipment. The better overall performance can be expected from the operation.
4. Departments that do not warrant a copier of their own can be served. Not every department may have the volume of copying or budget to justify a copier. Here the centralized site can provide service where there is a need.
5. The opportunity to use a good copier-duplicator mix is generally available. Because the centralized operation serves a larger and typically more diverse clientele, different types of equipment can be used. Spirit and stencil duplicators, offset presses, and copiers can all be more efficiently and practically used.

Determining Factors The nature of the work and the office layout have a great deal to do with determining which arrangement will work best. A good policy to follow might be to centralize as much as possible and to allow some equipment placement away from the centralized site. When deciding what approach or variation of each to use, the following factors might be considered:

1. How quickly are the copies required? If copies are needed immediately, then a convenience copier would probably be justified.
2. Would some type of pickup and delivery system be satisfactory? For a centralized arrangement, this type of system would keep employees from wasting time walking back and forth.
3. How far does the user travel to make a copy? If the employee leaves a building or goes over 150 feet to make a copy, then possibly a convenience copier should be placed nearer.
4. How long is the user away from his or her work station while making copies? To management, time is money. Employers can ill afford to have employees spend a lot of unproductive time making copies.
5. Would the use of a centralized site create pass-through traffic that would cause distraction? This should be looked at closely, since distractions create unproductive time, which increases costs.
6. Does the user have to wait more than a few minutes at the copier to make copies? Again, delays affect productivity. Moving a copier or acquiring another machine might help solve the problem. The situation should be closely observed before making a decision.
7. Does the type of work being done require that copies be made throughout the workday or possibly once in the morning or afternoon? A morning and afternoon copying schedule is good for convenience copying or a centralized operation. Often the work can be accumulated prior to making copies.

One should keep in mind that deciding to set up a convenience-copy unit, the factors leading to that decision may not always be economic. The payroll department, for example, might need a convenience copier because of the confidentiality of payroll records and/or the need to keep documents in the department. Even though the need seems reasonable and just, it should be looked at very closely to determine if some type of accommodation might first be worked out. These individual situations must be scrutinized and judged on their own merits.

Cost Comparisons

Few managers are in a position to order equipment without justifying their requests. To purchase a new piece of equipment, the manager must show that the combined expenses for the new copier (paper, toner, and so on) will probably be lower than for the copier being replaced. If the expenses are not less, then some tangible difference to be gained by the new copier should be shown. For example, the new copier may have capabilities (such as duplexing, reduction, or collating) that the present machine does not have.

To help compare costs, the records manager must develop some comparative figures. The items compared must genuinely be comparable. Paper, toner, maintenance charges, machine rental, or amortized purchase price are a few items to consider. Quality, for example, is subjective and should be put aside and used when making the final decision. When computing costs, one should use the largest sample for which data can be found. The records manager should total the charges for paper, toner, maintenance, machine rental or amortized purchase price for a one-month period. For example, assume the combined monthly charges are $860 for 22,000 copies. A simple computation ($860 ÷ 22,000 = .039) shows the cost per copy to be .039. This figure can now be compared with data on other copiers to help the records manager reach a decision. It is better to compare costs for identical periods, such as weeks or months, rather than on a per copy basis. Per copy costs frequently do not reflect changes that have occurred in the component charges over time.

According to an article on Copy Management, cost estimates for copiers should include:[3]

1. Copier: purchase, rental, leased cost amortized over the life of the equipment (accessories included).
2. Copier supplies: paper toner, developer, user oil, etc.
3. Installation and removal charges.
4. Electricity: power consumption on a large copier may cost $100 per month or more.
5. Waste: unreadable copies, poor quality copies can range from 1–8 percent.
6. Labor: full-time operators, time spent waiting in line, etc.
7. Miscellaneous: systems cost such as building and electrical modifications.

Purchase The outright purchase of copying equipment has become a growing trend. Vendors may have different types of purchase plans, which are generally designed to be more attractive than leasing. When equipment is purchased outright, maintenance is normally an extra expense. In most cases the cost per copy will be less for a copier that was purchased outright than for a leased machine. Typical purchase plans call for equipment to be paid off in two or three years. After the payoff period, copy costs drop sharply.

A form which analyses the lease/purchase of copier machines is shown in Figure 15-10.

[3]S.E. Thomas, "The Ins and Outs of Copy Management," *ARMA Quarterly*, July, 1990. Courtesy of ARMA International.

LEASE PURCHASE ANALYSIS FOR COPY MACHINES For use of this form see AR 25-30; Proponent agency is ODISC4		DATE October 31, 1989
1. ORGANIZATION	2. LOCATION	3. PROJECTED MONTHLY VOLUME 15,000
4. COPIER/DUPLICATOR MODEL XXXXX 1111 GS-00F-11111		5. COPY SPEED 20 CPM

6. RENTAL/LEASE			7. PURCHASE				
a. MONTHLY MINIMUM RENT/LEASE	NO COPIES 3,000	TOTALS $ 121.0	a. EQUIPMENT	b. No Months	c. Cost	b. Less Credit	c. Net Cost
c. Add: 12000 Copies @	$ 0.0090	$ 108.00	XXXXX 1111		$	$	$ 2,139.00
d. 0 Copies @	$ 0.000	$ 0.00	SORTER		$	$	$ 800.29
e. Copies @	$	$	SADF		$	$	$ 770.53
f. Accessories SORT @	$	$ 39.00	TRAY		$	$	$ 431.38
g. SADF @	$	$ 39.00	MISC		$	$	$ 0.00
h. TRAY @	$	$ 25.00	CRENT		$	$	$ 332.00
i. MISC @	$	$ 0.00			$	$	$
j. TOTAL MONTHLY RENT/LEASE ----→		$ 332.00	TOTAL EQUIPMENT COST -------→				$ 4,473.20

k. Per Copy Cost		g. Monthly Maintenance		
(1) Paper	$ 0.00580	(1) No. Copies 10,000		$ 94.16
(2) Toner	$ 0.00380	(2) Add 5,000 Copies @	$ 0.0094	$ 47.00
(3) Dev	$ 0.00080	(3) 0 Copies @	$ 0.0000	$ 0.00
(4) Total	$ 0.0104	(4) Copies @	$	$
(5) No. Copies 15,000 @ $ 0.0104	$ 156.00	(5) Accessories		$ 19.99
		(a) Total Monthly Maintenance		$ 161.15
		(b) Depreciation		$ 74.55
		(c) Supplies		$ 156.00
(6) TOTAL MONTHLY COST	$ 488.00	(d) TOTAL MONTHLY COST		$ 391.70

RENTAL/PURCHASE MONTHLY COPY COST Computation (Total Monthly Cost + Monthly Copy Volume)

	RENT/LSE	PURCHASE
(1) Total Mo. Cost	$ 488.00	$ 391.70
(2) Mo. Copy Volume	15,000	15,000
(3) Cost Per Copy	$ 0.0325	$ 0.0261

h. BREAK EVEN/PAY-BACK PERIOD COMPUTATION

(1) Monthly Rent/Lease $ 332.00	(2) Maintenance -$ 161.15	(3) Savings =$ 170.85
(4) Price (purchase) $ 4,473.20	(5) Savings / 170.85	(6) Mths to Brk Even/Pay Back =$ 26.20
(7) PRICE (purchase) $ 4,473.20	/ 60	(8) Mo. Deprecia-tion =$ 74.55

RECOMMENDED ☐ Lease ☐ Purchase	COMPUTED BY (Name and title)
	TITLE

DA FORM 4951-R(e), JUL 88

FIGURE 15-10
(Courtesy of ARMA International.)

Lease Pricing plans or leasing arrangements are generally on a yearly basis with a monthly minimum for a set number of copies. Some vendors have monthly, yearly, and two-year plans. There are also special price structures for local, state, and federal agencies.

Because of the advances in copying technology, the plain-paper copier has become less expensive to acquire. This trend, particularly in the low-volume market, has had a great deal to do with the increase in outright purchase of the equipment. Therefore, the user should take a hard look at many vendor's plans or options prior to making a final decision. In many cases, the decision to purchase can have a positive impact on equipment and supplies budgets.

Periodic Review

Once a piece of equipment is installed and running smoothly, it is important that one not just forget about it. "Out of sight, out of mind" is not an efficient and productive way to handle anything, particularly equipment that is crucial to a well-functioning office.

During the time period in which the machine was being selected, a *periodic review* schedule should also have been developed. It is simply a set of dates on which the copying operation is critically reviewed. Specifically, maintenance history, operational uses of the equipment, and any new office procedures running in concert with the operation should be reviewed. Finally, the general feelings of the user toward the equipment should also be taken into account.

The review should occur at least quarterly for the first half-year, then semiannually for a year, and finally once each year for as long as the equipment is used. For the review process to be effective, shortcomings found in the equipment and/or procedures should be corrected. For example, copies may look dirty, light, or dark. Perhaps the duplexing of copies may no longer be required. Vendors want return business and in many cases are willing to make whatever adjustments they can. Any necessary personnel and/or procedural changes are an in-house function and should be instituted for the good of the organization.

Controlling Copier Abuse

One business analyst estimates that 20 percent of copies made in the private sector are not work related. Abuse copying takes a large chunk out of the budget for reprographics. In some instances, it puts the budget "in the red" due to uncontrolled and not-work-related copying. Corporations are attempting to control abuse copying by using control systems such as key systems, cartridge systems, card systems, and digital touch pads. According to experts, these measures are cost-effective and help to counteract abuse copying. They do not entirely eliminate the problem since passwords can be borrowed and cards can be loaned. According to Records Manager S. E. Thomas, the following techniques can be used to limit unauthorized copying in corporations:[4]

1. Installing charge-back systems.
2. Holding users to an approved volume and increasing the charge back rate for copies over the volume.
3. Placing reminder posters near the copier.
4. Placing the copier near a key control operator or supervisor.
5. Implementing procedures for reviewing all documents to be copied.
6. Sending reports to managers on their copier costs.
7. Surveying the copier management program of each office on a scheduled basis.
8. Placing a thin, one line label on the inside of the copier glass which states "Reproduced at XYZ Corporation's Expense"
9. Reviewing copier logs to ensure that only business documents are being reproduced.

Quick Copy Centers

With the technological improvements in all types of reprographic processes, procedures, and equipment, an interesting phenomenon has occurred that affects both the business and the public sector. Quick copy centers have sprung up and become a viable alternative for many users of copying and duplicating equipment. Because of increasing employee salaries, equipment and maintenance costs, and supply costs, many companies have begun to use these copy centers. Business cards, invitations, forms, envelopes, letters, transparencies, and labels are just a few of the printing services provided. Some centers offer spiral, brief, and hardback book binding. Using offset presses, copiers, and some duplicating machines, these centers are able to provide rapid, diversified services to the business community and the general public. Color printing, pickup and delivery, and same-day services are also just a few of the reasons for the copy center's rapid growth.

Legal Considerations

With the ease and convenience of today's office copiers have come legal problems and restrictions never considered 30 years ago. People who might never have consciously broken a law in their lives may be doing so with a copier by reproducing books, pamphlets, magazines, and other material. These are violations of the copyright law. Before any copyrighted material can be repro-

[4]S.E. Thomas, "The Ins and Outs of Copy Machine Management," RECORDS MANAGEMENT QUARTERLY, July, 1990. Courtesy of ARMA International.

duced, the publishers' and/or authors' permission must be obtained. Since it is the records manager's task to retrieve and reproduce many types of material, they must be acutely aware of these legal limits.

In October of 1976 the president of the United States signed into law P.L. 94-553, which is known as the Copyright Revision Act of 1976. This act completely revised the copyright laws that had remained essentially unchanged since 1909. The part of the act that relates to this discussion is the concept of *fair use,* which was given statutory expression for the first time. To paraphrase, reproduction for purposes of criticism, comment, news reporting, teaching, scholarship, or research is a fair use of a copyrighted work and not a violation of the act.

The law has provided guidelines for determining whether or not the use made of a copyrighted work in a particular case is fair use. The act sets four factors to be applied to a case. These factors are:

1. The nature of the copyrighted work
2. The purpose and character of the use, including whether the use is of commercial nature or is for nonprofit or educational purposes
3. The amount and substantiality of the portion used in relation to the copyrighted work
4. The effect of the use on the potential market for, or the value of, the copyrighted work

In everyday terms, the law allows for reproduction of copyrighted material in situations where the individual reproducing the works does not stand to gain personally in any material way. This is considered fair use.

Not only must copyright restrictions be kept in mind, but also the many federal and state government regulations that prohibit reproduction of certain documents. Two of the obvious are stock and deposit certificates and paper money. A more comprehensive list is shown in Figure 15-11.

CHAPTER HIGHLIGHTS

- Reprographics machines can be categorized as follows: Personal copiers, 1 to 10 CPM; Convenience copiers, 11 to 45 CPM; and Copier Center Machines, 46 or more CPM.
- Cost estimates for copiers should include copiers, supplies, installation and removal charges, electricity, waste, and labor.
- Corporations can control copier abuse by using key systems, cartridge systems, card systems, and digital touch pads.
- Photocopying, which has made a big impact on today's office, is divided into two basic processes—wet and dry.

U.S. statutory law forbids the copying, under certain circumstances, the documents listed below. A fine and/or imprisonment may be imposed on violators.

1. Obligations or Securities of the United States Government, such as:

Certificates of Indebtedness	United States Bonds	Federal Reserve Bank Notes	Fractional Notes
National Bank Currency	Treasury Notes	Silver Certificates	Certificates of Deposit
Coupons from Bonds	Federal Reserve Notes	Gold Certificates	Paper Money

   Internal Revenue Stamps. (If it is necessary for a lawful purpose to copy a legal document on which there is a cancelled revenue stamp, this may be done.)

   Postage Stamps Cancelled or Uncancelled. (For philatelic purposes, Postage Stamps may be copied provided the reproduction is in black and white and is less than 3/4 or more than 1½ times the linear dimension of the original.)

   Postal Money Orders.

   Bills, Checks or Drafts for Money drawn by or upon authorized officers of the United States.

   Stamps and other representatives of value, of whatever denomination, issued under any Act of Congress.

2. Adjusted Compensation Certificates for Veterans of the World Wars.

3. Obligations or Securities of any Foreign Government, Bank or Corporation.

4. Copyrighted material, unless permission of the copyright owner has been obtained or the copying falls within the "Fair Use" or library reproduction rights provision of the copyright law. Further information on these provisions may be obtained from the Copyright Office, Library of Congress, Washington, D.C. 20559. Ask for circular R21.

5. Certificates of U.S. Citizenship or Naturalization.

6. Immigration Papers.

7. Badges, Identification Cards, Passes or Insignia carried by Military, Naval personnel or by members of the various Federal Departments and Bureaus, such as FBI, Treasury, etc., (unless ordered by head of such department or bureau).

   In some states, copying Automobile licenses, Drivers' Licenses or Automobile Certificates of Title is prohibited.

   The above list is not all inclusive, and no liability is assumed for its completeness or accuracy. In case of doubt, consult an attorney.

FIGURE 15-11
Documents that may be copied. (Courtesy of Xerox Corporation.)

- The wet processes include dye transfer, diazo, and diffusion transfer.
- The dry processes include thermographic, dual spectrum, and electrostatic.
- The electrostatic process, which if offered by most vendors, encompasses both the transfer or xerographic method and the direct method of copying.
- Copiers can be leased or purchased and come with many options, such as automatic feeders, enlarging and reducing capabilities, and color copying.
- Intelligent copiers are able to communicate with computers, word processors, and other office systems to produce copies.
- Facsimile, one of the new electronic mail options, scans documents and transmits images over telephone lines to the end users.

QUESTIONS FOR REVIEW

1. Distinguish between the "wet" and "dry" copying processes.
2. How is fiber optics used in copiers?
3. What function does a microprocessor serve in a copier?
4. What purpose would a color copier serve in the office?
5. How is a key counter used to control copying costs?
6. In what office environment will a facsimile device be most productive?
7. What items should be reviewed during the periodic reviews after the equipment has been installed?
8. Discuss the advantages of a centralized-copying operation.
9. When developing a cost comparison between equipment, what items should be considered?
10. What are five of the factors to consider when deciding to use convenience or centralized copying?
11. Discuss the four factors to be applied to a case in order to determine whether or not the use made of a copyrighted work was fair use.

THE DECISION MAKER

Case Studies

1. As the company's records manager, you are to write a memorandum to all company department heads, informing them that a planned move to centralized copying centers has been completed. The memo will contain a list of services and a brief description of each. You will also encourage the department heads to make full use of the centers' resources and ask them to notify departmental employees. Each copying center is equipped with one large-volume copier with collator and finisher, one low-volume convenience copier, a fluid duplicator, and an offset press. Spiral, brief, and hard-back binding equipment is also available.

MICROGRAPHICS

OBJECTIVES

Upon completion of this chapter, the student should be able to:

1. Discuss the different types of microforms.
2. Evaluate an office's need for micrographics.
3. Select the proper type of equipment for any given operation.
4. Explain the principles and methods of microfilm indexing.
5. Discuss the importance of computer-output microfilm.
6. Explain the records manager's role in micrographics.

A 1990 article titled, "Records Management: Making the Right Choices," in MODERN OFFICE TECHNOLOGY, cites microforms as the most economical choice for records storage as well as the best vehicle for vital records security. Microforms have many advantages over other forms of records storage:

Microforms offer 98 percent space savings over paper records.

Microforms are 98 percent more economical to mail than paper records.

Microforms are 10 times less expensive than optical disk systems.

Microforms, specifically computer-output-microfilm (COM), could save 87 percent of computer hard copy.

Thus, a micrographics system is an information system that utilizes microimages to record documents on film for preservation, file integrity, security, and legal purposes. Organizations are using micrographics in many ways. A few examples of records commonly stored on microforms include: parts inventories, police records, bank account balances, student records, and personnel files.

MICROGRAPHICS COMPONENTS

Film Types

Possibly the most important part of any micrographics operation is the microfilm used to store document images. Without a stable, long-lasting film, the process will not meet archival goals. The type of microfilm most commonly used today is *silver halide,* or *silver film.* This type of microfilm can be compared to the black and white film one might use in a standard photographic camera.

After the microfilm is developed, one will notice that a frame or image of a document on the microfilm will have light and dark areas. The areas of a document that are white or light in color will be black on the microfilm. Conversely, the dark areas of the document will show up as white or clear areas on the film.

Frequently, a duplicate roll of microfilm may be required. The duplicate can be generated from the original negative roll. The duplicating process produces a roll of microfilm with positive images.

Microfilm come in different sizes, widths, thicknesses, and lengths. The most common widths of microfilm used today are 16-, 35-, and 105mm. The thickness of microfilm varies from a minimum of 2.5 mil (.06mm) to 7 mil (.175mm). The most commonly used thickness is 5.5 mil. Microfilm is normally purchased in 100- and 215-foot rolls for the standard microfilm camera. The 16mm, 5.5-mil microfilm is wound on a standard reel in a 100-foot-long piece. On the other hand, the same standard microfilm reel will hold 215 feet of the 16mm, 2.5-mil "thin film" microfilm. The advantage of using thin film is that the user is able to get more than twice the number of images on the same standard-size reel.

The primary use of 16mm microfilm is to film smaller documents, ranging in size from checks to legal-size forms. Larger forms, such as maps, engineering drawings, plats, newspapers, and large books, are generally microfilmed on 35- and 105mm microfilm. The 105mm microfilm is also used for microfiche, which is discussed later in the chapter.

Diazo microfilm, which is used for contact printing, consists of a polyester or acetate base coated with a thin layer containing diazonium salt, dye couplers, and a stabilizing agent. Diazo microfilm may be used for source documents, continuous-tone copy, engineering drawings, and some computer-output microfilm processes.

Dry silver microfilm is a nongelatin silver film that is developed by a heat process. It is used primarily in computer-output microfilm (COM) cameras that use an electron or laser-beam recording method.

Vesicular film is another recent development used for duplicating microfilm. Generally, the film consists of a polyester base covered with a layer of light-sensitive material. The film is designed for copying computer-output microfilm, silver, and diazo masters. The standard sizes of 16, 35, and 105mm are available with thicknesses ranging from 2.5 to 7.0 mil.

Microfilm Quality Factors

Good-quality **lenses** are extremely important in microfilm cameras. The lens is the part of the camera through which light reflects from the document being filmed to the microfilm. The lenses are ground so that all light rays meet at the focal point, the position where the microfilm is placed.

The factors used to determine the quality of a microfilm image are resolution and density. In general terms, **resolution** is the ability of all aspects of a microfilm camera to record fine detail. More specifically, resolution is the sharpness of lines in a filmed image.

Density refers to the amount of light reflected and is used to measure the contrast between the dark and light areas of the film. The wider the variation in the darks and lights, the higher the contrast and the easier it is to distinguish images. A device called a densitometer (shown in Figure 16-1), which indicates the amount of light transmitted, measures the black or dark background. This is referred to as background density.

Cameras are designed to provide the user with an image a good deal smaller than the original document. This ability to give a reduced image is called the **reduction ratio.** In more precise terms, it is the ratio of the size of the original document to the size of the image on the microfilm. For example, a reduction ratio of 32 : 1 (pronounced "32 to 1") means that the original document was 32 times larger than the image on the microfilm. A few of the more common reduction ratios in use are 16 : 1, 24 : 1, 32 : 1, 42 : 1, 48 : 1, and 52 : 1. The higher the reduction ratio, the more images can be placed on a roll of micro-

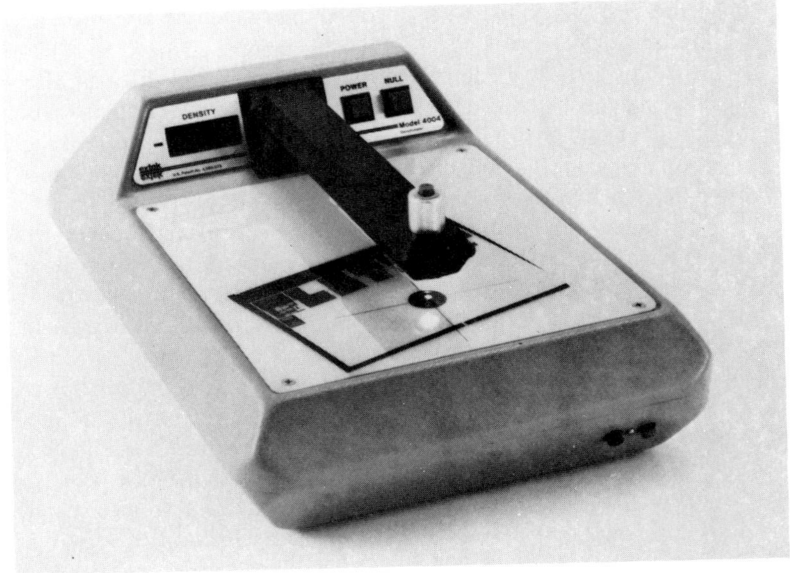

FIGURE 16-1 Extek Model 4004 densitometer. (Courtesy of Extek Microsystems, Inc.)

film. The micrographics industry has developed a shorter way of referring to reduction ratios. Instead of saying 48 : 1, for example, the term 48 × is used. As one can see from the document-size reduction chart (Figure 16-2), the size of a document also determines the size of the image

All of the images on roll microfilm will appear in either one of two directions. This is referred to as document **image orientation,** or mode (see Figure 16-3), which is the direction in which the images are positioned on the film. In comic mode, the images are positioned with the top of each image parallel to the edge of the film, like comic strips in the newspaper. Cine mode positions the top of each image perpendicular to the edge of the film, as on cinema film.

MICROFORMS

Microforms refer to the various forms in which one will find microfilm. The primary forms are aperture cards, microfilm chips, roll microfilm, microfilm jackets, microfiche, ultrafiche, and ultrastrip. The type of work being done dictates to a large degree what microform is used in any particular application.

Aperture Cards An **aperture card** is typically a keypunch card with a rectangular opening for a piece of microfilm. A card can hold a single 35mm frame or up to eight 16mm microfilm frames. The card can also be keypunched and processed on regular unit record equipment (the forerunner

FIGURE 16-2
Document size reduction chart.

Document Length (Inches)	Documents per 100-ft and 215-ft Rolls of Microfilm					
	18:1 Reduction Ratio		24:1 Reduction Ratio		42:1 Reduction Ratio	
	100 ft	215 ft	100 ft	215 ft	100 ft	215 ft
2½	6,172	13,274	8,229	17,692	14,000	30,100
3	5,400	11,610	7,200	15,480	12,600	27,090
4	4,320	9,285	5,760	12,390	10,080	21,660
4½	3,927	8,439	5,236	11,252	9,164	19,708
6	3,085	7,625	4,114	8,843	7,200	15,480
7	2,700	5,805	3,600	7,740	6,300	13,545
8½	2,290	4,925	3,053	6,571	5,060	10,870
10	1,964	4,228	2,618	5,626	4,580	9,850
11½	1,728	3,711	2,304	4,953	4,032	8,664
12	1,661	3,577	2,215	4,760	3,876	8,337
14	1,440	3,090	1,920	4,125	3,360	7,230
15	1,350	2,910	1,800	3,870	3,150	6,780

of computers). Aperture cards come in various sizes, with the standard being 3 1/4 by 7 3/8 inches (see Figure 16-4).

The versatility of the aperture card is reflected in the user's ability to retrieve images by referring to various types of keys (parameters) that are punched into the keypunch portion of the aperture card. Generally, the image

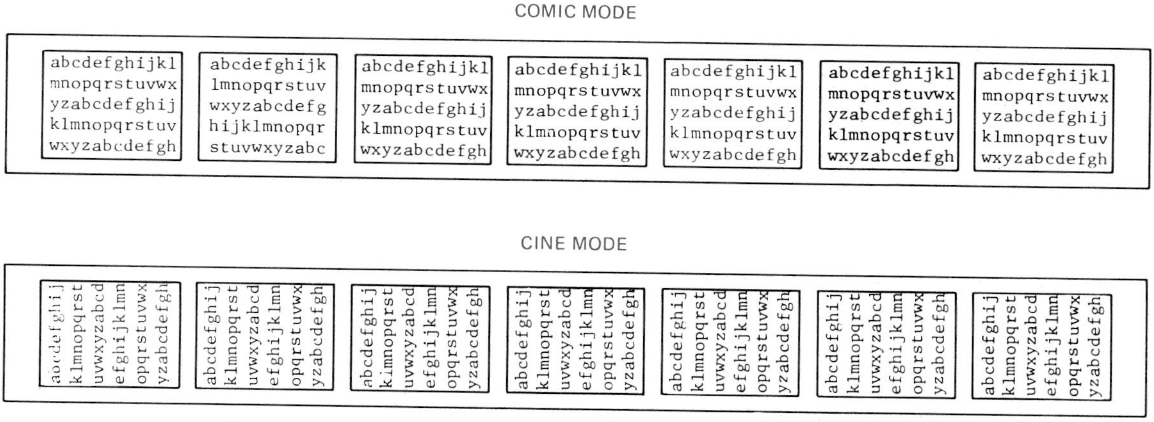

COMIC MODE

CINE MODE

FIGURE 16-3
Microfilm modes.

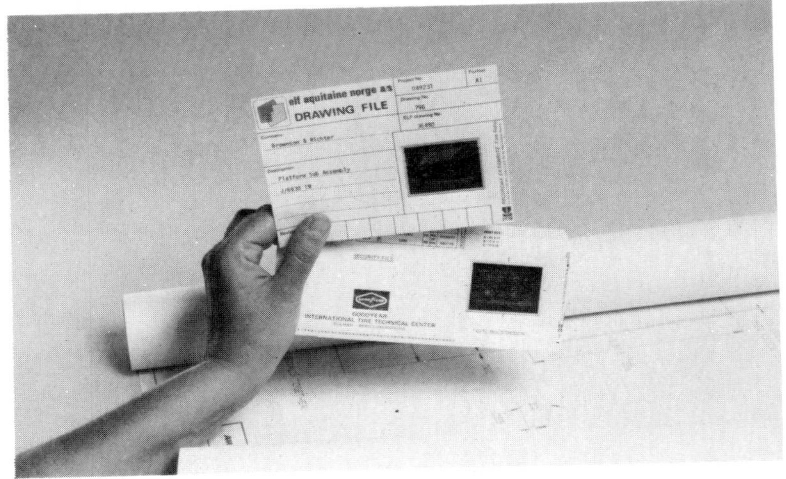

FIGURE 16-4 Microseal 35mm aperture cards. (Courtesy of Microseal Corporation.)

is placed between columns 54 and 75 on a standard 80-column card. This gives the user about 56 columns in which to enter data. The data then become the keys that are used to retrieve the aperture cards. For example, the engineering department of a large company has all of its engineering drawings stored on aperture cards with various types of data keypunched into the cards. The images for subassemblies, major assemblies, or any other breakdown can be retrieved within a very short time. The keys are used to sort out the required cards. The 35mm aperture card is commonly used for engineering drawings and other large documents. Generally, aperture cards are not used for the type of documents found in the typical office environment.

Roll Microfilm **Roll microfilm** is the most commonly used microform in use today. The microform is simply a length of microfilm in 16mm, 35mm, 105mm, or some other width, wound around a reel or spool. In many cases the reel or spool is encased in a cartridge or cassette (see Figure 16-5). This facilitates its loading and scanning in any particular manufacturer's equipment. A cartridge or cassette also provides a certain amount of security, since the film is protected from fingerprints, dust, and damage.

Roll microfilm provides the most economical method for storing sequentially organized documents and for referring to low-volume reference material. Since images are recorded serially, roll microfilm is an excellent choice for filming books, magazines, newspapers, reports, computer listings, or other materials where extensive updating is not required. The microform also allows for sequential additions to be spliced onto the roll of microfilm.

Microfilm Jacket The microfilm **jacket** is formed from two pieces of clear polyester material sealed at the top and bottom. This plastic carrier, or jacket, is subdivided horizontally into rows or channels. Into these channels are slid pieces of 16- or 35mm microfilm. Room is left at the top of the jacket for

FIGURE 16-5
Microfilm roll and cartridge.

Open Spool

Cartridge

coding information. Prepared adhesive labels or typing directly onto the area are the two most commonly used methods of coding. Jackets can be found in various sizes and configurations. The size most preferred is 4 by 6 inches, with five channels holding 12 frames each, for a total of 60 frames per jacket (see Figure 16-6). Some manufacturers have combined the aperture card and jacket to give the user a card with retrieval capabilities that can hold as many as 20 or 30 frames. This offers the user many more options and possibilities.

Jackets may be updated by simply inserting a frame or strip of microfilm into one of the channels. Frames that are no longer required may be removed. This updatability of the jacket, along with its inherent qualities, allows it to be considered a unitized microform. This means that because of its ability to hold many frames of like documents or records, a single unit or file can be formed. For example, a personnel department might use a jacket to store an

FIGURE 16-6
Microseal polyester microfilm jacket. (Courtesy of Microseal Corporation.)

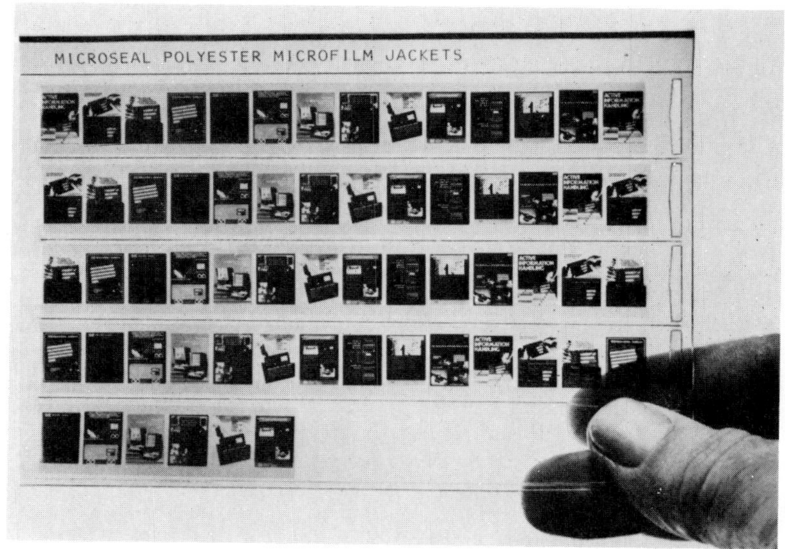

employee's personnel records. This allows all records to be available at one source. The entire file or individual frames may be viewed as the user requires.

Color coding and notching are the most common ways to code and retrieve jackets. The very top of the jacket can be color-coded to allow various parts of the storage file to be segregated. The procedure allows the jacket to be accessed and returned without being misfiled. Notching a jacket is a method where a small circular or square cut is made on the top of the jacket. This notch can be located almost at any point along the top. A jacket that is both color-coded and notched is noticeable if not filed in its proper place.

Microfiche **Microfiche** is similar to a jacket in that it has multiple images in a grid pattern. The piece of film may contain a few or several hundred images depending upon the reduction ratio used. Normally, the 4-by-6-inch size is used for computer-output microfilm (COM) and various duplicating processes. There are several ways to generate a sheet of microfiche. A

Microfiche Heading Area																	
A-1	A-2	A-3	A-4	A-5	A-6	A-7	A-8	A-9	A-10	A-11	A-12	A-13	A-14	A-15	A-16	A-17	A-18
B-1	B-2	B-3	B-4	B-5	B-6	B-7	B-8	B-9	B-10	B-11	B-12	B-13	B-14	B-15	B-16	B-17	B-18
C-1	C-2	C-3	C-4	C-5	C-6	C-7	C-8	C-9	C-10	C-11	C-12	C-13	C-14	C-15	C-16	C-17	C-18
D-1	D-2	D-3	D-4	D-5	D-6	D-7	D-8	D-9	D-10	D-11	D-12	D-13	D-14	D-15	D-16	D-17	D-18
E-1	E-2	E-3	E-4	E-5	E-6	E-7	E-8	E-9	E-10	E-11	E-12	E-13	E-14	E-15	E-16	E-17	E-18
F-1	F-2	F-3	F-4	F-5	F-6	F-7	F-8	F-9	F-10	F-11	F-12	F-13	F-14	F-15	F-16	F-17	F-18
G-1	G-2	G-3	G-4	G-5	G-6	G-7	G-8	G-9	G-10	G-11	G-12	G-13	G-14	G-15	G-16	G-17	G-18
H-1	H-2	H-3	H-4	H-5	H-6	H-7	H-8	H-9	H-10	H-11	H-12	H-13	H-14	H-15	H-16	H-17	H-18
I-1	I-2	I-3	I-4	I-5	I-6	I-7	I-8	I-9	I-10	I-11	I-12	I-13	I-14	I-15	I-16	I-17	I-18
J-1	J-2	J-3	J-4	J-5	J-6	J-7	J-8	J-9	J-10	J-11	J-12	J-13	J-14	J-15	J-16	J-17	J-18
K-1	K-2	K-3	K-4	K-5	K-6	K-7	K-8	K-9	K-10	K-11	K-12	K-13	K-14	K-15	K-16	K-17	K-18
L-1	L-2	L-3	L-4	L-5	L-6	L-7	L-8	L-9	L-10	L-11	L-12	L-13	L-14	L-15	L-16	L-17	L-18
M-1	M-2	M-3	M-4	M-5	M-6	M-7	M-8	M-9	M-10	M-11	M-12	M-13	M-14	M-15	M-16	M-17	M-18
N-1	N-2	N-3	N-4	N-5	N-6	N-7	N-8	N-9	N-10	N-11	N-12	N-13	N-14	N-15	N-16	N-17	N-18
O-1	O-2	O-3	O-4	O-5	O-6	O-7	O-8	O-9	O-10	O-11	O-12	O-13	O-14	O-15	O-16	O-17	INDEX

FIGURE 16-7
Computer-output microfiche format at 48× reduction ratio.

computer-output microfilm camera produces microfiche from computer data. This method is by far the fastest. The second method is to film documents with a step-and-repeat camera. This method gives the user complete control over the location of the images on the microfiche. The third way to produce a sheet of microfiche is to duplicate a jacket or another piece of microfiche onto a piece of copy film.

As can be seen in the microfiche sketch in Figure 16-7, the microfiche has uniform rows and columns. There are 15 rows, lettered *A* through *O*, containing 18 frames each, totaling 270 frames. This example is a typical COM microfiche arranged for 11-by-14-inch documents, produced at a 48× reduction ratio on standard 105mm microfilm. Frames are identified by their position in the grid pattern. For example, the D-4 location references row D, the fourth frame from the left. Generally, the last frame, O-18, is the index page for that particular sheet of microfiche. The index page contains a summary of the data contained on all other frames and gives the location of each.

Microfiche is an excellent application for large volume reports with frequent updates that are distributed to numerous locations. Such items as reports, catalogs, directories, manuals, and inventories are ideal subjects for use on microfiche. Updating is done simply by replacing the outdated microfiche, or sets, with the newly generated sets of microfiche.

Ultrafiche **Ultrafiche** is like microfiche, except that it is produced at a much higher magnification or reduction ratio. This microform may run from 90× up to 150× and 400× ratios. Because it must be prepared in a "clean-room" environment under strict conditions, ultrafiche has not gained wide acceptance. The two applications for which it is being used are large catalogs and micropublishing.

Ultrastrip A similar type of microform is the **ultrastrip,** which is also used in high-speed storage and retrieval units. The ultrastrip is a short length of microfilm containing highly reduced images. The microform is produced by refilming a roll of microfilm at a higher reduction ratio. This process also requires a clean-room environment and, like the chip system, is expensive and custom-designed.

Microfilm Cameras

A microfilm camera is the device that records miniaturized images from full-sized documents onto a piece of microfilm. To accomplish this task, microfilm cameras, in their many forms, are engineered and constructed to precise tolerances.

Rotary Cameras The **rotary microfilm camera** is designed to film at high speed such documents as checks, invoices, sales slips, memos, and so on (see

Figure 16-8). Documents are fed into the machine, filmed, and carried or rotated back out into the receiving tray. This movement of documents through the machine is normally done with rotating belts.

Documents are filmed as they pass over an open area in the camera called a slit aperture. A tripping device is activated as a document enters the camera, causing the shutter in front of the slit to open and begin filming. The shutter remains open until the entire document has passed by the slit. Both the film and the document are synchronized to travel at the same speed. This gives the effect of the document having come to a stop while being filmed.

The film unit is the part of the camera that contains and advances the film. Film units have fixed reduction ratios, with 24× and 32× being two of the more common ratios. The film unit may be equipped with a warning device or footage indicator. These mechanisms tell the operator how much film has been used and when the end-of-reel condition has been reached.

Lighting controls on cameras are manual or automatic. Since it is important to have good background density, the amount of light reflected from a document will vary with the paper's reflectiveness. With manually controlled lighting, the operator uses a dial, push button, or some like mechanism to change

FIGURE 16-8 3M Model 5000 rotary microfilm camera. (Courtesy of 3M Company.) An experienced operator can feed the rotary camera up to 1,000 documents per hour.

the light intensity to correspond to the color of the document being filmed. With automatic lighting controls, photoelectric cells scan the document before it enters the photographic field and electronically adjust the system to provide the right amount of light.

An automatic feeding device (see Figure 16-9) on rotary cameras is part of the entire system that gives the camera its high filming speed. Documents are fed through the throat, one at a time, by some type of friction mechanism. This automatic feeding allows the user to stack forms of uniform size and weight for rapid and continuous feeding. Some cameras have attachments that allow the user to film unburst computer printouts. In general the throat opening through which documents enter the camera is 12 inches wide. Some manufacturers provide wider throat openings with their cameras. The maximum document length that a camera will accept varies with manufacturers.

A receiving tray is the portion of the camera into which documents fall after being filmed. The tray may be located above or below the feeder portion of the camera. Some forms stack better than others. Those that have a tendency to slide or fly around may be stacked more uniformly with the help of a stacker. A stacker is particularly important when filming continuous computer forms

FIGURE 16-9 Kodak 800 rotary microfilm camera, showing automatic feeder and receiving tray. (Courtesy of Eastman Kodak Company.)

that have a tendency to stack poorly or not at all (see Figure 16-10).

Most rotary cameras can film both sides of a document (including odd-sized ones such as checks), and newer models when attached to a PC can index the document ID number, microfilm roll number, and the starting/ending frame numbers. Another option is to imprint a human-readable document ID number on the source document.

Some manufacturers provide a numbering device with their cameras. This piece of equipment sequentially numbers documents as they enter the camera. The imprinting or numbering mechanism can be set or reset to create an "address" for fast retrieval of images. For example, the first four digits of the number could be set to the roll number. The remaining digits could change as

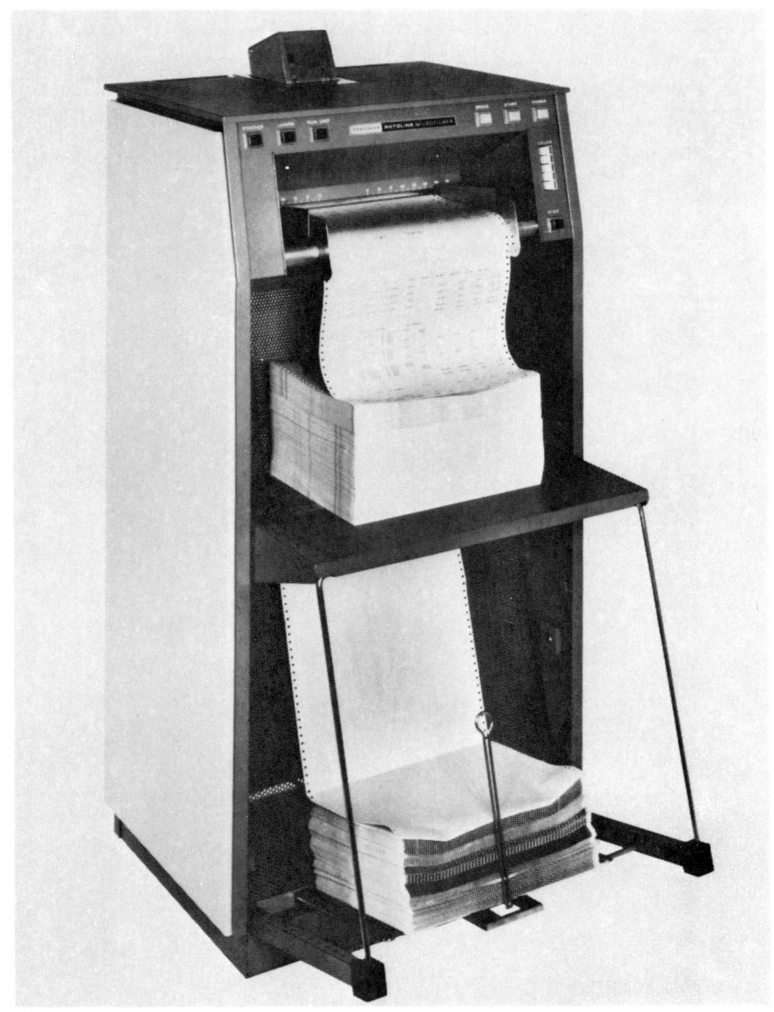

FIGURE 16-10 Kodak Rotoline Microfilmer shown with computer forms being fed and stacked. (Courtesy of Eastman Kodak Company.)

each document is filmed, creating a sequential number. These address numbers, which correspond to actual filmed documents on the microfilm roll, can be stored and retrieved by a computer. This in turn makes the addresses readily available to the user for rapid access.

Another extremely important device found on many microfilm cameras is a **blip-coding** mechanism. The blip is simply a square mark below each frame on a roll of microfilm. The coding mechanism causes a squaremark to be filmed at the same time as the document. When used on a microfilm reader capable of counting the blips, a roll of microfilm can be scanned automatically to find the required frame. In the process, the reader is first encoded with the number of the blip that the operator wants to view. The reader then counts along the film until the proper numbered blip is reached, stops, and displays the corresponding frame on the screen.

Planetary Cameras The standard **planetary camera,** shown in Figure 16-11, is generally considered to be an overhead flatbed camera. This camera differs from rotary cameras in that it can be used to photograph flat stationary objects. The lighting system is external. Reduction ratios can be fixed or variable, depending upon the type of camera. With the fixed-reduction camera, the camera head remains in a fixed position on a vertical column above the copyboard. The reduction ratio can be changed by using a camera head with different reduction ratio.

Variable-reduction cameras have the film unit or camera head attached to a mechanism that moves up and down a vertical column. By raising the camera head, higher reduction ratios can be achieved. Conversely, by lowering the

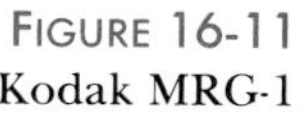

FIGURE 16-11
Kodak MRG-1

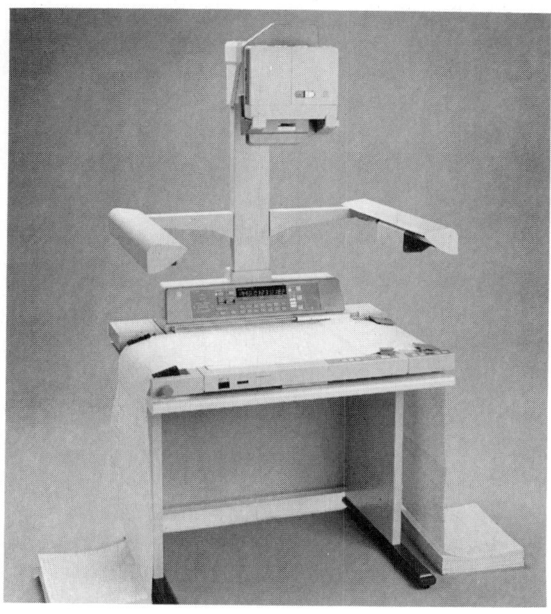

camera head, lower reduction ratios can be attained.

The planetary camera films up to 500 documents per hour and produces the highest quality images. As the camera moves vertically, it automatically determines the reduction ratio. Like the rotary camera, planetary cameras can be attached to a PC to record database information, and the source document can have its ID number printed directly on it.

A large rectangular surface called the copyboard holds documents in position for filming. Some copyboards can be so sophisticated that they are electrostatically charged to hold the document in place. Others use a vacuum system to pull the document to the table during filming. Metal or plastic strips are used on some copyboards to hold down documents. Copyboards are generally constructed of wood, glass, metal, or plastic.

Lighting controls may be either manual or automatic on planetary cameras. When using manual controls, the operator should first conduct a light test. The test helps to determine the optimum setting for each type of document to be filmed. Any necessary adjustments can be made during filming, according to the documents being filmed. Automatic exposure control is handled by photoelectric cells, which monitor the amount of light reflected from the documents.

A few manufacturers have developed small 16mm and 35mm planetary cameras for filming normal office documents. These units can also microfilm other types of documents that cannot successfully be filmed on a rotary camera. These small-document planetary cameras, like the one shown in Figure 16-12, are miniatures of the large planetary cameras, with many of the same features, but without copyboard backlighting.

The processor planetary camera shown in Figure 16-13 is specifically designed to microfilm engineering drawings and provide the film mounted in aperture cards. Because of its versatility, the equipment can be used in any application where 35mm microfilm-mounted aperture cards are required. Like the standard planetary camera, the processor planetary camera has a film unit, copyboard, and lighting system. Here the similarity ends. The copyboard is capable of moving up and down to change the reduction ratio; the camera completely develops the film and delivers a microfilm image mounted in an aperture card. The system uses premounted aperture cards.

The step-and-repeat camera seen in Figure 16-14 is a planetary camera designed to use 105mm microfilm to produce microfiche. Most step-and-repeat cameras have fixed reduction ratios. Two types of film may be used, depending upon the type of camera used. The microfilm used can be either film cut to size (105mm by 148mm) or roll microfilm.

A recent innovation in the step-and-repeat field is the ability of the camera to transfer frames from an already exposed microfiche onto a new microfiche along with regular document filming. This makes it possible for the operator to add new documents to an old microfiche, creating a new and updated microfiche.

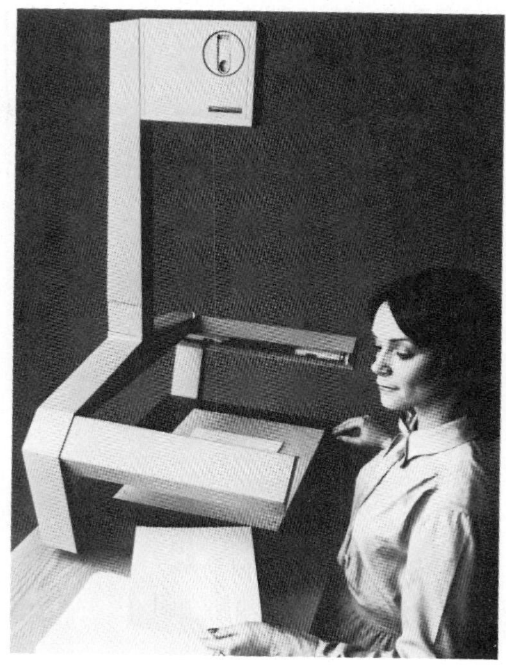

FIGURE 16-12 Kodak Starfile RV-3 small planetary camera. (Courtesy of Eastman Kodak Company.)

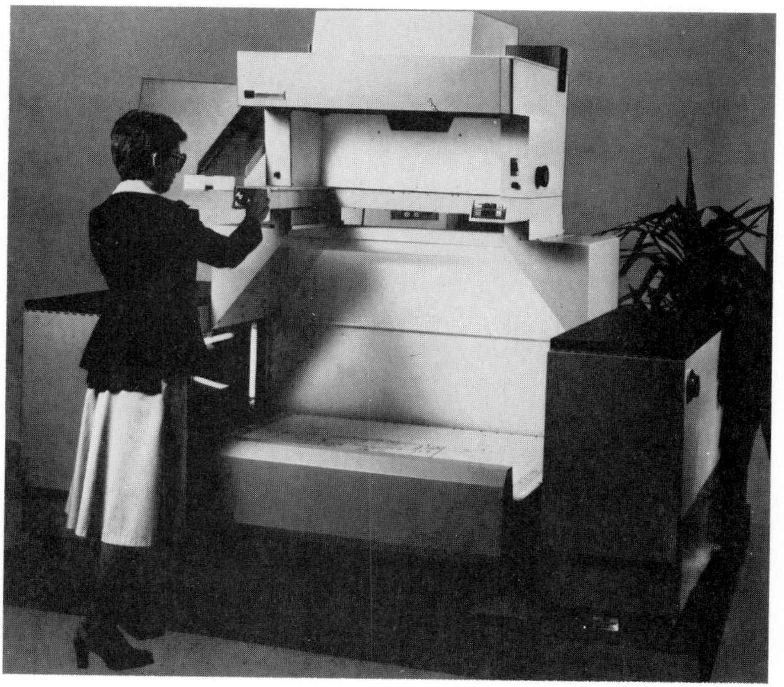

FIGURE 16-13 3M 2300 processor camera. (Courtesy of 3M Company.)

FIGURE 16-14 3M SRC 1050 step-and-repeat microfilm camera. (Courtesy of 3M Company.)

MICROFILM READERS/PRINTERS

Microfilm Readers

A microfilm reader is a piece of micrographics equipment designed to display an image from a microform onto a viewing screen. To do this effectively, a reader must have good illumination and optics. Many readers are now constructed with interchangeable lenses so that microforms with differing reduction ratios can be viewed on the same reader. The two basic types of readers are front projection and rear projection (see Figure 16-15).

Microfilm readers are found in all sizes and configurations. There are four basic designs: lap readers, portable readers, desk readers, and free-standing readers. The lap reader is designed for individual use. Portable readers are constructed to fit inside briefcases or portable cases. Desk readers are larger than both the lap and portable readers. These units are designed for use in the normal office environment and sit on a table, desk, stand, or work station. The free-standing readers are constructed with their own support units.

Roll-Film Readers Roll-film microfilm readers are constructed with two spindles, one for the take-up reel, and one for the supply reel. The supply reel is first mounted on the supply-side spindle. Then a small amount of microfilm is threaded between glass flats onto the take-up reel. The lens is normally located below the glass flats. Film is advanced by a hand crank or with an electric motor that rotates the spindles and moves the images across the screen.

A more recent development is the use of cartridge-, magazine-, and

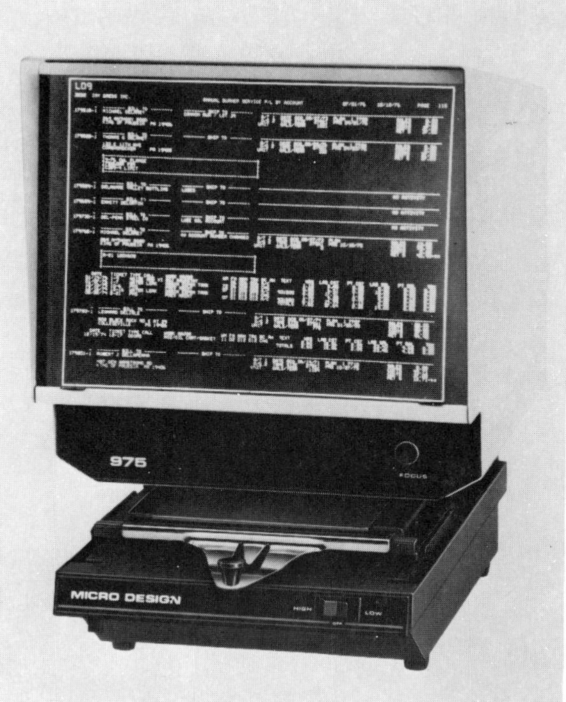

FIGURE 16-15
Front- and rear-projecting microfiche readers. (Courtesy of Micro Design.)

cassette-loaded film. In this method microfilm is preloaded by the film processor into plastic cartridges or cassettes. The cartridge contains a roll of microfilm that is automatically threaded by a motorized reader. The cassette is slightly different in that it has both the supply reel of film and the take-up reel encased in a single plastic case. The microfilm cassette is loaded by the user after it is returned from the film-processing source. To use a cartridge, magazine, or cassette, the reader must be specifically designed to operate with the particular case.

Microfiche Reader Many aperture-card and microfiche readers on today's market are designed to project images from microfiche, jackets, and aperture cards onto a screen. This additional capability gives the user more flexibility to mix microforms within their microfilm system.

Microfiche readers are designed with a carriage device formed from two glass flats mounted above a light source. The piece of microfiche or jacket is slid between the flats for viewing. Once the microfilm is in place, the pointer, which is located at the front of the carriage, is used to locate frames on the grid-pattern pad. The grid-pattern pad is a representation of the microfiche that has the same number of squares as the microfiche has frames. The grid squares are identified with letters and numbers. Grid position D-12 would equate to the twelfth frame in row D of the microfiche. To view an image on D-12, the operator simply moves the pointer to grid position D-12 on the pad and the image appears on the screen.

When the lens on a reader is changed to a different reduction ratio, the grid pattern pad must also be changed. This is because the number of frames on a microfiche depends upon the reduction ratio used to produce the microfiche. The higher the ratio, the greater the number of frames; for example, a 48× microfiche will have 270 frames, compared to 63 for a 24× piece of microfiche. Therefore, the pad (see Figure 16-16) must have the same number of grid positions as the microfiche itself.

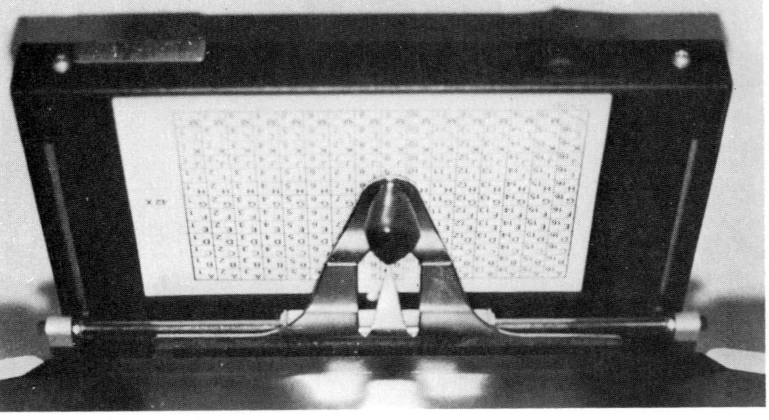

FIGURE 16-16 Microfiche reader pad.

Also important is a feature of some readers referred to as a "zoom lens." This device allows the operator to increase or decrease the magnification of a frame. The dual-lens system is required on all readers now purchased by the federal government and is used extensively in private industry. The reader is constructed with two lenses and a mechanism for moving easily from one lens to the other. This option is excellent for the operator who is using microforms with two different reduction ratios on the same reader. This type of versatility eliminates the necessity of having two readers with differing reduction ratios. Also avoided are frequent lens changes and the possibility of damage to, or loss of, the lenses.

Reader-Printers

Regardless of the type of microfilm system or application, there will come a time when the user will need a paper copy of the screen's image. When this happens, a reader-printer is used. This device, as seen in Figure 16-17, operates the same way as a regular reader; however, it also has the ability to produce a paper copy, or "hard copy," of the image.

The design principles of a reader-printer differ among manufacturers. But, generally, the device must have a paper supply, a process for getting the image viewed on the screen onto paper, and a mechanism for delivering the copy to the user.

There are five basic processes for creating an image on paper. Two of the processes are commonly referred to as the photographic processes. One uses dry-silver paper whereas the other uses liquid chemicals to develop the photographic paper. A third method, using paper coated with zinc oxide, is known as the electrolyte process. The fourth method is the direct method; the fifth method is the xerographic process. Both the fourth and fifth methods are based on the electrostatic copying process.

Indexing Systems

For any type of microfilm system to be effective, it must be able to retrieve images rapidly and efficiently. To do this, an index must be developed. In this context, an index is the address of an image on a microform or, in this case, on a roll of microfilm. Imagine the task of finding one particular frame out of 2,000 without any hint of where to look.

There are a number of ways to index microfilm. Some systems code the microfilm with blips or descriptive codes. Other less sophisticated systems might count images or use flash cards.

The **flash-card** coding system, as seen in Figure 16-18 can be compared to a file drawer with dividers separating sections of the drawer. Each section is titled so that one can easily find a subject. Flash-card coding makes use of batching or grouping, which is the grouping of documents into some predetermined order. An illustration would be filming of personnel records of all employees in a company. One method of batching is to group the documents by department and then alphabetically within the department. Prior to filming the documents, target flash cards are prepared with identifying information and placed in front of the batch to which each belongs. Identifying data should include, at a minimum, the type of document, batch identifier, and section of the alphabet. The batches are then filmed. The box or container in which the film resides is then marked to indicate the batch position and contents. Since the user knows in which batch the image to be retrieved is located, the flash targets can be counted and the microfilm stopped at the correct batch. The operator then advances slowly until the specific frame is found.

The **odometer** indexing method of retrieving images is one that associates frames with linear distances on the film. The microfilm reader must be constructed with an odometer that advances one position or "click" with the passage of some known distance of film (see Figure 16-19). For example, one click

FIGURE 16-17 3M EF6000 microfilm reader-printer. (Courtesy of 3M Company.)

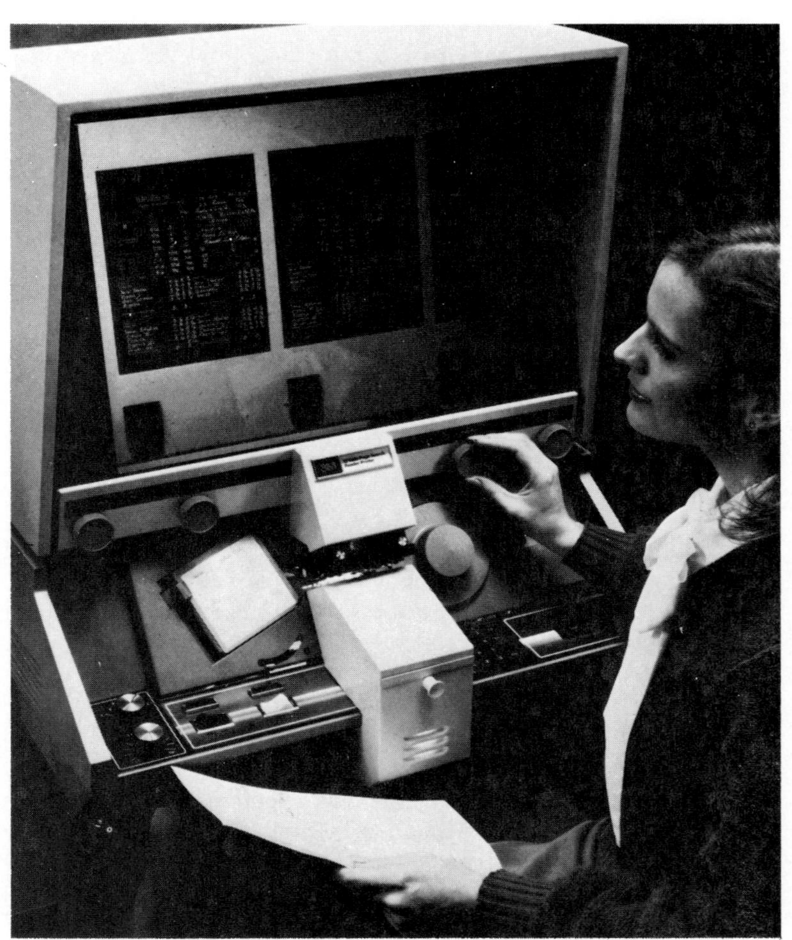

FIGURE 16-18
Flash cards.

might equal the passage of 5 inches of film. Therefore, the odometer would read 25 if 125 inches of film had been advanced by the reader.

To create an odometer index, the operator first chooses some index or meter points from which the contents of those frames are recorded. If the operator decides to index the film at every tenth metered or odometer position,

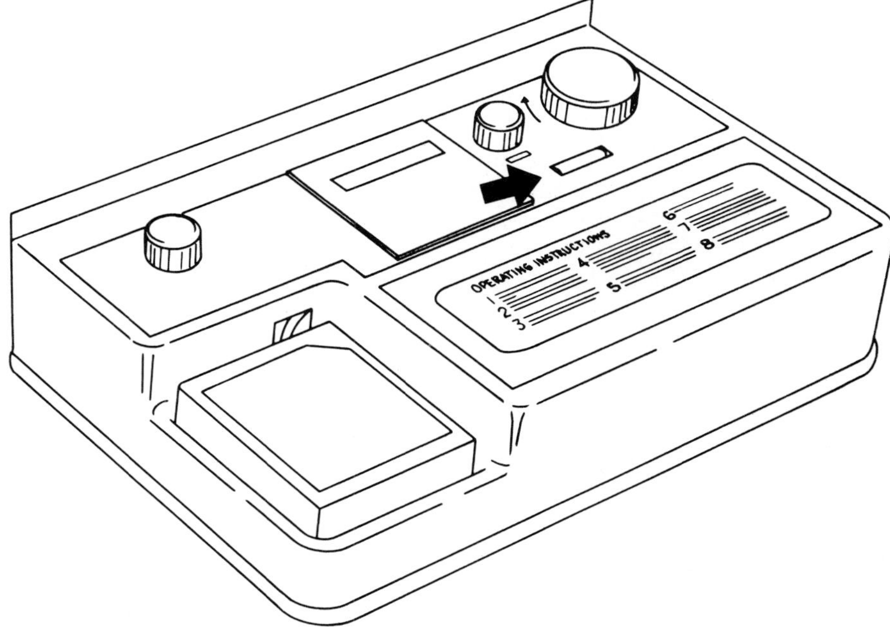

FIGURE 16-19
Odometer.

then the operator will start with meter position 10 and record pertinent data regarding that frame for the index, skip to position 20, and repeat the process. This procedure is used throughout the entire length of the roll of film.

For a roll of microfilm in which the documents were filmed in alphabetical or numerical order, the index-meter position can be based upon the location in which the alphabet or number sequence changes. In the case of the alphabet, there could be 26 index locations, one for each letter of the alphabet. The numerical locations could be based on any type of number sequence desired.

Retrieving images now becomes relatively simple. The operator first looks at the index to determine what odometer position is closest to the frame desired. The microfilm is then advanced rapidly to that odometer position or number. Finally, the microfilm is scanned slowly until the proper frame is reached.

Some vendors build microfilm cameras with odometers so the index can be recorded during filming. One should keep in mind that with odometer indexing, the index can be as comprehensive as the user wishes. But since this type of indexing is still a manual operation, most users tend to use it only to indicate major breaks or types of documents on the roll.

The **sequential-numbering** method of indexing requires that each document be numbered prior to filming. This may be done manually or by the camera during filming. The numbers are an integral part of the images and are seen whenever a frame is viewed on the screen. For this technique to be effective, an index must be developed that identifies the number assigned to a specific document or group of documents.

By using the batching method of filming, the sequential-numbering system of indexing can be developed into a powerful identifier. Assume that a six-digit number will be used to identify each frame. The first two digits from the left will be assigned to the film-roll number. The middle two digits will be the batch number. Finally, the last two digits will be the sequenced document number. Therefore, frame number 281376 will be located on film-roll number 28, in batch 13, in frame 76 in that batch. Since batches and documents within batches are filmed sequentially, the frame is rather simple to locate.

Code line is a method of coding film with horizontal lines at predetermined locations between the frames on the film. The code lines can correspond to batch or frame numbers. To retrieve frames using this method, the side of the microfilm reader next to the screen must be coded with numbers and lines. These lines correspond to the lines between the enlarged images on the screen. As the film is viewed, the magnified lines or bars on the film will line up with the index next to the screen. Once the index bar on the reader matches up with the index line on the screen, then the film is scanned slowly until the desired frame is found. With the newer methods of indexing and retrieving, the code-line method is used much less than in the past.

Auxiliary Equipment

In order to effectively store and retrieve microforms, the user needs to be concerned about using the proper equipment. Various storage devices are microfiche or jacket binders, books, and covered boxes. They are relatively inexpensive and provide minimum security and protection. Storage equipment for roll microfilm, jackets, and microfiche comes in various sizes, ranging from small portable desk-top units to work stations and free-standing carousel units, holding as few as 60 or as many as 600 rolls of film.

Of a more substantial nature are metal file cabinets designed specifically for roll microfilm, microfiche, or aperture cards. These units come with or without locks, are floor- or table-mounted and can be vertical or circular rotating units. The most expensive of these cabinets are the free-standing motorized rotary files, which come with lockable sliding covers and may cost as much as $45,000. Of more recent design are moderately priced work stations that resemble desks with storage drawers. The table portion is designed to accommodate a microfilm reader or reader-printer (see Figure 16-20).

Of all the equipment found in a jacket-oriented microfilm system, the reader-filler is certainly one of the more important (see Figure 16-21). This piece of equipment is designed to view and verify microfilm prior to inserting

FIGURE 16-20
BEA five-drawer file/work station. (Courtesy of Business Efficiency Aids, Inc.)

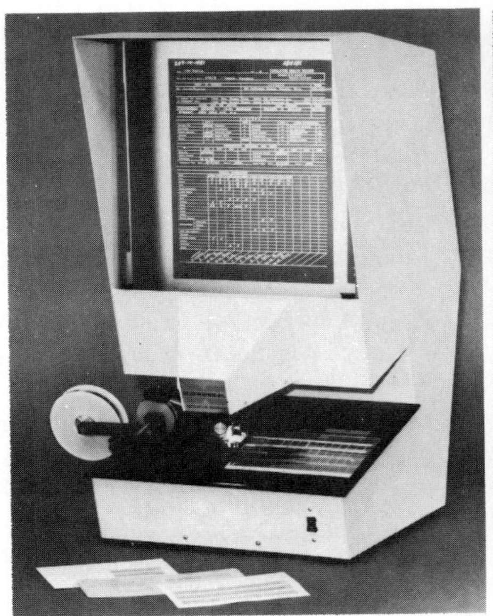
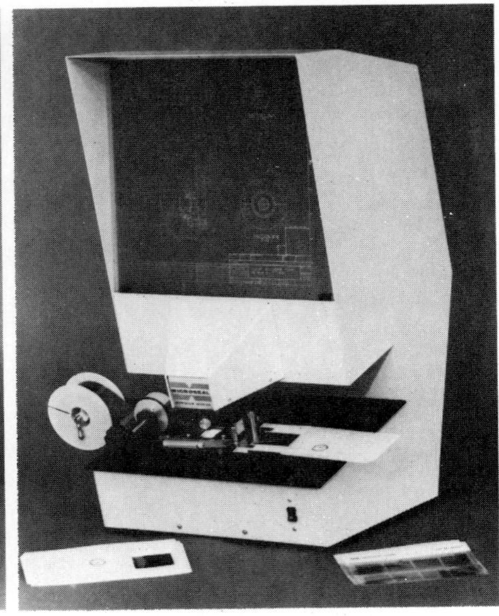

FIGURE 16-21 Microseal's 16mm and 35mm reader-filler. (Courtesy of Microseal Corporation.)

it into microfilm jackets. Earlier models were manually operated. Today, one manufacturer has developed a reader-filler that moves the film into the channels, cuts it, and moves to the next channel automatically. To use this device, the film is coded with large and small blips under the frames during filming. The large blip indicates to the device that a break in file or condition has occurred. Once the large blip is detected, the machine stops. The operator then puts a new jacket into the reader-filler, and the machine begins filling the channels until another large blip is detected. Reader-fillers are available for 16mm and 35mm jackets, and 16mm aperture-jacket combinations. Less expensive hand-held cutter-inserters are also available.

As mentioned earlier, the most common way to retrieve jackets is through the use of color coding and notching. This is a quick and easy technique for identifying a batch or group of jackets. The color-coding process is done during manufacturing by coloring the top portion of the jacket. With clear and 9 standard colors available, the user is able to segment a file in at least ten different colors or divisions. One vendor is able to provide, on a special-order basis, almost any color required. This expands the possibilities available for increasing the size of a jacket file.

Notching or notch coding is normally used in conjunction with color coding. This coding is done by cutting a small circular square piece from the top or bottom of the jacket (see Figure 16-22). The top cut is used with manual jacket systems, whereas the bottom cut is used with semiautomated retrieval systems.

With manual retrieval systems each notch position can be assigned a name, number, category, or similar subject. Given 10 color-coded jacket groups and a

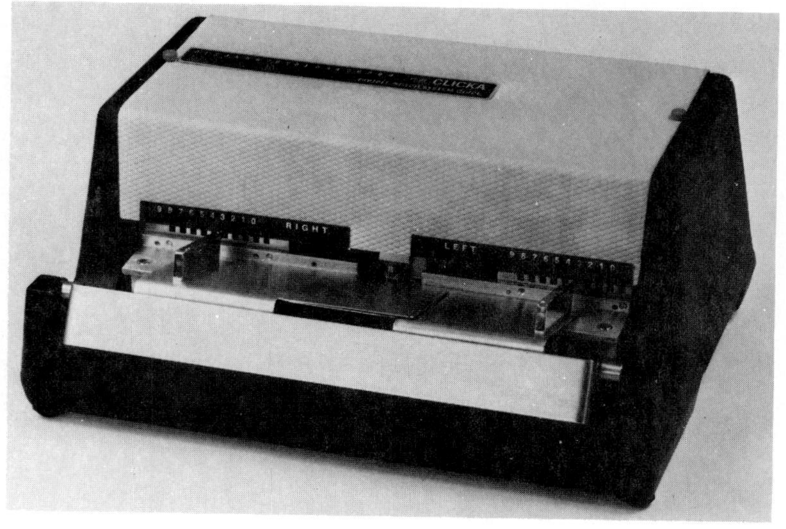

FIGURE 16-22
Clicka double-notch coder. (Courtesy of Click Industrial Automation, Inc.)

notcher than can notch in 10 different positions, there are 100 different batching or divisions possible. Depending upon the vendor, notchers can be found to notch 10, 20, and 26 positions. The 26 notching-position machine is constructed specifically for alphabetical notching.

Often the most important piece of microfilm equipment any operation can have is an editing-inspection station. This device is used to inspect and/or edit roll microfilm. Physically, an editing-inspection station has some type of light source over which the film passes. As light shines through the film it is inspected with a magnifying glass. A take-up reel and supply reel are mounted on either side of the light box. After processing, a roll of film is inspected to ensure that the film meets established standards. The inspection process is necessary so that such things as obliteration (partial or complete) of images, blurs, poor resolution, and so on, can be found and corrected. If a portion of the film is found to be unsuitable, those documents corresponding to the unusable film are refilmed, processed, inspected, and spliced into the roll. Splicing is the procedure where the unacceptable film is physically cut out and the reshot microfilm is spliced in place with a clear plastic tape.

It will often be necessary to have one or more duplicate copies of microfilm. The most common way to produce the copies is through contact printing (see Figure 16-23). This process involves bringing the emulsion side of the original film in contact with the copy film. Light passes through the original film to the copy film. Developing copy film depends upon the type of film used: silver, vesicular, or diazo.

Now that the various components of a microfilm system have been discussed, the reader should review Figure 16-24 to see how the various parts are pulled together to form a complete system.

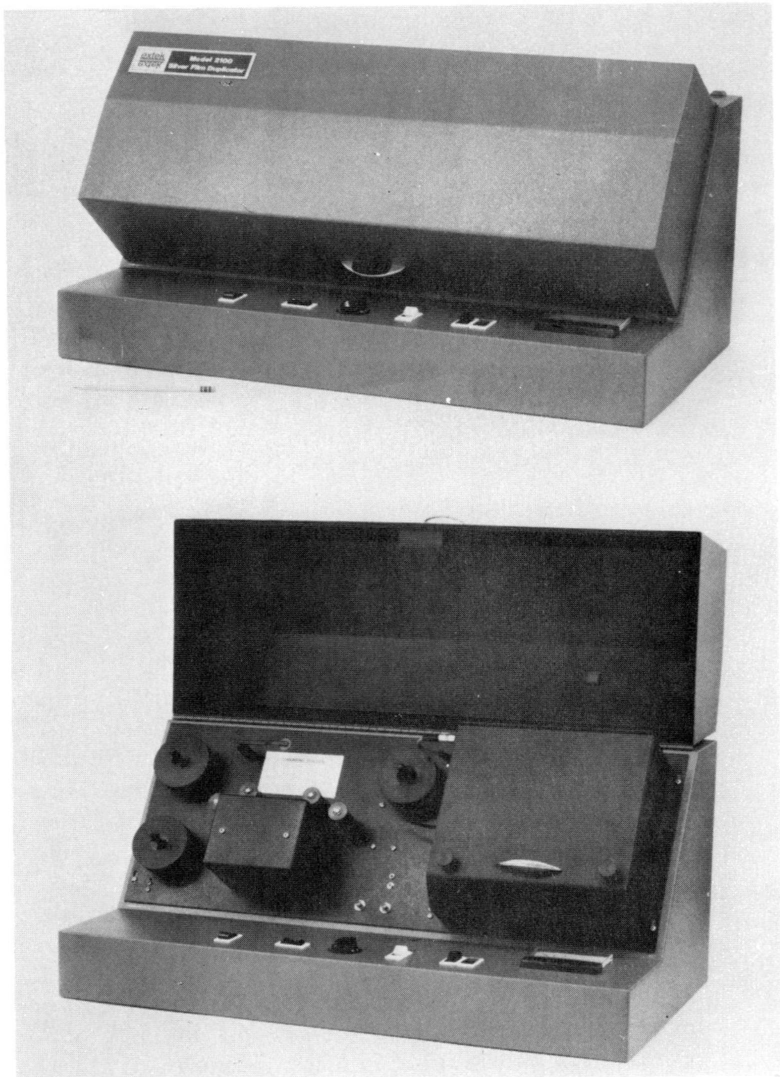

FIGURE 16-23 Extek silver film duplicator. (Courtesy of Extek Microsystems, Inc.)

Updatable Microfilm Systems

Updatable microfilm is a relatively new micrographics concept. This unique process is based upon the microfilm's ability to be reimaged many times. The A. B. Dick System 200, seen in Figure 16-25, uses a transparent electrophotography (TEP) film. Bell and Howell uses a slightly different process, called photoplastic, in its Microx system. The major difference in the two systems is in how images are affixed to the film.

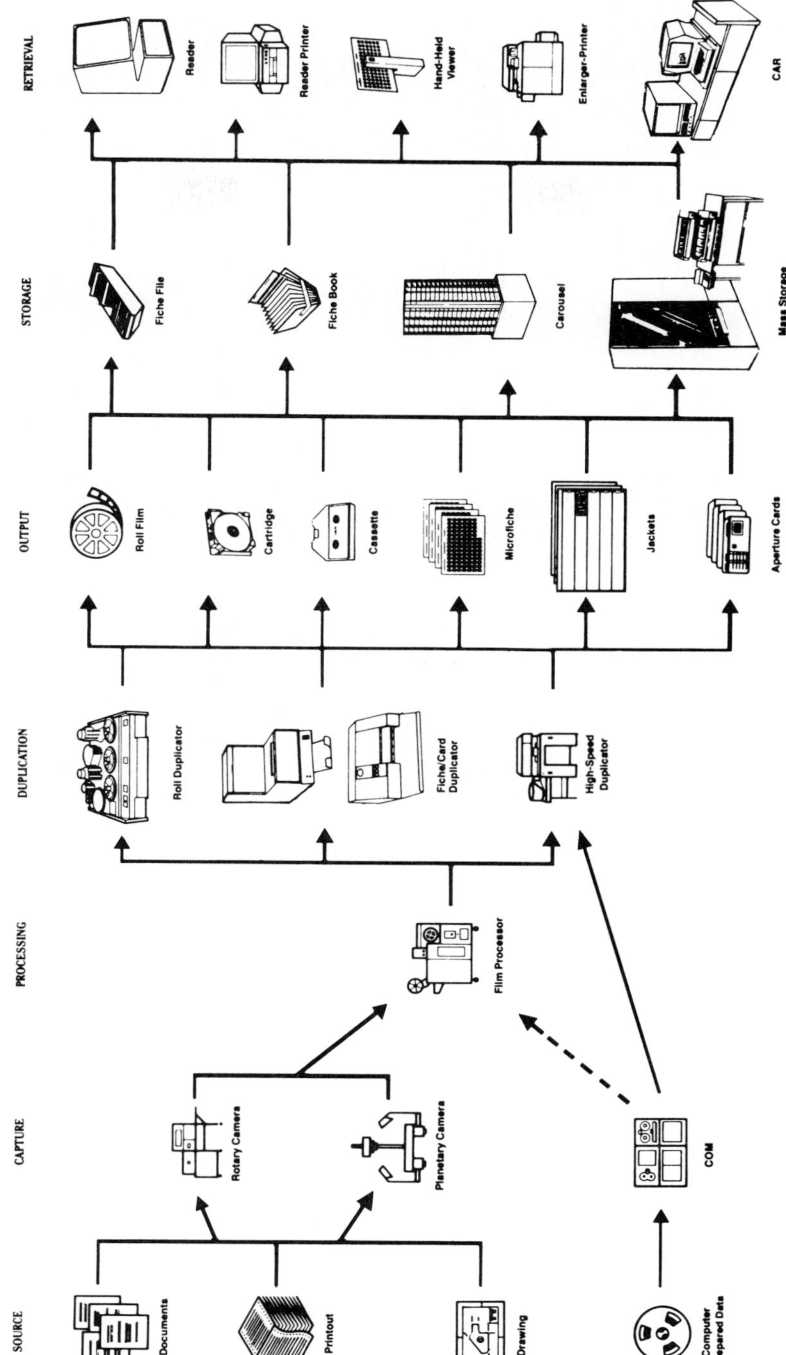

FIGURE 16-24
The seven different image-system steps in a micrographics operation. (Courtesy of International Information Management Congress.)

FIGURE 16-25
A. B. Dick System 200 processor (*top*) and file film (*bottom*). (Courtesy of A. B. Dick.)

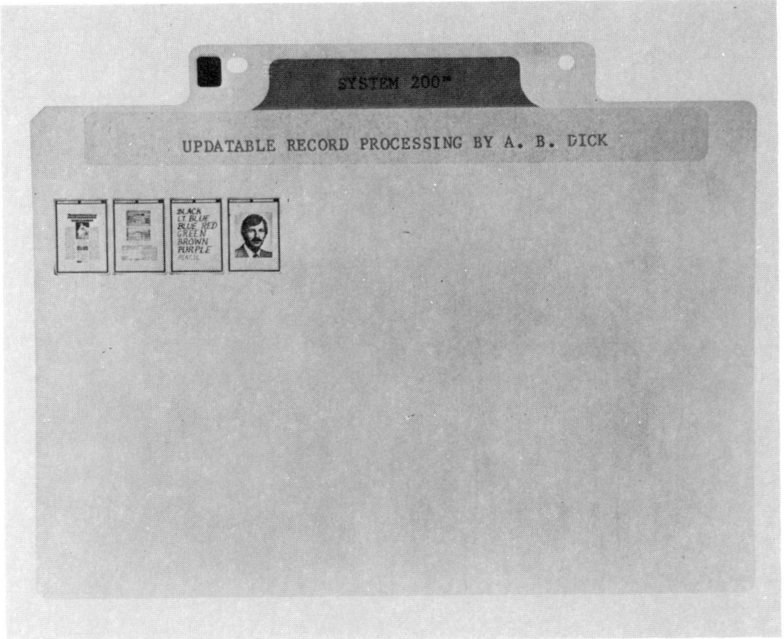

Both systems use a step-and-repeat planetary camera with a fixed reduction ratio to photograph documents. The System 200 microfilm is referred to as "file film." Depending upon which of the two A. B. Dick models the user obtains, the file film will hold up to either 60 legal-size or 98 letter-size images.

The Microx system, holds up to 98 images on its "master" film. The film used in both systems resembles a piece of microfiche with rows and columns.

The basic components of both systems are similar and consist of a camera-processor, a duplicating device, and a reader-printer. Either diazo or vesicular duplicates can be generated from the original film. To use the system, a piece of file or master film is inserted into the camera-processor and a document is placed on the copyboard. The operator then determines which of the 60 or 98 image positions is to hold the document's image. Once this has been done, the document can be photographed. Then, using special techniques peculiar to each system, the document's image is affixed to the film. If more documents are to be imaged on the same piece of film, the cycle continues. If not, the film is removed from the camera-processor and sent to a storage file.

The System 200 is designed to prevent inadvertent reimaging of a valid image or record. However, the system does permit the word *void* or *superseded* to be superimposed over an image. The Microx system is designed to allow the user to "erase" an image and place a new image over the erased one. This feature could lead to the unauthorized alteration of records.

The attractiveness of these systems lies in the fact that the film is updatable as well as being a unitized microform. Having both of these qualities in a single microform gives the records manager a flexibility not found in other microfilm processes.

Computer-Output Microfilm

Looking into a computer room, one will see reports being printed on paper by computer printers. The printer is just one of many devices to which computer-generated reports can be directed. Yet it is the only one that can provide a paper hard copy at high speed. The late 1960s saw computer printers that could print at 600 lines per minute. Now printers generate copy at more than 3,000 lines per minute. With its high speed and versatility, the computer has inundated the user with paper. Mountains of computer printouts helped to accelerate what has been called a "paperwork explosion." Never before have such critical storage and retrieval problems been encountered. Records managers have brought all the resources at their disposal to bear on the problems—with some success. According to Records Consultant, Jesse Clark, COM will save six cents per sheet over hard copy, and 87 percent of computer hard copy could be COM. Thus, COM offers significant financial savings.

General Characteristics

With the introduction and use of *computer-output microfilm,* also known as COM, these problems have become less critical. Remember that a single piece of microfiche can hold hundreds of pages of documents. By using COM, thousands of pages of paper can be reduced to a small handful of microfiche. For example, a 6-inch long card file will hold about 1,100 microfiche. At 48× reduction ratio, these 1,100 fiche will hold 297,000 pages, which is equal to about 100 cases of paper. Storing 100 cases of paper would take about 115 cubic feet of space. A standard 4-by-6-inch card file, 6 inches long, takes up less than one-half of 1 cubic foot. So one can readily see the vast difference that microfiche makes in storage. Retrieval is also simpler. Thumbing through a card file looking for a microfiche is faster and cleaner than looking through boxes of bound computer listings.

Computer-output microfilm is a method of converting computer-generated data into usable information on microfilm. All this is done at computer speed. For a better understanding, assume that a computer has just updated a company's inventory. Instead of printing the report on paper, it will be placed on microfiche. The computer first places the information onto a computer tape, which is magnetic recording tape. The information on the tape is transferred to the logic section of the COM device (see Figure 16-26). Here the information is interpreted and set up the way it will look on a microfiche frame. The data then travels to a converter section that changes information from computer language to alphanumeric or graphic information. Finally, the information arrives at the CRT, or cathode-ray tube. This device looks like a television screen. At this point, enough of the information is put onto the CRT screen to form a "page" or frame. Mounted in front of the CRT is a camera unit; as the camera unit takes a picture of the CRT's screen, it also records forms-overlay data. This data includes such items as column headings, lines, graphs, or anything that will appear on every frame. The camera and CRT are synchronized

FIGURE 16-26 3M Model 715 computer-output microfilm (COM) recorder. (Courtesy of 3M Company.)

so that the camera only takes pictures when the screen has all the information necessary for a frame. One should keep in mind that not every report should be put on COM. Not all users will want their reports on COM. In many cases, the user will have the option.

Advantages and Disadvantages of COM

As in most systems, COM has advantages and disadvantages that need to be recognized. Some advantages are:

1. COM's major advantage is volume and speed. A typical COM recorder can microfilm the equivalent of 200 pages of computer printout a minute.
2. Once in the user's hands, microfiche is cleaner to handle than paper, especially multiple-part forms that use carbon paper.
3. The amount of space required to retain records on COM is considerably less than the amount needed to store records on paper. Since storage space is at a premium in many locations, COM's size is certainly an advantage.
4. A COM report weighs much less than a paper report. A 500-page paper report can weigh many pounds. The same report on microfiche will weigh only ounces.
5. Materials costs with a COM system are lower than the costs of printing paper reports.
6. Duplicate copies of a COM-generated report are less expensive and are of a better quality than paper. Microfiche can be duplicated for pennies—far less than the cost of using multiple-part paper with carbon. Duplicate copies of COM are generally as good as the original, while the fourth, fifth, or sixth copies of a multiple-part report are often unreadable.

Some disadvantages of COM are:

1. The initial outlay for equipment acquisition is very high. A recorder and duplicator may cost as much as $280,000 and seldom cost less than $75,000.
2. The system requires skilled operators. Employees must be specially trained to operate the equipment.
3. The system requires additional equipment. Users must have microfilm readers and reader-printers for viewing and generating hard copy.

Recording Methods

When considering the purchase of a COM unit, one must first decide on its mode of operation. A COM system will function in either one of two modes—on-line or off-line. In the on-line mode, the COM system is connected directly into the computer. Data go directly from the computer to the COM unit, eliminating the intermediate step of storing data on computer tapes. In the off-line mode, the computer puts the data onto a computer tape, to be COM-recorded at some later time. The off-line mode is the one most commonly used, since not everyone who has a computer has a COM system. Because of high equipment cost, service bureaus make COM processing services available to users who cannot afford their own equipment.

Since scientists and engineers first developed COM, they have continually been searching for better methods of recording images. According to the report "Wang on Imaging" from Wang Laboratories (Lowell, MA), there are four ways to create images on COM:

With a CRT, which the COM camera photographs;

With a laser, which writes on the film like a laser copier;

With an electron beam, which creates the dots that make up the image;

With LEDs and a fiber optics bundle, which produces the image photographed by the COM camera.

Many COM records on the market today have the capacity to record directly onto 16mm, 35mm, and 105mm microfilm. Film recorded at 16mm can be loaded directly onto cartridges, cassettes, and jackets. Microfilm recorded on 35mm film can be inserted in aperture cards or left on the roll. Bulk 105mm microfilm is cut into microfiche after filming.

Choosing a Micrographics System

One might ask, why microfilm anything? This very basic question should be posed before considering any type of microfilm system. The first thing anyone with decision-making responsibility should do is verify that a need actually exists.

Reasons for Microfilming

The reasons for any company to microfilm its records will be many and varied. Probably the two most common are to save space and to provide records security. Other important reasons are the rapid retrieval of records, report replacement, and cost reduction.

The microfilming of records can usually be justified on the basis of saving space. In many organizations the records-storage function uses costly and desirable space for storage. Often, storage areas become crowded, necessitating some type of pruning program. For example, vault storage or restrictive (limited) wallbound storage areas do not allow for easy expansion. In this situation, records must be removed before others can be filed. Before the records are removed, a disposition program should be developed. This is particularly true for organizations that do not have records storage centers.

Firms with records centers may find it more expensive to film documents than to store the documents. This, of course, depends upon available space, filming costs, and retrieval costs. In situations where records may be too active for records center storage, they should be microfilmed. This has an advantage of releasing space and is less expensive, in the long run, than recalling documents from the center.

Securing records against unauthorized access, theft, fire, water, insects, and rodent damage is important. Microfilm is an excellent medium for providing records protection. After microfilming, documents can be stored or destroyed and the microfilm used for reference. Once documents are filmed, the images cannot be moved, altered, or otherwise changed. The microform provides excellent protection.

Just as individual documents need protection, so do microforms. Microfilm can be protected by storing it in a secure cabinet or by producing a duplicate copy. A roll of microfilm may be damaged, stolen, or destroyed. When this happens, it is crucial to the functioning of an office to have a duplicate copy. To ensure proper security, the duplicate copy should be stored off-site. This prevents both the original and the duplicate from being destroyed by the same disaster.

The rapid and timely retrieval of documents in an office environment can be crucial to any organization. Microfilming documents for rapid retrieval can save time in searching for records. Automated and semiautomated microfilm retrieval can provide information to the user within seconds. Less sophisticated and slower manual retrieval methods are not as effective. Searching through file drawers for documents can be time-consuming, frustrating, and often costly for a company. For example, a large gas and electric power company will microfilm all its monthly billing records. The microform is duplicated for all employees who answer customer billing inquiries. This permits each employee who answers customer inquiries to respond rapidly and efficiently. Imagine the delays and frustration if the employees had to look up records in file drawers. These retrieval systems function most effectively in areas of large files and high records-retrieval activity.

Whether microfilming for saving space, for security, or for ease of retrieval, a certain amount of cost savings will be realized. Because each firm's operation is individualized, no across-the-board savings can be cited. For example, the cost of floor filing space in a large city is generally more expensive than in medium and small cities. Cost savings realized through security may not be quite as apparent. Some years ago, a midwestern bank lost most of its records during a flood. Because it had microfilmed many of its records, the bank was able to recover in a reasonable length of time. In many cases, security cost savings are only realized in times of crisis.

The Records Manager's Role

Over the years top management has put little effort into developing effective microfilm functions. Generally, purchasing agents, comptrollers, or other middle- or high-level executives made equipment purchasing decisions. In many cases the vendor who had the best presentation made a sale. Little thought was given to how well the equipment would perform or actually meet the company's needs. This caused the microfilming operation to be designed around the equipment's capabilities. The equipment should have been ordered to meet specific operational requirements, not vice versa.

Management now realizes the need for competent study and planning before installing any microfilm system. Because of the impact a microfilm system can have on one's functions, the records manager must have the system's design responsibility. In many organizations the records manager is the one with the micrographics expertise and responsibility. As the knowledgeable individual, the records manager should be able to:

1. Determine if an organization needs to develop a microfilm function
2. Assist in determining which documents are to be microfilmed
3. Develop policies and procedures relative to the microfilm operation
4. Determine what microfilm equipment should be obtained to meet the organization's needs
5. Control the personnel responsible for operating the microfilm system
6. Review the policies, procedures, equipment, and personnel periodically and institute any necessary changes

Strategic Planning Process According to an ARMA publication, a four-step strategic planning process is recommended for planning conversions to micrographics. Authors Mark Langemo, CRM, and Daniel Brathal, recommend the following steps:

STEP ONE: Determine if a problem can be solved through the use of micrographics.

Is there a need to:

a. Speed information retrieval
b. Secure information in records
c. Improve file integrity
d. Speed distribution
e. Reduce storage space
f. Integrate document management into office automation systems
g. Reduce personnel costs
h. Save time and money

STEP TWO: Determine the appropriate microform.

a. Know the advantages and applications of each form of microfilm.
b. Evaluate characteristics of records to be filmed.
c. Determine how the records are and will be indexed, retrieved, and used.
d. Decide if archival quality film is necessary.
e. Consider budget, staff, user, and facilities restraints.

STEP THREE: Plan the conversion and training process.

a. Plan with the persons who will do the conversion.
b. Establish a step-by-step process for getting the work done.
c. Consider a test run to debug the process.
d. Set time frames and target dates.

STEP FOUR: Cost the job.

a. Personnel time
b. Equipment
c. Supplies
d. Facilities
e. Consultants' assistance
f. Any related costs
g. Expected return on investment

Source: Planning Conversions to Micrographic Systems by Daniel A. Brathal and Mark Langemo, CRM, ARMA, 1987. Courtesy of Arma International.

Feasibility Study Before developing a micrographics operation, the records manager must carefully review the company's need for a microfilm function. Therefore, a feasibility study should be conducted to present to management as a basis for the decision-making process (see Figure 16-27). A feasibility study should:

1. Identify all pertinent records
2. Determine purpose and use of the records
3. Establish the condition and size of records
4. Estimate the volume of the records and the amount of space they occupy
5. Determine the records retention periods
6. Compute the cost to store and retrieve the records

The study should begin by interviewing the responsible individual in each department, division, section, or office within the company. The objective is to learn the function of each area and how it interrelates with other areas. A careful review of pertinent records is also conducted. Each record is discussed with the document's originator, as well as with intermediate and end users. This gives the interviewer a good overview and understanding of the situation.

Along with these data, the records manager must consider the following facts:

1. The physical amount and annual cost of the space used by the present storage must be determined. This cost per square foot should be computed for only the space attributed to records storage.
2. The amount of time and dollars attributed to storing and retrieving documents must be computed.
3. The volume of records or number of documents to be microfilmed is important. These figures are used to compute filming costs, develop work schedules, and determine staffing needs.
4. Retention schedules for records should be used as an aid in determining whether a record should be filmed. Documents with short to intermediate retention periods (one to five years) should not normally be microfilmed. There are, of course, exceptions to this rule.
5. The physical size of the records must be considered when procuring equipment. Normal office documents can be filmed with a rotary camera. Engineering drawings are usually larger and generally require a planetary camera.
6. The physical condition of records should help determine how they are to be filmed. Documents may be torn, folded, or frayed; they may be disintegrating from age. These conditions prohibit satisfactory filming on a rotary camera. The amount and frequency of these records help to determine the type of equipment to obtain.

FIGURE 16-27 Flowchart of feasibility study and implementation of system.

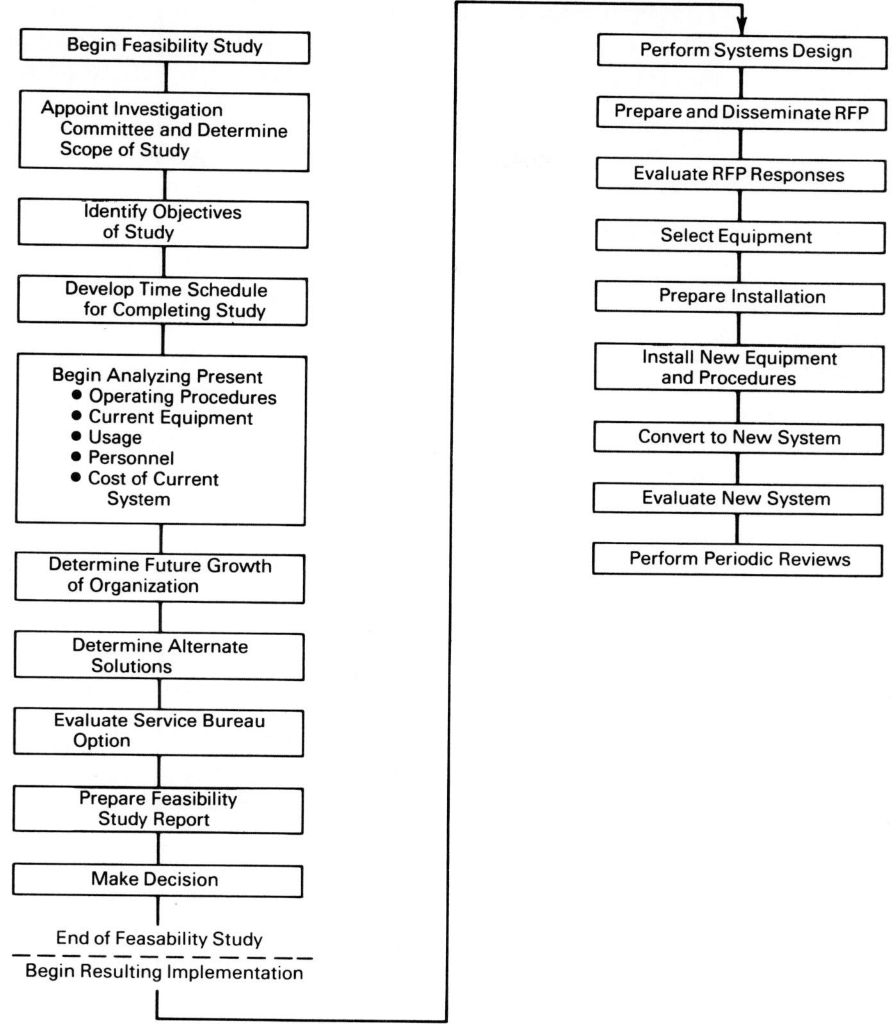

7. The need for paper copies of microfilm images should determine whether a reader-printer is required.

Service Bureaus Once all these data are assembled, a report to management should be developed. Before developing the report, the records manager should look into having the microfilming done by a service bureau. A microfilm service bureau is a firm that provides microfilming services for a fee. In many cases, a service bureau is an excellent alternative. Service bureaus serve both small and large firms. The benefits of using a service bureau are many and varied. A few of them are:

1. Service bureaus provide all the personnel necessary to complete the task.
2. A firm price on a per-image or per-file basis is guaranteed.
3. All equipment and supplies are provided by the service bureau.
4. The service bureau guarantees that all microfilm images will meet the user's standards.
5. Work can be done on-site or in the service bureau's shop.
6. Normally, service bureaus are able to provide additional equipment should the job requirements demand it. Microfilm turnaround time can be cut by using additional equipment.
7. The expertise of the service-bureau personnel can be used in an advisory capacity with no extra cost to the user.

Now the records manager is able to review the options and write a comprehensive management report with recommendations. The option of using a service bureau or setting up an in-house operation is developed and justified in the report. Management must be given enough information to make valid decisions. At this point a good records manager brings forth skills and expertise to help management reach the best solution.

Request for Proposal The records manager now drafts a request for proposal (RFP). This document, which is sent to interested vendors, asks for proposals or recommendations for solving the user's problems. The RFP should include all items that the vendor is to address in the recommendations. The document may be as detailed or as sketchy as the user wishes. The minimum number of items that any RFP should include are (1) the amount and type of equipment recommended, (2) the cost of the equipment, (3) the amount and cost of supplies, (4) delivery dates, (5) employee training requirements, (6) post-installation vendor support, and (7) total user costs. There may be more items the records manager wishes to cover, depending upon the comprehensiveness of the recommendations. The vendors should be given a deadline for responding to the RFP. This prevents the project from dragging on and losing momentum.

As the proposals are received, the records manager should critically review each recommendation. If any proposal does not satisfactorily answer the organization's needs, then it should not be actively considered. Once all the proposals have been received and reviewed, the records manager is ready to decide which proposal to select. In some cases, the records manager may provide recommendations to management for final proposal selection. Whichever method is used, a decision is reached based upon the criteria management feels are the most important. Such items as the cost of the system, customer satisfaction, vendor support, or equipment capabilities are often the deciding factors. Regardless of the reason, an order is placed with a vendor for the equipment and services required.

Preinstallation Planning After the equipment has been ordered and before it is delivered, the records manager must begin the preinstallation planning. Depending upon the task and the amount of time to complete it, the preparation might better have begun months or weeks before. Regardless of the lead time, some of the more important tasks to accomplish are:

1. Documents or files must be identified and prepared.
2. Working area must be located and, if necessary, utilities installed. Such items as water, electrical service, and telephone outlets might be needed.
3. Personnel to operate the system must be trained or hired and trained.
4. Normal operational policies and procedures should be developed.
5. Security arrangements and procedures should be developed.
6. Adequate storage space must be found.
7. Supplies not included with the equipment order must be procured.
8. Necessary office furniture should be obtained.

After the equipment has arrived and has been installed, the records manager begins using his or her organizational skills. Personnel, equipment, and procedures must now be pulled together to form an operational system. A team concept with everyone performing specific tasks can be developed. Definite lines of authority and responsibility are set forth. If the personnel operating the system are well motivated, the operation has a better chance of getting off to a smooth start. When problems arise, the records manager must be ready to respond in a timely and decisive manner. This helps to develop professionalism, respect for the operation, and, in general, a good feeling about one's position.

Periodic Review The records manager should review the system periodically to determine if any changes should be made. The equipment's performance and maintenance records should be studied carefully. Operational policies and procedures must be examined to determine if they are still appropriate. Employees' skills and tasks should be reviewed for effectiveness. An audit of the records will determine if costs are running at projected rates. Finally, the records manager must determine if the system as a whole is meeting organizational goals.

CHAPTER HIGHLIGHTS

- Silver halide microfilm is the most commonly used type of microfilm today.
- Diazo and vesicular microfilm are used for duplicating copies of original microfilm; dry silver microfilm is used as original microfilm in COM cameras.

- A standard reel holds 100 feet of 5.5-mil-thick microflim. If the same reel is loaded with thin film, which is 2.5 mil thick, the reel will hold twice as many images because there will be twice as much film on the reel.
- The reduction ratio of a camera is the ratio of the size of the original document to the size of its image when filmed. A 16× or 16:1 reduction ratio means that the original document was 16 times larger than its image.
- The various types of microfilm found today are called microforms and include roll film, microfiche, aperture cards, microfilm jackets, chips, and updatable microfilm.
- Microfilm cameras are of two general designs—rotary and planetary. Rotary cameras, designed for continuous feeding of documents, are considered high-volume equipment. Planetary cameras record flat stationary documents and, in general, produce a better-quality image.
- The processor planetary camera, which produces aperture cards, is designed to microfilm large engineering drawings or similar documents.
- Designed to produce 105mm microfiche, the step-and-repeat camera is a planetary camera.
- The microfilm readers that permit the viewing of microforms are of two basic types—front projection and rear projection.
- A reader-printer is a microfilm reader with a printing mechanism to generate a paper copy of the image.
- To help locate or retrieve a microfilm image, an index or address location must be developed. The more common types of index coding are flash card, odometer, sequential numbering, line code, blip coding, and descriptive codes.
- Other types of equipment necessary to an efficient microfilm operation are microfilm storage cabinets, reader-fillers, notching machines, editing-inspection stations, microfilm duplicators, and densitometers.
- Computer-output microfilm (COM) is a process that uses computer-generated data to produce microfiche, either on- or off-line. There are four basic methods of COM recording: cathode-ray tube (CRT), electron-beam recording (EBR), light-emitting diode (LED), and laser-beam recording (LBR).
- When selecting a micrographics system, the records manager should consider how crucial the need for a system is, what records center options are available, and whether the records need to be secured from damage and unauthorized usage.
- The records manager's role in selecting and operating a microfilm system is to advise, direct, and select. A records manager's expertise is extremely important in determining needs, developing policies and procedures, selecting equipment, training personnel, reviewing, and evaluating.
- Before making a firm commitment to any type of system, the records manager should consider contracting the work to a service bureau.

- Once the decision to purchase a micrographics system has been reached, the records manager should then draft a request for proposal (RFP).
- After equipment has been selected and ordered, the records manager must be sure to prepare the work site, order supplies, and train the employees.
- At some predetermined point after the system has been in operation, the records manager should review the entire system's operation. This allows for reevaluation and redirection where necessary.

QUESTIONS FOR REVIEW

1. What type of microfilm is most commonly used for business records?
2. Describe the differences among at least three types of microfilm.
3. Contrast rotary and planetary microfilm cameras.
4. List and describe four types of microforms.
5. What are four methods of indexing microfilm?
6. Why are jackets color-coded and notched?
7. How is a reduction ratio determined?
8. Briefly discuss some reasons for microfilming records.
9. What should be the records manager's role in the development and operation of a micrographics system?
10. Describe the advantages of using a service bureau for micrographics services.
11. Describe the advantages and disadvantages of COM.

THE DECISION MAKER

Case Studies

Three weeks ago you completed a research study for the records manager concerning a possible micrographics application for the company. Today you were notified that your report was favorably received and the company will begin making plans to develop a micrographics shop. Your first task is to prepare a recommendation for the type of microfilm camera(s) the company should purchase. The report should contrast both types, rotary and planetary, and make specific recommendations. The company will have the following amounts of work to microfilm on a weekly basis:

1. Newspapers, standard size: 500 pages
2. Magazines, various sizes: 1,600 pages

3. Shipping documents, 5-by-8-inch: 3,800 sheets
4. Continuous-form computer-generated reports, 11-by-14-inch: 7,000 pages
5. Various office memoranda and letters, various sizes: 600 sheets
6. Purchase order cards, 3-by-5-inch: 2,300 cards
7. Employee time sheets, 8 1/2-by-11-inch: 1,230 sheets

The recommendation should also include any accessory items needed by the camera(s). At this point, do not consider equipment costs or personnel; concentrate only on operational factors.

AUDITING THE RECORDS MANAGEMENT PROGRAM AND WRITING MANUALS

OBJECTIVES

Upon completion of this chapter, the student should be able to:

1. Describe the auditing process.
2. Describe the use of activity, accuracy, and retrieval time ratios in the auditing process.
3. Explain how to evaluate equipment, supplies, and procedures in the records system.
4. Describe how to prepare an auditor's report.
5. Describe the importance of the records management manual in attaining objectives.
6. Prepare a records management manual.
7. Explain basic concepts in writing the manual.
8. Identify the various types of company manuals.
9. Describe the FOG Index.

A records management program cannot function effectively and efficiently without control measures. This control is the result of the periodic *auditing process* which, through a thorough examination of the records management program, determines if established procedures and policies of the program are being implemented.

A records management manual documents such policies and procedures, and, in addition, serves as a training guide and a reference tool. A records manual encourages uniformity and standardization of job performance. Thus, the auditing process determines if policies and procedures are being followed while the records manual provides documentation of its existence.

The Records Audit

An effective records management program is made possible by an effective records audit program. Records retention schedules need to be enforced and monitored to insure compliance. An annual audit of retention schedules throughout an organization enables the records manager and staff to enforce retention decisions. Departments in large companies can be put on staggered audit schedules to distribute the workload of the records management auditors. Annual audits help to increase the credibility of the records program, and, in addition, assists in "fine tuning" the records retention schedule.

While top management authorization of audits is essential for success, some department heads may resist such an audit of their records. Records auditors can make noncompliance public knowledge by publishing the results of the audits to upper management. Public reports generally insure future cooperation. The use of positive motivation techniques increases the likelihood of continued compliance and cooperation in audits. Such techniques could include a notice in the company newsletter recognizing departments with good records management track records.

Audit Forms. For the audit to proceed efficiently, audit forms can be developed that will insure standardization and uniformity of departmental audits. Records Manager Jean Crary has developed several forms which she uses when auditing the records of the University of Delaware.[1] Figure 17-1 shows an Annual Records Retention Schedule Audit Report that is easy to complete. This form identifies what action has taken place over the past year with each record series. Figure 17-2 is an Audit Questionnaire which can be sent through interoffice mail or completed in interview fashion by an auditor. Generally, better results are obtained when in-person interviews take place. Figure 17-3 shows a Records Retention Schedule Compliance Audit Worksheet that helps to insure consistency about each records series selected for the audit. Records managers can utilize a variety of forms such as these to expedite the auditing process.

[1]Jean Crary, "The Teeth of the Program—The Records Audit," ARMA Quarterly, July, 1985. Courtesy of ARMA International.

FIGURE 17-1

RECORDS RETENTION SCHEDULE COMPLIANCE AUDIT
WORKSHEET

SERIES #__________

1. Is it necessary at this time to make any changes in the retention procedure? Yes____ No____

   If yes, what change(s) need to be made?

Retention period	Yes____	No____	N/A____
Change in wording	Yes____	No____	N/A____
Deletion of Series	Yes____	No____	N/A____

   What is the justfication for the change?____________________

2. Has the retention procedure for this series been followed as currently specified on the records retention schedule?

In-house review:	Yes____	No____	N/A____
In-house destruction:	Yes____	No____	N/A____
Transfer to Records Center:	Yes____	No____	N/A____
Review of records in R/C for permanent retention/destruction	Yes____	No____	N/A____

3. If records have been destroyed in-house, has a "Notification of Destruction of University Records" form been filed in the University Archives? Yes____ No____

   For records eligible for destruction in the Records Center, has the Unit Head signed the "Intent to Destroy University Records" form supplied by the University Archives?
   Yes____ No____

4. Is this series vital? Yes____ No____

   If yes, is there a vital records protection plan for these Records? Yes____ No____

   Has the plan been implemented? Yes____ No____

   If so, why not?____________________

5. Department is in compliance with the schedule for this series
   Yes____ No____

6. Audited by____________________

QUALIFICATIONS OF THE AUDITOR

The first step in the records management audit is to secure approval from top management. Once this approval has been given to the records manager, he or she must select the person who will perform the audit. One of the most important qualifications an auditor must have is an awareness and understanding of the federal, state, and local laws and regulations governing records retention.

Additional qualifications required for the records management auditor are basically the same as those needed by a qualified records manager, namely:

1. A strong academic background in such courses as business, accounting, economics, and history

FIGURE 17-2

AUDIT QUESTIONNAIRE

Department ______

Contact ______ Schedule # ______

1. Have any of your department's records been transferred to the Records Center since last year's records retention schedule audit? Yes____ No____

   If no, state reason

2. Have your department's records been weeded for destruction in-house since last year's records retention schedule audit? Yes____ No____

   If no, state reason

3. Does your records retention schedule need revision? Yes____ No____

   If yes, which of the following apply:

   Additions ______
   Deletions ______
   Rewording of existing series ______
   Total revision ______

4. Does your department currently have records stored in the Records Center? Yes____ No____

   If yes, do the records need to be reviewed for destruction or permanent retention in the Archives? Yes____ No____

5. Is your department's filing scheme effective? Yes____ No____

6. Does your records retention schedule reflect the filing scheme? Yes____ No____

   If no, would you like to schedule a consultation to discuss a revision to either the filing scheme or the records retention schedule? Yes____ No____

7. After reviewing your records and your schedule, please indicate on the attached page(s) what action has taken place during the past year.

Questionnaire completed by ______

Date ______

2. Experience as a records manager in an organization where all aspects of records management were implemented

External Versus Internal Auditors

The decision must be made whether to use an **external auditor** who is brought in from outside the organization or an **internal auditor** who is an employee of the firm. There are advantages and disadvantages upon each type of auditor.

Advantages of an External Auditor As a general rule, the advantages given here for the external auditor are those that are unique to a person brought in

FIGURE 17-3

RECORDS RETENTION SCHEDULE COMPLIANCE AUDIT
ENTIRE SCHEDULE REVIEW WORKSHEET

____________(total) series have been selected at random and physically audited. In addition, the following information is required to complete the audit.

1. Are there any problems with any of the other series on the schedule? Yes_____ No_____

   If so, what? Change in retention Yes_____ No_____
   Rewording of series Yes_____ No_____

   Which series are affected?

   Series Change

   ____
   ____
   ____
   ____
   ____

2. Is it necessary to make any additions to the schedule? Yes_____ No_____

3. Is it necessary to make any detentions from the schedule?

   If so, which series?____________________

4. What is the justification for the retention?____________
   ____
   ____
   ____

5. Have other series on the schedule been reviewed for any of the following?
   In-house destruction Yes_____ No_____
   Transfer to Records Center Yes_____ No_____

   If not, why not?____________________

6. Which series have not been reviewed this year?__________
   ____
   ____

7. Remarks?
   ____
   ____
   ____
   ____

8. Audited by____________________

for auditing the records. There are exceptions, of course, and a highly qualified person within an organization may possess these capabilities.

Listed here are the advantages that an outside auditor brings to an organization:

1. Expertise in the area of records management

2. Objectivity in assessing the problems that may be found in the records management program
3. Shortened time span for completing the audit, according to a prearranged agreement with management

The experience that an outside auditor acquires through his or her work with various organizations is invaluable. Many times a problem and its possible solutions are quite evident to the external auditors because of their having encountered similar situations in other organizations. It is unlikely that an internal auditor will have had such a varied experience.

The external auditor, also, can look at problems with complete objectivity and impartiality. For instance, each procedure and policy will be critically reviewed by the external auditor, who might then recommend updating, or in some instances, eliminating procedures and policies. The internal auditor, in many instances, may be so close to the problem that the policies and procedures will be accepted as hard-and-fast rules. The external auditor is more likely to review each policy and procedure to determine whether it is contributing to an efficient and cost-effective records management program.

In addition, the external auditor will devote full time to the task of auditing the records program. The internal auditor, on the other hand, may have to take care of routine duties and will be able to spend less daily time on the task of auditing.

Disadvantages of an External Auditor Depending upon such factors as the size and the scope of an organization, the disadvantages of using an external auditor could outweigh the advantages. Some of the disadvantages are:

1. Cost of the auditing services
2. Unfamiliarity with an organization's program
3. Employee resentment at having an outsider disrupting the normal routine

Using an external auditor will naturally be more costly to the organization than assigning an employee the task of auditing the system. Auditors and consultants command high salaries, and this fact may be the major deterrent in deciding against an external auditor.

Also, the time spent in becoming familiar with the organization's records program adds considerably to the cost factor.

Another problem faced by the organization that hires an external auditor is the resentment that employees may have toward an outsider who disrupts their work, and as the case may be, makes recommendations that may be objectionable to them for one reason or another.

Advantages of an Internal Auditor A small organization will probably look very favorably upon using one of its own employees as the internal auditor in order to avoid the disadvantages of an external auditor. The cost to the organization of using an internal auditor is minimal when compared with the cost for the services of an external auditor.

Another tremendous advantage is that an employee is already familiar with the records management program. In addition, the employee will be able to move unobtrusively among other employees while reviewing the activities in other departments.

Disadvantages of an Internal Auditor Few records management personnel will have the qualifications needed for a comprehensive audit of a records management system. A person may have great capabilities in specific areas of records management, but rarely in the total program. For a complete audit, expertise is needed in the total program of records management. Also, an internal auditor may find that routine duties interfere with the auditing process and prolong the completion of the audit.

Staff Function in the Auditing Process

Once the auditor has been selected, the records management personnel should take the necessary steps to prepare for the pending audit.

Preliminary Work

Space should be provided so the auditor will have a measure of privacy during the auditing process. The staff should plan for the auditor's work as carefully as possible to ensure that manuals, policies, procedures, forms, and relevant information are readily available before the beginning of the audit. One person should be assigned the responsibility of being an assistant to the auditor. The assistant, being familiar with the records management program of the organization, will expedite the work of the auditor. **Job descriptions** should be updated and available for the auditor's use. In addition, an **office layout** should be available that indicates communication patterns and work flow. Evaluating the office layout is an important factor in determining methods for cutting costs in an organization. Figure 17-4 is a checklist to be used in preparation for the auditor's visit.

The Auditor's Function in the Auditing Process

The duties of the auditor may be summarized as analyzing, checking, reviewing, and verifying the total program from *A* to *Z*; that is, from the creation of documents to their final retention or destruction.

FIGURE 17-4 Checklist to be used in preparation for the auditor's visit.

	Available for Auditor		Date Completed	Initialed by Person in Charge
	Yes	No		
Office Space for Auditor				
Records Manuals				
Policies and Procedures				
Retention Schedules				
Forms				
Job Descriptions				
Records Manager				
Assistant R/M				
Records Supervisor				
Records Clerks				
Office Layout				

Activities of the Auditor

The duties of the auditor are:

1. Determine that the objectives of the records management program are being carried out.
2. Confirm that written policies and procedures are available to all records management personnel.
3. Verify that the retention schedule is in compliance with the federal, state, and local regulations.
4. Analyze the layout of the records management area for greatest efficiency.
5. Review the procedures of the records management system.
6. Analyze the job description for each of the records management personnel.
7. Review the policies for classifying vital records.
8. Check filing equipment to determine its efficiency and possibly recommend replacement.

9. Inventory the electronic data processing tapes.
10. Check the charge-out procedure to make sure that it is effective.
11. Check the inactive files for materials that may have passed the destruction date.
12. Review the security methods used in housing vital records.
13. Recommend solutions to any problems that are revealed through the audit.
14. Write the report to management concerning the findings and the recommendations based on the audit.

Some or all of these activities will be carried out by the auditor, depending on the size of the organization.

USING EFFICIENCY RATIOS IN THE AUDIT PROCESS

To ensure that the auditor's final report is factual, the auditor should incorporate statistics on the records program. Three commonly used measures—activity, accuracy, and retrieval time ratios—are recommended for calculating how efficiently the records program is operating. This information gives the auditor, management, and staff objective data upon which to base their recommendations for improvement in the records program.

Activity Ratio

An activity ratio measures the number of records requested as a percent of the total number of records filed in the system. To compute the ratio, the auditor would use the following formula:

$$\frac{\text{Number of Records Requested}}{\text{Number of Records Filed}} = \text{Activity Ratio}$$

For example, if 10,000 records are in the system and 2,000 requests for those records are made, the activity ratio would be computed as follows:

$$\frac{2{,}000}{10{,}000} = 20\%$$

As a yardstick for interpreting the activity ratio when preparing an audit report, the following guidelines are suggested for active records:

From 10 to 20 percent	Records in the files are being used efficiently.
From 9 to 5 percent	Duplicate records might exist elsewhere.

Below 5 percent	Records are not being used. Retention schedules should be corrected to take records out of active files.

Accuracy Ratio

An accuracy ratio measures the ability of the files staff to locate records that are requested in the records system. Thus, it measures the efficiency of the files personnel as well as the efficiency of the records system. The formula for computing an accuracy ratio is as follows:

$$\frac{\text{Number of Records Located}}{\text{Number of Records Requested}} = \text{Accuracy Ratio}$$

Thus if 875 records were located out of a total of 900 records requested the auditor would compute the accuracy ratio as follows:

$$\frac{875}{900} = 97\%$$

Guidelines for interpreting an accuracy ratio are as follows:

99 percent and above	Files are well organized.
97 to 98 percent	Files are in satisfactory condition.
96 percent and below	Files should be reorganized.

Retrieval Time Ratio

A retrieval time ratio measures the time it takes to locate an individual record. Thus, this information provides management with an average time (expressed in seconds) that it takes to retrieve a record from the files. The formula for computing this ratio is as follows:

$$\frac{\text{Number of Minutes Required to Locate Records}}{\text{Number of Records Retrieved}} = \text{Retrieval Time Ratio}$$

For example, if 200 records were retrieved in 150 minutes, the retrieval time ratio would be calculated as follows:

$$\frac{150 \text{ minutes}}{200} = 0.75 \text{ minutes} \times 60 \text{ seconds per minute} = 45 \text{ seconds}$$

No set standards are available for evaluating retrieval times. Records managers set their own retrieval time standards based on the type of files system, the type of equipment (automated or nonautomated), the condition of the files, and the expertise of the records staff.

These three ratios will not be used on a daily basis, but conducting an evaluation periodically can help the records manager assess the efficiency of the records staff and of the retrieval process.

EVALUATING RECORDS SYSTEMS

An auditor must examine the internal contents of a records system to determine if the equipment, supplies, and procedures are appropriate for the record series being filed. To accomplish a comprehensive audit, the auditor should compile a list of questions like the ones that follow, to ascertain the condition of the files.

Evaluating Equipment

1. Is the equipment being used appropriate for the size and type of records being filed?
2. Is there appropriate aisle space for retrieval of records?
3. Is the equipment in good working order?
4. Is special records storage equipment being used for nonconventional records, such as magnetic tapes, microforms, and floppy disks?
5. Would a different type of storage equipment provide more filing efficiency or more efficient use of floor space?

Evaluating Supplies

1. Is the number of file guides per drawer adequate for easy location of requested records?
2. Can file labels be read without removing the file folders from the drawers?
3. Are individual folders overstuffed with papers? Are the scores on the bottoms of the folders being used?
4. Are uniform supplies being used throughout the records system?
5. Are file drawers correctly labeled to alleviate the need to open unnecessary drawers?

Evaluating Procedures

1. Is there adequate working space inside a file drawer for retrieval of folders and individual records?

2. Are charge-out forms and/or out guides being completed before distribution of requested records?
3. Are records being properly coded before filing?
4. Are records being cross-referenced correctly?
5. Are filing rules being followed as outlined in a records management manual?

The Periodic Audit

The organization that is having its first audit may find that a comprehensive audit is a tremendous, time-consuming task. Getting ready for the audit involves much time and effort on the part of records personnel. However, once the initial audit has been completed, the next audit will be less burdensome. Personnel will be more aware of materials that will be needed in future audits and will make sure that policies and procedures are kept up to date, that the manual is updated frequently, that job descriptions are also updated, and that forms are revised or eliminated whenever necessary.

Advantages of Routine Auditing

The organization that has its records management program audited routinely will find that there are several advantages:

1. Less time is needed to audit the program.
2. Staff members are more cooperative and willing to participate.
3. Problems may be more easily corrected when they have not had time to become routine policy.

Disadvantages of Routine Auditing

Probably the greatest disadvantage of routine auditing is the cost involved. This cost will be perceptibly high in the short term; but spread over the long term, the savings to an organization will be far greater than the cost. The dollar savings may not be measured with any degree of accuracy, but the obvious savings will be manifested in a much more efficient records program.

Another disadvantage of routine auditing, of course, is the amount of time spent by employees in keeping everything in readiness for the next audit.

The Auditor's Report

Once the auditor's report has been prepared, management, including the records manager, should review the findings and recommendations.

Significance of the Findings

An audit that has been thorough may reveal some surprises. The results may not necessarily be agreeable to the staff, and there could be resistance to change in the routine of the people concerned. The audit is of worth to an organization only if the findings and the recommendations are reviewed by management and, if feasible, implemented.

Writing the Report

The auditor who lacks writing skills will find that a course in report writing can be helpful. The report should be clear and concise and should follow the principles of effective business writing.

The length of the report will vary greatly depending upon the scope of the audit. For instance, a brief audit that simply verifies that the retention schedule is in compliance with regulations may be no more than one page in length. On the other hand, an audit that encompasses many of the auditor's activities will be much longer.

The report of the auditor will include several parts unless the report is very short. Usually, a report of 500 words or more will have a summary at the beginning, for quick perusal by management; an introduction that states the scope of the audit; facts and interpretation of the findings; conclusions based on the findings; and the recommendations that stem from the conclusions. The statements should be direct and forceful. Expressions like "It is the opinion of the auditor that the filing equipment is inadequate" will be more direct if stated "Filing equipment is inadequate."

The report should be objective and should use few adjectives. For instance, instead of reporting that "Staff are remiss in following procedures for protecting vital documents," the auditor would report, "Vital records must be protected according to written procedures."

Only the facts are presented in the report. There should be no effort to "sell" a program of the auditor's preference, although he or she should report the advantages and/or disadvantages of systems in relation to an organization's needs. The summary tells the reader what the report is about and is a condensation of the report. The auditor may find it a challenge to write the summary clearly and concisely, preferably filling no more than one page.

Report Format

To ensure the success of an audit report, the format should present the facts clearly, concisely, and attractively. Headings should be used to present the material in a coherent and organized fashion. Either side headings or paragraph headings can help the reader focus on the issues being addressed. Enumerations (numbered items) help to present conclusions and recommendations in a logical sequence. A suggested report format is shown in Figure 17-5.

FIGURE 17-5
Suggested report format.

POCONO REALTY CORPORATION

TO: Jessica Daniels, Records Manager

FROM: Matthew McCloskey, Records Consultant

DATE: June 22, 19--

SUBJECT: Records Management Audit

An audit of the central files of the Pocono Realty Corporation was conducted on June 15, 19--, to determine the operating efficiency of the records system. The conclusions and recommendations of this audit are presented below.

<u>Conclusions</u>

1. Job descriptions are incomplete and outdated.
2. Documents do not flow naturally from one work station to another.
3. Many inactive records have passed their destruction dates.
4. Vital records are not adequately protected.
5. The records manual is not available to all records personnel.
6. The filing equipment is inadequate.
7. The office space is seriously limited because of a tremendous increase in active records during the past two years.
8. Three electronic data processing tapes are missing.

RECORDS MANAGEMENT MANUALS

Who would be so unwise as to take a trip by automobile in an unfamiliar country without a road map? This is akin to launching a records management program without a records management manual. Traveling by automobile or attempting to manage the records of an office will end in chaos unless some sort of guide or chart is followed to keep on the proper path. In the office this guide is the records management manual.

Figure 17-5
continued

2

Recommendations

Based on the above conclusions, the following recommendations were drawn:

1. Complete and update job descriptions for each position.
2. Improve work flow between all work stations.
3. Dispose of inactive records as specified by the records retention schedule.
4. Improve vital records protection through the use of dispersal and microforms.
5. Distribute the records manual to all records management personnel.
6. Conduct a study to determine the type of files equipment that should be purchased.
7. Inventory active records and transfer inactive records to the central storage facility.
8. Create a charge-out system for electronic data processing records.

Incorporation of the above recommendations will help to improve the operating efficiency of the records management department of the Pocono Realty Corporation.

The records management manual documents policies and procedures, serves as a reference guide and a training tool, and encourages uniformity and standardization of job performance.

The Manual as a Communication Tool

Every office should provide a manual to guide personnel in making decisions concerning the filing, retention, destruction, and permanent storage of the documents originated by a business firm. The value of the documents and how long they should be retained cannot be determined by individual clerks. The length of retention and final disposition of records are determined carefully by the records manager together with other officials of a company. These regulations are written with care and become guidelines in the records management manual until they are superseded by more recent guidelines.

Importance for Attaining Program Objectives

The **records management manual** sets forth clearly the objectives of the records management program, as established by top management, the records manager, and staff. The manual serves as a guide in defining program objectives and in outlining the activities needed to attain those objectives. Clearly defined objectives enable the records manager to revise, update, or clarify areas of the records management program. For instance, one objective of the program may be to "reduce by one-fourth the floor space occupied by active records." This objective can be measured easily. If the objective is not attained, personnel must determine the reason and propose a solution. The solution may be to revise the retention schedule in the manual so that materials that are no longer needed may be discarded. On the other hand, a new system may be needed for storage and retrieval of the documents.

Training Guide for Employees

The records manual is an invaluable training guide for employees, both old and new. Employees who work with the records will keep the manual handy for easy reference. Even the employees who have been working in the same office for years will find that reference to the manual is needed frequently.

New employees will learn the procedures more quickly if they have the records management manual available. The written word is more complete and authoritative than the spoken word of a supervisor who may unintentionally omit detailed instructions during a training session.

New employees are quickly oriented to the records management program of an organization when they are assisted by a well-written manual. They will know, for instance, that documents are not to be removed from the files without a charge-out card being properly filled out and placed in the file, if the manual includes such instructions.

All employees, old and new, should be encouraged to review the instructions contained in the manual so that uniformity will be assured in day-to-day activities.

Advantages of the Manual

Probably the greatest advantage of adhering to the rules in the records management manual is that uniformity is guaranteed. Offices without such manuals will discover one day that their records have been filed without any consistency, often because of personnel turnover. Each newly hired individual brings a new set of rules; as a result, filing becomes a subjective matter. In such offices, personnel are often unable to locate quickly documents requested by management. After such an experience, the records staff realizes the necessity for rules and procedures governing the creation, management, and disposition of records.

Other advantages of a records management manual are as follows:

1. The records manager is freed from the repetitive task of training each new employee and can spend more time in the management and control of the records.
2. The chain of command is clearly defined in an organization chart. Supervisors are given responsibility for certain functions and the authority to carry out these functions. Staff members know that the supervisors are expected to delegate certain duties to them, and they realize that their activities entail such duties.
3. The precise documentation of information on policies and procedures saves time, and "time is money" as any manager knows. Time previously spent answering repetitive questions can now be spent in more productive ways. In addition, this documentation of policies and procedures reduces errors due to incorrect information.

Types of Manuals

Company manuals, and more specifically, records management manuals vary as to their type and purpose. The most common type of manuals found in business organizations can be grouped into the following categories:

1. *Organizational manuals* depict lines of authority and responsibility by showing how the various departments of an organization interact and relate to one another. Emphasis is placed on line and staff relationships throughout the organization. Departmental responsibilities and reporting relationships are clearly illustrated in such a manual.
2. *Policy manuals* describe broad managerial resolutions that establish the framework within which employees should perform their work responsibilities. Policy manuals state clearly the philosophy of top management, which should serve as a guideline for all departments in maximizing the goals of the organization. The stated policies also help employees understand the objectives of top management and how they can contribute to achieving the overall goals of the organization.
3. *Administrative procedures manuals* describe organization-wide procedures that all employees are expected to follow. These procedures might include such personnel policies as health benefits, vacation guidelines, and promotion information. Other procedures that the organization wishes to standardize for all employees should be included in the manual.

4. *Operating procedures manuals* detail the operating procedures, policies, and job responsibilities of one department of an organization. Records management manuals most appropriately fall under this category. Operating procedures manuals help employees, supervisors, and managers understand their role in the operation of an individual department of an organization. Operating procedures manuals also serve as ideal training aids, since department organization charts and individual position responsibilities are generally included.

Figure 17-6 shows a page from the RCA Corporation's records management manual.

THE SCOPE OF THE MANUAL

The records management manual must be all-inclusive if it is to serve its purpose. The purpose should be stated in the foreword of the manual to serve as an introduction to the content. Employees should see that the manual is a tool to be respected and used as a constant guide.

Contents of the Manual

The content of the manual will reflect the individual needs of the specific company. However, because there are common elements in handling paper flow and records cycles, the following sections should be included in any records management manual:

Contents of the Manual

1. *TITLE PAGE*—Serving as the first introductory sheet, the title page includes the name of the publication, the company name, department title, authorship, and date of publication.
2. *LETTER OF AUTHORIZATION*—An opening letter or message from the President of the organization establishes top-management support of the manual. Such an endorsement implies that the manual is an authorized company publication and encourages employee utilization.
3. *PREFACE*—The preface or foreword may include a welcome note to the employee and a short history of the company. This section should state the purpose of the manual, advantages derived from the use of the manual, and recognition of those who provided assistance in the preparation of the manual.
4. *TABLE OF CONTENTS*—The contents list provides a quick source of subject classifications contained in the manual. Following each subject heading, leaders—alternating periods and spaces—should guide the reader's

FIGURE 17-6 Sample page from RCA Corporation's records management manual. (Courtesy of RCA Staff Center, Princeton, NJ.)

RCA

Records Management Manual

Number VII
Issued 2/16/81
Supersedes All Previous

Subject TRANSFERRING, RETRIEVING, AND DISPOSING OF INACTIVE RECORDS
Page 1

A. General

1. All transfers to the Records Center are based upon the authority of an approved Records Retention Schedule. Records cannot be accepted at the Records Center if they are not specifically scheduled for inactive storage on an approved Retention Schedule.

2. The standard RCA Control System for transfer and control of records (RCA 844 System) is prescribed for use by all RCA Companies unless specific exemption has been given to employ another system.

3. Individual departments and activities are responsible for preparing records for transfer to the Records Center and will need the following materials:

   o Records Retention Schedule for the Department.
   o Supply of File Storage Control Cards (RCA 844).
   o Standard Records Center Storage Boxes.

   Because local handling procedures will vary among companies and divisions within companies, the Records Administrator is responsible for developing a transfer and control procedure based on local needs.

B. Preparing Records for Transfer

The activity transferring the records:

1. Consults the activity Records Retention Schedule and determines which records are to be transferred.

2. Obtains storage containers and RCA 844 control cards.

   Note: Three containers and control cards are needed for every two standard file drawers.

3. Completes form RCA 844, File Storage record as illustrated on the following page.

eyes to the appropriate page number. As an aid in locating information, staggered tabs can be utilized to separate the various topics contained in the manual.

5. *ORGANIZATION CHARTS*—A line and staff organization chart which clearly delineates reporting relationships company-wide is a prerequisite in the manual. In addition, a records management departmental chart should be included to illustrate typical job positions and lines of authority and responsibility.
6. *FUNCTIONAL TOPICS*—The manual should include all elements of the records management program in the organization. Topics such as vital

records, correspondence control, micrographics, and forms control are examples of subjects that should be included if they are an integral part of the records program. Some suggestions for manual inclusion appear below.

- *Retention schedule.* The next section will give precise information concerning the retention periods for the different types of records.
- *Coding system.* This section should give the method of coding the documents. For example, if the system is alphabetic, rules to be followed should be written in detail. In addition, information should be given on the filing procedure for foreign names where the surname is not easily determined or where to file names that include numeric words. Even experts who write filing rules do not agree on the correct way to file these names, so specific instructions need to be included in the manual. The important point is not where to file the record, but rather, to be consistent in filing.
- *Vital records.* The complete records manual will include information on storing records that are considered vital to the organization's operations. This section will identify the vital records, assign responsibility for the control of the vital records, and state where such records are located. Information also should be given on the procedure to be followed in case of an emergency.
- *Forms control.* Small offices may not have a formal forms control program, but even a very small office will have a few forms. Some of the forms may be reproduced in small offices on the typewriter. Instructions for designing and reproducing forms should be included in the manual. Larger offices may include information on forms analysis, forms inventory and appraisal, and the forms control file.
- *Records centers.* Organizations that maintain a records center will include information in the manual on the activities of the center, such as accessioning, transferring records, retrievals, refiling, interfiling, maintaining, and disposing of the documents.
- *Correspondence control.* Correct formats for letters, memorandums, envelopes, and electronic communications should be included in this section. In addition, instructions for reports and directives are an essential part of the manual, and standardized formats should be emphasized. Finally, information on grammar, style, punctuation, and proofreading is often included in correspondence control sections.

7. *SUPPLEMENTARY SECTIONS*—The last section of the manual can include a glossary and an index. A glossary defines all technical terms used in the records management manual, and it serves as a ready reference for all users. An index provides a page location for all keywords used in the manual.

Clarification of Policies The manual, if written clearly, will clarify policies concerning records management and identify the individuals who are responsible for the management of records. Instructions that are clear and uniformly interpreted will serve the organization as the authority for decision-making personnel.

Delineation of Duties and Responsibilities Job descriptions should be included in the manual for each member of the records staff. Initially, if such descriptions are not available, staff members should be requested to keep a record of their activities. The records manager will then review the job descriptions and make any necessary revisions before including this information in the manual.

Standardization of Procedures Standardization of procedures is the major purpose of the manual. Retrieval of records will be much improved if records personnel adhere to the procedures outlined in the manual. Without a standardization of procedures, not only is filing difficult, but retrieval of certain documents is nearly impossible.

Writing the Records Management Manual

Planning the Manual

Before any major undertaking in the office can succeed, top management must give its wholehearted support to the venture. Writing and using an office manual is no exception to this rule. The records management manual will be accepted and used if everyone in the firm is apprised of the task and if management supports the project 100 percent. If such support is not evident, the records manager has a selling job to do. Top management should be introduced to the project early in the planning in order to obtain budget approval for data gathering and final printing of the manual.

Cooperation and Support from Management and Staff Once management has indicated its cooperation and support, the same should be enlisted from the staff. The records manager should announce the plan to prepare a manual at a meeting of the entire staff. Each person should be asked to submit a detailed description of his or her job. Also, employees should be asked to note any items that they think would be helpful in a manual. If employees are hesitant about writing for such a purpose, samples of instructions will prove helpful in giving them the confidence needed to complete the task.

Gathering Ideas for Content Where do the ideas come from for a records management manual? Here are several sources from which material may be gathered:

1. Other manuals

2. Minutes of meetings
3. Policies of the organization
4. Top management (The foreword should be written by a person in a high-level position in order to lend authority to the manual.
5. Employees who will use the manual
6. Consultants
7. Handbooks on office management

Guidelines for Effective Writing

Writing for Readability The manual should be written in the simple, direct language of the business world. Stiff, wordy phrases are not natural and should be avoided. The rules for effective communication are applicable to the writing of the manual. The five recognized *C*s for *readability* should be employed while writing the manual: Writing should be *clear, concise, correct, complete,* and *courteous.* In manual writing, *courteous* should really take on the meaning of "not curt."

Sentences should have no unnecessary words. An instruction like "Please be certain that all documents are coded before they are filed" may be improved by stating simply, "Documents shall be coded before filed." Not only is the statement easier to read, but it also packs the authority and responsibility for the directive.

In addition, the writing should be on a level clearly understandable to all who will read it. The manual that stated, "The records manager is not a ubiquitous supervisor" probably did not communicate to the readers the intended message. How much more effective the statement would be if it said simply, "Staff are responsible for carrying out their assigned duties whether or not the records manager is present." The manual is intended to be a substitute for instructions that otherwise would be given vocally by a supervisor. This is one reason that instructions must be written in simple "talk" language. When the message becomes obscure, the rare individual may reach for the dictionary; however, too many readers skim over the unknown, and thus an important message may be missed.

Mechanical Means for Achieving Readability There are certain rules for effective communication that will be most helpful in achieving readability. One such readability factor is sentence length. Everyone does not agree on the desirable length of a sentence. Experts recommend between 15 and 20 words for the average sentence length.[2] Varying the length of sentences is a good practice; and in writing the records management manual, care should be taken to keep the sentences readable.

[2]Steven P. Golen et al., *Report Writing for Business and Industry* (New York: John Wiley & Sons, Inc., 1985), p. 139.

Robert Gunning has developed a formula he calls the "FOG Index." Gunning's FOG Index determines the readability of a passage. It should be an indication to the writer that revisions need to be made if the FOG Index exceeds a grade level of 12. The grade level can be easily reduced by shortening sentences and by using shorter words. For details on Gunning's FOG Index, see Figure 17-7.[3]

FIGURE 17-7
The FOG Index of readability.

THE FOG INDEX: COMPUTING READABILITY

1. *Determine the average sentence length.*

   Using a passage containing at least 100 words, count both the number of words and the number of sentences. Count each independent clause as a separate sentence. Divide the number of words in the passage by the number of sentences to arrive at the average sentence length.

2. *Determine the percentage of "difficult" words.*

   Difficult words are defined as words containing three or more syllables, except the following:

   a. Words that are capitalized
   b. Words formed by combining short words (such as *nonetheless* or *hereafter*)
   c. Verbs made into three syllables by adding *ed* or *es* (such as *disposes* or *confirmed*)

   Count the number of difficult words in the passage. Then divide the number of difficult words by the total number of words (counted in Step 1).

3. *Add together Steps 1 and 2.*

   Add the average sentence length to the percentage of difficult words.

4. *Multiply by 0.4*

   Multiply the result of Step 3 by 0.4 to obtain the reading grade level of the passage.

   Note: The general public can understand a fog index (grade level) of between 9 and 12. A higher Fog Index indicates that your communications are in danger of being misunderstood.

[3]Adapted from Robert Gunning, *The Technique of Clear Writing,* rev. ed. (New York: McGraw-Hill, 1968), pp. 38–39.

Common sense reveals that sentences that are long and filled with three- and four-syllable words will not be as clear to the reader as shorter sentences with one- and two-syllable words. However, sentences should not be choppy and confined to one-syllable words. Here again, the rule is simple—keep the writing natural. One would not say to a friend, for instance. "Would you do me the honor of accompanying me to the theater this evening?" It is more likely that the invitation would simply be phrased, "Let's go to the movies tonight."

Another factor in achieving readability is the use of words and terms that are understood by the reader. The records management manual will be used by the records staff. Therefore, readers should be acquainted with words and phrases such as *retention, archive, records center, integrity of the file,* and other terminology that is common in records management circles.

Instructions should be written carefully with attention given to every detail. Those who will be using the manual should be able to read the instructions and follow the step-by-step procedures for specific activities. Before printing the manual, employees who will use the manual should be used to **edit,** or correct and refine, the rough draft. This step will prevent the necessity of early revision that may be the result of not achieving readability.

Pitfalls in Writing Trite expressions are common among many writers and should be avoided in writing the manual. Stereotyped expressions and outworn phrases add nothing to the message. Instructions should be pared to the minimum to avoid verbiage.

Correct spelling and grammar are absolutely required. A manual that has misspelled words loses some of its respect. Amazingly, many business persons do not realize that the foreword of a book is not spelled *foreward* or *forward.* A good rule to follow in determining the proper spelling of a word is, "If in doubt, look it up in the dictionary."

Verbs should be expressed in active voice to strengthen sentences. Try to keep instructions impersonal. A statement such as "You should code the document" should be stated "Code the document."

Sentences beginning with "It is" are weak and should be avoided. Especially weak is the continuous use of "It is important to." Every instruction given in the manual is deemed important, and such a phrase is superfluous. Begin sentences with the main subject in order to avoid using expletives.

Sources for Reference

Manuals of Other Organizations These manuals are helpful in many ways. First, the cover and the format of the manual may be attractive and provide ideas for preparing new manuals. A new way of organizing the manual may also be found in another firm's manual. The sections may be divided in a unique fashion. Side tabs may be printed with a brief note of the contents. In many instances, manuals have different colored dividers to indicate what information will be found in that particular section.

The graphics found in another manual may be the source of a helpful idea. Graphics, such as pictures, maps, or graphs used for illustration of an idea, are effective tools for communication. Figure 17-8 shows a page from the Tenneco Inc. records manual, which depicts graphically the flow of records in that organization.

A simple drawing indicating how documents are to be placed in a folder can save many words of explanation. Figure 17-9 portrays graphically the procedure for placing a document in a folder.

Personnel In seeking help from others before preparing the records management manual, the records manager should not overlook top administrators who may have excellent writing skills. Help from such individuals is invaluable in writing the manual. A check on the skills and abilities of individual employees may reveal a latent talent heretofore undiscovered. Everyone in the organization who is able to contribute to the preparation of the manual should be asked to do so. Someone may be talented

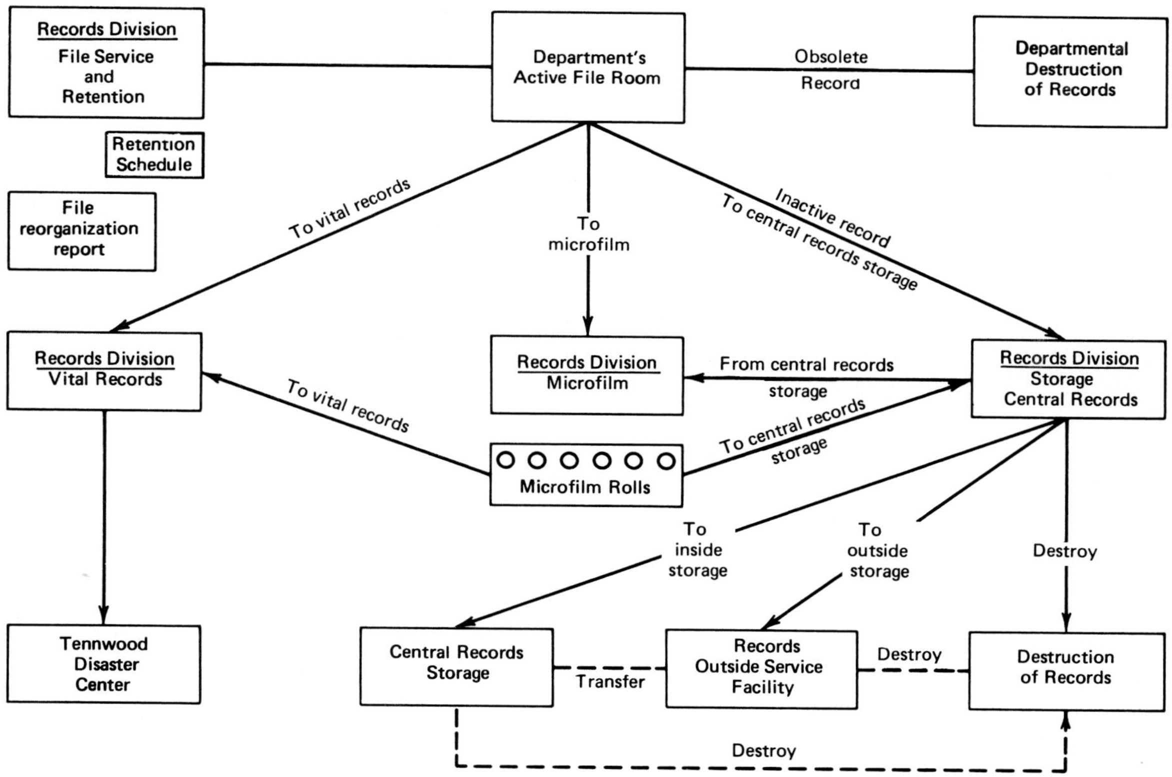

FIGURE 17-8
Tenneco Inc. records management flowchart.

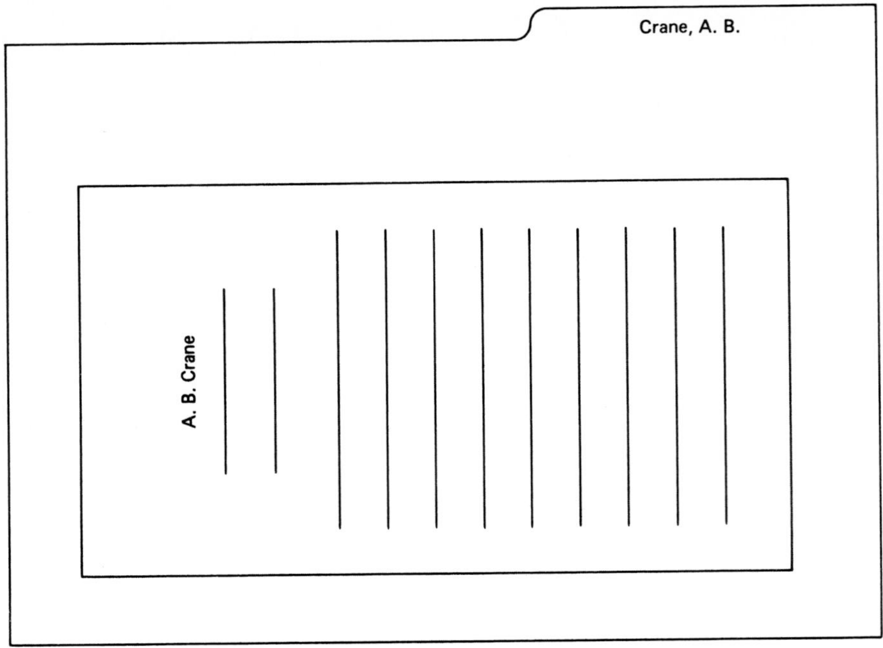

FIGURE 17-9 Drawing to illustrate placement of a document in a folder.

in the design of graphics. A few well-placed and relevant pictures or charts will increase the readability of the manual and help the reader grasp the message.

FORMATTING THE RECORDS MANAGEMENT MANUAL

Following the planning, gathering, and writing steps, the format of the manual must be considered. Since the manual is an important reference source, careful consideration should be given to the design of the manual. The manual, in most cases, will be distributed throughout the organization and should have a distinctive format. According to Wendy L. Chippie, a Records Manager for Hercules Incorporated, there are several formats from which to choose:[4]

1. *LOOSELEAF RING BINDERS*—usually have a high initial cost for the purchase of the binders, but the binders can be reused and the manual can be updated easily by just inserting pages.
2. *PLASTIC COMB BINDERS*—frequently used for binding small manuals. This format is not updatable but new copies are fairly low cost if updates are infrequent.

[4]Wendy L. Chippie, "A Procedure for Procedures," Records Management Quarterly, January, 1986, p. 39. Courtesy of ARMA International.

3. *ELECTRONIC FORMATS*—relatively new and practically eliminate the need for hardcopy circulation. Small and large organizations with compatible systems can access, search and sort to meet their individual needs.
4. *MICROFILM/MICROFICHE FORMATS*—alternatives to both hardcopy and electronic manuals. Depending on available viewing equipment, this format is ideal for distribution in large organizations with offices in various geographic locations.

Another important design element is the format of each individual page in the manual. Consistency is important. Identification information such as Chapter, Section, and Page number should appear on each page in the same position. This identifying information facilitates reference to the manual, and this should be a primary objective—making the manual easy-to-use.

In proofreading the manual, check to make sure that it is visually attractive. This is achieved by the use of white space, headings, bulleted items, and illustrations. These techniques promote ease of reading and reference. White space, in particular, is important. This simply means to avoid excessively long paragraphs by using spacing (white space) between paragraphs. When a paragraph is ten printed lines or longer, reading comprehension decreases.

Updating the Records Management Manual

Once the manual is completed, information in it will become outdated at varying points in time. Some statements in the manual could be outdated the day after it is printed. New laws, new procedures, or needed revisions of existing rules could outdate the manual very quickly. A member of the records staff should be charged with the responsibility of accumulating materials to add to the revised manual. Depending on the content of the revision, manuals may not need to be reprinted in their entirety. A few pages at a time can be easily inserted while superseded pages are removed from a manual that is in loose-leaf form. The person in charge of keeping the manuals updated should be responsible for seeing that the outdated or superseded material is removed from the manuals and destroyed. This task should be included in the job description of one of the records staff so that all will know whose job it is to keep posted on needed revisions.

Some specific suggestions for using and updating records management manuals are as follows:

1. Instruct manual users that written procedures are to be followed without exceptions.
2. Assign to manual users the responsibility of pointing out the need for revision. For example, they should notify the manager when they make changes in operating procedures that are not reflected in the current written instructions.

3. Establish a schedule for checking whether current practices are the same as the ones that are stated in writing.
4. Assign to one employee the responsibility of preparing, obtaining approval for, and issuing manual revisions.
5. Issue revisions frequently. Include a checklist giving the dates and topics of recent revisions so users can verify that their manuals are current.
6. Request that manual users check their manuals for completeness as they use them and inform the manager of any discrepancies.
7. Request that employees notify the manager of any changes in organizational structure, forms, equipment, and the like that change practices. Include these changes in the manual by issuing revisions.[5]

Records management manuals contained in a loose-leaf binder will be easy to revise and update.

The task of updating the manual is nearly as important as the initial writing. Only an updated manual will serve the records staff as (1) a training guide for employees, (2) a tool for orienting new employees, and (3) a continuing training aid and guide for all personnel.

CHAPTER HIGHLIGHTS

- The audit is a control measure that encompasses the entire records management program and all types of records.
- Obtaining top management approval and selecting an auditor are the initial steps to be taken in the audit process.
- The auditor must be aware of the federal, state, and local laws and regulations governing records retention; must have a strong preparation in business courses; and must have experience in the records management profession.
- The greatest advantage offered by an external auditor is the experience he or she had in auditing other organizations' programs, while the internal auditor's greatest advantage is the minimal cost to the organization.
- The greatest disadvantage of the external auditor is cost, while the difficulty of finding a totally qualified auditor among the employes is a major disadvantage of using an internal auditor.
- Forms, manuals, policies, procedures, and other relevant information should be made available to the auditor before the audit process begins.
- The activity ratio measures the number of records requested as a percent of the number of records filed in the system.

[5]Eleanor Hollis Tedesco and Robert B. Mitchell, *Administrative Office Management: The Electronic Office* (New York: John Wiley & Sons, Inc., 1984), p. 636.

- The accuracy ratio measures the number of records located in relation to the number of records requested.
- The retrieval time ratio measures the time it takes to locate an individual record (expressed in seconds).
- The auditor's report should contain statistics, facts, interpretation, conclusions, recommendations, and a summary.
- The records management manual sets forth the objectives of the records management program and serves as an invaluable training guide for all employees.
- Although company manuals vary in type and purpose, common types of manuals include: organizational, policy, administrative procedures, and operating procedures manuals.
- Robert Gunning's FOG Index determines the readability of a passage; the result of the index is expressed as a grade level.
- Varying sentence length, using terms that are understood by the reader, and using simple, concise words all help to improve the readability of the records management manual.
- Updating the manual should be the responsibility of a specific employee to ensure that outdated materials are removed when superseded and that new procedures are incorporated into the manual.

QUESTIONS FOR REVIEW

1. What qualifications should an auditor have in order to conduct a comprehensive audit of a records management program?
2. What preliminary steps should be taken by the records staff before the audit?
3. Identify the activities involved in the auditing process.
4. Indicate how activity, accuracy, and retrieval time ratios can be used in a records management audit.
5. Identify three important areas that should be reviewed during an evaluation of the records system.
6. Classify and describe the various types of company manuals.
7. State the advantages of using a records management manual.
8. Describe the factors that are helpful in achieving readability.
9. Explain the purpose of the FOG Index.
10. Discuss the pitfalls commonly found in writing.

THE DECISION MAKER

Case Studies

1. You have just completed an audit of an organization's records management program. You have listed your conclusions as follows:
   1. Job descriptions are incomplete and outdated.
   2. Documents do not flow naturally from one work station to another.
   3. Many inactive records have surpassed their destruction dates.
   4. Vital records are not adequately protected.
   5. The records manual is not available to all records personnel.
   6. The filing equipment is inadequate.
   7. The office space is seriously limited because of a tremendous increase in active records during the past two years.
   8. Three electronic data processing tapes are missing.

   Write your recommendations based on these conclusions.

2. As part of your audit of the Pocono Realty Corporation, you have collected the following statistics:
   1. Approximately 850 active records are listed on the records retention schedule.
   2. During a typical workday, approximately 50 records are requested.
   3. Generally, about 5 records out of the 50 requested cannot be located.
   4. It usually takes the records clerks an average of two hours to locate the records requested on a typical workday.

   Use the data above to compute accuracy, activity, and retrieval time ratios. Interpret your findings by applying the guidelines presented in the chapter.

3. You have been asked by the records manager to prepare a new section on correspondence control for the records management manual of the STARCO Corporation. Specifically, the new section is to address the composition of business letters. To complete this assignment, you must (1) prepare directions for writing business letters, and (2) prepare directions for letter formats. Accompany your written description with visuals to help the reader understand the directions.
4. As the records manager of Florida Federal Savings Association, you have been computing the FOG Index of various communications. Your findings reveal that almost 75 percent of communications to both employees and customers are written beyond the 12th grade level. Obviously, the reading level of FFSA's communications must be reduced. Review the components of the FOG Index and determine how such a reduction could take place. List your suggestions in an itemized form.

Records Management Technology and Trends

OBJECTIVES

Upon completion of this chapter, the student should be able to:

1. Discuss the role of the records manager in the future.
2. Explain the technological changes in the field of records management.
3. Cite the true impact of electronics on the office of the future.
4. Explain the concept of "the paperless office."
5. List issues and trends in records management in the 1990s.

Has the "Paperless Office" materialized? Will it become a reality in the 1990's? Most office automation experts now agree that the "Paperless Office" concept is an elusive goal. Paper is the preferred medium for many office employees; thus, the new goal is to streamline the use of paper and reduce its use where possible. Many office automation technologies have actually increased the production of paper rather than reduced it. For example, computers, printers, and reprographics machines all produce paper in large quantities.

AUTOMATION AND THE OFFICE

Office automation involves the use of technology in the creation, storage, manipulation, retrieval, reproduction, and dissemination of information. The primary objective of office automation is to increase the cost-effectiveness of office operations.

To function effectively in the planning, storing, and retrieving of company records, the records manager needs to be aware of the organization's commitment to office automation. Depending upon the breadth of the records manager's responsibilities, a more in-depth knowledge of the subject may be required. One must remember that a records manager's job content varies with each organization.

Office System Components

To appreciate the impact of automation on the office of the future, one needs to understand the individual components that make up the office. This discussion will be limited to specific areas: computers, reprographics, electronic mail, micrographics, and voice processing.

Computers Computers are the key to most office automation technologies. Computers come in a variety of sizes and types with varying speeds and capabilities, as noted in Chapter 9. Microcomputers, also known as micros, personal computers (PCs), or home computers, are small, low-cost computer systems that utilize application-specific software. Microcomputers also include portable and lap-top computers that are lightweight and transportable.

Minicomputers are fully functioning, general-purpose computers that are smaller than mainframes, but capable of storing and processing large amounts of data. Minicomputers take up less floor space than mainframes, but can handle payroll, inventory, accounting and shipping functions. An important function of the minicomputer is its ability to expand as an organization's computing needs increase. Minicomputers can be linked together and connected to a mainframe situated in another location.

Mainframe computers are designed to handle large multifunction tasks at fantastic speeds. Data can be sent around the office or around the world. Millions of characters of information can be available for immediate access.

Where does the records manager fit in this fast-paced world of the computer? Records managers in the 1990s need computer resources at their disposal to effectively control the records—paper, microform, and electronic—of an organization.

Reprographics Paper will remain an important element of the office of the future. Despite speculation about the paperless office, offices will continue to use paper to transmit information. Even though paper is the end result or end product of reprographic equipment, a bright future is expected for reprographics. Many believe that the industry has peaked and the future will be limited to refinements of current technologies.

Newly marketed reprographic equipment will continue to be more compact, efficient, and reliable. The equipment will produce better copies and exhibit desirable cost-effective benefits. Labor-saving devices, such as collators, staplers, automatic feeders, and copy counters will be more widely used. Possibly the one technological innovation with still a great deal of potential is fiber optics. Research is continuing in the use of fiber optics, which was first used in copiers in 1978 to replace mirrors and lenses.

With the ever-increasing integration of electronics into copiers and duplicators, "smart" copiers using microprocessors will become commonplace. Increased performance and versatility will be the by-product of computer technology.

Reprographics has been, and will continue to be, integrated with other automated office equipment. The prime example is the intelligent copier. This device can produce copies from digitized data via a computer or in the normal manner as a regular copier. Since the device is capable of receiving data electronically, the intelligent copier is capable of being integrated with computers, electronic-mail systems, some micrographic operations, and information processing.

Electronic Mail **Electronic mail** is one aspect of the office of the future that is currently being used. In simple terms, electronic mail is the delivering of messages via an electronic device, such as a computer or facsimile unit. A well-designed electronic mail system can handle most types of person-to-person communication within the office. These systems are designed to use a computer as an electronic mailbox so that messages can be prepared, edited, filed, retrieved, and distributed. The user has access to these resources through either a CRT or printing hard-copy terminal.

Some advantages of electronic mail are: (1) The message is sent instantaneously to the "mailbox" of the recipient. (2) Electronic mail can be sent 24 hours a day. (3) One does not need to know where the recipient is located to send a message, since the computer handles all the routing.

The type of electronic mail most often used today is facsimile. This is owing to its similarity to regular mail, as facsimile units are able to provide the user with a duplicate of the original message. The duplicate will contain all signatures, dates, drawings, or renderings exactly as on the original. With advances expected in electronics, facsimile has a bright future indeed.

Information processing systems, as well as large computers, are capable of being used for electronic mail. Communication devices must be obtained for information processing systems to function in the electronic mail environment. Large computers can serve as message-routing units, moving electronic mail around the office or around the world.

Micrographics When contemplating the future of micrographics, one must be aware both of the phenomenal growth in the industry over the last 20 years and of the technological changes expected in the future. There are actually two distinct areas in which the future use of micrographics will be important: (1) the fully automated office, and (2) those areas where automation will have less impact.

The recent history of micrographics has been marked by dramatic changes. During this period the micrographics industry has developed, refined, and marketed updatable microfilm computer-assisted retrieval systems, micropublishing, computer-output microfilm, a computer-input microfilm, and sophisticated retrieval devices, to name only a few advances. From this auspicious growth period, one might predict an exceedingly bright future. With the many different systems in the office of the future vying for resources, micrographic systems must be compatible, efficient, and of course, cost-effective.

In *Information and Records Management*, Don Avedon, in his article "Micrographics in the Office of the Future," discusses how micrographics will interrelate with other office functions. With the article is a drawing titled "The Office of the Near Future" that depicts these interrelationships (see Figure 18-1).

Avedon predicts that the high costs involved in storing records will make micrographics an important part of the office of the future. Micrographics offers a less expensive alternative for storing information than does either paper or electronic memory. The key to a well-functioning office in the future will be finding the right equipment combination to deliver information at the lowest cost.

Offices where automation has less impact will continue to require basic micrographics systems for such tasks as security microfilming, jacket systems, archival microfilming, and the like. Applications for this type of microfilming may include engineering drawings, student records, accounts receivable files, personal files, and so on. In this environment micrographics will be competing for resources with less sophisticated office systems.

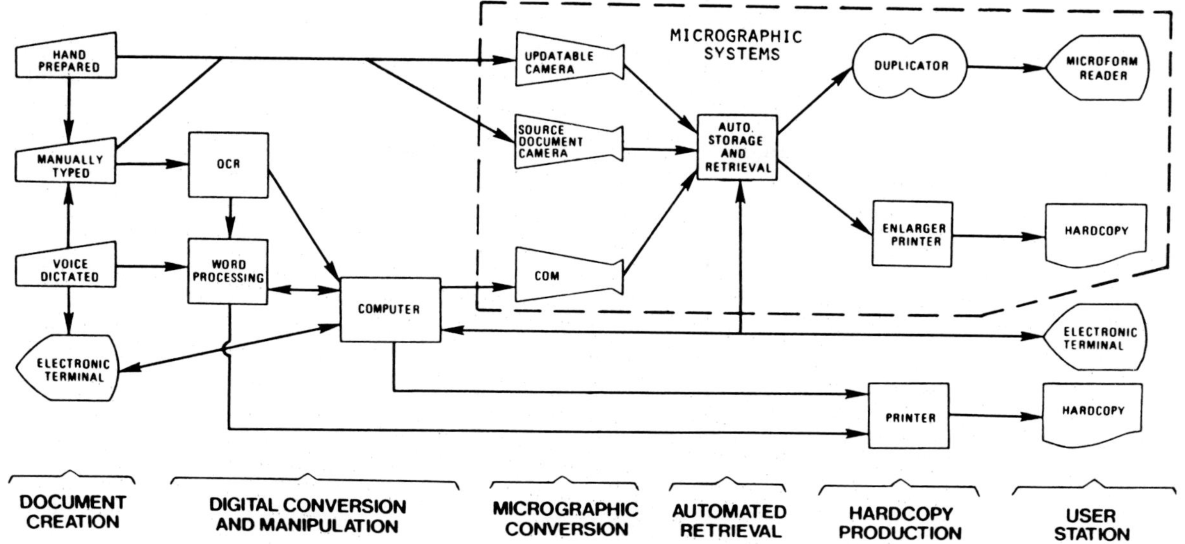

FIGURE 18-1
The office of the near future. (With permission of the *Information and Records Management Magazine.*)

Voice Processing Speech-processing technology made rapid gains in the late 1970s and early 1980s. Voice-recognition technology is widely used in the manufacturing industry for assembly and inventory applications. Current systems are used for command and instruction processing. An application that the public in general can probably associate with is the talking cash register used in many grocery markets to call out product prices.

Current technology is divided into two basic areas—input and output. Speech input is probably the more exciting because it uses machines that understand human speech. Speech-input systems use equipment that transforms voice input into a format that can be used by a computer. Voice-output systems are those that respond verbally to an inquiry.

Voice-based office equipment will be able to perform many tasks. Voice mail will function like electronic mail, but it will be more convenient for both the sender and the receiver of the message. Selective listening and transfer or deletion of messages can be handled easily. Dictation can be done from home, the office, or a mountain cabin by simply telephoning the letter or memo directly to the computer. Order-entry systems will fill orders more quickly and accurately, since the transaction will be processed directly by the computer. The system will be able to provide instant, up-to-date information on any particular order. Other services can include data entry, data retrieval, and transaction processing. Regardless of the particular application, office productivity will increase manifold when workers are able simply to converse with a piece of office equipment. With technology making rapid advances almost weekly, surely the day is not far off when anyone will be able to hold a business conversation with a computer.

Dictation in the 1990s differs from dictation in the 70s and 80s. No longer do secretaries sit with dictation pads and pens along side the boss' desk. Today most companies have hand-held recorders for dictation of correspondence, memorandums, and reports. The 90s will see an influx of digital dictation which essentially is voice processing.

According to MODERN OFFICE TECHNOLOGY, April, 1990, digital computer technology brings two fundamental characteristics to voice processing: voice information is stored in a randomly accessible form, and it is stored in a computer framework. In a digital dictation system, the speaker's voice is digitized and stored on a disk. Advantages of digital voice processing are:[1]

The system is accessible from any touch-tone phone;

Reports or messages can be listened to easily from a remote location;

Reports can be transcribed in any order, regardless of the order in which they were created;

Greater capability is offered in limited physical spaces;

Systems operate at higher speeds;

Systems exhibit higher reliability;

Systems can be customized to meet specific applications needs;

Systems can be upgraded easily via software;

Systems can be married with other technologies such as voice recognition, speech synthesis, telephony, information processing, word processing, etc.

The digital dictation systems of the 90s will be downsized to support smaller systems of two, three, and four-to-one author/secretarial groups. Such small systems will make it possible for businesses to minimize administrative support services for professional workers.

Records Management Technologies

Computer technology is becoming more prominent in records management systems in the 1990s. The creation, storage, and retrieval of information is greatly enhanced by the use of the computer.

Records management technologies that utilize the computer will be discussed in this section. These technological advances include CAR (Computer Assisted Retrieval) systems, EIM (Electronic Image Management) systems, Bar Code Scanning, and Records Management software.

[1]*Digital is Dictation's Future,* Francis J. Lavoie, MODERN OFFICE TECHNOLOGY, April, 1990, p. 82)

Computer Assisted Retrieval (CAR) Systems

Computer Assisted Retrieval systems represent the convergence of two separate but important technologies—micrographics and the computer. This joining of technologies is referred to as computer-assisted retrieval systems (CAR). According to industry analysts, CAR represents the most significant change in the micrographics industry over the past five years. While CAR systems have been around for years, they have come of age since 1985. While micrographics is a mature industry, the continual upgrading of standard, classic equipment such as cameras, film inserters, microfiche duplicators, readers, and reader/printers has kept the industry current.

In a CAR system, micrographics supplies sophisticated cameras and retrieval devices to this union, as well as an inherent ability to store vast amounts of information inexpensively. The computer brings its fantastic speed and data manipulation capabilities to handle indexes and associated information. Since the equipment used in these systems varies in capacity and performance, the user has a wide variety from which to choose. Figure 18-2 shows the Canon micrographics car system.

CAR Overview

The first process in a CAR system is the microfilming of records. These records are filmed by intelligent microimage cameras and the images are then

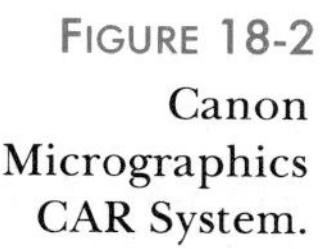

FIGURE 18-2
Canon Micrographics CAR System.

processed. The records are filmed in random order, and information identifying the records is captured and used to create computer indexes and databases. When the database is searched, individual records can be located by using their computer-generated names.

In a microfilm CAR system, the basic unit of data being managed is an index. The index is the location of records stored on microfilm. The index can contain a description of the document or record, as well as the actual microfilm frame and roll numbers.

There are two basic CAR systems for handling indexes and retrieving microfilm: on-line (direct access) or off-line (indirect access). Off-line CAR has indexes that are maintained by the computer, but retrieval is done manually. In this type of system, an operator inputs information into the computer to search for a specific record. The computer CRT screen displays the location of the record for the operator. Next, the operator manually loads the microfilm into a retrieval device to find the correct image.

On-line CAR (direct access) provides maximum assistance to the operator by offering automated indexing and retrieval of specific images. Here again the computer maintains an on-line index. In addition, a microfilm retrieval device is attached electronically to the computer terminal. This interface or attachment between devices allows the computer to direct the reader to find the correct image for the operator. Advancements in CAR systems over the years have contributed to a higher level of computer interaction while minimizing human intervention in the retrieval process.

Electronic Image Systems

Electronic image systems utilize optical disk technology for records storage, computers for communication and display, and database software for records organization and retrieval. Thus, image systems integrate several technologies to capture, store, and retrieve documents. As noted above, documents are "digitized" by a document scanner that converts paper documents into machine-readable, digitally coded images acceptable for storage on optical disks. This scanning process is called "document digitization."

Typical office correspondence such as letters, memoranda, and reports are all candidates for document digitization. Once scanned, the digitized documents are stored within an organization's computer system on read/write optical disks. The optical disk media can be divided into write-once/read many (known as WORM) and erasable disks. Write-once optical disks record information that cannot be altered while erasable optical disks act more like magnetic disks that permit recording over previously used segments.

A small image system would utilize a 5 1/4 inch optical disk while a large image system could utilize the 12-inch optical disk. One 12-inch optical disk can hold approximately 50,000 documents—8 1/2 x 11 inches. The optical disks are stored in jukeboxes. Jukeboxes are stored devices which provide on-line access to multiple optical disks for retrieval purposes.

Like micrographics, image systems have evolved into two types: archival systems and integrated systems. Archival image systems are utilized for long-term storage of document images offering quicker access to documents than micrographics. Integrated systems include magnetic disks, microfilm, and optical disks in the same system. Such integrated systems provide immediate access to documents stored. Suitable industries would include banks, insurance companies, and other financial industries which handle massive volumes of paper documents. An authorized user can simply view the image on a workstation to verify requested information. Thus, immediate turnaround time is available.

Figure 18-3 illustrates the Minolta MI^{3}MS 1000: The Minolta Integrated Information and Image Management System. The system consists of up to four workstations clustered around a 32-bit microprocessor. At each workstation, the operator can view and process images while performing word processing or other MS-DOS based programs as required. Each MI^{3}MS 1000 can be customized in hardware and software to the user's needs.

Electronic Image System Components

Hardware and Software Requirements. Imaging Systems require computer-based hardware and software to digitize documents and store them for retrieval. Such a system requires a central processing unit (CPU) which is usually a microcomputer or a minicomputer-based system, an input workstation with a copier-like scanner and a monitor attached on-line to the CPU, and both magnetic and optical disk drives. A retrieval workstation containing a monitor

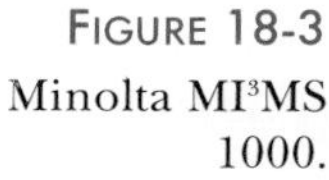
FIGURE 18-3 Minolta MI^{3}MS 1000.

and a keyboard may be utilized for large systems. Otherwise, the input workstation can support both input, indexing, and retrieval requests. If a hard copy of the image is needed, a laser printer is required to reproduce the image.

Indexing Documents. The scanned digitized documents are indexed at the input workstation's keyboard according to the parameters established by the records manager and/or information specialist. Indexing and retrieval software facilitates this process. Such software must accept the specific field and record structures established for the files. After the indexed information is keyboarded at the input workstation, the data is sent to the CPU for storage on magnetic disks. To retrieve document images, the user enters indexed information into the retrieval workstation where the image or images are viewed on the monitor and, if a hard copy is required, reproduced on a laser printer.

Figure 18-4 shows the Canofile 250 electronic filing system by Canon, Inc. The system utilizes Canon's newly developed Magneto Optical Disk which incorporates the latest in magnetic and laser technologies in a compact 5.25 inch disk. The Canofile 250 offers four indexing methods: Index Cell, File Name, File Number, and Date.

Document Scanning. As previously mentioned, all types of paper documents can be scanned and digitized. After this process, the digitized images are compressed to reduce computer storage space requirements. These compressed images can be immediately transferred to optical disks for permanent storage or go to magnetic disks for temporary storage prior to optical disk recording. Thus, both optical disk drives and magnetic disk drives are part of the hardware configuration requirements.

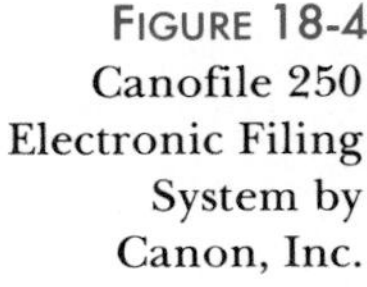
FIGURE 18-4 Canofile 250 Electronic Filing System by Canon, Inc.

Parameters for System Selection

As mentioned above, suitable applications for optical disk image systems include high volume paper handlers that require documentation for legal and/or business purposes. The TAB Products Company offers these suggestions for selecting an optical media filing system:

When you have voluminous amounts of documentation and high activity;

When you can't afford a misfile, lost file, or "out-of-file," a risk in 3 to 10 percent of paper-based filing systems;

When high security is required, such a system can lock out unauthorized personnel;

When you need an audit trail for verification;

When you need backup in paper or a duplicate optical system;

When space is a consideration;

When you need to maximize the efficiency of personnel;

When several people need to have access to the same document at the same time in order to make a business decision.

Benefits of Imaging Systems

A Consultant with the Coopers & Lybrand Consulting Group in Canada cites the following benefits from using imaging systems for records management applications:[2]

1. *ACCESS TIME*—Imaged documents are available in minutes (or seconds) compared to hours with a paper-based system.
2. *DOCUMENT SECURITY*—More rigorous controls can be built into the system. Users can be assigned various levels of access to documents. Thus, access can be restricted to certain users through security codes.
3. *MULTIPLE ACCESS*—Several users may access and view the document simultaneously. This is obviously not possible with paper records.
4. *PAPER DOCUMENTATION*—All signatures and handwritten notes are retained in the scanned image, and can be reproduced in print, if needed, by a laser printer.

[2]"Imaging Systems and Records Management, Monique L. Attinger, RECORDS MANAGEMENT QUARTERLY, January, 1990. Courtesy of ARMA International.

Turnkey Systems

While all the components mentioned above can be purchased separately by records managers wishing to implement a imaging system, such installations are likely to be time-consuming and technically frustrating. Thus, records managers have two options: purchase a turnkey system or a customized configuration. A turnkey system comes complete with all the hardware, peripheral devices and software required for the system operation. Some customization is available through a selection of various components offered by the vendor. For example, FileNet Corporation offers a range of imaging systems which allows companies to upgrade their existing system. One typical equipment upgrade might include a jukebox storage unit for multiple on-line optical disk storage. Turnkey systems provide convenient solutions to typical records management concerns while minimizing installation time and "new system quirks." Such a single-vendor approach, while limited to the vendor's preconfigured options, is a simplified approach to getting an image system "up and running."

Customized Configurations

Customized installations of electronic image management systems are available by contracting with systems integrators. These companies develop sophisticated document storage and retrieval systems for large-scale applications with unique requirements. Most of these customized contractors offer the latest in records management technologies, which currently is electronic imaging. While they do not generally manufacture their own products, they typically integrate various hardware and software configurations for customized applications. The first customized application by a systems integrator was for the Library of Congress in the mid-1980s. Other customized applications include the Internal Revenue Service, The National Archives, the U.S. Patent and Trademark Office, and the U.S. Army and Air Force.

Bar Code Scanning

Optical wand scanning of barcoded data provide a means for collecting data faster and more accurately. Barcodes are a method of encoding data which can be read quickly and interpreted accurately by an optical wand scanner.

Scanning Devices The most common types of scanning devices currently being used include laser scanners, OCR (optical character recognition) scanners, MICR (magnetic ink character recognition) scanners, and contact or "wand" scanners. Some typical applications are as follows:

Laser scanners: stationary devices used at grocery store check-out stations;

OCR scanners: used in general merchandising systems to scan character symbols;

MICR scanners: used primarily in the banking industry to automate the handling of checks;

Contact or "wand" scanners: portable scanners that are passed over a barcode symbol while reading information. Applications include files management, inventory control, accounting, etc. These scanners are used with portable data terminals which gives them added versatility.

Barcode Structures Most common barcodes are horizontal codes consisting of alternating vertical dark bars and spaces or light bars. The code is two dimensional having both height and width. Information is encoded into the bars and/or spaces by varying their individual widths. While the height of various barcodes may vary, there is no interpretive information gained from the height of either the bars or spaces. Thus, the height of a barcode simply allows an operator to move the tip of the scanner easily across the barcode to read the data.[3]

Records Management Applications According to Records Managers Susan Cisco, CRM, and William Wright, the following benefits can be gained from a barcode inventory system:[4]

Added value to the collection of records by making them more accessible to authorized users by (1) providing a reliable up-to-date listing of the company's information assets; and (2) helping management collect information for decision making purposes.

Minimized the growth of personal desk files by raising employee confidence in the centralized filing system by (1) providing a detailed inventory of what records were available; and (2) correctly identifying where records were physically stored.

Eliminated duplication of valuable technical work by (1) easy inventorying and quick retrieval of records; and (2) reducing replacement costs of records.

Reclaimed 25 percent of the filing equipment and floor space by disposing of unnecessary and obsolete records.

Provided a quantitative measure of work productivity.

Improved morale of records management staff by providing them with tools for faster records storage and retrieval.

[3]MSI Data Corporation

[4]ARMA Quarterly, April, 1990.

RECORDS MANAGEMENT SOFTWARE

Many companies have determined that the volume of paperwork is too cumbersome for manual records systems and have turned to records management software to computerize their records systems. According to Modern Office Technology, you should consider records management software when manual systems do not perform because of the following:[5]

1. the volume of activity is too large;
2. manual recordkeeping burden is cumbersome;
3. preparing summary reports for management is too expensive.

Thus, records management software will help to locate filed information quickly, reduce lost or misplaced records, track records requests, and analyze filing activity.

An article in the ARMA QUARTERLY states that the benefits to be gained from records management software are both direct and indirect. Direct benefits include increased productivity, decreased paperwork, greater internal controls, increased efficiency, better space management, greater flexibility, and improved customer service. The indirect benefits include enhanced department image, job enhancement for employees, and an upgraded marketability for the records staff.[6]

Software Choices. Basically, there are three selections that can be made:

1. *CUSTOMIZED OR IN-HOUSE SOFTWARE*—If an organization has unique needs and has in-house resources, then this approach is feasible. However, developmental costs usually run higher than commercially available RM packages. In addition, the time from development to installation is generally longer and many times more frustrating until the quirks are worked out of the system.
2. *DATABASE SOFTWARE*—General purpose database software packages can be purchased and customized to meet an organization's needs provided they are not too specialized. This approach provides a low-cost, quick implementation solution.
3. *RECORDS MANAGEMENT SPECIFIC PURPOSE SOFTWARE*—This software is usually made for IBM PC compatible equipment and can range from single application to integrated RM programs. Such integrated software can include active records, inactive records, vital records, records inventorying, destruction notifications, and general files management and tracking.

[5]Records Management: Making the Right Choices, MODERN OFFICE TECHNOLOGY, April, 1990.

[6]Skillman and Dmytrenko, "A Comparison of PC Based Records Management Software," RECORDS MANAGEMENT QUARTERLY, April, 1989.

Software Considerations A needs assessment should be undertaken to determine the RM software package that is right for a particular department or corporation. This needs assessment will include the records volume, user requirements, and the benefits expected from the software system.

Software Features After completing a needs assessment, a comparison of records management software should be undertaken. Consultant James V. Davis recommends the following criteria for judging such software:[7]

1. Vendor Support: check the vendor's track record for pre- and post-installation support
2. Vendor Stability: how long has the vendor been in business?
3. Quality of Documentation: well-written manuals and instructions
4. Ease of Use: software should be designed to handle both novice and expert users
5. Performance: speed of the software system to handle specific applications
6. Error Handling Ability: how easily a package recovers from problems and operator errors
7. Value: cost to benefit ratio of the package

Additional considerations include user friendliness, manual clarity, password security, speed and response times, software interfaces, and vendor training and support. A list of available software—both general systems and specialty systems—is listed in Appendix E.

Issues and Trends in Records Management in the 90's

Despite the dire predictions of a "paperless office" in the 70's and 80's, paper remains the primary choice for filing in the United States. Instead of dealing with a "paperless office," records managers are confronted with "information layering"—information appearing in various formats, i.e., paper, microform, floppy disk, and/or optical disk. Managers are faced with information overload due to this abundance of data.

According to an article in the *New York Times*, paper consumptions has grown more than twice as fast as the gross national product in the last decade. Indeed, according to author Lawrence Fisher, corporate managers have learned that the paper habit is harder to kick than they thought and, thus, are refining their vision of the paperless office. Rather than eliminate paper entirely, the new vision does away with paper where it is oppressive, such as when long-term storage is required, and utilizes paper where it is preferred, such as by employees when reviewing reports. Among the uses for which paper is still

[7]James V. Davis, "Choosing Records Management Software," ARMA Conference, Baltimore, Maryland, October, 1988.

preferred are formal letters, contracts requiring a signature, and other crucial correspondence. According to Fisher, "the line between an original and a copy blurs when documents are created and stored in electronic form, so if originality is an issue, paper is likely to be the medium."[8]

Today's records managers are addressing this issue of "Information Layering" as well as others in the decade of the 90s. A brief look at some of the more important issues and trends are presented below:

Legislation and Regulatory Issues. Records managers and professional organizations such as ARMA (Association of Records Managers and Administrators) must influence the government to reduce the paperwork burden. When more regulations are imposed on both the public and private sectors of business, the information burden increases. This burden translates to increased information costs which are eventually passed along to the consumer through increases in goods and services.

Downsizing Workforce and Tighter Budgets. Change is constant in organizations as acquisitions and takeovers force top management to justify every position as well as every department. Workload projections need to be scrutinized closely in the face of shrinking budgets. Organizations will be employing automated technology to manage an ever-increasing workload with fewer resources.

Technology and Systems Selection. Records managers must be willing to incorporate automated office technologies into their departments to remain productive and cost-effective. What new technologies should be implemented? What paybacks will accrue as a result of these new technologies? Currently, the "hot" technology for the 90s is imaging. Records managers must prepare a cost-benefit analysis to determine if imaging systems—or any other new technology—are appropriate for their organizations.

Human Resource Requirements. The records manager must be seen as the information resource manager, one who works with top management in interpreting data as well as in directing the total records program. Records managers need to be "proactive" by delineating responsibilities in the ever-growing information management arena. RM personnel need good oral and written communication skills, technical expertise, and human relations skills. Increasingly, companies are seeking college-educated information specialists knowledgeable in current technology with analytical abilities to "look at the big picture."

[8]"Paperless Office Evolves With Paper, but Less of it," Lawrence M. Fisher, THE NEW YORK TIMES, July 7, 1990.

THE RECORDS MANAGER AND THE FUTURE

Since the future office environment will require a total team effort to successfully install major office systems, the records manager needs to have a comprehensive background to be an effective contributor. To assume a leadership role, the records manager must be capable of understanding and successfully dealing with technological change.

The most obvious way for records managers to enhance their resourcefulness is through education, whether formal or informal. The training and upgrading of skills can be achieved through workshops, vendor-sponsored programs, professional seminars, and college- or university-level courses. Professional publications list vast numbers of available programs each month.

An area often overlooked, yet vitally important to any manager, is the management of people. This management skill is more important than all the other skills a manager may acquire. A manager cannot obtain the maximum productivity from his or her personnel without good human-relations skills. In many cases where office systems fail to function as expected, the non-machine-related problems can be attributed to personnel. It is well recognized in the business world that any system will fail if it does not have employee support.

Along with daily and weekly administrative duties, a records manager may also be challenged to work as a team member with other management personnel. A company might use the team approach to certain types of problem solving. Here the records manager will be working with data processing specialists as well as other skilled professionals. Clearly the challenge is for the records manager to assume a team-member role and to provide leadership and direction as circumstances dictate. How well the records manager performs in this role is a function of his or her individual personality and talents.

It should be evident that no matter what operational structure an organization may use, the records manager will need to be a skilled, intelligent, resourceful individual to function effectively in the automated office environment.

CHAPTER HIGHLIGHTS

- Computers have become an integral part of society; many records management functions have evolved into high-technology computer-assisted tasks.
- Micrographics has merged with computer technology to form computer-assisted retrieval (CAR) systems; there are two basic systems for handling indexes and retrieving microfilm: on-line (direct access) or off-line (indirect access).
- Computers are available in a variety of sizes and types, but they are generally classified into one of the following categories: microcomputers, minicomputers, or mainframe computers.

- Reprographics will continue to be important in the office; intelligent copiers using microprocessors will become standard office equipment.
- Electronic mail is the delivery of messages via an electronic device, such as a computer or facsimile unit.
- Micrographics will have a two-fold future. One area will see micrographics integrated with other high-technology systems. The other will see micrographics use in offices where automation has less impact.
- Voice Processing utilizes computer technology to store the speaker's voice in a digital format on a disk.
- Electronic image systems utilize optical disk technology for records storage, computers for communication and display, and database software for records organization and retrieval.
- Barcodes are a method of encoding data which can be read quickly and interpreted accurately by an optical wand scanner.
- Records management software helps to locate filed information quickly, reduce lost or misplaced records, track records requests, and analyze filing activity.
- In the 1990s, records managers are confronted with "information layering"—information appearing in various formats, i.e., paper, microform, floppy disk, and/or optical disk.
- Records managers need to be concerned with the following issues in the 1990s: legislation and regulatory issues; downsizing workforce and tighter budgets; technology and systems selections; and human resource requirements.

QUESTIONS FOR REVIEW

1. What technological changes have occurred in the field of records management?
2. Describe important issues and trends facing records managers in the 1990s.
3. Has the "paperless office" evolved? Why or why not?
4. What are the components of a CAR system?
5. Contrast the role of micrographics in the automated office vs. the traditional office.
6. How does indexing and retrieval occur in a CAR system?
7. How can records managers upgrade their skills?
8. What is office automation?
9. Describe the future of reprographics.
10. What is the "new vision" regarding the use of paper as a storage medium in offices in the 1990s?

THE DECISION MAKER

Case Study

The firm for which you work, the WWW Company, has all the company's records stored in file folders on open shelves in a small file room. The company's records have been growing at the rate of one open-file section per year. It is estimated that at the current rate of growth, the file room will be filled in about three years. As a records administrator, you have been asked to review the situation and propose a solution to the space dilemma. Assume that you will not be able to get more space by moving or enlarging the file room. Given the circumstances, you feel a CAR microfilm system would best serve the need. To justify your selection you should discuss the other options (new filing system, setup retention program, and so on) available. You may discuss systems covered in other chapters of the text. The written report you will prepare for the comptroller should be: (1) a review of the available options, (2) a thorough discussion of your choice, and (3) your reasons for selecting the CAR microfilm system. You may assume that all documents will be no larger than 11 by 14 inches, that no new personnel will be needed to operate the selected system, and that the storage and retrieval equipment will be placed in the file room. Conversion from the old system to the new system will have a minimal effect on the department's ability to respond to requests for assistance.

APPENDIX A

ARMA Job Descriptions

POSITION TITLE
Records & Information Clerk
FUNCTION
The Records & Information Clerk assists in processing incoming information, sorts and classifies material for integration into systems. Retrieves/references information for users. Maintains logs and indexes to provide status of information. May type and perform other clerical duties as assigned by supervisor.

POSITION TITLE
Senior Records & Information Clerk
FUNCTION
The Senior Records & Information Clerk distributes incoming information to Records Clerks for integration into systems. Retrieves/references information for users. Maintains logs and indexes to provide status of information. Accu-

Source: Association of Records Managers and Administrators, Inc., 4200 Somerset Drive, Suite 215, Prairie Village, KS 66208.

mulates statistical data, performs special data gathering projects, acts as coordinator between records center and other records areas. Assists in training personnel and performs other office duties as assigned by supervisor.

POSITION TITLE
Records Center Clerk
FUNCTION

The Records Center Clerk assists in the operation and maintenance of the Records Center. Assists in reference, use, and disposal activities of the Center. Maintains current status of information for accurate retrieval. Assists in maintenance of vital records program.

POSITION TITLE
Records & Information Technician
FUNCTION

Records Technician operates and is knowledgeable in the maintenance of specialized records systems, i.e., medical records, engineering documentation, personnel records, and the like.

POSITION TITLE
Records & Information Supervisor
FUNCTION

Supervise operations of Records and Information organization. Responsible for handling all incoming requests for information and retrieval of data. Plan and coordinate special projects associated with the access, usage, and disposition of Records and Information. Assist in developing organizational procedures manual. Responsible for training personnel in Records and Information and organizational policies and procedures. Apply Records & Information Automated Technology applications relevant to achieving goals and objectives.

POSITION TITLE
Records Center Supervisor
FUNCTION

Operate and maintain all activities of Records Center. Responsible for receipt, storage, retrieval, use, and disposition according to Records and Information Center Procedures. Responsible for maintenance of vital records program in accordance with established procedures. May assist in developing records retention schedules. Train and supervise all Records Center personnel. Apply Records and Information Automated Technology applications relevant to Records Center Operations.

POSITION TITLE
Records & Information Systems Analyst
FUNCTION

Review existing and potential systems and prepare recommendations for change and improvement. Design and develop manual and/or automated Records & Information systems. Prepare and assist in preparation of retention schedules. Write procedures and provide training. Other duties may include but are not restricted to special projects involving: Forms Management, Micrographics, Copy Management, Word Processing, and Mail Management.

POSITION TITLE
Senior Records & Information Systems Analyst
FUNCTION
Directs work projects, acts as a team leader or work director to other Records & Information Systems Analysts. Reviews existing and potential systems and prepares recommendations for change and improvement. Direct, design and development of manual and/or automated Records & Information systems. Directs and/or assists in preparation of retention schedules. May lead and direct other Records & Information Systems Analysts in special projects. May have supervisory responsibility. Writes procedures and provides training. Other duties may include but are not restricted to special projects involving: Forms Management, Micrographics, Copy Management, Word Processing, and Mail Management.

POSITION TITLE
Records & Information Administrator
FUNCTION
Interprets and administers already developed forecasts and long-range organizational plans and translates them into specific plans and schedules at the lower organizational level for the records and information program. Prepares periodic reports to the Records & Information Manager for the Records & Information Management program. Assigns individuals with requisite abilities to already defined positions. Direct organization-wide Records and Information Management program. Must possess strong supervisory and leadership capabilities to lead and direct subordinates. Responsible for protection of organization assets through systematic review and control of information. Maintains knowledge of laws affecting Records & Information Management. Evaluates concepts and techniques for coordination of manual and automated records systems.

POSITION TITLE
Records & Information Manager
FUNCTION
Manage long-range plans and necessary resource projections approved by top management for the organization-wide Records and Information Management program. Prepare annual reports to top management on the Records & Information Management program. Plan long-range organizational needs for employee development and education. Prepares fiscal budget and has fiscal planning responsibilities for the organization-wide Records & Information

Management program. Provides technical expertise and supervisory staff necessary in maintaining a Records & Information Management program for the organization. Possesses and demonstrates strong supervisory and leadership skills in managing the Records & Information Management program. Responsible for protection of organization assets through systematic review and control of information. Maintains knowledge of laws affecting Records and Information Management. Evaluates concepts and techniques for manual and automated Records Systems.

APPENDIX B

CRM EXAMINATION INFORMATION

Historical Background

The Institute of Certified Records Managers (ICRM) is a nonprofit certifying organization of professional records managers and administrative officers who specialize in the field of Records and Information Management Programs.

The concept of the Institute and of Certification for professional records managers was developed by the American Records Management Association in 1966. Their committees spent nearly ten years developing and testing the structure, principles, and practices underlying the qualifications and examinations for professional certification of records managers.

The Association of Records Executives and Administrators (AREA) joined with ARMA to initially finance and staff the Institute. Sponsors of the ICRM now include: the Association of Records Managers and Administrators (ARMA), the National Association of State Archivists and Records Administrators (NASARA), the Society of American Archivists (SAA), and the Association for Information and Image Management (AIIM).

The Institute of Certified Records Managers was incorporated in 1975. The Institute is a separate and independent organization from its sponsoring associations.

Institute Objectives

1. To develop and administer a program for the professional certification of records managers, including the granting of appropriate recognition.
2. To promote the value of certification of records managers to the various national, state, and local governments and the private sector.
3. To develop and administer certification examinations in records management.
4. To work with educational institutions in the development and improvement of records management courses.
5. To define, promote, and advance records management concepts.
6. To support the professional recognition of records managers.

Membership

The ICRM membership is composed of individuals experienced in information requirements, records and information systems, and the related office operations and technologies. All members have met certification requirements set forth in the ICRM Constitution and By-Laws and have received the Certified Records Manager (CRM) designation.

Members in good standing are expected to adhere to the Code of Ethics of the Institute, comply with standards for high-quality performance in professional undertakings, and participate in the Institute's activities to improve the records management profession.

Qualifications

The Candidate for Certification:

1. Need not be a member of a sponsoring organization of the Institute.
2. Must have a minimum of three years full-time or equivalent professional

experience in records management in two or more of the following categories:

Records Management and Principles and Program Organization
Records Generation and Control
Active Records Retrieval, Systems, and Equipment
Records Retention, Scheduling, Protection, and Records Centers
Technology of Records Management

3. Must have a baccalaureate degree from an accredited institution.

(The ICRM Board of Regents may authorize substitution of additional qualifying professional experience for some of the required education.)

Examination Required

The Candidate for Certification must pass within a consecutive 5-year period the CRM Examination as administered by the ICRM.

The examination covers all categories mentioned in the Qualifications section in paragraph 2.

All educational and experience qualifications must be met prior to sitting for the examination. Qualification details, including required education and qualifying professional experience, are set forth in the information materials available to applicants from the ICRM Secretary.

Personal Opportunities

CRM's meet and confer with professionals having common interests and concerns. They may join in research projects on records and information management or assist on committees to further the profession and the Institute. They share their experience and knowledge through writing, teaching, and speaking.

CRM's receive the ICRM Newsletter and Directory of Members. They attend the Annual Meeting of members and are eligible for the Invitational Essay Competition and prizes. They enjoy the camaraderie and recognition of peers and have new opportunities to excel professionally.

Examination Application

The Certified Records Manager Examinations are offered every Spring and Fall, usually in mid-May and mid-November. The deadline for submission of examination applications is at least two months before the exam, to provide time to establish the exam proctors and locations and for the ICRM Certification Evaluation committee to review candidate credentials and qualifications. Application forms are available from the ICRM Secretary.

Institute Information

For applications and additional information about the Institute and CRM Examinations, write to:

ICRM Secretary
P.O. Box 8188
Prairie Village, KS 66208

Source: Institute of Certified Records Managers, 1985.

APPENDIX C

PROFESSIONAL ORGANIZATIONS

Administrative Management Society
1101 Fourteenth St., N.W.
Suite 1100
Washington, DC 20005

Association of Commercial Records Centers
P.O. Box 20518
Raleigh, NC 27619

Association of Information and Image Management
1100 Wayne Avenue
Silver Spring, MD 20910

Association of Records Managers and Administrators, Inc.
4200 Somerset
Suite 215
Prairie Village, KS 66208

Association for Systems Management
2487 Bagley Road
Cleveland, OH 44138

Business Forms Management Association
519 S.W. Third
Suite 712
Portland, OR 97204

Computer and Business Equipment Manufacturers Association
1828 L Street, NW
Washington, DC 20036

Data Management Association
505 Busse Highway
Park Ridge, IL 60068

Institute of Certified Records Managers
P.O. Box 8188
Prairie Village, KS 66208

International Information Management Congress
345 Woodcliff Drive
Fairport, NY 14450

International Records Management Council
22243 Miston Drive
Woodland Hills, CA 91364

National Business Forms Association
433 E. Monroe Avenue
Alexandria, VA 22301

National Office Products Association
301 North Fairfax Street
Alexandria, VA 22314

National Records Management Council
60 East 42nd Street
New York, NY 10017

Office Automation Society International
P.O. Box 374
McLean, VA 22101

Office Systems Research Association
Western Kentucky University
501 Grise Hall
Bowling Green, KY 42101

Society of American Archivists
600 S. Federal
Suite 504
Chicago, IL 60605

Society for Management Information Systems
Illinois Institute of Technology
10 West Thirty-first Street
Chicago, IL 60616

APPENDIX D

Records Management Publications

Administrative Management
Dalton Communications Company
1123 Broadway
New York, NY 10010

American Archivist
The Monumental Printing Co.
3110 Elm Avenue
Baltimore, MD 21211

Disaster Recovery Journal
2712 Meramar Drive
St. Louis, MO 63129

Form
National Business Forms Association
300 North Lee
Alexandria, VA 22314

Format
Association of Business Forms Manufacturers
19034 Mills Choice Road
Gaithersburg, MD 20760

Forms and System Professional
P.O. Box 12830
Philadelphia, PA 19108

IMC Journal
International Information Management Council
P.O. Box 34404
Bethesda, MD 20817

Information Management
Information and Records Management, Inc.
101 Crossways Park West
Woodbury, NY 11797

Journal of Data Management
Data Management Association
505 Busse Highway
Park Ridge, IL 60068

Inform
1100 Wayne Avenue
Silver Spring, MD 20910

Management World
Administrative Management Society
1101 14th St, N.W.
Suite 100
Washington, DC 20005

Microfilm Techniques
250 Fulton Avenue
Hempstead, NY 11550

Modern Office Technology
1100 Superior Avenue
Cleveland, OH 44114

The Office
Office Publications, Inc.
1600 Summer St.
Stamford, CT 06905

Office Systems
941 Danbury Road
Georgetown, CT 06829

Prologue: The Journal of National Archives
National Archives Building
Washington, DC 20408

Records Management Quarterly
Association of Records Managers and Administrators, Inc.
4200 Somerset, Suite 215
Prairie Village, KS 66208

APPENDIX E

RECORDS MANAGEMENT SOFTWARE

VENDOR	SOFTWARE NAME
Andrews Records Management 1 Andrews Circle Cleveland, OH 44141	Corporate Keeper
Assured Information Systems P.O. Box 947 Chadds Ford, PA 19317	AIS-CCFS AIS-CDFS AIS-CRMS
Automated Records Management 23011 Moulton Parkway Suite J-10 Laguna Hills, CA 92653	A.R.M.S. Active System A.R.M.S. Commercial System A.R.M.S. Corporate System A.R.M.S. Legal System A.R.M.S. Retention System

Bechtel 50 Beale P.O. Box 3965 San Francisco, CA 94119	CCR Communication Control Register DDR Design Document Register
BETADATA Systems, Inc. System 4100 North First Avenue Tuscon, AZ 85719	BETADATA Inactive Record
Chase Technologies, Inc. 82 Peace Valley Road Chalfont, PA 18914	FASTTRACK
Creighton Mackay Management 515 E. Third Street North Vancouver, B.C. V7L 1G4	Record Master
Datafile Wrightline 130 Sparks Willowdale, Ontario Canada, M2H 2S4	FROLIC
Document Control Systems 616 S. State College Fullerton, CA	ColorBar Image Trax
Electronic Cottage, Int. 700 East 800 South Green River, UT 84525	Librarian
Image Source, Inc. 801 Front Street Toledo, OH 43605	BoxTrax
Infologics, Inc. 77 N. Oak Knoll Suite 101 Pasadena, CA 91101	ERS III Electronic Record System
JVL Systems, Inc. 1834 Ridge Avenue Evanston, IL 60201	RECCS Custom
Michigan State University Main Library EG-13 E. Lansing, MI 48824	MicroMARC: amc
Minicomputer Systems, Inc. 2037 Sixteenth Street Boulder, CO 80302	InfoTrax

O'Neil Software/Electronics 15251 Alton Parkway Irvine, CA 92718	O'Neil Record Storage System TRACKER
SARD Enterprises, Inc. P.O. Box 13079 Las Vegas, NV 89112	SARDONYX
Shurgard Records Management 55 Union Street Seattle, WA 98101	Records Manager
Software Strategy, Inc. 185 Sound Beach Avenue Old Greenwich, CT 06870	ARC-Plus InARC
Spacesaver Software Systems 155 Executive Drive No. 104 Brookfield, WI 53005	RTS Record Tracking System
Guy Thomas & Associates, Inc. 5107 Lodge Creek Houston, TX 77066	FIRMS
Triad Software Corporation 18127 22nd Drive, S.E. Bothell, WA 98012	GAIN
Zasio Enterprises 1755 Parkview Green San Jose, CA 95131	Versatile

GLOSSARY

A

Accession book or register A book or register, arranged numerically by the code or file numbers used in a numeric filing system, that shows the customer or correspondent to whom each number has been assigned.

Active records Those records that are referenced frequently in the daily operations of the business.

Administrative procedures manual A manual that describes organization-wide procedures that all employees are expected to follow.

Administrative value The value attached to a record by virtue of its role in helping an organization perform its current short- or long-term work.

Air space The space above eye level, up to the ceiling, that can be used for records storage equipment.

Aisle space The amount of space required for a worker to gain working access to stored records in file cabinets.

Alphabetic classification system A system in which records are filed by names of individuals, businesses, institutions, government agencies, subjects, or geographic locations—all according to the sequence of letters of the alphabet.

Alphanumeric classification system A system in which records are filed by a combination of either a personal or business name and a number or a subject and a number.

AMS simplified letter style A letter style endorsed by the American Management Society, in which the salutation and closing are omitted.

Aperture card A keypunch card with a rectangular opening into which a piece of microfilm can be inserted.

Appraisal Assessment of the value of records to an organization, used to determine which records possess historical or research value and should be preserved in a company's private archives.

Archival management Records management field that is concerned with the selection, preservation, and storage of archival documents in both the public and private sectors.

Archives A facility that houses records retained for historical or research value after their primary purpose has been fulfilled.

Archivist One who selects, appraises, and preserves documents that an institution or organization judges to have historical value.

Ascending order The arrangement of records in a numeric filing system in consecutive sequence from the lowest number to the highest number.

Auditing process A thorough examination of the records management program to determine whether the established procedures and policies of the program are being implemented.

Automatic exposure control A copier feature in which a microprocessor monitors the original document and adjusts the amount of light and toner to ensure a high-quality copy.

Automatic feeder A photocopying equipment option that allows the operator either to feed individual originals or to stack groups of originals for automatic feeding.

B

Backup copy An extra copy of a record—especially a vital record—kept as a precautionary measure.

Barcodes Horizontal codes consisting of alternating vertical dark bars and spaces or light bars.

Barcode scanning A method of encoding data that can be read quickly and interpreted accurately by an optical wand scanner.

Blanket ordering A purchasing practice in which forms that are not subject to frequent revision are ordered for a specific period of time from a single vendor.

Blast freezing A freezing technique that minimizes the size of ice particles in documents.

Blip coding An automatic process on many microfilm cameras, in which a square mark (or "blip") is filmed below each frame on a roll of microfilm so the film can be scanned by a microfilm reader to find a specific frame.

Block letter style A letter style in which all lines begin at the left margin.

Built-in dispersal The practice of storing a second copy of a record in another location as a matter of procedure.

C

Carbonless paper Specially sensitized paper forms that do not require carbon paper to make copies.

Centralized copying An arrangement in which photocopying or other reprographic service is provided from a single site or a few central locations.

Centralized purchasing A type of purchasing in which all divisions of an organization combine their forms requirements for each form into one large volume order.

Centralized records storage Storage system in which records for an entire business are gathered and stored in one location within the company.

Charge-out request form A form completed by an authorized employee to borrow records from the files.

Check boxes A method of gathering information on forms by providing boxes that can be checked to indicate the appropriate data.

Checklist form letters Form letters that provide optional statements preceded or followed by a box or space for checking.

Chronological sequence Arrangement by date; filing records with the most recently dated item in front or on top of the file.

Classification control file A control file for forms, in which forms for related functions or uses are grouped together.

Classification system System used to classify records based on how they will be referenced, or called for; examples are alphabetic, numeric, or alphanumeric.

Code line A method of coding microfilm with horizontal lines at predetermined locations between the frames of the film.

Code of Federal Regulations A guide to federal regulations, published by the National Archives and Records Service.

Coding records Writing or otherwise marking a record with the name or number under which it should be filed.

Color copying Using copiers that make copies in color.

Combination ordering Ordering at one time all printed forms that have the same basic construction, but different designs.

Combination storage Storage system that combines features of both centralized and decentralized storage systems within the same company.

Commercial records center A public records storage center that takes responsibility for housing and maintaining inactive records for various companies.

Compact disk read-only memory (CD-ROM) An optical disk, the equivalent of a 5 1/4 inch floppy disk, that stores general purpose digital data for computers.

Compound name A name formed by joining two words or a prefix and a word.

Computer-assisted retrieval systems (CARS) Automated systems that combine micrographics and the computer for records storage and retrieval.

Computer-output microfilm (COM) A method of converting computer-generated data into usable information on microfilm.

Computerized storage and retrieval systems Systems that operate with the aid of a computer or microprocessor in storing, retrieving, and controlling records.

Continuing (perpetual) method A method of transferring records to the records center continually as each file is closed; used most effectively where unit or job files are maintained.

Convenience copying The placing of photocopying equipment in sites where it is easily accessible to users.

Conveyor or elevator-type files Motorized storage units that rotate, bringing the desired set of records to the worker.

Copier/duplicator mix The ratio of the number of copying machines to the number of duplicating machines used in a reprographics operation.

Correspondence manual A guide for all personnel who are responsible for the creation and control of correspondence.

Cross-referencing Coding a record with a second filing caption and creating a special cross-reference sheet under the second caption.

D

Database An organized collection of related information.

Database management system (DBMS) Specific purpose software that is used to maintain the data of a business or an individual.

Database programs Allows information to be entered and stored in random sequence, accessed sequentially or randomly according to the user's needs.

Decentralized records storage The practice of storing records within their respective departments in a company.

Decimal classification system A numeric classification system based on numeric groupings of 10.

Density A measure of the contrast between the dark and light areas on a microfilm.

Diazo A copying and microfilming process that uses ammonia gas, heat, or pressure to develop the image.

Dictionary system A method of subject and geographic filing in which records are filed in alphabetic sequence with no grouping of related topics, similar to the way words are listed in a dictionary.

Diffusion transfer A method of copying in which a document to be copied and a piece of negative paper are exposed to a filtered light.

Digital computer A device that performs numerical calculations using numbers in a sequential manner.

Direct-access system A filing classification system in which a person can locate a particular record by going directly to the files and looking under the coded name of the record.

Directive A communication from management that instructs, informs, or guides employees in performing their work responsibilities.

Disaster Flood, fire, earthquake, or hurricane where there is destruction of property.

Disk packs Hard disks placed in a stack inside a computer.

Dispersal The practice of duplicating hard copies and storing them in another location.

Double-file (duplicate equipment) method A method of transferring records in which the previous period's year's files are retained in file cabinets or next to the current files.

Dry silver film A nongelatin silver microfilm that is developed by a heat process.

Dual-spectrum process A copying process that uses heat and light to produce copies.

Duplexing A printing and copier option that allows both sides of a sheet of copy paper to be imaged without having the paper leave the machine between cycles.

Duplex-numeric classification system A numeric classification system that uses two or more sets of code numbers on its records.

Dye transfer A wet-copying method better known as Verifax or Ready-print.

E

Edit To correct or refine information or data on a record.

Electronic file A database of records that can be accessed electronically.

Electronic image systems A record storage system that utilizes optical disk technology for records storage, computers for communication and display, and database software for records organization and retrieval.

Electronic mail A computer-based electronic message that provides a hard copy of the message and can be accessed from remote terminals; the delivering of messages via an electronic device.

Electronic media Includes floppy or flexible disks, hard disks, magnetic tape and optical digital disks.

Electronic records Information or data recorded in digital form on a magnetic medium or optical disk and that can be read by or retrieved from a computer.

Electrostatic process A photocopying process encompassing two methods—transfer (or xerography) and direct.

Encapsulation A method of preservation in which a document is placed between two sheets of plastic that are then fastened together at the edges with adhesive.

Encyclopedia system A method of subject and geographic filing in which records are filed under major topic names or geographic locations and then according to subheadings for related subtopics or geographic subunits.

Engraving A method of printing in which the design or lettering to be printed must be engraved or cut into the surface of a plate.

Enlargement A feature of copiers that permits an original image to be increased in size.

Evidential value The value attached to records because of the evidence they contain about the company organization and function.

External auditor A person brought in from outside the organization to conduct an audit.

Facsimile (FAX) A copy of a record; a system of transmitting document images over telephone lines from terminal to terminal.

Fair use Reproduction of a copyrighted work for purposes of criticism, comment, news reporting, teaching, scholarship, or research.

Feasibility study A survey of all functions performed by both management and support staff in the records management department.

Federal Register A daily update of the *Code of Federal Regulations.*

Fiber optics The use of extremely small light-transmitting tubes in copiers to replace the conventional lenses and mirrors used to transmit images.

Field A category for the grouping of related information in a database.

File A collection of related records.

File capacity A measurement of the storage capacity per square foot of floor space of records storage equipment.

File-drawer cabinet Standard vertical or lateral file-drawer units; steel-constructed cabinets with the capacity to store 60–70 pounds of letter-size records per drawer.

File folder Kraft, manila, plastic, or pressboard container used to store records pertaining to one correspondent or customer, one account or case, one subject or topic, or one geographic region, depending on the filing classification system used.

Filing Placing records in their appropriate file drawers, cabinets, shelves, or other records storage equipment.

Fill-in form letters Preprinted form letters that have spaces for names, dates, or amounts to be filled in.

Fine sorting The process of sorting records from large alphabetic or numeric groups into smaller, or finer, groups in preparation for filing.

Fiscal value Records that provide evidence of a company's financial condition.

Flash card A microfilm coding system that uses filmed dividers to batch or group documents in some predetermined order.

Fluid duplication The earliest type of office-machine duplicating; more commonly known as "ditto" or spirit duplicating.

Fog Index A reading formula developed by Robert Gunning that determines the readability of a passage by determining average sentence length and the percentage of difficult words.

Following up records Checking on records that have been charged out and not returned by the due date; usually done via the charge-out request form.

Form letters Messages of similar nature composed in advance of their use.

Forms analysis The process of determining how a new form is to be used or how a form to be revised is currently being used.

Forms design The process of designing a form, based on forms analysis, that meets the requirements of the potential user(s).

Forms register An index of all forms in numerical order.

Form title, name, or number Identification information for forms; should be located in the upper-left section of a form.

Freeze drying A document restoration technique that removes frozen water in water-damaged documents before it returns to a liquid state.

G

Geographic filing A classification system in which records are arranged alphabetically according to the names of geographic locations.

Given name An individual's first name.

Gravure process Printing process that uses a copper plate etched with depressions of different depths for holding ink; an economical process for long runs.

Guide letters and paragraphs Form letters that are written for specific purposes, but which can be used or adapted to answer routine correspondence.

Guides Dividers used in file drawers or shelves to identify specific groups of records and to support the file folders.

H

Hard copy Data or information printed in paper form.

Hard disks Flat circular plates housed within a computer that spin at high speed, permitting rapid reading and writing of information.

High-density storage Equipment and systems used to store large volumes of highly active records.

Historical value Evidential or informational records that are permanently preserved due to their secondary or inactive value to researchers.

Holding file A special file box or tray, a specially marked folder, or a special drawer in the desk or file cabinet in which records are housed temporarily until filed.

Hollinger carton A gray fiberboard storage box.

I

Identifying elements City, state, and street names that are used to place identical individual names in proper sequence for filing.

Image orientation The direction in which images are positioned on the film; can be either comic mode or cine mode.

Important records Records that contribute to the smooth operation of a company and can be replaced or duplicated if lost or destroyed in a disaster.

Improvised dispersal The duplication of an extra copy especially for storage in a second location.

Inactive records Records referred to less than once a month per file drawer.

Incineration Disposition of records by burning.

Indexing records Determining the name, subject, location, or number under which a record should be filed.

Indexing (filing) unit Each part of a name or number that is considered in determining the proper filing location of a record.

Indirect-access system A filing classification system in which an index must first be consulted in order to determine the special code assigned to a record; numeric filing classification systems are examples.

Informational value The value that attaches to records because of the information they contain.

Information management The managing of words or data generated by computer-oriented and other related systems.

Information processing A system that uses electronic equipment and specialized procedures to prepare correspondence, as well as to maintain personnel, legal, and financial records.

Information-resource management The managing of all organizational information resources.

In-house records center An area within the company used to store inactive records.

Inspection task The task of checking each item of correspondence, report, business form, or other such record to be sure it has been released for filing.

Instructions and routing information Information included on a form to aid the user in completing and distributing copies of the form.

Intelligent copier A copier that is able to communicate with computers, information processors, and other office systems to produce copies; combines the technologies of data processing, photocopying, and phototypesetting.

Interfiling The procedure of placing records within stored files.

Internal auditor A company employee who performs auditing functions.

Inventory control A program used to maintain a forms inventory.

Item arrangement The proper placement of items on a form.

J

Jacket A plastic carrier for microfilm, formed from two pieces of clear polyester material sealed at the top and bottom.

Job description A specification written to describe the duties and responsibilities of a particular position.

K

Key counter A device for counting the number of copies produced by a copying machine.

L

Lamination A method of preserving documents by placing them between layers of plastic and using heat and pressure to fuse the layers.

Lateral file cabinet A lengthwise file cabinet whose drawers or shelves are opened broadside.

Layout The arrangement of information on forms to achieve efficiency in space utilization.

Leaf-casting The process of restoring deteriorated paper records by bonding fibers to the document to reinforce the worn areas.

Legal value The value attached to a record that contains evidence of the legal rights and obligations of an organization.

Letterpress printing A printing process in which ink is applied to paper as it is pressed against a raised surface printing area.

Life cycle of records The period from a record's origination or receipt to its final disposition, whether that disposition is permanent retention or destruction.

Local area network (LAN) A group of interconnected processing devices used to distribute data or information throughout a given geographic area.

M

Mainframe computer Large computer designed to handle large multifunction tasks at fantastic speeds.

Management by objectives (MBO) A management tool to encourage employees to establish goals and to formulate objectives that are practical in attaining those goals.

Manual storage and retrieval systems Systems that store and retrieve records without the use of mechanical or automated devices.

Master retention schedule An alphabetical listing of all records with specific retention and disposition data.

Mechanical storage and retrieval systems Systems that use some type of mechanical or electrical assistance in the storage and retrieval of records.

Media The floppy disks, paper tapes, magnetic tapes, cassettes, magnetic disks, or cartridges on which information is stored.

Memorandum Short, informal messages used to communicate to employees within an organization.

Microcomputer A desktop microprocessor system that consists of a central processing unit, a keyboard, and a video display terminal; magnetic floppy disks or diskettes are used for auxiliary storage.

Microfiche A sheet of microfilm on which many pages of greatly reduced printed matter in the form of microimages are recorded.

Microform records Data or documents whose images have been photographed in highly reduced form and stored on a microform.

Micrographics The filming, storage, and retrieval of information, data, or records in a miniaturized image form.

Microimage A highly reduced photographic image on microfiche, roll film, jacket, ultrafiche, or aperture card.

Microprocessor A miniature integrated circuit chip consisting of a thin wafer of silicon; comprises basic element of microcomputers, copiers, small appliances, etc.

Middle-digit numeric system A numeric filing system in which records are filed by using the middle digit(s) of the number as the primary indexing unit.

Minicomputer A small, fully functioning, general-purpose computer.

Mobile storage files High-density storage units that require construction of permanent floor tracks on which several rows of separate open-shelf lateral file units can be rolled.

Modified-block letter style A letter style in which each line begins at the left margin, except the date and closing, which begin at the center.

N

National Archives and Records Service (NARS) The federal agency responsible for record-keeping activities.

NCR paper "No carbon required" paper.

Nonessential records Records that are not essential to the restoration of business and should be destroyed once their purpose has been fulfilled.

Nonrecords Documents or copies of documents made for convenience are disposed of after use.

Numeric control file A control file for forms, arranged numerically by form number.

Numeric classification system An indirect-access classification system that relies on the use of code numbers assigned to businesses, individual names, subjects, or geographic locations.

O

Odometer An indexing method for retrieving microimages; the device associates frame numbers with linear distances on the film.

Office automation The process of employing technology in the creation, storage, manipulation, retrieval, reproduction, and dissemination of information.

Office layout The arrangement of people and equipment in an office to facilitate effective communication and work flow.

Offset A printing process that produces high-quality volume printing with good color and halftones; also known as offset printing, lithography, multigraph, and multilith.

Off-site records center A center in an off-site location used to house inactive records.

Open-shelf file units File cabinets or shelves that are not entirely closed or protected, unlike traditional file-drawer cabinets.

Operating procedures manual Manual that details the operating procedures, policies, and job responsibilities of one department of an organization.

Optical character recognition (OCR) A method where printed text, photographs, and other images in hard copy format are scanned electronically and stored on a computer disk or tape.

Optical disks Rigid disks that record digital data in the form of microscopic pits etched in a spiral on a plastic surface.

Optical disk system A records storage system that consists of a disk, a scanner-printer, a high resolution video display terminal, and a microcomputer.

Optical read-only memory (OROM) A prerecorded, nonerasable optical disk used for recording and distributing high-density, high-capacity digitally encoded information; also used for maintaining massive databases that are accessible through microcomputers.

Organizational manual Manual that depicts lines of authority and responsibility by showing how the various departments of an organization interact and relate to one another.

Organization chart A diagram of the lines of authority and the span of control in a firm.

Original order Arrangement of archival records with evidential value in the sequence in which records were originally arranged.

Out folder A substitute folder used when an entire file is temporarily removed; used to house incoming records that subsequently need to be placed in the file.

Out guide A special guide that is substituted for a folder or for a record within a folder that has been temporarily removed from a drawer or shelf.

Oversized file drawer cabinet Cabinet similar to, but larger than, those used for ordinary paper-based records, which is designed to store oversized records and can extend from floor to ceiling.

P

Paper-based records Information generated and stored on paper or paper card stock.

Paperless office An automated office that combines many of the latest high-technology devices into a single, integrated office system in which all incoming information is converted into electronic or micrographic form, then edited, indexed, stored, and retrieved when required.

Periodic review A critical review of a specific operation conducted on pre-established dates.

Periodic transfer method A method of transferring files in which all files for a given period are transferred, usually annually or semiannually.

Perpetual inventory An inventory control method in which changes in stock level are recorded on an inventory control card as stock is received or issued.

Physical inventory A physical search of all records, records storage equipment, and facilities.

Plain form letter A form letter that is completely printed and does not require any fill-ins.

Planetary camera An overhead flatbed camera used in micrographics to photograph flat stationary objects.

Platen The top portion of the copier upon which the original is placed for copying.

Policy manual Manual that describes broad managerial resolutions that establish the framework within which employees should perform their work responsibilities.

Primary guides Guides used to highlight the major divisions and subdivisions of records stored in file drawers, cabinets, or shelves.

Primary value The active value or records for an organization's current operations including the administrative, fiscal, legal, and scientific uses.

Provenance order Arrangement of archival records with evidential value according to their initial use.

Pulverizer Machine used for complete records destruction; may also be called a disintegrator.

Q

Questionnaire A survey instrument used in a records inventory to obtain information about records storage equipment.

R

Random access A method of recording data in a random sequence.

Read-only memory (ROM) Section of computer that holds permanent instructions needed by the computer to function.

Record A collection of related data fields.

Records analysis An examination of the information about existing records, records storage equipment, and facilities that results from the records inventory.

Records center A low-cost storage facility for housing the inactive and semi-active records of an organization; the center may be in-house, either on-premises or off-premises, or in commercial storage.

Records clerk A clerical worker whose primary function is to perform routine duties under supervision, such as sorting and filing correspondence and other records.

Records disposition The final stage of a record's life cycle, concluding with either disposition or permanent storage.

Records inventory A complete and accurate listing of file contents, including the type of equipment used, the classification system, descriptive data on the records, location of the records, and the cubic feet of space used.

Records inventory form A form on which information about records and records storage equipment is recorded during the physical inventory.

Records life cycle The time span from the origination of a record until its final disposition, whether that disposition is permanent retention or destruction.

Records maintenance The process of categorizing records according to their nature and use; gathering, preparing, sorting, and storing records; charging out records; following up records; and locating lost or misplaced records.

Records management The systematic management and control of records from the time of their creation or origination of their storage, use, transfer, and disposition.

Records management manual A guide that sets forth the objectives of the records management program, as established by top management, the records manager, and the staff.

Records manager One who plans, develops, and administers the company's records management policies and coordinates these efforts with other personnel, equipment, and systems.

Records retention schedule A document that outlines specific periods set by government regulations and company policies as to how long records should be retained and when certain records can be disposed of.

Records retrieval The removal of records from storage for referencing or updating information in the files.

Records storage The equipment and systems used to file records during their useful lifetime in an organization; also refers to the process of filing records.

Records supervisor One who supervises records clerks and reports directly to the records manager.

Records system The equipment, materials, and staff necessary to maintain effective and efficient control and management of the records of an organization.

Records transfer The moving of records from active to inactive storage, as specified in a records retention schedule and based on legal requirements and administrative decisions.

Records transfer document A form used to record the transfer of specific records for storage.

Records vault A storage place for vital records, appropriate for an organization with a large volume of vital records.

Reduction A feature on a copier that permits an image to be reproduced at a fraction of its original size.

Reduction ratio The ratio of the size of an original document to the size of its photographically reduced image on a microform.

Reference filing and retrieval Retrieval system that requires entire files to be located and removed from the records storage area periodically for review, editing, or updating.

Reference number form letter A form letter in which optional statements are referred to by number.

Refiling The process of returning to the files records that have been temporarily removed from their storage places.

Relative index An index listing in alphabetic order all topic names that are used in a subject filing system; a cross-reference index used in a numeric filing system.

Reports functional file A file that contains a copy of each type of report generated in an office.

Reprographics The field dealing with the facsimile reproduction of graphic material by duplicating, printing, and photocopying processes.

Resolution The ability of a microfilm camera to record fine detail; the sharpness of lines in a filmed image.

Rolled-plan files "Pigeonhole" storage cubicles or shelves for storing rolled-up oversized plans or maps.

Roll microfilm A length of microfilm wound around a reel or spool; may be encased in a cartridge or cassette.

Rotary card file A small desk-top revolving file tray or a large motorized storage unit that stores cards and revolves to bring the desired set of records to the operator.

Rotary microfilm camera A camera designed to film documents at high speed as a rotating belt carries them past a slit aperture.

Rough sorting Sorting or arranging records into alphabetic or numeric groups in preparation for filing.

S

Safe deposit vault A storage place for vital records, appropriate for a small organization with few vital records.

Scientific value The value that attaches to a record that contains technical data gathered as a result of scientific research.

Screening The use of shading or color to highlight areas, offset captions from blank fill-in spaces, or separate areas of a form.

Screen printing Printing process that can be used for printing on a wide variety of materials; also referred to as silk screening.

Secondary (auxiliary) guides Special guides used in file cabinets, drawers, and shelves to highlight frequently referenced sections of records.

Secondary (inactive) value The value attached to records that have a historical or archival use.

Sequential access A method of recording data in a one-after-the-other sequence.

Sequential numbering A method of indexing microfilm that requires that each document be numbered prior to filming.

Shared-logic system Type of word processing system in which several terminals share the processing, printing, and/or storage facilities of a single computer.

Shredding A records disposal process that cuts records into shreds.

Silver halide film The type of film most commonly used for microfilming records; the image is retained by the emulsion.

Software programs Instructions that tell a computer what to do.

Sorting The process of arranging documents into some sequence before filing; the sequence depends on what filing classification system is used.

Spot carbon Carbon paper manufactured with uncoated areas for use when there are data on the form that the user does not want printed on the additional copies.

Standard A measure of quality and quantity.

Stand-alone system Type of word processing system in which individual work stations operate independently of other equipment.

Stencil A porous sheet of tissue paper coated with a waxlike, ink-repellent material, used in the mimeograph duplication process.

Straight numeric filing A numeric classification system in which files are arranged consecutively in ascending order, from the lowest number to the highest number.

Structured-functional subject system A specific subject classification system based on the six basic organizational functions, i.e., finance, manufacturing, marketing, information systems, human resources, and engineering.

Subject filing An alphabetic classification system in which records are arranged by the names of topics or categories.

Surname An individual's last name.

Suspension files Specially designed wall-hung or free-standing storage units of either open shelves or cabinets, in which records can be hung on rods that extend along the width of the shelf or cabinet; also specifically designed file drawer frames on which records inserted in special folders are hung.

System A series of interrelated tasks or procedures followed to perform a major activity.

T

Tabs The protruding top or side edge of file folders and guides, positioned in one-fifth, one-third, or one-half "cuts" across the guide.

Terminal-digit numeric system A numeric classification system in which records are filed by using the last digit(s) in the number as the primary indexing units.

Thermographic process A heat transfer copying method that is based on the principle that images absorb more heat than do areas without images.

Tickler file A file that is referred to regularly as a reminder about items that need attention on specific dates.

Time-shared system Type of word processing system in which customers purchase operating time on a computer from a commercial service.

Transaction filing Retrieving active records from storage so information can be removed, added, or refiled regularly as transactions occur.

Typewriter duplication The process of making copies on the typewriter by using carbon paper.

U

Ultrafiche Similar to a microfiche but with microimages of printed matter that are reduced 90 times or more.

Updatable microfilm Microfilm that can be reimaged many times.

Useful records Records that are convenient to have on hand to prevent a delay in resuming normal operations after a disaster, but not considered essential because the data can be easily replaced or obtained from other sources.

V

Vertical file A type of records storage equipment.

Vertical file-drawer A conventional upright steel-constructed file-drawer cabinet.

Vertical filing The practice of storing individual file folders or cards upright, or vertically.

Vesicular film A microfilm generally consisting of a polyester base covered with a layer of light-sensitive material and used for duplicating microfilm; designed for copying computer-output microfilm, silver, and diazo masters.

Visible card file File in which information printed on the protruding edge of a card can be referred to without having to handle the card or remove it from its position in the card file.

Vital records Records essential for the continuous operation of a business.

Vital records manual A manual that identifies the records that are classified as vital to the continuous operation of a business.

Voice mail Telephone communications system that allows messages to be stored, retrieved, and relayed to various recipients.

Voice processing Voice information stored randomly in a computer system; also known as digital dictation.

W

Wide-area network (WAN) Nationwide networks of telephone lines, microwave relays, and satellites used to communicate over long distances.

Work flow The organization of people, equipment, and work within an office.

Write-once read many (WORM) A one-time use optical disk where the user, rather than the manufacturer, writes information on the disk.

X

Xerography A transfer copying process; one of the two electrostatic processes.

INDEX

A

B

C

D

E

F

G

H

N

O

P

Q

R

S

T

U

V

W

X

Z